AMERICANS ALL

Race and Ethnic Relations in Historical, Structural, and Comparative Perspectives

Second Edition

Peter Kivisto
Augustana College

Wendy Ng
San Jose State University

OXFORD
UNIVERSITY PRESS

OXFORD
UNIVERSITY PRESS

Oxford University Press, Inc., publishes works that further Oxford University's
objective of excellence in research, scholarship, and education.

Oxford New York
Auckland Cape Town Dar es Salaam Hong Kong Karachi
Kuala Lumpur Madrid Melbourne Mexico City Nairobi
New Delhi Shanghai Taipei Toronto

With offices in
Argentina Austria Brazil Chile Czech Republic France Greece
Guatemala Hungary Italy Japan Poland Portugal Singapore
South Korea Switzerland Thailand Turkey Ukraine Vietnam

First published by Roxbury Publishing Company
Published by Oxford University Press, Inc.
198 Madison Avenue, New York, New York 10016
http://www.oup.com

Oxford is a registered trademark of Oxford University Press

Library of Congress Cataloging-in-Publication Data available

ISBN 978-0-19-533053-3

Dedication

To my children, Sarah and Aaron

—PK

In memory of my father, Henry Ng
December 20, 1923–June 13, 2003

—WN

To be an American is to be constantly transforming oneself.

—Bharati Mukherjee

Table of Contents

Preface xiv

Part I
Thinking About Race and Ethnicity

1. Ethnic and Racial Dimensions 3
    History and Social Structure 4
    Five Lives: Identities and Experiences 6
        An Italian American 6
        A Mexican American 7
        An African American 8
        A Chinese American 8
        A Native American 9
        Generalizing From the Specific Case 10
        Making Visible the Invisible 12
        Why Can't They Be Like Us? 13
        Nobody Knows the Trouble I've Seen 13
    Ethnic Groups 14
        Group Definitions and Boundaries 15
        Choosing Names 16
    Intergroup Relations 16
    The Big Picture: What Is Ethnic America? 18
        The Melting Pot 19
        Cultural Pluralism 22
        Alternative Images of Ethnic America 23
    Summary 24
    Key Terms 25
    Questions for Discussion and Critical Thinking 25

2. Toward a Conceptual Map of Ethnic Relations 27
    The Emergence of Ethnic Studies 27

Clarifying Concepts 29
   Nations, Nationality, and Nationalism 30
   Minority Groups. 31
   Race. 33
Ethnicity and Ethnic Groups. 37
   Religio-Ethnic Groups 39
   Racial Groups 39
Ethnic Relations 41
   Assimilation 42
   Pluralism. 43
Toward a New Model 46
   Marxism and Social Classes 46
   Rational Choice Theory 47
The Social Construction of Ethnicity 49
   Ethnogenesis 49
   Ethnicization 50
   Emergent Ethnicity 50
   The Invention of Ethnicity. 51
Contemporary Diversity: Multiculturalism
and Transnationalism. 54
Ingroups, Outgroups, and Group Position 56
   The Psychology of Prejudice 57
   The Sociology of Prejudice and Discrimination . . . 58
Explaining Ethnic Differences 60
Summary. 63
Key Terms 64
Questions for Discussion and Critical Thinking 64

Part II
Sociology Meets History

3. **Constructing WASP Hegemony and the Racial
'Other' From Colonial America to the Civil War** 67
  Nation Building 67
   Albion's Seed 70
   Transplanting the Old World to the New 71
   Nineteenth-Century Migration 71
   The Core Society: Anglo-Saxon Protestant 72
  Erin's Children in America. 72
   Immigrant Adjustment 73
   Communal Activities and Organizations 75
   Nativism 76
  Germans in America 77
   The Early Ethnic Community 78

Intraethnic Conflict 79
Interethnic Encounters 80
Coercive Pluralism and the Politics of Exclusion 81
The First of This Land 82
   The Market Period (1600–1775) 83
   The Conflict Period (1775–1850) 84
   Relocation Policies 85
Beyond the Middle Passage 86
   The Ideology of Racism 87
   Slavery and the Plantation 88
   The Origins of an African American Culture 89
   The Community of Slaves 91
   Slave Revolts 92
   Free Persons of Color 93
   Challenges to the Peculiar Institution 94
The Politics of Conquest 95
Travelers to Gold Mountain 96
Summary 98
Key Terms 99
Questions for Discussion and Critical Thinking 99

4. **Reconfiguring the Racial Divide: Immigration and**
   White Supremacy, 1865–1950 . . . . **101**
Becoming Ethnic Americans 101
Peasants No More: The Italians 103
   The Ethnic Community 104
   Roman Catholicism 106
   Education and Upward Mobility 106
   Ethnic Stereotypes and the Mafia 107
   Politics 108
   Generational Change 108
The Birth and Maturation of Polonia in America 109
   Emigration 110
   The Immigrant Community Takes Shape 111
   Cultural Values 113
   Generational Change 113
The Jewish Diaspora 114
   The Early Community Presence 115
   The Ethnic Community Evolves 116
   Religious Divisions 117
   Political and Labor Organizations 117
   Anti-Semitism 118
   Upward Mobility 119
The Color Line From the Civil War to the
Civil Rights Movement 119

From Emancipation to Jim Crow:
  African Americans 120
    Reasserting White Domination 121
    Leadership in the African American Community . . 122
    Southern Race Relations 124
    The Promised Land 127
    The Development of the Black Community 127
  The Latino Presence in the United States 128
    Mexicans in the Southwest 129
    Cubans and Puerto Ricans 133
  The Chinese and Japanese: A Comparison 133
    The Chinese and Immigration Restriction 134
    Emigration and the Role of the
      Japanese Government 138
  Native Americans During the Reservation Era 142
    Reservations as Total Institutions 143
    The Dawes Act and Acculturation Policies 144
    Responding to Defeat 145
    Stereotypes 146
    The Indian New Deal 146
  Summary 147
  Key Terms 148
  Questions for Discussion and Critical Thinking 148

Part III
Yesterday, Today, and Tomorrow: From 1950 to the Twenty-First Century

5. European Americans: The Twilight of Ethnicity? . . . 151
  Suburbanization and White Ethnics 152
  Does Ethnicity Matter? The Case for
    Cultural Transmission 154
    The Polish Americans 156
    Italians 157
  The Debate Over an Ethnic Revival 157
    The Hansen Thesis 158
    Political Ethnicity 158
  Symbolic Ethnicity 160
    Evidence From Census Findings 161
    Ethnic Options 162
    The Privatization of Ethnicity 163
  The Invention of Ethnicity 164
    Regional Identities 165
    A European American Identity? 166

Jewish Exceptionalism? 167
    The Core Jewish Population 168
    Continuity and Change. 169
    Intermarriage 171
The Specter of Race 173
    White Attitudes About Governmental Actions . . . 175
    The Politics of Hate and Racial Divisiveness 176
Summary 178
Key Terms 180
Questions for Discussion and Critical Thinking. 180

6. African Americans: The Enduring American Dilemma . 181
The Civil Rights Movement: 1940–1970 183
    Phase I: Nonviolent Confrontation and
        Legislative Lobbying 184
    Phase II: Militancy and Black Nationalism 189
Two Controversies. 191
    Busing and School Desegregation 191
    Affirmative Action 195
    Improvement or Decline?. 204
Housing and Residential Segregation 206
    Public Housing. 206
    Alternatives to Public Housing 208
    Equal Housing Opportunity. 209
The Enduring Significance of Race. 212
    The Black Middle Class 214
    Poor Blacks 217
Into the Future 221
Summary 222
Key Terms 223
Questions for Discussion and Critical Thinking. 223

7. American Indians: The Continuing Plight of the
First of This Land 225
The Indian Reorganization Act 225
Termination 226
Searching for Alternatives to Termination 227
Urbanization 228
    Adjusting to Urban Life 230
    Intermarriage 231
    The Ethnic Community in the City 233
Political Activism 234
    The Red Power Movement 235
    Competing Political Goals 237
Ongoing Conflict With White America 238

The Chippewa Spearfishing Dispute 238
The Blackfeet and Oil Exploration:
    Limiting Development 240
Land Disputes: The Legacy of Treaty Violations. . . 242
Development Plans on Native American Reservations . . 243
    Exploiting Natural Resources 243
    Tourism and Gaming 244
Quality of Life on Reservations 246
    Housing. 246
    Health Issues. 247
Native Americans in the White Mind 248
Uncertain Futures. 250
Summary 251
Key Terms 252
Questions for Discussion and Critical Thinking. 252

8. Latino Americans: Into the Mainstream or on
the Margins? **253**
Latino Panethnic Unity or Ethnic Distinctiveness? . . . 256
The Bilingual Issue 257
Cuban Americans 260
    Settlement Patterns 263
    The Enclave Economy 264
    Political Participation 266
    Are Cubans Assimilating? 267
Puerto Ricans 268
    Settlement Patterns 270
    Economic Status 271
    The Impact of Return Migration 273
    The Ethnic Community 274
    Integration or Isolation? 276
Mexican Americans 277
    Chicano Politics 280
    Socioeconomic Status 286
    Current Economic Problems 288
    The Problem of Marginalized Youth 289
New Latino Immigration: Central and South America
    and the Caribbean 290
Summary 292
Key Terms 292
Questions for Discussion and Critical Thinking. 293

9. Asian Americans: The Myth of the Model Minority . . **295**
The Model Minority: Myth and Reality 296
Japanese Americans 299

The Third Generation and Beyond 300
Changes in the Ethnic Community 301
The Future of the Japanese American Community . 303
Chinese Americans 305
Pre-1965 Developments 305
Post-1965 Developments 308
Korean Americans 312
Immigrant Entrepreneurs 313
Interethnic Conflict 314
Korean Ethnic Churches 315
Adhesive Adaptation. 316
Scenarios for the Future 317
Filipino Americans 318
Immigration Since 1945 320
The Ethnic Community 322
Other Asians 323
Education and Occupation 326
Prejudice and Discrimination 327
Summary 328
Key Terms 329
Questions for Discussion and Critical Thinking. 330

10. **Multicultural Prospects in Comparative Perspective . . 331**
The United States in Comparative Perspective 333
Settler Nations 334
Canada: The Vertical Mosaic 335
Australia: From Settler Country to
Multicultural Nation 339
Western Europe 341
Britain in a Postcolonial World 342
Germany: The Challenge of a 'Blood-and-Soil'
Conception of Citizenship 348
The French Melting Pot 350
A Multicultural America in the
Twenty-First Century 353
Key Terms 356
Questions for Discussion and Critical Thinking. 356

References 357

Photo Credits 401

Author Index 402

Subject Index 409

Preface

R ace and ethnicity have played and continue to play crucial roles in shaping our nation's social, cultural, and political character. The sheer complexity of race and ethnic relations over time, the passions that they evoke, and the problems they have produced make it vitally important for students to expand their understanding of the multicultural world they inhabit. We have written this book with the belief that sociology can perform a vital role in facilitating greater understanding. These assumptions are the basis of this book, which will introduce students to the central importance of race and ethnic relations in America's past and present.

During the past three decades, a veritable flood of work has been published on this subject, which indicates the dramatic escalation of interest in racial and ethnic differences within the academic community as a whole. Not surprisingly, this interest coincides with profound changes in the nature of race and ethnic relations, brought about most dramatically by the civil rights movement and the resumption of mass immigration since 1965. We attempt to make sense of these changes by using the new body of scholarship in an interdisciplinary manner.

In particular, we review recent trends in social history and historical sociology, especially the emphasis among practitioners in these fields to write history "from the bottom up," which is to say, to write about ordinary people who with limited resources and power were nonetheless agents in shaping their own lives. We have used an interpretive theoretical approach to the topic, treating racial and ethnic identities, cultures, communities, and relations as socially constructed and variable. We use this general approach in addressing the long-standing debates between assimilation theory and pluralism, as well as in exploring the more recent scholarly debates over such topics as the ethnic revival, symbolic ethnicity, multiculturalism, and transnationalism.

This book differs from other texts in the field because it is far more historically grounded. In some texts history is simply ignored; in others history functions as essentially a backdrop to the present. This book shows how the past continues to impinge on the present by using in-depth case studies of major racial and ethnic groups. Moreover, the book is structured in terms of historical periods, which allows you to revisit various groups in different sections of the book and trace their particular historical trajectories. Specifically, the book examines three periods, which roughly run from (1) the founding of the republic to the Civil War, (2) the end of the Civil War to the immediate aftermath of World War II, and (3) the middle of the twentieth century up to the present.

A second difference from other texts is that this book has a genuinely comparative perspective. Not only are specific similarities and differ-ences between and among groups highlighted, but also the attention given to distinct differences in terms of time, place, and circumstance will help you comprehend the reasons for differing contemporary situ-ations. For example, this approach is important in understanding the reality of the current Asian experience that makes possible the "myth of the model minority." In addition to these comparisons of ethnic groups within the United States, the concluding chapter explores national comparisons by looking at a number of similar advanced industrial na-tions.

This book is also unique because of the attention given to the inner workings of racial and ethnic communities, including extended discus-sions of aspects of particular groups' cultures, institutions, leaders, re-sources, and internal divisions. This connects to the concept of seeing members of groups as makers of their own lives and histories. The book pays considerable attention to the impact of prejudice, discrimination, and exploitation. But unlike some texts, it resists the reductionist temp-tation to view racial and ethnic minorities as mere victims. Ample evi-dence of legacies of oppression is complemented by extensive inquiries into the various ways that individuals have responded and groups mo-bilized to combat oppression and discrimination and to improve their situations.

One aspect of internal differences within groups revolves around other important social divisions, particularly class and gender differ-ences. This book is distinctive in its attempt to reveal the interconnec-tions and the tensions that exist between race and ethnicity and both class and gender. Thus, rather than viewing women as a distinct minor-ity group, accorded a chapter in a manner parallel to chapters on Afri-can Americans and Jewish Americans, this book seeks to understand, for example, how the experiences of Irish women differ from those of both Irish men and women from other groups. Another division—that of age or generation—is also discussed in greater detail here than in other texts.

We believe that W. E. B. Du Bois was in fundamental ways right when he wrote, in 1903, the "problem of the twentieth century is the problem of the color-line." This book, unlike most textbooks, has a thematic core, one that seeks to indicate the continuing validity of Du Bois's claim as we proceed through the first decade of the twenty-first century. Understanding is a prerequisite for any attempts to create a more equitable and just social order. Without preaching or indoctrinating, this book will help you better understand our highly diverse society. This book is a sustained attempt to illustrate the continuing significance of sociology in identifying and assessing both the dynamics of racial conflicts and the forces that might serve to create a more harmonious society.

Acknowledgments

Peter Kivisto would like to single out two people who were, in their own ways, especially helpful. Werner Sollors, from Harvard University, has not only commented on various parts of the first edition of this work but has also been generous in the extreme in responding to both versions of previous work and to numerous queries. He is chiefly responsible for providing us with the title of the book. Second, the late Stanford M. Lyman was Kivisto's mentor at the New School for Social Research. For almost 30 years, Peter benefited from his critical insights and his unflagging support. A number of other scholars have helped clarify issues pursued in this book. Some have done so by engaging in ongoing dialogues and debates over the years. Others have provided useful comments on various sections of the book or related work. Among those Kivisto would like to single out for thanks are Richard Alba, Thomas Archdeacon, Raymond Breton, Rose Brewer, John Bodnar, Martin Bulmer, Kathleen Conzen, Thomas Faist, Herbert Gans, Philip Gleason, Steven J. Gold, Melvin Holli, James McKee, Fred Matthews, Tariq Modood, Ewa Morawska, Joane Nagel, Alejandro Portes, Moses Rischin, Rubén Rumbaut, Rudy Vecoli, Arthur Vidich, and R. Stephen Warner.

On the home front, Peter's wife, Susan, and children, Sarah and Aaron, have been involved in the everyday routines of writing for many years and have been consistent sources of both inspiration and diversion. Although they may not always realize it, they have made it all worthwhile.

Wendy Ng would like to acknowledge the support of the College of Social Sciences at San Jose State University. In particular, she would like to single out two colleagues in the Sociology Department, Peter Chua and Scott Myers-Lipton, for their support in the revisions of this edition. More important, she would like to extend special thanks to her students at San Jose State, particularly those who have taken her Sociology of Race and Ethnic Relations course and who continue to provide useful comments and engage in stimulating dialogues about issues related to race and ethnicity in today's world.

Wendy's husband, Roger Jue, and her children, Justin and Natalie, always know that she is doing nonstop "homework," and in fact her children have concluded that having a college professor for a parent means a lifetime of "homework." Their support has been invaluable. Finally, in the final months of her writing revisions, Wendy's father, Henry Ng, passed away. During his last weeks in hospice care, he continued to take an active interest in this book project, continually asking her how it was going. Henry was a merchant seaman by trade, traveling the world to provide for his family. He valued education and provided the support and encouragement Wendy needed to succeed at university. The dream of a college education for himself eluded him until after he retired, but his love of education led him to work on a degree late in life. He received his diploma in 1994, when he was 69 years old.

Margaret Abraham, Hofstra University; Peter Adler, University of Denver; Donna Barnes, University of Wyoming; James Button, University of Florida, Gainesville; Joseph Carroll, Colby-Sawyer College; Valerie Carter, University of Maine; Grant Farr, Portland State University; Clarence Lo, University of Missouri, Columbia; David Musick, University of Northern Colorado; and C. Gray Swicegood, University of Illinois, Urbana, provided perceptive and extremely helpful reviews for the first edition of this book. Richard Alba, State University of New York, Albany; Rose M. Brewer, University of Minnesota; Delores Cleary, Central Washington University; Rodney Coates, Miami University; Mary Yu Danico, California State University—Pomona; Kevin Delaney, Temple University; Jo M. Dohoney, Stanford University; Martin Eisenberg, City University of New York, Staten Island; Thomas D. Hall, DePauw University; Allen Martin, University of Texas—Tyler; Theresa A. Martinez, University of Utah; Amy J. Orr, Linfield College; Matthew Oware, DePauw University; Silvia Pedraza, University of Michigan; Anne Rawls, Bentley University; Alan Siman, San Diego State University; Rachel Sullivan, University of Connecticut; Hector Velez, Ithaca College; and Lynne M. Woehrle, Wilson College offered similarly insightful reviews for this second edition.

Finally, Danielle Romano served as our editorial assistant. A sociology major at Augustana College and editor of the campus newspaper, Danielle proved herself to be a diligent and highly skilled editor, researcher, and fact checker. We deeply appreciate her contribution to this project. ✦

Part I

Thinking About
Race and Ethnicity

Chapter 1

Ethnic and Racial Dimensions

The United States has always been a nation of nations—a society composed of numerous and diverse ethnic, racial, and religious communities. Long before the birth of the nation the continent served as a magnet for settlers from Europe and as the final destination for African victims of the slave trade. For 500 years the indigenous peoples of North America confronted wave after wave of sojourners and settlers, first from a select number of western European countries and later from the rest of Europe, from various points in Asia, from Africa, from Latin America, and from virtually every other place on the face of the globe (Hughes and Hughes, 1952). Though the ebb and flow of immigration has varied over time, immigration has never completely ceased, and the result is a composite population that is perhaps more heterogeneous than that of any other nation in the world (Handlin, 1959). One upbeat commentator characterized America as the "first universal nation" (Wattenberg, 1991). However, the ability of the many groups inhabiting the nation to live in relative harmony has always been precarious, requiring individuals and groups to engage in a constant renegotiation of their rights and obligations. Americans have had to define and redefine what it means to be a citizen in a pluralist society (Williams, 1977).

For example, what did citizenship mean for black Americans denied the right to vote in many southern states prior to the 1960s? What does it mean now that the right to vote has been extended to them and is in fact backed up by federal law? What do white southerners think about this change? Similarly, why were Native Americans denied citizenship rights until 1924, even though their ancestors had inhabited the land long before the arrival of Europeans? What does it mean for them today to be simultaneously citizens of the United States and of various tribal nations? What do nonIndians think about such "dual allegiances"? Why were the Chinese denied the right to become naturalized citizens until 1943, despite the fact that they had arrived in the United States as early as the mid-nineteenth century? What does citizenship mean for contemporary transnational immigrants? Asking these kinds of questions is essential if we are to understand the powerful impact that race and ethnicity have had throughout the history of the United States.

History and Social Structure

This book provides you with the tools needed to arrive at a better understanding of the ethnic dimension of America's collective social life. These tools include a variety of concepts and a theoretical perspective that can serve to make sense of what would otherwise be a mind-boggling mountain of facts. The conceptual map in Chapter 2 provides a way to look at both history and social structure.

Unlike many sociological studies of ethnicity, this book pays considerable attention to history because, as we shall see, the past continues to exert its influence on the present in many ways that people often fail to appreciate. Social historians and historical sociologists have attempted to bring sociology and history into fruitful contact in an effort to better understand the past. We extensively review the works of many scholars operating in this interdisciplinary arena, especially in Part II.

Social structure refers to persistent, orderly, and patterned institutional arrangements of a society, including the systematic distribution of power and various resources possessed by individuals and groups. Social structure entails constraints, and those constraints are more burdensome for those with the least power and the fewest resources. For example, if discrimination prevents some categories of people from obtaining jobs that pay well, those people will be forced, because of economic circumstances, to live in inadequate housing in ghetto neighborhoods. There, among other things, they will find schools inferior to those located elsewhere. Their children will thus be prevented from obtaining an education that would allow them to work their way out of poverty. Clearly, social structure can and does perpetuate social inequalities over time. But social structure also enables people to act: It makes possible certain kinds of activity that would otherwise be impossible. For example, in a country with democratic values and the rule of law, disenfranchised groups can challenge existing social arrangements. Legal challenges to job discrimination can be mounted, and political campaigns can be mobilized to elect officials committed to social change.

Social structure has a profound impact on the lives of members of a society, and it is a central focus throughout this book. But social structure should not be seen as simply determining the outcomes of individual opportunities, with people as mere puppets, pulled by the strings of powerful social forces. Individuals are the products of their social world, but they also have a say in what that world will look like. Thus, it is not enough to look only at social structure. We must examine how people—as individuals and also as members of collectivities—go about the business of shaping, changing, preserving, and otherwise responding to their social environment.

This chapter highlights a number of problems that confront anyone trying to comprehend the role played by ethnicity and ethnic relations in American life. Problems arise when we try to (1) understand ethnicity as a lived phenomenon that is experienced differently by different people; (2) define the nature of the ethnic group; (3) identify the characteristic patterns of interethnic relations in the nation; and (4) depict ethnic America as a whole. Each of these problems will be explored in the remainder of this chapter.

We see at the outset an extraordinarily complex picture. Making sense of that picture requires that we pay attention to several levels of analysis. It is essential to study both individuals and the circumstances in which they find themselves. One level focuses on individual social actors in the process of creating and defining their own lives. Here we are interested in their beliefs, their desires, and the motives behind their actions. The second level locates individuals in concrete historical and geographical circumstances. Here we are interested in how changing circumstances serve either to constrain or to enable individuals in their social interactions. The focus shifts to the group and to both intergroup and intragroup relations.

In sociology, both individual and group analyses are seen as operating at the micro level. In contrast, the third, or macro, level is primarily concerned with the whole rather than with the parts—with American society in general rather than with the discrete ethnic pieces that constitute it. The macro level entails examining the impact of the state, economic conditions, and cultural factors on ethnics and ethnic groups, as well as the impact that the ethnic factor has on the society as a totality. As we will see in Chap-

Howard Chandler Christy's World War I poster promoted the idea of national unity despite ethnic differences.

ter 2, these levels interpenetrate each other, and such analytic distinctions should not be equated with a view that sees them as empirically discrete or autonomous.

Five Lives: Identities and Experiences

Ethnic and racial backgrounds can be a benefit or a burden and are more or less important to different individuals. People attempt to embrace their ethnic ancestries or repudiate them. Ethnic and racial identities are a source of pride or shame. People accept their identities as givens that cannot be changed or attempt to modify them in some respects. In short, people experience race and ethnicity in a multiplicity of ways. Consider the following examples, which are not meant to be representative but rather are intended to suggest something of the wide range of possible encounters with the ethnic factor and with racism in America.

An Italian American

Jerre Mangione was born in 1909 and grew up in Rochester, New York. His parents were Italian immigrants who, with relatives and other acquaintances from their native Sicilian village, immigrated to America in search of economic opportunities that did not exist at home. In his memoirs, Mangione relates what it was like to grow up in a world that was at once a southern Italian village transplanted in urban, industrial America and at the same time a bustling metropolis inhabited by an incredibly diverse array of people.

For some, the Old World remained a source of solace and comfort because traditional values and modes of conduct were preserved. For Mangione, and others like him, his parents' world was increasingly too parochial, and the lure of America created a gulf between him and his parents. He recalls, for example, that he "became increasingly resentful of my parents for being more foreign than anyone else. It irked me that I had not been born of English-speaking parents" (Mangione, 1978: 14). For their part, his parents wanted their children to remain close to them and their culture while being successful.

These dual goals caused a complicated bind for his parents but also provided them with a way of reconciling their differences with their children. In school, Mangione found himself identifying with Jews more than fellow Italians because in his view the former were more interested in intellectual pursuits and the latter were too boisterous. His route out of the transplanted village was accomplished not by open rebellion, however, but by entering Syracuse University. Though his parents and relatives felt a sense of loss when he departed for the university, they also felt a sense of pride and expectation regarding their son's future. Thus, coming of age for Mangione entailed maintaining a relationship with his family while distancing himself from his inherited immigrant culture.

A Mexican American

In a different place and a generation later, echoes of this narrative are heard again. Richard Rodriguez grew up in Sacramento, California, the son of Mexican immigrants. Sent to Roman Catholic parochial school by his parents, he began his education knowing very little English. The nuns at the school told his parents that to be successful he would have to learn English. His parents and the school encouraged Rodriguez to break with his native tongue, and he became a scholarship student. As a beneficiary of affirmative action programs, he went to Stanford University and then on to graduate school at Columbia University and the University of California at Berkeley.

As with Mangione, education was a vehicle for Rodriguez's upward mobility and for entry into a cosmopolitan American society. In his autobiography, poignantly titled *Hunger of Memory* (1981), Rodriguez reflected on the painful side of this move. A major consequence of his educational success was his growing distance from the Spanish language and with it the ability to communicate freely and easily with his parents. This situation led to a "bewildering silence" that served to separate parent from child, a state of affairs that was never overcome—Rodriguez's mother later referred to him as "Mr. Secrets" (Rodriguez, 1981: 5, 173–195). There is, in short, a tragic dimension to this account that is lacking in the preceding one.

This autobiography introduces another dimension: race. Although many things contributed to childhood insecurity, perhaps none was more significant than skin coloration. Rodriguez's dark skin was a source of shame and inferiority, partly the result of racial slurs directed at him but also the result of his reaction to the way Mexican Americans viewed complexion. He knew about home remedies designed to lighten skin color (a mixture of egg white and lemon juice concentrate), and he understood the aesthetic implications of such efforts: Beauty was associated with fair or light skin. He also realized that his mother saw dark skin as the "most important symbol of a life of oppressive labor and poverty" (Rodriguez, 1981: 119).

Rodriguez became alienated from his body: the scholarship boy would develop his mind to compensate for the inadequacies of his body. In adulthood, Rodriguez continued to wrestle with the social implications attached to such physical attributes as skin color. In subsequent writings, such as *Days of Obligation* (1992), he also reflected on other elements of his identity, including his relationship to Roman Catholicism and his homosexuality.

An African American

For Maya Angelou, a black woman growing up in the American South, race loomed large as a force shaping her life. Like Rodriguez, she was a victim of the aesthetic view that valued whiteness, and she sometimes fantasized about waking from her "black ugly dream" and finding her "kinky mass" of hair replaced by long blonde locks (Angelou, 1969: 2). Unlike Rodriguez, however, she also confronted a virulent form of racism. Far from the heterogeneous ethnic milieu of Mangione's Rochester, the segregated South was defined by a much simpler divide: the "color line" separated black from white.

Furthermore, it was understood that white supremacy was challenged only at great risk. Angelou relates an incident in which the grandmother who helped raise her was informed that "[a] crazy nigger messed with a white lady today" and therefore night riders would be combing the countryside in search of a black male who would likely be the victim of a lynching. Angelou was forced to participate in the indignity of hiding her crippled uncle Willie to protect him from such vigilante "justice" by covering him with potatoes and onions in a storage bin. The precariousness of black life was an everyday reality, though she learned to hold in check any public expression of contempt for many whites, whom she saw as "cement faces [with] eyes of hate" that exhibited a perverse desire to perpetuate the "ugliness and rottenness" of racial oppression (Angelou, 1969: 14–15).

In many ways, Angelou's early life paralleled that of Richard Wright, who, in his powerful chronicle of his formative years, *Black Boy* (1937), concluded that active resistance to oppression was futile and that the options available to him were inadequate: being the "genial slave," internalizing anger and directing it toward other blacks, or seeking escape in sex and alcohol. Rejecting each of these, he decided that his only chance to succeed on his own terms entailed migrating to the North. The important difference between Angelou's and Wright's respective experiences was gender. At age 8, Angelou was raped. In reflecting on this and subsequent events, she concluded that

> [t]he Black female is assaulted in her tender years by all those common forces of nature at the same time that she is caught in the tripartite crossfire of masculine prejudice, white illogical hate and Black lack of power. (Angelou, 1969: 231)

A Chinese American

Jade Snow Wong was born in San Francisco's Chinatown. Her father was a businessman in the Chinese enclave, who, as a Christian convert, was not as traditional as some of his contemporaries. Nonetheless, his wife had had her feet bound in childhood, and he considered both her and their six daughters inferior to men. After 15 years of anxious waiting by the father, the first male child in the family was born, named Forgiveness from Heaven. Then Wong clearly understood the subservient role of women in the Chinese family (Wong, 1945). Despite this role and the rather rigid demands for filial obedience and respect for elders, her early years were far less traumatic than those of Maya Angelou.

Jade Snow Wong's family sought to preserve much of Chinese culture, including language, while collectively partaking of such aspects of American mass culture as the newspaper comic sections and movies, where "they shared the excitement of six-shooters, posses, runaway stagecoaches, striking cobras, the unconquerable Tarzan, and organized apes" (Wong, 1945: 71). Only as she got older did Wong begin to feel the tension between the world of Chinatown and that of the larger host society.

While attending college (a decision she made that was viewed ambivalently by her parents), she began to distance herself from Chinatown. Upon learning in a sociology class that in America children are considered individuals with rights and an ability to make their own decisions, she came to the stark realization that her parents "had not left the Chinese world of thirty years ago." This provoked her into an act of rebellion when she decided to accept an offer to go to the movies with a young man without first asking for her father's permission. This seemingly inconsequential challenge to authority was of major significance for Wong insofar as it provided her with what she would describe as "a measure of freedom" (Wong, 1945: 125–129).

Subsequently, Wong learned that gender discrimination, though manifested differently, existed in American society. For her, it was overlaid with racial discrimination. Ultimately, Wong established her independence by becoming a potter, but she set up a shop in Chinatown, preserving her ties to the ethnic community in contradistinction, for example, to Mangione.

A Native American

N. Scott Momaday is an American Indian, or Amerindian—a member of the Kiowa tribe. His memoir, *The Names* (1976), is both an autobiographical account of his childhood and adolescence and an act of recovery and imagination. It is a lyrical portrait of the author's sense of connectedness with his ancestors and with the lands they inhabited. In stark contrast to Angelou and Wong, there is no discussion of prejudice and discrimination. He describes matter-of-factly the world of his grandfather: "the Kiowas had been routed in the Indian wars, the great herds of buffalo had been destroyed, and the sun dance prohibited by law." He describes his grandfather's understanding that in the wake of this tribal catastrophe, he "had his own life to live" and he sustained himself as a farmer (Momaday, 1976: 28–29).

Actually, Momaday's mother was not a full-blooded Native American, and she only gradually came to see herself as an American Indian, a journey undertaken later by her son. Momaday grew up in a middle-class home. Both his parents were college educated and, like their son, were artists and teachers. Because Momaday's mother had a tense relationship with her parents, the family decided to move from Oklahoma to the Southwest, and so Momaday grew up among Navajo and Jemez peoples rather than the Kiowa. Momaday's embrace of his heritage was thus not restricted to a particular tribe but was decidedly pan-Indian.

Momaday's description of his relationship with his parents suggests an idyllic childhood in which many of the anxieties and generational conflicts noted in the previous vignettes appear to have been absent. Similarly, his relationships with other Native Americans, as well as with nonIndians, are depicted as being remarkably unproblematic. Perhaps because his parents had already, by entering the middle class, established a bridge between the two cultures, Momaday conveys in the memoir a sense of his ability to live comfortably in both Indian and nonIndian worlds. Momaday planned for his college education with parental help, not resistance, which Mangione and Wong faced. Thus, Momaday described a scene in which he pored over college catalogues with his father and mother. Like his parents, he evidently thought that moving into the societal mainstream did not mean that being Indian would lose its relevance.

Generalizing From the Specific Case

What can these brief synopses of five lives reveal about the ethnic experience? First and foremost, they provide insights into the subjective character of ethnicity, illustrating differing influences on the creation and maintenance of personal identities. Second, these vivid and poignant writings permit us access to the inner world of these writers, providing us with an opportunity to understand the pain, joy, anger, ambiguity, and sustenance that ethnic identity and affiliation can provoke. These stories help us appreciate the varied and complicated nature of this phenomenon. For this reason, autobiographies are an invaluable resource. So are other documentary resources, such as letters and oral histories, as well as literary sources, for the fiction and poetry of ethnics can be read not simply for their artistic merit but also as social-historical documents (Skardal, 1974; Early, 1993; Ferraro, 1993). Finally, the ethnographic tradition in sociology and anthropology has made considerable contributions, such as *Street Corner Society* (1943), William Foote Whyte's classic study of an Italian slum, and *Tally's Corner* (1967), Elliot Liebow's highly acclaimed study of black ghetto men. This tradition continues today, as can be seen in the influential work of scholars such as Elijah Anderson (2000) and Katherine Newman (2000).

These sources reveal much, but they also raise questions that are not easily answered. The initial question covers the representativeness of these five examples: How typical are they? For example, to what extent can Mangione be seen as typical of the Italian immigrant? Did most second-generation Italians seek liberation from the confines of America's Little Italies the way he did, or were most intent on preserving their ties to the ethnic community? As a Sicilian, and thus the offspring of parents from Italy's most economically underdeveloped region, did Mangione have experiences similar to or profoundly different from the experiences of northern Italians, who migrated from a region that had witnessed greater industrialization?

Similar questions can be directed at the other four examples. Can we speak about Rodriguez's case as an instance of the Hispanic experience (thereby including Mexicans, Puerto Ricans, Cubans, and other Latin Americans), or should we limit the scope of generalization only to the Mexican American experience? How is Wong's account of life in Chinatown similar to or different from the experiences of Japanese, Korean, and Filipino Americans? Does the pan-Indian sensibility conveyed in Momaday's memoir capture the worldview of the far less cosmopolitan, poor American Indians who have spent their lives on isolated reservations? Does Angelou's life in the rural South dovetail with or significantly diverge from the lives of African Americans resid-

---

Voices   **Chief Fomoaley**

I am Chief Fomoaley, of the Bontac Igorrotes, and I have come to the United States with my people in order to show the white people our civilization. The white man that lives in our town asked me to come, and said that Americans were anxious to see us. Since we have been here great crowds of white people have come and watched us, and they seem pleased.

We are the oldest people in the world. All others come from us. The first man and woman—there were two women—lived on our mountains and their children lived there after them, till they grew bad and God sent a great flood that drowned them, all except seven, who escaped in a canoe and landed, after the flood went down, on a high mountain.

Three times a year our old men call the people together and tell them the old stories of how God made the world and then the animals, and lastly men. These stories have been handed down in that way from the very beginning, so that we know they are true. The white men have some stories, too, like that. Perhaps they may have heard them from one of us. At any rate, they are wrong about some things.

Chief Fomoaley was a leader of a tribe from the Philippines who, in the early twentieth century, worked at the amusement park at Coney Island (Holt, 1991: 139–140).

ing in inner-city ghettos in northern cities? How typical is her portrait of the role of the extended family for African Americans? The questions about ethnic identity go on and on.

We must note that each of the five people presented are or were skilled writers whom we have come to know based on their books. All five are considered professionally accomplished. This fact suggests that in some fundamental way these individuals are decidedly atypical.

Making Visible the Invisible

Many ordinary people also provide documentation of their lives, sometimes at the behest of interested journalists or scholars. One autobiographical collection of particular note exists because of the initiative of social reformer and journalist Hamilton Holt, who commissioned a diverse array of individuals to write or to narrate for transcription brief autobiographical sketches, or what he called "lifelets." First published in 1906, *The Life Stories of Undistinguished Americans, as Told by Themselves* (Holt, 1991) is a collection that includes, in the language of the time, the life stories of a Polish sweatshop girl, an Italian bootblack, a Negro peon, a Chinese man, an Irish cook, and a Syrian clerk. This vivid and often blunt work illustrates the ability of ordinary people to provide articulate and compelling accounts of their lives. Nonetheless, even here the same questions must be raised, though these individuals are probably more representative of their peers than our five cases.

Some suggest such documents should not be considered serious resources for social scientific or historical inquiry. But just like any other type of data, this kind of material can be used beneficially only if its limitations are appreciated and if interpretations are made with great care. The best way to ensure that autobiographical material is used appropriately is to juxtapose it with other data. Assessments of any first-person document require determining whether the person in question is unique or even idiosyncratic or is in some important ways typical of many other members of an ethnic group. The person must be placed into context, by considering the historical time frame, the particular place, and the circumstances and events in which (and often in response to which) a document was created.

Most ordinary people, however, have not left documentary traces that could help elucidate the character of their lives and the distinctive role of ethnicity in shaping those lives. The limited quantity of evidence available to scholars has produced, at least in part, what historian Anne Firor Scott (1984) has referred to as the "historical invisibility" of such people. Because ordinary people are often viewed as objects of history rather than as subjects who have a role in shaping their social world, ethnicity was for a long time a relatively neglected dimension in history and the social sciences (Vecoli, 1970).

The considerable body of scholarship produced during the past quarter century by sociologists and historians, and particularly by those operating at the boundary between the disciplines—historical sociologists and social historians—has done much to remedy this neglect (Kivisto, 1990; Morawska, 1990; Archdeacon, 1985; Vecoli, 1979). Furthermore, by treating ordinary people as subjects of history, as authors of their own lives, such work has sought to make visible that which was heretofore invisible.

Why Can't They Be Like Us?

Two pitfalls in the study of ethnicity must be identified. The first pitfall—borrowing from a title of one of sociologist Andrew Greeley's (1971) books—is reflected in the question, "Why can't they be like us?"

Although generalizations about the constituent members of different groups and comparisons between and among groups are essential, they become distorted when ethnocentrism intrudes. The term **ethnocentrism** was coined by the early American sociologist William Graham Sumner (1940 [1906]: 13–15) to refer to the tendency to use one's own group as a standard or norm by which to assess other groups. This practice yields invidious comparisons. Insofar as the individual's membership group is viewed as a positive ideal, all other groups are judged by how far they deviate from this ideal; groups relatively similar to the membership group are evaluated more favorably, whereas groups manifesting greater differences are judged negatively. Ethnocentrism can affect any study of ethnicity. It is frequently a problem when members of privileged or dominant groups in a society seek to describe and assess less privileged and relatively powerless groups.

Nobody Knows the Trouble I've Seen

Conversely, the second pitfall emanates from members of groups who are less privileged and relatively powerless, from groups falling victim to ostracism and oppression. Some members of such groups argue that the essence of what it means to be a member of that particular group can only be lived and experienced; it cannot be comprehended from the outside. Ethnic identity is therefore fundamentally ineffable, its meaning and significance being accessible only to insiders. This pitfall, which stems from what sociologist Robert Merton (1972) has called the **insider-outsider debate,** denies the social scientist or historian the ability to provide valid interpretive accounts of ethnic group life and the beliefs and actions of members therein—unless that scholar also happens to be a member of that particular group.

Accepting this position means denying the possibility that the human condition is sufficiently universal to transcend ethnic differences. This position, which Merton dubbed "extreme insiderism," also implicitly denies that the tools used by social scientists and historians can actually add to our ability to know or to understand. This view suggests that the questions posed after the five brief autobiographical glimpses presented earlier are unanswerable.

Peter Rose (1978: 25) has responded to the "extreme insider" position by suggesting that scholars can overcome the difficulties of being an outsider insofar as they are able to "experience things vicariously." Scholars cannot provide first-person accounts, and they should not be apologists for their subjects. Scholars contribute distinctive modes of inquiry that emphasize comparative studies that constantly move back and forth between the particularities of distinct groups or subgroups and more general patterns of social action and interaction. As Rose (1978: 27) notes, all groups

> institutionalize their behavior patterns, set criteria for the conferring or denying of status, indicate the tolerance limits of accepted and expected behavior, and maintain social systems of great intricacy even when they, themselves, have great difficulty articulating their character.

Social scientists and historians can use their methods and theories to assist all of us—insiders as well as outsiders—in comprehending how these processes occur for different groups at various times and places.

Ethnic Groups

Rose's discussion shifts the focus of analysis from the individual to the ethnic group. Individuals as members of varying ethnic groups are shaped by the distinctive character of those groups. Therefore, we must understand the dynamics of ethnic group formation, maintenance, transformation, erosion, revival, and the like. Indeed, in the chapters that follow, intergroup and intragroup relations will receive more attention than the individual's experience of ethnicity. Underlying each level of analysis, however, is an appreciation that all groups are the creations of social actors acting in complex ways with others.

What groups are we interested in examining? Because ethnic groups are socially constructed and defined, what is and what is not an ethnic group can change over time and in different places. Definitions will be contested, with some opting for one definition and others for an alternative definition. Two examples can help explain this situation. First, consider a man who immigrates to America directly from Spain (that is, not via Latin America). He might consider himself to be a Spaniard or a Spanish American. This perception might be reinforced by those around him in America and by officially sanctioned definitions. If, however, he came from the Basque region in Spain, not only might he prefer to be seen as a Basque, but if he supports the claims of

Basque nationalism, he might vehemently deny that he is a Spaniard and might prefer to use the term *Euskaldunak*, which refers to those who speak Euskera (Guibernau, 1999; Douglass and Bilbao, 1975).

Second, consider a woman departing from Sicily in the nineteenth century. Her understanding of who she is may well revolve around the village or region she came from. Thus, she sees herself as Sicilian, not Italian. Once in America she may slowly come to redefine her self-image—aided and abetted by the definitions imposed on her by those she encounters in America. Her sense of being a Sicilian may give way or merge first with a sense of being an Italian and still later be transformed into being an Italian American (Foerster, 1919).

Group Definitions and Boundaries

Although the boundary parameters of a particular group may not be disputed, there may be a question about whether it is an *ethnic* group. The *Harvard Encyclopedia of American Ethnic Groups* (hereafter the *HEAEG*, Thernstrom, Orlov, and Handlin, 1980) includes in the list of groups represented the following: Amish, Copts, Hutterites, and Mormons. The advisory editors of this volume concluded that these groups met the criteria for inclusion in the encyclopedia as bona fide ethnic groups, although some might protest that these are religious groups and not ethnic groups. Appalachians, however, are not accorded an entry, though some have contended that an ethnic group is emerging out of this region of the United States (Marger and Obermiller, 1983).

The matter of who gets included within the boundaries of a group and who gets excluded introduces further complications. Who in America is black? What if one quarter of an individual's ancestry is white? Is that person black? What about the person whose ancestry is half black and half white? What about the person whose ancestry is $\frac{1}{32}$ black and $\frac{31}{32}$ white (Davis, 1991)? Where do we locate in America's racial definitions those people described in the *HEAEG* as "tri-racial isolates," peoples with ancestries derived from white, black, and American Indian origins (Berry, 1963)? Why, in contrast to most of the rest of the world, does this country not recognize any mixed racial categories between black and white—such as the designation "mulatto" (Starr, 1992: 274; see also Perlmann and Waters, 2002)?

The related issue of the relationship between race and ethnicity poses further problems. Those today referred to as African Americans are also referred to as blacks (and have been designated at other times as Negroes and Afro-Americans). Two of these definitions—Negroes and blacks—emphasize race, whereas the other two find their parallel with other ethnic groups: Irish Americans, Chinese Americans, Mexican Americans, and so forth. Is a person with ancestry derived from Africa necessarily an African American? For instance, what about such a person who happens to have been born and raised in the Dominican Republic? Is that person black? Is that person an African American?

Choosing Names

Finally, what we call various ethnic groups has changed over time, and there is often a lively debate over which name is preferred, as the example of black Americans illustrates. For people of African descent, *Negro* was the most commonly used label up to the 1960s, when the term *black* came to replace it. In the late 1960s, a majority of African Americans preferred Negro over black, but that changed. Now if one sees the word *Negro* in print, it is a good indication that the publication was written prior to 1970. The term *Afro-American* also received some popularity, though it gave way by the 1980s to *African American*. Today both *African American* and *black* are widely used both inside and outside of the group.

Similar shifts can be seen for Hispanics, partly because some ethnics prefer to use a particular national identity, such as Cuban or Mexican, rather than the more pan-ethnic label *Hispanic*. The term *Latino* vies at present for general acceptance with *Hispanic*.

The indigenous peoples of the North American continent have also carried different labels. Through much of the past, the term *Indian* was imposed on them by Europeans. During the 1960s this term was held in disrepute, and the term *Native American* gained in popularity and general usage. More recently, the term *Indian* has gained a comeback in usage, along with the related designations *American Indian* and *Amerindian*.

These examples show the fluid, imprecise, ambiguous, and sometimes contradictory character of group definitions. We are studying social constructs that human beings are continually renegotiating and articulating.

An immigrant barber from Trinidad in his shop.

Intergroup Relations

Groups undergo this continual process of redefinition, and their members seek to advance their individual and the group's interests by interacting with other groups. Thus, the next dimension we'll consider is that of intergroup relations.

Although not the whole story, submerged tensions and overt conflicts have characterized much of the history of ethnic relations. From

Benjamin Franklin's condemnation of the use of the German language in America during the nation's founding period to the current acrimonious debates concerning bilingual education in the public schools, the future of transplanted cultures in general, and language maintenance in particular, has been an open question. From the first concerted attempt to curtail open immigration—the passage of the Chinese Exclusion Act of 1882—to the incarceration of the Mariel boat people (refugees from Communist Cuba), ethnic factors have been at the core of the discourse about who should and who should not be accepted into American society. From the first treaties enacted between American Indians and the United States government to the current court cases brought by various tribes demanding the enforcement of nineteenth-century treaties permitting tribal governments to claim sizable areas across the country, North American native peoples have sought to deal with the consequences of conquest. From the many slave revolts and conspiracies that occurred prior to the Civil War to the numerous urban riots of the 1960s, African Americans have challenged the persistent legacy of racial oppression and injustice.

Competition for jobs has historically been an important source of friction among groups. This can be seen in the rise of the labor movement in the twentieth century, when nonwhites were frequently denied union membership (racial animosity thereby serving as a barrier to class solidarity) and in the current battle over affirmative action programs to redress past discrimination.

Paralleling competition in the economic arena is the recurring quest for political power. For example, at the local level, the political machines that became a crucial force in many American cities during the late nineteenth and early twentieth centuries pitted various ethnic groups against both the native-born and other ethnic groups, meanwhile ensuring that others were effectively denied the political franchise. Today, in the process of ethnic succession (in which ethnic groups that have obtained sufficient rewards exit declining cities for the suburbs), the groups have changed, but the struggle for what is perceived to be an equitable piece of the pie continues.

In the cultural realm, newcomers, outsiders, and marginalized peoples have always wrestled with the implications for their own culture of various modes of adaptation to and acceptance of the dominant culture. Whether they opted to embrace incorporation into the larger culture (and thereby forsake their inherited cultural tradition), resist such incorporation, or blend ancestral with American cultures is and has been an ongoing decision that members of ethnic groups have had to make. Doing so means responding to the demands imposed by political and cultural elites intent on Americanizing the diverse peoples of the nation in an image solely defined by these elites.

Although much has changed over time, these examples suggest that the potential for conflict remains and imply that understanding the present requires understanding the past. The problems generated by ethnic differences have not been resolved. Some groups have improved their lot in America with each succeeding generation, while for others the picture is not so clear. Some groups have a vested interest in preserving the status quo, whereas others are intent on effecting various kinds of social change. In the continuing drama of social reality, the ethnic dimension of that drama continues to be a powerful divisive force.

Mutual hostility and conflict, however, do not tell the whole story. Ethnic history amply illustrates the myriad ways in which many people from differing ancestral backgrounds have managed to forge cooperative and harmonious relationships with many outside of their own ethnic group. In towns and cities where ethnic groups have lived and continue to live side by side with other groups, what historian Rudolph Vecoli (1991) refers to as a "spirit of neighborliness" became a common characteristic of everyday social life: People care for their neighbors' sick children, help neighbors through tough economic times, and so on, regardless of ethnic identities. Similarly, in the workplace and in schools, various modes of mutual accommodation and working together have been established. Ethnic differences have not prevented friendships from developing, and the willingness to marry across group boundaries is a powerful testament to people's abilities to transcend ethnic divisions.

On the other hand, another way that group members have related to others is simply by avoiding contact. Many new immigrants report confronting neither overt hostility nor cooperation but rather a sense of isolation from people outside of their own group, combined with a feeling that they are being kept at a distance.

The Big Picture: What Is Ethnic America?

Earlier we asked what it meant to be an ethnic in America. An equally crucial question is this: What does it mean to be an American? Can we speak about a typical American as, for example, the principal characters do in Gish Jen's (1991) novel about an extended Chinese family in post-World War II America? In the novel, the immigrant protagonists find themselves talking about the "typical American" when they want to criticize people and their behaviors. When irritated, they complain about a "typical American no-morals" or a "typical American just-dumb." What is interesting in this fictional illustration is that the characters find it increasingly difficult to decide what is and what is not "typical" the longer they are in America. They have learned to appreciate the complexity and the diversity contained within what can be called the American character.

Perceptive outsiders who have traveled throughout the country—from Alexis de Tocqueville in *Democracy in America* (1981 [1835]) after his visit to America a century and a half ago to the more recent visitor Jean Baudrillard (1988: 82)—have commented on this phenomenon.

Discussions about ethnicity in America often rely on metaphors and evocative images designed to capture the social relationships created by an extraordinarily heterogeneous population. Anselm Strauss (1991: 287) explained this tendency:

> The early decision to throw the country open to virtually all peoples of the world was fateful for the nation, and consequential for the development of American imageries, including those pertaining to mobility, rurality, cities, frontier, and industrialization.

The United States has been described in numerous ways, including as a melting pot, a mosaic, a symphonic orchestra, a salad bowl, and a kaleidoscope. The "first new nation," a "nation of nations," and the "first universal nation" are only a few of the images used at various times. Why do we so frequently use these and similar characterizations of America's ethnic character? Two primary reasons account for this. First, the sheer complexity of America encourages, and perhaps even demands, attempts to generalize and to provide an overarching picture of the American scene. Second, these metaphors and images have built into them not only descriptions about what America looks like but also evaluations about how it ought to look.

The Melting Pot

Without doubt the **melting pot** has been the most powerful and enduring metaphor, but as historian Philip Gleason (1964) suggested, this symbol of fusion has also been a source of considerable confusion. To a greater or lesser extent, our thinking about ethnicity has been shaped by this particular metaphor; we should examine it to better understand its impact on our thought (Rumbaut, 2005; Jacoby, 2004).

The notion of America as a place where diverse peoples are melded, blended, or fused has a long history. Perhaps the first person to use this imagery in print was the French immigrant farmer J. Hector St. John de Crèvecoeur, who has been described as the first spokesperson of our national consciousness (Rischin, 1990: 64). In his *Letters From an American Farmer* (1904 [1782]: 39), composed shortly after the nation achieved independence from Britain, de Crèvecoeur saw America losing its nonAmerican past as "individuals of all nations are melded into a new race of men" (we can assume that he included women in this process as well). Out of this would emerge a new culture (including a new religion) and a new society. De Crèvecoeur believed that all of the people residing in the new nation—Europeans, Africans, and what he referred to as Polynesians—would intermix in what he called a "smelting pot," yielding something novel and precious. The metaphor thus refers to metallic compounds like brass that are the unique creations of combining unlike metals.

Although this imagery did not gain general acceptance in the nineteenth century, others, such as Ralph Waldo Emerson, the American frontier historian Frederick Jackson Turner, and Theodore Roosevelt, used this metaphor. The person most responsible for popularizing the melting pot metaphor, however, was Israel Zangwill, a Jewish playwright residing in England. On October 5, 1908, his play, *The Melting-Pot*, opened in Washington, D.C., in the midst of the most wide-scale immigration that the country had ever witnessed. This immigration brought large numbers of eastern and southern European immigrants, groups whose religion and culture differed significantly from the older American stock. Many earlier immigrants made invidious comparisons between established Americans and the newcomers. They questioned whether the new arrivals were competent to become citizens and whether it was appropriate to include them in the social fabric. Others, especially from the ranks of social reformers and political progressives, were quick to defend the immigrants.

In short, Zangwill's play entered into, and became a centerpiece of, an intense national debate on immigration and American citizenship. One of the members of the audience on opening night was President Theodore Roosevelt, who proclaimed it a great play (Mann, 1979). Roosevelt saw the play as an endorsement of his faith in the ability of the nation to absorb the new arrivals and as support for his call to abandon immigrant cultures. Opposed to the "hyphenated American," he promoted a process of rapid and complete Americanization. Those more sympathetic to and supportive of immigrant heritages—such as Jane Addams, the social worker chiefly responsible for the establishment of Hull House in Chicago—also responded favorably to the play.

The critics noted that *The Melting-Pot* was not an artistic success. It was, however, popular with audiences, chiefly because of its optimistic view of America's capacity to incorporate diverse peoples. Something of a melodrama, the play is a love story whose protagonists are David Quixano, a Russian Jew, and Vera Revendal, a Christian also from Russia. David emigrated after an anti-Semitic campaign resulted in the massacre of Jews from his home community. He meets and falls in love with Vera, who works at a settlement house where David goes for help in getting established in his new surroundings. David is convinced that their love can overcome their cultural differences in America, though it would have been doomed in Russia, but his beliefs are tested when he learns that Vera's father was the military officer responsible for the massacre. After breaking off the relationship, he ultimately concludes that a fresh break with a painful past is possible, and in the climax of the play the two are reunited on a tenement rooftop in the immigrant enclave in lower Manhattan, with, according to Zangwill's stage directions, the Statue of Liberty's torch twinkling in the background. David's concluding speech is described by the playwright as prophetic:

> There she lies, the great Melting-Pot—listen! Can't you hear the roaring and the bubbling? There gapes her mouth [he points east]—the harbour where a thousand mammoth feeders come from the ends of the world to pour in their human freight. Ah, what a stirring and a seething! Celt and Latin, Slav and Teuton, Greek and Syrian,—black and yellow—["Jew and Gentile" Vera interjects]. Yes, East and West, and North and South, the palm and the pine, the crescent and the cross—how the great Alchemist melts and fuses them with his purging flame! Here shall they all unite to build the Republic of Man and the Kingdom of God. Ah, Vera, what is the glory of Rome and Jerusalem where all nations and races come to worship and look back, compared with the glory of America, where all races and nations come to labour and look forward! (Zangwill, 1909: 198–200)

For at least the first half of the twentieth century, this emotionally charged symbol became the dominant way in which Americans thought about the relationships of the many ethnic groups in the country to one another and their bearing on national unity. The symbol is, as Philip Gleason (1964: 34–35) has indicated, ambiguous and confusing. First, it is not clear whether the melting pot should be seen as descriptive or prescriptive. Second, does it refer only to cultural fusion or to biological fusion (that is, intermarriage) as well? Third, is it only the immigrant who is changed, or does the host society change, too? Because people can answer these questions in various ways, many could claim to support the symbol while disagreeing with other supporters about the actual concrete implications of the melting pot.

Clearly, many cultural, economic, and political elites during the two decades after Zangwill's play reacted in one of two ways to the idea of the melting pot. On the one hand, those who manifested a nativist hostility to the European newcomers (usually combined with an equally or greater hostility to racial minorities) feared that American culture—seen as a product of western European, and particularly British, influence—would be irreparably damaged by unbridled immigration (Solomon, 1956). In a particularly influential book, *The Passing of the Great Race* (1916), Madison Grant sought to prove scientifically that southern and eastern European immigrants were intellectually, morally, and physically inferior to native-born stock (see also Stoddard, 1920; Fairchild, 1926). The newcomers were seen as contributing to increases in social problems such as poverty, illiteracy, and crime, and they were blamed for undermining the standard of living of the working class by accepting lower wages than Americans (Billington, 1938).

On the other hand, those with a more optimistic view about the transformative capacity of American society urged on the immigrants' Americanization campaigns. These campaigns were intended to eradicate all vestiges of the new arrivals' cultural heritages (language, folkways and mores, and so forth) while instilling in them what were deemed to be genuinely American attitudes and behaviors. Perhaps nowhere was this position more vigorously pursued than by the automobile industrialist Henry Ford. Ford established language and citizenship training schools for workers in his plants, and in graduation ceremonies, workers entered a large pot dressed in native garb, only to emerge in American attire, holding their naturalization papers and American flags and singing the national anthem. Central to this viewpoint is the element of loss, specifically the loss of one's past. American culture would be forged at the expense of old-world cultures.

Cultural Pluralism

The melting pot was not universally accepted. Those who embraced diversity and the preservation of ethnic allegiances and heritages were opposed to the creation of a homogeneous American culture and society. Culture critics welcomed the infusion of new cultural influences on America. For example, in 1916 Randolph Bourne (1977) called for the establishment of a "trans-national America." What Bourne envisioned by this is not entirely clear, but he certainly intended to preserve and integrate foreign cultures into American culture, thereby transforming and rejuvenating the latter (Blake, 1990).

The most sustained and influential early critique of the melting pot thesis came from philosopher Horace Kallen. In an article published first in 1915, titled "Democracy *Versus* the Melting Pot," Kallen (1924: 122–123) contended that the demands for "100 percent Americanization" were antithetical to democratic ideals. Moreover, they were contrary to an important sense of self-identity, which he saw as based on an appreciation of and identification with one's ancestral background. Defining his position on **cultural pluralism,** he provided an alternative to the melting pot metaphor by suggesting that America could be seen as an orchestra. He wrote,

> As in an orchestra every type of instrument has its specific *timbre* and *tonality,* . . . so in society, each ethnic group may be the natural instrument, its temper and culture may be its theme and melody and the harmony and dissonances and discords of them all may make the symphony of civilization. (Kallen, 1924: 125)

The melting pot came under increasing attack after 1960. Nathan Glazer and Daniel P. Moynihan voiced their conviction in *Beyond the Melting Pot* (1963) that the metaphor was wrong. At the outset of their study, which focused on five major groups in New York City (Irish, Italians, Puerto Ricans, Jews, and African Americans), they boldly proclaimed, "The point about the melting pot . . . is that it did not happen" (Glazer and Moynihan, 1963: v). Michael Novak, a polemicist and self-proclaimed advocate of ethnics of eastern and southern European origin, issued a more provocative attack in *The Rise of the Unmeltable Ethnics* (1972). Arguing for a deeply rooted psychic need to maintain ethnic attachments, Novak argued that the forced efforts to destroy ethnic attachments had been a decided failure. He concluded that white ethnics would be an important political force in the foreseeable future.

Alternative Images of Ethnic America

In short, the melting pot, as description and as prescription, was under attack. Any number of alternatives were offered in its place. Some, such as a cultural rainbow or a kaleidoscope, suggest an aesthetic perspective that values diversity. Another example is the image of a mosaic, in which the individual pieces of colored tiles are placed in various relationships to other tiles to produce an integrated whole based on maintaining distinctiveness. This image has served Canada—also a heterogeneous, immigrant-receiving nation (and thus like America in many respects)—as its most powerful symbol of identity. It has been used less frequently in America, though when David Dinkins was elected New York City's first African American mayor, he proclaimed the city to be a "gorgeous mosaic" (*New York Times*, 1990: 20). The imagery of a tapestry conjures up a similar perspective.

Although these images have gained increased currency in recent years, images from the kitchen appear to be the most popular, perhaps because food remains one of the most important artifacts of ethnic and racial groups. America has been characterized as a soup, stew, or salad bowl. No one has analyzed the relative popularity of each of these alternatives, but we suspect that the salad bowl has become the most frequently used metaphor. What is implied by this image, and related alternatives to the melting pot? Quite simply, they portray America as a nation in which different groups maintain their distinctive identities: a tomato is always a tomato; it does not become part of the lettuce. The salad dressing is the part of the civic culture that holds these diverse elements in a palatable harmony.

The salad bowl is, however, as confusing a metaphor as is the melting pot for several reasons. First, some foods simply do not go well in a salad. Does this mean that some foods should be excluded from the salad bowl? Second, some parts of a salad are clearly dominant while others offer little more than a subtle garnish. Should this be taken to suggest that for a proper harmony of tastes, careful limits need to be established, with some items in the salad being introduced only in small doses? Third, as with the melting pot thesis, it is not clear whether those who prefer the salad bowl view it as descriptive or prescriptive.

Clearly, this image offers a rather static view of how groups interact with one another. If the melting pot overlooks continuity and resistance to change, treating every group as being fused in the great cauldron, the salad bowl suggests the opposite. Artichokes and tomatoes will not blend or fuse to create something new. In the world of ethnic groups, this metaphor glaringly fails to address the reality and the consequences of intermarriage, which is an extremely important contemporary phenomenon.

These metaphors are all problematic because they each fail to capture the complexity of America's heterogeneous population. We consider these metaphors because they are frequently used in everyday characterizations of ethnicity and are related to major theories concerning the dynamics of ethnic relations.

Summary

In the simplest circumstances, ethnicity is an extremely complicated factor in social life. Given the ethnic diversity that characterizes the United States, the complications become even more daunting. Indeed, the task of understanding the significance of ethnicity over the course of the nation's history can be formidable. This chapter introduced readers to the many dimensions of ethnicity that must be considered. These dimensions range from the micro level to the macro level. On the micro level, we introduced the impact that ethnic identities have on different individuals and how individuals respond to those identities. From the macro level, we looked at the overarching impact of ethnicity on American society at large and the reciprocal impact of American society on ethnics and ethnic groups. The significance of the ethnic group was explored, with emphasis given to its role as a mediator between the micro and macro levels.

The dilemmas of studying ethnicity as an outsider were reviewed, including the problems brought about by ethnocentrism. The insider-outsider debate revealed another facet of the problem by raising the issue of whether outsiders are capable of understanding what it means to be an insider. We also discussed the tendency in much research to ignore the lives of certain categories of relatively powerless people. Throughout the chapter the importance of examining ethnicity in historical and structural terms was stressed. The next chapter builds on this discussion by providing a conceptual map that is intended to assist in the quest to more fully comprehend ethnic America.

Key Terms

cultural pluralism   melting pot
ethnocentrism   social structure
insider-outsider debate

Questions for Discussion and Critical Thinking

1. Discuss your family's background, looking at the points of origin of your ancestors and the length of time your family has lived in the United States. Look also at the amount of intermarriage that has occurred over time. How did race and ethnicity affect the family and their lives? In what ways has this heritage had an influence on your own life?

2. Identify ways that social structure (for example, educational, legal, or religious institutions) reinforces cultural pluralism or assimilation in American life. Give examples of how this process works and evaluate its positive and negative consequences.

3. Various metaphors used to characterize racial and ethnic relations in the United States were reviewed in this chapter. Two of the most popular are the melting pot and the salad bowl. What are the respective strengths and weaknesses of each metaphor? ✦

Chapter 2

Toward a Conceptual Map of Ethnic Relations

E thnic groups exist because a sufficient number of individuals with similar ancestral backgrounds identify with like others and exhibit a willingness to engage in collective behaviors that create the group. Ethnic relations are not possible in culturally homogeneous societies (for example, Iceland), because ethnic relations depend on the interactions of two or more ethnic groups. The study of ethnic relations covers three related topics: interethnic relations, intraethnic relations, and ethnic identity.

When we speak about ethnic relations, we also are speaking about race relations. The latter is a subset of the former. The relationship between ethnicity and race is often a matter of considerable confusion, so in this chapter we will clarify how these and other related terms are used in the social sciences in general and sociology in particular. To place this discussion into historical context, we shall first look briefly at the way in which ethnic studies developed in America during the first half of the twentieth century.

The Emergence of Ethnic Studies

Sociology's contribution to the study of ethnicity derives from two key features of its approach: first, the careful examination of behavioral, cultural, and organizational differences among groups, and second, the search for sociocultural factors that contribute to these differences and that furthermore contribute to shaping the character of interethnic relations (Morawska, 1999). By searching for sociocultural factors—such as economic competition for scarce resources, political conflict, or cultural differences—sociology directs us away from explanations that rely on biology. By turning to the social world to explain group differences and relations, sociology repudiates efforts to use in-stincts, genes, or other biological notions to study ethnicity.

A thumbnail sketch of the history behind the sociocultural ap-proach introduces it as well as some of the central figures associated with its advance. A major reaction to biological racism began to be evi-dent early in the twentieth century, and although it derived from several sources, historian Carl Degler (1991) considers the anthropologist Franz Boas to be the most important scholar in this reorientation of the social sciences.

Clearly, Boas had a profound impact on the development of cultural anthropology, including the training of such well-known scholars as Al-fred L. Kroeber, Ruth Benedict, Robert Lowie, and Margaret Mead. But Boas's thought extended beyond anthropology to other disciplines. In sociology, important scholars of African Americans who came under Boas's influence, such as Howard Odum and Edward B. Reuter, revised their earlier views which were based on biological racism and em-braced sociocultural interpretations on matters related to race. Psy-chologists were slower to make the shift—because the discipline was so attached to the notion of instincts—but by the 1920s change was appar-ent here as well (Cravens, 1978; Gossett, 1965; Wiley, 1986; Barkan, 1992).

In sociology this shift was most visible among the members of the sociology department at the University of Chicago, or what came to be known as the Chicago School (Matthews, 1978, 1987; Wacker, 1983; Persons, 1987). The two major figures behind this shift were W. I. Thomas and Robert E. Park. Thomas was the major force at Chicago until his departure because of an unfortunate scandal. His monumen-tal study (written in collaboration with the Polish émigré sociologist Florian Znaniecki) on *The Polish Peasant in Europe and America* (1918) was a landmark work that set the stage and served as a model for subse-quent empirical research (Wiley, 1986; Creelan and Granfield, 1986). This study replaced the concept of instinct with that of attitude and used Thomas's social psychology, which was based on what he referred to as the "four wishes"—for experience, security, response, and recogni-tion. In interpreting the Polish immigrants' responses to their new envi-ronment, he used such concepts as personal disorganization, social dis-organization, and reorganization.

Robert E. Park used and adapted these concepts in his work and was perhaps the first sociologist to state that the study of the European immigrant and the study of racial groups should proceed in the same manner (Wacker, 1983: 9). Although Park's work was not always consis-tent and he made no particular attempt to be systematic, he was per-haps the principal force in severing the sociology of ethnic studies from explanations based on presumed innate hereditary dispositions. The generation of graduate students he trained reflected this perspective, as evidenced in works of his students that became classics in the field. A short list of contributions includes St. Clair Drake and Horace Cayton's *Black Metropolis* (1962 [1945]), Louis Wirth's *The Ghetto* (1956 [1928]), Everett Hughes's *French Canada in Transition* (1943), and E. Franklin Frazier's *The Negro Family in the United States* (1939) and *The Negro in the United States* (1949). What these studies had in common was an appreciation of the "complexity and fluidity of ongoing group life" and a refusal to employ theories that imposed overly rigid or oversimplified interpretations (Lal, 1986: 281; Lal, 1990; Kivisto, 1990).

Voices   **Robert E. Park**

I t was at this moment that Booker Washington invited me to visit Tuskegee and start my studies of Africa in the southern states. I think I probably learned more about human nature and society, in the South under Booker Washington, than I had learned elsewhere in all my previous studies. I believe in firsthand knowledge not as a substitute but as a basis for more formal and systematic investigation. But the reason I profited as much as I did from this experience was due, I am sure, to the fact that I had a long preparation. As a result I was not, as I found later, interested in the Negro problem as that problem is ordinarily conceived. I was interested in the Negro in the South and in the curious and intricate system which had grown up to define his relations with white folk. I was interested, most of all, in studying the details of the process by which the Negro was making and has made his slow but steady advance.

Robert E. Park worked as Booker T. Washington's personal assistant and later became the head of the Chicago School of Sociology (Park, 1950: vii–viii).

Race, racial groups, and race relations were thus to be construed as ethnicity, ethnic groups, and ethnic relations. But what did Park and the Chicago School mean by these terms? What do we mean by them? Our purpose here is not to provide a detailed history of these concepts. Instead, we seek to clarify them to provide working definitions. Before addressing these particular questions, we will turn first to two related terms: nationality groups and minority groups.

Clarifying Concepts

Ethnicity has received considerable attention in recent years from scholars in the social sciences and history. This attention is a virtue insofar as contemporary discussions of a perplexing topic can build on a substantial body of research and of theory development. For a variety of reasons, however, including imbalances regarding which groups do or do not get studied (Lavender and Forsyth, 1976), scholars have taken widely divergent approaches. Not only do the ways we look at this subject vary considerably, but the precise parameters of what it is we are studying are unclear (Petersen, 1982).

Some scholars define the subject matter somewhat differently than others: many prefer to speak about ethnic groups, whereas others have defined their subject matter as the study of nationalities, minorities, or racial groups. Sometimes the term *ethnic group* is used as a virtual synonym for these terms. Although they are related, there are important differences. As Michael Banton (2001) has recently argued, ethnic studies today is a considerably broader field compared with a half century ago, because of the increase in the amount of empirical research devoted to the subject. However, he contends that there remains a need to improve sociological theory by clarifying and adding precision to the concepts we use.

Nations, Nationality, and Nationalism

Nationalities are groups with a sense of peoplehood and with a political agenda that calls for creating or preserving a nation-state. **Nationalism** provides the ideological justification for, among other things, the territorial claims of the group and the implications such claims have relative to other groups (Gellner, 1983; Horowitz, 1985; Kedourie, 1985; Smith, 1986; Hobsbawm, 1991). Nationalism is a potent force in the modern world, especially in areas where political, cultural, and social boundaries have been subject to dramatic changes in complex histories over long periods of time (Kristeva, 1993).

Thus, the recent conflict in the Balkans that pitted most centrally Serbs against Croatians, but also included Slovenes, Macedonians, Albanians, and Montenegrins, developed from nationalist aspirations. From this perspective, nationality refers to a politicized form of ethnicity, which political scientist Walker Connor (1994) has described as **ethnonationalism.** The fragmentation of the Soviet Union into the Baltic areas of Lithuania, Latvia, and Estonia and the Asian republics that include Azerbaijan, Tadzhikistan, Kirgizistan, Turkmenistan, and Uzbekistan provides another vivid indication of nationalism's central significance. In Western Europe as well, nationalist movements have risen to prominence in numerous places in this century. Examples include the Welsh and Scottish in Britain, the Basque and Catalonian in Spain, and the Breton and Corsican in France. Throughout much of the Third World, nationalism has been a divisive force. Recent examples include the strife in Lebanon, the civil war in Sri Lanka that involves the Sinhalese and Tamils, and the numerous conflicts in Africa that are based, at least in part, on tribal differences, including the genocidal campaign in Rwanda. In North America, the Québecois separatists have recurrently during the past quarter century demanded that the province of Quebec remove itself from the Canadian confederation and declare itself an independent nation.

In the United States, nationalism is a relatively insignificant force—especially when viewed in comparative perspective. This situation is not surprising, because the United States is largely a nation of voluntary immigrants, and immigrants are usually not in a position to make the territorial claims that underpin nationalism. Nonetheless, this particular designation has been applied to the United States, more commonly several decades ago, as seen in the titles of such books as Louis Adamic's *A Nation of Nations* (1944), Oscar Handlin's *Race and Nationality in American Life* (1948), and Brown and Roucek's *Our Racial and National Minorities* (1937). Nationalist ideas can be seen among relatively small segments of the African American population and among American Indians (two groups not composed of voluntary immigrants), though not as especially significant features of intragroup relations and ideologies.

Fundamentally, this country is unique because nationalist ideologies have generally not been advanced by societal subgroups. Somehow America differs from the rest of the world—or at least most of the world—in patterns of interaction across and among the diverse groups that make up the nation's citizenry. The term *nationality group* is too restrictive: In global terms, nationality groups should be seen as a subset of ethnic groups, the former being seen in some multiethnic nations but not in others (Calhoun, 1997: 40; see also, Connor, 1978; O'Brien 1991).

Minority Groups

Although nationality group is too restrictive a term to capture the character of the American situation, the more commonly used designation *minority group* is too expansive. As the Brown and Roucek title cited earlier illustrates, this term can be linked to that of nationalities. Indeed, as Philip Gleason (1991) has indicated, the earliest use of the term *minority*, in the nineteenth century, linked it with nationalities. In the United States, however, the term acquired a new definition that severed this connection: *minority* gained popularity as an alternative to the term *race*. Race tended to be used in a biological sense, and minority was intended to emphasize the centrality of social and cultural factors. Gleason saw the publication of sociologist Donald Young's textbook *American Minority Peoples* (1932) as the beginning of the widespread utilization of the term *minority*. Indeed, the authors of some textbooks on this topic continue to define their subject matter in terms of minority groups (e.g., Vander Zanden, 1973; Newman, 1973; Farley, 1982; Schaefer, 1988).

Although attempts to delineate what constitutes a **minority group** vary somewhat, most definitions share the view that minority groups occupy a subordinate position in a society in the allocation of wealth, prestige, and power (Schermerhorn, 1978; Francis, 1951; Rose and Rose, 1948; Wirth, 1945). Differential markers identify minority groups, and on this basis they are denied full participation in the institutions of the society. Minority groups are thereby perceived to be victims—the objects of prejudicial attitudes and discriminatory actions by the majority group. Parenthetically, note that discussions of minority groups imply the existence of a majority group, which is the dominant group in a society, usually depicted as benefiting from its ability to force other groups into the role of subordinates.

Several problematic features are inherent in the concept of the minority group. The first point is that the term conjures up the numerical representation of the group in a society. When the concept was first applied to the United States, two groups in particular were singled out for designation as minority groups: African Americans and Jewish Americans. Both were, in fact, numerical minorities. If we look at South Africa, however, we discover that apartheid entailed a relatively small minority oppressing a sizable numerical majority of the population. Since Wirth's (1945) discussion of this issue, most of those using this term have contended that majority and minority do not refer to absolute numbers and can be seen as synonyms for dominant and subordinate (Blalock, 1967).

The second, and more serious, point is a lack of attention paid to defining what constitutes the majority group and who should and who should not be included. To take one example, contemporary discussions of the current dilemmas of African Americans often lack clarity concerning the dominant group they confront. At one extreme, a restrictive definition suggests that the majority is limited to White Anglo-Saxon Protestants (WASPs). At the other extreme, the majority is white America. But in this instance, should Latinos be included under the rubric of the white majority? What about American Jews, who have a long history of confronting anti-Semitic exclusion?

The third point is related to the second: majority-minority terminology encourages examining a society in an essentially dichotomous fashion. In a highly complex and heterogeneous society such as the United States, attempting to depict its social character by utilizing these terms encourages an oversimplification that can obscure some important issues while distorting others. That is to say, as we focus attention on the relationship that exists between a subordinate group and a dominant group, we fail to pay sufficient attention to the relationships between and among subordinate groups. For example, the dominant-subordinate relationship diverts attention from the often strained relations between African Americans and Jews, as well as the tensions that exist between African Americans and Korean Americans. Further, we tend to overlook the very significant differences that persist among various European-origin groups (Greeley, 1974).

The fourth point addresses the matter of what counts as a minority group. The examples cited above could suggest that the term is roughly equivalent to *ethnic group*. However, *minority group* is used by most practitioners to include a variety of other groups as well, including women, religious sects, homosexuals, and both the physically and mentally disabled. Although broad generalizations can include these and perhaps other groups, they can only be made by ignoring that which is distinctive about each of the groups. This is a mistake in the study of ethnic relations, for which a considerable amount of theoretical work has been produced that is based on features of ethnicity that make it a relatively unique phenomenon. Parallel to this, an ever-expanding literature on feminist theory proceeds with a similar desire to recognize and comprehend features that are unique to gender issues (Harding, 1987; Smith, 1990).

Race

In our view, *nationality* is too restrictive for our use and *minority group* is too expansive or general. But what about *race?* Throughout its history, American society has been permeated by race relations issues and by the consequences of racism. Thus, we must examine the varied ways in which race and racial groups have been defined and acted on by different social actors in differing times, places, and circumstances. Does this mean that race is a useful analytic tool for exploring these issues, and if so, how should we conceptualize the connection between race and ethnicity?

The general consensus among sociologists is that race fails as a useful theoretical concept. The reason for this failure can be seen by a brief look at the history of the use of racial theory. The classificatory list of races by the Swedish taxonomist Linnaeus in the eighteenth century was the first of numerous attempts to identify the varieties of *Homo sapiens* and determine what should and what should not be considered truly human. Linnaeus divided humankind into four major varieties: white, red, yellow, and black. He argued that these physical differences were correlated with personality differences (Rose, 1968).

Nineteenth-Century Racialist Thought. By the time Comte de Gobineau published *The Inequality of Human Races* (1915 [1853–1855]) in the middle of the nineteenth century, the pattern was set. Thereafter, repeated efforts were made not only to classify but also to illustrate the inferiority of various races and the superiority of others. Gobineau divided the races into the strong and the weak, with whites or Aryans constituting the former and other groups located in the latter category. He contended that the strong, because of their tendency to migrate, would inevitably conquer the weak and in the process would provide the weak with the benefits of civilization. He warned, however, of the dangers that racial mixing would bring about. In his view, racial differences were rooted in human nature and not in social conditions. Thus, the domination of some races by others was not only inevitable but also in a perverse way beneficial to superior and inferior races alike (Bolt, 1971; Banton, 1987; Stone, 1985). Gobineau described the age of the European colonization of much of the rest of the world, and his quasi-scientific theory served well as an ideological justification for conquest.

As William Stanton (1960) indicated, similar thinking was used by Southern slaveholders in the United States to justify the institution of slavery. But such thinking extended beyond African and Asian origin groups. During the peak of mass immigration from eastern Europe in the early part of the twentieth century, race theory was used to discredit the new arrivals. As Madison Grant's diatribe against these newcomers, *The Passing of the Great Race* (1916), illustrates, this mode of thinking was extremely pliable. Where predecessors might have viewed all Europeans as members of the same race, Grant provided a new classificatory schema that delineated the superior races (the Nordic peoples from western Europe) from the inferior, which he identified as originating from the "Mediterranean basin and the Balkans." Here, racial theory was used in the interest of the immigration restriction movement. As Grant (1916: 92) argued, "Our jails, insane asylums, and almshouses are filled with this human flotsam and the whole tone of American life, social, moral, and political, has been lowered and vulgarized by them."

Darwinism and Eugenics. Several important figures in the early history of American sociology were deeply influenced by this kind of thought. Like Edward Alsworth Ross, they frequently sought to apply Darwin's theory of natural selection to human society. They were also influenced by the hereditary arguments of eugenicist Sir Francis Galton, who defined **eugenics** as the improvement of the human race based on genetic policy. Perhaps aware of the scientific shortcomings of previous racial theories, they came up with approaches intended to redress the deficiencies of earlier expressions. The conclusions they drew, however, differed little from those less influenced by Darwin and Galton. Ross could have been parroting Grant when he concluded, in *The Old World in the New* (1914), that the fit were not surviving and as a result American society was experiencing a "certain decay of character." Franklin Henry Giddings, Ross's contemporary, thought that many new immigrants could not be incorporated into American society. Like Ross, Giddings felt that their presence was detrimental to the well-being of American society, fearing the superior Anglo-Saxons would end up "sinking to the level of their more brutal competitors" (Giddings, 1893: 237). This conviction led Giddings to active participation in the Immigration Restriction League; he even served for a time as its vice-president.

Racialist Thought Challenged. By the 1920s, race theories that were purported to be rooted in biology had come into disrepute (Benedict, 1959). Although they never entirely disappeared from the social sciences, racial theories ended up occupying an extremely marginal position. As the examples just presented illustrate, the reasons are twofold: They are based on bad science or pseudoscience, and they carry racist political implications (Tucker, 1994; Graves, 2001). These reasons were evident during the heyday of the eugenicist movement around the turn of the century, and they can be seen in the more recent claims by figures such as Arthur Jensen and Richard Herrnstein that black IQs are lower than those of whites and that this difference can explain differences not only in academic achievement but in occupational status as well. As Troy Duster (1990: 9) has observed,

> In this century, the empirical research on the genetics/IQ controversy and the attendant policy injunctions have had a remarkably varied history. However, one consistent pattern emerges: the more privileged strata have at each juncture raised the "genetic" question about those at the lower end of the socioeconomic ladder.

In recent decades, scholars have been highly suspicious of the "received truth" about racial differences. Anthropologist Frank Livingstone (1962), for example, emphasized the lack of clear-cut divisions among human population groups, which led him to conclude that "if races have to be discrete entities, then there are no races." In other words, racial classifications have no scientific basis. This conclusion led to the call for a nonracial approach to the understanding of human diversity. Not all have agreed with this conclusion, but few dispute the assertion that the boundaries distinguishing groups are at best imprecise (Dunn and Dobzhansky, 1952; Coon, 1965; Banton and Harwood, 1975).

Geneticists have continued to study the differences in gene pools in humankind. The prevalence of illnesses such as sickle-cell anemia among African Americans and Tay-Sachs among Jews can be viewed as indications of the validity of the biological approach. In contrast to these physical maladies, however, attempts to apply the findings of biology to explain social and cultural differences, particularly to explain inequality, have failed (Yinger, 1985). As geneticist N. P. Dubinin (1956: 69) wrote in a book published by UNESCO that summarized the status of research on race 50 years ago, "Theories of the alleged inequality of human races have no scientific basis."

Thus, to a large extent Elazar Barkan (1992) is correct to claim that since the middle of the twentieth century, scientific racism has been in retreat. Indeed, the controversy surrounding the publication of Richard Herrnstein and Charles Murray's *The Bell Curve* (1994) reveals that scientific racism has lost much of its credibility. Treating racial differences in IQ scores as evidence of the lower intelligence of blacks, the authors contended that nothing could be done to redress these differences, as much of the cause was genetically based. Although published by a reputable press and well funded by foundations committed to reviving the eugenics movement, the book was widely condemned for its shoddy scholarship and reactionary political implications by natural and social scientists and by political figures—including many mainstream conservatives (Lane, 1994; Fischer, 1996).

Sociobiology. Before leaving this topic, we should note one significant effort to resuscitate a biological understanding of race (and ethnicity), because it comes from a prominent scholar in the field. Pierre van den Berghe, who in his early career used a historical approach quite at odds with the biological (1965, 1967, 1970), later shifted his thinking as a result of the impact of **sociobiology,** an approach that applies biological evolution to human behavior (1978, 1981, 1986, 1990; see also Lopreato, 1990; Lopreato and Crippen, 1999). A self-fashioned iconoclast and anarchist, van den Berghe (1981) became disenchanted with a perspective that, in his estimation, was too dismissive of biology's role in the sociocultural realm. He faulted this view for severing the link between the social and the cultural approaches on the one hand and the biological on the other; then he united them so that biology plays the central role in explaining group attachments and intergroup relations. He wrote, "My basic argument is quite simple: ethnic and racial sentiments are [an] extension of kinship sentiments" (van den Berghe, 1981: 18).

With this simple assertion he attempted to establish a model that assumes that human beings seek to maximize their fitness for survival by favoring, through nepotism, those who share their genes. Therefore, genetics influences the construction of ingroup and outgroup definitions, which means that there is something immutable about the problematic, conflict-ridden character of race and ethnic relations.

Van den Berghe does not argue, as the racial thinkers noted earlier do, that some races are inferior and others superior. He does not seek to justify racial oppression on the basis that the members of some racial groups will, because of their favorable genetic inheritances, inevitably obtain more power, wealth, and status than members of groups not so favorably endowed. Instead, he challenges those who assume that it is possible to create social environments conducive to racial harmony. He believes that individual self-interest is bound up with the interest of the racial group, which leads to competition and conflict among groups for scarce resources. This rather fatalistic view limits the role of human consciousness in effecting social change and also limits (or denies) the relative autonomy of social and cultural factors.

In this respect, van den Berghe's work bears a remarkable similarity to that of William Graham Sumner, who in an earlier period of American sociology was convinced that efforts at societal reform and improvement were largely doomed to failure (Sumner, 1940 [1906];

Kivisto, 1978). Sumner used the term *ethnocentrism* to account for what he saw as the universal tendency to advance the interests of one's own group at the expense of others. In effect, van den Berghe attempts to use what he sees as the contributions of sociobiology to explain the underlying cause of ethnocentrism.

Conceptual models, however, should not be judged by whether one agrees or disagrees with their political implications. Rather, they should be assessed on their usefulness or lack of usefulness in helping to make sense of aspects of our world. Van den Berghe is too reductionist. That is to say, he used biology to explain too much, at the expense of explanations that are rooted in social and cultural factors. Criticisms of sociobiology in general, such as Marshall Sahlins's (1976), have made the same point in considerable detail. Like any other grand theory, van den Berghe's overgeneralizes and thus oversimplifies. He is not willing to consider history—which is muddled, complicated, and subject to varied and partial interpretations—seriously enough.

As a result, the sociobiological approach does not help us understand ethnic phenomena. That no studies to date have fruitfully employed van den Berghe's model is perhaps the best indication of its limited utility. An approach rooted in the social and cultural sciences, which does not need to avail itself of biology, provides a far more promising basis for dealing with this subject.

Ethnicity and Ethnic Groups

Most definitions of *ethnicity* have two central features: a shared culture (see, e.g., Ware, 1940) and a real or putative common ancestry. The ethnic group should be seen as a distinctive type of group. E. K. Francis (1947) saw the ethnic group as a subtype of *Gemeinschaft* groups. *Gemeinschaft*, which can be roughly translated as "community," implies a type of group characterized by its involuntary nature (that is, you are born into it) and by the member's familiarity with and emotional bonds to other group members. As such, Francis considers the ethnic group to be a secondary group with some of the features of primary groups.

Werner Sollors (1981) noted that the term *ethnicity* is of relatively recent origin: the first use appeared only 50 years ago. Sollors locates its initial use by W. Lloyd Warner, an anthropologist at the University of Chicago. Warner used the term in his famous community studies, particularly "Yankee City" (Newburyport, Massachusetts), to highlight cultural differences he observed in the city.

The adjective *ethnic* was used at least a century earlier, but not widely until the publication of William Graham Sumner's *Folkways* in 1906. Since then, both *ethnicity* and *ethnic* have gained wide acceptance, but no consensus has been reached about precisely what they mean. In a study intended to discover the various ways that ethnicity has been defined in major social science journals, Wsevolod Isajiw (1979) found that a sizable majority of writers on the subject simply avoided dealing with the matter of definition.

The editors of the *Harvard Encyclopedia of American Ethnic Groups* (*HEAEG*; Thernstrom, Orlov, and Handlin, 1980) presented the following list of features that in varied combinations can be seen as defining **ethnicity:**

- Common geographic origin.

- Migratory status.

- Race.

- Language or dialect.

- Religious faith or faiths.

- Ties that transcend kinship, neighborhood, and community boundaries.

- Shared traditions, values, and symbols.

- Literature, folklore, and music.

- Food preferences.

- Settlement and employment patterns.

- Special interests in regard to politics in the homeland and the United States.

- Institutions that specifically serve and maintain the group.

- An internal sense of distinctiveness.

- An external perception of distinctiveness.

This is a loose and broad listing. The editors cast their net widely, which resulted in a selection of 106 groups for inclusion in their volume and a sense that this was to be seen as a minimum number of ethnic groups. Two features are actually consequences of ethnicity rather than attributes of the phenomenon: migratory status and settlement and employment patterns. Furthermore, some features seem to be more important than others. Since the editors do not provide criteria for the implementation of these features to concrete ethnic groups, an ambiguity (that they admittedly recognize) remains about what, in essence, ethnicity is.

Isajiw (1979: 25) offers a particularly parsimonious definition of the **ethnic group** when he describes it as an "involuntary group of people who share the same culture or the descendants of such people who identify themselves and/or are identified by others as belonging to the same involuntary group." This definition combines, as he notes, both a subjective and an objective component. With the provisos that follow, this definition will be used throughout this book.

Religio-Ethnic Groups

Isajiw finds fault with definitions that include religion as one of the attributes of the ethnic group (cf. Gordon, 1964, and Schermerhorn, 1978). Although Isajiw is right to argue for preserving an analytic differentiation between religious groups and ethnic groups, religion is often a critical aspect of culture. Along with language, common folkways and mores, and a shared history, religion should be considered as one of the building blocks of culture. Thus, Baptists do not constitute an ethnic group, because their religion is open to people regardless of their ethnic background. For some groups, such as Jews, the ethnic cannot be separated from the religious, and they might properly be viewed as **religio-ethnic groups.** The editors of the *HEAEG* included Mormons, but it is more appropriate to consider Mormons as a religious group like the Baptists. The editors also included the Amish and Hutterites, and here the religio-ethnic designation is correct, for members of these groups trace their ancestry to Germanic sources as well as to particular dissident religious movements. Greeks, given their connection with Orthodox Christianity, might also be appropriately seen as a religio-ethnic group. To some extent, a similar description might appear to apply to Muslims from various Middle Eastern countries. However, given that immigrants from such nations also include members of faiths other than Islam, including Christians, Jews, Baha'is, and Zoroastrians, the religio-ethnic label must be used cautiously.

Racial Groups

As religio-ethnic groups are a subset of ethnic groups, so racial groups should be considered a subset of ethnic groups. Racial definitions are socially constructed and use differentiating physical features such as those associated with skin color to serve as markers of identity. Racial markers are used to define relationships of dominance and subordination. Based on a person's particular racial markers, others may attribute favorable or unfavorable personality characteristics: the person will be seen as intelligent or unintelligent, industrious or lazy, rational or emotional, trustworthy or untrustworthy, and so forth. Based on a person's racial markers, others may be more or less willing to enter into social relationships with the person.

Racial definitions vary according to time and place. Some societies do not make sharp distinctions between racial groups but see them as fluid, taking into account the impact of interbreeding. By developing definitions of mixed-bloods (mulatto, sambo, and so forth), such societies portray racial definitions along a continuum. In contrast, other societies—and the United States falls into this category—make especially sharp distinctions between groups (Cross, 1991).

Robert Park (1950), in an insightful essay titled "Behind Our Masks," argued that in the latter case a great deal of importance is attached to racial differences. These societies are generally characterized by considerable racial hostility and conflict. The reason is that by forcing individuals to, in effect, wear their race like a mask, it becomes difficult for members of one group to see people of other groups as individuals. Instead, people are nothing more than representatives of their race. If people cannot view members of another race as individuals, with distinctive personalities, fears, desires, aspirations, and so forth, they cannot develop harmonious relationships with them. Race has been the most divisive force throughout the entire history of the United States.

Given this situation, does it make sense to make a sharp contrast between ethnic groups and racial groups? M. G. Smith (1982) thinks so, and he argues that it is a mistake to subsume race under the more general concept of ethnicity. His reason is that race is a reality in nature, or in other words that somehow biology actually counts.

Other theorists argue for the need to maintain an analytical distinction between race and ethnicity because they think the respective dynamics of interethnic relations and race relations differ appreciably. Michael Omi and Howard Winant (1986), for example, refer to European-origin groups as ethnic but use race to refer to African Americans and American Indians. Eduardo Bonilla-Silva (1997) makes a similar claim by noting that these groups have vastly different histories rooted in their distinctive locations in the modern capitalist world system. The problem we see with this position is that it confuses historical differences with analytical ones.

This book proceeds with a different understanding. Racial groups are ethnic groups. When race is socially defined as important, those definitions carry with them real and profound consequences. We will employ the definitions used in the society but will not mistakenly consider these definitions as rooted in, and thus determined by, biology or nature. In this regard, we embrace the position of Oliver C. Cox (1948; see also McAuley, 2004), who viewed racial groups as a subset of ethnic groups. Similarly, we concur with Susan Olzak (1992: 25) when she writes that, "*race* is a specific instance of ethnicity, defined by membership based on what are *assumed to be* inherited phenotypical characteristics" (Olzac's italics). Likewise, we agree with Steve Fenton's (1999: 4) claim that the "term 'ethnic' has a much greater claim to analytical usefulness in sociology because it is not hampered by a history of connotations with discredited science and malevolent practices the way the term 'race' is."

However, as Randall Collins (2001: 18) has written, "Race is a folk concept, a popular mythology that elevates particular kinds of ethnic distinctions into an absolute break." Given that race is used in everyday language, it is the task of sociology to make sense of how people define situations and to determine the implications of those definitions for social relations. An important part of this project involves the examination of racism as ideology, the racism of everyday life, institutional racism, and racialist social movements—in short, all facets of the racialization of ethnicity. We should not view these concepts in an overly rigid manner, because the definitions we use are secondhand, based on the logics-in-use of social actors who are constantly defining and redefining their world and the people who inhabit it. To use the phrase of sociologist Herbert Blumer (1954: 3–10)—a product of the Chicago School and the original spokesperson for a tradition of sociology that he referred to as "symbolic interactionism"—we need to use "sensitizing concepts" that assist us in comprehending how people interpret the social world.

Ethnic Relations

In one of the more systematic attempts to develop a general theory of ethnic relations, R. A. Schermerhorn (1970: 12) emphasized that the ethnic group must be seen as a "collectivity within a larger society." The ethnic group must be considered in relation to other groups as well as to the society at large.

But what is the range of possible relations? At one extreme is the unwillingness on the part of a more powerful group to permit a less powerful group of people to exist. **Genocide,** the programmatic extermination of a people, has been an altogether too frequent occurrence in the modern world. In the twentieth century, two genocidal campaigns—the Turks against the Armenians in the second decade (Dadrian, 1989) and the Nazi Germans against Jews and Gypsies, or Romanies—have left bitter memories for survivors and their children, many of whom now live in the United States. The only group in America, however, to have confronted what can be seen as genocidal campaigns is the American Indian. Though these campaigns may not have achieved sufficient political or public support to have become a coherent governmental policy, the net result of the treatment of the Native American has appropriately been described by Russell Thornton (1987) as a holocaust.

Another possible response of a more powerful group to a less powerful one is either to deny entry or to expel the less powerful from the territory controlled by the more powerful group. Many have advocated this option at various points in American history. Furthermore, it has been implemented on several occasions, beginning with the rise of anti-

Chinese sentiment in the nineteenth century. Asian-origin groups have been the principal targets of such efforts, although Latin American, Middle Eastern, and selective European-origin groups have also been subject to such attempts. Although immigration laws have been used to deny entry to various groups, wide-scale, governmentally sponsored policies of ethnic expulsion have not been characteristic of American ethnic relations.

A third option, which has not shaped ethnic relations in this country in a significant way, is secession. Ethnic groups with territorial claims sometimes attempt to leave an existing nation-state to establish a new one. Secessionist movements are nationalist movements. The Québecois separatists in Canada are a contemporary example. In other cases, what are called "irredentist" movements attempt to promote the voluntary exodus from one nation to another or to fuse a territory with a nation. The rationale used by movement adherents is that the territory is the natural homeland of the group. Such movements often elicit challenges from ethnic groups and political forces opposed to such an undertaking. This situation has been seen in eastern Europe among some Albanians in the Kosovo region of Serbia. These attempts cause much of the ethnic conflict in the world today. In the United States, because an overwhelming majority of Americans are voluntary immigrants or the offspring of voluntary immigrants, this phenomenon has been limited to only two groups, African Americans and American Indians. Moreover, in both cases, such movements have attracted only limited support within the group.

This leads us to two types of ethnic relations that are applicable to the American setting: assimilation and pluralism (Abramson, 1980; Gleason, 1992). Assimilation is a theoretic articulation of the melting pot metaphor; pluralism is a parallel conceptualization of the salad bowl. Both have been used as key explanatory concepts in discussions of American ethnicity and have been the objects of extensive theoretical discussions and elaborations.

Assimilation

Assimilation can be defined as the incorporation of an ethnic group's members into the larger society. This definition, however, raises a number of questions, because the term *incorporation* is unclear. Milton Gordon (1964) cites, in his seminal study on the topic, seven types of assimilation. Three do not actually refer to assimilation but rather to preconditions for assimilation. They have to do with the absence of various impediments to harmonious or cooperative social relations: *attitude receptional assimilation* refers to the absence of prejudice; *behavioral receptional assimilation* signifies the related absence of discrimination; and *civic assimilation* is based on a situation free of institutional conflict in the political and cultural arenas.

The four remaining types do signify aspects of incorporation. One, *identificational assimilation,* addresses the subjective or social psychological dimension of assimilation, whereas the other three deal with objective, external aspects of inclusion: *cultural assimilation* concerns modeling behavioral patterns after those of the dominant society; *structural assimilation* refers to the entry of ethnic group members into the institutions, neighborhoods, and primary groups of the dominant society; and *marital assimilation* refers, quite simply, to intermarriage.

Gordon did not claim that these types of assimilation were necessarily connected in a series of stages. He avoided depicting assimilation as an inevitable course of events. This approach set him apart from a perspective held by many of his predecessors, such as Robert Park, who at one point in his career spoke about a four-stage *race relations cycle,* which was portrayed as moving inevitably from contact through conflict and accommodation to assimilation (Park, 1950; Lyman, 1972; Matthews, 1978; Lal, 1983, 1990). Gordon's main objective was to construct a typology for comparative purposes, but he did suggest that if these modes of assimilation were to occur in sequential order, marital assimilation would be the last to occur.

In discussions about assimilation, two somewhat different versions of assimilation are frequently depicted. William Newman (1973) summarized the two possibilities diagrammatically. A + B + C = D describes a situation in which cultural, structural, and marital assimilation take place. This is the purist expression of the melting pot, for the groups that enter the cauldron are transformed into something new—a heretofore nonexistent entity. This subset of assimilation might properly be called, as Gordon does, *amalgamation.*

A + B + C = A (where A is the dominant group) describes a situation in which all groups are transformed except the dominant one, which becomes the template used to reshape the identities of the other groups. This situation has been referred to as Anglo-conformity and as Americanization. In this model, the dominant model and the host society in general are not changed by the process of ethnic group interaction. This has a peculiarly one-sided character: change for subordinate groups, and stasis for the dominant group.

Pluralism

Similarly, two variations of **pluralism** can be distinguished. Again, Newman (1973) provides a useful schematic portrait. A + B + C = A + B + C portrays a situation in which ethnic groups maintain their distinctiveness and their separateness. In contrast to the changes that occur in both the amalgamation and the Anglo-conformity models, ethnic persistence over time and in spite of interaction is the central defining feature of this version of pluralism. This is the most pristine expression of the salad bowl: Distinctive identities and boundaries are preserved, just as lettuce is even after its interaction with the tomatoes, peppers, olives, and artichoke hearts.

A second, somewhat modified form of pluralism sees group identities preserved but simultaneously changed via interaction with other groups and the dominant society: $A + B + C = A1 + B1 + C1$. Borrowing from the title of the book by Nathan Glazer and Daniel P. Moynihan (1963), Newman refers to this scenario as "beyond the melting pot." In this version of pluralism, African Americans remain different from Italian Americans, but African Americans are also different from Africans and Italian Americans are different from Italians. The difference is the product of the shared civic experience that both groups—and, of course, all others—have had as a result of their ongoing contact with society at large and the complex patterns of interaction with other groups.

Just as the public arguments of proponents and opponents of the melting pot concept have been heated, so frequently have been the scholarly debates between assimilationists and pluralists. In the midst of these exchanges, however, a substantial body of empirical research has been produced, particularly in sociology and history, that helps clarify and put into perspective these theoretical discussions. Neither extreme position—amalgamation or radical cultural diversity—can provide compelling overarching descriptions of America yesterday, today, or in the foreseeable future. Evidence can and has been amassed to support and to critique both of the modified alternatives. Moreover, recent efforts have been undertaken to assess both the conceptual strengths and weaknesses of these positions.

The modified assimilationist position is, in effect, a model of change. However, the dynamic factors that produce the predicted change have not been sufficiently developed by assimilationist theorists. Modernization theorists, including Marxists, have seen industrialization as a destroyer of ethnic attachments and, indeed, of all attachments rooted in tradition. From this perspective, ethnicity's demise leads to the emergence of powerful class-based allegiances. But, as we shall see, the empirical evidence provides compelling proof that a simple analysis of a progressive shift from ethnicity to class does not adequately capture the relationship between the two.

Force can only account in part for a decision to abandon ethnic attachments. Indeed, the demand to renounce one's ethnicity can lead to an intensified commitment to ethnic identity. Ethnic commitment can be a form of resistance to enforced compliance with the dictates of a dominant group or societal elites. Surprisingly little attention has been paid both to factors that stimulate a desire to leave the confines of the ethnic group and to the lures of the host society in attracting people to it. Furthermore, assimilationists often underplay the persistence of ethnic antagonism and the power of forces intent on ensuring that assimilation does not occur.

The research agenda pursued by assimilationists tends, not surprisingly, to focus attention on measuring the perceived degree of assimilation. They use a variety of indicators dealing with rates of socioeconomic mobility, civic participation, social integration, cultural accommodation, and intermarriage rates, and they have paid scant attention to indicators of ethnic persistence.

By contrast, pluralists address precisely those issues that assimilationists ignore. The persistence of markers of cultural identity (language, values, behavior, and so forth) and the continuing impact of ethnicity on political orientation, educational achievement, and socioeconomic status have been explored extensively by pluralists (Greeley, 1974; Parenti, 1967).

The Primordialist Perspective. An important question that divides pluralists concerns the reasons for ethnic persistence. Some theorists, such as Clifford Geertz (1973), Edward Shils (1975), Harold Isaacs (1975), and Pierre van den Berghe (1981), adhere to what has been described as a **primordialist** perspective, which sees ethnicity as a deeply rooted, and immutable, universal given. Most primordialists do not agree with van den Berghe's biologically based version of primordialism. Instead, they treat ethnic persistence as a mysterious given. Shils (1975: 122) states, simply, that ethnicity is predicated on a "certain ineffable significance [that] is attributed to the tie of blood." In a similar vein, Geertz (1973: 259) writes that ethnic allegiance manifests a powerful coercive force because of "some unaccountable absolute import attributed to the very tie itself." Primordialists do not quite put it in these terms, but they seem to see ethnicity as the result of a not fully understood, but nonetheless extraordinarily powerful, psychological attachment to the group.

This view is problematic because it devalues the role of historical and social structural conditions that act to either reinforce or undermine ethnic loyalties. Ethnic identity may meet certain psychological needs, but it is not an immutable given, a basic part of the human condition (Glazer and Moynihan, 1975; McKay, 1982; Scott, 1990). Furthermore, primordialists cannot account for why ethnic identities wane and even disappear.

The Circumstantialist Perspective. "Circumstantialists," a term that gained currency when used by Glazer and Moynihan (1975), or "optionalists" (Gleason, 1983), provide a more compelling sociological basis for understanding ethnicity. They contend, quite simply, that societal, cultural, and environmental factors combine to create conditions that either sustain or undermine ethnic attachments for particular groups at different times. Ethnicity can wax or wane, depending on the circumstances. This particular perspective will be the basis of our discussion of ethnic identity and ethnic group formation and maintenance.

Toward a New Model

Until recently, theoretical discourse about ethnicity has been limited chiefly to polemics that pitted assimilationists and pluralists against each other. The sterility of these debates has become increasingly apparent, and efforts are under way to develop alternative theoretical models that can account for both persistence, which is the focus of pluralists, and change, which is the central concern of assimilationists (Kivisto, 1989; see also Higham, 1982). As the longtime student of ethnicity J. Milton Yinger (1986: 39) commented, "neither the assimilationist thesis nor the persistence-of-ethnic-difference antithesis is adequate."

Thus, we have arrived at a situation aptly described by Ewa Morawska (1990: 218) in the following way: "The assimilation paradigm in its classical version has been abandoned on account of its excessive simplicity, and the 'ethnicity-forever' approach that replaced it is also passing away." If both of these theoretical perspectives can be faulted for seeing only part of the larger picture, one might think that a successful alternative model would meld both approaches into its overarching theoretical model that can account for the incorporation of diversity in a pluralist society (Kivisto, 2004). This has been attempted by a variety of reductionist theorists intent on identifying a single analytical factor in the study of ethnicity and ethnic relations.

Marxism and Social Classes

Some Marxists, particularly those who see themselves as the most orthodox, have made a persistent attempt to use class as the pivotal concept in defining various types of social relations, thereby reducing ethnic differences to class differences (Cox, 1948; Parkin, 1979; Bonacich, 1980; Steinberg, 1981; Miles, 1993). Thus, Alex Callinicos (1993: 52–57) views the riots that erupted in Los Angeles in the aftermath of the trial of the police officers accused of beating Rodney King as a "class rebellion, not a race riot." A related danger is "to subsume ethnicity, not to class but to power" (Zunz, 1985: 61). In both instances, ethnicity is epiphenomenal: it is a mystified version of class relations (Anthias, 1990; Solomos and Back, 1995; Winant, 2000). In other words, this thinking holds that ethnic divisions are actually superficial and do not reflect the most important kinds of social divisions. Moreover, to the extent that people view ethnic divisions as central, they do not see that the real underlying social divisions are class based or are a matter of who has and who does not have power. Marxists are not alone in advancing this position. Around the turn of the century, the German sociologists Ludwig Gumplowicz and Gustav Ratzenhofer suggested that in the modern Industrial Age ethnic conflict (actually, they used the term "race conflict") would progressively give way to class conflict. This view was embraced by many American sociologists, including Robert Park during the earlier phase of his career (Matthews, 1978; Lal, 1990; Lyman, 1992).

The problem with this view is that the empirical evidence does not bear it out. Although class divisions are certainly a major form of societal differentiation and the consequences of social class location are profound, other divisions are also important in their own right. Attempts to minimize their importance illustrate a failure to appreciate the actual character of self-identity in the modern world. Sociologist Georg Simmel (1955) contended that the individual in the contemporary world is enmeshed in what he referred to as a "web of group affiliations," each making various demands of allegiance.

Among the most important affiliations are those based on ethnicity, social class, gender, and religious affiliation. Others include place of residence (urban, rural, or suburban), regional location, occupational status, and marital and family status. Ethnicity should thus be seen as one potential mode or aspect of individual identity (Dashefsky, 1976). Ethnicity can be a more or less significant aspect of identity, depending on the combined role of several variables; Table 2.1 provides a summary of some of the most significant variables.

Anya Peterson Royce (1982: 1) wrote, "[Ethnicity] is developed, displayed, manipulated, or ignored in accordance with the demands of particular situations." Ethnicity can interact in complex ways with other aspects of identity, at times in a mutually reinforcing manner, but at other times it competes with these other modes of identity in terms of the relative importance or salience attached to them. For example, middle-class blacks might highlight features of their class identity when they are at work, since that environment would bring them into contact with many middle-class whites. Their shared class identities would serve as a basis for commonality. On the other hand, if middle-class blacks live in a predominantly black neighborhood, with many working-class and poor blacks, they may accentuate their racial identity and downplay their class identity, again to accentuate that which these middle-class residents share with the people around them at the moment.

Rational Choice Theory

Another recent attempt at a general theory to account for ethnic identity and behavior is **rational choice theory** (Hechter, Friedman, and Appelbaum, 1982; Hechter, 1986; Banton, 1983). Derived from economics, rational choice theory assumes that people act to maximize their economic and social positions. They weigh their actions in terms

Table 2.1	Variables Affecting the Importance of Ethnic Group Affiliation	

Tend to Increase Importance	Tend to Decrease Importance
1. Large group (relative to total population)	Small group
2. Residentially concentrated by region and community	Residentially scattered
3. Short-term residents (high proportion of newcomers)	Long-term residents (low proportion of newcomers)
4. Return to homeland easy and frequent	Return to homeland difficult and infrequent
5. Different language	Dominant language
6. Different religion from dominant group(s)	Share religion of dominant group(s)
7. Different race	Same race
8. Involuntary immigrants	Voluntary immigrants
9. Culturally different society	Culturally similar society
10. Attracted to political and economic developments in land of origin	Repelled by those developments
11. Homogeneous in class and occupation	Diverse in class and occupation
12. Low average level of education	High average level of education
13. Victim of a great deal of discrimination	Little discrimination
14. Resident in a society with little social mobility	Resident in open-class society

Source: Adapted from Yinger (1985).

of the costs involved and the potential benefits that might accrue. This theory has considerable appeal insofar as it can help us understand that ethnic affiliation and ethnic competition (as opposed to individual competition) can be based on rational calculation. In other words, when individuals perceive ethnic bonding as personally advantageous, collective ethnic action is likely to result, and when other groups are viewed as impediments to goals, interethnic competition and conflict will occur.

This perspective has considerable merit but does not provide an overarching explanation of ethnicity. Instead, it must be combined with a view that considers the nonrational character of ethnic phenomena. This is not to suggest that the "blood-and-guts" perspective of the primordialists (including the sociobiologists) should somehow be grafted onto this paradigm. Rather, we need to recognize that the historically embedded character of ethnicity produces nonreflective, habitual forms of identification and action that cannot be construed as rational (Thomas, 1909; Lyman, 1990a).

Ethnicity can produce powerful attachments that do not elevate the economic or social status of the individuals but instead connect people to a past. This aspect can, when ethnicity is not a particularly important part of identity, manifest itself as a form of nostalgia for a past that had largely disappeared. To the extent that factors such as nostalgia can reinforce ethnic identity, we can appreciate the limitations of rational choice.

Ethnic identity can thus be influenced by rational considerations, but not necessarily so. Ethnic identity can also be shaped by traditional modes of conduct, whose habitual character is not rational. Ethnic studies must consider both possibilities and attempt to sort out their respective roles in particular instances. This approach demands that careful attention be paid to how people shape their own lives. Careful attention must also be given to the muddle of historical contingency and the complexities of relevant concrete historical events. Grand theories cannot be sustained. As Herbert Gans (1985: 303) has suggested, paradigms that can profitably guide ethnic research must be "more situationally sensitive" than most of those employed in the past.

The social construction of Swedish American identity, circa 1900.

The Social Construction of Ethnicity

In this book, we use an approach that builds on some of the most compelling insights of earlier theories. We begin with the rather simple sociological assumption that ethnicity is a social construction, and we incorporate strands from a variety of theories into this general orientation. The social construction of ethnicity has been referred to by a number of terms, which we'll discuss in the following sections.

Ethnogenesis

Anthropologist Eugene Roosens (1989) has defined the social construction of ethnicity as **ethnogenesis.** His position is essentially an instrumentalist one that is indebted to a perspective similar to that of rational choice, and with its inherent limitations. In his view, ethnicity emerges and is sustained over time when leaders make rational choices—based on self-interest—that require efforts to mobilize ethnic identity and collective action. Although not providing the whole picture, Roosens is instructive insofar as he indicates that the role of ethnic leadership must be considered, and thus we must carefully examine the inner workings of ethnic communities.

Ethnicization

Jonathan Sarna (1978) describes a process that he calls **ethnicization.** Referring specifically to immigrant groups in America, he argues that at their time of arrival these groups were highly fragmented with little communal unity. This changed over time as a result of two factors: ascription and adversity. *Ascription* refers to the definition of group identities and the assigning of individuals to particular groups by outside agents, particularly by political and economic elites in the larger, host society. The connection between ascription and adversity is a reciprocal one insofar as those chiefly responsible for defining the ethnics also confront ethnics from a position of power and are frequently a source of hostility and exploitation.

Hostility and exploitation cause the creation of ethnic communities that are designed to meet the immediate social, political, and cultural needs of the ethnics. Sarna's characterization of this process may place too much power in forces outside the ethnic group, thus overstating the powerlessness of the ethnics in defining who they are and in confronting the dominant society. In other words, the ethnic is viewed too simply as a victim, thereby downplaying the active role ethnics had in shaping their own lives. Nonetheless, the virtue of Sarna's perspective rests with its call to locate or contextualize the ethnic group in relation to the larger society.

Emergent Ethnicity

This perspective is echoed in William Yancey, Eugene Ericksen, and Richard Juliani's (1976) **emergent ethnicity** thesis. The authors downplay the impact of cultural heritage and argue that rather than being an ascribed attribute, ethnicity is structurally conditional. Of central importance are the intersecting influences of occupational location, residential patterns, and institutional affiliations. The result is that, "As society changes, old forms of ethnic culture may die out but new forms may be generated" (391). Douglass and Lyman (1976) concur with this position but concentrate on individual actors, rather than the ethnic group, in exploring the strategies actors use in accepting or rejecting aspects of ethnicity while creating a self-identity.

The Invention of Ethnicity

A social constructionist term that has been developed recently originates with Werner Sollors (1989): the **invention of ethnicity.** His choice of words derives from a similar notion put forward by historian E. J. Hobsbawm, who has written about the "invention of tradition." Hobsbawm (1983: 1) defines invented tradition as a

> set of practices, normally governed by overtly or tacitly accepted rules and of a ritual or symbolic nature, which seeks to inculcate certain values and norms of behavior by repetition, which automatically implies continuity with the past.

Speaking about *invention* is a problem for some scholars because of connotations that they see in the word. Herbert Gans (1992) believes that the term can lead one to think that the act of ethnic invention has no connection with the past but is simply conjured up in the present. Moreover, he thinks the word places too great an emphasis on agency, which is to say on individual actors creating their world, and not enough on the role of social structure. In any case, those who have used invention built on earlier social constructionist theories while remedying some of the earlier versions' shortcomings.

Sollors uses this particular term to challenge the primordialist belief that ethnicity is at bedrock an irrational or preconscious form of cultural attachment, rooted in either blood or a past lost in the fog of time. Ethnic identity necessarily appeals to tradition, and tradition is something created, sustained, and refashioned by people. However, Sollors also wants to avoid those who see ethnicity as merely a rational construct of those intent on manipulating it for political or economic ends (cf. Glazer and Moynihan, 1975). Although he does not dismiss this instrumentalist position completely, he does not want to reduce all of what counts as ethnic to such means-ends calculations.

An interdisciplinary group of historians and social scientists has further developed this concept by suggesting that

> ethnicity itself is to be understood as a cultural construction accomplished over historical time. Ethnic groups in modern settings are constantly recreating themselves, and ethnicity is constantly being reinvented in response to changing realities both within the group and the host society. Ethnic group boundaries, for example, must be renegotiated, while the expressive symbols of ethnicity (ethnic traditions) must be repeatedly reinterpreted. By historicizing the phenomenon, the concept of invention allows for the appearance, metamorphosis, disappearance, and reappearance of ethnicities. (Conzen et al., 1990: 38)

This process of invention must be seen in a dialectical or reciprocal way, for not only do immigrants and indigenous peoples shape ethnic definitions and boundaries, but so does the dominant group in the society and so do the other groups that make up the societal totality. Differences in political, economic, and cultural power must be considered in analyzing this ongoing process of constituting and reconstituting ethnicity. Some groups have found themselves in an advantageous position by having greater resources—financial, social, and human capital—that can be used to construct a favorable and pragmatically useful identity. Other groups have had fewer resources and less power and, as a result, have had far less say in this process. Their identities have, to a comparatively greater extent, been imposed from the outside. In this regard, this approach is congruent with the racial formation approach advocated by Howard Winant (2000: 182), wherein he suggests that by viewing race and racial identities as "unstable and politically contested," we are able to see the meanings imputed to race as being "open to many types of agency, from the individual to the organizational, from the local to the global." For example, ethnic groups from eastern and southern Europe were often depicted as being members of distinct racial groups when they first arrived in the United States. As recent research by scholars such as David Roediger (1991) and Theodore Allen (1994) indicates, for these groups the process of gaining an economic foothold and being accepted into the mainstream of the host society entailed a process of *becoming* white.

Furthermore, within and outside of different groups, two or more versions of ethnic identity and group definition usually compete. The invention-of-ethnicity perspective calls attention to this situation and to the intragroup struggles for dominance that generally result. Moreover, given the assumption that this process of group definition is never completely accomplished, the invention-of-ethnicity perspective demands that we pay careful attention to changing circumstances.

Finally, the invention-of-ethnicity model questions the extent to which we can speak about a clear and singular American cultural and societal core or center. The process of ethnicity is a two-way street. Ethnics adapt to American culture. At the same time, ethnics influence and transform that core culture. Almost three quarters of a century ago the historian Arthur Schlesinger, Sr., made a case for a research agenda that studied not only the impact of America on the ethnics but also the impact of these diverse groups on America. To date, historians and social scientists have too frequently ignored the latter part of this equation. Those arguing for a new theory of ethnicity, however, have echoed Schlesinger by contending that "what is distinctively American has been itself a product of this synergistic encounter of multiple peoples and cultures" (Conzen et al., 1990: 54).

The invention, or construction (a term some prefer), approach is not an example of grand theory (Nagel, 1994). It does not seek to be predictive or to develop propositions from which lawlike patterns of behavior can be derived. Instead, the model is conceived in a manner that fully accords with Blumer's (1954) "sensitizing concept" in that it orients us to an appreciation of the place of human agency in creating social worlds. Given this character, it is appropriate to complement this perspective with other conceptual tools.

Ethnic Boundaries. One concept particularly relevant to the invention of ethnicity is that of **ethnic boundaries.** Fredrik Barth (1969) is generally credited with establishing the singular importance of boundaries in the definition of ethnic groups. He rather bluntly contends that "[t]he critical focus of investigation from this point of view becomes the ethnic *boundary* that defines the group, not the cultural stuff that it encloses" (Barth, 1969: 15). He is referring to social, rather than territorial, boundaries. Boundaries can be rigid or flexible, expansive or constrictive, permeable or impenetrable. They are subject to change. For example, Hasidic Jews and the Amish have rather rigid, constrictive, and impenetrable boundaries. Outsiders cannot easily enter, and insiders leave only with difficulty and often at the expense of ending all relationships with group members. On the other hand, in situations where intermarriage rates are high, boundaries are flexible, expansive, and permeable. Through intermarriage, a person may be one-eighth Irish, and on this basis may choose to identify with and participate in Irish American organizations for either limited or extended periods of time.

The ethnic boundary "canalizes social life—it entails a frequently quite complex organization of behavior and social relations" (Barth, 1969: 15). The boundary is seen as both enabling certain kinds of relationships to exist and constraining or limiting others. The ethnic boundary is the principal device that distinguishes the respective character of intragroup and intergroup relations (Carling, 1991).

We disagree with Barth's dismissal of the "cultural stuff" (behaviors, attitudes, traditions, and so forth), because this "stuff" is the source of the rationale for defining boundaries in one way or another. Rather than posing this situation in an either-or manner, as Barth does, the relationship between ethnic boundaries and cultures can be viewed as interconnected and mutually reinforcing. Indeed, as Joane Nagel (1994) has pointed out, part of the very process of constructing ethnic identity and culture involves the continuing renegotiation of ethnic boundaries.

Institutional Completeness. Similarly, Raymond Breton's (1964) concept of **institutional completeness** is valuable because it calls attention to the fact that an institutional presence is an essential ingredient for the creation and maintenance of *collective* ethnic identity (which, in turn, is a prerequisite for the preservation of individual ethnic identities). Ethnic institutions perform a number of valuable services for members of ethnic communities, including functions related to employment, the acquisition of political rewards, welfare, ethnic cultural expression, recreation, the adjudication of conflict within and outside of the ethnic enclave, and so on.

Some groups have had the ability to create institutional networks that perform a wide range of tasks on behalf of constituents, thereby binding them to the community. These are institutionally complete ethnic communities. Two good examples are the Chinese throughout their history in America and the Italians during the periods of mass immigration. Other groups have, for various reasons, been less successful in achieving institutional completeness. The English and the Danish are two examples.

Breton (1964: 204) speaks about "social entrepreneurs" who attempt to fulfill what they see as the needs of an ethnic "clientele." Another way of posing this is in terms of ethnic leaders and the mass of the ethnic community. Recently, attention has been paid to the role of ethnic leaders (Higham, 1978; Bodnar, 1985; Greene, 1987). Their backgrounds, especially their social class backgrounds, their bases of support, the resources at their disposal for mobilizing ethnic-based action, and the nature of the coalitions they form are topics that help answer questions related to the particular character of an ethnic community.

Connected to analyses of leaders must be an examination of the ordinary members of the ethnic group. How internally unified or divided are they? To what extent do they act as either supporters or detractors of potential candidates for leadership? What reasons underlie differing exhibitions of loyalty to leaders? What are the bases of loyalty—or, in other words, what kinds of appeals to legitimation are made, on traditional, charismatic, or legal-rational grounds? How important is territorial clustering (Zelinsky, 2001)? What role do social class divisions within a group play? What is the role of gender (Nagel, 2000; Pedraza-Bailey, 1991)?

Contemporary Diversity: Multiculturalism and Transnationalism

During the past two decades, the term **multiculturalism** has gained currency and has become the focus of considerable controversy. One of the problems with the term is that, as David Pearson (2001: 129) has noted, it is a "chameleon-like neologism," meaning quite different things to different people. In part, this variation is due to the fact that, like *assimilation* and *cultural pluralism*, multiculturalism frequently involves an unspoken mixing of what is and what ought to be. In other words, it is used as both an analytic term and a politically normative precept. Critics of multiculturalism, such as Arthur Schlesinger, Jr. (1992), fear that multicultural politics fuels a "cult of ethnicity" that is leading to the disuniting of the nation. Supporters, such as Ronald Takaki (1993a), contend that multiculturalism can become the basis for a meeting ground for members of diverse ethnic cultures. Some commentators have suggested that *multiculturalism* is essentially a contemporary synonym for *pluralism* (Parrillo, 1996: 157–158). Others have pointed out that there are "hard" and "soft" versions of multicultural-ism. The hard version promotes separatism and lacks an interest in finding a center where diverse groups have shared values, whereas the soft version wants to allow diversity to exist within a unified national culture. Nathan Glazer (1997) has concluded that it is because of the failure of the nation to assimilate all of its ethnic groups—and African Americans in particular—that "we are all multiculturalists now."

Given these competing views, it is difficult to disentangle the theo-retical use of the term from its ideological aspects. Perhaps a useful starting point is to observe the distinction that political theorist Bhikhu Parekh (2000a: 7) has made: "The term 'multicultural' refers to the fact of cultural diversity, the term 'multiculturalism' to a normative re-sponse to that fact." With this distinction in mind, we would suggest that *multiculturalism* refers to the quest on the part of ethnic groups to preserve and enhance their distinctive ethnic identities. Those who em-brace multiculturalism are engaging in what political philosopher Charles Taylor (1992) has referred to as the "politics of recognition." Multiculturalism in its soft version is about finding a way to preserve discrete identities while simultaneously finding in a larger sense of na-tional identity a countervailing identity that unites disparate groups. Parekh (2000a: 219) succinctly summarizes this dual-edged project:

> Like any other society, a multicultural society needs a broadly shared culture to sustain it. Since it involves several cultures, the shared culture can only grow out of their interaction and should both respect and nurture their diversity and unite them around a common way of life.

Multiculturalism is, thus, a political project. Impediments to its realiza-tion include resistance from the dominant groups to the incorporation of ethnic minorities or to a willingness to recognize (in Taylor's sense of the term) those cultures, as well as resistance from hard multicultura-lists who exhibit little interest in finding the common ground of a shared national culture.

Related to contemporary discussions of multiculturalism, a grow-ing number of immigration scholars have begun to speak about the rise of transnational immigrant communities. Such communities are treated as a parallel phenomenon to other manifestations of transna-tionalism, such as those related to global corporate capitalism, the emergence of transnational NonGovernmental Organizations (NGOs), and the increasing hybridization of popular culture. Linda Basch, Nina Glick Schiller, and Christina Szanton Blanc (1994: 7) define **transna-tionalism** as the "processes by which immigrants forge and sustain multistranded relations that link together their societies of origin and settlement." Put simply, transnational immigrants are seen as attempt-ing to live with one foot in their homeland and one foot in the host society, and in the process create an ethnic community that transcends national boundaries. This is akin to the idea of an ethnic global village (Faist, 2000; Portes, 1996). Whereas ongoing involvement in homeland concerns was common among immigrants from earlier immigration periods, theorists of transnationalism contend that today's immigrants are better able to remain involved as a result of improved communications technologies and transportation systems.

Alejandro Portes, Luis E. Guarnizo, and Patricia Landolt (1999: 221) identify three types of transnationalism: economic, political, and sociocultural. Economic transnationalism involves entrepreneurs whose network of suppliers, capital, and markets crosses national borders. Political transnationalism refers to "the political activities of party officials, governmental functionaries, or community leaders whose main goals are the achievement of political power and influence in the sending or receiving countries." Finally, sociocultural transnationalism entails activities designed to reinforce homeland culture and adapt it to new circumstances.

Theorists of transnational immigration have attempted to provide an account of contemporary immigration that can be viewed as a new type of socially constructed ethnic identity based on the ability of immigrants to create transnational social spaces (Faist, 2000). They have also created the conceptual framework for a research agenda that is currently being pursued by many immigration scholars (Portes et al., 1999). In coming years, this research will determine the extent to which transnational immigrant communities have actually developed among immigrant groups during the past few decades. Likewise, research will determine whether transnationalism is essentially a phenomenon of the immigrant generation or whether it will be capable of persisting over time as the subsequent American-born generations come of age (Kivisto, 2001; Waldinger and Fitzgerald, 2004).

Ingroups, Outgroups, and Group Position

The invention of ethnicity, ethnic boundaries, institutional completeness, multiculturalism, and transnationalism are concepts that assist in comprehending the internal dynamics of ethnic groups. Ethnic groups, however, never exist in a vacuum and are possible only insofar as the definition of "we" is linked to definitions of "they." This section focuses on prejudice and discrimination—the processes by which some groups are accepted by the larger society (ingroups) while others are excluded (outgroups). We'll also look at negative attitudes toward outgroup members and actions taken that are designed to prevent their full and equal inclusion into the larger society.

The Psychology of Prejudice

As See and Wilson (1988) have contended, in an earlier period in ethnic studies much attention was devoted to the psychological dimension of intergroup boundaries, with most of the focus on prejudice. **Prejudice** refers to individually held negative attitudes about a group of people that are often accompanied by a strong emotional aversion to members of that group. Rupert Brown (1995: 8) succinctly defines prejudice (and in the process links it to discrimination) as

> any or all of the following: *the holding of derogatory social attitudes or cognitive beliefs, the expression of negative affect, or the display of hostile or discriminatory behaviour towards members of a group on account of their membership in that group.* (Brown's italics)

Arnold Rose (1951: 11) sees prejudice as "nearly always accompanied by incorrect or ill-informed opinions." This view was shared by psychologist Gordon Allport, who in his book *The Nature of Prejudice* (1958: 7) treats prejudice as "thinking ill of others without sufficient warrant." This definition suggests that prejudice is the product of a lack of knowledge and that therefore education can be a valuable tool in eradicating such attitudes.

Allport, however, along with many other psychologists of his generation, viewed prejudice as more problematic than this lack-of-knowledge perspective would suggest. Allport attempted, in his notion of the "prejudiced personality" (1958; see also Rokeach, 1960), to incorporate psychoanalytic theory into research on ethnic prejudice. This approach also is seen in T. W. Adorno and his colleagues' (1950) thesis of the "authoritarian personality" and in related versions of frustration-aggression theory (e.g., Dollard, 1937). Despite differences, these approaches owe a shared debt to Freud. In the first place, they placed great emphasis on early childhood socialization. In the second, they viewed prejudice as the product of pathology.

This view holds that the prejudiced person manifests a personality disorder that involves intense insecurity and anxiety, a feeling of powerlessness, and internalized rage against parental authority. The result is an outlook that considers the external world to be threatening and evil and that reacts to this generalized perception in an often rigid and superstitious manner. Central to these psychoanalytically inspired theories is the concept of *projection:* the process by which an individual externalizes aggressive attitudes onto a group that functions as a scapegoat. The scapegoat becomes the object of prejudicial beliefs (Kovel, 1970; LeVine and Campbell, 1972).

Beyond the specific shortcomings that some psychologists have found with psychoanalytic theories of prejudice, more far-reaching limitations have been noted. First, the theories fail to account for the societal contexts in which prejudice appears. Second, by defining prejudice as pathological, these theories fail to consider the possibility that prejudice might also be the result of normal socialization into a world characterized by intense ethnic rivalries and animosities (cf. Sherif and Sherif, 1953; Pettigrew, 1958).

The Sociology of Prejudice and Discrimination

Concerns with the limitations inherent in the psychology of prejudice have been voiced frequently (Park, 1950; Schermerhorn, 1978; Francis, 1976). Recent work by social psychologists has tended to abandon this earlier psychoanalytic approach in favor of cognitive and learning theories (Tajfel, 1969, 1978, 1981), which consider the impact of larger societal forces on individual prejudice. Such a perspective emphasizes the socially constructed nature of prejudice, suggesting that it must be understood as an intergroup phenomenon (Brown, 1995).

To the extent that these theorists treat individual prejudice as essentially derivative, they agree with Herbert Blumer's (1958) definition of *prejudice* as a "sense of group position." In this deceptively simple formulation, Blumer shifts the focus of attention from individual attitudes to history and politics (Esposito and Murphy, 1999). As Stanford Lyman (1984: 110) said in commenting on this move: "Attitudes in turn were merely the lowest form of expression of these historically established positions, and were not irremediably correlative with conduct." Without referring explicitly to Blumer (Killian, 1970), most scholars in ethnic studies today work with a similar understanding of the psychology of prejudice.

The significance of Blumer's definition can be seen in the analysis of derogatory expressions, stereotypes, and humor. Different groups have been variously characterized as lazy, miserly, drunken, morose, happy-go-lucky, cunning, inscrutable, hot tempered, or stupid (Allen, 1990). These **stereotypes** are not interchangeable. Why is it that African Americans are stereotyped as lazy while Japanese Americans are not? Why is it that Jewish Americans are depicted as miserly while Italian Americans are not? As an illustration of a derogatory expression directed at Irish Americans, why did the vehicle used by the police to transport arrestees to jail become known as the "paddy wagon"? In the realm of ethnic jokes, why does one ask how many Polish Americans it takes to change a light bulb and not how many German Americans? The answer rests, not in the psychological proclivities of the individual using such negative expressions, but in the location of these groups in relation to each other and the society at large.

Stereotypes, derogatory expressions, and jokes are invidious distortions of a sociocultural truth. Those groups least successful socioeconomically are often deemed to be lazy if they are more highly represented in the ranks of the unemployed than the general population.

Those who are employed in unskilled, low-paying, dead-end jobs may be deemed stupid. The stereotype addresses a truth: These groups are not as successful as other groups. The stereotype is invidious because the members of the group are blamed for this state of affairs. This kind of stereotyping is prevalent in America because of the high premium placed on individual achievement.

In a parallel way, the view of people as cunning or miserly is applied to groups that have been more, rather than less, successful than the general population. The invidious distortion here questions the means by which such groups got ahead, viewing their advancement as being based on less than scrupulous means. This stereotype, too, serves to justify a person's own place in the social hierarchy, for the implicit message is that the person is more morally upright than those who are more successful.

Discriminatory actions reinforce existing ethnic relationships by denying outgroup members equal access to jobs, homes, neighborhoods, education, income, political power, influence, and status. Such actions can be crude or subtle, overt or covert. A person, for example, may be denied a job interview because her address identifies her as a resident of a black ghetto. A realtor may tell a middle-class black couple that a suburban home they want to see has already been sold, only to show the house to a white couple a few hours later.

Sometimes such **discrimination** is the intentional result of prejudicial attitudes. At other times it may be unintentional. A person who does not harbor prejudicial attitudes may be pressured into acts of discrimination. The connection between prejudice and discrimination is not a simple matter of cause and effect. Robert Merton (1976) illustrated this fact by identifying four different types of individuals. Unprejudiced nondiscriminators, or "all-weather liberals," are willing to act on their beliefs even in the face of pressure to do otherwise. At the other extreme, the prejudiced discriminator, or "all-weather bigot," is equally consistent and will continue to discriminate even when confronted by societal demands to end discrimination. In contrast, the other two types reveal an inconsistency between attitudes and actions. In both cases, the individual gives in to social pressure. Unprejudiced discriminators, or "reluctant liberals," give in to social pressure to discriminate, and prejudiced nondiscriminators, or "timid bigots," yield to opposite pressures.

The owners of a Chinese-Vietnamese herb shop.

Beyond individual manifestations of discrimination is the issue of *institutional discrimination.* This term refers to patterns of discrimination at the societal rather than individual level and includes widespread practices, laws, and customs that perpetuate existing inequalities. The most powerful expression of institutional discrimination in this nation's history was the institution of slavery.

Explaining Ethnic Differences

What, then, are the causes of the differences in group position in America? What contributes to ethnic stratification (Shibutani and Kwan, 1965)? Some, such as the neoconservative social theorist Thomas Sowell (1981a), believe that the differences are due to differing cultural characteristics. Simply put, some groups are seen as having cultural values that synchronize with the dominant cultural values of America, permitting them to achieve success. Other groups harbor values at odds with the dominant culture's values and consequently are unable to be upwardly mobile.

College students at their graduation in Los Angeles.

Focusing on the role of culture in explaining perceived differences across ethnic groups has considerable merit. Ethnic cultures must be investigated as potential sources for inequalities. For example, early in this century Jews—for a variety of reasons rooted, at least in part, in cultural differences—used education as a vehicle for upward mobility, whereas Italians were suspicious of education's virtues. Jews were also more successful economically than their Italian counterparts.

When, however, cultural explanations are not linked to social structural explanations—Sowell's unfortunate tendency—the result is something like blaming the victim. The analysis resembles a morality play in which those presumed to be possessing the proper virtues (hardworking, emotional control, family oriented, and so forth) are justly rewarded, while the morally deficient have only themselves to blame.

The equally shortsighted reverse perspective, common among many sociologists, is to ignore culture and attempt to use social structural factors alone as causal variables. In an influential work, Stephen Steinberg (1981) provides what amounts to an antithetical explanation to that of Sowell. Steinberg looks at Jewish success and attempts to disparage the cultural elements central to that success by focusing instead on such factors as the level of urbanism and occupational skills derived from the premigration milieu.

The point is obvious: Both culture and social structure must be considered. Moreover, they need to be viewed in a reciprocal manner: culture shapes social structure, which in turn shapes culture. Moreover, both social structure and culture must be linked to the role of individuals as active agents engaged in creating their social worlds (Pedraza-Bailey, 1990). Individuals confront their cultures and social structures as both constraining their ability to act and as enabling them to act (Giddens, 1984).

That being said, what must be considered in determining the precise ways in which both culture and social structure manage to constrain or enable certain courses of action? What, in short, would be contained on a conceptual map that plotted the different life courses of individuals who happen to be members of different ethnic groups?

Though by no means a complete map, we would include the following crucial considerations: How groups became a part of American society relates to the amount of power and resources (financial, social, and human capital) they have to influence their position in the social hierarchy (Kinlock, 1974; Kuper, 1975). Voluntary migration, involuntary migration, and colonial domination constitute the three ways in which ethnic groups have been incorporated into America. The differences have had pronounced differential impacts (see Table 2.2), and therefore consideration of these differences is an essential starting point. The ability of each group to preserve its inherited culture and social institutions is important, as this ability provides an important mechanism for individuals to adapt to and become part of America.

Most Americans live in this country because they or their ancestors voluntarily migrated. These immigrants include the Swedish peasant who left home in the nineteenth century to acquire farmland in the Midwest, the Jew who fled religious persecution in czarist Russia, the Cuban who fled to Miami after Castro's victory, and the Dominican who left last year to find employment in New York City. We must consider the forces that pushed voluntary immigrants out of their homeland, as well as timing and migration patterns, including chain migration, individual versus family migration, and so on (Thistlethwaite, 1960; Tilly, 1990). We must ask, who left: the poorest of the poor or a middle stratum? Did they leave for economic, political, or religious rea-

Table 2.2	Types of Ethnic Groups Based on Mode of Incorporation Into the United States

I. Voluntary immigrants
  A. Economic immigrants
    1. Skilled immigrants (including "brain-drain" immigrants)
    2. "Middlemen minority" or trader immigrants
    3. Poor immigrants
  B. Political refugees
II. Imported slaves
III. Victims of colonial conquest

sons? Did they view their migration as permanent or temporary? The reverse side of this equation involves determining the pull factors that brought immigrants not simply to America, but to particular places in America. Settlement location (that is, urban or rural, established communities or frontier settlements, and so forth) plays a key role (Conzen, 1991), as do the skills and educational levels that immigrants brought to America. We need to explore the role of distinctive mixtures of various forms of capital—financial, social, and human—in propelling immigrants into entrepreneurial, professional, or low-skilled factory and service-sector occupations (Nee and Sanders, 2001).

Although some similar considerations pertain to involuntary immigrants and colonized peoples, these immigrants had far less freedom of initiative than the voluntary immigrants. The term *involuntary immigrants* describes Africans who were the victims of the international slave trade; the term *colonized peoples* refers to Native Americans. African slaves were unfree and powerless. They were stripped of much of their cultural heritage and denied the resources or opportunities to create a new communal institutional presence in America. Native Americans found their worlds undermined by the desire of the more powerful European colonizers to acquire their lands. Both involuntary migrants and colonized peoples had less power than voluntary immigrants, and the implications must be taken into account. Without ignoring how such groups sought to shape their own lives, we must determine the nature of and the reasons for the constraints imposed by more powerful groups (Rex, 1983; Williams, 1990).

The nation's economy has changed from an agrarian one to an industrial one to what some call a postindustrial or advanced industrial society. Concurrently, these changes transformed the class structure. Different kinds of employment possibilities exist depending on the particular historical period. The working class, for example, has often been divided between skilled and unskilled workers, sometimes leading to what Edna Bonacich (1972) has referred to as the "split labor market." Such split labor markets have often been defined in terms of racial differences, with blacks, Asians, and Hispanics disproportionately located among the ranks of the unskilled. Here class and ethnicity or race turn out to be mutually reinforcing. In addition, some industries exhibit what can be termed *ethnic succession*. The meatpacking industry, for example, was once an important source of employment for Europeans, especially Poles, Lithuanians, Germans, and Irish. Although such groups are still represented, the workforces at packinghouses today include large numbers of Mexicans and Southeast Asians. Earlier generations left for other jobs because the work is hard and dangerous and pay levels have declined in recent years, whereas these are perhaps the first jobs the newly arrived can find (Lamphere, 1992).

Economic changes also contribute to different entrepreneurial possibilities. Economic niches in various industries or businesses have characterized many groups (Light, 1972; Bonacich, 1973). For example, prior to the 1960s, Jews were prominent merchants in black ghettos, whereas today they have been replaced in many major cities by Koreans. Jews have been historically prominent in the garment industry; today in Miami the same industry is an important source of ownership and employment opportunities for Cubans. The relationship between class and ethnicity is important—and sometimes mutually reinforcing. Employment discrimination, which has proven to be especially burdensome to some groups but not to others, is related to class and ethnicity (Light and Gold, 2000).

The political realm, particularly citizenship, is linked to the ways in which the economy shapes ethnic relations (Shklar, 1991). Some groups whose members were permitted to become citizens easily did so quickly, whereas others did not. Some groups involved themselves in the political process, whereas others distanced themselves from it. For others, especially Native Americans, Africans, and Asians, citizenship was long denied, and even when it was granted, the remnants of institutional discrimination remained (Lyman, 1997). Understanding why these observed differences occurred is essential.

The culture of America has evolved from its primarily Anglo-American roots to reflect the multicultural character of the nation. Ethnic cultures have also transformed over time. Some have all but disappeared, and others remain alive. Some have had a significant impact on American culture; others have had little or no effect. Some ethnic cultures made the transition into American society relatively painlessly; for others a profound culture conflict ensued. This conflict was sometimes generational, as first-generation immigrants hung on to their old-world cultures, while their children, who grew up in America, rejected much of the ancestral heritage, identifying instead with American culture (Hansen, 1938; Kivisto and Blanck, 1990; Ueda, 1992; Higham, 1999; Gerstle, 2001).

Summary

We began this chapter with an overview of sociology's repudiation of biological explanations and its development of a sociocultural approach. This chapter included discussions of the limited utility of two concepts: nationality groups and minority groups. We have defined ethnicity and ethnic groups and have indicated their relationship to race and racial groups. After discussing central forms of intergroup relations, we analyzed the two most important types for the United States: assimilation and pluralism. A review of their respective strengths and weaknesses led to a discussion of various alternatives to both positions, culminating in a discussion of variations in the social constructionist approach and including discussions of multiculturalism and transnationalism. We then explored the issues of prejudice and discrimination. With all of these pieces in place, we presented a brief conceptual map that included a number of things that must be examined in attempting to understand the big picture.

What this overview indicates is that a wide range of variables must be considered if one is to begin to comprehend the continuing role of ethnicity in America. Furthermore, to understand the present, we must consider the past. To this end, Chapters 3 and 4 provide a historical survey that will inform the remainder of the book, which focuses on the present and possible futures of America's main ethnic groups.

Key Terms

assimilation	*invention of ethnicity*
discrimination	*minority group*
emergent ethnicity	*multiculturalism*
ethnic boundaries	*nationalism*
ethnic group	*nationalities*
ethnicity	*pluralism*
ethnicization	*prejudice*
ethnogenesis	*primordialist*
ethnonationalism	*rational choice theory*
eugenics	*religio-ethnic groups*
genocide	*sociobiology*
institutional completeness	*stereotype*

Questions for Discussion and Critical Thinking

1. Discuss your understanding of the relationship between race and ethnicity. Do you think that these terms refer to different types of identities, or should race be seen as an aspect of ethnicity? Defend your position.

2. Define assimilation and pluralism. Which of these two perspectives seems to provide the most accurate portrait of contemporary ethnic group relations in the United States? Should we view assimilation and pluralism in either-or terms, or can they be reconciled?

3. What is transnationalism? Do you think that many of today's new immigrants can be described as transnational? Can transnational immigrants assimilate, or does transnationalism function as a new and qualitatively different type of immigrant adaptation? ✦

Part II

Sociology Meets History

Constructing WASP Hegemony and the Racial 'Other' From Colonial America to the Civil War

In this chapter we begin by examining the major social processes that formed the nation between the colonial period and the Civil War and their relevance for the peopling of America by Europeans during this time. We then discuss the three major European immigrant groups of this period: the British, Irish, and Germans. We look both at the ways that these social forces affected each group and at how the groups responded to those forces.

Tzvetan Todorov (1984) has argued that the European conquest of America raised what he refers to as "the question of the other." In other words, it forced a consideration of how to define nonEuropeans in the process of deciding who would and who would not be included in full societal membership. Racialized ethnicity was used to differentiate those deemed fit for inclusion in the new nation versus those viewed as unqualified. It soon became clear that Native Americans, Africans caught up in the slave trade, and voluntary immigrants from Asia and Latin America were made to confront barriers of exclusion that distinguished their experiences in the new nation from those of European settlers.

Nation Building

The period from 1760 to the Civil War was critically important to immigration and its impact on American society. Economic, political, and cultural forces shaped the experiences of those already in America as well as the experiences of new immigrants. The impact of these societal forces continued long after the Civil War ended.

The first of these processes was economic. Given the obvious economic success of the United States in the nineteenth and twentieth centuries, it is ironic, Rowland Berthoff (1971: 3) observed, that "American society began in a long series of business failures." During the seventeenth century, mercantilist policies encouraged state-chartered business ventures in the Americas. Major European powers sponsored a variety of undertakings prior to American independence.

The British met all challengers and became the dominant economic force in North America. As Table 3.1 illustrates, in the 1790 census, 82.1 percent of the white population originated from England. The British colonial empire actually extended from Newfoundland to Barbados and Tobago (Wells, 1975). Franklin Scott (1963: 9) aptly described the British in North America as "the shock troops and the pace setters of European occupation." In the settlements along the Atlantic seaboard, the British dominated major businesses such as shipping and steel production and were the major group in banking and finance. Furthermore, on the frontier they had more influence than any other European group.

The economic domination of the British coalesced with political domination. British laws, institutions, and political sensibilities were transplanted to North America. In a more philosophical sense, the political ideals of those who shaped the American Revolution derived from Enlightenment thought in its various forms and was, therefore, not simply British. Nonetheless, the concrete political form of the new republic was most indebted to the way in which these ideas developed in a British setting (Commager, 1977; Bailyn, 1986).

But the United States's political self-definition was based on its anticolonialism and, therefore, on its ability to distance itself from its origins. Unlike Canada, which has continued to maintain its ties to Britain, the United States became, in Seymour Martin Lipset's (1963) phrase, "the first new nation." He meant that the United States was the first large colony to successfully free itself from the domination of a colonial power via revolution. The revolution's challenge to monarchical government meant that the new nation had to wrestle with competing definitions about what representative government meant and what form it should take.

Table 3.1	European Origin Population in 1790 by Nationality	
Nationality	Number	Percentage
English	2,605,699	82.1
Scotch	221,562	7.0
German	176,407	5.6
Dutch	78,959	2.5
Irish	61,534	1.9
French	17,619	0.6
Jewish	1,243	0.1
All Other	9,421	0.3
Total	3,172,444	100.0

Source: U.S. Bureau of the Census (1909).

'You can't come in. The quota for 1620 is full.'

Particularly important to ethnic and racial groups was how notions about democracy emerged. As historian Bernard Bailyn (1967) has indicated, for colonists hostile to British rule, a "contagion of liberty" swept the new republic, but at the same time many influential revolutionary leaders expressed their fears about the dangers that would result if political power was granted to "weak or ignorant" people. Thus, although the nation was conceived as a democracy, who was and who was not eligible for citizenship became an important question. Citizenship, and how it was granted and denied, became a major means of incorporating some groups into not only the American polity but also social life in general, while excluding others. Although the history of incorporation and exclusion is a complicated one, as we shall see in this and subsequent chapters, race became the most powerful determinant of inclusion and exclusion, as whiteness and citizenship became intertwined (Jacobson, 1998).

Cultural development was related to these economic and political forces. Two aspects of culture concern us here. The first relates to the identification of certain core values that are deeply embedded in American culture. Although a number of values could be noted, none have had the enduring impact on national identity as the following trio: freedom, equality, and individualism. When the French traveler Alexis de Tocqueville visited the United States during the 1830s and subsequently presented his impressions in his now classic *Democracy in America* (1981 [1835]), he identified these three as central to what differentiated America from Europe. In his opinion, America represented an entirely new kind of society, seen, for instance, by de Tocqueville's need to coin a new word—*individualism*—to describe one of the nation's core values.

The second important issue related to culture is the extent to which culture is dynamic and open to outside influences or is static and closed. Obviously, this would affect the extent to which a culture chiefly shaped by its British origins in the seventeenth and eighteenth centuries was either preserved or transformed by the waves of immigrants—voluntary and involuntary—as well as by the indigenous people. Put bluntly, would America always be a white Anglo-Saxon Protestant culture, or would it continue to refashion itself into what the early twentieth-century social critic Randolph Bourne (1977) referred to as an ever-changing "transnational America"?

Albion's Seed

To assess the extent to which America is stamped by the British imprint, we must first answer the following question: Who are the British? In one sense, the answer appears simple: they are people who originated from the British Isles. Yet, as with all national, ethnic, and racial definitions, what appears self-evident actually has a historical dimension that makes it far more complicated (Furer, 1972). The British were not always British. In fact, as David Hackett Fischer (1989) has observed, the earliest recorded name of Britain was *Albion*. The Greeks used this name as early as the sixth century BCE. Though it was used for another thousand years, it gave way to *Britain*. Those we refer to as the British are, however, a remarkably heterogeneous people whose sense of collective identity has changed extensively over time.

Fischer (1989) has argued that America's folkways—the values, customs, and meanings that make up a normative structure—bear the heavy imprint of the nation's British founders. These influences can be seen in a wide range of human activities and attitudes, including our language; religion; education; cuisine; work and leisure habits; attitudes regarding wealth and inequality; views about marriage, the family, and sexuality; architectural preferences; and general political orientations (including views of power, freedom, and social order). Fischer doesn't see a unified culture derived from British roots, however. Instead, he sees in pre-Revolutionary America four distinct folkways based on the different socioeconomic, political, and religious orientations of four large waves of emigration from Britain that occurred between 1607 and 1775.

The first wave involved the Puritans, who originated in eastern England and arrived in America between 1629 and 1640. Central to Puritan theology was its understanding of a covenant with God and the need for the commonwealth to be composed of members who had found redemption. The second group, arriving between 1640 and 1675, came from southern England to Virginia and consisted chiefly of cavaliers (a royalist elite) and their indentured servants. Far less democratic and far more elitist and traditionalist, the cavaliers became a central force among the slaveholding class. The third group came from the North Midlands of England and Wales and entered the Delaware Valley (especially Pennsylvania) between 1665 and 1725. These were largely members of the dissident pacifist sect known as the Society of Friends, or Quakers, who in the following century founded the first antislavery society in the Western world (Bailyn, 1967). The final group to arrive from Britain (1717 to 1775) did not originate in England but rather came from Scotland and Northern Ireland. The Scotch-Irish clustered in a region known today as Appalachia, where they had a pronounced influence on frontier politics, particularly in their promotion of aggressive campaigns of forced relocations of American Indians.

Transplanting the Old World to the New

The obvious differences among these four groups make it difficult to speak about British America as a singular, coherent culture. Bonds such as language and a shared (if contested) history allow us to speak at another level about British culture in America. From the seeds of this culture we can find the tensions—the ambiguities and the contradictions—that have existed and continue to shape our national culture: a belief in equality versus a justification of the unbridled accumulation of wealth by individuals; a premium placed on liberty versus a systematic denial of liberty to people because of their skin color; theocracy versus religious freedom; and the belief in democratic participation versus the demand that decisions be made by elites.

The multifaceted British culture rather quickly and rather decisively became dominant, and all immigrant groups that followed had to respond to this cultural imprint (Hansen, 1940b). For example, the English language became the language of the nation in both politics and commerce, an achievement reached without legislation mandating English as the country's official language.

Nineteenth-Century Migration

After the Revolution, British settlers continued to come to America. Though there was relatively little migration between the American Revolution and the War of 1812, when the two nations entered into a more cooperative political relationship, the increase in immigration was unprecedented. Charlotte Erickson (1980) estimates that the figure was around 410,000. The main motive for emigration was economic. One of the most persistent rationales for migrating was economic independence.

British immigrants entered a country whose language and culture was far more familiar to them than to any other immigrant group. This did not mean, however, that the world they entered was a mirror image of the old country. Wilbur Shepperson (1965) has studied English immigrants who became disenchanted with America and chose to repatriate, and he argues that assimilation into the new world for these settlers was not as easy as is popularly assumed. Some returned home because they harbored such a romanticized portrait of America that they could not bear the harsher realities. Others returned because they were unwilling to accept features of American life that were different from British life.

Nonetheless, most of the British adapted to the new environment with far greater ease than any other settlers did. Although they founded ethnic societies similar to other immigrant groups, these organizations were relatively short-lived, as the British soon opted to join American voluntary organizations. Doing so was easier because no language barrier existed. Thus, a distinctive ethnic community did not emerge and maintain itself over time as was typical with most other groups. To be sure, elite organizations such as the St. George's Society served as a mark of identity for Anglophiles, and numerous self-help associations—fraternal societies, trade unions, and cooperatives (based on the Rochdale model)—were founded, but many did not survive past the first generation. By blending into the host society as rapidly as they did, the British became, in Charlotte Erickson's (1972) words, "invisible immigrants."

The Scots, including those from Ulster, the Lowlands, and the Highlands, could also be called invisible immigrants. Their transition, however, occurred more slowly because of their outsider status in relation to the English. Scots counted for approximately half a million people by the end of the colonial period, constituting almost 15 percent of the population (Anderson, 1970). In occupational status, they were second only to the English and Welsh, being well represented among the merchant class as well as among artisans, clerks, politicians, and officers in the military (Graham, 1956).

The Core Society: Anglo-Saxon Protestant

Although there was considerable diversity among the various components of British America, these immigrants were melded into what Charles Anderson (1970: 41) described as "the larger Anglo-Saxon Protestant core society." Furthermore, British Americans, because of this cultural hegemony and their dominant location in the American economy and polity, were in a position to attempt to dictate the terms of entrance for other ethnic groups. Other groups were forced to react to this situation in a reciprocal process of adaptation to British American folkways while seeking to preserve aspects of their own cultural heritages. As Thomas Archdeacon (1983: 94) suggested, "The pattern of combining cultural accommodation with resistance was common to all nonBritish European immigrant groups."

This pattern can be seen in the two largest nonBritish groups in America during the first half of the nineteenth century, the Irish and the Germans.

Erin's Children in America

The Irish had a powerful presence in the United States during the nineteenth century. In stark contrast to the Scotch-Irish, Irish Catholics did not migrate in significant numbers until after 1815. Migration prior to that time was quite common, but the destination was primarily England, with some Irish moving to the continent. Those who arrived in America during the colonial period were often either indentured servants or criminals who had first been sent to the West Indies (Lockhart, 1976). Some settled in Maryland because of its reputation for greater religious tolerance than the other colonies, only to find that this tolerance had limits—a law was passed that limited the number of Irish Catholic servants admitted into the colony (Blessing, 1980).

From their first encounter with America, the Irish confronted anti-Catholic and anti-Irish prejudice and discrimination. Most of the Irish in America were poor, though they brought various skills that helped them obtain work. A small contingent of wealthy Irish Catholics also resided in some colonial cities, particularly New York and Philadelphia. The poor Irish settled in residential concentrations in some cities and formed the beginning of the Irish ethnic enclave or ghetto. Thus, what would later be characterized as the "shanty Irish" and the "lace curtain Irish" were in evidence at an early date. In everyday parlance, the latter were described by the former as those who had fruit in the house when nobody was sick and flowers in the house when nobody had died.

An ever-expanding stream entered this embryonic ethnic community between 1815 and 1845; after 1845 the stream became a major river. The increase was partially due to Irish population growth. In a century's time the population had expanded from 3 million to more than 8 million. Although demographers have indicated that population growth occurred throughout all of Europe during the eighteenth and early nineteenth centuries, the growth was higher in Ireland (Connell, 1950).

As late as 1845, the number of Scotch-Irish continued to outnumber the number of Irish Catholics in America (Miller, 1985). But this proportion changed as a consequence of the extremely destructive potato blight that struck Ireland in 1845—when the Great Famine began. In the wake of successive crop failures, widespread starvation and disease took a terrible toll. Between 1845 and 1851 an estimated one million people died as a result of starvation or disease. An equal number emigrated, most going to the United States. Within half a decade the population of Ireland was reduced by a quarter. Many believed that the British government had failed to respond adequately to the crisis, which further fueled anti-British sentiments (Wittke, 1956).

Immigrant Adjustment

The exodus had a major impact on the receiving country, as well: Between 1841 and 1860, Ireland supplied more immigrants to the United States than any other country. In the first of these two decades Irish immigration accounted for 45.6 percent of all immigrants entering the United States. In contrast with those who had arrived prior to 1845, this cohort was decidedly poorer and, lacking economic resources or marketable skills, they found themselves in impoverished conditions that were rife with crime, disease, various social pathologies, and human misery. They became, in effect, America's first truly impoverished ghetto dwellers.

Though Irish immigrants settled virtually everywhere throughout the country, including the rural agricultural communities of the Midwest and the Pacific Coast states, they were heavily concentrated in the northeastern states. They settled principally in urban rather than rural areas. Large concentrations of Irish could be found in New York, Philadelphia, and Boston, as well as in smaller cities throughout the region. They were also well represented in the mining centers of Pennsylvania.

Irish immigration was distinguished from that of many other groups by the relative parity in the sex ratio of immigrants. While other groups were overwhelmingly male—a ratio of 9:1 was not unusual—more Irish females than males entered the United States between 1880 and 1910. No other large European-origin group counted so many women among its ranks (Daniels, 1990). This was not because the Irish emigrated as family units. Instead, unmarried females, like their male counterparts, exhibited a willingness to make the journey alone. As Hasia Diner (1983: 50) points out, "it indicates that economic motives for migration remained paramount. Irish women did not migrate primarily to find the husbands they could not find at home." As in Ireland, many men and women remained celibate, and others entered matrimony only late in life. Though women found employment in a variety of places, two types of work stood out (the women exhibited less occupational diversity than their male counterparts): factory work, especially textiles and clothing manufacturing (some had prior experience), and domestic service as maids. For Irish women, who were less intent than their counterparts from other groups on getting married and establishing a family, domestic service afforded a security they could not get from factory work. Irish women maintained a remarkably high degree of identification with and participation in Irish America. Diner (1983: 153) concluded that ethnicity proved to be more powerful than gender, and, in the final analysis, "[Women's] economic assertiveness and strong sense of self did not jar with those cultural traditions but proved instead to be the mechanism for blending old-world ideals with American needs."

One striking feature of the economic status of the Irish as a whole was the lack of upward social mobility they experienced during the nineteenth century. This was evident during the period up to the Civil War and persisted throughout the century. Blessing (1980: 531) observed that, unlike any other immigrant group arriving during this period, their "occupational mobility during the late nineteenth century appeared almost as small as that of American blacks." As a result, the Irish poor were confined to inner-city ghettos, where levels of crime, violence, alcoholism, poverty, and social disorganization helped create a growing perception among other Americans that the Irish were a social problem. The perceived threat of what was known at the time as the "dangerous class" within the ethnic community concerned both

nativists who were hostile to the Irish and more sympathetic social reformers (Wittke, 1956: 40–51).

Communal Activities and Organizations

The Irish became involved in politics soon after they arrived in the
United States. Many have argued that the Irish had a unique penchant
for politics (Levine, 1966; Erie, 1988). Clearly, the Irish had certain advantages compared with other immigrant groups, such as facility with
the English language and familiarity with Anglo-American laws and
customs (Shannon, 1963). They also had a keen interest in homeland
politics (Brown, 1966).

The Irish leaned toward the Democratic party because they felt the
Republicans harbored deep-rooted anti-Catholic attitudes. The result
of this conviction was that from the 1840s the Irish began to be incorporated into big-city political machines, although the Irish did not control those machines until after the Civil War. According to sociologist
Steven Erie (1988: 31), the Irish attraction to machine politics stemmed
from their "intense group solidarity, and the high value they placed on
the economic rewards of politics."

Irish voluntary organizations began during the colonial period
when the first, known as the Charitable Irish Society of Boston, was
founded in 1737. Like a number of subsequent organizations, the early
groups were largely dominated by Protestants and by "lace curtain"
Catholics. Early leaders of these organizations—some of whom were
local political functionaries, newspaper publishers, clerics, or business
owners—played an important mediating role between the ethnic community and the host society. They sought to reduce the level of animosity directed against Irish Catholics. At the same time they served as
mentors for the rank-and-file immigrants, helping them see themselves
not as Irish exiles in America, but as Irish Americans (Greene, 1987).
One further type of voluntary organization that appeared in the 1840s
had a somewhat different purpose: the workers' association. The American union movement was still in its formative stages, but the Irish involvement was pronounced. Although some of the early voluntary organizations were distinctly ethnic in character, the Irish also became
involved in transethnic organizations.

The Irish immigrant entered a world that was overwhelmingly
Protestant, but the Irish had a greater impact on American society in
the area of religion than in any other area. The Irish dominated the development of Roman Catholicism in nineteenth-century America, and
they were chief contributors to the leadership of the church (Fallows,
1979). The number of Catholics rose fourfold in the decades between
1830 and 1860, exceeding 3 million by 1860. Although other groups accounted for some of this growth, a majority of the church at this time
was Irish (Clark, 1977). Furthermore, priests and nuns emigrated from

Ireland to establish and maintain parishes and related religious institutions.

While the Irish Catholic church leaders created a position for themselves in which they could be the arbiters of competing efforts to shape American Catholicism, they also saw themselves struggling against the forces of Protestantism's "righteous empire." To prevent their offspring from losing their attachment to their heritage, the Irish Catholics established parochial schools at great financial cost, as alternatives to public schools. Public schools were seen as powerful forces promoting Americanization. The Irish were not opposed to Americanization per se. Rather, they sought to have a role in defining what was entailed in becoming an American. They believed that public schools were controlled by Protestant elites who were generally hostile to Catholicism and desirous of eradicating all traces of old-world cultures, except the British. Thus, the Irish feared that the future of their religion and culture was at stake, and parochial schools could provide them with the ability to dictate the terms of Americanization for Irish immigrants.

Nativism

This defensiveness partly reflects the conservatism and traditional character of the immigrant heritage, but it also reflected the attitudes of the larger society. The Irish were the first among the voluntary mass immigrant groups to confront intense antipathy. **Nativism**—negative reactions to new immigrants—grew in the nineteenth century. Hostility occurred not only as individual prejudice and acts of discrimination but also through an organizational presence from such anti-Irish groups as the Native American Party, the Order of United Americans, the Order of the Star-Spangled Banner, and the Know-Nothing or American Party.

Given the impact of Irish mass immigration in the 1840s, it was not entirely surprising that, as Philip Taylor (1971: 239) observed, "Opponents of immigration became vociferous in the second quarter of the nineteenth century." The Irish were not the only target, although they were recipients of the most intense and sustained nativist animosity, which frequently characterized the Irish as nonwhite and thus not capable of being incorporated into the mainstream (Ignatiev, 1996). Anti-Irish agitation had three components. First, the Irish were viewed as a social problem. They were accused of being prone to alcoholism, brawling, and crime, and they were condemned for placing a heavy burden on charitable institutions because of their poverty. However overstated, there was obvious truth to these charges. The problem with such nativist complaints was that they failed to adequately analyze the social roots that had spawned such problems. Instead, the nativists engaged in a campaign of blaming the victim. The second component was political. The swelling numbers of Irish in major cities combined with their tendency to engage readily in political activities fueled anxiety about their potential impact. The Irish were seen as ignorant people susceptible to manipulation by scheming political operatives. Their attachment to machine politics, with its fraud and violence, suggested to nativists that the Irish were not capable of becoming responsible citizens.

The third component was religious. Anti-Catholicism was directed at other groups as well, but as the Irish position in the church solidified, the Irish and Catholicism were closely identified. Hostility to Catholicism was partly political: The Catholic church was viewed as authoritarian and antidemocratic, and the Vatican's support of various oppressive regimes in Europe suggested to some that it posed a threat to political freedom (Jones, 1960). Furthermore, charges were often made that the papacy was intent on extending its political influence in the United States.

The combination of these components of anti-Irish animosity created a heightened potential for conflict. Interpersonal contact with Irish Catholics was avoided, so when they began to enter a neighborhood in significant numbers, established residents exited—an early instance of neighborhood succession in American cities. Attacks on Irish homes and Irish Catholic institutions occurred with regularity throughout the country, but perhaps the two most dramatic events were the 1834 burning of the Ursuline convent outside of Boston and an 1844 riot in Philadelphia.

Germans in America

The Germans arrived in the Americas during the colonial period, but under somewhat different circumstances than those of most other European sojourners. Germany did not become a unified nation-state until 1871, so what we refer to as "Germany" was actually several autonomous principalities. As a result of this situation, there was no colonizing nation-state encouraging settlement in the New World. The German immigrants, therefore, established themselves in colonies founded by the European colonial powers and, as a consequence, were an ethnic minority.

The first distinctly German settlement in North America was Germantown, Pennsylvania, founded by Mennonites in 1683. Germans were attracted to Pennsylvania because of the religious tolerance that its founder, William Penn, made the hallmark of the colony. These early arrivals were followed later by other religious dissenters, Pietists, and various nonconformist groups, including the Schwarzenau Brethren (commonly referred to as the Dunkers) and the United Brethren, or Moravians. This early emigration took place chiefly among groups, rather than only individuals or families, because so much emigration was prompted by a quest for religious freedom (Rippley, 1984). Economic motives also played a part in pushing people out of Germany and into the American colonies (Conzen, 1980).

These immigrants were quite diverse economically. Few were very poor, and most possessed at least limited skills. Some were actually rather well off economically, reflective of their flight to America being prompted primarily by religious and not economic concerns. These arrivals included various kinds of artisans and entrepreneurs. Most Germans, however, were farmers intent on acquiring land in America so they could continue farming.

The Germans developed a reputation as successful farmers, often where others had failed; many bought land from English and Scotch-Irish farmers. Thus, the Germans became an important force in the settlement of the Midwest, moving from Ohio to Nebraska in an effort to remain in farming. Early observers, such as Benjamin Rush, Benjamin Franklin, and J. Hector St. John de Crèvecoeur, depicted them as practical, hardworking, and thrifty. This assessment appears to have been widely held. The Germans not only proved to be efficient farmers but also were innovators in the crops they planted and the methods they used (Billigmeier, 1974).

The Early Ethnic Community

Germans generally lived in ethnic enclaves. Although some religious sectarians preferred to limit contact with outsiders, most German immigrants were not opposed to living in close proximity to nonGermans. They were nevertheless criticized for their presumed tendency to be clannish and for their intense desire to preserve their culture. Franklin was not alone in voicing a fear that not only would German culture persist in areas of high concentration but would also absorb British American culture (Billigmeier, 1974). Nonetheless, because of their advantageous socioeconomic position and because they were willing to mingle with British Americans, the members of this first stage of German immigration assimilated quickly.

A distinctly German presence did not disappear, however, partly because of some Germans' efforts to maintain aspects of their traditional culture. The proliferation of German-language newspapers (a reflection of the immigrants' high rate of literacy), the creation of organizations intent on raising ethnic consciousness, and the establishment of a system of parochial schools checked the assimilative trend.

Mass immigration began relatively slowly in the decade of the 1820s, when fewer than 6,000 Germans arrived. The number swelled to nearly 125,000 during the following decade. The decadal numbers continued to grow until the peak decade of the 1850s, when 976,072 immigrants arrived. Between 1820 and 1859, nearly 1.5 million German immigrants arrived in the United States. Moreover, during the three decades beginning with 1830, German immigration was 31.1 percent of total immigration (U.S. Bureau of the Census, 1975).

Intraethnic Conflict

Some immigrants left Germany for political reasons. Known as the "Forty-eighters," these were victims of the abortive revolutions that convulsed Europe in 1848. In German-speaking Europe, these revolts resulted in considerable bloodshed, especially in major cities such as Berlin and Vienna. Initiated by a loosely held together coalition of liberals and radicals of various strains, ranging from communists to anarchists, the uprisings were somewhat spontaneous attempts to overthrow reactionary and oppressive regimes. The battle cry echoed the ideals of both the American and French Revolutions, with core values centering on notions of liberty, equality, and fraternity. When the revolts were crushed, many Germans were forced into exile, among them several thousand Germans who fled to America. Though they were a very small part of the pre-Civil War mass migration, their impact was felt both within the German American community and, to a lesser extent, in the larger society as well (Wittke, 1952).

The Forty-eighters constituted an intellectual stratum that was not only more politically radical but also more politically outspoken than most of their fellow countrymen and countrywomen. These political émigrés' anticlericalism and secularism compounded tensions. Religious Germans, regardless of their form of religious expression, took offense at this Enlightenment-inspired challenge to the Christian faith.

Germany contained a complex array of political, religious, regional, and class differences. Given the immense size of the immigrant population, it is not surprising that virtually the full spectrum of differences could be observed in the United States. This ethnic community's deep internal divisions made it impossible to forge institutions that included members from every quarter. Instead, institutions reflected various ideological orientations and competed with other institutions for the allegiance of the immigrants (Conzen, 1980).

The "Germantowns" or "little Germanies" provided immigrants with a transplanted version of the Old World in the new. Mutual aid societies, dramatic associations, singing clubs, athletic associations, lodges and fraternal orders, and a variety of other organizations catered to this clientele. Restaurants, saloons, and cafes became vital places for socializing, and German-owned businesses provided the immigrants with goods and services that reminded customers of the homeland. The German-language press offered a wide selection of newspapers, and papers often catered to particular religious or political segments of the ethnic community. Attending to the cultural and social needs of its residents, the ethnic enclave was, to use Raymond Breton's (1964) term, "institutionally complete."

Religious divisions played perhaps the greatest role in preventing a unified community from arising. Within Protestantism, Lutherans had pronounced differences with Reformed churches and with the Pietist sects. The arrival of German Catholics further complicated the religious picture. The relationship between German Protestants and Catholics can be characterized as one of mutual antagonism. Catholics were forced to confront a nation in which anti-Catholicism was rising. Furthermore, they had to stake out a place in the American Catholic Church and address the challenge posed by growing Irish domination.

Besides religious differences, political divisions precluded German American unity and harmony. The Germans willingly engaged in the political controversies of the day, and they were especially vocal over the issue of slavery. Except for small pockets of German America in the Southern slave-owning states, the German American community was overwhelmingly opposed to slavery. This viewpoint did not, however, establish a basis for unity. Germans who had arrived prior to the Forty-eighters were often aligned with the Democratic party because, in their opinion, it best advanced the Jeffersonian ideals of freedom and equality. They were not attracted to the Republican party, which they associated with nativism and with temperance advocates.

These religious and political differences resulted in a system of parallel ethnic institutions, as "church" and "club" Germans competed with each other to forge a German American identity (Conzen, 1980). Both were able to play off of the comparatively favorable stereotypes of Germans: industrious, efficient, innovative, and the like. The former, however, sought to meld such positive images with notions of Christian devotion and obedience, while the latter wanted to incorporate views related to rationalism and freethinking.

In a country that was, as historian Jon Butler (1990) described, "awash in a sea of faith," religiously inclined Germans were in a strategic position to advance their particular construction of German America and be assured it would be well received by the larger society. Indeed, some of the negative stereotypes that arose about the Germans centered on agnostic and atheistic tendencies. Linked to this image was a condemnation of their political radicalism. In short, precisely those features of the Germans that served to distinguish them from their contemporaries helped ensure that their version of German America would be less attractive to the host society.

Interethnic Encounters

German workers began to be involved in the embryonic trade union movement in the United States and in political activities. Those arriving in the wake of 1848 and later often brought with them a familiarity with, if not an explicit endorsement of, socialism and also practical experience in political activism. Because many were skilled workers, they proved to be a source of leadership in both leftist political organizations and the more militant trade unions. In this regard, the Germans were quite different from their Irish contemporaries, who as peasants and unskilled workers were far less likely to embrace socialism or the more radical versions of trade unionism (Trommler and Shore, 2001).

On the eve of the Civil War, the Germans were well positioned in the hierarchy of ethnic groups in America. Since the Scandinavians were all Protestant and were less inclined to be active in freethinking, radical, or labor activities, their general image in the larger society was perhaps a bit more positive than that of the Germans. The Germans had a decided edge over the Irish, however, and their active involvement on the Union side in the war enhanced their position. Thus, during the immigration hiatus brought about by the war and attendant economic conditions, the Germans were poised to enhance their social status in America when mass migration resumed.

Coercive Pluralism and the Politics of Exclusion

Lawrence Fuchs (1990) has referred to the nation's collective response to nonEuropean groups as one that entailed various forms of **coercive pluralism.** For American Indians, he described the form of pluralism as **predatory,** by which he meant that the original occupants of the continent were defined as outsiders who, insofar as they stood in the way of European settlement, were to be pushed aside. The integrity of the American Indians' traditional ways of life was thoroughly disregarded.

In contrast, Africans confronted a system of **caste pluralism.** Africans were forcibly brought into the country and consigned to a particularly oppressive place in the economic system (Fuchs, 1990). In an otherwise class-based economy that permitted individual mobility, Africans were relegated to a subordinate position based on race-specific ascriptive criteria.

The third type of coercive pluralism Fuchs (1990) defined was **sojourner pluralism,** which characterized the situation of two particular groups in the antebellum period, Mexicans and Chinese, and later was applicable to other Hispanic and Asian groups. As the term suggests, members of these groups were perceived as temporary residents in the country, individuals who wanted to come to America for a limited time to take advantage of economic opportunities. The expectation was that they would eventually return to their respective homelands (Saxton, 1990).

The historical experiences of these groups differed appreciably based on the differential consequences of these three types of pluralism. When compared with the histories of the European-origin groups we have been discussing, we can appreciate the gulf that separated those inhabiting a world of **voluntary pluralism** (Fuchs, 1990) from those forced into any of the three coercive pluralisms.

The First of This Land

We turn first to Native Americans. Care is required in generalizing about American Indian social organization because of limitations in anthropological knowledge and because of the diversity among tribes across the continent. For example, some tribes—including the Iroquois and the Pueblo—permitted only monogamous marriages, while others allowed men to have more than one wife. Nonetheless, some broad general statements can be made. Extended families were common, and especially with the death of a spouse, it was usually assumed that the dead person's family would care for the surviving spouse and children. *Clans* were organizations that linked kin members in even larger extended kinship networks. *Associations* performed many of the mutual aid activities characteristic of clans but were not based on kinship. *Moieties* were tribe subdivisions similar in their social utility to clans or associations (Leacock and Lurie, 1988). *Tribes* refer to what might be seen as governmental units.

Indians' contact with Europeans exhibited considerable variation, ranging from tranquillity and cooperation (some whites even opted to assimilate into tribal cultures) to duplicity, violence, exploitation, and extermination. In part, these variations were based on the proclivities of differing Native American tribes: Some were warlike and others essentially peaceful; some had the power to resist outsiders while others were forced by necessity to accommodate to newcomers (McNickle, 1962). Europeans differed in their general orientations toward the indigenous peoples they encountered. The French were perhaps the group that was, comparatively speaking, freest from racist attitudes and the least hostile. The Spanish were the most hostile and exhibited the most intense expressions of racism. The British and the Dutch manifested more varied and ambiguous responses.

The nature of Native American-European interaction was dictated by differing historically conditioned circumstances. Several periods of political and economic relationships linking American Indians and Europeans can be identified between the initial European contact with the Americans and the time by which competing European nations established permanent settlements in the New World. We will use the classificatory scheme of Stephen Cornell (1988), who has identified six stages, two of which concern the period under discussion in this chapter: (1) the market period, which persisted into the latter part of the eighteenth century; and (2) the conflict period, which ran from the end of the eighteenth century to the middle of the nineteenth or shortly past that time.

The Market Period (1600–1775)

During the earliest period, European interests in the Americas were chiefly motivated by economic considerations, and political interests associated with permanent settlement overlaid the economic. The first period brought European mercantile interests into contact with new goods and raw materials. Native Americans were allowed to enter into relationships with European commercial interests. The fur trade, which was prompted by prosperity and fashion in Europe, was the glue that held American Indians and Europeans together (Bolt, 1987).

In exchange for furs, Native Americans received European goods, including such practical items as blankets, woolen goods, cooking utensils, knives, axes, and firearms. They also obtained glass beads and alcohol. These items increasingly entered tribal life, where they replaced many of the more traditional goods and caused considerable change in the material culture (Jennings, 1976). Cornell (1988) observed that although it is a mistake to view Native American cultures prior to European contact as static, the arrival of these settlers set off an unprecedented process of economic change. Thus, the American Indian population began to be incorporated into a European-centered world economic system (Wallerstein, 1974). Furthermore, since the economy was integrally linked to the rest of tribal society, the effects filtered throughout all facets of the society (Sahlins, 1972).

During this period, warfare between Indians and Europeans broke out at some junctures, but the desire on both sides to establish trade links promoted diplomacy. The potential for conflict should not be underestimated. For example, in the Pequot War of 1637, the Pequots, located in the Connecticut River Valley, suffered a debilitating loss, which included 600 to 700 Indians being burned alive and countless others sold into slavery in the West Indies (Hauptman and Wherry, 1990). Overall, however, this period was characterized by something of a symbiotic relationship between Native Americans and Europeans.

Political developments brought this period to an end. Specifically, the British triumph over their European counterparts undid the ability of American Indians to negotiate with various competing interests. The Treaty of Paris, signed in 1763, was a watershed event because it provided for British domination of all lands heretofore held by the French. If this development was not sufficiently problematic, the fur trade served as a basis for permanent European settlements in which the Native Americans increasingly became superfluous, their hunting roles taken over by the offspring of immigrants. By the time the colonies freed themselves from British rule, a new era of relations between Indians and Americans was dawning.

The Conflict Period (1775–1850)

This period was defined by conflict over land. The primary factor generating this conflict was the increased demand for land by the citizens of the new republic. The Revolutionary War had placed a heavy strain on the new nation's treasury, and political leaders saw westward expansion as a way of alleviating these financial woes. The desire to push the U.S. boundaries toward the Pacific was shared by a wide range of the American citizenry, including farmers, land speculators, and entrepreneurs interested in exploiting new areas for their valuable raw materials. Furthermore, immigration began to grow, and many of the newcomers believed that their chances for success were better if they settled somewhere other than the Atlantic seaboard. Increasingly, Native Americans were seen as being in the way, and a process of displacement began.

Europeans found an ideological justification for their policy of Indian removal from ancestral lands in the **Manifest Destiny** doctrine. In part, this term reflected the belief that the United States was destined to control the continent from the Atlantic to the Pacific. To some this meant incorporating Canada and Mexico into its ultimate boundaries. The concept was also based on the religious belief held since the Puritan period that the United States had a providential mission to tame the continent and Christianize it (Dinnerstein, Nichols, and Reimers, 1990).

Roy Harvey Pearce argued in his study of white images of the American Indian, *Savagism and Civilization* (1967), that the American Indian was seen as religiously and morally incomplete and as an impediment to civilization. Although some Europeans—Catholics earlier than Protestants—saw it as their Christian duty to convert these nonbelievers, others were less sanguine about the prospects of "civilizing" them and sought merely to remove or eliminate the American Indians. For example, troops sent by George Washington to pacify the Iroquois uttered the following toast: "Civilization or death to all American savages" (Wax, 1971: 15).

Andrew Jackson, whose actions were especially important in expropriating Indian land, prominently displayed this thinking. Jackson became U.S. president as the champion of common folk, an egalitarian democrat. Yet his political rise was based in no small part on his vicious campaigns against Native Americans. Jackson first came into national prominence as the commander of troops in the Creek War of 1813–1814, during which time he characterized the American Indians as "savage bloodhounds," "blood-thirsty barbarians," and "cannibals"

(Takaki, 1979). During the decades leading up to his presidency, open conflict and warfare escalated. The most violent wars pitted Americans against two formidable tribal confederations: the Iroquois in the Northeast and the Creek in the Southeast. The campaign against the American Indians was intended to remove any who were perceived to be in the way of westward expansion.

Relocation Policies

During Jackson's presidency, this process led to the forced relocation of a number of tribes in the eastern United States, including Cherokees, Seminoles, Ottawas, Potawatomis, Shawnees, Kickapoo, Delaware, Peorias, Miamis, and the Sauk and Fox. As early as the Louisiana Purchase in 1803, the possibility of exchanging Indian lands in the eastern part of the country for land west of the Mississippi had been contemplated.

In continuity with British law, the Americans proceeded with a view that recognized the right of Native American ownership. For the Cherokee, a series of 13 treaties extending from 1721 to 1798 resulted in the loss of about 82,000 square miles of tribal lands (Thornton, 1990). Although in practice treaty rights were often not considered, such violations were in defiance of the law. Thus, governmental policy had to consider the law in establishing **relocation policies** that effectively removed Indians from their lands. What cannot be underestimated was the inordinate amount of pressure placed on Native Indians, combined with interference in the internal affairs of tribes, that was designed to encourage relocation. Relocation was frequently a wrenching process that brought misery, starvation, and death, as with the case of the move of the Cherokees to Oklahoma from the southeastern states across what became known as the "Trail of Tears."

During this time the status of the American Indians was uncertain. They were neither citizens nor aliens. They were neither persons nor slaves. Murray Wax (1971) made the interesting observation that since the late eighteenth century American Indian affairs had been under the purview of the War Department. He noted that had their affairs been located in the Commerce Department, Native Americans would have been seen as a purely domestic issue. On the other hand, had they been located in the State Department, Indian tribes would have been defined as sovereign foreign nations. The choice of the War Department reflected the ambivalence of the situation: it "implied that, in the last analysis, the relations were those of control and subjugation of peoples [within the boundaries of the United States but] outside of the frame of the Union" (Wax, 1971: 47).

This situation did not mean that the United States government refused to enter into treaties with tribes. The government did so without explicitly recognizing the tribes as independent nations, although treaties by definition are transacted between autonomous nations. Congress ended this activity in 1871, but it was common practice during the late eighteenth and first half of the nineteenth centuries, reflecting the considerable uncertainty about the Indians' place in American society.

In one of the first sympathetic accounts of Native Americans written by a white person, Helen Hunt Jackson (1881) aptly characterized this period as "a century of dishonor." Cornell (1988: 45, 50) described the period as the Indian's "descent into powerlessness" and claimed that by the end of the Civil War "the Indians were rapidly disappearing as major actors on the intergroup stage." This set the stage for the development of the reservation system—an institution in which Native Americans were defined as wards of the nation.

Beyond the Middle Passage

The institution of slavery decisively shaped the lives of all Africans in the United States, free persons as well as slaves (Berlin, 1974, 2003; Williams, 1990). Slavery was by no means unique to the United States, or to Western civilization. Indeed, it has been practiced in virtually every part of the world, including Africa. Wherever slavery has taken institutional form, it has operated in similar ways. Slavery has been succinctly and accurately defined by sociologist Orlando Patterson (1982) as "human parasitism." The motivation behind slavery is to subjugate another person or persons. The reasons behind such practices vary but usually entail an economic impetus to get others to do burdensome work at minimal cost, status considerations, and sometimes political factors. Slavery operates through a process of systematic degradation of the slave, who, by being reduced to property owned by another, experiences what Patterson (1982) refers to as "social death."

African slaves were imported into the Americas from the seventeenth century on, where, as Figure 3.1 reveals, most ended up in the Caribbean and South America. All of the principal European colonizing nations engaged in the slave trade, and in British North America slaves were found along the entire Atlantic coastal area, in urban centers as well as in rural sections. In colonial America, as with the rest of the Western hemisphere, slavery was practiced for decidedly economic reasons: slavery provided an abundant source of cheap labor.

Africans, by being violently uprooted from their homelands, were controlled by slaveholders far more readily than other groups would have been. Thus, Native Americans were not enslaved in large numbers because their familiarity with the environment meant that escape and return to their tribe was a distinct possibility. Africans had nowhere to go in America (Stampp, 1956; Fredrickson, 1981).

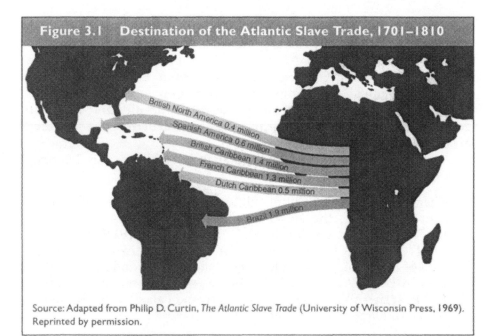

Figure 3.1   Destination of the Atlantic Slave Trade, 1701–1810

British North America 0.4 million
Spanish America 0.6 million
British Caribbean 1.4 million
French Caribbean 1.3 million
Dutch Caribbean 0.5 million
Brazil 1.9 million

Source: Adapted from Philip D. Curtin, *The Atlantic Slave Trade* (University of Wisconsin Press, 1969). Reprinted by permission.

The Ideology of Racism

Why were Africans singled out for slavery? A number of rationalizations have been offered by apologists for the practice of slavery, including the argument that the southern climate demanded Africans since Europeans could not survive as laborers in that environment. George Fredrickson (1981) contends that racial prejudice was not the primary cause of slavery; rather, economic considerations were the primary causal agents. The planter class in the Southern states determined that it was economically advantageous to use slave labor rather than indentured servants or wage laborers. Race prejudice justified slavery but did not produce it.

Two intertwined features of the ideology of racism involved the claims that Africans were intellectually inferior and were barbarians incapable of becoming civilized on their own. This latter aspect derives from deeply rooted images that link blackness to evil in Judeo-Christian thought (Jordon, 1968; Wood, 1990). Thus, the ideology of race characterized the African as the eternal "other," standing outside of and being fundamentally hostile to civilization. A modified version of this thesis viewed African cultures as simple and primitive, incapable of contributing to the construction of major historical civilizations (see Bernal, 1987, for a powerful critique of this view).

Politicians and civic leaders in the South offered powerful ideological rationales to protect the slave system from the challenges posed by those opposed to it, as well as by those ambivalent about its existence. Perhaps the most sophisticated were those articulated by two Southern slavocrats, Henry Hughes and George Fitzhugh, who invoked the newly emerging discipline of sociology for their respective theses. In 1854 Hughes published his *Treatise on Sociology;* Fitzhugh's work was also published that year, titled *Sociology for the South.* Both works were designed to establish an intellectual justification for slavery. In other words, these writers viewed slavery as both morally and politically good; they saw it as essential for the preservation of morality and social order.

With this conviction, Hughes (1854: 292) concluded his *Treatise* in glowing fashion:

> Then, in the plump flush of full-feeding health, the happy war-rantees [that is, the slaves] shall banquet in PLANTATION-REFECTORIES; worship in PLANTATION-CHAPELS; learn in PLANTATION-SCHOOLS; or in PLANTATION-SALOONS, in the cool of the evening chant old songs, tell tales, . . . and after slumbers in PLANTATION-DORMITORIES, over whose gates Health and Rest sit smiling at the feet of Wealth and Labor, . . . [here] shall be the fulfillment of Warranteeism.

Of course, the reality of slavery was far different from this ideological portrait. Nonetheless, this portrait of a *Gemeinschaft* world, in which owners and slaves engaged in a system of reciprocity where owners not only had rights but obligations and slaves could find contentment on the plantation, had a profound impact on racial thought well into the twentieth century. We see a version of this worldview articulated in Margaret Mitchell's best-selling novel, *Gone With the Wind.* This genre of literature, written after the Civil War, has been dubbed the "moonlight and magnolia" school, a romanticized portrait of the antebellum South produced by apologists for the "lost cause."

Slavery and the Plantation

Slavery has been described by historian Kenneth Stampp (1956) as "the peculiar institution"—despotism in a country that defined itself as democratic. Although slavery was practiced in Northern states, and although urban slavery existed in both the North and the South, slavery is most intimately associated with the plantations of the South. Who were the slaveowners? Almost three-quarters of slaveowners were relatively small farmers who owned fewer than 10 slaves. Only 3,000 families throughout the South owned more than 100 slaves (Stampp, 1956). Slaves were concentrated in relatively large agricultural units. The majority lived on plantations containing more than 20 slaves. In short, slavery and the plantation were integrally connected.

The plantation can be seen as an instance of Erving Goffman's (1961) **total institution.** Goffman used this term in *Asylums* to describe a mental hospital he had studied, but he saw it as an apt characterization of a variety of similar institutions ranging from prisons to monasteries. Such institutions circumscribe the entire life of individuals who are part of them: people work, play, eat, and sleep in the institution. Furthermore, the subordinate members of such institutions are forced to undergo rituals of incorporation into the institution that are intended to sever their connections with their pasts—rituals appropriately characterized as "degradation ceremonies." Individuals in these institutions are the recipients of discipline and authority designed to ensure that they do not challenge their subordinate status (Goffman, 1961; Foucault, 1979). For historian Stanley Elkins (1959), the Nazi concentration camp served as an analogy to the plantation.

The peculiarity of the plantation was that it operated internally as a "total institution" while being part of an international economic system. The Industrial Revolution in England, for example, would not have been possible without the availability of cotton (Hobsbawm, 1969). So the emergence of modern capitalism was connected to a noncapitalist form of labor exploitation—slavery. "In this essential respect, the Old South emerged as a bastard child of merchant capital and developed as a noncapitalist society increasingly antagonistic to, but inseparable from, the bourgeois world that sired it" (Fox-Genovese and Genovese, 1983: 5).

The Origins of an African American Culture

Within these oppressive conditions Africans constructed a community. As did other migratory peoples, they used aspects of their ancestral cultures. The problem for Africans was that the involuntary character of their migration, combined with slaveholders' efforts to repress expressions of African culture, resulted in a greater degree of uprooting than was the case for voluntary migrants. Furthermore, unlike most other groups, Africans were not able to maintain communication links to the homeland.

Some scholars have concluded that African Americans had their pasts thoroughly eradicated, thereby making them simply and totally the products of their American experience. This was Robert E. Park's opinion. His student, the African American sociologist E. Franklin Frazier (1963: 23), summarized this position when he argued that "because of the manner in which Negroes were captured in Africa and enslaved, they were practically stripped of their social heritage."

This conclusion was challenged by anthropologist Melville J. Herskovits in his trailblazing study, *The Myth of the Negro Past* (1941). He argued that he had discovered remnants of African culture in the Americas and specifically in the United States in a number of relatively isolated enclaves in coastal regions of South Carolina, Georgia, and Florida. The best known is the Gullah community on coastal islands off the South Carolina mainland, where linguistic, religious, and artistic evidence of Africanisms is apparent (Creel, 1988).

Although Herskovits rebuts the view that all vestiges of African culture disappeared in America, subsequent research indicates that Africans lost far more of their ancestral culture than did voluntary immigrants. The extent to which Africanisms survived is testimony to the ability of those cultures to address the hardships confronted by the slave community as well as the tenacity of slaves in their attempt to hang on to aspects of their past despite intense repression and acute social disruption and deprivation (Holloway, 1990).

Lawrence W. Levine (1977) has gone beyond the Frazier-Herskovits debate to argue that what should be explored are not African survivals but rather how African culture was transformed by its interaction with the culture of white Southerners. Particularly important to him are the many and complex ways in which slaves sought to subvert or to resist oppression and exploitation. For example, Levine found that the trickster in African myths was also a common feature of slave tales. Depicted in stories in divine, human, or animal guise, the trickster succeeded in a contest of wills against those more powerful by using deceit and cunning. Slaves became tricksters as they sought to practice the frequently repeated aphorism, "White folks do as they pleases, and the darkies do as they can." Reports from the era indicate the prevalence of slaves who "lied, cheated, stole, feigned illness, loafed, pretended to misunderstand the orders they were given," and did damage to the masters' property, crops, and livestock (Levine, 1977: 122).

These expressions of discontent reinforced the slaveowners' view of Africans as "a troublesome property" and served as an inducement "to make them stand in fear" (Stampp, 1956: 86–191). Indeed, the Sambo stereotype cast the slave as fundamentally infantile and therefore in need of stern "parental" control (Elkins, 1959).

Moreover, such modes of resistance did not challenge the status quo by articulating an ideology of liberation. Many scholars have recently acknowledged that the quest for freedom—individual and collective—was powerfully expressed by slaves and was fueled chiefly by religion. The Africans' desire for liberation en masse had begun early as members of various African tribes quickly came to see their fates intricately intertwined. The horror encountered on the slave ships was so profound that these vessels are appropriately seen as the first "incubators of slave unity across cultural lines" (Stuckey, 1987: 3).

Though slaveowners sought to inculcate a Christianity designed to convince the slaves that they should accept their fate on earth and concentrate on a heavenly reward—encouraging slaves to be docile, obedient, and respectful—slaves found a message of freedom in this religion. Actually, the slaves' religious expression was a mixture of African religious tradition and Christianity. Scholars continue to debate the relative importance of Protestant Christianity and African religions in this syncretistic religious expression (Blassingame, 1972; Genovese, 1972; Levine, 1977; Lincoln and Mamiya, 1990).

Out of this mutual influence of African folk religion and Christianity emerged a rhetoric of resistance to racial oppression. Christianity proclaimed a message of salvation that provided a rationale for activist involvement in political and social struggles for liberation. Perhaps the most important feature of African folk religion in shaping the religious character of the slave community was its emphasis on a communal rather than an individual orientation. African American religion was exceedingly complex and ambiguous, as various tensions persisted between what Lincoln and Mamiya (1990) refer to as dialectical poles, including otherworldly versus this-worldly, communal versus privatistic, and resistance versus accommodation.

The Community of Slaves

Slaves were not able to construct an institutional community similar to those created by voluntary immigrant groups. Slaves could not establish mutual benefit societies, fraternal organizations, businesses, political associations, and the like. So it is not surprising that one central institution stood out as crucially significant in defining the slave community: the family. Unfortunately, our understanding of the slave family is limited and subject to considerable controversy because the African American has too often been reduced to what was referred to earlier as "historical invisibility."

Because slaves could be sold at will, owners could dissolve marriages. The extent to which this practice of separating family units at the slave-trading block was actually used is uncertain. Historians Eugene Genovese (1972) and Herbert Gutman (1976) saw this as a relatively infrequent occurrence, although they understood that its very possibility generated uncertainty and anxiety in slaves. John Blassingame (1972), however, believes the practice to have been very common and estimates that perhaps as many as one-third of all marriage unions were terminated by the sale of one of the partners. Since no consensus has emerged among scholars about the respective merits of these two positions, it is difficult to know the extent to which the typical African family that emerged from slavery was or was not a stable, dual-parent nuclear family (Fogel, 1989).

A lack of clarity about gender roles and the respective impacts of African culture versus the conditions imposed by servitude also affected Africans' family lives. What was clear to early students of African America, such as W. E. B. Du Bois (1970 [1909]) and E. Franklin Frazier (1939), was that the out-of-wedlock birth rate for blacks in the post-Civil War period was much higher than the white rate. Both attributed this situation to the demoralization brought about by slavery. Frazier further talked about what he saw as a dual-family structure in the African American community: male-headed families and female-headed households. In his view, this division was the consequence of "widespread illegitimacy" (Frazier, 1939: 483).

However different in form from white families and from the families of free Africans, the slave family managed many of the usual functions, especially those associated with child rearing. Blassingame (1972: 79) writes that because slave parents were chiefly responsible for raising their children, "they could cushion the shock of bondage for them, help them to understand their situation, teach them values different from those their masters tried to instill in them, and give them a referent for self-esteem other than their master."

Abolitionist leader Frederick Douglass.

One persistent challenge to the integrity of the family and to monogamous relationships was the sexual exploitation of African women by whites. The African man, whether or not he was a husband, was powerless to ward off the advances of the master or his sons or employees. Doing so would put the slave's life at risk, which instilled in him a profound sense of powerlessness (Blassingame, 1972). The slave-owner's power was not confined to the sexual realm; it also shaped all facets of slave life. Both kind and cruel masters sought to perpetuate the subordination of their slaves. The former did so by attempting to elicit consent and compliance, while the latter did so by instilling fear and by punishment.

Slave Revolts

Herbert Aptheker (1943) provided the first attempt to assess the prevalence of slave revolts, and in this benchmark work he contended that more than 200 revolts occurred during the era of legal slavery. Subsequent scholarship has questioned that number, but clearly slaves were willing to revolt and a number of major rebellions or conspiracies occurred (Genovese, 1972, 1979). Although all revolts failed, they reflected the desire of slaves to be free and revealed the fear of revolt felt by slaveowners. Every aborted or failed insurrection was met with renewed repression. Religion's role in challenges to the legitimacy of slavery was sufficiently pronounced that free Africans were either forbidden by law to preach to slaves or were forced to register and preach under the surveillance of whites (Genovese, 1972). As the early historian of the American South, and an apologist for slavery, Ulrich B. Phillips (1918) concluded, white Southerners had considerable anxiety about the potential for violent slave uprisings. Nonetheless, slavery did not cease to exist because of the slaves' efforts alone.

Free Persons of Color

Not all Africans were slaves. At the onset of the Civil War, a half million "free persons of color" lived in the United States (Berlin, 1974). Some were descendants of the earliest African arrivals in America, who had been defined as indentured servants rather than slaves and had worked through their indentured period and become free. Others, like Denmark Vesey in Charlestown, South Carolina, managed to become free in their own lifetimes. In most instances this freedom was due to the abolition of slavery in Northern states or to the manumission of slaves by individuals who could no longer live with the incongruity of democratic ideals and despotic practices. For example, the Quakers made a collective decision after the American Revolution to uphold the ideals of the new nation by freeing their slaves (Sowell, 1981a). Many slaveowners, torn by what they perceived to be economic necessity and morality, chose to manumit their slaves on their deathbeds.

Free Africans found employment in cities; many had craft and artisanal skills, but others worked chiefly as unskilled laborers. They differed from slaves in many ways. For instance, although no more than 2 percent of slaves could read, most free persons of color were lit-

---

Voices	**Frederick Douglass**

I was born in Tuckahoe, near Hillsborough, and about twelve miles from Easton, in Talbot County, Maryland. I have no accurate knowledge of my age, never having seen any authentic record containing it. By far the larger part of the slaves know as little of their ages as horses know of theirs, and it is the wish of most masters within my knowledge to keep their slaves ignorant. I do not remember to have ever met a slave who could tell of his birthday. They seldom come nearer to it than planting-time, harvest-time, cherry-time, spring-time, or fall-time. A want of information concerning my own was a source of unhappiness to me even during childhood. The white children could tell their ages. I could not tell why I ought to be deprived of the same privilege. I was not allowed to make any inquiries of my master concerning it. He deemed all such inquiries on the part of a slave improper and impertinent, and evidence of a restless spirit.

Frederick Douglass escaped from slavery and became one of the most important anti-slavery spokespersons in the black community (Douglass, 1993 [1845]: 39).

erate (Woodson, 1968). Free Africans were often racially mixed. They were not accepted by white society, but they often sought to distance themselves from the mass of Africans. They lived, as Adele Logan Alexander (1991) has written of the free women of color who were her ancestors, "ambiguous lives." They sought to emulate the mores of white society and to distance themselves from the world of the slaves. This did not prevent some mulattos from owning slaves, however.

Challenges to the Peculiar Institution

Slavery cast a powerful shadow over free Africans' lives, even if they resided in antislavery Northern states (Pinkney, 1987). There were forces in the larger society urging the abolition of slavery, however. Opponents of slavery in European America were heard prior to the American Revolution, but the ideology of the revolution itself served as a powerful stimulus to abolitionism. As Gary Nash (1990) suggested, "The revolutionary generation drank deeply from the wells of antislavery ideology," but their abolitionist efforts in the years just after the revolution failed to put an end to the "peculiar institution."

During the nineteenth century the **abolitionist movement** continued to challenge the slavocracy. Throughout the Northern states slavery was progressively abolished. In 1807, further slave importation was prohibited by federal law (Du Bois, 1969 [1896])—a fact that did not in actuality stop the illicit slave importation until the very eve of the Civil War. As new states became part of the union, a political conflict ensued over whether they should be free or slave states. Ira Berlin (2003: 244) writes, "Rumors of the demise of slavery elsewhere in the world and the upswell of abolitionist strength in the North entered the slave quarter in fragments. . . ."

The Underground Railroad was a sophisticated and well-financed operation that defied the Fugitive Slave Law (which granted slaveowners the right to repossess slaves who had fled to freedom in the North) and may have helped as many as 100,000 Africans escape from involuntary servitude (Franklin, 1967). The abolitionist movement gained in militancy with the ascendance of such powerful leaders as William Lloyd Garrison, the important black abolitionist David Walker, and the leading spokesperson for African Americans, Frederick Douglass (Stuckey, 1987).

Historians continue to debate the factors that finally resulted in the end of slavery. Particularly important to the debate is the question of whether or not slavery was profitable. Eugene Genovese (1972) viewed slavery as inefficient and thought that plantation owners tended to exhaust the soil, compelling a perpetual quest for new land. In addition, he saw slaveowners as essentially precapitalist, antibourgeois aristocrats willing to subjugate profit to honor, luxury, and leisure.

Economic historians Robert W. Fogel and Stanley L. Engerman (1974), using the sophisticated quantitative methods of cliometricians, presented a powerful argument that suggests slavery was highly profitable, and not moribund, prior to the Civil War. Indeed, they considered the plantation economies, due to economies of scale and the intensive utilization of cheap labor, to have been more profitable than Northern agriculture. Their findings imply that the institution of slavery did not end because of economic shortcomings. Rather, the reasons must be sought in the political and social realms (cf. Smith, 1987; Lyman, 1991).

The Politics of Conquest

Mexicans were incorporated into the United States as the nation pushed its borders westward, so the initial population of the West was not composed of voluntary immigrants. Actually, the indigenous peoples of what became Mexico confronted two different conquests. The first was the invasion in the sixteenth century by the Spanish conquistadors, who were primarily motivated by the riches they thought could be provided by the mineral wealth of the Americas. They established permanent settlements, and with the help of missionaries, sought to introduce Spanish culture into the region (Stoddard, 1973).

In the process they confronted the matter of whether their policies toward the indigenous peoples would entail incorporation, pluralism, or some form of exclusion. Certainly, there was tension among Spaniards about this issue, as reflected in the famous debate between Bartolomé de las Casas and Juan Ginés de Sepúlveda in the mid-sixteenth century. Sepúlveda, using Aristotle's understanding of the "natural slave," argued that domination of Indians was just, because of their sins (especially the sin of idolatry) and what he referred to as their "rude nature." Las Casas argued that the Indians were fully human and therefore equals of the Spaniards. Although he did not disagree with the proselytizing efforts of Catholic missionaries, he forcefully challenged the arrogance of those who, in his view, failed to realize that nobody is born enlightened. Las Casas argued that all must be guided and taught—in short, he urged the colonizers to have a sense of humility and compassion.

This debate occurred in Spain, and although some suggest that Las Casas was the more persuasive of the two, a ruthless campaign of subjugation continued to characterize the Spanish relationship to the Indians. The indigenous population declined precipitously, and over time interbreeding resulted in mixed bloods, or *mestizos*, making up a substantial majority of the Mexican population.

Spanish control of territory north of the present Mexican-United States border included all or part of Texas, New Mexico, Arizona, California, Nevada, Utah, Colorado, and Wyoming. Hispanic settlement in these regions was sparse. At the end of the seventeenth century, the Pueblo revolt in what is now Arizona and New Mexico provided temporary relief from an oppressive system of forced labor and cultural suppression. Although resistance did not entirely disappear, and pockets of autonomy persisted, the Spaniards were successful over time in tightening their control of the Indians.

Mexicans were confronted with the escalating incursion of Anglo-Americans into their northern territory, especially in Texas and California. As early as the Louisiana Purchase of 1803 it became increasingly clear to government officials that the United States, and not the European powers, posed the greatest threat to the region. Nonetheless, little was done early on to stop Anglos, who took advantage of commercial opportunities. As a consequence, by 1828 Anglos were the majority of the population in Texas, and their numbers continued to rise there and elsewhere (Chavez, 1984).

Actually, both demographic and political factors created different relations between Americans and Mexicans in each of the border states (Hraba, 1979). Tensions between the United States and Mexico intensified over time. Texans revolted against Mexican rule and established the Republic of Texas in 1836. A decade later, American rebels in California, under the "Bear Flag" banner, attempted to found the California Republic. Also in 1846, the Mexican War began. It concluded two years later with the signing of the Treaty of Guadalupe Hidalgo, which ceded Mexico's northern frontier to the United States. As a consequence, the United States expanded by more than 525,000 square miles. When the Gadsden Purchase was signed in 1853, additional land was acquired from Mexico, establishing what are today the boundaries between the two nations.

Shortly thereafter, gold was discovered in California, which set off a gold rush that brought thousands of Anglo settlers into the frontier. The decade of the 1850s saw increasing conflicts over the control and ownership of land, resulting in the progressive displacement—through legal and extralegal means—of Latinos. Chavez (1984: 43) captured the significance of the Mexican War and its immediate aftermath when he wrote, "We can date to 1848 the modern Chicano image of the Southwest as a lost land."

Travelers to Gold Mountain

The mass immigration of Chinese to America did not begin until 1849, the year gold was discovered in California. In the ensuing decade, 34,000 Chinese immigrated to the United States, settling almost entirely in California (Kitano and Daniels, 1988).

Most of the immigrants came from two southeastern provinces, Guangdong and Fujian (Chan, 1991). These coastal Chinese have historically been a diaspora people, willing to leave their homeland and settle in other lands. This was evident in two earlier waves of emigration: during the seventh century and during the Ming era (1368–1644). During the nineteenth century Chinese settled in Hawaii and in coastal areas from Canada to Peru (Lyman, 1974). The push factors propelling Chinese out of China included such natural disasters as floods and crop failures, which resulted in famine conditions. The fear and devastation caused by the Taiping Rebellion (1850–1864), which resulted in perhaps as many as 10 million deaths, was an additional stimulus.

New York's Chinatown in the nineteenth century.

The initial pull factor was remarkably singular: the quest for gold. For this reason, the typical Chinese immigrant was an adult male traveling alone. Indeed, more than 90 percent of those seeking the "Gold Mountain," as they referred to California, were male. Whether they were unmarried or married with a family left behind in China, their general goal was to get rich quickly and return to China, where they could live as wealthy individuals. Thus, the Chinese have been described as "sojourners" or "birds of passage" (Daniels, 1988: 16).

During the 1850s, most Chinese were involved in mining. Not until the beginning of the transcontinental railroad construction would the Chinese find an alternative employment for a significant number of workers. They began to settle in cities, the most important being San Francisco. In these urban settings, they moved into ethnic enclaves that became known as Chinatowns. Soon after the first wave of immigrants, a merchant stratum developed. Settling both in mining locales and in cities, the merchants opened stores and restaurants that provided provisions imported from China as well as American-made products. In addition, merchants played an important role in meeting the social needs of immigrants, assisting with health care and death benefits, leisure time, and so forth.

During the decade beginning in 1850, the foundation of the Chinese ethnic community was in place. The community was dominated by the business elite, which over time created powerful coordinated organizations that enhanced their position in the community. The Chinese also transplanted an institutional structure from the homeland in which three types of organization were most prominent. Two performed similar functions: clan associations and speech or territorial associations (*hui kuan*) were involved in mutual aid, employment, recreation, and commerce. The third type was secret societies, criminal bands, and what E. J. Hobsbawm (1959) has called "primitive rebels"—nonideological and opportunistic outsiders who were willing to work for the highest bidder. They, too, provided goods and services to the immigrants, the three most important involving gambling, drugs, and prostitution (Lyman, 1974). In this overwhelmingly male community—a "bachelor society"—many of the women were prostitutes, often living, according to Roger Daniels (1988: 16), "in a condition of semislavery."

The Chinese were subjected to intense prejudice. They were described as being superstitious, dishonest, cruel, lacking in courage, intellectually inferior, lecherous, and xenophobic. One clergyman went so far as to characterize them as "marginal members of the human race" (Lyman, 1974). This hostility resulted in concrete actions to stem the flow of immigration almost as soon as the Chinese arrived. Within this context of isolation and simmering hostility the Chinese community in America grew and developed.

Summary

In this chapter we have seen that the quest for economic opportunity was a prime cause of the Atlantic migration of western European immigrants, although many were attracted to North America by the promise of religious and political freedom. The British were by far the most numerous and the most powerful. In all areas of social life, they established themselves as the principal architects of the new nation.

The two largest nonBritish groups to arrive during this period were the Irish and the Germans. The Irish had a long history of conflict with the British, and this spilled over into the New World. The Irish were the primary victims of anti-Catholic sentiments, and religious conflict continued well beyond the Civil War. In contrast, the Germans advanced economically rather quickly. While the English more readily accepted the Germans than their Irish counterparts, the Germans did have their own problems. In particular, they had to deal with far more internal divisions within the ethnic community than did the Irish. Indeed, a variety of political, religious, regional, and economic differences characterized the German American community, and these differences frequently led to intraethnic conflicts. Both of these groups shared one important thing with the British: they came to be defined as white.

When examining nonEuropeans, we have seen the barriers that race posed to the fulfillment of the democratic ideals of the American republic. We have seen how race has determined who would and would not be caught up in coercive forms of pluralism: predatory, caste, or so-journer. Native Americans suffered from the perception that they stood in the way of the nation's westward expansion. Blacks, in contrast, were economically vital for the growth of the nation's economy. The institution of slavery defined a long legacy of the oppression of blacks by whites. The involuntary migration of Africans and their subjugation was motivated by a simple economic need: the need for labor. Racism served as an ideological justification for slavery, and though not all whites embraced racialist thought, the vast majority did. It took whites more than a century after the Civil War to begin to seriously consider the possibility that biological notions of inherent inferiority were mistaken.

The black-white division cast a shadow over white relationships with other people of color. This was true for the first Asian group to arrive in America: the Chinese. Such racist ideas were also evident with Mexicans, although not quite as pronounced because Mexicans could to some extent claim European origins and were not perceived to be quite as "foreign" as the Chinese. The imposition of racial definitions on all Asian and Latino groups took a heavy toll on group members and made their ability to gain a foothold in America more difficult than whites' ability to do so.

Key Terms

abolitionist movement	*predatory pluralism*
caste pluralism	*relocation policies*
coercive pluralism	*sojourner pluralism*
Manifest Destiny	*total institutions*
nativism	*voluntary pluralism*

Questions for Discussion and Critical Thinking

1. Compare and contrast the experiences of the Irish and the Germans in gaining a foothold in the United States and in dealing with the power of the British. Can you draw any parallels between these groups and today's immigrants?

2. What is the difference between predatory pluralism and caste pluralism? Identify the groups for which these terms are most appropriate, and compare and contrast the types of oppression and exploitation they experienced.

3. Compare and contrast the experiences of Mexicans and the Chinese. Are there any groups in today's immigrant mix that appear in some ways comparable to either of these groups? ✦

Chapter 4

Reconfiguring the Racial Divide: Immigration and White Supremacy, 1865–1950

The United States was quickly transformed into an urban industrial society shortly after the Civil War. As a consequence, the nation's economy, politics, and culture changed dramatically during this period. Immigration underwent an unprecedented rise as millions of newcomers entered what they perceived to be a land of opportunity, resulting in considerably more ethnic heterogeneity than the nation had known earlier. In this chapter, we will look at the three largest new immigrant groups: Italians, Poles, and Jews.

At the same time, a new racial formation emerged with a rearticulation of the black-white racial divide in what became known as the Jim Crow era. During this era, the promise of Reconstruction failed to materialize as whites managed to reassert their dominance. As our discussion will indicate, the implications of this racial formation had a profound impact not only on African Americans but also on other groups that were defined as nonwhite, particularly major Latino and Asian groups.

Becoming Ethnic Americans

The largest wave of immigration in the country's history occurred between 1880 and 1930, during which time 27,788,140 immigrants entered the United States. By 1910 the foreign-born constituted 14.7 percent of the total population, a level that has not subsequently been reached (Gibson and Lennon, 1999; U.S. Bureau of the Census, 2003). The vast majority came from Europe (U.S. Bureau of the Census, 1975).

This immigration brought millions of eastern and southern Europeans who differed in many respects from the western European immigrants who had preceded them. These new immigrants entered an unfamiliar world in search of employment opportunities that had eluded them at home (Gabaccia, 2002). They frequently confronted not only economic exploitation but nativist hostility.

Sympathetic scholars characterized these immigrants as alienated. Oscar Handlin's Pulitzer Prize-winning history of these new arrivals, *The Uprooted* (1973), contains a classic portrait of alienation. The book attempts to provide an ideal typical portrait of the southern and eastern European immigrants, whom Handlin viewed (mistakenly, as we shall see) as primarily peasants.

Handlin saw these new immigrants as politically and culturally conservative, religiously devout, and attached to the intimate and familiar world of the village and to an agricultural way of life. He considered their worldview to be defined by a hierarchical conception that not only placed them near the bottom of the pyramid but required them to defer to those at the top who were in positions of authority. Handlin argued that migration would occur only under conditions of extreme duress, such as dire economic crises in the homeland.

The majority of immigrants entered an urban industrial world diametrically different from the world they had previously inhabited. The dislocations proved disorienting. The immigrants' old values and ways of life no longer worked in America. Communal attachments were destroyed by an all-pervasive and previously unknown individualism. The **uprooted** metaphor reflected this situation, for these immigrants had lost their Old World but were not yet established in the new. They confronted an existential crisis that Handlin (1973: 97) described in the following manner:

> Loneliness, separation from the community of the village, and despair at the insignificance of their own human abilities, these were the elements that, in America, colored the peasants' view of the world. From the depths of a dark pessimism, they looked up at a frustrating universe ruled by haphazard, capricious forces.

Although Handlin captured much of the anxiety and the misery of the immigration experience, subsequent scholarship has challenged his portrait. Three major problems mar his ideal type: (1) it is too general; (2) it depicts the immigrants solely as victims and not as actors involved in constructing their own lives; and (3) it fails to appreciate the powerful impact of the ethnic communities that sustained and nourished their respective members.

John Bodnar's *The Transplanted* (1985) challenged the general thrust of Handlin's work. As the choice of metaphors in the title suggests, Bodnar downplayed the alienating consequences of migration and offered, instead, a perspective that stresses the role of the family, ethnic institutions, the church, labor unions, and political organizations in promoting the interests of immigrants. This perspective looks carefully at the role played by leaders, who frequently developed from the ethnic community's middle class. Bodnar did not simply dismiss Handlin's work. Rather, he provided a corrective to Handlin's overemphasis on alienation. Bodnar urged appreciating the extent to which immigrants were able to effect a **transplantation** that brought elements of the Old World into the new while adapting aspects of the New World into their everyday lives.

Peasants No More: The Italians

Although Italians were present in colonial America, and a growing stream of immigrants arrived during much of the nineteenth century, large numbers of Italians did not immigrate until after 1880. Between 1820 and 1830, for example, only 439 Italians entered the United States; between 1881 and 1890, the number was 307,309. The subsequent three decades brought even more immigrants, with 2,045,877 Italians arriving in the peak decade of 1901–1910 (U.S. Bureau of the Census, 1975).

Italians migrating prior to the Civil War tended to originate from northern Italy. During the mass Italian migration period, an overwhelming majority came from the Mezzogiorno and settled primarily in the northeastern United States, with the heaviest concentrations in

---

Voices   **Rocco Corresca**

Now and then I had heard things about America—that it was a far-off country where everybody was rich and that Italians went there and made plenty of money, so that they could return to Italy and live in pleasure ever after. One day I met a young man who pulled out a handful of gold and told me he had made that in America in a few days.

I said I should like to go there, and he told me that if I went he would take care of me and see that I was safe. I told Francesco and he wanted to go, too. So we said good-bye to our good friends. Teresa cried and kissed us both and the priest came and shook our hands and told us to be good men, and that no matter where we went God and his saints were always near us and that if we lived well we should all meet again in heaven. We cried, too, for it was our home, that place. Ciguciano gave us money and slapped us on the back and said that we should be great. But he felt bad, too, at seeing us go away after all that time.

Rocco Corresca worked at a shoeshine stand in New York City in the early part of the twentieth century (Holt, 1991).

New York, New Jersey, and the industrial cities of New England. Many also settled in the Midwest in cities such as Chicago, St. Louis, Kansas City, and Cleveland (Barton, 1975). These individuals moved from an agrarian world to an industrial one. As early as 1919 Robert Foerster observed that the Italians in America tended to avoid farming. In fact, the Italians were among the least likely European group to move into American agricultural occupations (Hutchinson, 1956).

Italians found work in a wide range of industries and provided the economy with a large supply of unskilled labor, working in factories, mines, and on "pick and shovel" jobs. Women were well represented in the garment industry (Caroli and Kessner, 1978; Gabaccia and Iacovetta, 2002). One distinctive feature of Italians in the labor market was the role played by the labor boss, or padrone. This was an adaptation of practices common in southern Italy, where the padrone served as a labor broker in what has been described as a form of indentured servitude (LaSorte, 1985). The padrone often exploited the newcomers by demanding kickbacks and overcharging workers for such things as transportation fees to work sites and for provisions at those sites. Since the immigrant paid a fee for a job, padrones had an incentive to discharge workers routinely to ensure additional fees from new workers (Alba, 1985a).

Not all immigrants chose to remain in America. Many were commonly seen as birds of passage—primarily single young men who planned to work in America just long enough to earn capital that could improve their economic status back home. More than 4.5 million Italians arrived in the United States between 1880 and 1930, and some estimates place the return migration at about 50 percent (Caroli, 1973; Nelli, 1980). Although some migrants returned home and stayed, others made more than one voyage to America. Cinel (1982b) observed that some Italians were seasonal migrants, coming to America to escape springtime poverty in Italy only to return home in the winter. Because official statistics do not make it easy to determine whether and when this was occurring, we cannot easily differentiate those who left America for good from those who went to Italy for visits. Clearly, women and children became a more prominent feature of the latter phase of the great migratory wave, which began the ethnic community shift from a male-dominated one to one with an increasing number of families (Gabaccia, 2000).

The Ethnic Community

Italians were heavily concentrated in large cities, but they also settled in smaller towns and cities. They formed an integral part of the iron mining communities in Michigan and Minnesota, for example (Vecoli, 1987). **Ethnic enclaves** emerged in both large and small cities.

In the larger cities, such as New York, Chicago, Philadelphia, Balti-more, Boston, and St. Louis, these enclaves often were dubbed "Little Italies" (Nelli, 1970; Harney and Scarpaci, 1981). Within these "foreign colonies" much of the first and second generation resided. The smells, sounds, and sights of these enclaves indicated the Italians' ability to transplant elements of their homeland to America.

In some cities the region, or even the village, of origin determined residential patterns. Harvey Zorbaugh (1929) described village affilia-tions of the Sicilians in Chicago's Little Italy by the streets in which they lived. Those from Altavilla resided on Larrabee Street, those on Townsend came from Bagheria, those on Milton came from Sambuca-Zabut, and so on. Thus, the immigrants and their offspring remained connected with their cultural origins (Kessner, 1977; Harney, 1976).

Two additional points are necessary to avoid a tendency to romanti-cize these communities. First, Little Italies were slums. The tenements provided substandard housing units for residents, and conditions were unsafe, unhygienic, and overcrowded (Brace, 1872; Riis, 1971 [1890]; Woods, 1903; Tomasi, 1978). In general, this was the only kind of hous-ing available to poor immigrants. Second, many nonItalians resided within these communities. In some quarters Italians lived next to Irish families, and in other cities Jews and Italians experienced considerable residential mixing. The ethnic community allowed the continuation of Old World cultural patterns while providing opportunities for social in-teraction with members of other ethnic groups (Yancey, Ericksen, and Leon, 1985).

Within the institutional matrix of Little Italy an ethnic community was forged. Families developed as women followed men and as the mi-grations of entire families became more common. The family proved to be a resilient institution, and in a new environment it enabled immi-grants to negotiate cultural differences and economic obstacles (Yans-McLaughlin, 1977).

Mutual aid societies, churches, Italian-language newspapers, and banks contributed to various facets of group welfare. Rudolph Vecoli (1964) argued that the family in Mezzogiorno culture was a selfish in-stitution that demanded such devotion that nonfamilial institutions were necessarily rather weak; he also contended that he could see the imprint of this cultural trait on the contadini (peasants) in Chicago. Al-though this may be an accurate depiction of the traditional family, forms of mutual aid emerged even before migration, and once in Amer-ica they developed quickly. These efforts were designed, as Humbert Nelli (1983: 115) wrote, to "deal with sickness, loneliness, and death" in a setting where the family could not undertake such welfare functions alone.

The centrality of work led to the close connection between mutual aid societies and incipient labor unions. The development of working-class consciousness melded with traditional notions of cooperation to encourage collective solutions to economic problems rather than notions of individual mobility. Labor union involvement was one way in which immigrants interacted with nonItalians. Most Italians did not embrace political radicalism, so their attitudes regarding labor unions tended to have a moderate, reformist orientation (Gabaccia, 1988).

Roman Catholicism

The church's role in the immigrant community is debated, but the general consensus is that, comparatively speaking, the church was weak. The pietism that characterized the Irish was uncharacteristic of the Italians. Italy had a long history of hostility to the Roman Catholic church; some of this enmity came from secular ideals, some from the continuing impact of magic in place of religion, and some from anticlerical sentiments. This attitude does not mean that the church was irrelevant, for Italians used it to mark the major events of life (baptism, marriage, and funerals) and as the focus of religious festivals, which were communal celebrations (Lopreato, 1970; Tomasi, 1975). Over time, these rituals were transformed and modified by new social patterns that arose in America, but they also served as a powerful source of connectedness with the Old World (Cowell, 1985).

Two facts conspired to further weaken the role of the church in the immigrant community. First, Italian priests and nuns did not migrate in large numbers, which deprived the first generation of a sufficient number of Italian-speaking priests. Second, by the time of mass Italian immigration, the Irish had ascended into positions of control of Catholicism in this country. The church thus became an institution that fueled hostility between the two groups (Femminella, 1985). As a result, the Italians did not send their children to parochial schools in great numbers. Although the Irish did so to avoid the impact of Anglicization in the public schools, the Italian aversion to parochial education was partly due to a desire to protect their children from "Irishization."

Education and Upward Mobility

A more general aversion to public education was also evident, part of a legacy from the homeland. In southern Italy peasants were suspicious of education, and most children spent very little time in school. A compulsory education law passed in 1877 met stiff resistance, widespread noncompliance, and even riots and the burning of schoolhouses. Alba (1985a) characterized the tension between peasant culture and mandatory state-sponsored education by the contrasting values accorded to being *buon educato,* or knowledgeable about society's mores and folkways, and being *ben instruito,* or knowledgeable from book learning. The former, based on the preservation of tradition, was considered unreservedly good, while the latter was viewed with considerable suspicion.

As a result of this general dislike of educational institutions, Italians in America did not use education as a vehicle for upward mobility until the emergence of the third generation, after World War II. Instead, truancy and dropping out were common through the first four decades of the twentieth century and were characteristic of both the first and second generations (Oliver, 1987). Although many immigrants and their children from all ethnic groups left school early, the Italians appear to have done so to a far greater extent. Richard Gambino (1974) reported that in 1931, while the graduation rate for all students in New York City had risen to 42 percent, only 11 percent of Italians graduated from high school. In a study of a mining community in the upper Midwest, a similar pattern emerged. Throughout the 1930s, the Italians (and French Canadians) had lower rates of high school completion than the three other large ethnic groups in the community: English, Swedes, and Finns (Kivisto, 1991; see also Smith, 1969). This attitude toward education affected upward mobility.

Ethnic Stereotypes and the Mafia

Italians confronted considerable negative imagery in their attempt to become a part of the larger society. In a study of ethnic **stereotypes** conducted by Daniel Katz and Kenneth Braly (1933), Princeton University students saw Italians as artistic, impulsive, passionate, quick-tempered, musical, and imaginative. In short, Italians were seen as being guided by their emotions and not their intellects. As such, they were seen as fit for manual but not mental labor. Some of this imagery is not inherently negative, so it is not surprising that when Emory Bogardus (1933) conducted his first study of social distance in the 1920s, Italians fell somewhere in the middle of the 30 groups studied: not as readily accepted as groups such as the English, Germans, and Swedes, but far more accepted than blacks, Chinese, Turks, and various racial minorities.

One part of the negative stereotype not mentioned in the Katz and Braly study involves crime. Overall, Italians had a lower crime rate than many other ethnic groups and were not as readily identified with many other social problems (for example, the alcoholism rate was comparatively low). Nonetheless, the existence of the Mafia colored perceptions of the association of ethnicity and criminal activity. During this era organized crime grew in power and influence, in no small part due to Prohibition, and many prominent gangsters came from various ethnic groups, including Irish, Jews, and Germans. The public, however, believed there was a powerful link between Italians and organized crime, which was seen in the Mafia.

Politics

Italians were slower to enter the political arena than the Irish were. Although most Italians were, especially by the New Deal era, Democrats, a segment of the more prosperous, especially northern Italians, had identified with the Republican party and had, at least for a time, brought some southern Italians into the fold. Democratic allegiance was affected by the class location of the majority of Italians—the working class ravaged by the Depression endorsed Roosevelt's policies.

A small but important segment of Italians continued to support various radical political positions. Carlo Tresca was the most important radical outside the ethnic community. He was a prominent organizer in two of the era's most famous strikes, the 1912 textile workers strike in Lawrence, Massachusetts, and the 1916 Patterson, New Jersey, silk workers strike. The celebrated case of Nicola Sacco and Bartolomeo Vanzetti—two anarchists tried, convicted, and, in 1927, executed for murder—highlighted the efforts the government was willing to make to get rid of immigrant radicals (Pernicone, 1979). On the 50th anniversary of their execution, the state of Massachusetts officially declared that justice had not been served by the trial that led to their conviction (Nelli, 1983).

Both interethnic and intraethnic conflict were produced by Benito Mussolini's rise to power in Italy and the ascendance of fascism (Salvemini, 1977; Bayor, 1978). During the 1920s support for Italian fascism among Italian Americans was widespread, as it was in many other quarters. Many Italians thought that Mussolini would solve the social and economic problems besetting Italy while gaining respect for Italians from Americans. This latter aspect of support suggests that events in the homeland were perceived to have a direct bearing on acceptance in America. During the 1930s, when the character of fascism became clearer, support waned considerably. Conflict intensified between antifascists and sympathizers. At the eve of World War II, despite the continual erosion of fascist support, some questioned the "divided loyalties" of Italian Americans.

Generational Change

While these political events were transpiring, larger changes occurred. In the interwar years the second generation came of age and tensions arose between children and parents. For example, in Caroline Ware's (1935) study of Italians in New York's Greenwich Village, she discovered pronounced generational differences regarding values and beliefs about the family. Although 88 percent of older Italians thought that divorce was not permissible in any circumstances, only 39 percent of younger Italians agreed. Similarly, the younger were more willing to question the authority of fathers, large families, and traditional strictures about young women being in the company of men. In some instances, it seems that the immigrant generation had already abandoned some elements of traditional mores, and the second generation merely took that trend further. For example, fully 70 percent of older Italians disagreed with the practice of arranged marriages, while the figure soared to 99 percent for their younger counterparts.

Throughout this entire period American mass culture began to have an impact, simultaneously shaping the perceptions of Italians and the larger society. The dance and musical tastes of the new ethnics and those who had been in America for generations served as a basis of commonality. Movies were a primary vehicle for creating what Elizabeth Ewen (1980: 46) has referred to as "a new visual landscape of possibility." The silent film, Ewen points out, transcended language barriers.

This change reflects a transformation, which is not to suggest that the ethnic community had outlived its usefulness. William Foote Whyte's (1943) classic ethnographic study of "Cornerville" (Boston's North End) indicated that as the second generation came of age in the 1930s, other Italians continued to be the individual's primary reference group, and the ethnic world defined such central norms as honor, respectability, and duty. But youth increasingly desired to move out of the ghetto and into the mainstream. In commenting on the youth that were Whyte's focus, Arthur Vidich (1992) wrote that they were not rebels hostile to American society but rather "sought a way to get into it." The opportunities to do so considerably improved after midcentury.

Italian American shopkeepers in the early twentieth century.

The Birth and Maturation of Polonia in America

The first sustained sociological study that sought to interpret the lived experiences of immigrants in America was William I. Thomas and Florian Znaniecki's *The Polish Peasant in Europe and America* (1918). Their analysis of the immigrant world is not unlike that of Oscar Handlin's uprooted thesis—not surprising, since Handlin was influenced by their work. Thomas and Znaniecki spoke about the **disorganization,** both personal and social, that migration brought about. The authors devoted sections of their multivolume work to such topics as marital breakdowns, unemployment and welfare dependency, youth delinquency, murder, "sexual immorality," and "demoralization." In short, they paid considerable attention to immigrants as a social problem and as victims of circumstances.

Emigration

As Poles left their homeland for various destinations, Germany, because of its proximity, was one important country to receive them. For many Poles this was a step in a series of migrations that culminated in a final move to America. Others made the Atlantic migration directly, especially after the first arrivals had settled and began sending those back home information about opportunities in the United States. Letters—written by a third party if the immigrant was illiterate—were commonplace. They kept the new arrivals in touch with events back home and provided a vital link with others contemplating emigration. In addition, many Poles reported traveling back and forth at least once, thereby providing firsthand accounts of America (Balch, 1910; Thomas and Znaniecki, 1918). Steamship lines and labor recruiters also encouraged Poles to emigrate because of the increased demand for labor in industrializing America.

Beginning in the 1850s Poles from Prussian-controlled territory began to arrive in a steady stream that continued to grow until 1890. Then the numbers of immigrants from western Poland declined and they were replaced by Poles migrating from Russian and Austro-Hungarian Poland. In all, between 1850 and the end of World War I, approximately 2.5 million Polish immigrants came to America, 2 million of whom arrived after 1870 (Greene, 1980).

These overwhelmingly economic immigrants frequently saw themselves as temporary sojourners ultimately intending to return to Poland. They were described at home as *za chlebem* (for bread) emigrants. Although this term suggests that they were motivated

1921. The First Quota Act limited the admission of each nationality to 3 percent of its representation in the U.S. Census of 1910.

by abject poverty, and thus had extremely low expectations, Ewa Morawska's (1985) community study of Poles in Johnstown, Pennsylvania, suggested that they had a higher, though realistic, sense of what they could obtain. She titled her book *For Bread With Butter* to convey an appreciation of their vision of a better life.

Immigrant destinations depended on the pull factors associated with job availability combined with the forces of chain migration networks (Golab, 1977). Approximately 95 percent of Poles worked in industry as unskilled laborers and were heavily concentrated in coal mining, steel production, and slaughtering and meatpacking (Morawska, 1989).

The Immigrant Community Takes Shape

Chicago became the undisputed center of Polonia in America, as 400,000 Poles had settled in the city by 1920. Along with Chicago, six other cities became major Polish destinations: New York, Pittsburgh, Buffalo, Milwaukee, Detroit, and Cleveland. Early in the twentieth century half of the nation's Poles lived in one of these seven cities, with another 20 percent in mining communities in Pennsylvania (Balch, 1910; Morawska, 1989; Daniels, 1990).

In these burgeoning urban industrial cities, Polonia was born. One central institution in these ethnic communities was the Roman Catholic church. Like the Italians, Poles had to contend with a church already dominated by the Irish, but unlike the Italians, the Poles made demands for Polish-speaking priests and for representation in the ranks of the hierarchy. The majority of Poles were particularly religious, partly because religion and nationalism were intertwined in Poland, and religion was a key ideological source of resistance to external domination (Greene, 1975; Wrobel, 1979; Parot, 1981).

Besides churches, Poles built numerous ethnic institutions, including two large national organizations, the Polish National Alliance and the Polish Roman Catholic Union. Both actively engaged in homeland issues, with the former seeking a secular Poland while the church played a central political role in the latter. In addition, countless local mutual aid societies, social clubs, and culture centers arose. Still another institution was the tavern, a preserve of workingmen often located in the shadow of the factory. In the early period of the colonies, the tavern was the most important place for single men, who frequently resided in boarding houses, to socialize. Even after other institutions developed and the community was transformed by the presence of women and children, the tavern remained important. The tavern owners, like other small businessmen in Polonia—primarily the owners of butcher shops, markets, restaurants, small merchandise stores, and the like—were community leaders (Bukowczyk, 1987).

Polish support for organized labor was a critical prerequisite in many unionization attempts. Indeed, as Victor Greene (1968) illustrated in his study of striking miners in Pennsylvania, Poles were often an especially militant group among the workers. This has also been pointed out more recently in James Pula and Eugene Dziedzic's (1990) study of the role of Poles in the 1912 and 1916 textile strikes in New York Mills, New York.

Poles were also actively engaged in intraethnic political involvements. Although slow to develop their own municipal leaders, Poles were a force to be reckoned with in urban machine politics, if for no other reason than the sheer force of numbers. Polish involvement in Chicago's political life illustrates a similar process elsewhere (Kantowicz, 1975). In the early twentieth century both Republicans and Democrats vied for the votes of immigrant groups who were being incorporated into the body politic. But after the watershed election of Anton Cermak, the Democratic party dominated because of its ability to capture the loyalty of large ethnic constituencies, among them the Poles.

The Chicago Democratic machine, which survived longer than other machines throughout the country, extended through the "glory days" of Richard Daley's long tenure as mayor and functioned, according to Dianne Pinderhughes (1987), as a "static hierarchy" of ethnic and racial groups. In this hierarchy blacks were consistently located at the bottom, the Irish generally at the top, and eastern and southern European groups in the middle. A group was accorded differentially distributed selective rewards depending on its location in the hierarchy. In this way, the Polish community in Chicago found a niche in the political arena, one that placed them solidly in the Democratic camp.

Poles were an active force in the formation of the Congress of Industrial Organizations (CIO), which achieved considerable success in organizing low-skilled industrial workers during the 1930s. More militant than the American Federation of Labor (AFL), which primarily attracted skilled workers, the CIO sought to avoid the mistakes of the Industrial Workers of the World, which identified too closely with socialism. This approach was important for nonsocialist Poles who had a history of labor activism but who were opposed to radical political ideologies. Bukowczyk (1987: 79–80) stated that Poles "played a central role in sparking the wave of union-organizing activity that virtually remade industrial America between the early 1930s and the early 1940s." Indeed, during the critical years of 1935–1937 about one quarter of the CIO membership was composed of Slavs, and Poles were by far the largest Slavic group. By the next decade approximately 600,000 Poles were members of the CIO.

Most Poles were members of the industrial working class, operating at its lower tiers, which resulted in a situation in which class identities and ethnic identities proved to be mutually reinforcing. As Lizabeth

Cohen (1990) has argued, workers' organizing activities were based on a desire for economic security; neither conservative nor radical anti-capitalists, they sought a form of "moral capitalism" that provided due compensation for their labor and protection during economically troubled times.

Cultural Values

The immigrant worldview transplanted into Polonia affected attitudes regarding work. Poles tended to believe that humankind had to engage in ceaseless hard work (Lopata, 1994). Work was to be endured rather than being a means toward upward mobility. They were also suspicious of secular education in public schools as a means for individual advancement. Instead, they understood education to be, according to John Bodnar (1976: 1), "for the purpose of retaining the cultural, linguistic, and religious values of the group." For this reason Poles created their own educational institutions, such as Alliance College in Pennsylvania, and they pressured local school boards to provide Polish language classes.

More than anything else, Poles were motivated by what John Bodnar (1982, 1985) terms "pragmatism." They were motivated not by political ideologies but rather by which potential course of action would achieve steady employment and economic well-being. One particularly important manifestation of this pragmatic orientation was homeownership. Commentators frequently observed that Poles saved money, even if doing so created hardships, so they could purchase homes. Poles exceeded all other ethnic groups in homeownership rates in the interwar years (Bodnar, Simon, and Weber, 1982). Helena Lopata (1994) sees property ownership as a culturally transplanted "status competition." It is probably primarily related to a quest for security and a stake in urban neighborhoods. Home purchases were like union efforts: Both promoted security and stability (Slayton, 1986).

Generational Change

Although continuity with cultural traditions characterized the Polish American community through the decade of the 1930s, after World War II changes emerged that powerfully transformed Polonia and Polish American ethnic identity. Poles had confronted their share of nativism, and during the 1920s community leaders fought to enhance the status of Poles in America. By the 1930s, the more vehement anti-Polish sentiments had begun to subside. The stereotype that persisted was that of the "dumb Pollack," an invidious distortion of a social reality: Poles were overwhelmingly located in the ranks of unskilled workers, and as a group they were relatively slow to climb the socioeconomic ladder into the middle class.

By the 1930s, the second generation came of age, and as with other groups, generational conflict intensified. Although most of the second generation still participated in the institutional life of Polonia and many continued to speak Polish at home, they were different from their parents. John Bukowczyk (1987: 71) wrote of the second generation, "The majority did not object to the idea of ethnic intermarriage; and most, while retaining Polish customs, had absorbed a great deal of American culture." Parents and ethnic leaders alike shared a growing concern that they were losing their offspring to America, and they increasingly voiced the fear aptly characterized by the title of Bukowczyk's book: *And My Children Did Not Know Me.*

The Jewish Diaspora

In *The Transformation of the Jews* (1984), Calvin Goldscheider and Alan S. Zuckerman observe that in less than a century, the center of world Jewry shifted from Europe to America. Indeed, there are currently more Jews in the United States than there are not only in Europe but also in Israel, the Jewish state founded in 1948 after the Holocaust. How and why did this movement take place?

Jews have been a diaspora people for centuries, living in exile from their homeland in the Near East. Scattered throughout the world, they were principally located throughout Europe and northern Africa. Wherever Jews settled, they were a minority group and were thus forced in various ways to adapt to the cultures of the dominant society. The result was considerable diversity, as seen in language differences. Jews located in the Iberian Peninsula spoke Spanish or Portuguese. Those residing in central and eastern Europe spoke various regionally distinct dialects of Yiddish, a language produced by the interplay of Middle High German, Hebrew, Aramaic, and the language of the host culture, which included, for example, Hungarian and Polish (Lavender, 1977; Goren, 1980).

Prior to the period between 1880 and 1924, during which time mass immigration brought nearly 2.5 million Jews into the United States from eastern Europe, two distinct settlements had already occurred involving the Sephardim and the Ashkenazim. Sephardic Jews, who originated in Spain or Portugal, arrived first. They had been expelled from both countries after 1492 as a result of the Inquisition, and they moved in large numbers to Holland and England. Although their numbers never exceeded more than a few hundred, Sephardic Jews exerted considerable influence over the Ashkenazic Jews emigrating from Germany in the eighteenth century. By the second decade of the eighteenth century this latter group outnumbered the Sephardim (Sklare, 1971).

During the first half of the nineteenth century German Jews continued to enter the country. By 1880 the numbers had reached approximately a quarter million (Glazer, 1957). They were still, it should be noted, a distinct minority in the country, constituting only about 0.5 percent of the population as a whole. They settled in established cities on the Atlantic seaboard, in the emerging commercial cities in the Midwest, and in hundreds of small towns (Sharfman, 1977). Many began their American life modestly as peddlers, expanding when successful to shop ownership, and, from there, for the most successful, to owning a chain of stores or a major department store. They also played a key role in merchant banking (Sklare, 1971).

The Early Community Presence

In the United States, German Jews attempted a balancing act, seeking acceptance and even incorporation into the larger society while maintaining a sense of Jewish identity. The Reform movement was a reflection of this effort. Orthodox Jews were traditionalists and therefore hostile to rationalism, liberalism, and the various currents of modernist thought. Many of the more educated Jews who were not prepared to abandon religious belief sought to incorporate these ideas into Judaism rather than using their religion as a bulwark against them (Sarna, 2004).

Although Reform Judaism had its origins in Germany among higher-status Jews, it proved to be far more successful in America, where it did not have to confront a powerfully entrenched traditional community. In addition, various fraternal and mutual aid societies, or what were called *Landsmannschaften*, were established. One notable organization, B'nai B'rith, was founded in 1843 to enhance the social status of Jews and to challenge anti-Semitism.

The Jewish community changed appreciably after 1880 as a result of the mass immigration of Jews from eastern Europe, especially Poland, Russia, Lithuania, Hungary, and Romania (Perlman, 1991). These Jews came from far more difficult circumstances than their western European counterparts. They were poorer and had resided in the part of Europe that was least changed by industrialization (Kahn, 1978). Furthermore, anti-Semitism was a greater problem for them during the nineteenth and early twentieth centuries. Religious hatred was a key to prejudicial attitudes, as Jews were depicted by Christians as "Christ-killers." Moreover, their enemies viewed them as economic adversaries.

Emigration was prompted by a combination of factors. Economic changes had undermined the economic livelihood of small merchants, artisans, and similar members of the group. Furthermore, political conflict intensified the always latent anti-Semitism and a number of pogroms occurred, particularly in Russia—in Odessa as early as 1871, followed by attacks elsewhere in 1881, 1889, and over an extended period from 1903 to 1907. As a result, Jews were political as well as economic migrants and moved to the United States with the intention of remaining. In contrast with many groups, the return migration rate for Jews was very low.

The Ethnic Community Evolves

Central to the ethnic community were four institutions: the family, fraternal and mutual aid societies, religious institutions, and labor organizations. The family in eastern Europe was an integral part of the *shtetl* (the Jewish village in eastern Europe), and the *shtetl* was seen as a kind of extended family. The nuclear family was embedded in a larger network of socially prescribed kin obligations. Gender roles were rigidly defined, with men's worlds involving both economic pursuits and religiously defined scholarly learning. Women were confined to the domestic realm, where they often assumed a dominant role. Mothers' expressions of love for their children embodied the "notions of suffering and sacrifice for the sake of the children" (Farber, Mindel, and Lazerwitz, 1988: 407–408). Marriages were typically arranged, and the matchmaker (*shadchen*) had considerable power, but with the sometimes-daunting responsibility of ensuring that marriages remained intact over time.

Change took place in America. For instance, nonreligious Jews rebelled against the idea of arranged marriages, opting for the romantic love that they saw in the Gentile world. Arthur Hertzberg (1989a) also contends that because fathers had such a difficult time in the workplace, their authority eroded at home. The mother became the central figure in the family unit, the "source of family loyalty for her children because she was their protector."

New fraternal organizations and mutual aid societies emerged. Because of the divisions within the community, this often entailed a dual system of halls and enterprises because neither religious nor radical Jews were willing to participate in social activities with those from the other camp. Actually, there were several cross-cutting currents of intragroup conflict: between political radicals and conservatives; between the religiously devout and the secular; between German and nonGerman Jews; between the economically well off and the poor (in New York they were described respectively as uptown and downtown Jews); and between the greenhorns and those who had been in America for some time. Despite these cleavages and the problems—personal and social—that resulted, a vibrant ethnic community based on Yiddish culture arose. Credit-lending institutions, *Landsmannschaften*, neighborhood organizations, educational enterprises, and the like grew rapidly. Yiddish-language newspapers proliferated (Jaret, 1979). In New York City alone, 20 daily Yiddish papers were published between 1885 and 1924 (Waxman, 1983).

A thriving Yiddish theater sought to entertain and sometimes to edify. As Irving Howe (1976: 460) wrote, "It was a theater superbly alive and full of claptrap, close to the nerve of folk sentiment and outrageous in its pretensions to serious culture." Drama, music, and comedy were an integral part of this milieu, and it later became a training ground for entertainers who ultimately found national popularity: Al Jolson, Eddie Cantor, George Jessel, Sophie Tucker, Jack Benny, Fanny Brice, and many others.

Religious Divisions

Religious Jews were divided into three major expressions, and they created an institutional presence that reflected these theological differences. The religiously devout from eastern Europe did not embrace the German-dominated Reform movement, and after 1880 Orthodox Judaism gained momentum and became the main vehicle for an anti-accommodationist stance toward the dominant culture. This served as the institutional home of traditionalists, that part of the Jewish community intent on not developing social relationships with Gentiles, while demanding the strict observance of Jewish law (*halacha*). The Orthodox founded *yeshiva* to educate their children, avoiding public schools for the same reason as those Catholics who sent their children to parochial schools (Glazer, 1957; Heilman and Cohen, 1989; Sarna, 2004).

Reform Judaism, although representing a minority of the Jewish religious, was particularly influential because of the higher socioeconomic status of its adherents. Modeling themselves after Protestant Christians, Reform Jews established a system of Sunday schools for religious instruction, and they founded a seminary for rabbinical training. They sought accommodation with the outside world rather than segregation from it.

The Conservative movement established a middle ground, which became an attractive alternative for many post-1880 immigrants. Unlike Reform Judaism, which had its origins in Germany, Conservative Judaism was a distinctly American phenomenon. The Jewish Theological Seminary, founded in 1887, became a center of theological life for Conservative Jews. This was the religious choice of middle-class or lower-middle-class nonGerman Jews, and because eastern Europeans far outnumbered German Jews by the end of mass migration, this was the fastest growing branch in the twentieth century (Sklare, 1972 [1955]; Woocher, 1986).

Political and Labor Organizations

The final institutional component of the Jewish community involved radical political organizations and labor organizations. Although not all Jews attached to the union movement were radicals, it is true that socialists, communists, anarchists, and labor-Zionists played a crucial role in forming and leading many organizations. Gerald Sorin

(1985) argued that the proletarianization of the majority of immigrants was a necessary but not sufficient cause to explain the significance of radicalism for a sizable segment of the Jewish community. He argues that radicalism was a secular substitute for the Jewish religion that preserved a religiously rooted sense of social justice. Jewish radicalism was deeply connected to the Jewish past, while having a tense relationship with central elements of the traditional culture (Liebman, 1979). In terms of Breton's (1964) institutional completeness thesis, radical political organizations and militant trade unions served the part of the ethnic community that was disaffected with the religious side.

Anti-Semitism

From these key institutions, a vibrant Jewish community arose. From the outset it confronted nativist hostility. Although there was a rising general antipathy toward essentially all of the new immigrant groups, according to John Higham (1970) no other group was subjected to as much hatred as the Jews. For example, the Ku Klux Klan was not only hostile to blacks; it was also intensely anti-Semitic. The link between antiblack and anti-Semitic attitudes was poignantly seen in the 1915 lynching of Leo Frank. Frank was a Jewish businessman in Atlanta who was unjustly accused of the murder of Mary Phagan, a 14-year-old girl who worked in his pencil factory (Lindemann, 1991).

In addition to the hostility of violence-prone hate groups, a pervasive genteel animus toward Jews could be seen in the thinking of political, business, and religious leaders, as well as among academics and intellectuals. The old stereotypes of Jews originally involved the image of Christ-killers. This aspect persisted but was not the most prominent facet of stereotypes during this era. Instead two contradictory images arose. The first expanded on the long-held characterization of Jews as Shylocks seeking power through money. This image translated into a fear of Jews controlling government and the banks. Prominent in this perspective was the notion of the "International Jew." Henry Ford, for instance, embraced as the truth an infamous tract titled "The Protocols of the Learned Elders of Zion," which had presumably been written by Jews in Russia but was actually a fabrication of Russian monarchists. The tract purported to outline a conspiratorial plan for establishing a worldwide Jewish dictatorship (Ribuffo, 1986).

The second image singled out the Jews as being particularly prone to radicalism. Although this was true, anti-Semitism fused with anti-radicalism in the United States, especially after the Russian Revolution and the Red Scare era in America (Higham, 1970). Not bound by logical consistency, anti-Semites condemned the Jew both for presumably controlling Wall Street and for fomenting communism. The irrationality of this view can be seen in Ford's writings in his newspaper, *The Dearborn Independent*, in which he blamed Jews not only for capitalist and communist conspiracies but also for short skirts, bootleg liquor, and the corruption of baseball (Wirth, 1956 [1928]).

Upward Mobility

Despite this hostility, during the interwar years upward mobility was evident as Jews moved out of the working class and into the middle class. Some did so via business success. Others used higher education and joined the emerging white-collar workforce. Many entered teaching and government service. The trend from business to the professions began at this time, although it became far more pronounced after World War II. As Jews applied to professional schools—law, medicine, and so on—they confronted discrimination based on the fear that if merit were the sole criterion for admission into these institutions, Jewish enrollment would overwhelm that of Gentiles. Thus, major universities, such as Harvard, Yale, Chicago, and Columbia, implemented quota systems whereby Jewish admissions were limited to a certain percentage of class size.

Other changes that signaled the beginning of a new relationship with the nonJewish world were linked to this occupational shift. Jews began to move out of the ethnic enclave during this period for dwellings in better neighborhoods of cities, and later this became a mass migration to the suburbs (Sklare and Greenblum, 1967).

In both the workplace and neighborhoods, interaction between Jews and nonJews increased and afforded the possibility of new relationships. This period also witnessed an exodus from Orthodoxy, and Conservative Judaism was the major beneficiary. Linked to this was a trend toward overcoming the cultural differences between German and east European Jews (Swatez, 1990; Sarna, 2004).

Although poised for more dramatic changes, Jewish America remained more insular than other European-origin groups because of anti-Semitism and the desire among Jews to preserve a distinctive ethnic identity. Jews, for example, had a considerably lower rate of intermarriage than other new immigrants.

The Color Line From the Civil War to the Civil Rights Movement

In an oft-quoted passage, W. E. B. Du Bois (1961 [1903]: 23) contended, "The problem of the twentieth century is the problem of the color-line—the relation of the darker to the lighter races of men in Asia and Africa, in America and the islands of the sea." In other writings he suggested that white workers were "compensated in part by a public and psychological wage" that was based on the racist belief in the inferiority of people of color (Du Bois, 1973 [1935]). Thus, white workers refused to join with Africans, Asians, and Hispanics in establishing a class consciousness that transcended racial boundaries because they derived a benefit from their racial identity. Similarly, white citizens frequently sought to deny the rights and benefits of citizenship to nonwhites. Whites excluded nonwhites from their neighborhoods, social organizations, unions, athletic clubs, churches, schools, and other institutions. Transracial friendships were infrequent and, when they occurred, often involved risks and a price for both parties. Interracial marriages were even less likely and were, in fact, banned by antimiscegenation laws in many states.

The color line operates along two axes: first, that of dominance and subordination; and second, that of inclusion and exclusion (Blumer, 1965; Lyman, 1994). We will illustrate these axes by providing an overview of how the color line was drawn during the first four decades of the twentieth century. In doing so, we will see the implications of this line for people of color in America.

From Emancipation to Jim Crow: African Americans

On January 1, 1863, President Lincoln signed the Emancipation Proclamation, which declared that slaves in all areas under the control of the Confederacy were free. The Reconstruction Acts provided for governmental actions in the immediate aftermath of the Civil War, during what became known as the Reconstruction era. After the Confederacy's defeat, several critical matters related to reintegrating the South into the Union had to be addressed. These matters included the terms under which Confederate states would be readmitted, who among Confederate supporters should be punished, whether rebels should be barred from seeking public office, and a host of related matters. Another facet of Reconstruction dealt with the rebuilding of the Southern economy. The central issue of freed slaves revolved around redefining the role and status of Africans in American society (Frazier, 1949; Franklin, 1967; Litwack, 1979; McPherson, 1982).

The first action, in January 1865, was the proposal for the Thirteenth Amendment to the Constitution, which would abolish slavery throughout the nation. Two months later Congress passed legislation establishing the Freedmen's Bureau, which was intended to protect the interests of former slaves. By the time the Amendment was ratified, at the end of 1865, Lincoln had been assassinated and Andrew Johnson, a Southerner, undertook a policy of Reconstruction that was designed to enhance the interests of the white small-holder farmers. He did not press for citizenship for blacks and was not opposed to the passage of "black codes" in several Southern states that were intended to both revive the Southern economy and reassert the role of the white landowning class. These laws required former slaves to sign labor contracts, permitted whipping, and allowed jail sentences for unemployed blacks (Foner, 1988).

Johnson's efforts to avoid policies aimed at integrating blacks into the political system and into a new position in society were challenged by radical Republicans in Congress. Not only was Johnson impeached and missed being forced out by one vote, but Congress also passed the Civil Rights Act of 1866 over Johnson's veto. This act granted various rights to African Americans and provided a role for the federal government in protecting these rights. Congress also succeeded in passing both the Fourteenth and Fifteenth Amendments to the Constitution. The Fourteenth granted citizenship to all African Americans and provided for equal treatment under both federal and state laws. The Fifteenth made it unconstitutional to deny citizens the right to vote on the basis of race.

African Americans attempted to assert their autonomy and to stake out a new place in American society (Du Bois, 1973 [1935]). One important legacy of the Freedmen's Bureau was the creation of schools to educate former slaves. From this program developed what became some of the most important institutions of higher education for several generations of African Americans: Atlanta University, Fisk University, Hampton Institute, and Howard University. Taking advantage of these opportunities, a cadre of educated blacks emerged and formed the basis of a black middle class and a leadership stratum.

Not only were attempts to re-create a labor system based on caste temporarily curtailed, but also many reform policies, such as those related to education and taxation, benefited poorer whites and blacks. This, however, did not last, and when Reconstruction came to an end, a new system of racial oppression replaced the former system (Scott, 1994). Before this happened, African Americans asserted themselves in ways that established the foundation for a distinctive black community. One important underlying feature of this gestation period of the free black community was its social distance from the white world. Two interrelated phenomena accounted for this situation: white resistance to racial equality and the black "quest for self-determination" (Foner, 1988: 89; Williamson, 1986).

Reasserting White Domination

The first challenge to blacks occurred in the political arena, as efforts were made to disenfranchise them. Blacks were, beginning in the 1890s, excluded from running for elective office and from voting. Because the Fifteenth Amendment prohibited denying citizens the right to vote on the basis of race, other criteria were used to circumvent this prohibition. The two most widely used devices were literacy tests and the poll tax.

Reducing African Americans to political powerlessness was just the first step in efforts to institute a new form of **caste society** predicated on race. Next came laws that mandated racial segregation. Although de facto segregation was actually more characteristic of the North than the South, what became known as the era of Jim Crow in the South redefined race relations far differently than advocates of Reconstruction had in mind. In a somewhat piecemeal fashion, a series of laws were enacted in Southern states that required the **segregation** of blacks and whites in public accommodations, schools, residences, streetcars, and the like. Thus, around the turn of the century began what historian C. Vann Woodward (1974) has termed the "strange career of Jim Crow." **Jim Crow** referred to a series of laws passed in the South that were designed to repress blacks. The origin of the term is uncertain. However, the intention of these laws was quite clear: to impose on blacks a "constriction of possibilities" (Royce, 1993).

African Americans found that, in spite of white supporters in both the North and South (White, 1990), there was not enough support to prevent the institutionalization of Jim Crow. In fact, such laws were found to be constitutional in the 1896 Supreme Court case *Plessy v. Ferguson.* The plaintiff, Homer Adolphus Plessy, argued that because he was only one-eighth black, the state of Louisiana's laws pertaining to railroad segregation should not apply to him. The court did not rule in his favor. Rather, it declared that racial segregation was constitutionally permissible if segregated facilities were equally provided to both races. This doctrine of "separate but equal" remained the law of the land for more than a half century.

Plessy also permitted states to determine who was and who was not to be defined as a "Negro." Thus, a school reserved for whites could deny admission to a young girl who was one-sixteenth black. In short, a color line divided the races into two discrete camps (Baker, 1964 [1908]; Lyman, 1991). The problem with this situation, as the two examples in the preceding paragraph attest, is that there was a long history of racial interbreeding (Williamson, 1980). In some cosmopolitan parts of the South, such as Charlestown and New Orleans, the antebellum period witnessed racial definitions expressed in very subtle distinctions. Categories in use included *mulatto* (one-half black), *quadroon* (one-quarter black), *octoroon* (one-eighth black), *sambo* (three-fourths black), and *mango* (seven-eighths black). This changed in the age of Jim Crow.

Leadership in the African American Community

Three black leaders rose to national prominence during the early part of the twentieth century: Booker T. Washington, William Edward Burghardt (W. E. B.) Du Bois, and Marcus Garvey. They presented three different leadership styles and different, if sometimes overlapping, programs for responding to the new racial order in America.

Washington was by far the most powerful and influential of the three. Born in slavery, Washington later founded Tuskegee Institute, a vocational training school in Tuskegee, Alabama (Washington, 1963 [1901]) that was financially supported by Northern progressives and had on its board several ranking Protestant reformers who were part of the Social Gospel movement (White, 1990). From this base, Washington became an adviser to Presidents Theodore Roosevelt and William Howard Taft, members of Congress, and governors (Harlan, 1983).

Washington's success came because he did not directly challenge the system of institutionalized racial inequality. In his famous "Atlanta Compromise" speech of 1895 he set the terms for a racial peace that resonated well with many whites. It called for a situation of "mutual progress" in which blacks could expect increased opportunities for economic advancement. In turn, African Americans would demand neither racial equality nor integration. He sought to accommodate to what he viewed as the realistic limitations that existed in the nation. This approach explained the emphasis of Tuskegee on vocational training in such areas as carpentry, farming, and teaching. Recent evidence has indicated that this portrait of Washington as the consummate "Uncle Tom" who capitulated to the whites rather than challenge their moral authority was not entirely accurate. Behind the scenes, Washington funneled money to support legal challenges to segregation and political disenfranchisement (Harlan, 1983).

The moderate accommodationist position articulated by Washington was challenged most forcefully by W. E. B. Du Bois, who many saw as the heir of Frederick Douglass (Lewis, 2001). DuBois was born and raised in Massachusetts, and his life was quite different from that of the Southerner Washington. Du Bois, for example, became the first African American to receive a doctorate from Harvard University. Like Washington, he wanted to bring African Americans into the mainstream, but he refused to limit their socioeconomic positions to the working class and lower middle class. To do so, he believed, would result in the consignment of blacks to permanent servility. Instead, he urged the promotion of what he termed the "Talented Tenth," a stratum that he wanted to be provided with the best education possible (Du Bois, 1961 [1903]). From their midst would come intellectuals, educators, clergymen, lawyers, doctors, and other professionals who would collectively function as a vital leadership for the African American masses (Broderick, 1959).

Through the organization of the Niagara Falls Conference of 1905, out of which sprang the National Association for the Advancement of Colored People (NAACP), Du Bois posed a direct challenge to Washington's leadership and racial policies. The NAACP was a liberal assimilationist organization that advocated, according to Joel Williamson (1986: 68), the "immediate assimilation of black people as equal citizens in the Republic." Its economic stance basically supported laissez-faire capitalism. Although Du Bois moved from this position over the course of his career, embracing first socialism and later Pan-Africanism (he died in Ghana in 1963 shortly after becoming a citizen of that country), the NAACP maintained its liberal reformist orientation.

A third approach to remedying the subservient position of African Americans was found in the program advanced by Marcus Garvey. Born in Jamaica, Garvey offered a version of black nationalism that encouraged the belief that blacks could not develop within the confines of a white-dominated society. Indeed, Garvey advocated an exodus to Africa and was seen by followers as a "black Moses" (Cronon, 1955; Redkey, 1969). He founded the Universal Negro Improvement Association (UNIA), which was based on the quest for self-respect and dignity; in this, his approach was indebted to Washington, under whom he studied, and Du Bois would not have disagreed.

Garvey differed, however, from the other two major black leaders by opposing integration, instead endorsing a nationalism that mandated racial separatism. Garvey's quest for "racial purity" elicited support from such white supremacist groups as the Ku Klux Klan and Anglo-Saxon Clubs. Sometimes leaders from these white supremacist groups were invited as speakers at UNIA meetings; they found common ground in their advocacy of racial separatism (Cronon, 1955).

Another aspect of Garvey's nationalism was its hostility to socialism. His economic policies called for the development and expansion of black capitalism. He did not believe that African Americans had a future in America, so he urged their return to Africa, calling first upon pioneers with skills to build new societies on the African continent. He created a shipping company, the Black Star Line, which was intended to facilitate the anticipated migration out of America. Garvey's organization was inherently unstable, built on personal charisma and on slippery financial footing, so it is not surprising that it failed. He was convicted of fraud and was ultimately deported to Jamaica. As with the approaches of Washington and Du Bois, however, Garvey's nationalist ideals were revived again in subsequent decades.

Southern Race Relations

Throughout the period between the Civil War and World War I, African Americans remained heavily concentrated in the South (Geschwender, 1978). Black and white farmers confronted similar economic difficulties, including high interest rates, mortgage debt, and the cost of shipping their crops by rail. Populism in the Midwest and the South was a political response to economic distress caused, populists argued, by financiers and industrialists. The populists' political objectives included a more egalitarian society that challenged the capitalists' economic power (Goodwyn, 1978). In the Southern states, this populist vision took form in the Southern Farmers' Alliance. Race became a bar-

An ex-slave couple residing in the rural South in the early twentieth century.

rier to a unified alliance of tenant farmers, however, because the Alliance excluded blacks from membership (Geschwender, 1978; Schwartz, 1988).

The failure to develop a biracial populist movement served the interests of the economically powerful. They were in a position to play race against race, and their domination of the region not only kept African Americans in a position of caste subordination but also helped "to maintain a captive force of tenant labor, [and] to control agricultural labor costs" (Schwartz, 1988: 286). The racial division also mitigated the efforts of some in organized labor to mobilize the Southern workforce.

Underpinning this new social system in the South was the perpetual threat of violence and terror. The actions of groups such as the Ku Klux Klan and the Knights of the White Camellia were clearly intended as an extralegal reinforcement of a social order stratified along racial lines. The burning of property, beatings, and lynchings became an integral part of the social order. The result was the reestablishment of an interracial "etiquette" code in which blacks were expected to conduct themselves in a manner of servile politeness in the presence of whites. As Bertram Doyle (1936: 205) commented, this race-specific etiquette was "a form of social control." Indeed, violations of the code could result in serious consequences, up to and including lynching—which became an endemic feature of Southern life (Raper, 1933; Shapiro, 1988).

Two classic community studies of Southern cities were conducted during the 1930s, John Dollard's (1937) study of "Southerntown" and the monograph of Allison Davis, Burleigh Gardner, and Mary Gardner (1941) on "Old City." Both provide compelling documentation that the communities were divided along both class and caste lines, with a white class structure and a black class structure each further divided along caste lines. In Figure 4.1, derived from Davis and her colleagues (1941), it is clear that the upper class in the black community—professionals and businesspeople serving the black community—are higher than the lower echelon of the white caste in socioeconomic position.

Nonetheless, the caste barrier was erected to ensure that there were advantages to being white, regardless of location in the class hierarchy. Dollard (1937) singles out three ways in which whites benefited at the

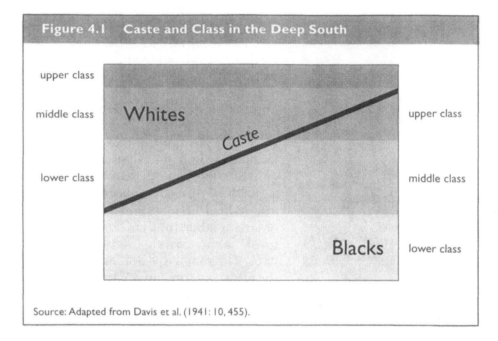

Figure 4.1   Caste and Class in the Deep South

upper class

middle class   Whites   upper class

                    Caste

lower class   middle class

                            Blacks lower class

Source: Adapted from Davis et al. (1941: 10, 455).

expense of blacks: economic, social status, and sexual. The last actually applied only to white men, who were described as having sexual access to both black and white women. Because a central tenet of the caste system revolved around the prohibition of black men engaging in sexual relations with white women, this obviously meant that white women also were restricted in their access to potential sexual partners (Dollard, 1937; see also Davis, Gardner, and Gardner, 1941: 25).

Within the black community, an emerging class structure was based on occupation. The small upper class and the middle class were composed of owners of businesses that serviced a black clientele, professionals such as doctors and lawyers, and members of the clergy. Overlaying and reinforcing these internal economic divisions was the prestige attached to light skin by African Americans. Those in the upper and middle classes were disproportionately light skinned, while poor blacks were more often dark skinned. Dollard (1937: 69) observed, "Consciousness of color and accurate discrimination between shades is a well-developed Negro caste mark; whites, of course are not nearly so skillful in distinguishing and naming various shades." Color consciousness in the black community played a significant role in upward mobility, choice of marital partners, and the like.

The economy of the South continued to be dominated by the importance of three major crops: cotton, tobacco, and rice. Changes in Southern agriculture, especially felt in the cultivation of cotton, progressively undercut blacks' ability to remain on the land. Until 1910, cotton production expanded chiefly because of westward movement and led to the migration of blacks within the South. After 1910, however, expansion ceased. Several factors produced severe economic hardship for blacks engaged in cotton production. The boll weevil infestation destroyed crops and reduced the amount of acreage under tillage. A worldwide depression in cotton prices during the 1920s added to the problems, followed by the advent of increased mechanization and the payment of government subsidies to farmers. The combined impact of these changes served as a powerful migratory push force (Wilhelm, 1970; Fligstein, 1981; Daniel, 1985).

The Promised Land

However, economic factors alone do not entirely explain the move out of the South. Intertwined was a desire to escape the subordination of the caste system and the ever-present reality of violence perpetuated by whites. In a sense, African Americans exiting the South were "refugees," and not simply workers moving to improve their economic condition (Tolnay and Beck, 1992). Many African Americans looked to the North as a "promised land" (Grossman, 1989; Marks, 1989; Lemann, 1991; Hirsch, 1998).

A northern migration began to occur about the time of World War I, produced partly by the demand for labor in war industries. This migration expanded during the 1920s, as the immigration restriction law passed in 1924 dried up the supply of immigrant labor. The Depression reduced, but did not entirely stop, this flow northward, and World War II fueled the movement of even greater numbers into Northern cities (Fligstein, 1981). In many respects, the African American migration was akin to the transoceanic migrations of many other ethnic groups. Blacks migrated not by steamship but by rail. Whatever economic opportunities the "Great Migration" afforded, it did not result in entering anything that remotely resembled the "promised land." Indeed, African Americans quickly learned that much of the racial exclusion and discrimination they had experienced in the South would be replicated in the North. In fact, the movement north sparked racial hostilities. Around the time of World War I, for example, there were serious race riots in numerous cities, including Chicago, Philadelphia, Washington, D.C., Omaha, and East St. Louis. Similar events occurred during World War II; riots in New York's Harlem and Detroit were among the most severe and destructive. As in the South, African Americans were forced to reside in separate worlds in Northern cities (Lynd and Lynd, 1929, 1937).

The Development of the Black Community

The most systematic and richly detailed study of black life in the North between the world wars is found in St. Clair Drake and Horace R.

Cayton's *Black Metropolis* (1962 [1945]), a community study of a major destination for Southern blacks: Chicago. Between 1900 and 1940, the African American population of Chicago increased more than tenfold. Referring to the black enclave as "Bronzeville," the authors depict it as a "world within a world." Bronzeville developed a rich institutional complex, including churches, businesses, voluntary associations, and newspapers. This community was connected to African Americans nationwide.

Furthermore, there were countless ties to the outside world of whites. For one thing, social reformers set up operations in Bronzeville to address a variety of social problems. Schools were another connection. In addition, the local political machine brought blacks into its fold, albeit in a subordinate position (Pinderhughes, 1987). During the 1930s, the organizing efforts of the Congress of Industrial Organizations (CIO) and of the political left, especially the Communist party, sought class alliances that transcended racial boundaries, with limited success (see Naison, 1983, for a look at communist influence in New York's Harlem).

In this milieu a distinctively black musical idiom emerged—the blues—that played a major role in shaping a distinctively American popular music (see, e.g., Jones, 1963). Rooted in the rural South, this secular music (as compared with spirituals) took instrumental form in Southern cities, especially New Orleans, as jazz was born in the teens and took off in the 1920s. In Northern cities this music was central to the rise of rock and roll. But the crossover from the black to the white world took time.

In this general context a cultural movement arose within African America, centered not in Chicago but rather in the nation's intellectual capital, New York City. The Harlem Renaissance was the first great blooming of a distinctly African American culture, a literary movement that had both cultural and political implications. Principal figures such as Alain Locke, Langston Hughes, Countee Cullen, Zora Neale Hurston, Jean Toomer, and Claude McKay reflected the heterogeneous character of this largest of the African American communities. Its inhabitants included African Americans from both the North and the South and also the West Indies (Huggins, 1971; Lewis, 1981). The writers associated with the Harlem Renaissance tried to articulate a common consciousness of what it meant to be black in America.

The Latino Presence in the United States

Latino immigration was chiefly a Mexican phenomenon until after 1940, with relatively small numbers of Puerto Ricans and Cubans also entering the country during this time (Burma, 1954). After the Mexican-American War, about 80,000 Mexicans resided in the United States, chiefly in border regions. Although a few thousand Mexicans opted to repatriate to Mexico after the conquest, most remained and were joined by a small but steady stream of immigrants. Mexican migration from the middle to the end of the nineteenth century was quite small.

Mexicans in the Southwest

Although Mexicans in the United States were accorded citizenship rights, the rapid settlement of Anglos on the western frontier jeopardized their socioeconomic and cultural positions. Demographic change reduced the Mexican population to a minority in regions of the Southwest, although New Mexico was an exception (Moore, 1970). Political conquest was followed by economic domination and a challenge to Hispanic culture. The Anglo exploitation of the Southwest's natural resources in mining, lumbering, and agriculture combined with the growth of business ventures and industrial development.

Viewing the Hispanic and Anglo frontiers as increasingly "interlocked," Sarah Deutsch (1987: 13) argued, "This renewed Anglo assault posed an even greater challenge to the territory's Hispanics." It resulted in the loss of substantial amounts of land, sometimes through legal means and other times through outright fraud. Some land went to private interests, but the federal government also appropriated substantial holdings into the national forest system. Although wealthier Hispanics often managed to hold onto their land, the poorer and less educated did not (Cortés, 1980).

This challenge did not occur without resistance to the Anglo incursion. Some secretive societies, such as the Mano Negro (Black Hand) and Gorras Blancas (White Caps), engaged in guerrilla tactics, destroying telegraph lines and railroad ties, but they were also willing to use the courts and public opinion in their struggle to protect their interests (Cortés, 1980). Despite this struggle, the Mexican position in the Southwest eroded considerably. Anglo domination entailed a progressive marginalization of Mexicans into what some scholars have referred to as a colonized status that produced the barriozation of the Mexican populace (Camarillo, 1979; Barrera, 1979; Romo, 1983). Thus, Mexican Americans can be viewed in terms of Robert Blauner's (1969) **internal colonialism** thesis. Blauner argued that when a group is subjugated by a more powerful and numerically larger group, the colonized group ends up economically and politically weakened and its indigenous culture is threatened. Confined to a residential ghetto, Mexican Americans became isolated politically and religiously as control of the Roman Catholic church slipped from them (Griswold del Castillo, 1979; Weber, 1973; Daniels, 1990).

Mexican Immigration in the Early Twentieth Century. In the twentieth century immigration increased dramatically. The border's permeability allowed Mexicans, especially those living near the border, to respond rapidly to job opportunities in the United States. Seasonal and temporary work was attractive to workers because it did not require permanent migration. Employers increasingly came to appreciate the benefits of a "reserve army of the unemployed." These workers' labor power could be exploited during labor shortages, while they could just as easily be dismissed during economic downturns (McWilliam, 1948).

Mexicans departed their homeland for chiefly economic reasons, but economic factors were overlaid with political ones, especially as a result of the Revolution of 1910 in which Porfirio Díaz's dictatorship was overthrown. In the ensuing chaos, Mexicans poured into the United States. Some estimates suggest that as much as 10 percent of the population emigrated during this period. In the second decade of the twentieth century, 219,004 Mexicans immigrated and were followed by 459,259 during the 1920s (U.S. Bureau of the Census, 1975).

Responding to opportunities in the American labor market, Mexicans began to move into urban industrial settings. The largest populations were located in the following southwestern states (ranked in descending order of size): Texas, California, Arizona, New Mexico, and Colorado. In addition, Mexicans moved into the burgeoning industrial cities of the Midwest, particularly Chicago and Detroit (Bogardus, 1934; Moore, 1970).

Mexican industrial workers were received ambivalently by Anglo workers. Mexicans were sometimes imported by industrialists as strikebreakers, which produced anti-Mexican hostility from organized labor. This divide-and-conquer strategy tended to be a rather effective way for employers to stymie labor organizing (Barrera, 1979). The Mexican American situation supports Edna Bonacich's (1972) **split labor market** theory, which sees recent immigrants and racially marginalized groups excluded from higher-paid jobs and as a source of cheap labor. Like blacks and Asians, Mexicans were often not welcomed into the union movement. But when Mexicans were involved, they were often actively involved.

The border communities from Brownsville, Texas, to San Diego acquired distinctive features because the border between the two nations allowed considerable movement back and forth (Garcia, 1981; Heyman, 1991). Illegal immigration was common, and attempts to control it resulted in an adversarial relationship between Mexicans and the Immigration and Naturalization Service's Border Patrol, along with local authorities such as the Texas Rangers. Illegal immigrants were vulnerable to abuses from these agencies. Many illegal immigrants were dependent on the padrone system for employment because of their legal status and their unfamiliarity with the language and culture. In this, they were like Italians and Greeks: victims of the system's exploitive character.

The Depression and Repatriation. Despite the problems, Mexicans continued to come to the United States in response to job opportunities. Communication networks between Mexican Americans and those in the homeland provided would-be migrants with information and advice. World War I and the end of the European mass migration meant that opportunities for Mexicans existed over an extended period of time. The depression finally stopped large-scale migration. With the rise in unemployment, many Mexicans voluntarily returned to Mexico. Few were admitted to the United States, with the number of Mexicans obtaining visas in the hundreds rather than thousands for most years of the 1930s. It became routine practice to deny visa requests by identifying Mexicans under the bureaucratic designation LPC (that is, "liable to become a public charge," or in other words, a recipient of welfare or unemployment relief). Scapegoating was common as Mexicans were blamed for filling up relief rolls (Stoddard, 1973).

As one means of dealing with the crisis of unemployment during the 1930s, Secretary of Labor William Doak advocated ousting aliens from the country. Many counties and municipalities agreed. Abraham Hoffman (1974) documented the forced repatriation policies of the County of Los Angeles. Concluding that it was cheaper to pay transportation costs than to maintain Mexicans on relief rolls, the county chartered trains and paid for one-way tickets, generally shipping individuals to Mexico City—far from the border where reentry would be possible (Romo, 1983). The result of the combined effects of voluntary and forced repatriation was that the Mexican-born population in the United States declined from 639,000 in 1930 to 377,000 a decade later (Moore, 1970).

Prejudice and Discrimination. Economically troubled times generally intensify prejudice and discrimination. For Mexican Americans the repertoire of negative stereotypes included persistent images of laziness and corruption. There was a generalized perception of Mexicans as being present oriented, complacent, subjugated to nature, seekers of immediate gratification, nonintellectual, emotional, superstitious, and traditional (note that many of these resemble stereotypes of Italians). In addition, the notion of *machismo* was applied to males. Linked to machismo was the representation of Mexicans as prone to violence.

Not surprisingly, in Bogardus's (1959) social distance studies, Mexicans were located in the bottom third of the 30 groups he studied in both 1926 and 1946. Their social distance score was only slightly better than those of African Americans, Asians, and Turks.

The Bracero Program. Nonetheless, the value of Mexican labor became increasingly obvious, especially to employers in the Southwest, in both agriculture and manufacturing. With the outbreak of World War II, the demand for workers grew, and it was hoped that Mexicans would temporarily meet that demand, as they had done during World War I. Unlike in the earlier wartime period, however, the Mexican economy in the 1940s was doing well, so migratory push forces were not strong. This situation led to the implementation of a program of contract labor known as the "bracero program."

Begun in 1942, this program enticed Mexicans with the offer of higher wages than could be obtained at home if they would temporarily migrate. It carried the explicit expectation that when their services were no longer needed, they would return to their homeland (Moore and Pachon, 1985). Suspended after the war, as soldiers returned home and again entered the workforce, the bracero program was later resumed because it gave employers considerable flexibility in meeting labor needs. Although this program was a boon to these temporary workers, it was not viewed favorably by Mexican Americans, many of whom thought that they were being passed over for jobs because the immigrants, it was believed, worked for less than American workers (López, 2003).

The Ethnic Community. In this context, characterized by considerable fluidity within the Mexican American population, an ethnic community emerged. For a variety of reasons the community was less developed than those among European immigrants. Mutual aid societies were relatively slow to develop into formal organizations, as Mexicans were inclined to rely more on informal kin networks. The Roman Catholic church was quite weak. The pervasive poverty combined with the relative ease by which Mexicans could return home also contributed to the underdeveloped state of the ethnic community.

During the interwar years, however, a middle class arose and developed a sense of self-identity and an organizational presence. Its leaders sought to develop a mentality within the entire Mexican American community that stressed a dual consciousness—Mexican in culture, but politically American. They invested in various local community institutions, especially the Roman Catholic church, and they got involved in political affairs at the local level. Political and economic concerns were also pursued in a national organization that represented middle-class interests, the League of United Latin American Citizens (LULAC). Essentially a civil rights organization, LULAC's objectives and tactics resembled those of the NAACP and B'nai B'rith. LULAC waged an ongoing campaign against Anglo prejudice and discrimination (Garcia, 1991).

Although middle-class leaders played a major role in shaping Mexican American consciousness, Mario T. Garcia (1989: 145) argues that "they did not monopolize it." El Congresso del Pueblo de Habla Espanola (the Spanish-Speaking Congress) was a working-class counterpart to LULAC that had ties to left-wing political organizations, including the Communist party. It was concerned with discrimination, jobs, housing, education, and the problem of youth crime and delinquency in the barrio. In addition, Mexican American workers joined with other border proletariats in the CIO's International Union of Mine,

Mill, and Smelter campaign to unionize the lead, gold, silver, zinc, and copper mines and refineries in Arizona, New Mexico, and Texas (Garcia, 1989).

Cubans and Puerto Ricans

As the Mexican American community evolved, the two other Hispanic groups under consideration, Cubans and Puerto Ricans, remained relatively small. Cuban immigration remained very low until the 1960s, despite the island's close proximity to the mainland and the U.S. role in Cuban history since the Spanish-American War. The impetus for emigration in the 1960s was the revolutionary overthrow of the corrupt dictator Fulgencio Batista. The small contingent of Cubans arriving in the late nineteenth and early twentieth centuries settled in a few small enclaves in southern Florida, and many found employment in cigar factories owned by fellow Cubans. The heaviest concentration was in the Ybor City section of Tampa (Pozzetta and Mormino, 1986).

Puerto Rico became a commonwealth of the United States in 1900, which in essence means that it is a colony. This situation led to the birth of a nationalist movement that sought independence (Duany, 2002). After 1917, Puerto Ricans were granted U.S. citizenship (and thus became subject to the military draft). Citizenship meant that they could legally move to and from the mainland freely. Nonetheless, until 1930 the numbers were low. The early immigrants were largely political exiles. Labor migrants began to arrive in the 1920s and continued during the Depression years, due to a long-term drop in world prices for the island's two main export crops, sugar and tobacco. Migratory pressures were heightened by the destructiveness of two powerful hurricanes that hit Puerto Rico in 1928 and 1932.

By 1940 there were nearly 70,000 Puerto Ricans on the mainland. Unlike Cubans, they did not opt for Florida but instead settled in New York City and its immediate environs. Women in particular found work in the textile industry in that city, while many others—both male and female—found employment as migrant farm workers in New York State. In 1940, 87.8 percent of all Puerto Ricans in the continental United States lived in New York City (Fitzpatrick, 1980). Only the beginnings of an institutional presence were evident during the interwar years. This situation changed after 1945, as cheap airfares provided easy access to the mainland and resulted in a dramatic increase in immigration.

The Chinese and Japanese: A Comparison

As Figure 4.2 indicates, the Chinese population in America reached a peak of 107,488 in 1890. Thereafter, the population declined, its nadir being in 1920, when U.S. Census data report a total of 61,639. From this

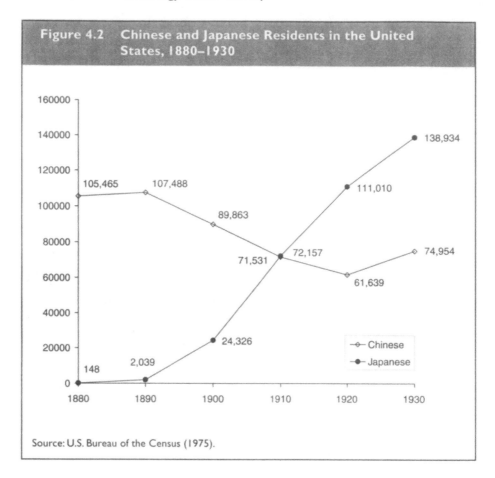

Figure 4.2   Chinese and Japanese Residents in the United States, 1880–1930

Source: U.S. Bureau of the Census (1975).

low point, the population again began to grow slowly (U.S. Bureau of the Census, 1975).

The Chinese and Immigration Restriction

This demographic overview reflects a unique feature of the Chinese experience: The Chinese were the first group to be singled out by immigration restriction forces (Barth, 1964). Organized labor played a particularly important role in restriction efforts. White workers in the labor movement viewed the Chinese in racial rather than class terms—whites saw Chinese workers as a competitive threat rather than as allies in the struggle against capitalist exploitation. Samuel Gompers, the head of the American Federation of Labor, was a vocal spokesperson for the demand: "The Chinese must go" (Saxton, 1971). But organized labor was not alone in this call. When President Rutherford Hayes called for a stop to "the present Chinese invasion," he reflected a widely held public sentiment for restrictive legislation (Takaki, 1989: 103; Gyory, 1998).

In 1882, a national Chinese exclusion act became law. It prohibited further Chinese immigration of laborers for a period of ten years. Despite protests by the Chinese government and spokespersons in the United States, the prohibitions were not merely extended a decade later, but the Geary Act imposed even harsher burdens on the Chinese (Tichenor, 2002; see also E. Lee, 2002, and Lyman, 1974). A decade later immigration restriction was again continued, and it persisted until the national legislation of 1924 that halted mass migration across the board.

Actually, migration did not cease altogether. By getting themselves classified as merchants or students, some would-be immigrants were admitted under false pretenses. In addition, though precise figures are hard to come by, illegal immigrants found their way into the country. The 1906 earthquake in San Francisco destroyed records on Chinese immigration and citizenship, so authorities could not dispute Chinese claims that they had been born in America. Because it was permitted to bring relatives to the United States, it was possible to claim that a child born in China should be permitted entry papers. This led to a practice known as the "slot racket" or "paper son" migration (Wong, 1988).

The Bachelor Society. The Chinese community in America continued to be heavily male dominated (Lyman, 1977). As a consequence of the imbalance, throughout this period the family had difficulty developing as an integral part of the ethnic community. Most Chinese women in America were either the wives of merchants or prostitutes (Hirata, 1975; Nee and Wong, 1985). Most men were either single or married with families in China, forced to live in a "bachelor society" (Siu, 1952; Nee and Nee, 1973; Lyman, 1977). Those who were married and forced to live apart from their wives and children were members of what Betty Lee Sung (1967) has called "mutilated" families.

Chinatown as an Ethnic Island. Ordinary Chinese were heavily dependent on clans and *hui kuan* for many facets of everyday life: jobs, housing, socializing, adjudicating conflicts, relationships with the host society, and welfare. In turn, these institutions (and more indirectly, this was true for the secret societies, as well) were controlled by the merchant class, which over time solidified its position as the ruling elite in the community. Although conflict was common within the community, it was not permitted to threaten the power of the merchant class (Lyman, 1977). Overarching merchant associations were established to help ensure cooperation, with San Francisco's Chinese Consolidated Benevolent Association, or Six Companies, serving as the model for similar ventures.

The immigrants' dependence on the ruling elite and the community institutions meant that it was in the interest of that elite to preserve the Chinese ghettos as something approximating what Ronald Takaki (1989: 230) termed "ethnic islands." The elites' position was based on an ability to control a highly dependent group. They were aided and abetted by intense racism on the part of the host society.

Anti-Chinese Activity. The Chinese were heavily concentrated in the western part of the United States. Although San Francisco quickly became the undisputed center of Chinese America, many Chinese found employment in rural areas and small towns on the frontier. Economic survival was precarious because of the intense discrimination they confronted.

In this inhospitable climate, Chinese carved out an economic niche in two business enterprises: restaurants and laundries. Ronald Takaki (1989) noted that laundries did not exist in China, so this cannot be seen as an instance of transplantation. These two areas provided opportunities because of the gender imbalance on the frontier. Both occupations were construed as being "women's work." The shortage of women in this region permitted the Chinese men to assume these roles, thereby establishing a form of structured ethnic subordination circumscribed by an understanding of a gender division of labor.

Even here, however, if the Chinese were perceived as a threat to white businesses, they could confront harassing laws. Thus, in response to the pleas of white-owned laundries, the San Francisco City Council passed an ordinance that mandated the use of a horse and buggy for the delivery of laundry. This meant that it was a misdemeanor to carry baskets suspended on a pole over the shoulder for the same purpose. This legislation was an explicit assault on the Chinese laundry business.

These were not the only expressions of anti-Chinese attitudes. The Chinese were the victims of mob violence in numerous places. In several cases they were forcibly driven from localities. For example, in California they were expelled from Humboldt County and from Eureka. In Washington, they were similarly cast out of Seattle and Tacoma (Lyman, 1974). In Los Angeles in 1871 somewhere between 18 and 21 Chinese immigrants were killed by hanging or burning. In 1885, 31 gold miners were murdered on the Idaho-Oregon border. Two years later in Rock Springs, Wyoming, at least 28 coal miners were killed (Kitano and Daniels, 1988; Storti, 1991).

The animosity directed at the Chinese was evident after the San Francisco earthquake of 1906. Although the city was the recipient of an unprecedented outpouring of aid from around the country, city leaders thought it an opportune time to rid themselves of the Chinese. Thus, they refused to direct any aid to the rebuilding of Chinatown. The Chinese managed to rebuild on their own.

Given that the African American population in the West was quite small, that part of the country developed a racial sensibility that pitted Asians against white Europeans. It was a bifurcated understanding in which the Chinese were readily lumped together with other Asians. In numerous states marriages between whites and "Orientals" were prohibited. Because of prohibitions against immigrants becoming citizens, by 1920 over two thirds of the Chinese remained aliens, disenfranchised from participation in the American political system (Chen, 2002).

Chinatown and the Outside World. Despite their social isolation, the economic pursuits of the Chinese brought them into contact with members of other ethnic groups and with the larger economy. In addition, Chinatown itself was not economically isolated, because Chinatown relied on the tourist trade. It played off of the outsider's image of Chinatown as a world inhabited by the "exotic other." This imagery continued to be tinged with a negative cast, replete with notions of lurid tong wars, opium dens, and prostitution. Nonetheless, the merchant class managed quite successfully to sanitize these images to make the gilded ghetto attractive to tourists.

Within Chinatown, business enterprises often got their start from a system of rotating credit, whereby individuals received necessary capital to begin a business from a collectively funded supply of capital. This system provided the ethnic community with a measure of autonomy from external economic interference and with a sense of internal mutual interdependence (Light, 1972). Over time this system served the merchants of Chinatown well, and by the third and fourth decades of the twentieth century, it enabled the socioeconomic elevation of a sector of the Chinese American community.

Very few individuals, however, left the ethnic island for the larger society. A few Chinese had acquired college educations; some of this group had actually entered the United States from China as students and for one reason or another had not returned. Part of the student group has been referred to as the "stranded" educated. They chose educational training for entry into fields such as medicine, pharmacy, dentistry, chemistry, and engineering (Kwoh, 1947; Lyman, 1974). Because of their educational credentials, they were poised to exit Chinatown—and the control of its ruling elite. Prejudice and discrimination, however, made it difficult to sever these ties—as was seen in the case of Jade Snow Wong.

World War II proved to be a watershed event for Chinese America. When Pearl Harbor was attacked and war was subsequently declared against Japan, the United States' war propaganda machinery redefined the Chinese. Because China was under siege by Japan, the Chinese became our de facto allies. Thus, Americans had to learn how to distinguish, as a headline from *Time* magazine (December 22, 1941) put it, "your friends from the Japs." Although such repugnant distinctions actually do little to define ethnic differences, the net result of this event was that it reduced the level of prejudice directed at the Chinese in America. This provided breathing space that, in the immediate postwar years, allowed the emergence of a middle class that was no longer intimately tied to the ethnic community (Hsu, 2000).

Of course, Pearl Harbor had profound, devastating consequences for the Japanese in America. Although in many ways Americans had been unwilling to distinguish among the various Asian groups in the country, the differences are in fact pronounced. From the outset, the Chinese and Japanese migrations exhibited considerable differences. The Japanese did not begin to arrive until late in the nineteenth century, some four decades after the arrival of the first wave of Chinese.

Emigration and the Role of the Japanese Government

Japan emerged from a self-imposed isolation that had extended over two centuries to become an increasingly powerful nation-state, and in this regard it was different from China. By the end of the nineteenth century, Japan had made considerable strides in expanding the economy, doing so chiefly by developing agriculture and the rural-based silk and textile industries (Lockwood, 1954; Dore, 1959). The government played a central role in developing communication and transportation systems, in introducing new technologies into the country, in establishing a new comprehensive educational system, and in founding new industries. The government also strengthened the military and, in the 1890s, initiated a policy of imperialist expansion that led to war with China in 1894 and with Russia in 1905. The latter elevated Japan to major world-power status.

Within this context emigration to the West started. Economic dislocations for many peasants, combined with demographic pressure brought about by rapid population growth fueled the desire to emigrate. Japan's inheritance system was based on primogeniture, which meant that the oldest son acquired the land of the parents, and younger sons had to look elsewhere for an economic livelihood. Given Japan's land scarcity, agriculture could not support most of these sons, and Japan's industrial development was not sufficiently advanced to absorb them either (Takaki, 1989). Thus, they became prime candidates for emigration. Unlike most other governments, the Japanese government played an active role in shaping and controlling emigration. This often took the form, especially in the early phase, of governmentally arranged terms of contract labor (Daniels, 1988).

After 1885, because of an exacerbation of economic problems, the number of emigrants increased, with Hawaii and California being the two major destinations. Two features of the Japanese government's role in emigration were significant. First, because of concerns about outsiders' perceptions of the Japanese, the government did not send the poorest peasants but rather those from the middle strata, often with agricultural skills that would serve them well in the future. Second, the Japanese took an active interest in the well-being of their expatriate community, intervening when they thought it necessary. Between 1885 and 1924, approximately 480,000 Japanese emigrated to either Hawaii or the U.S. mainland (Takaki, 1989).

Getting a Foothold in America. The Japanese found work in a wide range of occupations, including mining, mill work, lumbering, cannery work, and railroad labor. More than 40 percent were employed in agriculture. As a consequence, the Japanese were more rurally based than the Chinese. Furthermore, those who did reside in cities tended to be more residentially dispersed than the Chinese. Cities did not experience the proliferation of Japantowns or Little Tokyos in the same way that Chinatowns emerged, though in the center of Japanese America—Los Angeles—such an enclave grew (Lyman, 1986). In 1920, the three cities with the largest Japanese communities were Los Angeles, San Francisco, and Seattle.

Immigration was possible because the restrictive acts of 1882 and 1892 did not apply to the Japanese. In fact, they would not confront similar restrictive legislation until 1907. They did, however, face racism similar to that experienced by the Chinese, although they were spared from some of the negative imagery. In this regard, the Japanese government, acutely aware of anti-Chinese sentiments, sought to ensure that this would not be repeated for the Japanese.

When Theodore Roosevelt was president, one issue that Japan raised with the United States was the admission of women to redress the unbalanced sex ratio. This request addressed both the issue of prostitution and the ability of the Japanese in America to create a viable ethnic presence. The so-called "Gentleman's Agreement" was entered into in 1907. Among its terms, Japan voluntarily limited the number of immigrants, to stem the tide of restrictionist demands (Kitano, 1969). This agreement permitted the admission of relatives of immigrants. Arranged marriages were common in Japan, and this practice was used to join women in Japan with men in America, with "picture brides" arriving in the United States to see their husbands for the first time. This practice was condemned by the anti-Oriental lobby, but it proved the basis for a second, American-born generation (Wakatsuki, 1979).

As Evelyn Nakano Glenn (1986) has shown, a substantial number of women entered the U.S. labor force as domestics. They worked for a variety of reasons: to build up a nest egg in case they wanted to return to Japan; to add to the family's finances, especially after the arrival of children; or as the sole wage earner if a spouse died or for whatever reason became unemployed. Domestic service provided opportunities for women with family responsibilities and with limited English-language and marketable job skills.

Because of the skills Japanese American males brought to agriculture and the ability to use a rotating-credit system, some Japanese acquired prime agricultural land, and many others found success as tenant farmers. Ivan Light (1972) suggests that their success in this area was due to their familiarity with Japanese methods of intensive cultivation and because they were responsible for introducing some crops to the regions where they resided.

Prejudice and Discrimination. Whatever the reasons, conflict with white landowners was quickly apparent. California passed an Alien Land Act in 1913 that prohibited the Japanese from owning land. Because Japanese agricultural workers were needed during World War I, little was done to stop the Japanese from circumventing the law. When competition between Japanese and whites was renewed after the war, however, a new act was passed in 1920 that prohibited "aliens ineligible for citizenship" from both owning and leasing agricultural land. There is an ongoing debate among historians about whether or not the law was effective (Higgs, 1978). What is clear is that the Japanese were the victims of considerable discrimination during this period.

The Japanese not only found ways to minimize the impact of discriminatory legislation but were willing to challenge it in court. Race became the focal point of a 1922 Supreme Court decision, *Ozawa v. U.S.* Takao Ozawa was a legal immigrant who had resided in the United States for two decades, graduated from high school, attended college, was employed, spoke English even at home, and went to church. He was also, according to the government, ineligible to be naturalized. Ozawa's challenge was a novel one, for rather than disputing the racially exclusionary intentions of the law, he argued that he should be exempt because in his view Japanese were actually Caucasians. The Supreme Court was not persuaded (Lyman, 1991). Sojourner pluralism continued to describe the Japanese situation.

The Ethnic Community and Generational Differences. Despite prejudice and discrimination, the Japanese were remarkably successful in various entrepreneurial ventures. Two fields, related to agriculture, stand out as especially important: produce markets and gardening. By 1929 there were more than 700 Japanese-owned markets in Los Angeles (Light, 1972). The Japanese gardener was so common that gardening was to the Japanese what restaurants and laundries were to the Chinese. A willingness to undertake business risks and use of an ethnic-based credit system were common. Moreover, the Japanese got into businesses that required little initial capital investment and that were portable and easily liquidated. All these features made the Japanese quite successful. They did not limit themselves to a few areas, but ran hotels, restaurants, dry-cleaning establishments, and numerous other businesses (Sowell, 1981a).

The Japanese were culturally and socially distinct, but they were economically interdependent with the larger society. When the second generation came of age between 1920 and 1940, a considerable amount of intergenerational tension resulted. The use of terminology to distinguish the generations—*Issei* for the first and *Nisei* for the second—highlighted the differences. Although, as we have seen, tension was characteristic of most groups, it was perhaps more pronounced in the

Japanese case. Exacerbating the typical differences in generational experiences was the fact that the immigrant generation was consigned to alien status while their children were citizens. Furthermore, while Buddhism was the dominant religion among the *Issei,* Christianity became more attractive to the second generation, especially to those intent on assimilating. This difference caused considerable conflict. The *Nisei* acquired English-language skills, and over time it became clear that many had not retained a working knowledge of Japanese (Kitano and Daniels, 1988).

A dramatic change in Japanese America occurred over a two-decade period beginning in 1920, as those born in the United States became a sizable majority. The *Nisei* were inclined to define themselves as neither "too Japanesy" nor "too American" (Lyman, 1977), and they were intent on preserving aspects of their ancestral past. At the same time they chose those elements of American culture that they found most appealing and conducive to maintaining a distinctive Japanese American identity.

World War II and Internment. World events conspired against an easy or gradual melding of the two cultures. Prior to the attack on Pearl Harbor, many young Japanese American males had already enlisted. In various ways the community sought to dispel the suspicion that they harbored "dual loyalties." Japanese Americans feared the worst, and after Franklin Delano Roosevelt signed Executive Order 9066, these fears were realized. The order granted to the Secretary of War the right to declare any region of the country a military region. If deemed necessary, the Secretary had the authority to remove any or all persons from the area. There was no explicit mention of the Japanese, but they, and not the Germans or Italians, were singled out for wholesale removal from their homes on the West Coast. General DeWitt, the military official in charge of the removal, believed that the Japanese continued to harbor allegiances to the Japanese government. He crassly declared, "A Jap is a Jap, and it makes no difference whether he's a citizen or not" (Daniels, 1972).

Not surprisingly, the decision to remove Japanese Americans to internment camps in remote regions of the plains and Rocky Mountain states was greeted with delight by the political right and by those who had earlier supported immigration restriction. Japanese Americans discovered that they could find no solid sources of support anywhere across the political spectrum. Most liberals and even political radicals joined conservatives in approving relocation (Daniels, 1972). Devoid of outside support, some resisted, some challenged the decision in court, and some opted to go to Japan, but most relocated with no overt resistance (Ng, 2002).

The camps, 10 in all, were constructed like military barracks and were located in desolate and isolated areas: Manzanar and Tule Lake in California, Poston and Gila River in Arizona, Amache in Colorado,

Topaz in Utah, Minidoka in Idaho, Heart Mountain in Wyoming, and Jerome and Rohwer in Arkansas. Over time, increasing numbers of Japanese were permitted to leave the camps, because they were needed in the labor force or to fight in the European theater. About 22 percent of *Nisei* males refused to affirmatively answer loyalty questions and were not considered for military service. These "no-no boys" did so as a protest against internment. Seeking to prove their loyalty to America, despite its act of injustice, many others served with valor. One of the most highly decorated units in American military history was the *Nisei*-composed 442nd Regimental Combat Team (Takaki, 1989).

Internment caused the loss of jobs, savings, homes, and status. Tetsuden Kashima (1980) argued that the evacuation legacy also resulted in a deep sense of personal inferiority, a proclivity to noncommunication and inarticulateness, and a shying away from any discussion of this hurtful topic. The aversion to talking about this devastating event resulted in a kind of social amnesia in Japanese America. From this nadir in Japanese American history, the victims of internment were forced to rebuild their lives in the postwar era.

Native Americans During the Reservation Era

Cornell (1988) refers to the third period (the earlier periods were the market and conflict periods) of Indian relations with European-Americans as the *reservation era*. Although reservations had been set up before the middle of the nineteenth century, and continue to exist up to the present time, Cornell believed they were central to the Indian experience after 1850 and extending to the 1930s.

During this period, the subjugation of the Indians was completed (Spicer, 1962). The process moved westward: To establish military control over the frontier regions, a series of forts were constructed to quell resistance. Although no one event spelled the final defeat of the Indians, the surrender speech of Chief Joseph of the Nez Perce tribe, after being caught trying to flee to freedom in Canada, spoke to the situation of other tribes as well. He said:

> I am tired of fighting. Our chiefs are killed . . . The old men are all dead . . . It is cold and we have no blankets. The little children are freezing to death. My people, some of them, have run away to the hills, and have no blankets, no food; no one knows where they are—perhaps freezing to death. I want to have time to look for my children and see how many I can find. Maybe I shall find them among the dead. Hear me, my chiefs. I am tired; my heart is sick and sad. From where the sun now stands I will fight no more forever. (quoted in Nabokov, 1991: 180–181)

> **Voices**   **Cochise**
>
> When I was young I walked all over this country, east and west, and saw no other people than the Apaches. After many summers I walked again and found another race of people had come to take it. How is it? Why is it that the Apaches wait to die—that they carry their lives on their fingernails? They roam over the hills and plains and want the heavens to fall on them. The Apaches were once a great nation; they are now but a few, and because of this they want to die and so carry their lives on their fingernails.
>
> *Cochise, a member of the Chiricahua Apaches, took part in a guerrilla campaign against white settlers and soldiers until his death in 1874 (Brown, 1970).*

Reservations as Total Institutions

The conquered were relocated to reservations, which, like plantations, can be viewed as "total institutions" (Goffman, 1961). The differences, however, were pronounced. Plantations were founded for economic reasons and were connected to an international marketplace; such was not the case with reservations. Generally established on the most arid and inhospitable land, Native Americans had little success with their agricultural endeavors. They were isolated and cut off from larger markets. They were frequently unable to make the reservations even into subsistence economies, thereby furthering the notion that American Indians had to be treated as wards of the state.

Reservations were constructed as a means of political containment—not as a means to allow American Indians to acquire economic self-sufficiency (McNickle, 1962; Vogel, 1972). Tribes found themselves in a dependency relationship with agents of the federal government. These agents constituted the real power on reservations. Not all Native Americans lived on reservations, but the tentacles of the federal government held in place even those who did not. For example, the Oklahoma Cherokee did not reside on a reservation, but the Principal Chief of the Cherokee Nation was appointed by the President of the United States, not by the Cherokee themselves.

A Native American family outside their home, circa 1920.

Denied the right to become citizens, regulated in their movements off the reservations, stifled from engaging in many traditional religious practices, and victimized by unscrupulous Indian agents, the indigenous peoples of the Americas and their social world reached their nadir (Lurie, 1968; Josephy, 1969). The American Indians' lack of power and inability to engage in self-determination combined with the fact that their population reached its low point in 1890. At this time governmental policy changed by directing attention to the issue of what Cornell (1988: 56) refers to as the "cultural transformation" of the Indian. The Bureau of Indian Affairs (BIA) was the primary governmental agency responsible for this task, and it did so by implementing policies that were underpinned by a combination of coercion and co-optation. The goal was the acculturation of Indians into the dominant culture.

The Dawes Act and Acculturation Policies

Policymakers saw tribal organizations as the major impediment to acculturation and pressed for legislation that would end collectively held land by making the American Indians into individual property owners. A severalty law, formally the Indian Allotment Act but generally known as the Dawes Act, was passed in 1887, despite the objections and apprehensions of many Indians. In general terms it was designed to allot to Native American families title to 160 acres of reservation land, with smaller parcels granted to single individuals. The land was to be held in trust by the federal government for 25 years, during which time it could not be sold or leased. Reformers believed that by replacing tribal identities with the centrality of the autonomous individual, Native Americans were being prepared for citizenship (Bolt, 1987; Cornell, 1988: Foster, 1991).

The Bureau of Indian Affairs initiated various actions that undermined traditional tribal practices. For example, it used its authority to force schoolchildren to attend boarding schools on reservations, thereby separating them from their families. The bureau established courts, set up new forms of social organization, and suppressed practices the bureau found offensive, such as polygamy. Certain Indians willing to work with the BIA were rewarded and elevated to leadership positions. In conjunction with missionaries who moved onto reservation lands to convert Native Americans to Christianity, the BIA attempted to instill white culture.

One other feature of the act compounded the American Indian's plight. A provision built into the law allowed a land grab on Indian territory. The provision in question allowed any "surplus" land after allotment to be held by the government and allowed the government the right to sell it to anyone. As a result, between 1887 and 1934, 86 million acres of land, more than 60 percent of the total, was purchased by nonIndians (Wax, 1971; Cornell, 1988). Outright fraud and deception, combined with debt payments that Indians could not meet, also contributed to the loss of land. Thus, by the 1930s Native Americans were more impoverished and were considerably more land poor than before the Civil War (Bolt, 1987).

Responding to Defeat

The response of Native Americans to this situation reflected their plight. Several religious movements emerged, the most significant being the Ghost Dance movement. Beginning sometime in the 1870s and extending into the twentieth century, the Ghost Dance movement proved to be a recurring if sporadic feature of many Indian tribes. It was particularly prevalent among Plains Indians. In defeat, many Indians held views similar to that of a Blackfeet named Flint Knife, who banefully commented, "I wish that white people had never come into my country" (quoted in Nabokov, 1991).

This wish took the form of a chiliastic cult after a Paiute Indian named Wovoka had a revelation and began to expound a millennial prophecy based on what he claimed he had seen in the world of the dead. He contended that dead ancestors were alive and would be reunited with the living if Indians participated in a mystical ghost dance. In addition, prosperity would return (the bison that had been killed off were with the dead), and whites would disappear. The movement was generally pacifistic, because advocates believed that the end was near and active struggle against whites was not necessary (Wax, 1971).

Under the emotional influence of the cultic ritual dance, some American Indians felt that they had acquired mystical powers that led them to believe that they were immune from the destructiveness of U.S. Cavalry bullets. In the tragic case of the Oglala Sioux in South Dakota, a confrontation between Native Americans empowered by the ghost dance and frightened, inexperienced soldiers led to the massacre at Wounded Knee, in which 150 defenseless Indians were gunned down (Niehardt, 1961; Brown, 1970; Wax, 1971).

Related religious practices developed elsewhere, including the Dreamer movement and the Drum Cult (Josephy, 1971; Spindler and Spindler, 1984). Another religious response was the peyote cult (LaBarre, 1975). This particular cult took institutional form in the Native American Church, a syncretistic religion using Christian imagery as well as traditional tribal religions. It appealed to a population that was impoverished and seminomadic (Wax, 1971).

These religious expressions have been depicted by some as essentially apolitical and thus as a form of passive acquiescence to circumstances. As with the Christianity of the slave quarters, however, they provided the basis for active resistance that occurred later. In addition to offering a semblance of an alternative to their present condition, millennial religions were a vital stage in the emergence of a pan-Indian consciousness. This consciousness did not deny the distinctiveness of various tribal identities, but fused that identity with a larger identity. An overtly political response to oppression was not felt until after World War II.

Stereotypes

Throughout this period, American Indians confronted numerous problems related to employment, housing, health care, education, and other issues. The most enduring social problems within the Native American community were connected to the persistence of poverty, chronic unemployment, and alcoholism. These problems shaped the two most powerful negative stereotypes of the Indian: lazy and drunken.

Hollywood's outpouring of western movies generally portrayed the American Indian as the savage enemy of white settlers on the frontier. In fact, most films, from D. W. Griffith's *America* (1924) to John Ford's *Stagecoach* (1939) and *Drums Along the Mohawk* (1939), were fixated on the frontier period. Although this image generally did not extend to views regarding contemporary Indians, it made it difficult to appreciate the incredible destructiveness that the conquest of the Indians entailed. Furthermore, little room was left to explore more positive relationships between Indians and whites (Woll and Miller, 1987).

The Indian New Deal

All American Indians became citizens in 1924, thereby permitting them the right to vote and other involvement in the political process. This act reversed the Supreme Court decision of four decades earlier in the case of *Elk v. Wilkins*, in which John Elk was denied the right to revoke his tribal membership to become a citizen of the United States. The Indians' response to this act of Congress was decidedly ambiguous. Although some welcomed it, others saw it as a threat to the future of tribal organizations. This ambivalence was obvious in the differing reactions to military service during World War II. On the one hand, both individuals and tribes were willing to challenge the legitimacy of efforts to draft Native Americans. On the other hand, many Indians volunteered to serve in the military (Bolt, 1987; Lyman, 1991). The tragic death of Ira Hayes, brought about by alcoholism, is recounted in a song by Bob Dylan. Hayes was a soldier decorated for valor at Iwo Jima but condemned to second-class citizenship after the war. This example poignantly illustrates that even if Native Americans were expected to serve the nation at war, they would have to, in Stanford Lyman's (1991: 229) words, "wait for a long time before being granted the full measure of their citizenship and civil rights."

The most deleterious effects of the Dawes Act were amended during the first term of Franklin Roosevelt's administration. John Collier, the

Commissioner of Indian Affairs, had a long history of involvement in progressive activities as executive director of the American Indian Defense Association. Collier proposed legislation that would have ended the land grab allowed under Dawes, promoted tribal home rule, and validated the desire to preserve American Indian culture by encouraging such activities as school courses in native history (Collier, 1945).

Although the Indian Reorganization Act of 1934 (IRA) proved to be a watered-down version of Collier's proposal, it nonetheless set the stage for a renewed orientation toward a central role for tribes in political and economic affairs. Not all Indians embraced the plan, including those who were assimilationists and those who simply distrusted any policy initiated by the federal government. Some Indians and non-Indians accused the policy of being a form of socialism (Collier, 1945). This charge was echoed a half century later by Ronald Reagan's extreme right-wing Secretary of the Interior, James Watt.

The shifting policies of the federal government, combined with the varied responses of Native Americans, led to considerable ambiguity. This is reflected in the decision to remain on the reservation or to move into the larger society. Although a sizable majority of American Indians resided on or near Indian lands, a growing number began to leave, generally in the quest for work. This movement ebbed and flowed based on employment opportunities. In the long run, substantial Indian settlements developed in a number of major cities. Despite this movement, the urbanization rate of Indians lagged far behind that of the general population (Steiner, 1968).

Summary

This chapter showed that what W. E. B. Du Bois referred to as the "color line" has served as the major obstacle to social harmony and to the possibility of extending freedom and equality to all people. After the Civil War a new form of racial oppression was established that ensured the domination of white Americans and the subordination of all peoples of color. The color line was used to determine who would and would not be incorporated into the American political process and into the civic culture. Race was the principal criterion for determining who would be insiders and who would remain outsiders. Its rigid application allowed all white ethnics to develop bonds across ethnic boundaries with other whites. Quite simply, the differences between white ethnics became less consequential as the differences across the racial divide became more pronounced.

The stark division between blacks and whites—implicitly denying the reality of extensive racial mixing—was used by whites after emancipation to reassert a caste system. How white Americans thought about blacks shaped the nature of racial definitions for the other racial minority groups considered in this chapter: Hispanics, Asians, and Native Americans. These groups experienced racially motivated actions from whites that were designed to ensure their subordination and exclusion.

All of the nonwhite groups considered in this chapter responded to the challenges posed by racism. All attempted to improve their position in America. They had fewer financial and human capital resources than white ethnics had. Nonetheless, like European-origin groups, each created an ethnic community, established a leadership, created alliances with other groups, and in other ways responded to its particular circumstances.

Key Terms

caste society	*segregation*
disorganization	*split labor market*
ethnic enclaves	*stereotypes*
internal colonialism	*transplantation*
Jim Crow	*uprooted*

Questions for Discussion and Critical Thinking

1. The role of religion in various ethnic groups varied considerably. Compare and contrast the role of organized religion among Italians, Poles, and Jews.

2. Describe the way that white racial domination was reestablished after the failure of Reconstruction. What were the main ways that the African American community sought to respond to racial oppression?

3. Provide an overview of the ways that whites attempted to ensure the subordination and exclusion of Latinos, Asians, and American Indians. In what ways did these groups respond to racism? ✦

Part III

Yesterday, Today, and Tomorrow: From 1950 to the Twenty-First Century

Chapter 5

European Americans: The Twilight of Ethnicity?

According to the 2000 Census, European Americans constitute 11 of the 16 largest ancestry groups in the United States (see Table 5.1 for the rank order of groups by size). During the past half century, profound changes have occurred within and among these groups. This chapter explores the most significant of those changes.

In the second half of the twentieth century, America underwent changes as far-reaching and all-encompassing as those during the earlier transformation from a rural-agrarian to an urban-industrial nation. The new epoch is reflected in some of the terminology used to describe contemporary society, such as *advanced industrial* or a *postindustrial* society (Bell, 1973; Giddens, 1973). Although scholars disagree about the extent to which a distinct break with the earlier phase of industrialization occurred, there is nonetheless general agreement about some of the implications of these changes.

Beginning in the late 1940s the American economy grew, and heightened productivity levels resulted in a two-decade period of unprecedented prosperity. The growth of large-scale national (and later, international) corporations and the simultaneous decline of smaller local and regional industries were connected to this prosperity. The new corporations were huge bureaucratic enterprises requiring a large cadre of educated workers in white-collar positions—legal, accounting, advertising, design, administrative, and so on. At the same time, due chiefly to automation, relatively fewer blue-collar workers were needed. In addition, because of government's new role in the Keynesian welfare state created during the New Deal and because of the military's expanded role in American society during the Cold War, huge government bureaucracies also provided job opportunities for the new middle class.

C. Wright Mills (1951) was one of the first sociologists to systematically explore this reshaping of the class structure. His study was an indictment of the middle class's conformity in its quest for financial security and status. He, like other social critics of the immediate postwar era (e.g., David Riesman et al., *The Lonely Crowd* [1950]), stressed the shift to an increasingly homogenized mass society. According to these critics, one consequence was a decline in the significance of both class and ethnic identities. Rather than being class conscious, the new middle class was portrayed as opportunity conscious. If an individual thought his or her ethnic background was an impediment to upward mobility aspirations or to chances for social inclusion, ethnicity was downplayed or repressed as much as possible.

The ranks of the new white-collar class swelled as the children of the working class acquired college educations, the credentials that permitted their ascent in the social hierarchy. Many college students had served in the armed forces, which proved to be a training ground in improved intergroup relations, at least among white ethnics (blacks and Asians were forced to serve in segregated units). Veterans were able to take advantage of the GI Bill, which provided them with student assistance payments. College became a means to leave urban ethnic ghettoes and, in the process, helped those with a desire to forget their ethnic past to do so (Bensman and Vidich, 1971). According to Richard Sennett (1998), these trends have become even more pronounced in recent decades, because among the consequences of work in the "new capitalism" is the lack of a sense of a shared history, which is connected to the erosion of ethnic communities.

Table 5.1	Ancestry in the 2000 U.S. Census
The Top 16 Ancestry Groups	
German	46.5 million
Hispanic or Latino*	34.3 million
Afro-American	33.9 million
Irish	33.1 million
English	28.3 million
American	19.6 million
Italian	15.9 million
Asian	11.7 million
French	9.8 million
Polish	9.0 million
Scottish	5.4 million
Scotch-Irish	5.2 million
Dutch	5.2 million
Norwegian	4.5 million
Swedish	4.3 million
American Indian	4.1 million

*Includes Mexican (21.5 million), Puerto Rican (3.5 million), Cuban (1.2 million), and "Other Hispanic or Latino" (8.1 million).

Source: U.S. Bureau of the Census (2000).

Suburbanization and White Ethnics

The sons and daughters of working-class ethnics departed the ethnic enclave in droves for the suburbs. Policies of the federal government, particularly those relating to housing and transportation, encouraged the rapid expansion of American suburbs. The American housing stock in cities had declined because of a lack of investment during the Depression and war. Furthermore, the urban infrastructure needed large-scale upgrading, particularly in older cities in the East and Midwest. The Federal Home Administration (FHA) and Veteran's Administration (VA) guaranteed home mortgage programs and, combined with the Department of Transportation's expressway system construction financing, propelled white-collar workers into the suburbs, where they built new homes. The result was a gulf between those ethnics who went to college, entered the middle class, and moved out of the city and those who did not go to college but remained in both the blue-collar work force and the city.

The connection between ethnicity and class suggests that for blue-collar workers, ethnic and class identities had been mutually reinforcing, while for the middle class, the connection between class and ethnicity was less clear. The importance of ethnic identity did not disappear, but changes were clearly under way in both cities and suburbs, with somewhat different results. Some differences can be seen by comparing two ethnographic studies conducted during the 1950s and early 1960s by the same sociologist, Herbert Gans (1962, 1967)—one in an Italian neighborhood in Boston, and the other in the suburban Long Island tract development known as Levittown.

In Levittown, ethnicity continued to shape interactional patterns. Ethnic subcommunities were one basis for friendship, which meant that for the small number of Chinese, Japanese, and Greek families that did not have a developed subcommunity, Levittown could be a lonely place to live. Anti-Semitism, though not seen as especially problematic, nonetheless was evident and did limit interaction between Jews and Gentiles. In many ways, however, ethnicity was increasingly a less consequential factor in defining attitudes and everyday behaviors. Gans pointed to areas in which ethnicity continued to play a role while identifying areas where it did not. For instance, German names were in evidence in the local Lutheran Church and Irish names in the Catholic parish, indicating the persistence of an ethnic character related to religious affiliation, but ethnic divisions did not determine patterns of interaction in many other realms of social life. The spirit of neighborliness often served as a catalyst for friendships based on shared professional or leisure-time interests (Gans, 1967).

Gans's study of the Italians in Boston's West End suggests a more pervasive persistence of ethnicity in the lives of these "urban villagers," when compared with their suburban counterparts. Noting the retention of the Italian language by the second generation, the continuation of the immigrant generation's relationship with Roman Catholicism, and the survival of food and drinking habits, Gans (1962) observed that

> Social relationships are almost entirely limited to other Italians, because much sociability is based on kinship, and because most

friendships are made in childhood, and are thus influenced by residential propinquity. Intermarriage with nonItalians is unusual among the second generation, and is not favored for the third.

An aversion to politics at the local level and a lack of interest in state and local politics further reinforced the relative isolation of the West End from the outside world.

But change took place here, too. The second generation did not pass the Italian language on to the third. Neither generation expressed an interest in Italy. Italian names were Anglicized. Outside institutions intruded into the everyday lives of West Enders. Of particular importance was the public school system, which introduced youth to a world outside of the ethnic enclave. Gans (1962) saw the impact of consumerism and the mass media, especially television, in drawing West End residents into the larger society, although he saw a "selective acceptance" of consumer goods and the media (for further discussion of this general pattern of change during the 1950s, see Vidich and Bensman, 1958; Berger, 1960; Cohen, 2003).

In his rich ethnographic accounts Gans provided an awareness that both ethnic persistence and change can be detected. He indicated that ethnic identity and ethnic affiliation were destined to not remain the same as they had been at an earlier historical period. But it is not clear whether this meant that ethnicity was fading into oblivion or merely adapting to new circumstances. Gans's snapshot of a specific point in time cannot by itself reveal future trends. Furthermore, as with all ethnographic accounts, we must question how much we can generalize from this particular case.

Does Ethnicity Matter? The Case for Cultural Transmission

Sociologists have engaged in a sustained debate over whether a process of straight-line assimilation is under way among European ethnics or, to use the phrase of Richard Alba (1981), whether these groups are witnessing the **twilight of ethnicity.** In a series of books and articles, Andrew Greeley (1974, 1975, 1988; Greeley and McCready, 1975; Greeley, McCready, and Theisen, 1980) challenged this conclusion, arguing that ethnicity continues to shape people's values and behaviors.

Greeley's work was meant to challenge those who, like Gans, saw a fading role for ethnicity among the third and subsequent generational offspring of European immigrants. Unlike Gans, Greeley did not rely on ethnographic research but used National Opinion Research Center surveys of relatively large national samples, many of which were conducted during the 1960s and 1970s. Thus, his work has a scope that is lacking in community studies.

Greeley explored a wide range of attitudinal and behavioral topics. These topics included such personality attributes as conformism, anxiety, authoritarianism, moralism, and trust, as well as attitudes regarding such diverse topics as families and children, politics, race relations, and religion. Behaviors investigated ranged from political participation to drinking patterns. In addition, Greeley looked at ethnic differences in educational attainment and socioeconomic mobility. Throughout this ongoing research, one recurring question was constantly posed: Does ethnicity matter?

The results of Greeley's investigations do not provide a simple response to the question. For example, in a comparison of individuals with Irish, Italian, and British ancestry, several hypotheses based on an assumption of differences in cultural heritages on various personality traits were not supported (e.g., that Irish would be more "trusting" than Italians because the former were more religious than the latter). Other hypotheses were supported. At some level, as Greeley (1974) observed, the Italians are more like the British than like the Irish, perhaps suggesting that they were assimilating while the Irish were not. Despite the mixed findings that emerged from his research, Greeley (1974: 319) argued that ethnicity *does* matter, although he qualified his answer: "to some extent some dimensions of the ethnic culture do indeed survive and enable us to predict some aspects of the behavior of the children, grandchildren, and great-grandchildren of immigrants." He suggested, though with little empirical support, that people tend to look to the ethnic community in establishing a variety of interpersonal attachments, including marital partners, close friends, recreational partners, and informal associates (Greeley, 1974).

If Greeley is right, why is this the case? He attributed ethnic importance to differential socialization processes brought about by differing ethnic family structures (Greeley, 1974). He did not assign a role to nonfamilial institutions of the ethnic community and paid scant attention to changes within ethnic communities. This lack of attention is a product of the research strategy he pursued. His data did not address the issue of change versus continuity within ethnic institutions. He paid virtually no attention to the particular historical experiences of specific groups. In short, he did not attempt to locate ethnic identity in either social structural or historical contexts.

During the second half of the twentieth century the institutional network of most European American ethnic communities eroded considerably. This process was under way earlier, but it accelerated. Mutual aid societies, athletic clubs, cultural organizations, and the like all declined in membership. The immigrant generation died off, and their children and grandchildren did not need these institutions to assist them in their quest for economic security, a political voice, or enhanced status. Foreign-language newspapers ceased publishing as native-born ethnics no longer maintained what Joshua Fishman (1966) termed "language loyalty." In an ecumenical era, many Christian churches lost their distinctively ethnic character and consciously downplayed their ethnic origins. Thus, what was once the Swedish Evangelical Lutheran Church might be renamed the First Evangelical Lutheran Church.

It is not surprising that the pace of change varied both across and within groups. Among the particularly relevant factors cited in Chapter 2 are group size, degree of residential concentration, length of time in the country, religious affiliation, homeland concerns, and degree of educational and occupational mobility. Looking just at the Scandinavian groups in America, differences in the pace of ethnic erosion occurred. The Danish presence faded rather quickly and, although somewhat more slowly, the Swedish presence did too. At the other extreme, Finns, and to a lesser extent Norwegians, preserved an institutional presence and a stronger sense of ethnic identity for a longer period of time. Even so, the movement for all four groups was in the same direction. Relatively little empirical research has been conducted on particular groups, especially earlier-arriving groups and Protestant groups. Large European American groups such as the English, Germans, Irish, French, Swedes, and Norwegians have not been the objects of sustained sociological inquiry.

The Polish Americans

Poles have not been widely studied, but Neil Sandberg (1974) studied the Polish Americans in Los Angeles (not a representative community because of the continuing clustering of Poles in the Great Lakes region), and his findings challenged Greeley's persistence of ethnicity theory. Rather, Sandberg saw a progressive decline in the intensity and significance of ethnic identity from the immigrant generation to the third and fourth generations. He also saw a connection between a decline of ethnic identity and affiliation and the Poles' move out of the working class and into the middle class. Sandberg traced the decline in ethnic institutional affiliations, which was seen even in the area of religion. Recalling that, in comparative terms, Polish immigrants had exhibited a higher level of religiosity than a number of other immigrant groups, this is an especially significant change. Sandberg saw decline in ethnic church attachment as well as religious attendance. Linked to this has been a decline in parochial education support. This is not to say that ethnicity has disappeared, because it can be detected even in the fourth generation.

We can look at certain cities, most notably Chicago, and still find evidence of a functioning Polish American community, so Polish American ethnicity might be more salient than is the situation for most European Americans. In part, this difference can be attributed to events in the Polish homeland. Actually, since Sandberg conducted his study, the rise of the Solidarity Movement in Poland and the eventual demise of communist rule were potent issues that mobilized the Polish American community, and in this regard it may exhibit some similarities to both the Irish (for whom Northern Ireland is an ongoing concern) and Jews, for whom the fate of Israel is an important concern. In addition, a new wave of Polish immigrants arrived in Chicago during the 1980s, many forced to leave Poland because of their political involvement with Solidarity. While this served to revitalize Polish identity to some extent, Mary Patrice Erdmans (1998) reports that it also led to internal conflicts as more assimilated Polish Americans confronted new immigrants with different values, modes of conduct, and needs.

Italians

James A. Crispino (1980), in his research on the Italians of Bridgeport, Connecticut, and its suburban environs (a representative site for Italians), came to conclusions similar to those of Sandberg. Crispino chronicled the demise of mutual aid societies, neighborhood bars, athletic clubs, and the like in the city and noted that there was no evidence of re-creating the ethnic enclave in the suburban ring of the city. Acculturation was evident. For instance, in areas related to the traditionalism investigated by Greeley, such as the prevalence of distrust of others and fatalism, Crispino's research indicated generational decline in traditional attitudes. His subjects overwhelmingly supported legalized abortions under certain circumstances and so disagreed with the official teaching of the Roman Catholic church. In addition, he discovered a decline in ethnic identification.

Perhaps most problematic for Greeley's cultural transmission thesis is the fact that structural assimilation is also apparent. Crispino (1980: 94) reported a "decline in strong attachments to kin, especially those at some distance, and ethnic friends, and their replacement by considerations of class and presumably common interests in the selection of close associates." A linked issue is **intermarriage.** Although neither Sandberg nor Crispino directly addressed intermarriage, a study conducted by B. R. Bugelski (1961) of Poles and Italians between 1930 and 1960 in Buffalo, New York, found that both groups had a precipitous drop in ingroup marriages during these three decades. For Italians, the ingroup marriage rate fell from 71 percent in 1930 to 27 percent in 1960; the corresponding figures for the Poles are 79 percent in 1930 and 33 percent in 1960. These findings led Bugelski to suggest that by 1975 ingroup marriages would be rare. This and related forms of structural assimilation led Richard Alba (1985a) to conclude that Italian Americans were entering "into the twilight of ethnicity."

The Debate Over an Ethnic Revival

The ethnicity perspective, which derived from the work of sociologists like Greeley, gained popular expression during the early 1970s in the writing of Michael Novak (1972), who described "unmeltable ethnics." In contrast, a different argument reflected a contemporary resurgence of interest in ethnic identity that presumably involved a return to various modes of ethnic affiliation.

The Hansen Thesis

Actually, there are two different, though not necessarily mutually exclusive, versions of the **ethnic revival** theory. One focuses on the dynamics of generational change and is essentially psychological, whereas the other is political. The generational theory was initially formulated by historian Marcus Lee Hansen (1938) and is summarized by the pithy claim that "what the son wishes to forget the grandson wishes to remember." Hansen's **principle of third-generation interest** was based on his understanding of the social psychology of second- and third-generation ethnics. Whereas the former were seen as insecure about their place in America and therefore sought to abandon their ethnic past to fit into the society outside of the ethnic world, the third generation was at home in America. Their secure status permitted a curiosity about and a pride in their ancestry.

If Hansen is read literally, the evidence overwhelmingly suggests that his hypothesis is incorrect (Appel, 1961; Lazerwitz and Rowitz, 1964; Nahirny and Fishman, 1965; Abramson, 1975; Greene, 1990). If freed from its generational formulation, however, Hansen's thesis suggests that ethnicity must be treated as a flexible and variable phenomenon. This general perspective could account for the growth of ethnic celebrations; genealogical interests; travel to the ancestral homeland; interest in ethnic artifacts, ethnic cuisine, and ethnic language and literature; and the dramatic expansion of interest in ethnicity by scholars from a variety of disciplines (TeSelle, 1973; Tricarico, 1984, 1989; Archdeacon, 1985; Fishman et al. 1985; Knottnerus and Loconto, 2003). Although these manifestations of ethnicity must be acknowledged, it is difficult to determine the extent to which this "voluntary" interest in one's ethnic background has permeated large sectors of European America. Actually, it appears that this voluntary ethnicity is limited to a rather small sector, generally composed of the more highly educated members of the middle class.

Political Ethnicity

Numerous ethnically based nationalist social movements exist elsewhere in the industrial world, including the Welsh and Scottish in Britain, the Occitan in France, the Flemish in Belgium, the Basques in Spain, and the Québecois in Canada. According to Anthony Smith (1981: 156), what is distinctive about the United States that makes this ethnic revival weak and politically ineffectual is the "lack of an autonomist, let alone separatist, nationalist component of the ideology of 'neo-ethnicity.'" Simply put, this revival in the United States was not linked to land—it entailed no territorial claims. Given the steady erosion of ethnic communities, ethnic solidarity did not prove to be an especially viable source of collective action (Rothschild, 1981; Nagel and Olzak, 1982; Nielsen, 1985; Pearson, 2001).

A more political, interest-based form of resurgent ethnicity did occur at approximately the same time as this more apolitical, nostalgic form of ethnic return, however. Nathan Glazer and Daniel P. Moynihan, in their seminal work *Beyond the Melting Pot* (1963), considered the five major groups in New York City that they scrutinized, including three European-origin groups (Jews, Italians, and Irish), as constituting in effect political interest groups that vied competitively in the political arena. Although Glazer and Moynihan did not highlight this in their work, emergent ethnicity was closely connected to racial politics, especially in major American cities with large black populations (Weed, 1971; Yancey, Ericksen, and Juliani, 1976; Polenberg, 1980).

In a study of Italians and Irish in Providence, Rhode Island, during the height of the civil rights movement, John Goering (1971) discerned a reemergence of ethnic identification as a crucial form of self-identification. He observed that this identification had little effect in terms of concrete actions aimed at political mobilization. Instead, it was largely associated with a questioning of the American dream brought about by the belief that the civil rights movement had granted blacks government-sponsored benefits at the expense of white working-class ethnics. Although the first form of ethnic interest derived from the educated middle class and often suburban offspring of European immigrants, this conservative defense against perceived challenges to their neighborhoods and jobs came from working-class and lower-middle-class urban ethnics—that is, those who have not gotten out of the ethnic enclave.

Jonathan Rieder's (1985) ethnography of the Jews and Italians in the Canarsie section of Brooklyn provided a vivid account of how these two ethnic groups, different in history and politics, managed to find common ground in their collective quest to protect their neighborhood. They are united by a fear that their neighborhood is vulnerable to the pathologies of the ghetto (crime, drugs, teen pregnancies, and a general decline in civic responsibility) brought about by the incursion of blacks and Hispanics into a predominantly white section of the borough. Both ethnic groups, although they expressed it in different ways, viewed affluent liberals as being unconcerned or outright hostile to them. Although these white ethnics had been an important component of the liberal coalition that made up the Democratic party since the New Deal, they have shifted to embrace conservatism. Rieder provides ample evidence of the racist thinking of many of these white ethnics, including some violent and other unpleasant acts by a very small minority, but he also indicates that the obvious discontent and anxiety they feel about their future is not entirely unfounded. However romanticized their collective descriptions of the neighborhood a generation ago might be, it was once a haven and it might not be so in the future (see also Sleeper, 1990).

What is at stake here is not Italians and Jews returning to their ethnic roots, but European ethnics finding a common cause against changes in the city that they believe have occurred because of the increased proximity of nonEuropean ethnics. If, earlier in the century, Italians had conflictual relations with Jews, Irish, or other European ethnics, today those things that generated such conflicts have either disappeared or become inconsequential compared with forces that have produced or reinforced racial tensions and hostilities. Moreover, the boundaries that historically separated these groups have become considerably less consequential (Waters, 2000).

Symbolic Ethnicity

The notion of an ethnic revival in America is problematic, even though there are clear cultural and political manifestations of ethnic interests (Stein and Hill, 1977). Ethnicity has not disappeared for many if not most European Americans, as the earlier assimilationists predicted. But neither has it exhibited an ability to resist change. Most evidence suggests that the salience of ethnicity for these groups has declined in recent years. There is little to suggest that this trend will be reversed.

The theory of **symbolic ethnicity** accounts for both the indicators of the persistence of various manifestations of ethnicity and its simultaneous, more pervasive gradual decline. This concept was formulated by Herbert Gans (1979) and is applicable to ethnics from the third generation and beyond. Gans saw ethnicity for most European Americans as having a low level of intensity, thus occupying an individual's attention only sporadically. The decline in ethnic organizations and cultures does not permit more substantive manifestations of ethnic identity or affiliation. Rather than relying on community or culture, the third generation and beyond uses symbols, primarily out of a sense of nostalgia for the traditions of the immigrant generation. According to Gans (1979: 203–204),

Elderly Jewish immigrants at a California synagogue.

Most people look for easy and intermittent ways of expressing their identity, for ways that do not conflict with other ways of life. As a result, they refrain from ethnic behavior that requires an arduous or time-consuming commitment, either to a culture that must be practiced constantly, or to organizations that demand active membership. Second, because people's concern is with identity, rather than with cultural practices or group relationships, they are free to look for ways of expressing that identity which suit them best, thus opening up the possibility of voluntary, diverse, or individualistic ethnicity.

Until 1980 government census takers did not question members of the third and later generations about ethnic background, categorizing them as "native white of native parentage." The 1980 census, however, did incorporate questions that permitted an inquiry into the relevance of ethnic background for such variables as residential location, cultural differences, economic attainment, and intermarriage (Hout and Goldstein, 1994).

Evidence From Census Findings

Stanley Lieberson and Mary C. Waters (1988) believe these data show a progressive decline of the ethnic factor in shaping European Americans' lives. For example, although differences persist regarding the spatial distribution of groups, in part based on length of time in the country, the trend for all groups is to spread out across regions of the United States over time. Conceding that census data are not the most useful for considering cultural issues, they nonetheless found that in terms of three culturally shaped issues—fertility, marriage rates, and educational attainment—a clear convergence has occurred or is under way. Although some differences remain in the propensity to marry, these differences are fading. No statistically significant differences were observed across groups for both fertility patterns and educational attainment. Similarly, "for the most part socioeconomic inequalities among white ethnic groups are both relatively minor and unrelated to patterns of ethnic inequality found earlier in the century" (Lieberson and Waters, 1988: 155).

Lieberson and Waters (1985, 1988) concluded that there is a trend toward increased intermarriage among European Americans, seen especially among younger cohorts, and involving ethnic groups from both northwestern Europe and those from south central Europe. This conclusion supports Richard Alba's work (1985b), which also utilized data from the 1980 census. Alba found intermarriage among native-born nonHispanic whites to be widespread. It is more widespread among those individuals of mixed rather than single ancestry, but since more and more people are of mixed ancestry, this trend suggests increased intermarriage rates in the future. Alba (1985b: 17) noted one irony in this trend: As people acquire ever-more complicated mixed ancestries, multiple ancestry actually "increases the probability of sharing some common ancestry with a spouse."

So what do these trends mean for ethnic identity? There is evidence of a considerable amount of flux in terms of ethnic identification (Lieberson and Waters, 1986). For the 13.3 million respondents who identified their ancestry as "American" or "United States" in the 1980 census, national origins were either unknown, unimportant, or both. One's ethnic ancestry had no apparent relevance for current sociopolitical matters. Such "unhyphenated whites" may constitute a new ethnic group that "is in the process of forming" (Lieberson, 1985: 179). Although this may be, the percentage of unhyphenated whites did not rise appreciably in the years that followed, although the overall number did by 2000, as 19.6 million individuals answered the ancestry question by defining themselves as "American" (U.S. Bureau of the Census, 1992b, 2002).

Ethnic Options

Most respondents did opt to identify with, by claiming ancestry in, one or more European ethnic groups. The census data did not reveal what this identification meant to these individuals. Was it merely a fact of birth that a person was, say, Irish and German, or did these identities mean something to the individual? Mary C. Waters (1990) explored this question through a series of in-depth interviews with third- and fourth-generation ethnics in suburban Philadelphia and San Jose, California.

Her general conclusion was that ethnicity did mean something for her subjects. She discerned in their attachment to ethnic identity a desire for a sense of community, while they were also intent on preserving a sense of individualism. Thus, their ethnicity took on a voluntaristic cast. Taking part in a St. Patrick's Day parade and preparing ethnic dishes for holiday meals are examples of ways of connecting intermittently with an ethnic past without great outlays of time and energy. People pick and choose features of the ethnic tradition to valorize, while ignoring or abandoning others, such as a tradition that is sexist. Although the immigrant culture might have demanded that a woman's role be in the home, a dual-career household composed of third- or fourth-generation ethnics will not perpetuate the values that endorse that particular gender division of labor (Waters, 1990).

Waters (1990) concurs with Gans that the behavior of her subjects can be seen as symbolic ethnicity, which, she believes,

> is not something that will easily or quickly disappear, while at the same time it does not need very much to sustain it. The choice itself—a community without cost and a specialness that comes to you just by virtue of being born—is a potent combination.

Voices   **Joyce Hoffman**

When I was about 8 years old my mother suddenly discovered that we were German. Up until that time she always thought my father was Irish. She thought he was Irish when she married him. But then this letter came to the house with an extra *n* on the end [of the family name] and my father told her that that was the German spelling of the name and that it was a German name and that his grandparents were German. So my mother really got into this and told us all that we were German. She started serving sauerkraut and putting sour cream on top of everything and at night we would get out the atlas and look up Germany and know that we had come from there. It was really sort of bizarre. . . .

Joyce Hoffman is a 49-year-old teacher (Waters, 1990: 65).

Furthermore, Waters (1990) provides evidence of what she refers to as "cultural syncretism." By this she means the tendency by ethnics to consider various interethnic marriage combinations as decidedly positive because they establish a healthy and beneficial balance between the differing imputed emotional traits of various ethnic groups (for example, the "emotional" Italian and the "reserved" Irish). Although her subjects made frequent use of such ethnic distinctions, she noted that when asked to describe how the traditional values of their own ethnic group differed from others', respondents routinely argued, regardless of which group they were from, that their particular group placed a high premium on family, education, hard work, religiosity, and patriotism (Waters, 1990).

The Privatization of Ethnicity

The symbolic ethnicity thesis was further confirmed in a survey research project undertaken by Richard Alba (1990) in New York State's capital region, which includes Albany, Schenectady, and Troy. In his sample, two thirds of respondents identified ethnically, and of this group only one quarter said that ethnicity was very important to them, about two fifths said it was somewhat important, and one third attached no importance to it. The older immigrant groups (English, German, Dutch, and French) attached less importance to ethnicity than the newer immigrant groups, such as Italians and Poles. Alba found that women tended to attach greater importance to ethnicity than men did (cf. di Leonardo, 1984).

Moreover, those who attached some importance to their ethnic identity, the largest category, believed that ethnicity must be consciously nurtured if it is to survive. In other words, they thought that ethnicity was at risk of fading away into insignificance.

Alba (1990) documented the progressive unlinking of ethnic identity from ethnic social structure. The erosion of ethnic institutions and neighborhoods, the declining role of ethnic culture, the expansion of intermarriage, the prevalence of nonethnic bases for friendships and other modes of social interaction, and the lack of discrimination based on one's ethnic background all contribute to this unlinking. Like Gans, Lieberson, and Waters, Alba did not conclude that ethnic identity will entirely disappear for these white ethnics in the foreseeable future. Rather, he contended that as ethnic identity is severed from ethnic social structure, it increasingly becomes privatized, and (echoing Waters) as such resonates with American notions of individualism. This conclusion suggested to him the possibility that what Thomas Archdeacon (1990) referred to as an "ethnic hum" might persist for many generations.

The Invention of Ethnicity

Ethnicity for European Americans has not disappeared, but it is undergoing various reformulations, taking at least three different forms. We have only focused on one: symbolic ethnicity, which entails an attempt to remain at least nominally connected to a particular European-origin group. Some manifestations of symbolic ethnicity illustrate the profound erosion of ethnic tradition. Two related examples will suffice to illustrate this point. In the center of Helsinki, Finland, a drinking establishment, "St. Urho's Pub," is named after the patron saint of Finland, who, according to legend, saved farmers by casting the grasshoppers out of the country. No one in Finland celebrates St. Urho's Day, however—not surprisingly, since he dates only to the 1950s. Rather, this holiday was the invention of a small band of Finnish Americans in northern Minnesota. They decided to create a counterpart to St. Patrick as a source of pride in things Finnish (Kaups, 1986). Clearly, the original signs of Finnish ethnicity no longer served as meaningful markers of ethnic identity. However contrived this attempt was, it also indicated the presence of a conviction about the need for preserving ethnic allegiance and for enhancing the status of the group vis-à-vis other groups.

St. Patrick was a real historical figure, and although a considerable body of legend surrounds him, he was the patron saint of Ireland, the person primarily responsible for Christianizing the nation. The Irish in America have celebrated St. Patrick's Day since 1737, but over time the celebration has been transformed. Once a religious event, it is now secular. Some use it as a political event to show support for the Irish Republican Army. But for most people of Irish descent, it is merely an occasion to engage in a nostalgic tribute to one's ancestors. Furthermore, in recent decades it has increasingly taken on the character of a panethnic celebration: Organizers of parades and related festivities frequently refer to March 17 as a day during which everyone can be Irish.

Moreover, as events in recent years in New York City (the site of the nation's largest St. Patrick's Day parade) indicate, precisely what it means to be Irish is a matter of controversy. The Irish Lesbian and Gay Organization was banned from participating in the 1992 parade by the sponsoring organization, the Ancient Order of Hibernians. Although members of the homosexual group argued that one can be both gay or lesbian and Irish, the Hibernians countered by arguing that homosexuality was an affront to Irish Catholic tradition (*New York Times*, 1992b: A16). In short, one group wanted to change and the other preserve an inherited cultural orientation.

Regional Identities

Regional cultures, such as Cajuns in Louisiana, remain important into the twenty-first century (Griswold and Wright, 2004). Related to this fact, a second type of invention involves the emergence of new ethnic groups based chiefly on geographic region. This can be seen most clearly in Appalachia and among people from Appalachia who have moved to cities, such as Cincinnati, Pittsburgh, and Chicago, to find work. Although one can identify various European ethnic groups that make up this population—the most predominant being Scotch-Irish—their relative isolation fused ethnic groups into a new regionally based identity. Elements of the traditions of several ethnic groups compose part of the Appalachian identity. But the identity is also shaped by shared features of life in the hollows—the remote and self-contained valleys—of this region, which have been characterized by being both economically disadvantaged and isolated from the outside. This self-construction of Appalachian identity is reinforced by outsiders, who often refer to the residents of Appalachia with the pejorative term "hillbillies." Marger and Obermiller (1983) argued that what is occurring here is an instance of "emergent ethnicity."

One can see a similar process developing in the Upper Peninsula of Michigan, another geographically remote region whose people are composed of a variety of ethnic groups, including Finns, Swedes, Norwegians, Poles, Irish, Italians, and Cornish. The regional identity there is a product of the composite impact of the various ethnic groups. A sense of distinctiveness and alienation from the more urban Lower Peninsula has fueled regional consciousness. A distinctive speech dialect serves as a marker of identity when residents travel "downstate." When the state's tourist bureau began a campaign to promote the state a few years ago, it distributed red bumper stickers with the slogan: "Say yes to Michigan!" Almost immediately, green bumper stickers began to appear on cars in the Upper Peninsula with their response: "Say ya to da U.P., eh!" During the past two decades, there has been increased usage of the self-identification term "Yooper." Some residents of the region embrace its use while it is decried by others.

A European American Identity?

The third trend is based on the assumption that among European-origin groups we may be witnessing not merely the lingering vestiges of past inherited ethnic identities but the construction of a new one. Alba (1990) pointed to the emergence of a new ethnic group that he refers to as the European Americans. Although he does not use the language of the "invention of ethnicity" perspective, this process is clearly what was involved when he (1990: 292–293) wrote:

> Ethnic distinctions based on European ancestry, once quite important in the texture of American social life, are receding into the background. Yet this development does not imply that ethnicity is any less embedded in the social fabric, but rather that the ethnic distinctions which matter are undergoing a radical shift. The transformation of ethnicity among whites does not portend the elimination of ethnicity but instead the formation of a new ethnic group: one based on ancestry from anywhere on the European continent. The emergence of this new group, which I call the "European Americans," with its own myths about its place in American history and the American identity, lies behind the ethnic identities of many Americans of European background.

Although Alba did not stress it, the manner in which many European Americans forge this panethnic identity is based on their conceptualization of other nonEuropean groups—on their understanding of "we" versus "them." Micaela di Leonardo (1984: 234) made this connection when she wrote of a symbolic ethnicity that uses "rhetorical nostalgia" in celebrating one's own past, while criticizing or denigrating other ethnic groups. Such nostalgia becomes a substitute for an appreciation of the differences in historical experiences of various groups. For example, to argue, as so many European ethnics do, that their culture placed a high premium on close-knit families is to implicitly criticize groups such as African Americans because of the prevalence of single-parent households in that group. Similarly, the belief that one's ancestors imbued subsequent generations with a willingness to engage in hard work can be used as a way of blaming those groups who suffer from persistently high levels of unemployment and underemployment for their economic circumstances. Charles Gallagher (2003) refers to this as "playing the white ethnic card."

This approach fails to recognize, among other things, the historical impact of exclusionary hiring practices and organized labor's opposition to inviting some groups into its ranks. Mary Waters (1990: 147) detected a similar underside to symbolic ethnicity and bluntly concluded that one of the reasons that symbolic ethnicity persists is because of "its ideological 'fit' with racist beliefs." We shall return to this issue of race relations later, but before doing so, we will look at one ethnic group that does not fit these general trends: Jews.

Jewish Exceptionalism?

Because the U.S. Census poses its ethnic ancestry questions in terms of national identity and not religious identity, Jews are not identified by their religio-ethnic identity. Instead, they are lumped into such national groups as Poles and Russians. In addition, Alba's Capital Region study contained relatively few Jews, while Waters did not include Jews in her project. Thus, the question arises: Might the trends described in the preceding section be inapplicable to Jews? Substantial research that attempts to answer this question has been devoted to Jewish Americans.

What might contribute to the persistence of differences between Jews and nonJews? First, the lingering power of anti-Semitism has made discrimination and exclusion more problematic for Jews than, for instance, anti-Italian or anti-Polish sentiments have been for Italians or Poles. At the same time, Jews have been, as a group, remarkably successful in socioeconomic terms. This success has provided them with the resources to combat anti-Semitism while undertaking actions to preserve the strength of their ethnic community. The fusion of religion and ethnicity for Jews differentiates them from other European-origin groups (the Greek Orthodox community may be an exception). The memory of the Holocaust and the ongoing concern with the future security of Israel have bolstered a sense of group allegiance and have overcome many of the divisions within the ethnic community. In combination, these factors raise the possibility that the future of the Jewish community and of a distinctive ethnic identity might be different from that of other European Americans.

Sections of Jewish America that show continued vitality are intent on remaining in fundamental ways aloof from the larger society. This can be seen in the Hasidic community, which has its center in Brooklyn (Mayer, 1979). In addition, there has been a modest return to religious Orthodoxy (Danzger, 1989; Kaufman 1991). Furthermore, during the Carter presidency and again after the collapse of the Soviet Union, Jews emigrated from Russia. An enclave located near Coney Island in Brooklyn is referred to by local residents as "Odessa by the Sea," while immigrants from Israel have taken up residence in the borough of Queens (Shokeid, 1988). The presence of new arrivals can inject vitality into an ethnic community. Steven Gold (1995: 66) has pointed out that, with a desire to preserve historic Jewish enclaves because many elderly remain in them even though their children have moved out, many Jewish organizations have played roles in assisting in "the settlement of recent Jewish immigrants from the former USSR as well as Israel and Iran." In the case of Israeli Jews, many maintain ties with family, friends, and business interests in Israel and thus have many of the characteristics of transnational immigrants (Gold, 1997, 2002). They show evidence of being economi-

A Russian immigrant wedding party.

cally successful in a relatively short period of time (Cohen, 2003). Taken together, however, all of these Jews compose a very small percentage of the total Jewish American population.

The Core Jewish Population

According to the 1990 National Jewish Population Survey (NJPS), 6.8 million American Jews were identified by ethnic background or by religious preference. Of this number, 1.3 million had either converted to another religion or were children currently being raised with another religion. Of the 5.5 million that constitute what the survey authors referred to as the "core Jewish population," 77 percent were born Jewish and identified with the Jewish religion, 3 percent were nonJews who converted to Judaism, and 20 percent were secular Jews, born Jewish but claiming no religious identity (Kosmin et al., 1991). Between 1980 and 1998, Jews have consistently represented about 2 percent of the total population of the nation (Princeton Religious Research Center, 1998).

The results of the 2000 NJPS revealed that the Jewish population remained relatively stable during the intervening decade. The core population dropped slightly to 5.2 million people. The population is aging, with the mean age rising from 37 in 1990 to 41 in 2000. Meanwhile, 9 percent of the Jewish population is 75 or older, compared with only 6 percent of the general U.S. population (United Jewish Communities, 2002).

The difference in size between the core Jewish population and the total ethnic background and religious preference figure illustrates that changes have occurred within American Judaism. These changes have been brought about mainly by expanded opportunities for inclusion into the larger society in recent decades. Since the 1950s, as Jews were incorporated into the fabric of America's civil religion, which was seen as rooted in a shared Judeo-Christian heritage, their place in America seemed more assured. Since that time, the level of anti-Semitism has markedly declined. This situation has permitted structural and cultural assimilation and raised questions about the possibility of integrating into the larger society while preserving a unique group identity (Waxman, 1983; Cohen and Fein, 1985; Glazer, 1985; Silberman, 1985; Hertzberg, 1989b).

Continuity and Change

There is growing evidence of changing patterns of institutional affiliation and religious observance, heightened levels of geographic mobility and residential dispersal (Goldstein and Goldstein, 1996), shifts in attitudes on political and social issues, a lessening of support for Israeli policies toward the Palestinians and their Arab neighbors, changes in interpersonal relations, and rising rates of intermarriage.

Some scholars argue that these changes point to assimilative patterns not unlike those experienced by other European American groups (Glazer, 1985; Hertzberg, 1989b). Gans thinks that symbolic ethnicity is increasingly an apt term to characterize Jewish America, and, before he wrote about symbolic ethnicity in general terms, he had argued that what was occurring as early as the 1950s in the suburbs was the development of "symbolic Judaism" (Gans, 1956, 1979). While others agree that assimilation is occurring, they contend that the role religion continues to play casts doubt on the extent to which the contemporary situation can be characterized as symbolic ethnicity (Kivisto and Nefzger, 1993; Winter, 1996).

At the other extreme are those who, like Calvin Goldscheider (1986), contended that "the American Jewish community is a powerful and cohesive community. It has strong anchors of social, religious, and family life; it is neither diminishing demographically nor weakening Jewishly." This position sees American Judaism changing but not eroding, transforming itself to meet the particular circumstances and demands of the present. This transformation is depicted as being resistant to the corrosive impact of the assimilative process.

A major research project directed by Steven M. Cohen (1988) contains a careful and systematic attempt to assess the merits of these two positions. The study, conducted in 1981, entailed a survey by mail and phone of 4,505 Jewish households in the greater New York area.

As Table 5.2 indicates, New York currently has a considerably larger Jewish population than any other city. Such has been the historic pattern, and thus Cohen studied the largest and most highly concentrated Jewish community in the nation. He examined a variety of attitudinal and behavioral topics, dividing them into three major categories: religious ritual observance, Jewish communal affiliation, and interpersonal relations (friendships and marriage). The conclusions distilled from these data provide a somewhat mixed picture.

In terms of ritual observance, Cohen noted that across generations there are patterns of both declining and increasing practices, indicating a considerable amount of what he terms "intergenerational flux." This fluidity is seen in other aspects of Jewish social life as well. The role played by inter-marriage in prompting assimilation has, in Cohen's view, been overstated. He contended that although intermarriage rates continue to grow, the rate of growth has tapered off since the 1960s. According to Cohen, the effect of inter-marriage on involvement in Jewish life has been minimal. Furthermore, he saw conversion by a nonJewish spouse as a remedy to the problem that inter-marriage poses to Jewish identity and group affiliation.

Cohen (1988) constructed what he calls a "typology of Jewish commit-ment," which derives from combining the findings from his three indices. He defined five categories and cited their respective sizes in the population: ob-servant (10 percent), activists (17 per-cent), affiliated (49 percent), holiday (15 percent), and inactives (10 per-cent). On the basis of this overall por-trait, Cohen concluded that a modified, "moderate transformative" view most adequately captured the character of Jewish life in greater New York (where 30 percent of the nation's Jews re-sided). He further suggested that these conclusions can be extrapolated to the country at large. This conclusion tends to overlook the role of Jewish population density and propinquity in shaping attitudes and be-haviors. Does it apply to Jews in other parts of the country, where they are a smaller minority of the overall population?

A study of a midwestern city with a considerably smaller Jewish population was modeled after Cohen's New York study to see whether such extrapolation was warranted (Nefzger and Kivisto, 1990; Kivisto and Nefzger, 1993). The findings also provided somewhat mixed re-

Table 5.2 The 20 Largest U.S. Jewish Communities	
Community	Jewish Population
New York, NY	1,900,000
Los Angeles, CA	585,000
Miami, FL	535,000
Philadelphia, PA	315,000
Chicago, IL	250,000
Boston, MA	228,000
San Francisco, CA	210,000
Washington, DC	165,000
Baltimore, MD	100,000
Detroit, MI	95,000
Rockland County, NY	83,000
Orange County, CA	75,000
San Diego, CA	70,000
Atlanta, GA	67,000
Cleveland, OH	65,000
St. Louis, MO	53,000
Phoenix, AZ	50,000
Denver, CO	46,000
Houston, TX	42,000
Dallas, TX	35,000

Source: World Jewish Congress (2003).

sults. For example, in the area of ritual observance, although this community did not have an Orthodox institutional presence and therefore did not contain those that Cohen identified as highly observant, there were still clear parallels between the two communities. In the other two indexes, however, there were important differences. In the area of communal affiliation (which includes involvement in both religious and secular Jewish organizations) the midwestern Jews ranked significantly higher than those in greater New York. The situation is reversed for the interpersonal index, where New York Jews ranked higher. The midwestern community showed a voluntaristic affiliation with Jewish religious organizations and a growing tendency to choose friends and marital partners without regard to ethnic background.

In terms of friends, 63 percent of respondents reported that at least two of their three closest friends were Jewish, a figure considerably lower than that obtained in Cohen's study but similar to that found in numerous other community studies (Fishman, 1987; Cohen, 1988). Particularly noteworthy is that the figure for 25- to 34-year-olds is lower in every city studied, and outside of the New York area, it drops appreciably. As the proximity to other Jews diminishes by geographic region, so does the likelihood of having mainly Jewish friends.

Intermarriage

Similar patterns are evident for intermarriage. Cohen's dismissal of the implications of intermarriage for Judaism are not reflected in other regions of the United States. According to Marshall Sklare (1971), intermarriage did not become a particular topic of concern for Jews until the 1960s. Between the 1950s and the 1970s, the intermarriage rate of Jews increased from 3.7 percent to 11.8 percent (Glenn, 1982). This was quite low in comparison with the rates for other European Americans. Evidence from a number of community studies shows that the intermarriage rate has increased since the 1970s, and one study argued that a "sharply rising incidence of intermarriage among Jews" is seen in the Midwest and West (Sandberg, 1986: 557). The National Jewish Population Survey released in 2003 indicates that if we look at the identity of the spouse by year of marriage, the differences over the past four decades are profound. As Figure 5.1 indicates, only 12 percent of pre-1970 marriages involved Gentile spouses, but the number soared to 47 percent by 2001 (NJPS, 2003; Kosmin et al., 1991: 13–14). Calvin Goldscheider (2003: 18) has argued that the rising rate of intermarriage has "become an obsession with Jewish community leaders, [who] fear the disappearance of Jews in America." However, he and others disagree with this pessimistic prognosis, noting that intermarriage does not necessarily lead to a decline in the salience of Jewish identity or Jewish communal activities (Winter, 2002; Cohen, 2003; Goldscheider, 2003).

The overall figure remains lower than that for other European Americans (Spikard, 1989). Religion appears to play a role in keeping the rate of outmarriage lower than that for other groups. Jewish parents have historically been more opposed to their children dating or marrying Gentiles than Gentile parents have been opposed to their children dating or marrying Jews. Egon Mayer (1980) has argued that this opposition by Jewish parents has waned considerably, however, and he attributed the rise in intermarriage, in part, to what he refers to as "Jewish default."

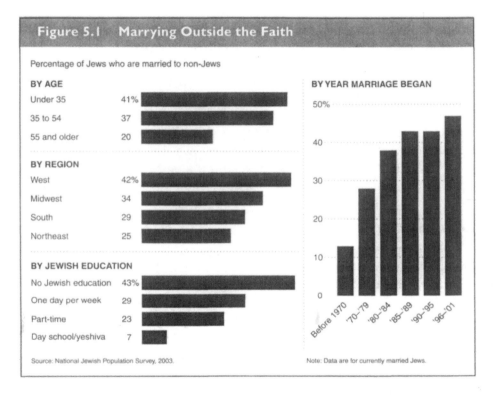

Figure 5.1   Marrying Outside the Faith

Percentage of Jews who are married to non-Jews

BY AGE

Under 35	41%
35 to 54	37
55 and older	20

BY REGION

West	42%
Midwest	34
South	29
Northeast	25

BY JEWISH EDUCATION

No Jewish education	43%
One day per week	29
Part-time	23
Day school/yeshiva	7

BY YEAR MARRIAGE BEGAN

(Before 1970, '70–'79, '80–'84, '85–'89, '90–'95, '96–'01)

Source: National Jewish Population Survey, 2003.

Note: Data are for currently married Jews.

Although marital indicators imply increased assimilation, there are other indications that Jews still retain a distinctive identity. Jews have traditionally been more liberal than many other white ethnics, and they remain so. Similarly, they remain closely identified with the Democratic party at a time when many other white ethnics from the former New Deal coalition have bolted to the conservatism offered by the Republican party. In addition, the question of the Jewish homeland, Israel, still remains a potent stimulus to ethnic identity. Anti-Semitism has not disappeared, and in the late 1980s and early 1990s various white supremacist groups ranging from the KKK to the Aryan Nation, replete with their skinhead youth contingents, have justifiably revived concerns among Jews. This situation intensified ethnic identities and boundaries.

In short, it appears that Jews *might* follow the pattern of other European ethnics, but it is by no means clear that they *will* do so. There is also evidence of vitality, and the intertwining of religion and ethnicity may maintain a distinct Jewish American presence. It should be noted that this takes place within the context of changes in the racialized ethnicity of American Jews. Once seen as racially distinct, as Jews have assimilated, they have also "become white" (Brodkin, 1998).

The Specter of Race

The Jewish example points to the fluidity of racial boundaries and definitions (Omi, 2001). What is clear is that those boundaries have shifted by becoming more inclusive, but the divide between whites and nonwhites persists. Moreover, the dynamics of constructing racial differences implies a quest on the part of those already defined as white and those seeking to be so defined to benefit from "whiteness" (Lipsitz, 1998; Winant, 1999, 2001). At the same time, following the end of World War II, when the United States emerged as the most powerful nation in the world, what Howard Winant (2001: 148) has called its "racial theater" fused domestic and international politics. The leader of the "free world" was under scrutiny: How could it claim to be the land of freedom and equality when it denied both to nonwhites? At the same time, this was also the era when the civil rights movement commenced (a subject we shall discuss in the next chapter). The combined impact of these global and domestic challenges to the existing racial order was profound. However, as Winant (2001: 6) observes, since the mid-twentieth century, the United States—like many other nations—has been able to effect only "a partial shift away from formally avowed white supremacy. The demolition of the racial subjugation that created the modern world is far from over."

Public opinion polls capture something of the changes that have transpired during this period. What has happened to the color line while boundaries dividing different white ethnic groups have eroded considerably? Changes in white racial attitudes since the 1940s are difficult to summarize both because the trends are ambiguous and because different analysts can and do interpret changes in various ways.

There is rather clear evidence that a substantial majority of whites have come to endorse equality and integration in principle (Taylor, Sheatsley, and Greeley, 1978). For example, in 1942, 54 percent of whites believed that blacks should be required to occupy separate sections on streetcars and buses, but by 1970, 88 percent of whites disagreed with this stance. Subsequent public opinion polls dropped this question, reflecting the fact that the number of whites accepting integrated transportation systems was approaching 100 percent. The percentage agreeing that whites and blacks should attend the same schools rose from 32 percent in 1942 to 90 percent by 1982, reaching 96 percent by 1995 (Schuman, Steeh, and Bobo, 1985; Bobo, 2001).

Questions about residential segregation suggest a more favorable attitude about open housing than in the 1940s, but the change is not as pronounced as in other areas. This is partly because this issue has often been posed in terms of rights, including the rights of whites to sell their homes to whomever they want. Given the importance attached to individual rights in America, it is not surprising that the rights of whites and the rights of blacks could conflict. Nevertheless, in a 1982 National Opinion Research Center (NORC) survey, 71 percent of whites either disagreed or disagreed strongly with the statement that whites have a right to keep blacks out of their neighborhoods if they want to (Schuman, Steeh, and Bobo, 1985).

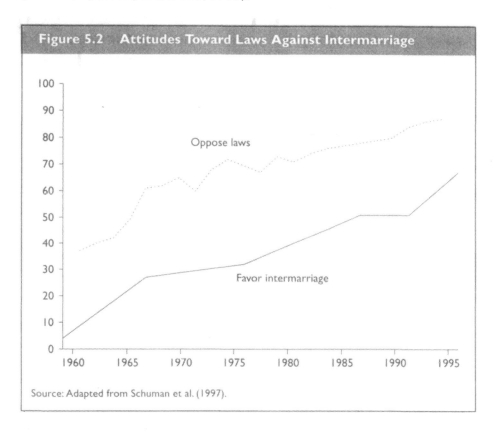

Figure 5.2   Attitudes Toward Laws Against Intermarriage

Source: Adapted from Schuman et al. (1997).

These principles are not as overwhelmingly supported in areas of intimacy in social relations, although even here the trend during the past several decades has been toward greater acceptance. For example, as recently as the 1980s, 34 percent of white Americans agreed that there should be laws prohibiting racial intermarriage, but that figure declined to around 20 percent by the 1990s (see Figure 5.2). A majority of whites—60 percent—disapproved of marriages between whites and nonwhites during the 1980s (Schuman, Steeh, and Bobo, 1985), but that figure declined to about one third of whites a decade later (Bobo, 2001; see also Schuman et al., 1997). Despite these positive changes, what Robert Park saw as the last major barrier to assimilation remains a significant feature of white attitudes about race.

Looking at the preferred kind of social contact with blacks, it is clear that in matters related to residential and school integration, whites are far more comfortable in situations with small numbers of blacks. This finding suggests that whites prefer to interact with blacks in a context in which whites are in the majority and black interactants find themselves in a situation where they must conform to white expectations and work at fitting in. Although some analysts have concluded that this is an indication of persistent racism, that would be a gross oversimplification. Issues related to social class also have an effect, as whites manifest a greater willingness to interact with blacks from the same class background than with blacks from a lower class background than their own (Hartigan, 1999).

White Attitudes About Governmental Actions

When turning from principles to ways of effecting changes that promote equality and integration—or, in other words, to questions related to implementation—whites are far more divided. In general, the majority of whites do not support the federal government having a major role in initiating policies to remedy problems such as school and residential segregation, inequitable treatment in the labor market, and related issues (Schuman, Steeh, and Bobo, 1985). As we shall see in greater detail in the next chapter, in two areas—busing to achieve school integration and affirmative action policies—the pronounced split in white opinions has made these implementation practices highly charged political issues.

Although public opinion surveys provide valuable data, there are limits to their utility. They fail to reveal some of the complicated reasons for people's attitudes. Furthermore, attitudes do not necessarily translate into behaviors. For example, although 86 percent of whites in 1982 said they would vote for a black presidential candidate if he or she were qualified, whites have been far less willing than this suggests to cast their votes for black candidates in local and state races. The reason for this reluctance is not easy to unravel. Is it because of latent racism or because the voters genuinely believe the candidate is not as qualified as the opponent? Is it due to disagreement over the candidate's platform and general political orientation?

Whites constitute a majority of the nation's population and as such are characterized by a great number of divisions. They cannot be seen in monolithic terms. The opinion polls reviewed above indicate, for example, the differences that persist between southern whites and whites elsewhere in the nation—the former remain more conservative in their racial attitudes than the latter. Similarly, more highly educated people have more liberal racial attitudes than those with less education.

Michael Omi and Howard Winant (1986) pointed to a shift in the configuration of race relations since the 1960s. A conservative reaction not only to the civil rights movement but also to the loss of the Vietnam War, the transformations brought about by the 1960s counterculture, and the growing stagnation of the American economy led to electoral victories first by Richard Nixon and then, in 1980, by the most ideologically motivated president of the century, Ronald Reagan. The backlash that was part of this shift to conservatism was frequently motivated by what can be seen as the politics of resentment. White ethnics, especially poor and working-class whites, felt that liberal politicians had left them behind. The Reagan administration contended that the federal government did not have a legitimate role in promoting social change and sought to roll back the government's role in matters related to racial and class inequality. Omi and Winant (1986: 113) wrote, however:

> There were clear limits to any attempt to undo the effects of the "great transformation." In the aftermath of the 1960s, any effective challenge to the egalitarian ideals framed by the [civil rights movement] could no longer rely on the racism of the past. Racial equality had to be acknowledged as a desirable goal. But the *meaning* of equality, and the proper means for achieving it, remained matters of considerable debate.

The implications of this transformation for the politics of the recent past and the present will be discussed in the following four chapters. Particular attention to the theoretical debates over the issue of the role of racism in shaping life chances of nonwhite groups is treated in the next chapter's section on "The Enduring Significance of Race."

The Politics of Hate and Racial Divisiveness

A resurgence of white supremacy marks the far-right-wing response to black advancement and takes a number of organizational forms. All of these groups combine a virulent racism with an equally virulent anti-Semitism. With a view of racial boundaries as properly fixed and unchanging, these groups exhibit paranoia about mixed-race people. Racial intermarriage is viewed as a form of racial suicide on the part of the white race (Daniels, 1997; Ferber, 1998; Blee, 2003). The Ku Klux Klan has experienced something of a revival since the early 1970s, especially in the South and along the entire Atlantic coast, under the leadership of David Duke. West of the Mississippi has the greatest concentration of various neo-Nazi groups, including Tom Metzger's White Aryan Resistance (WAR) and many loosely organized skinhead youth gangs with names such as Youth of Hitler and Confederate Hammerskins. Several groups see themselves as "Christian patriots," including Posse Comitatus, the Golden Mean Society, the Order, and Identity Christians. They are alike in their hostility to what they refer to as the ZOG (that is, Zionist Occupied Government). They are convinced that they are a "chosen people" engaged in a righteous war against blacks, whom they refer to as "mud people" (Omi and Winant, 1986; Aho, 1990; Langer, 1990). These groups are small in number but nevertheless dangerous. They have been responsible for terrorist acts throughout the country, including shootings, lynchings, and beatings (Marable, 1983). They have also attempted to use the mass media to attract a larger audience, such as Metzger's efforts to use public access television shows.

These extremists are largely outside of the conventional political process, although David Duke has made an effort to enter electoral politics. After being elected to the state legislature in Louisiana, he ran unsuccessfully for the governorship of the state. He lost the election but garnered the majority of the state's white vote—despite his connection with the Klan and the American Nazi movement. He proved to be an embarrassment to the Republican party, which sought to disassociate itself from him.

Voices   **Chris Berlet**

We didn't change the nature of the neighborhood fundamentally except in one area. The Klan and neo-Nazis went away.

It was absolutely imperative that we live in the neighborhood to do this work. I don't think that white folks who want to fight racism have any idea how irrelevant it is to drop into a community after some crisis or event and decide that they're going to do something about racism. . . . Having been inside the neighborhood, I can tell you if you want to fight racism in a white community, live in it. That gives you a stake; you have a place at the table. You have neighbors and no matter how much they hate your ideas, they'll still give you coffee and pie when you talk to them about what's going on because you're a neighbor.

Chris Berlet is an antiracist activist who works for an organization that studies right-wing racist organizations (Thompson, Schaefer, and Brod, 2003: 97).

Indeed, whereas right-wing racists seek to hold on to the old Jim Crow racism, with its biologically deterministic claims about the inferiority of blacks and other nonwhites, today's mainstream neoconservatives—the New Right—repudiate this racism. For example, the Reagan administration and both of the Bush administrations, as the major exemplars of the New Right, publicly repudiated the racism that characterized, for example, Southern politics well into the 1960s. They espoused ideals of racial equality and harmony, and they appointed conservative blacks to highly visible governmental posts. But they achieved victory by driving a wedge into the New Deal coalition, one that split the Democratic party chiefly along racial lines.

Moreover, far from signaling what neoconservative writer Dinesh D'Souza (1995) has called the "end of racism," new forms of racist discourse have emerged based on culture rather than biology. In the case of the New Right, Amy Ansell (1997) has written about the new racial discourse suggesting that the cultural shortcomings of the least successful minority groups, not white resistance, account for the fact that they have not achieved socioeconomic parity with whites. The Democrats have been increasingly seen as the party of racial minorities and the poor, but no longer as the voice of the white working class. Conservatives have played on white resentment and a sense that governmental intervention on behalf of blacks has been at their expense. As with the Willie Horton advertisements of George H. W. Bush's 1988 election campaign, conservatives fueled the public's growing fear of crime and reinforced the association of violent crime with black males. Frequently, conservatives relied on subtle codes that aroused racial animosity without resorting to overt racist appeals. The charge that affirmative action was in reality a form of "reverse discrimination" is a key example of this tendency—a topic we discuss more fully in the next chapter.

Although the electoral victories of conservatives since 1980 have been the result of a combination of factors, with racial issues being only one, the repudiation of many liberal policies of the 1960s by a significant portion of the white voting population should temper the generally optimistic findings of the opinion polls reported above (Edsall and Edsall, 1991; Franklin, 1991). The fact that during its eight years, the Clinton administration did very little to address the problems of race testifies to the extent to which the New Right has managed to reorient political discourse. By seeking a centrist path, President Clinton avoided the positions or policies that would be opposed by whites and thus would be divisive. This approach reflected a more general retreat on the part of liberals and moderates from tackling issues related to racial justice, leading commentators such as Stephen Steinberg (1995) to conclude that the nation was turning its back on the civil rights agenda that had emerged after World War II. However, George W. Bush's opposition not only to affirmative action but also to many of the other legacies of the civil rights era (including the popular Head Start program) has served to mobilize many liberals.

Summary

This chapter has surveyed the profound changes that have occurred within European-origin ethnic communities during the past half century. As earlier chapters have illustrated, these communities have often been at odds with one another. Conflict related to job competition, political control, or cultural, religious, and linguistic differences has pitted one group against another. Throughout American history, however, these groups have also constructed bridges to overcome differences. In short, from an early date one could point to various indicators that suggested assimilation was occurring.

The pace of change accelerated dramatically after 1950. Interethnic conflict declined precipitously. Ethnic communities and cultures eroded, ethnic allegiances declined in strength, and intermarriages increased among white ethnic groups. Although the way change occurred varied for each group, with some groups assimilating more quickly than others, for all Gentile groups abundant evidence suggests the validity of Richard Alba's characterization of them entering the "twilight of ethnicity." For a number of reasons, Jewish assimilation remains distinctive. There is evidence of assimilation, especially during the past quarter century, but it is difficult to speculate about what the future holds for the Jewish American community.

Ethnicity has not disappeared for most European-origin Americans. Rather, several new forms of ethnicity may be emerging. The invention-of-ethnicity perspective calls attention to how ethnicity is currently being reshaped, whether in the form of symbolic ethnicity, the creation of new regional and ethnic identities, or the emergence of the European American.

The chapter also examined how race plays a role in this redefinition of ethnicity for European Americans. Although racial attitudes have improved, racism is a continuing problem. The majority of whites are opposed to governmental actions designed to overcome the legacy of racial oppression. There is a tendency to think that blacks are to blame for their problems. Most whites live in worlds apart from blacks, especially in the intimate worlds of friendships and marriages. In this regard, we are indeed, as David Shipler (1997) has posed it, "a country of strangers."

Nonetheless, this situation does not mean that all whites are, in effect, closet racists. Many, perhaps most, are not. Their orientations toward race relations are highly varied and often ambiguous. Some simply want to avoid the issue as much as possible. Its seeming intractability leads them to a fatalistic view of race relations or to mere indifference. Others overestimate the extent to which inequality has been overcome and the amount of opportunity actually available to blacks. For many well-intentioned people, one can point to countless acts, small and large, that are intended to do something to improve race relations. For all, race continues to cast its shadow over their definition of the American situation as we proceed along in the twenty-first century (Franklin, 1991; Gerstle, 2001; Winant, 2001).

Key Terms

ethnic revival

intermarriage

*principle of third-generation
   interest*

symbolic ethnicity

twilight of ethnicity

Questions for Discussion and Critical Thinking

1. What does symbolic ethnicity mean? How is it related to assimilation and pluralism? Do the Italian and Polish cases provide evidence to support or reject the concept?

2. A major question about Jewish Americans is whether they are going to experience changes similar to other European-origin groups. Do you think the Jewish case is unique? Why or why not?

3. White racism continues to persist, although it has changed over time. Review the discussion in the chapter on racism and provide an assessment of what you consider to be the most likely future trends. ✦

Chapter 6

African Americans: The Enduring American Dilemma

In 1944 the Swedish economist Gunnar Myrdal published a monumental study on African Americans. Encyclopedic in its effort to cover all aspects of black life, *An American Dilemma* included analyses of major political, economic, and cultural forces that shaped the black experience in America. Furthermore, it provided extended discussions of social inequality and the persistent role of prejudice and discrimination. After presenting a vast body of data regarding the past and present circumstances of blacks in America, Myrdal provided tempered, but nonetheless generally optimistic, conclusions about the future.

The study was commissioned by the Carnegie Corporation, a philanthropic organization established by the estate of industrialist Andrew Carnegie, which wanted to derive implications for social policy from the study. Although it is not entirely clear why the corporation hired a foreigner who had conducted no prior research on race relations in America, a primary reason was the desire to get a fresh, outsider's perspective on the topic of race relations. Myrdal had ample monetary support and involved many prominent American scholars, including several black activists and intellectuals (Southern, 1987).

The overarching thesis advanced in the study was noteworthy in several ways. Despite the range and complexity of the topics treated, Myrdal's conclusions about the future of race relations derived from a remarkably simple claim: The dilemma produced by the conflict between the American ideals of freedom and equality and the reality of black oppression would be resolved in favor of the realization of American values. Myrdal was an assimilationist who based his assessment of the future of race relations on the assumption that America had a unified cultural system with commonly shared core values. The race problem was located in the white mind, which, as long as it harbored prejudicial attitudes that were translated into discriminatory actions, would ensure that the dilemma persisted. Thus, the solution to the race problem would occur when whites rooted out their own racism and treated blacks in a manner congruent with the core cultural values.

But Myrdal did not think that a mass therapy session was all that was necessary to cure the nation of white racism. On the contrary, he understood that the historical legacy of racial oppression had to be remedied. He called for the government to play a central role in improving the social condition of African Americans. Having been a central figure in the creation of Sweden's welfare state, Myrdal was an exponent of social engineering. This position had not been a particularly prominent feature of earlier American social science, but it was congruent with the expanded role of the state being advanced by advocates of the New Deal (Lyman, 1972; Wacker, 1983). This position contrasted with the laissez-faire views of one of the founders of American sociology, William Graham Sumner. Sumner contended that mores cannot be legislated—or, in other words, laws do not change the way people think and feel. Myrdal's position starkly refuted this claim. In his opinion, government could and should involve itself in improving the living conditions and life chances of blacks, through expanded educational opportunities, job training, and the like.

Moreover, Myrdal called for racial integration. He abandoned Booker T. Washington's approach, which opted for developing blacks within the confines of a caste society. Prior to Myrdal commencing his research, Roy Wilkins of the NAACP expressed his concern that Myrdal might promote a renewed commitment to the Washingtonian position of development within the framework of a segregated world (Southern, 1987: 10; Lyman, 1998). Instead, Myrdal endorsed the quest most closely associated with the views of W. E. B. Du Bois for the dual objectives of advancement and integration.

Myrdal placed relatively little emphasis on black activism as a means for changing the subordinate place of African Americans in American society (Smith and Killian, 1990). When he discussed the presence of protest organizations within the black community, especially the NAACP and the Urban League, he stressed the importance of their interracial character. He was sympathetic to such organizations and suggested that more organizations with somewhat different political orientations would be welcomed. Nonetheless, his general view was that because of their lack of power and experience, such organizations would ultimately play an essentially secondary role in the move to redefine the place of blacks in American society.

But an event that Myrdal mentions can be seen as signaling the beginning of a social movement that was far more consequential than he was able to imagine (Myrdal, 1944). The event was a proposed march on Washington, D.C., orchestrated by the political and labor activist A. Philip Randolph. The planned march was motivated by Franklin D.

Roosevelt's refusal to desegregate the armed forces but was called off when Roosevelt signed Executive Order 8802, by which he established the Fair Employment Practices Commission. According to Doug McAdam (1982: 84), "That order marked the official termination of the earlier policy of executive inaction, and as such established an important, if largely symbolic, precedent."

The Civil Rights Movement: 1940–1970

Randolph was the most important black leader during the 1940s, an interstitial figure who bridged two generations of leadership. Although he was a unique leader in his own right, with a distinct operational base and political stance, he was in many respects the heir to Du Bois. Randolph was also a model for the new generation of protest organizers, most notably Martin Luther King, Jr. Randolph's success in pressuring the Roosevelt Administration to take a more active role in the affairs of black America or risk a confrontation set in motion repeated attempts to stimulate change. Segregation continued as official policy of the military until after the conclusion of World War II. But in 1948 President Truman signed an executive order that was designed to end segregation—although integration did not occur immediately.

The **civil rights movement** intensified and grew during the 1950s, during a period of heightened international tensions brought about by the struggle between the United States and the Soviet Union. Because both superpowers were intent on serving as a model for peoples throughout the world, racial oppression in the bastion of the "free world" proved increasingly to be an embarrassment and a political burden. Mass communications permitted the rapid dissemination of unsavory events such as the lynching of Emmett Till in 1955. Till was a teenage black from Chicago who, on a visit to relatives in the South, failed to understand the region's perverse "racial etiquette." After allegedly making a sexual remark to a white woman, he was kidnapped, tortured, and murdered by two white men. Because the Soviet Union made quick and effective use of this and similar events in their propaganda war, it became increasingly evident to some government officials and politicians that steps had to be taken to prevent racism from further tarnishing America's image abroad. In addition, given the centrality of racism to Nazi ideology, progressives were able to link the rationale for our participation in the war against fascism to the struggle for black rights at home.

This was also a period of unprecedented economic prosperity and one in which the middle class expanded. A growth economy demanded workers and resulted in low unemployment rates. This meant a reduction in the competition for jobs, which allowed a lowering of interracial tensions. There were decided limits to who benefited from these new

economic circumstances, however. Poverty did not disappear, as some
thought it would. Instead, an affluent society was forced to confront the
existence of those who stood outside—those whom Michael Harrington
(1962) depicted as residents of the "other America." Blacks were disproportionately represented in the ranks of the other America, and their
concentration in inner-city ghettos made them a highly visible feature
of the urban landscape that highlighted both the gulf between comfort
and want and the divide between blacks and whites.

Phase I: Nonviolent Confrontation and Legislative Lobbying

In this climate, the modern civil rights movement developed during
the 1950s and 1960s, built partly on already existing black organizations. The church played a key role, as did black colleges and the oldest
civil rights organizations, particularly the NAACP and the National
Urban League (Morris, 1984; Haines, 1988; Lincoln and Mamiya,
1990).

In addition, several new organizations emerged. These included the
Congress of Racial Equality (CORE), founded in 1942, which was an
offshoot of the Fellowship of Reconciliation, a Christian pacifist group
(Meier and Rudwick, 1973). Another key organization created in the
midst of movement activism was the Southern Christian Leadership
Conference (SCLC), founded in 1957. It began after discussions among
some influential northern blacks, including A. Philip Randolph, Ella
Baker, and Bayard Rustin, and southern clergy, the most prominent of
whom would soon be seen as its leader, Martin Luther King, Jr. Aldon
Morris (1984: 77) has described the SCLC as "the decentralized political arm of the black church." CORE and SCLC were alike in their advo-

cacy of nonviolent protest, and in this they differed from the NAACP, which was more inclined to seek redress for injustice and racial inequality through the courts and the legislative system. The former groups were thus more militant than the NAACP but not as militant as the Student Nonviolent Coordinating Committee (SNCC). A spin-off of SCLC, SNCC was construed at its inception in 1960 as a place for student activists to be connected to the larger movement while being able to act creatively and independently. Within a few years of its founding, this organization was transformed from having a reformist integrationist stance similar to these other groups into a radical, black nationalist one (Haines, 1988).

The civil rights movement was, until the second half of the 1960s, quite unified in terms of its objectives. For example, considerable overlap in organizational support and membership existed. The major differences that generated conflict revolved around tactics, which ultimately involved conflicting assessments about the appropriate speed of change and the desirability of compromise with whites. Related to this conflict were two relevant facts regarding the movement's relationship with whites. First, wealthy liberal whites and various foundations contributed financially to movement organizations. Parenthetically, J. Craig Jenkins and Craig Eckert (1986) suggested that wealthy Jews, out of a longstanding concern about discrimination, may have been disproportionately represented among the contributors. Certainly this is true for one of the most important sources of foundation support: the Julius Rosenwald Fund. Movement organizations also derived support from prominent law firms, media executives, and liberal politicians. Movement organizers also found political backing from well-placed government officials in the central corridors of power, especially after the election of John F. Kennedy.

Although much of the black leadership came from the middle class, it succeeded only insofar as it connected with the black working class and poor, which, as became increasingly clear, were far from docile. Blacks from all socioeconomic backgrounds pressed for dramatic social change. Although much of what transpired during two tumultuous decades involved considerable spontaneity and innovation (Killian, 1984), it was also encouraged by professional social movement organizers and paid staffs who utilized, through rational calculation, strategic resources (McCarthy and Zald, 1977; McAdam, 1982; Bloom, 1987).

Because of the middle-class leadership base, the professional cast, and the role played by white elites, some have argued that the militancy of the civil rights movement was effectively contained by those who sought change, but only change within certain circumscribed limits. Some have argued that elite sponsorship amounted to a form of social control (Piven and Cloward, 1971). Recent historical studies of the movement have disputed this contention, reporting such support as essentially reactive rather than as controlling—playing, in other words, a secondary role (McAdam, 1982; Morris, 1984).

The first phase of collective action began in the South, where the Jim Crow system was challenged. Direct action took varied forms of peaceful confrontations with white rule. For example, in 1953 a boycott of city buses in Baton Rouge, Louisiana, challenged the "back of the bus" requirement. The local chapter of the NAACP was involved in this early, and partially successful, attempt to end segregation in public accommodations. Two years later a similar effort to end segregation on municipal buses began in Montgomery, Alabama. When Rosa Parks refused to take a seat in the back of the bus, she was arrested. Out of this not entirely spontaneous action, an ad hoc committee was formed to boycott the bus line. Through his early involvement in the Montgomery Improvement Association, Dr. Martin Luther King, Jr., was catapulted into national prominence. The boycott was a year-long struggle that sought to make a moral argument while exhibiting the economic clout of black consumers. Since 75 percent of the public transit riders were black, the boycott put the bus company in financial jeopardy and had a direct impact on city tax revenues. The movement combined protest tactics with court challenges, which proved to be successful as the federal courts ruled against segregated busing (Blumberg, 1984; Haines, 1988; Valocchi, 1996).

In varied ways in different locales, similar nonviolent actions were undertaken throughout the 1950s and into the early 1960s. These included sit-ins at segregated lunch counters, beginning with an initial demonstration at the Woolworth store in Greensboro, North Carolina. Several major episodes of this period occurred in a relatively short span of time. Among the most important was the CORE-initiated Freedom Rides. CORE sought implementation of the federal ban on segregated interstate buses and organized an unsuccessful attempt in Albany, Georgia, to desegregate public facilities and a similar campaign in Birmingham, Alabama, which was a success.

Closely linked to these efforts was work designed to overcome barriers to political involvement, particularly impediments to voting. Thus, in 1958 a voter registration drive was started in Tennessee's Fayette and Haywood counties. Similar drives were conducted in many places after 1960, especially in the Deep South. This activity culminated in 1964 with the implementation of Freedom Summer, a massive voter registration project in Mississippi that was made possible by an interracial coalition of civil rights volunteers, chiefly recruited from the North.

As Figure 6.1 indicates, the number of movement-initiated events grew slowly during the first half of the 1950s and increased thereafter; a dramatic escalation of activities occurred during the first half of the 1960s. In 1963 a massive march on Washington, D.C., took place, a little more than two decades after A. Philip Randolph had initially proposed such a protest. Two years later, with the voting rights struggle in Selma,

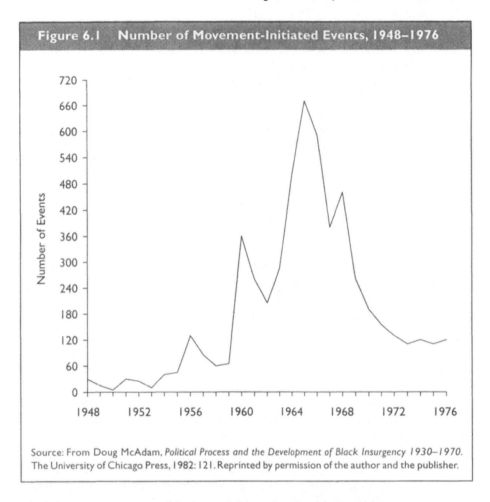

Figure 6.1   Number of Movement-Initiated Events, 1948–1976

Number of Events

Source: From Doug McAdam, *Political Process and the Development of Black Insurgency 1930–1970.* The University of Chicago Press, 1982: 121. Reprinted by permission of the author and the publisher.

Alabama, this phase of the civil rights movement, for all intents and purposes, came to an end (Garrow, 1978; Powledge, 1991).

White Responses to the Civil Rights Movement. Throughout this phase, the movement evoked varied responses from whites, but the challenge to the caste system began to undermine the paternalism that permeated it. For instance, wealthy whites who traditionally made donations to buy gifts for poor black children stopped doing so (Bloom, 1987). Their benevolence had been based on a sense of their own superiority and on the legitimacy of the "racial etiquette" of the South. The assertiveness of blacks was an indication to wealthy whites that these taken-for-granted assumptions were being seriously challenged.

On the one hand, black protest met stiff white resistance. This opposition to change entailed legislative challenges such as the gerrymandering law that was designed to prevent blacks from acquiring political power in Tuskegee, Alabama. It also involved defiance of court orders by southern politicians. The two most prominent challenges were Arkansas Governor Orval Faubus's attempt to stop the integration of Little Rock's Central High School and George Wallace's similar stance against the introduction of black students to the University of Alabama. Citizens Councils were founded in many communities to provide an organizational base for white resistance. Moreover, the Ku Klux Klan underwent a revival. Along with other white supremacist organizations, the Klan was responsible for a wave of violence, taking form in the beatings of Freedom Riders; numerous murders, including those of three volunteers—James Chaney, Mickey Schwerner, and Andrew Goodman—working for Freedom Summer; and bombings of churches and homes (Blumberg, 1984; McAdam, 1988).

On the other hand, many whites, especially outside of the South, began to react to the incidents of violence directed at unarmed, nonviolent protesters. The unleashing of police dogs on demonstrators, the wanton beatings, and similar events were documented and reached national (and international) audiences in daily newspapers, magazines, and television news. The leadership of the movement understood that if they were to be successful they had to dramatize racial injustice to what was a "conscience constituency." In appealing to an otherwise passive public, leaders hoped that citizens would demand that their elected officials undertake policies that would advance equality. Indeed, part of this constituency was composed of elected officials and, perhaps more indirectly, members of the judiciary.

Legislative and Judicial Decisions. The first major governmental decision came from the judiciary, and it occurred at the initial stage of protest activity. That decision was *Brown v. Board of Education of Topeka, Kansas* (1954), in which the segregation of public schools was declared to be unconstitutional. The Court argued—for the first time in its history basing a decision partly on the evidence amassed by social scientists—that segregated schools were inherently unequal. Therefore, the Court argued, the constitutional guarantee of equal treatment had been violated. Thus, the Supreme Court reversed *Plessy v. Ferguson* and with it the doctrine of separate but equal. A year later the court ruled that the implementation of this decision should occur "with all deliberate speed."

A decade later, the legislative centerpiece of the civil rights era became law: the 1964 Civil Rights Act, which contained a number of bans on discrimination, focused attention on employment discrimination (as well as discrimination by labor unions) and provided mechanisms to enforce educational integration. Although several other pieces of legislation and judicial decisions had a bearing on civil rights, two other acts combined with the Civil Rights Act to provide the most important bases for ending the Jim Crow era. These were the Voting Rights Act of 1965 and the Housing Act of 1968. The former banned the discriminatory use of literacy tests in voter registration (the poll tax was prohibited by a 1966 Supreme Court decision) and provided for the use of federal marshals to enforce voting rights (Haines, 1988). Title 8 of the latter act, or the Fair Housing Law, established provisions designed to promote open housing, although its enforcement mechanism was weak (Goering, 1986).

Phase II: Militancy and Black Nationalism

While these pieces of legislation were enacted into law, a second, far more militant phase of the movement commenced. Rod Bush (1999: 193) has referred to this as "the transformation from civil rights to black liberation." The militancy of the second half of the 1960s is partially attributable to the mutual reinforcement of the civil rights struggle with other social movements. Together they represented a generalized legitimation crisis. Thus, the black struggle for racial justice influenced the emergence of parallel movements in the Hispanic and American Indian (and, to a lesser extent, the Asian) communities. In addition, both the anti-Vietnam War movement and the youth counterculture attracted increased numbers of adherents and sympathizers. Not only were there important interconnections among these movements (for example, Martin Luther King, Jr., became increasingly vocal about his opposition to the Vietnam War during the last years of his life), but also their overarching impact on the nation presented a significant challenge to the status quo (Rollins, 1986). This is not to suggest, however, that there was a unified and coherent opposition. Serious and persistent tensions and conflicts existed among movements and within each movement.

Within the black community militancy was expressed in the form of Black Power, which was based ideologically, at least partially, on the position earlier espoused by Marcus Garvey. Some African American clergy were influenced by the powerful critique of American society offered by the black theology movement (Baer and Singer, 1992). The Black Power idea was first expressed by Stokely Carmichael in 1966 when he was working within the integrationist framework of the earlier phase. The two organizations most closely associated with the idea—the Black Muslims (the Nation of Islam) and the Black Panthers—were opposed to integration. They opted, in somewhat different ways, for separatism and **black nationalism** (Carmichael and Hamilton, 1967; Blumberg, 1984; Bush, 1999). Rather than attempting to break the barriers that had been erected during the Jim Crow era, black nationalists sought to achieve power and economic development while preserving racial autonomy. The Black Muslims, led by Elijah Muhammad, had been in existence for some time, but they were revitalized when Malcolm X rose to prominence. To the dismay of many Muslims, he split from the movement while rethinking his earlier positions and possibly moving to a new rapprochement with whites and with the mainstream of the civil rights movement. His assassination in 1965 ended this reevaluation and repositioning of his political views.

The Black Panthers were a product of the 1960s, formed by Huey Newton and Bobby Seale in Oakland, California, in 1966. The Panthers defined themselves as a self-defense organization, especially intent on protecting urban ghetto residents against police brutality (Blumberg, 1984). Their ideological position changed rapidly, to embrace a Third World perspective and, contrary to Garvey, condemn capitalism. Nonetheless, the actual program they advanced was reformist, replete with breakfast programs for schoolchildren and a presidential campaign by one of their chief figures, Eldridge Cleaver. In contrast, their style was that of the resistance fighter, and their leather jackets, berets, and weapons gave the public appearance of a militia. Their message was clear: they did not want in on the American dream, which they considered to be a nightmare (Killian, 1975; Bush, 1999).

The Panthers became the focus of intense political repression. According to Doug McAdam (1982: 219), "In the late 1960s law enforcement officials at all levels of government responded to what they perceived to be the growing threat posed by insurgents by initiating a stepped-up campaign of repression designed to destroy the black-power wing of the movement." The Panthers were a major object of the FBI's Counter-Intelligence Program (COINTELPRO) and the victims of various police assaults. One notorious case was the 1969 killing of Mark Clark and Fred Hampton by the Chicago police, who fired between 800 and 1,000 rounds of ammunition into the victims' apartment (Blumberg, 1984).

At the same time, a wave of urban riots swept the country, beginning as early as 1964 in Rochester, Harlem, and Philadelphia. Riots first acquired widespread national attention with the 1965 civil disorder in the Watts section of Los Angeles. During the next few years riots ultimately encompassed hundreds of cities, large and small (McPhail, 1971). These essentially spontaneous outbursts constituted a form of political theater acted out by relatively powerless people who had concluded that despite the changes that had occurred, their most basic grievances remained unmet. Hundreds of deaths and thousands of injuries resulted, and vast numbers of ghetto dwellers were arrested for violence and looting. Millions of dollars worth of property were destroyed or stolen during these uprisings, and in many places local and state police were joined by the National Guard, equipped with tanks and other military hardware reflecting an army occupation.

By the end of the decade the movement was winding down. Internal conflicts between various expressions of moderate support for integration and radical nationalism escalated and splintered the movement. Moderate organizations suffered from declines in outside financial support. The assassination of Martin Luther King, Jr., in 1968 robbed mainstream civil rights organizations of their most important national spokesperson. Repression and white backlash took a toll. The inability to achieve consensus about goals made cohesiveness impossible, mainly because the objective of ending Jim Crow had succeeded and a legislative apparatus was in place that provided mechanisms for addressing the legacy of the past (McAdam, 1982).

Two Controversies

Although white attitudes toward the issue of justice and equality for blacks changed appreciably between the 1940s and the end of the twentieth century, the principle of fair play did not necessarily translate into support for various policies to redress the legacy of segregation. This is evident in two highly controversial policies: busing and affirmative action.

Busing and School Desegregation

Busing was a mechanism for assisting in the **desegregation** of public schools. The initial phase of school desegregation entailed prohibiting legally mandated, or de jure, segregation. The focus was on the South. When the *Brown* ruling was made, less than one tenth of 1 percent of black students in eleven southern states attended school with whites. Although many southern white elites determined that change would occur and began to develop desegregation plans, resistance to **integration** was intense in many places. The conflict was felt throughout the South, but racial politics in Little Rock, Arkansas, riveted the attention of the nation and reflected the dilemmas of change in the face of resistance. In Little Rock, local school administrators, with the support of some white business elites, began a plan to integrate the all-white Central High School. The plan was opposed by many whites. By 1956, however, some in the black community decided that the school system was not moving with "all deliberate speed." So they filed a lawsuit in federal court to bring the power of the federal courts into the dispute.

The school superintendent went forward with his plan, but as it was to be implemented in 1957, Governor Orval Faubus intervened to prevent the plan from being carried out. This resulted in a conflict between the state and federal governments and culminated in President Eisenhower's decision to send National Guard troops to enforce the desegregation order. The citizens of the city responded the following year by voting to close the schools to terminate the integration policy. Ultimately, a coalition of influential and powerful white moderates intent on a peaceful transition from segregation waged a successful campaign, and the schools were reopened. Integration proceeded without widespread disruption. This leadership entered into a working relationship with the black community, and during the next few years, according to Irving Spitzberg, Jr. (1987: 9), the local economic elite, "on its own and apart from the public governmental system, desegregated many sectors of the economy as well as maintained modest desegregation in the schools."

This local initiative occurred in many other southern communities, but where it did not, involuntary, court-ordered integration plans were enacted. By the time the Civil Rights Act had passed in 1964, the percentage of blacks attending schools with whites stood at only 2 percent. Desegregation plans were enacted throughout the South by utilizing a provision of the act that granted to the Department of Health, Education, and Welfare the ability to impose financial sanctions on noncompliant school systems by cutting federal funding. By 1973, 46 percent of blacks in the South attended integrated schools.

Judicial Decisions. The trend toward integration was further enhanced by several Supreme Court decisions. In *Green v. New Kent Co.* (1968), the Court ruled that freedom-of-choice plans were an unacceptable remedy to segregation, and in *Alexander v. Holmes* (1969) the Court moved beyond the "with all deliberate speed" framework to order the immediate desegregation of all southern schools (Jaynes and Williams, 1989). Finally, the *Swann v. Charlotte-Mecklenberg* (1971) case addressed the link between residential and school segregation, arguing that desegregation plans could not be limited to schools a student could walk to. Therefore, busing was an appropriate tool for achieving integration. This decision also raised the possibility that busing could go beyond established school district lines if residential segregation was so pronounced that the goal of integration could not be achieved within a district. Specifically, this idea introduced the possibility of incorporating suburbs into the desegregation plans of cities.

This particular court case had implications that went beyond the South. Included in the mandate to promote racial integration in American schools was the elimination not only of de jure segregation but also of de facto segregation. In many northern cities, residential segregation was more pronounced than in the South, and where neighborhood schools existed, segregated schools were the inevitable result. De facto segregation was specifically declared to be unconstitutional in *Keyes v. Denver School District No. 1* (1973).

White Opposition. Nowhere was the conflict between the opponents and supporters of busing more acrimonious than in Boston, where Federal District Court Judge W. Arthur Garrity developed a plan that met with stiff resistance. Many lower-middle-class and working-class white ethnics, especially Italians and Irish, felt that they were being treated unfairly because the impact of busing would be felt at their local schools and on their children. They argued that it would not have an impact on the children of affluent middle-class citizens who either sent their children to private schools or lived in suburbs that would be untouched by the plan. For their part, white supporters of the plan often viewed the opponents as uneducated bigots.

Certainly, racism was a major factor in the busing controversy. Thomas Cottle (1976: 2) reported the reaction of one white student, who argued, "Nobody's busing me just so some niggers can get a better deal." As Ronald P. Formisano's (1991) case study of Boston indicated, however, the reality was more complicated, and the conflict cannot be reduced solely to racism. A core of anti-busing activists caught the attention of the media, and they had a constituency in white ethnic enclaves such as South Boston. According to Formisano, however, many whites were willing to give busing a chance. In addition, reasons other than simple racism accounted for a position against busing. For residents of working-class neighborhoods, the local school was seen as an integral part of the local community, a community that residents did not want to leave or see their children leave. Busing was seen as an assault on the neighborhood.

For white parents, the prospect of their children being shipped into lower-class black neighborhoods evoked fears of crime and drugs. Formisano (1991) observed that black-on-white crime was a troublesome reality and not simply a rationalization for racist hostility. Moreover, many blacks were at best ambivalent about busing. In one black neighborhood, there was dismay over the fact that an excellent school would have introduced whites, while many blacks in the area would have been bused elsewhere in the city. Some blacks argued that what they wanted was local neighborhood control of schools, not integration.

Social Contact or White Flight. Although the conflict in Boston was more intense than in many other places—where, in fact, integration plans were implemented without controversy—Boston nonetheless served as a microcosm of national patterns. It reflected the dilemmas caused by the unintended consequences of busing. The purpose of busing was to facilitate racial harmony by overcoming social distance between the races. Research had tested the hypothesis that increased social contact yielded more positive race relations over time (Zeul and Humphrey, 1971). This assumption underpinned school integration plans. In addition, research initially conducted by James Coleman and his associates (1966), and confirmed by subsequent studies, concluded that students from lower socioeconomic backgrounds benefited from the presence in schools of students from higher socioeconomic backgrounds. Meanwhile, the latter group did not perform less well because of the presence of the former. Together, these findings seemed to confirm the beneficial nature of policies designed to promote integration.

What policymakers had not foreseen, however, was the exodus of whites from urban public schools. In Boston, for example, 60 percent of students were white in 1973. By 1988 that figure had plummeted to 26 percent, and a disproportionate number of those whites attended a few prestigious schools in the system rather than being dispersed throughout the city. This phenomenon became known as **white flight,** and it took two main forms: moving from urban to suburban school districts and enrolling students in parochial schools or, especially in the South, in newly created "Christian academies." James Coleman, Sara Kelly, and John Moore (1975) concluded that white flight was so pervasive that it rendered busing a failed remedy.

Although the relationship between white flight and busing is complicated and somewhat uncertain, by 1980 in many urban public schools whites made up a small minority of the student population (Pettigrew and Green, 1976; Rossell, 1976, 1988; Farley, Richards, and Wurdock, 1980). For instance, the white student population in the nation's capital was only 4 percent, and it was only 8 percent in Atlanta, 9 percent in Newark, and 12 percent in Detroit (Orfield, 1983; Jaynes and Williams, 1989). Even within schools a form of "resegregation within desegregated schools" often occurred as special academic programs effectively created what amounted to two schools within one, and each was racially quite distinct (Jaynes and Williams, 1989).

The reason for white opposition to busing has been the object of scholarly debate. David Sears and Donald Kinder (1985: 1141) contended that opposition is an expression of what they refer to as **symbolic racism.** They saw symbolic racism as having "its roots both in early-learned racial fears and stereotypes," and therefore having "little to do with the direct, tangible threats blacks might pose." In short, opposition is the consequence of early childhood socialization and does not derive from a perception of real intergroup conflict.

This position has been challenged by others. Lawrence Bobo (1983) did not deny the lingering impact of prejudicial attitudes derived early in life, but he argued that this is not a sufficient explanation. Rather, he concluded that when whites perceive black demands and potential gains as detrimental to white self-interest, they resist change. In effect, if whites think that their lifestyle and well-being are being jeopardized in a zero-sum game—one in which black gains necessarily are made at the expense of whites—they will be opposed to the demands put forth by the civil rights movement. Bobo (1983: 1208) argued that group conflict can best explain opposition, for whites opposed to such policies as busing "need not hold blatantly stereotypical beliefs or hostile orientations toward blacks."

Bobo's claims were supported by two carefully documented case studies of the school districts in Los Angeles and Baton Rouge conducted by Christine Rossell (1988). She found that real costs are attached to school desegregation for some whites. When the costs are weighed, a decision is made to either comply with the requirements of a busing plan or exit the school system. For example, white parents are less willing to permit their child to be bused to another school if that school has (or is perceived to have) lower average achievement scores or if such a move puts them with a student population from a lower social class than that of their previous school.

Because of the controversy generated by busing, black support declined from 78 percent in 1964 to 55 percent in 1978. Nonetheless, by that latter date, much of the tension had appreciably subsided. Many blacks have argued that they would prefer to see greater attention paid to improving the quality of public school education than to integration. Jaynes and Williams (1989) noted that the major strides toward school integration took place between 1966 and 1973, during which time conflict was at its highest. Rossell (1976; 1988) found that white opposition to busing was at its highest during the first year of desegregation. A decade later, both black and white parents of children being bused found busing to be generally satisfactory, while a majority of students nationwide believed that busing improved race relations and black academic achievement (Hochschild, 1985; Jaynes and Williams, 1989).

The federal government shifted its orientation toward school desegregation during the Reagan Administration. Not only did its Justice Department refuse to support pending desegregation litigation, it sought to undo existing desegregation plans. With the Supreme Court's 1991 ruling in *Oklahoma City v. Dowell,* the legal hurdle for desegregation plans was raised. Reagan's successor George H. W. Bush continued the neoconservative policies of Reagan. Although Bill Clinton's administration was more supportive of desegregation, it had little to show for it, and the current Bush administration has expressed no inclination to promote school integration. Not surprisingly, a recent study conducted by Harvard University's Civil Rights Project found that during the past two decades schools have begun to resegregate (Frankenberg, Lee, and Orfield, 2003). As Figure 6.2 reveals, in 2000 over 70 percent of black students attended predominantly minority schools, including 38 percent that attended intensely segregated schools. Thus, a half century after the *Brown* decision, the evidence points to losing ground in the quest to integrate schools, leading Gary Orfield, one of the authors of the report, to conclude, "We are not back to where we were before Brown, but we are back to when King was assassinated" (Dobbs, 2004: 1).

Affirmative Action

The busing issue had become a less burning issue by the end of the twentieth century, but affirmative action continues to spark intense debate (Skrentny, 1996). Those supporting the policy viewed **affirmative action** as a means for redressing past inequities. This position was aptly reflected in President Lyndon Johnson's 1965 speech at Howard University, where he said, "You do not take a person who for years has been hobbled by chains, and liberate him, bring him up to the starting line, and then say, 'You are free to compete with all the others.' " On the other hand, opponents perceived it as a form of **reverse discrimination.** They felt that affirmative action permits unwarranted compensa-

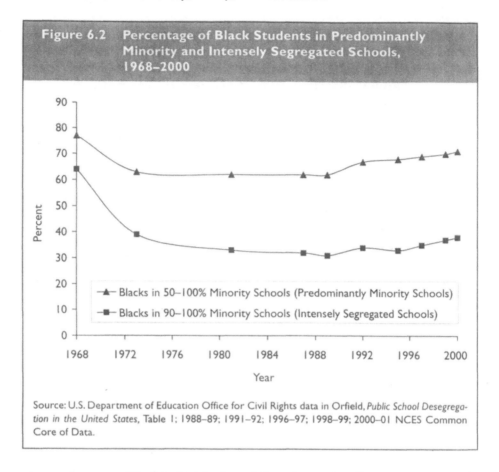

Figure 6.2   Percentage of Black Students in Predominantly Minority and Intensely Segregated Schools, 1968–2000

Source: U.S. Department of Education Office for Civil Rights data in Orfield, *Public School Desegregation in the United States*, Table 1; 1988–89; 1991–92; 1996–97; 1998–99; 2000–01 NCES Common Core of Data.

tion to less qualified individuals, while adversely affecting individuals who have not practiced discrimination (Glazer, 1975; Pinkney, 1984; Sowell, 1989).

Affirmative action is not concerned with racial integration per se but rather with improving the socioeconomic status of blacks (and other minorities). The rationale behind affirmative action plans is that merely terminating discriminatory laws and policies does not result in racial equity. This is because over time such historical practices have enhanced the position of whites in their socioeconomic location at the expense of blacks. Indeed, in many instances after the Civil War blacks were forced out of skilled jobs that they held. They thereby became victims of downward social mobility caused by racism and not by merit. The argument by supporters of affirmative action is that if parity is ever to be achieved, it will have to directly confront and remedy this historical legacy. Affirmative action reflects a shift in concern from equal rights to genuinely equal opportunity (Ezorsky, 1991).

The focus of affirmative action plans has been on employment and education. The constitutional basis of affirmative action is part of the debate. In the opinion of Stanford Lyman (1991), the abolition of slavery by the Thirteenth Amendment to the Constitution carries a mandate to

> remove the badges of slavery from all those to whom they are still affixed. The forms of race discrimination that derive their authority from the more than two centuries of involuntary servitude are the evil manifestation of such badges, and are, hence, the proper objects of legislative attention with respect to effecting the public interest. (200)

Although this argument can serve as a persuasive constitutional rationale for general plans of affirmative action, the legal basis for the specific shape of current affirmative action policies is exceedingly complex. Efforts at enforcing nondiscrimination were evident as early as the presidency of Franklin D. Roosevelt, who during World War II issued an executive order that opened defense-plant jobs to blacks. His successor, Harry S. Truman, proposed an expanded federal policy requiring equal employment opportunities. John F. Kennedy, through Executive Order 10925, prohibited racial discrimination by contractors doing business with the federal government and set up guidelines that were designed to encourage the hiring of blacks. During this administration the phrase "affirmative action" first came into use.

Implementation. The most important legal basis for affirmative action, however, derived from Title VII of the 1964 Civil Rights Act. The act was not limited to the government or to businesses that have government contracts. Rather, it banned discrimination in all aspects of employment and established the Equal Employment Opportunity Commission (EEOC) to investigate complaints and to refer violators to the U.S. Department of Justice, which had the charge of prosecuting violators of antidiscrimination laws. This legislation was soon linked to President Johnson's Executive Order 11246, which mandated the creation of affirmative action plans that were to indicate the steps an employer

Black and white college students reacting to the announcement of the O. J. Simpson verdict.

was going to take to correct existing deficiencies (Jaynes and Williams, 1989). Affirmative action applied not only to employers but also to labor unions and to colleges and universities.

One way of designing affirmative action plans was to establish concrete goals and timetables for achieving those goals. This approach was first advanced during Richard Nixon's administration. The administration's "Philadelphia Plan" required contractors doing business with the federal government to set numerical goals in the hiring of minority workers. In 1972 legislation was enacted, amending the 1964 Civil Rights Act, that granted to courts the power to enforce affirmative action measures. Implementation of this enforcement provision occurred during the same year, as the state of Alabama was required by federal court order to hire one black state trooper for each white hired. This policy was to continue until blacks held one-fourth of the positions on the force (Hacker, 1992). This particular shift in policy raised the politically controversial debate over quotas (Glazer, 1975; Fullinwider, 1980; Sowell, 1989).

Legal Challenges. Not long after the implementation of affirmative action plans throughout the nation, opponents filed a series of court challenges. They argued that these plans, especially those with numerical quotas, constituted a form of reverse discrimination in which whites who themselves had not discriminated were being unfairly made to pay the price for the policies of the past. What such arguments tended to avoid addressing was that whites as a group had been the beneficiaries of historical practice. Although not always explicitly stated, underlying the charge of reverse discrimination was the belief that blacks were being given unjust preferential treatment insofar as less-qualified blacks obtained positions at the expense of higher-qualified whites.

A series of important early court challenges to affirmative action occurred during the 1970s. These included *Anderson v. S.F. Unified School District* (1971), which questioned San Francisco's plan for increasing the number of minority school administrators, and *DeFunis v. Odegaard*, a case that challenged the University of Washington's law school minority recruitment plan. The most significant case was decided in 1978, however, in *Allan Bakke v. Regents of the University of California*. Bakke had been denied entrance to the medical school at the University of California, Davis. The basis for his complaint that he had been unfairly denied admission derived from the fact that 16 of the 100 slots available at the school were targeted for "economically and/or educationally disadvantaged persons," which could have included whites but in practice had meant racial minorities (Sindler, 1978). Bakke contended that such preferential treatment amounted to illegal discrimination. The university countered with the claim that their admissions plan increased the number of heretofore underrepresented groups in the student body.

Implicit in Bakke's position was the conviction that the sole criterion for admissions should be merit. This position raises two issues. The first involves what is and what is not an appropriate test of merit. Although some would argue that standardized tests, such as the Medical College Admissions Test (MCAT), are a valid measure of aptitude, others see such tests as biased in various ways. Critics see standardized tests as not only racially biased but also biased toward people who have a facility for this particular form of testing, which places a premium on multiple-choice rather than essay questions and on factual retention rather than reflective thinking (Hacker, 1992). In any event, blacks as a group do not fare nearly as well as whites on standardized tests.

The second issue concerns the range of factors that institutions of higher education use in admission decisions. Colleges and universities have used and continue to use a variety of selection criteria that are not based on merit. To create a more cosmopolitan atmosphere, considerations are given to applicants based on their location in the country. Thus, a midwestern school might be particularly interested in students from either coast. College athletes are admitted partly by athletic ability, permitting their admission despite the fact that they are less academically qualified than others. Moreover, the children of privilege have often been granted special dispensations at elite institutions. As Andrew Hacker (1992) wrote,

> For years, so-called selective colleges have set less demanding standards for admitting children of alumni. (This by itself should show that affirmative action has a venerable history.) These privileged offspring know full well that other applicants with better records received rejection letters. Yet few of them are seen slouching around campus, their heads bowed in shame. (129)

In the *Bakke* case, the Supreme Court ruled against the school's special admissions program and ordered Bakke admitted. In a second part of the ruling, however, the Court concluded that ethnic and racial background could be one factor among others in determining admissions. Seen by most observers as a compromise, the ruling did not deny the constitutionality of affirmative action.

Bakke was followed by several other court decisions that addressed various other aspects of affirmative action plans. An important case in the area of employment was *Weber v. Kaiser Aluminum and Chemical Corporation* (1979). The company and the United Steel Workers Union had formulated a plan to increase the number of blacks in skilled labor positions. Brian Weber, a white worker, filed suit on the grounds that he had been denied admission to a skilled crafts on-the-job training program despite having more seniority with the company than many black candidates. The court did not rule in his favor but instead concluded that voluntary goals and timetables such as those established jointly by the company and union were constitutionally permissible (Feinberg,

1985; Pinkney, 1987). Together, these two decisions were hailed by supporters of affirmative action and decried by opponents.

A conservative political agenda gained the upper hand in 1980, when Ronald Reagan was elected to the presidency, and continued into the Bush administration. One centerpiece of this agenda was a call for the elimination of affirmative action programs. Throughout the 1980s the executive branch urged the judicial branch to reverse earlier court decisions that legitimated this remedy to racial inequality. During this time a number of aging liberal members of the Supreme Court retired and were replaced by conservatives chosen by Presidents Reagan and Bush. The culmination of this process occurred when Justice Thurgood Marshall was replaced by Clarence Thomas. Marshall was an appointee of Lyndon Johnson. He had worked earlier as a lawyer for the Legal Defense Fund of the NAACP and served as their counsel in the *Brown v. Board of Education* case. In contrast, Thomas, who as a graduate of Yale University's law school had been a direct beneficiary of affirmative action, became an ardent neoconservative and quickly made his mark as one of the relatively few blacks appointed to important positions in the first Bush administration.

Although the Supreme Court now has a clear conservative majority, it did not during much of the 1980s. Instead, it was a deeply divided body, which was reflected in the affirmative action cases. On the one hand, several decisions upheld the constitutionality of affirmative action. Included in such decisions was *United States v. Paradise*, a challenge to the previously noted Alabama state police hiring plan. On the other hand, in the 1984 *Firefighters Local Union No. 1784 v. Stotts* case, the court ruled that the city of Memphis, Tennessee, was within its rights to maintain a seniority system that meant that blacks, as the last hired, would be the first fired.

During the 1990s the future of affirmative action was severely tested. In 1995, the U.S. Court of Appeals for the Fifth District ruled in *Hopwood v. Texas* that the affirmative action plan at the University of Texas Law School had discriminated against a white woman who had been denied admission while some black and Mexican applicants with lower test scores and grades were admitted (Swain, 2001). In the following year, the voters of California passed Proposition 209, an anti-affirmative action state constitutional amendment, by a 54 to 46 percent margin (Chávez, 1998). Around the same time, two cases at the University of Michigan—one at the undergraduate level and the other in the law school—presented further challenges. Unlike *Hopwood*, which the Supreme Court declined to hear, both of these cases were accepted by the Court for consideration.

Supporters and opponents of affirmative action mobilized in an effort to influence the decision. The administration of George W. Bush sided with opponents of affirmative action. In contrast, a huge number of friend of the court briefs were filed not only by civil rights organiza-

Black firefighters in Detroit demonstrating firehouse cooking.

tions and churches but by universities, corporations, and the U.S. military. This support is a reflection of John David Skrentny's (2000: 282) claim that by the beginning of the twenty-first century affirmative action had become "a taken-for-granted way of doing things in our nation's largest corporations, in many universities, and for policy-makers working in civil rights."

In June 2003 the Supreme Court handed down its decisions in the two cases. In *Gratz v. Bollinger,* the undergraduate case, the Court ruled by a 6-3 margin in favor of the plaintiff, contending that the university's plan was too formulaic and thus like a quota system, which had been forbidden by the *Bakke* decision. However, in *Grutter v. Bollinger* the Court concluded by a 5-4 margin that the law school plan, because the decision-making process was more individualized, was constitutional. Moreover, the majority opinion powerfully endorsed the continuing need for affirmative action in order to address the legacy of racism. Opponents on the Court were equally assertive in their criticism of the decision, reflecting the highly contested nature of affirmative action. The mixed responses of the Supreme Court are also an indication of the legal complexity of these issues. Despite this, to date affirmative action remains a constitutionally permissible means of redressing a legacy of racial inequity.

Changes in Public Opinion and Political Orientations. The American public is deeply split over whether or not policies that entail preferential treatment are acceptable. Prior to the civil rights movement, the majority of white Americans did not agree with the claim that blacks should have the same chance as whites to obtain any job. In 1944, for example, only 45 percent of whites agreed. In the ensuing several decades, that assessment changed dramatically, so that by 1972, 97 percent of whites agreed (Lipset and Schneider, 1978; Schuman, Steeh, and Bobo, 1985; Beer, 1987; Sigelman and Welch, 1991). Thus, there appears to be a consensus about the ideal of equal opportunity.

The conflict derives from disagreement over the appropriate mechanisms for ensuring equal opportunity. Sigelman and Welch (1991) analyzed a variety of survey results on this issue. They concluded that it is difficult to provide a simple assessment of white or black attitudes regarding the appropriateness of affirmative action. Depending on the question and on what the respondent considers is and is not contained under this rubric, responses vary widely. They noted that some surveys suggest widespread support for affirmative action among both blacks and whites, citing respective levels of support as 96 percent for blacks and 76 percent for whites. Other surveys paint a very different picture, with low levels of support reported for both races: 23 percent for blacks and 9 percent for whites. For both races, the word *quota* conjures up negative reactions. Blacks are far more likely to conclude that without affirmative action blacks would not have fared as well as they have in recent years; furthermore, they are only half as likely as whites to conclude that affirmative action inevitably leads to reverse discrimination.

The specter of quotas provided conservative politicians with an effective racially divisive weapon. When George Bush the elder ran for the presidency, he persistently proclaimed his opposition to quotas. (Although he did not choose to broadcast this fact in 1988, in the 1960s he—like his predecessor, Ronald Reagan—had also opposed the 1964 Civil Rights Act.) Part of the electoral success of Ronald Reagan and George Bush can be attributed to the defection from the Democratic party by a bloc of working-class whites who believed that they, and not those higher on the socioeconomic ladder, were paying the price of black advancement. George W. Bush has been even more critical of affirmative action than his father, even though he was the beneficiary of the legacy program at Yale, which might reasonably be defined as an affirmative action program for the rich and powerful.

The unraveling of the New Deal coalition, which had, among other things, brought blacks and blue-collar whites into the Democratic party, was a consequence of the perception that American society was addressing its racial problems by constructing what amounted to a zero-sum game: black gains were being achieved at the expense of whites. This attitude was exploited by the conservative Senator Jesse Helms, in his close electoral race in 1990 with Harvey Gantt, who was black. Helms ran a television advertisement that depicted a white who had been denied a job, and it asked the question: "You needed that job, and you were the best qualified. But they gave it to a minority because of a racial quota. Is that really fair?" Despite limited empirical evidence that whites have in any significant way lost out to racial minorities in the quest for jobs, this belief is deeply held by many conservatives, and for this reason it continues to contribute to opposition to affirmative action (Steinberg, 2000; Pincus, 2003).

The Unintended Consequences of Affirmative Action. Some liberals who support affirmative action in principle have been concerned that the unintended conflict it has generated can work against black advancement in the long run. Therefore, they have called for efforts to pursue alternative policies that would unite rather than divide the potential coalitions in the American political arena (Killian, 1991). Stephen Steinberg (2000) has referred to this reaction as "liberal capitulation." On the other hand, some individuals who at one point had questioned affirmative action have, on further reflection, revised their position. Thus, Harvard University sociologist Nathan Glazer, who had earlier leveled the charge of reverse discrimination, changed his mind by the beginning of the new century. African American sociologist William Julius Wilson (1978) concluded a quarter of a century ago that it would be better to place a premium on what he refers to as universal entitlement programs than to maintain race-specific governmental social welfare policies. His assessment was based on the assumption that across-the-board entitlement programs—a good example being Social Security—are far more popular and more immune to attack by opponents of the welfare state than are programs targeted to particular audiences, such as racial minorities or the poor. It should be noted that Wilson was not opposed to affirmative action per se. Rather, he was concerned that it can produce a political impasse that, by generating a powerful white backlash, might result in stymieing reform. Policies aimed at full employment would, in Wilson's view, have more beneficial consequences than race-specific policies. At the same time, the persistence of racially based inequalities also led him to conclude that class-specific policies are not adequate substitutes for race-specific ones. He has suggested that by reframing the very idea of affirmative action to one of "affirmative opportunity," it might be possible to elicit greater support from whites (Wilson, 1999).

An important question is: Who among blacks are the main beneficiaries of affirmative action? Andrew Hacker (1992) argued that in the competitive quest for jobs, whites in highly trained and well-paid occupations face little threat to their economic livelihood from policies designed to grant preferences in job allocation to blacks. Rather, this threat is confronted by working-class and lower-middle-class whites. He wrote, "One of the chief effects of affirmative action has been to pit whites with modest aspirations against blacks who want better lives for themselves" (131). Wilson (1978) would not agree, though his position should not be seen as a total rejection of Hacker's. According to Wilson, blacks already in the middle class and those poised to enter it, as well as more highly skilled working-class blacks, are those in a position to benefit from affirmative action. Poor blacks have not benefited. This position was supported by Feinberg (1985), who considered the economic growth of the 1950–1970 period (when a tight labor supply forced employers to hire blacks) to have been the primary cause for economic gains experienced by poor blacks. The growth of the black middle class since 1970 is attributable, in part, to the role of affirmative action. We will consider the connection between class and race in more detail later.

The idea of **stigmatized achievement** is noted by opponents and allies of affirmative action alike (Carter, 1991; Steele, 1990; Sowell, 1981b). This idea refers to the belief held by many that blacks have succeeded because of two standards, one based on achievement for whites and the other on racial criteria for blacks. The result is that the genuine achievements of blacks are not appreciated, and blacks are forced to confront suspicions that they are not really as qualified as their white peers. Although how white peers perceive them is no doubt a real concern to many blacks, in a recent study of 100 black men and women in professional and executive positions, Lois Benjamin (1991) did not see this concern translated into feelings of inferiority. On the contrary, her respondents viewed themselves not only as capable, but as having to overcome obstacles that whites did not have to confront in achieving success.

Improvement or Decline?

All of this discussion leads to a simple question: Have the conditions of blacks improved in terms of educational attainment, occupational location, and income? It is not surprising to learn that blacks have a less optimistic assessment than whites about the extent to which improvement in the black community has occurred since the civil rights era. For one thing, blacks believe that prejudice and discrimination remain a far more consequential force in their lives than whites assume to be the case. Furthermore, although blacks as a group indicate a positive assessment about change during the past two decades, not all blacks concur. Many believe the situation of black America has either remained unchanged or has gotten worse (Tuch and Martin, 1997; Sigelman and Welch, 1991; Jaynes and Williams, 1989; Schuman, Steeh, and Bobo, 1985).

These differing perceptions are partly due to very different life experiences, but the course of change has also produced mixed results. Since 1940 a sharp increase has been seen in the percentage of both blacks and whites completing high school, and during this period the gap in years of school completed by blacks and whites born since the late 1950s has nearly disappeared. Black rates of enrollment in college rose from the 1950s to the late 1970s, but since then have declined. The rate of college enrollment peaked in 1977 as slightly less than one out of two black high school graduates entered college. Furthermore, at that time, the figure for blacks was only a few percentage points lower than that for whites. Within half a decade, however, the gap had reappeared as white rates of enrollment rose to around 60 percent, while black rates dropped to about 40 percent (Farley and Allen, 1989; Jaynes and Williams, 1989; Farley, 1984).

Blacks continue to be educationally disadvantaged. Less money is spent educating black children compared with white students (Nettles and Orfield, 2000). Early intervention to assist disadvantaged children, seen especially in the Head Start program, has been quite successful. Unfortunately, such programs are underfunded and cannot meet the need. Moreover, intervention programs to address the problems of older students at risk of dropping out are inadequate, with the result being that black dropout rates exceed those of whites (Nettles and

Orfield, 2000). Various standardized measures of educational achievement indicate blacks do not do as well as whites, although there is evidence that the achievement gap between whites and blacks has narrowed during the past three decades (Ferguson, 2001). Research by James Coleman, Thomas Hoffer, and Sally Kilgore (1981), which indicated that students in private and parochial schools were more successful than public school students, suggests part of the problem. Black children are far more likely to attend public schools than whites, and in these institutions achievement is lowest. Conservatives have argued that a remedy is to force public schools to operate in a marketplace in which students are treated as consumers who can pick and choose among the schools in the area. These are generally referred to as *choice* or *voucher* plans.

This view fails to consider one important fact. School integration was only partially successful, which means that in many instances blacks and whites continue to attend racially segregated schools. Integration has occurred in many areas of the rural South and in the region's smaller and medium-sized cities, as well as in areas where school districts are county systems that link urban and suburban schools. Elsewhere, most blacks attend urban schools, while most whites in public schools reside and go to school in the suburbs (Farley, 1984). Be-

---

Voices	**Robert Moses**

We're now confronted by the fact that the whole society has invested in education as our main opportunity structure, and we're trying to get our own group in. I think we've got a couple more generations if we are able to make this strategic change.

There is a legacy from slavery and afterwards where the country agreed to set up sharecropping and sharecropper education tied to work in the fields and low expectations for black children. This was exported around the country during the 40s and 50s. The goal of The Algebra Project is to put a floor under all the children in the country, so that they have the option, when they graduate, to go to college if they exercise that option, and not have to remediate any subject area.

This is the goal, and I think it is necessary to get people ready for citizenship. The sharecroppers we worked with in the 60s were serfs of the industrial economy. The country is growing with a city-serfdom now, with young people who either graduate or drop out without the tools needed to access the economic opportunities sufficiently to support themselves and their families.

We want to end that.

Robert Moses, an important SNCC leader during the 1960s, is today a key organizer of a math literacy program called The Algebra Project (<http://www.blackdigital.com/archives/algebra.project/html>).

cause public schools are funded primarily by local property taxes and because the class character of suburbs means that they have a far more solid tax base than cities, considerably more is spent per student on suburbanites than on their urban counterparts. Suburbanites have resisted attempts to bring urban blacks into their schools, and there is no reason to assume that various choice or voucher proposals would change that.

The economic status of blacks as a whole improved compared with that of whites between 1940 and 1970, but since then black incomes have leveled off or declined (Jaynes and Williams, 1989). There is a bifurcation within black America between a now relatively sizable middle class and a remaining core of poor blacks, who have a poverty rate more than twice the national average (Ferguson, 1996; Farley, 1990).

Housing and Residential Segregation

Housing policies have also been the source of intense political conflict. An important connection exists between race and economic status when it comes to the provision of decent, safe, and affordable housing, which is a right of all Americans according to the Housing Act of 1949. Actually, the topic of housing must be sorted into two related but nonetheless distinct issues. The first involves the link between race and poverty and raises the topic of subsidized housing. This issue concerns the extent to which poor blacks are or are not able to obtain and pay for housing that meets certain minimum quality standards. The second issue deals with housing discrimination and pertains not only to poor blacks but also to working-class and middle-class blacks seeking housing in white neighborhoods.

Public Housing

The United States was slow to establish laws aimed at improving the housing conditions of its citizens. Furthermore, to this date the United States has resisted creating universal entitlement programs, despite the ideal set forth in the 1949 housing legislation. Throughout the nation's history, powerful economic interests have resisted state intervention in housing markets. There has been little support for the public ownership and management of housing (Fisher, 1959; Friedman, 1978). Only during the Depression did a coalition of labor, social reformers, religious leaders, and the construction industry push successfully for the passage of the United States Housing Act of 1937. This legislation provided only a limited role for governmentally run housing. Such housing was designed for the poor alone, and in this regard the public housing program differed from those in other industrial nations, such as Great Britain, where council estates were also intended to meet the housing needs of the middle class.

The reason for this limited government role was that the real estate industry convinced Congress that the government should not compete with private industry for tenants. Considering the poor to be incapable of generating profits for the industry, industry representatives were willing to concede that part of the market to the government. Public housing was built with federal monies, but the projects were managed by local housing authorities, who were required to charge rents high enough to cover operating costs. As a result, the poorest of the poor were excluded from the program because they could not afford the rents. Because blacks were overrepresented in the ranks of this lowest socioeconomic stratum, this policy had a negative impact on them.

The majority of public housing residents during the 1940s and 1950s were white. Moreover, segregated public housing projects were customary. New Haven, Connecticut, was one of the first cities to open public housing projects, and its approach was typical of cities throughout much of the country. At essentially the same time, three projects were built. Elm Haven in the black ghetto around Dixwell Avenue was solely occupied by blacks, while both Farnham Courts and Quinnipiac Terrace were located in white ethnic neighborhoods and were occupied entirely by white ethnics, predominately Italians and Irish.

By excluding the middle class from participation, public housing never gained the level of public support that council housing did in Great Britain (Bredemeier, 1955). A consequence of the limited scope of public housing was that during the post-World War II prosperity period, the program was vulnerable to attack by political critics. A submerged white working and middle class came out of the Depression and the war and, in this period of unprecedented affluence, found opportunities to purchase homes, largely by moving out of cities and into growing suburbs. Thus, throughout the 1950s and into the 1960s, the tenants of public housing were increasingly black and were poorer than before (Kivisto, 1986). As such, public housing is an example of what Kevin Fox Gotham (2002: 27) refers to as the "racialization of space."

Hundreds of thousands of substandard housing units were demolished in slum clearance efforts. Urban renewal was an attempt to rejuvenate center cities, and linked to the plan was a call for constructing more public housing. Actually, Congress called for a 1:1 equation: For each unit of housing demolished, one should be built to replace it. Construction fell far short of this goal. Moreover, instead of the low-density, low-rise projects built in the first decade of the program, new units tended to be high-density, high-rise developments. This approach was seen as a cost-cutting mechanism—large projects suggested economies of scale. A second factor was that by building more low-density scattered sites, many public housing projects—now increasingly occupied by blacks—would have to be located in white neighborhoods. White resistance to residential integration stymied such efforts. Mayors and other local officials thought it would mean political suicide to push such proposals. They found it expedient to build huge developments, such as Chicago's Robert Taylor Homes, in black ghettos.

These projects proved to be failures. Instead of being seen as part of the solution to the problem of poverty, public housing acquired the reputation of being part of the problem. By 1965 a majority of public housing residents were black (Freeman, 1969). Their poverty made it impossible for them to pay rents that would cover operating costs, so maintenance suffered. This period saw a dramatic increase in the number of female-headed households, who were generally supported by Aid to Families with Dependent Children (AFDC) payments. Such social problems as truancy and school dropouts, child abuse, alcohol and drug abuse, and crime escalated.

Public housing projects were increasingly described as "vertical ghettos," "federal slums," and "warehouses for the poor" (Moore, 1969; Rainwater, 1970; Savas, 1979). Perhaps the most dramatic indication of this view was the fate of the Pruitt-Igoe project in St. Louis. This high-rise development, built in the 1950s, was the recipient of a major architectural award. Within a decade, however, the project experienced such serious problems that the only solution the city concluded was reasonable was to demolish it. Nonetheless, public housing remains an important source of housing for very poor families, particularly those headed by women. The political struggles of tenants in these housing developments is shaped by the combined impact of racial exclusion, class-based inequalities, and gender (Williams, 2004).

Alternatives to Public Housing

President Lyndon Johnson attempted to expand the welfare state legacy that first emerged during the New Deal in his call for a Great Society and in his War on Poverty. This period yielded the second major wave of welfare legislation. It took various forms that affected blacks because they were disproportionately poor (Patterson, 1981; Katz, 1989). The Great Society called for the expansion of older programs and the development of new ones. The Johnson Administration, and later the Nixon Administration, began efforts to find alternatives to conventional public housing rather than increase new construction for poor families.

The alternatives relied in various ways on a greater role for the private sector. These included the Section 23 Leased Housing Program, which used existing housing owned by private landlords. The program provided qualified applicants rent subsidies that made up the difference between the rent they could afford to pay (30 percent of the tenant's net income) and a market rent that provided the owner with a reasonable return on investment. This program became the model for its successor, which is still in place: the Section 8 program. Like Section 23, housing in the private sector is used, but unlike the earlier program,

Section 8 provided incentives for new construction and housing reha-
bilitation. Finally, this program led to a major experiment that was designed to further reduce government's role in housing provision. This
took the form of the Experimental Housing Allowance Program
(EHAP), which gave recipients direct cash outlays. Participants were
provided greater flexibility compared with other programs (they could
choose to move to better quality housing, invest in home improvements, or use the money for other needs). Additionally, many administrative responsibilities were removed from the purview of local housing
agencies.

The effects of these programs are somewhat difficult to determine.
Clearly, blacks have participated in Section 23, Section 8, and EHAP.
But reliance on private-sector landlords has meant that blacks have encountered housing discrimination—partly because, in the private sector, blacks confront more competition from low-income whites for the
limited number of available housing slots in these other programs.

Nonetheless, this trend set the stage for the aggressive privatization
campaign undertaken during the Reagan Administration. Thus, *The
Report of the President's Commission on Housing* (1982) called for the
"deprogramming" of a sizable portion of the current public housing
stock through sale, conversion, planned deterioration, or demolition.
As critics argued, however, such efforts posed serious problems for
poor blacks. First, the evidence pointed to the shortage of decent, safe,
and affordable housing for such families that privatization schemes did
not address. Second, no adequate mechanisms are available to handle
cases of housing discrimination. Existing tools designed to do so are
weak. The result is that alternatives to public housing fail to meet the
shelter needs of poor blacks, especially for certain categories of families, such as female-headed large families. Coupled with cuts in benefits
to poor people, the result of the conservative policies of the 1980s
meant, according to researchers at the Urban Institute, that "beneficiaries will be increasingly impoverished" (Struyck, Mayer, and Tuccillo,
1983: 67). Moreover, it has meant that government policies have contributed to the increasing concentration of the very poor in highly segregated neighborhoods (Farley, 1999; Massey and Denton, 1993).

Equal Housing Opportunity

A large majority of whites agree that blacks should have **equal
housing opportunity,** while the majority also are opposed to any laws
that prohibit discrimination (Levitan and Taggart, 1976). These contradictory responses can be explained by noting that whites are far less
likely than blacks to believe that blacks are, in fact, the victims of housing discrimination. Thus, 52 percent of blacks believe that blacks are
generally discriminated against in attempting to obtain decent hous-

ing, while only 20 percent of whites agree (Sigelman and Welch, 1991; Schuman et al., 1997).

An early challenge to housing discrimination came in the 1948 *Shelley v. Kramer* case, in which the Supreme Court banned restrictive covenants in the sale of property. Such covenants had been inserted into sale transactions in an effort to ensure that homes were not sold to certain ethnic groups, with blacks and Jews being singled out most frequently. Despite this ruling, the Federal Housing Administration (FHA) and the Veteran's Administration (VA) mortgage insurance activities willingly condoned such covenants, following the practice of the real estate industry.

During the 1960s, several additional measures to combat discrimination were introduced. They included President Kennedy's Executive Order 11063, which banned discrimination in federally subsidized or financed housing. Title VI of the 1964 Civil Rights Act extended these provisions even further. The Civil Rights Act of 1968 provided the most sweeping changes for fair housing: Title VIII of the act prohibited discrimination in the sale, rental, and financing of all housing. In the same year, in *Jones v. Mayer*, the Supreme Court ruled that racial discrimination in housing had been outlawed more than a century earlier, in the Civil Rights Act of 1866. For 102 years after the passage of this post-Civil War legislation, the government had chosen to ignore it in practice. Thus, although the newer act appeared redundant, the 1968 act differed from the its predecessor because it added enforcement provisions that were heretofore missing.

But what has been the impact of this legislation on residential segregation? During the 1970s, residential segregation in 20 of the 25 cities with the largest black populations declined; some cities (including Houston and Los Angeles) saw substantial declines, but for most, it was very modest. Three cities remained unchanged, while Cleveland and Philadelphia ended up more segregated by 1980 (Taeuber, 1983). The cumulative change reflected a minor decline in residential segregation in cities.

During the same period, suburbs continued to grow. The black suburban population grew during the 1970s at an annual rate of 4 percent, in contrast to 1.5 percent for the white population (Long and DiAve, 1981). In the 16 Standard Metropolitan Statistical Areas (SMSAs) with black populations of at least 250,000, an overall modest decline in segregation was observed. The reduction was equal to that seen in central cities. There was still a high level of racial separation, however. In 1980, only 20 percent of blacks lived in suburbs, compared with 42 percent of nonblacks (Farley and Allen, 1989). A decade later that figure had risen to 26 percent (Farley, 1999). The unanswered question today is whether the suburbanization of blacks will lead to integration or whether we will continue to have, as Farley, Schumun, Biachi, Colasyto, and

Hatchett (1978) have described the situation, "chocolate cities and va-nilla suburbs."

Although increasing numbers of middle-class blacks have moved out of center cities to the suburbs, they are not necessarily now living in integrated neighborhoods. In fact, the white flight from cities that be-came so pronounced during the 1960s has a contemporary equivalence in recent years. Some suburbs that were once entirely or predomi-nantly white are experiencing white flight with the arrival of blacks. For example, Matteson, Illinois, a suburb on Chicago's southwest side, went from 84 percent white in 1980 to only 33 percent white by 2000 (Terry, 1996; U.S. Bureau of the Census, 2003). This change is a reflection of the fact that blacks and whites differ in terms of the racial ratio they prefer in their neighborhoods, with blacks preferring 50-50 areas, a much higher percentage of blacks than found in white preferences (Krysan and Farley, 2002).

However halting and limited, the black middle class has experi-enced enhanced housing opportunities, even though the obstacles to further integration have not disappeared (Farley and Frey, 1994). Blacks are moving to suburbs at a lower rate than Hispanics and Asians, and furthermore, within suburbs, blacks are more residentially isolated than other racial minorities (Massey and Denton, 1988, 1993). Blacks have greater difficulties in achieving entry into desirable neigh-borhoods than other racial minorities, even though the disadvantage of middle-class blacks is not as pronounced as it was in the past (Massey and Fong, 1990). Middle-class blacks tend to live in neighborhoods with whites who have lower socioeconomic characteristics than they do (Alba, Logan, and Stults, 2000; Horton and Thomas, 1998).

For those not in the middle class, the situation is quite different. Within segregated neighborhoods in central cities, blacks confront a number of problems. Those seeking to purchase homes in predomi-nantly black neighborhoods often encounter lending institutions en-gaged in the practice of **redlining**—a tacit practice of denying mort-gages to would-be homeowners when the property is located in an area where such financial investment is deemed to be too risky (Gotham, 2002). The National Committee Against Discrimination in Housing has concluded that neither the Department of Housing and Urban Develop-ment (HUD) nor the National Association of Realtors has established adequate strategies for combating redlining (Blackwell, 1985).

An additional dilemma has resulted from the gentrification of some neighborhoods and from the conversion of rental apartment buildings to condominiums (U.S. Department of Housing and Urban Develop-ment, 1980; Sumka, 1978). In both instances, these trends have re-sulted in the displacement of low- and moderate-income families and have had a disproportionately negative impact on blacks. To date, nei-ther the federal government nor local governments (who stand to bene-fit from these changes through increased revenues from property taxes) have taken substantial steps to control these processes or to address the problems of those most adversely affected. Unfortunately, little empirical data exist on the fate of the displaced. Aside from impressionistic evidence, we know little about whether families have found alternative housing and, if so, what it is like in terms of quality, cost, overcrowding, and related indices.

The Enduring Significance of Race

To what extent is a black person's fate shaped by racial identity? To what extent is it shaped by the individual's location in the American class structure? These are complex and controversial questions. Many social scientists of ethnicity have seen race as being a far more important determinant of a black person's life chances than class location. Challenging this claim, some Marxist-influenced sociologists going back to the seminal work of Oliver Cox (1948) have placed a premium on class relations. For them, race is merely a subterfuge for what is at bedrock class exploitation. Clearly, class and ethnicity (including race) are intertwined. Milton Gordon (1964) understood the importance of wrestling with this interconnection when he called for the analysis of what he termed **ethclass** relations.

Although few would dispute the interconnectedness of race and class, explicit attempts to unravel the connections have elicited considerable debate. Nowhere was this more evident than in the thesis advanced by sociologist William Julius Wilson in his book *The Declining Significance of Race* (1978). Wilson attempted to historicize the connections by identifying three historical periods, each of which is defined in terms of differences in the respective salience of race and class. The periods he identified are roughly the same as those used throughout this book.

During the first period—the antebellum era—racial oppression was paramount as blacks were consigned to a subordinate location in a caste system. The underlying rationale was economic: blacks provided a cheap and compliant supply of labor. Class differentiation among blacks was minimal and quite inconsequential. This gave way during the period from the end of the Civil War to the demise of Jim Crow to

The owner stands outside of his Afrocentric bookstore.

a new form of economic exploitation in which class acquired a significance that it did not previously have. Although race was still more important in determining the life chances of blacks than class was, it was no longer the sole determinant. One of the changes that occurred during this period was the emergence of an internal class structure within black America, one that largely paralleled, while standing outside of, the class structure of white America.

Since 1965, the thesis continued, this second period has been superseded by a third in which race is no longer as powerful a force as class in determining blacks' life chances. First, as we have seen, white attitudes toward blacks have improved since the 1940s. Second, Wilson (1978) stressed, the federal government played a new role in the drama of race relations. Previously it had served as a prop to the maintenance of economic subordination. Increasingly since World War II, however, the federal government has been a key force in the promotion of racial equality. Government action was instrumental in eliminating legal barriers to black incorporation into the mainstream of the American economy and to active political involvement.

At the same time, changes in the American economy transformed the labor force. The white-collar, professional middle class expanded, which provided opportunities for upwardly mobile blacks. Simultaneously, because of a variety of factors that together can be referred to as processes of deindustrialization (for example, the expansion of automation and the export of factory jobs to plants in the Third World), structural unemployment grew, and poorer blacks were most adversely affected. In contrast to the economic expansion period from 1950 to 1970, these blacks, confronting a situation in which real purchasing power was actually declining, found limited opportunities for economic advancement. These blacks included the working poor and a core of impoverished people at the bottom of the socioeconomic ladder that some have referred to as the "underclass." Wilson (1987) chose to call them the **truly disadvantaged.** Wilson depicted a profound split within black America along class lines and described this bifurcation in the following manner:

> On the one hand, poorly trained and educationally limited blacks of the inner city, including that growing number of black teenagers and young adults, see their job prospects increasingly restricted to the low-wage sector, their unemployment rates soaring to record levels (which remain high despite swings in the business cycle), and their labor-force participation rates declining, their movement out of poverty slowing, and their welfare roles increasing. On the other hand, talented and educated blacks are experiencing unprecedented job opportunities in the growing government and corporate sectors, opportunities that are at least comparable to those of whites with equivalent qualifications. (Wilson, 1978: 151)

This thesis has been criticized by those who thought that Wilson underplayed the continuing importance of racism in determining black opportunities. Thomas Pettigrew (1979), for example, argued that though change had occurred, the significance of race had not necessarily declined. Charles Vert Willie (1979) argued that we can speak about an "inclining significance of race" (actually undermining his counterthesis by relying on limited data derived primarily from the pre-1965 period). Wilson did not claim that racism had been eradicated. He contended, however, that though racism was instrumental in the historical oppression of blacks, it had become less consequential than class factors in shaping life chances. He made a case for looking carefully at the internal class stratification of black America, in particular the middle class and the poverty class.

Wilson's thesis would be more convincing if he had been more attentive to the shifting nature of racism. As attitudinal research has indicated, what Lawrence Bobo (2001) calls "Jim Crow racism" has declined in significance, replaced by what he refers to as **laissez-faire racism.** Instead of overt bigotry and calls for segregation and discrimination, the new form of racism refuses to look at the structural causes of racial inequality and rejects a governmental role in attacking it. The result is that we have a situation characterized by, as Eduardo Bonilla-Silva (2003) somewhat ironically puts it, "racism without racists." In other words, in the current climate, rather than hearing a person say, "They all look alike to me," one will instead hear, "I'm not a racist, but, . . ."

The Black Middle Class

Two major and interconnected changes have occurred in recent decades: The black middle class has grown, and it no longer finds itself confined to the black ghetto. Between emancipation and World War I the black middle class was very small—no more than 3 percent of the total black population, compared with 23.8 percent for the white middle class. In 1910, 89.1 percent of blacks were either farm workers or unskilled industrial workers. The comparable figure for whites was 47.1 percent (Landry, 1987). Most members of the black middle class were part of the old mulatto elite, and they owned businesses in service industries. They worked as barbers, caterers, and tailors, and in other small business enterprises. Many served a white clientele (Katzman, 1973).

A half century later, with the expansion of urban ghettos brought about by migration from the rural South, the middle class grew. As Figure 6.3 indicates, it accounted for 13.4 percent of the black population. In addition, 25.7 percent of blacks were in the skilled working class. Although these figures lagged behind those recorded for whites, this statistic nonetheless reflects a greater class differentiation within the

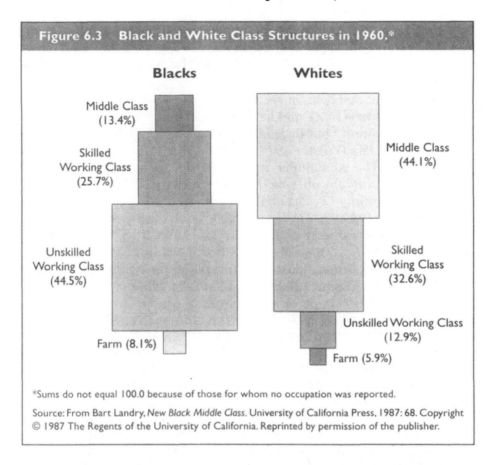

Figure 6.3   Black and White Class Structures in 1960.*

Blacks

Middle Class
(13.4%)

Skilled
Working Class
(25.7%)

Unskilled
Working Class
(44.5%)

Farm (8.1%)

Whites

Middle Class
(44.1%)

Skilled
Working Class
(32.6%)

Unskilled Working Class
(12.9%)

Farm (5.9%)

*Sums do not equal 100.0 because of those for whom no occupation was reported.

Source: From Bart Landry, *New Black Middle Class*. University of California Press, 1987: 68. Copyright © 1987 The Regents of the University of California. Reprinted by permission of the publisher.

black community than in the earlier period. Among the important professions in the middle class were doctors, lawyers, accountants, undertakers, and similar occupations. What made their professional lives different from the preceding era was that they were largely restricted to serving a black clientele. Black sociologist E. Franklin Frazier described this middle class in highly critical fashion in his controversial book *Black Bourgeoisie* (1957).

In a world of enforced or de facto segregation, middle-class blacks lived in isolation from the white middle class. They generally obtained their educations from historically black colleges and universities. When they entered professional life, they both worked and lived in a largely all-black world. This, according to Frazier, had a profound impact on the worldview of the black middle class. He criticized them for their tendencies toward conspicuous consumption and the pretentiousness of their "high society." He saw these behaviors, however, as manifestations of the inferiority imprinted on this stratum by racism. Theirs was a world of make-believe in which "the masks which they wear to play their sorry roles conceal the feelings of inferiority . . . that haunt their lives" (Frazier, 1957; see also Drake and Cayton, 1962 [1945]; Landry, 1987). This world has not entirely disappeared, as shown in Spike Lee's devastating critique of the mores of the children of these black bourgeoisie in *School Daze,* his film about the social world of a black college.

Nonetheless, one consequence of the civil rights movement was the emergence of a new black middle class—one that was no longer tied to the black community but instead was integrated into the fabric of the larger middle class (Wilson, 1978; Kilson, 1983; Landry, 1987; Banner-Haley, 1994). The educational attainment levels of blacks increased after the 1960s, thereby offering the credentials that were a prerequisite for upward mobility (Zweigenhaft and Domhoff, 1991). According to Martin Kilson (1983: 86–87), the overall growth of the white-collar professional class permitted the rapid entry of blacks. They found employment "in national job markets—in national (white) banks, insurance companies, retail firms, industries, universities, and government agencies. The last employs the heads of 30 percent of white-collar black families, compared with 16 percent for whites."

Furthermore, from this middle class has come the new black suburbanites, with the purchasing power to acquire homes in such communities and the desire to integrate into the mainstream. Like their white middle-class counterparts, many middle-class blacks have fled the problems associated with urban life for the relative security, better schools, and related amenities offered by the suburbs.

Wilson (1978) and Kilson (1983) contended that the black middle class had become sufficiently secure that their opportunities were now determined chiefly by economic and not by racial factors. That is, racism had not disappeared, but while "persistent racist practices by police, business firms, unions, and by hoodlums like the Ku Klux Klan continue to threaten all blacks, these practices are now a weaker constraint upon Afro-Americans than they were ever before" (Kilson, 1983: 90). This is what Wilson meant when he spoke of the "declining significance of race."

Others have questioned this conclusion. Bart Landry (1987), for example, in the first comprehensive study of the black middle class since Frazier, cautioned against what he saw as an overly optimistic assessment of the black middle class. Although he believed that this

Black revelers celebrating Halloween in New York City.

class would continue to grow during the last quarter of the twentieth century, there are many reasons to be concerned about this class in the future. The black middle class lags behind the white middle class in earnings, and some evidence indicates that blacks tend to get locked into middle-range managerial positions, so their chances of rising to the top of an organization are considerably more limited than those of whites. Furthermore, blacks are more adversely affected by economic recessions. Black entrepreneurs, aside from a small number of highly successful people, continue to earn less than whites and their businesses are often precarious; the failure rate is quite high. Thus, genuine parity with whites does not appear to be attainable in the near future (see also Thomas, 1993).

If the difference between blacks and whites in terms of income is cause for concern, the gap between the races in terms of wealth is even more disturbing. In research conducted by Melvin Oliver and Thomas Shapiro (1995, 2001), it became evident that middle-class whites own considerably more wealth than their middle-class black counterparts. The authors observe that the main source of wealth for ordinary citizens is found in homeownership. The persistence of housing discrimination means that many blacks do not have the same access to this form of wealth as their white counterparts. This is significant insofar as it is wealth that serves as the basis of intergenerational shifts of resources. In other words, whites have much more capital to pass on to their children, who can draw on this resource in their quest for economic success. Black children can count on far fewer such assets.

Moreover, the impact of discrimination may have been understated in the declining significance of race thesis. Joe R. Feagin (1991), in a study of middle-class blacks in a number of cities, has documented the extent to which his respondents confront various discriminatory actions in their daily lives in public places—actions ranging from threats and harassment by strangers or the police to verbal epithets, rejection or poor service, and avoidance (for example, crossing the street to avoid passing a black male on a sidewalk). Such actions are far more common than many whites appreciate, and they take a heavy toll on blacks because, as Feagin (1991: 115) puts it, "You cannot accomplish as much as you could if you retained the energy wasted on discrimination." Similar findings have been reported by Bonilla-Silva (2003). The result is that there is good reason to conclude that while one can speak about the privileges that have become available to middle-class blacks, their situation is also one characterized by what Mary Pattillo-McCoy (1999) refers to as "peril."

Poor Blacks

One of Wilson's (1978) concerns was that the exodus of middle-class blacks from urban enclaves had further impoverished such communities, both financially and culturally. The middle class served as leaders of black ghettos prior to the 1960s and as role models for more disadvantaged blacks (Wilson, 1987). Life in the inner city is shaped by poverty in the midst of an affluent society, an impoverishment that is characterized by high levels of unemployment and underemployment, a high percentage of female-headed households, high levels of crime and violence, low levels of educational attainment, substandard housing combined with relatively high rents, inadequate health care, and the like.

Although most inner-city adults work, they do so at low-paying, unskilled jobs, which offer few, if any, fringe benefits, little opportunity for advancement, and frequently little job security. There is also a stratum of nonworking poor. In the 1960s, two now-classic ethnographic studies, both conducted in Washington, D.C., explored the everyday lives of groups of men from this stratum: Elliot Liebow's *Tally's Corner* (1967) and Ulf Hannerz's *Soulside* (1969).

Both captured features of the everyday lives of groups of "streetcorner men." Hannerz observed that those inner-city residents with relatively stable lives were oriented toward the mainstream of society. The main reference of streetcorner men, however, is the immediate peer group. Hannerz (1969: 54–55) wrote that they

> usually return day after day to the same hangout. There they talk and drink, play cards, and shoot craps, or just do nothing. . . . There is continuous drinking. . . . If they are not already alcoholics, they are well on their way. . . . Many of the men have some kind of police record.

Liebow's (1967) account reinforced Hannerz's portrait. Liebow emphasized that although these men often fathered children, they tended to have little or no contact with them and were not inclined to provide financial support to them. These men often drifted from job to job, exploited women financially and sexually, and had tenuous and violent relationships with other streetcorner men. They were concerned primarily about the present, viewing their futures as too unpredictable for them to shape or influence. Liebow (1967: 70) contended that for these men, "the constant awareness of a future loaded with 'trouble' results in a constant readiness to leave, to 'make it,' to 'get out of town,' and discourages the man from sinking roots into the world he lives in."

The Moynihan Report. Women with children were increasingly forced to rely on various governmental support programs, the most notable being Aid to Families with Dependent Children (AFDC) and public housing. A rising percentage of women were forced to confront the dilemmas of raising children in poverty without a partner to share those responsibilities. This situation is what is meant by the "feminization of poverty." This increase in female-headed households prompted discussions about the "matrifocal black family," a line of inquiry that culminated in the 1960s in a highly controversial debate over what became known as the "Moynihan Report." This document was prepared in 1965 by sociologist Daniel Patrick Moynihan, then employed by the U.S. Department of Labor, and went by the title *The Negro Family: The Case for National Action.* Pointing to the dramatic increase in single-parent households in black America and the connection between such households and poverty status, Moynihan paid considerable attention to what he referred to as a "tangle of pathology," which included academic failure, crime and delinquency, unemployment, and out-of-wedlock births. Government policy, it was argued, needed to address family instability as part of the effort to combat poverty (Moynihan, 1965).

Critics countered the report's conclusions. Some argued that the report was based on a bias that saw the dual-parent nuclear family as superior to other family forms. For example, Carol Stack (1974) sought to illustrate the strengths of families that were headed by women. What others depicted as unstable family arrangements, she saw as flexible, exhibiting a creative reliance on extended kin networks. Others argued that by focusing on the family and on the behaviors of poor blacks, Moynihan's approach tended to blame the victims of poverty for their plight (Rainwater and Yancey, 1967; Valentine, 1968; Ryan, 1971). The role of culture and of behaviors emanating from cultural values was seen as derived from the underlying structural conditions that were the true cause of poverty: racial oppression, economic exploitation, enforced segregation, and exclusion from meaningful participation in civic life.

Inner-City Poverty Today. Three decades later, inner-city poverty continues to be a serious unresolved problem. Recent research has documented the continuing significance of the problems that afflicted similar communities a generation earlier. For poor blacks, especially those at the bottom of the socioeconomic ladder, whom Wilson (1987) characterized as the truly disadvantaged, the world continues to be as segregated—in some instance even more so—as it was during the Jim Crow era. Inner-city blacks live in segregated neighborhoods, attend segregated schools, worship in segregated churches, shop in segregated stores, and so forth (Massey and Denton, 1993). They continue to confront discriminatory practices such as redlining (Gotham, 2002).

The economic situation for this segment of the African American community has become increasingly precarious. Deindustrialization has reduced the number of manufacturing jobs, and new jobs have moved to the suburbs. The result is that large numbers of inner-city residents end up unemployed, underemployed, working at dead-end, low-paying jobs, or working in the illicit underground economy (Wilson, 1996).

Elijah Anderson's (1990) study of young people in a Philadelphia neighborhood does not provide grounds for optimism concerning the future. Differences between earlier studies and his suggest an intensification of old problems, such as teenage pregnancy, and the arrival of new ones, particularly those associated with drugs—especially crack—and, related to this, violent crime. Furthermore, he saw a deterioration of stabilizing social networks, largely because of the erosion of authority of what Anderson called the "old heads," mature men who traditionally served as role models for young men.

In a series of films directed by prominent black filmmakers, including *Boyz N the Hood, Straight out of Brooklyn,* and the parts of Spike Lee's *Jungle Fever* concerned with the main character's crack-addicted brother, the ravages of crime and drugs and the sense of isolation from the larger society are poignantly and forcefully depicted. In the inner city, as Anderson's (2000) more recent work indicates, a powerful "code of the street" is based on a constant demand for respect and on a defiance of white middle-class values and standards. He focuses on black males who constitute the hard-core street culture that is at odds not only with the values of the larger society but with the values of what he calls "decent" people. If Anderson focuses on the code of the street, anthropologist Katherine Newman (2000) examines those young people in inner cities who struggle against the odds to survive by working in legitimate businesses, which often means in fast-food restaurants and similar businesses that rely on unskilled workers and pay minimum wage. Taken together, these writers paint a portrait of areas of concentrated poverty where people are torn between trying to embrace the values of white middle-class America and entering into an oppositional culture.

Results from these and similar case studies are reflected in national-level data. Social problems—including drug use, violent crime, gangs, teen pregnancy, and low academic achievement—have had a devastating impact on inner-city neighborhoods. For example, although blacks compose no more than 13 percent of the general population, they account for 47 percent of prisoners in state and federal prisons and 40 percent of death-row inmates (Hacker, 1992). The leading cause of death among black male youths is murder, usually committed by other black youths. Drug addiction is far more problematic among ghetto dwellers than outside such communities. Furthermore, AIDS has hit inner cities especially hard. Not surprisingly, many poor blacks have concluded that the American Dream has eluded them, and they see themselves several decades after the civil rights movement as still victims of the "scar of race" (Sniderman and Piazza, 1993; Hochschild, 1995).

What accounts for the persistence of poverty and the exacerbation of the problems it produces? Why does an affluent society have in its midst an underclass that finds no significant place in the larger economy (Auletta, 1982; Wilson, 1996)? The debate begun during the War on Poverty era continues unabated. Traditional liberals still argue that two factors are chiefly responsible: racism and a lack of governmental support for social programs. Conservatives have challenged this view by arguing that it is precisely because of government programs that the cycle of poverty has not been broken. They contend that government programs have generated a dependency that has caused the inner city to be actually worse off than before the existence of significant government intervention (Murray, 1984). Although liberals focus on social structural factors, conservatives tend to pay greater attention to the cultural attributes and behaviors of the poor.

Wilson (1987, 1991, 1999) offered an alternative explanation. He called it a social democratic account, one that stressed changes in the nation's occupational structure that limit upward mobility by the poorest poor. Like liberals, he stressed social structure, although unlike them he minimized the current impact of racial prejudice and discrimination. He gave conservatives their due, however, by also considering culture's role.

He viewed the effort to pit culture against social structure as a simplistic distortion of what is, in fact, a complex interplay between the two: "Poverty, like other aspects of class inequality, is a consequence not only of differential distribution of economic and political privileges, but of differential access to culture as well" (Wilson, 1991: 1). As a consequence, no simple solution is possible. Rather, what is needed includes increased job opportunities and increased access to political power as well as a renewed connection between the ghetto poor and the cultural beliefs and attitudes of the larger society. A sense of futility and fatalism reinforces a lack of success in the job market. Only when such views are replaced by a conviction that work is a means toward economic betterment will efforts to combat the problems of the truly disadvantaged succeed.

Into the Future

Although Wilson's analysis dealt with social policy shaped largely by whites, blacks have acquired a political voice in the wake of the civil rights movement. Blacks have been elected to the United States Congress, and many cities, including the nation's five largest—New York, Los Angeles, Chicago, Philadelphia, and Detroit—currently have or have recently had black mayors. Although these electoral victories signal empowerment, they have not necessarily indicated genuine integration of black candidates into the political process. Most black members of Congress represent predominantly black constituencies. In many major cities that have elected black mayors, a majority or large plurality of the citizenry is black.

The 1988 presidential candidacy of Jesse Jackson highlighted the dilemmas of black involvement in the political process (Reed, 1986,

1999). A veteran of the civil rights movement, Jackson portrayed himself as not only a candidate of blacks but of other racial minorities as well as blue-collar workers and the poor regardless of race, dubbed the "Rainbow Coalition." His candidacy failed to get off the ground, due to its inability to attract not only sufficient numbers of white votes but also the votes of other minority groups. But the Jackson presence was an indication of the effort needed to move from social protest to participation in the political mainstream without abandoning the objectives of the former. For this reason, some political commentators have argued that a black not associated with the civil rights movement, such as Colin Powell, might have a better chance of becoming the first black U.S. president.

Summary

The civil rights movement was one of the most important sources of social change in twentieth-century America. In this chapter we have reviewed its various stages, beginning with the work of A. Philip Randolph, turning to the early phase in the 1950s in the South, the subsequent move North, and its culmination in the militancy of the Black Power movement. We surveyed the central organizations and key leaders that played a role in this history, examining the types of resources that they had at their disposal, as well as the resistance that they confronted.

A number of legislative and judicial decisions came out of this period that were intended to overcome the legacy of racial oppression. After reviewing the most important of these, we turned to their net impact on the lives of black Americans. Going beyond general black-white differences on a number of quality-of-life measures, we discussed the increasingly different life chances of middle-class blacks and poor blacks. Although there is considerable debate about the levels of gains made by middle-class blacks, few would dispute that for poor blacks in the inner cities, life has gotten more difficult, not less so. Poor blacks are not misreading the situation when they conclude that social change has not improved their lives for the better.

Cornel West (1993) noted that a distressingly pervasive nihilism can be seen in these quarters of black America. Spike Lee's film *Do the Right Thing* depicted deep conflict-ridden fissures in contemporary race relations. Beneath any surface comity he sees the ever-present potential for venomous and destructive exchanges. The film implicitly indicts white America for a lack of will, while depicting the ambiguities and uncertainties in black responses to racial inequality: Malcolm X and Martin Luther King, Jr., advanced two very different responses to the condition of blacks, but in the end the viewer is left with both options—which is to say, with a lack of certainty about how to proceed. All of this was forcefully illustrated in the 1992 Los Angeles riot following the Rodney King decision. Black frustration was acted out in attacks on whites, Korean merchants, and others, while millions of dollars of property were destroyed. This is vivid testimony that a half century after Myrdal's monumental work, the American dilemma clearly continues to bedevil the nation.

Key Terms

affirmative action　　　　　*laissez-faire racism*
black nationalism　　　　　*redlining*
civil rights movement　　　*reverse discrimination*
desegregation　　　　　　　*stigmatized achievement*
equal housing opportunity　*symbolic racism*
ethclass　　　　　　　　　*truly disadvantaged*
integration　　　　　　　　*white flight*

Questions for Discussion and Critical Thinking

1. Summarize the various stages of the civil rights movement, from the initial work beginning during World War II through the Black Power movement. Compare and contrast the goals and tactics of various organizations and leaders. What were the major accomplishments of the movement, and what were its chief failures?

2. Review and analyze the current status of the African American community, paying particular attention to the divide between the middle class and the poor. What are the implications of this divide on the black community in general and on the poor in particular?

3. Affirmative action has been a controversial policy during the past four decades. Review the origins and the key judicial cases that have shaped it as public policy. What do you make of the claim that we will not need affirmative action a quarter of a century from now? ✦

Chapter 7

American Indians: The Continuing Plight of the First of This Land

N ative Americans occupy a unique place in the United States. Previous chapters have chronicled the important role played by the federal government in defining the subordinate relationship of Indians to
European Americans. Their relative lack of power has meant that
American Indians have had to learn to respond to shifting governmental goals and policies. This chapter traces the history of those shifts
from the Indian Reorganization Act (IRA) of 1934 to the present. During the past several decades, Indians have mobilized resources in ways
that were not possible earlier. The result has been gains for some Native
Americans. However, many others remain both impoverished and political and social outsiders.

The Indian Reorganization Act

The **Indian Reorganization Act** was hailed by advocates as the
"Indian New Deal." It was intended by its supporters to preserve and
strengthen Native American cultures. As such, it was designed to encourage resistance to assimilation. Proponents saw the IRA as a way to
preserve tribal organizations and identities and to stop the loss of Indian lands that resulted from the allotment acts of the 1880s. In at least
two ways this legislation and the underlying rationale advanced by
John Collier has been subsequently called into question (Prucha, 1985;
Cornell, 1988).

First, by the 1930s many Native Americans had only tenuous, if any,
connections with tribal entities, and in many instances tribes had
changed considerably due to acculturation. Thus, preserving traditional tribal organizations was frequently unrealistic. The second point

is, ironically, a reflection of the government's willingness to impose on tribes nontraditional forms of government. Collier proposed a democratic process for electing tribal representatives and even drafted a constitution that many tribes adopted without revision. As Francis Paul Prucha (1985: 66) observed, "These tribal governments, with councils and tribal chairmen elected by majority vote, were Anglo-American inventions, which did not accord with traditional Indian ways." Actually, in some instances, such as the case of the Apache, the IRA constitution looked rather similar to traditional Apache government. However, if traditional government and IRA-defined government were markedly different, as in the case of the Pine Ridge Lakota, the legitimacy of tribal government proved to be problematic (Cornell and Kalt, 1998).

As with other New Deal programs, the IRA expanded the role of the federal government. This led critics both within and outside of Native American communities to accuse the government of embarking on a new form of paternalism. Washington became more, rather than less, involved with the internal workings of Native American affairs. Indeed, the Bureau of Indian Affairs (BIA) and the secretary of the interior did play a determinative role in tribal decision making. Traditional tribal religious leaders, whose importance in tribal life was challenged as a result of these policies, frequently considered the elected leaders to be mere pawns of the federal government. They often referred to elected leaders disparagingly as "BIA Indians" (Prucha, 1985; Deloria, 1985). Nonetheless, the IRA ended the allotment system, stimulated economic development on reservations, and promoted cultural preservation, including the centrality of tribal organizations to Native American identity.

Termination

The IRA was followed, during the Eisenhower Administration, by a concerted effort to undo the Indian New Deal. The context for the policy shift included key economic and political features of the post-World War II landscape. The nation's economy grew dramatically, and the public generally believed in expanded opportunities for members of heretofore disadvantaged groups. However, success was assumed to be an individual, not a collective, matter. In other words, individual Native Americans might be economically successful, but tribal units might not. This rather pervasive belief, stemming in part from the Cold War ideology of the 1950s, "placed particular value on national unity and conformity, and special groups, especially if they emphasized communal values, were considered out of line" (Prucha, 1985: 69). In fact, such groups were sometimes accused of embracing communistic ideals.

A new governmental approach to Native Americans was developed that became known as **termination.** The head of the BIA, Dillon S.

Myer, argued that the relationship of Native Americans to the land, as reflected in the **reservation** system, had worked against their desire to achieve economic well-being. He contended that if the health, education, and economic situation of the Native American were to improve, that would have to occur outside of the tribal context. Termination entailed eliminating the reservations and severing the unique relationship that existed between the federal government and Native Americans (Burt, 1982; Fixico, 1986). In short, this new response by the federal government constituted an aggressive campaign of assimilation. Many liberals were sympathetic to this campaign because they considered reservations to be "rural ghettos" (Cornell, 1988: 121).

Most Native Americans were vehemently opposed to termination. In particular, the National Congress of American Indians (NCAI), a pan-tribal political organization formed in 1944, waged a battle against the policy. The NCAI was opposed to termination because of the threat to tribal entities posed by assimilation and because of the loss of land and federal protection that termination would bring about. The amount of opposition to termination is illustrated by the fact that only 3 percent of the total Native American population terminated its relationship with Washington. Furthermore, only 3 percent of Native American land was removed from the trust status accorded to reservations. Still, in two notable cases, the Menominee tribe in Wisconsin and the Klamath Indians in Oregon, Native Americans approved termination laws. Native American land in these instances was no longer held in trusteeship, and all federally funded services, including health and educational ones, ceased. The economic and social consequences were disastrous. Menominee tribal members concluded it was in their best interest to return to the previous status quo: After a long legal battle their tribal status was finally restored in 1973 (Spicer, 1980; Prucha, 1985; Cornell, 1988). The Klamath tribe has never been reinstated.

Searching for Alternatives to Termination

Termination was abandoned by the Kennedy administration in the early 1960s, and since that time no administration, liberal or conservative, has attempted to revive the assimilationist strategy of the Eisenhower years. During the Great Society initiatives of the Johnson presidency, policymakers revived aspects of the IRA. They emphasized programs designed to strengthen communities and facilitate economic development. The new approach differed because Native Americans were accorded a far greater role in decision-making. This was an attempt to avoid the charges of governmental paternalism and forced subservience of Indian communities. Community action programs were often funneled through the Office of Economic Opportunity (OEO) and other government agencies, such as the Administration for

Native Americans, and not the highly criticized BIA. These alternative sources of funding provided avenues for Native Americans to challenge tribal councils too dependent on the BIA. Not infrequently, these programs served as training grounds for a leadership that used confrontational tactics to advance Native American issues (Prucha, 1985; Cornell, 1988). During this period, economic development became increasingly linked to the politics of self-determination (Riggs, 2000).

The Nixon administration scuttled the activist element contained in OEO programs, although it urged enhanced possibilities for Native American involvement in community development. The slogan of this administration was inherited from the Great Society era: "self-determination." It took legislative form in the 1975 Indian Self-Determination Act. The argument was made by administration spokespersons that Native American independence should occur without ending tribal allegiances or withdrawing federal support (Spicer, 1980). This was an attempt to steer a course between assimilation and total separatism. It was an ambivalent course.

This ambivalence has been evident in every subsequent administration. The Reagan administration made a concerted attempt to reduce the size of the federal government's involvement in domestic affairs, but Native Americans found a confusing situation. On the one hand, the administration contended that it was going to treat tribal governments with respect, relating to them on a "government-to-government" basis. This approach was viewed positively by most Native Americans. At the same time, however, draconian budget cuts were proposed, and Native Americans were understandably fearful of the negative consequences of these cuts on already impoverished reservations (Cornell, 1988).

An overall lack of interest in domestic affairs by the first Bush administration meant that no new initiatives directed at Native Americans were undertaken. Little changed in this regard during the Clinton or second Bush administrations. Thus, at present, self-sufficiency remains the goal for Native Americans. Concrete workable policies that can advance that goal have not yet been formulated, however. Later in this chapter we shall explore how Native Americans have responded to the various shifts in governmental policies from the IRA to the present (Fixico, 1998).

Urbanization

Because of the centrality of the reservation system to the ongoing existence of tribes, Native Americans have lagged far behind the general population in their level of **urbanization.** Nonetheless, after 1945 the number of Native Americans seeking employment in cities in-

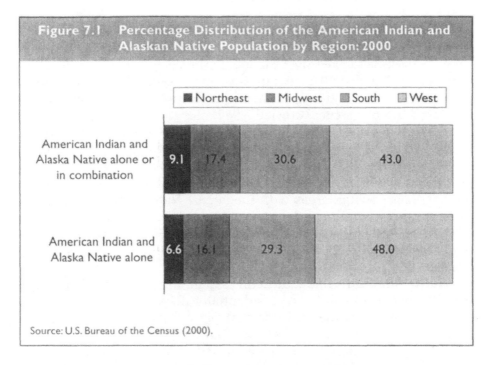

Figure 7.1   Percentage Distribution of the American Indian and Alaskan Native Population by Region: 2000

■ Northeast   ■ Midwest   ■ South   □ West

American Indian and Alaska Native alone or in combination: 9.1 | 17.4 | 30.6 | 43.0

American Indian and Alaska Native alone: 6.6 | 16.1 | 29.3 | 48.0

Source: U.S. Bureau of the Census (2000).

creased. Partly voluntary, this migration resembled the labor migrations of immigrant groups but perhaps resembled more the migration of African Americans from the rural South to northern cities. Like the African Americans, Native Americans had other reasons to leave reservations, including to serve in the armed forces and attend college. But there was something unique about the Native American experience: By the 1950s, urban migration was actively encouraged by the federal government. During the termination period, relocation to cities was seen as a way of breaking down tribal allegiances and promoting the incorporation of Native Americans into the national economy (Waddell and Watson, 1971). Furthermore, as Edward Spicer (1980: 113) observed,

> The movement of Indians into cities has proceeded on a quite different basis from the urbanization of European or Asian immigrants. It is not characterized by the growth of extensive contiguous neighborhoods in which thousands of persons of similar cultural backgrounds live in subcultural enclaves. The urbanization of Indians in the United States has been a relatively small-scale movement of individuals and small family groups from quite different tribal cultural backgrounds.

Native Americans in cities were no longer under the direct jurisdiction of tribal governments or of the BIA, although the government established relocation centers designed to assist Native Americans in acquiring jobs and adjusting to their new environment. During the early

1950s field relocation offices were set up in a number of cities that had become major destinations for Native Americans: Los Angeles, Chicago, Denver, Salt Lake City, Oakland, San Jose, Cleveland, and Dallas. Between 1950 and 1960, as the urban population of the whole country increased by almost 30 percent, the urban Native American population increased by 160 percent (Cornell, 1988).

According to the Census Bureau, at the end of the twentieth century about half of the nation's Native American population resided in rural areas, with the other half located in metropolitan areas; this latter group was divided about equally between residents of cities and suburbanites. Metropolitan areas with the largest Native American populations are, in descending order of size, Los Angeles, Phoenix, New York City, Tulsa, San Francisco-Oakland, Oklahoma City, Seattle, Albuquerque, Flagstaff, Arizona, and Minneapolis-St. Paul (U.S. Bureau of the Census, 1999).

Native Americans find it difficult to maintain ties with other Native Americans because they are residentially dispersed in many cities. Churches often provide an important place for maintaining contact. Many Native Americans are Roman Catholic, although various Protestant denominations have also attracted members. Some religious groups have helped establish community centers for Native Americans. For example, in San Francisco the Society of Friends (Quakers) founded the Intertribal Friendship House. The center provided various social services to recent arrivals in the city and functioned as a gathering place. Although this particular center was run by whites, Native Americans also created their own organizations, such as the Bay Area American Indian Council, which offered similar services but also promoted political involvement (Spicer, 1980).

Adjusting to Urban Life

Native Americans had to overcome a number of obstacles to be successful in an urban setting (Lobo and Peters, 2001). They confronted some discrimination in hiring, although the level of discrimination is not generally as high as that experienced by blacks (Mucha, 1984). Their initial poverty meant that they tended to locate in ghetto neighborhoods, which had poor-quality housing and lacked adequate community services and social amenities. Urban migrants also brought with them some social problems, the most troublesome of which was alcoholism. In the pre-1970 period, some Native Americans were either monolingual and had to learn English or were bilingual but their English-language skills were not well developed. In either case, the acquisition of functional English-language skills was a prerequisite for occupational success.

Sociologist Janusz Mucha (1984), in an ethnographic study of Native Americans in Chicago, pointed to the cultural adaptations that had to take place for the Native Americans to succeed economically. He offered one particularly revealing case, that of a person who after many years in Chicago had become an electric plant designer. The individual had a difficult time during his early years in the city coming to terms with the competitiveness of the white employment world. He disliked what he referred to as the "dog-world" of whites, where everyone "barked and bit." He also had to learn to deal with a different conception of time (recall the similar reorientation many European immigrants from agrarian backgrounds also had to make at an earlier time in American history). Mucha (1984: 333) summarized the change that occurred in the following way:

> The "white" concept of time is a situation in which people are ruled by their watches, and it was very difficult to understand. Eventually, this person got used to the white concept of time and even came to the conclusion that it was the only correct concept when large groups of people who have to work together are involved. For about ten years, however, he was on the edge of being fired because of [persistent] lateness, and only his very good work record saved him.

Despite these various obstacles to economic betterment, because the job opportunities in cities far surpass those in rural areas, whether on or near reservations, urban Native Americans have a higher standard of living than rural Native Americans; furthermore, that difference will probably increase over time (Snipp, 1989). Urban Native Americans can be found throughout the socioeconomic hierarchy. They are located in the middle and upper middle class, in the solid blue-collar working class, in the unskilled working class, and in tenuous circumstances of underemployment and chronic unemployment (Jarvenpa, 1985).

This class diffusion has had an impact on various shifts in ethnic identity. Those at the top of the socioeconomic ladder often have limited contact with other Native Americans and with Native American institutions. Those at the bottom of the ladder are often recent arrivals from reservations, and their contact with the tribe is usually intact. For the latter, frequent trips to the reservation are common. Indeed, many Native Americans show considerable movement to and from reservations.

Intermarriage

Connected to this internal class differentiation is the issue of **intermarriage.** Since intermarriage is seen as perhaps the key indicator of social acceptance, the contrast between blacks and Native Americans is instructive. The Native American standing was only slightly higher than that of blacks (and Mexicans and Puerto Ricans) in social distance studies. This being the case, the pronounced difference in intermarriage rates for Native Americans and blacks is remarkable. As we noted in the preceding chapter, the historically low rates of black-white intermarriage still persist. For Native Americans, however, the rate is very high (Sandefur, 1986).

The rate has been high for quite some time. Data from the as far back as the 1980 census indicate that 53 percent of married Native Americans were married to nonIndians. To appreciate how unique this figure is, compare it with the rates for both blacks and whites. Only approximately 4 percent of

Native American college students promoting cultural awareness.

blacks are married to nonblacks, and the figure for whites married to nonwhites is only around 2 percent. This situation has prompted some in the Native American community to question whether this tendency to marry nonIndians means that Native Americans will, "in the not too distant future, marry themselves out of existence" (Snipp, 1989: 165; see also Vogt, 1957).

The city has been a crucible for intermarriage. As Table 7.1 reveals, by the last quarter of the twentieth century only one in five married Native Americans in metropolitan areas was married to a Native American, while for those residing on or near reservations the figure was closer to one out of two. Furthermore, Native Americans on or in close proximity to reservations have a variety of communal institutions that can assist intermarrieds maintain contact with the Native American community. In contrast, many intermarrieds in cities have few if any ties to Native American communities. This lack of ties can be due to choice, as Native Americans seek to distance themselves from their Native American past—or perhaps merely from poor Native Americans in cities—as they assimilate into white society. But it can also be partially caused by the relative weakness of ethnic institutions in urban settings.

Whatever the precise reasons, clearly a segment of urbanized Native Americans are not part of the Native American community and do not choose to accentuate, or even claim, their Native American identity. Others are not part of the community but choose, when they think it advantageous, to claim their Native American ancestry. For this segment of the population, Native Americanness becomes a form of symbolic ethnicity. This segment of the population tends to be intermarried and

Table 7.1 Marital Choices of American Indians by Place of Residence				
Place of Residence	**American Indian Husband and Wife**	**Indian Husband, NonIndian Wife**	**NonIndian Husband, Indian Wife**	**Total**
Metropolitan	20.6%	39.5%	39.9%	100.0%
Nonmetropolitan	48.6	24.3	27.1	100.0
Off Reservation	20.6	39.5	39.9	100.0
On or Near Reservation	46.2	25.6	28.2	100.0

Reprinted from *American Indians: The First of This Land*, by C. Matthew Snipp, 1989: 160 © The Russell Sage Foundation. Used with the permission of the Russell Sage Foundation.

more highly educated than the Native American population as a whole (Eschbach, Supple, and Snipp, 1998).

Insofar as intermarriage leads to mixed-race children, it creates a dilemma. On the one hand, the children can contribute to the growth of the Indian population by increasing the number of people who can lay claim to some Indian heritage (Shoemaker, 1999: 88). However, intermarriage comes into conflict with the one-quarter blood quantum rule employed by the federal government and many tribes. As historian Patricia Limerick (1987: 338) notes, "Set the blood quantum at one-quarter, hold to it as a rigid definition of Indians, let intermarriage proceed as it [has] for centuries, and eventually Indians will be defined out of existence." This situation has led to a vigorous debate within the Native American community about what it means to be an authentic Indian (Churchill, 1999; Fogelson, 1998).

The Ethnic Community in the City

For those who remain attached to the Native American community—especially those in the ranks of working-class and poor Native Americans—an institutional presence has developed. Such institutions have actually existed in cities since at least the 1920s, and their numbers have grown since the 1950s. But distinctive features have a bearing on ethnic identity. Most important, these institutions have tended to promote pan-Indian organizations and ethnic identity. Although pan-Indian ethnicity is not new, it is a more pervasive feature of the Native American population today, largely because of urbanization.

Although urban organizations have been established on a tribal basis, many community centers and organizations formed to advance the interests of urban Native Americans have been constructed across tribal boundaries. The connection between tribes and the federal government has been severed in cities, opening up the possibility of new forms of organization. This process has been further encouraged because white society has tended to be oblivious to tribal differences among urbanized Native Americans, defining native people by the supratribal designations "American Indian" or "Native American."

Robert Thomas (1968) considered pan-Indianism as an instance of the invention of a new ethnic group, one that replaces tribal identity with a more inclusive one. He believed that this is a way for Native Americans seeking inclusion in an urban-industrial society to preserve a sense of ethnic identity. For Thomas, the root motives for this invention are psychological and cultural. Cornell (1988: 146) disputed this claim by pointing to the political character of pan-Indianism: It provides Native Americans with the resources needed to mount effective campaigns to advance their political interests and improve their economic conditions.

In a study of the Native American community in Los Angeles, Joan Weibel-Orlando (1991) documented both the cultural preservation and the political activities of these institutions. Thus, this in-depth empirical study lent credence to both positions. It also pointed out something that both Thomas and Cornell tended to overlook: Only a small minority of urban Indians actually involve themselves in these institutions—only about 4 percent of the approximately 48,000 Native Americans in the Los Angeles area actually participate in the social world of the ethnic community.

Political Activism

The main vehicle for pan-Indian political activity until the 1960s was the National Congress of American Indians (NCAI). Its political stance was moderate and its tactics were nonconfrontational. The NCAI operated primarily by lobbying in Washington, and its chief objective was to fight termination. As such, the organization was committed to protecting the existing relationship between tribes and the federal government. Thus, supratribalism was designed to be a political means to protect the integrity of tribes and preserve the reservations. Of course, the NCAI also tried to find ways to foster economic development on or near reservations (Wax, 1971).

Given this general orientation, it is not entirely surprising that the leadership of the NCAI was publicly hostile to the black civil rights movement and to the tactics of nonviolent civil disobedience. In part this was due to their belief in the appropriateness of conventional political activities. It can also be seen as a way of making invidious comparisons between blacks and Native Americans in an effort to display Native American activism in a more favorable light.

This stance was challenged during the 1960s. The National Indian Youth Council (NIYC), formed in 1961 by Native American college students, argued for more militant opposition to white society and to the detrimental effects of government policy. In contrast with the NCAI, the NIYC was inclined to be sympathetic to the black civil rights movement. In many ways the NIYC modeled its activities after the civil rights movement's more militant wing. The NIYC gave way to several other militant groups, the most influential being the American Indian Movement (AIM), which not only engaged in confrontational politics but also endorsed the use of violence in some instances. Like the Black Panthers, AIM was founded in a city (Minneapolis in 1968) as a response to police mistreatment and harassment.

The Red Power Movement

Direct political confrontation dramatically escalated during the 1960s (Nagel, 1995, 1996), although there were actually activist stirrings in the late 1950s. These included the attack by Lumbee Indians of Robeson County, North Carolina, on a Ku Klux Klan rally in 1958, and a pan-Indian march on the Washington, D.C., headquarters of the BIA in the following year. In the 1960s numerous local actions reflected a growing willingness to engage in civil disobedience and in political theater. For instance, the "fish-ins" and hunting in defiance of state laws were responses to what were seen as violations of treaties that had guaranteed special hunting and fishing privileges to Native Americans. Contestations over land ownership and the use of land by loggers and other developers was yet another early focus of conflict (Cornell, 1988).

Voices	Tim Giago

Afrer all was said and done, things became worse for the long-suffering people of the reservation. The media packed up and left as did the occupiers. The people of Pine Ridge were left to clean up the mess. Because of the violent actions of a few, a backlash of hate and anger came down on the Indian people left behind in the wake of the takeover . . . legal cases the Oglala Sioux should have won in court suddenly went against them. Funds vital to the survival of the Lakota people were slashed and cut by a Congress bent on revenge. . . . The takeover was not a good thing then and it is not a good thing to remember now.

Tim Giago, a resident of the Pine Ridge reservation and editor of the Lakota Times, *reflecting on the AIM takeover at Wounded Knee (Nagel, 1996: 173).*

Such activism was a precursor to what became known as the **Red Power** movement. As Joane Nagel (1996: 130) observed, "Red Power borrowed from civil rights organizational forms, rhetoric, and tactics, but modified them to meet the specific needs and symbolic purposes of Indian grievances, targets, and locations." The three most dramatic events that captured the attention of the national media during this period were the occupation of Alcatraz in 1969, the Trail of Broken Treaties march in 1972, and the takeover of the community of Wounded Knee in 1973. The first action involved the occupation of the San Francisco Bay island that had formerly served as a federal prison. An ad hoc organization called Indians of All Tribes claimed that the island legitimately belonged to Native Americans. Its leaders proclaimed their intention of establishing a training school and a center for Native American culture and education. Several thousand Native American supporters and whites sympathetic to the movement visited the island during the 19-month occupation. But the government held its ground and finally, in June 1971, without achieving their demands, the Native Americans withdrew from the island (Spicer, 1980; Prucha, 1985).

The other two events were initiated by AIM. The Trail of Broken Treaties march was in some respects a parallel to the 1963 civil rights movement march on Washington. By highlighting the long history of injustice suffered by Native Americans and the failure of whites to abide by treaties, protest organizers appealed to a moral constituency. AIM's goals and tactics were more militant, however. The demands, contained in the "Twenty Points" proposal, included abolishing the BIA and reinstituting the ability of tribes to enter into treaties with the federal government. Thus, AIM's objectives were far different from those of the NCAI and called for a complete reorganization of Native American relations with the U.S. government (Cornell, 1988).

The Trail of Broken Treaties march culminated in the weeklong occupation of the BIA headquarters, during which demonstrators hung a sign from the building proclaiming it to be the American Indian Embassy. When threatened with expulsion, occupiers vandalized the building. The subsequent reaction to this dramatic event has been summarized by Prucha (1985: 82): "The BIA was dispersed and reorganized, and Congress investigated possible foreign influence in AIM. No one any longer doubted that Indian conditions were serious enough to lead to violence."

The site chosen for the third action was symbolic. On February 27, 1973, activists occupied the village of Wounded Knee—the site of the 1890 massacre of some 150 Native Americans participating in the Ghost Dance—located on the Oglala Sioux's Pine Ridge Reservation. The government surrounded the Native Americans with several hundred heavily armed FBI agents, U.S. marshals, and BIA police. For 10 weeks the nation witnessed a violent siege that took the lives of two Native Americans and resulted in many injuries on both sides. The demands of the occupiers included the restoration of lands that, it was claimed, had been taken by whites in violation of treaties. AIM called for an end to government involvement in Native American affairs and condemned the purported corruption among tribal officials (Prucha, 1985; Cornell, 1988). When the occupation finally ended, none of these goals were met, but, as with the actions that preceded it, AIM had captured the spotlight and drawn public attention to the situation of reservation life.

Competing Political Goals

The Red Power movement forced the government and the general public to ask, "What do Indians want?" The social movement elicited varied responses from white society, ranging from an intensified hostility toward Native Americans to growing support for their cause. Needless to say, within the Native American community, this movement also caused considerable debate and conflict. The Native American population is not a single, homogeneous group but rather consists of peoples of great diversity, as we have seen in terms of geographic and social class locations, tribal identities, mixed versus full-blooded Native Americans, and so forth. Native Americans do not always agree on what they want collectively.

Cornell (1988) makes two distinctions in classifying the variations in Native American goals. The first distinction deals with the structure of Native American-white relations. He distinguishes two different orientations: *reformative* and *transformative*. Reformative goals basically accept the existing structure of Native American-white relations but seek to improve the welfare of Native Americans through a redistribution of resources, services, and rewards. Transformative goals seek not only a redistribution of rewards but also a fundamental restructuring of Native American-white relations.

The second distinction lies in differences between *integrative* and *segregative* goals. Integrative goals essentially accept the presence and appropriateness of European-American institutions in Native American communities. This approach promotes the assimilation of Native Americans into the mainstream American culture and into the larger society's institutions. In contrast, segregative goals challenge the benefit of permitting the dominant group's economic and political institutions to take root within Native American communities. As such, segregative goals are "antiassimilationist and antiacculturational" (Cornell, 1988: 153).

In the aftermath of the militancy of the 1960s and 1970s, transformative goals gained adherents at the expense of reformative goals. Although advocates for reform are still a powerful presence in Native American communities, they are not nearly as powerful as they were prior to 1960. Thus, Native Americans are currently far more critical of the status quo than they were a few decades ago. Native Americans remain deeply divided, and quite ambivalent, about the appropriateness of primarily integrative goals versus essentially segregative ones. While activism during the last two decades of the twentieth century often operated in conventional political channels, it was nonetheless shaped by the impact of the Red Power period. Moreover, AIM continued to be a presence in numerous political protests (Johnson, Champagne, and Nagel, 1997).

Ongoing Conflict With White America

In recent years Native Americans have combined confrontational tactics with increased court challenges. Tribal and supratribal organizations have been created or strengthened (Legters and Lyden, 1994). These organizations rely on a cadre of educated Native Americans with leadership skills, supporters outside of Native American communities, and the media. They operate with better financial resources than in the past. Although a number of important transformative organizations exist, the Native American Rights Fund, founded in 1971, has been particularly instrumental in undertaking numerous court cases.

The 1975 Indian Educational Assistance and Self-Determination Act and related legislation and court rulings transformed the issue of tribal sovereignty. These developments permitted tribal control of mineral and other natural resources and provided the legal basis for Indian gambling casinos. Many legal battles were based on claims of violations of treaty agreements between various tribes and the U.S. government. To capture the flavor of some of the areas of greatest conflict, we will briefly review a few examples, looking at three areas of dispute: hunting and fishing rights, control of natural resources, and land claims.

The Chippewa Spearfishing Dispute

The Chippewas, located near Lake Superior, had ceded lands in what is now eastern Minnesota, northern Wisconsin, and northern Michigan to the United States government in a series of treaties entered into in 1836, 1837, 1842, and 1854. The Chippewas did not relinquish their rights to hunt, fish, and gather on these lands; they sold the land to the government but did not give up their right to the resources that had been essential to their economic survival. In Wisconsin, the Chippewas have historically harvested fish, deer, furbearing animals, waterfowl, and wild rice (Terry, 1991). During the ensuing century and a half, the Chippewas have not consistently exercised these rights. It is important to note that the right to harvest is not held by individual Native Americans, but by the tribe.

Beginning in the 1970s, a controversy arose in northern Wisconsin over the right of the Chippewas to engage in spearfishing, a practice that is illegal for nonNative Americans. Opponents of the practice complained that Native Americans were given special rights not granted to others. Furthermore, opponents contended that old treaties could not possibly be applicable to present circumstances and thus should no longer be legally binding. They also argued that when Native Americans became United States citizens in 1924, they gave up their tribal citizenships and thus such special privileges. Finally, they argued, treaties applied only to full-blooded Native Americans, not to individuals who are only part Chippewa. Actually, these arguments are wrong on all counts. The Chippewas were not granted privileges: they never relinquished them in their treaties. The age of the treaties does not void them. Native Americans did not give up their tribal citizenships when they also became U.S. citizens. Instead, tribes are the arbiters of who is and who is not eligible for membership in the tribe. They use varying criteria for making such determinations, including the use of blood quantum or birthright.

Native Americans had confined their spearfishing to reservation land until 1974, when the Tribble brothers of the Lac Courte Oreilles Band of Chippewas crossed reservation boundaries to fish. They were subsequently arrested by Department of Natural Resources wardens. This act of defiance set the stage for a legal battle—a test case to challenge the legality of the state's right to enforce Wisconsin law against tribal members in areas under which treaty rights superseded state law. The Chippewas, in a report titled "A Guide to Understanding Chippewa Treaty Rights," indicated their conviction that by the 1970s they had acquired the necessary sophistication and skill to deal with the complicated legal system of the white world. The report stated, "Time and familiarity with the system eventually provided the Chippewa with the ability to assert their rights within the legal forum of the dominant society." Indeed, after a nine-year legal battle, the Chippewas won their case in the U.S. Court of Appeals.

This case set the stage for the intensification of conflict with whites, who argued that the decision was a direct threat to the economic livelihood of all nonNative Americans. The economy of the area was dominated by tourism and the timber industry. Whites feared that the ability of the Chippewas to exploit the region's natural resources would undermine their economic position. Spearfishing was only one example of how Native Americans were seen as having a potentially disruptive impact on the local economy.

Out of this economic conflict emerged an organized anti-Native American presence that included such local efforts in Wisconsin as Equal Rights for Everyone, Wisconsin Alliance for Rights and Resources, and Protect American Rights and Resources. These groups waged both legal and media campaigns to halt spearfishing. Their members picketed and used high-speed boats to disrupt the Chippewas when they sought to exercise their fishing rights. There were also scattered threats of violence, including shooting in the vicinity of spearfishers and the planting of pipe bombs. The threat of violence was associated with manifestations of racism, seen for example in bumper stickers that read "Save a Walleye, Spear an Indian" or "Spear a Pregnant Squaw, Save a Walleye." Native Americans were referred to as "Indian niggers" or "Red niggers" (Ivey, 1990; Terry, 1991; Gedicks, 1993).

On the other hand, the Chippewas not only were well organized but also received support from a variety of nonNative American organizations, ranging from the regional chapter of the environmentalist Green party to the human rights office of the Evangelical Lutheran Church in America. The end to this dispute occurred in March 1991, when the Chippewas agreed to a court settlement that reaffirmed their traditional treaty rights. The Native Americans agreed to drop a $325 million lawsuit and to a limitation on the number of fish they could take from nonreservation waters. They also agreed to refrain from harvesting timber off of reservation land, thereby protecting the economic interests of whites in the timber industry. The agreement pleased some Native Americans and whites, but it was received with either hostility or ambivalence by others (Gedicks, 2001).

The Blackfeet and Oil Exploration: Limiting Development

A conflict over oil development of a vast tract of land in Montana known as the Badger-Two Medicine region, part of the Lewis and Clark National Forest, pitted the Blackfeet Indians against the combined forces of the oil industry and the U.S. government's Forest Service. The Chevron Oil Corporation and Fina Oil and Chemical Company obtained the lease to this land and over several years worked to acquire the government's approval to conduct exploratory drilling. The result was an ongoing conflict between those favoring exploration and those opposed to it (Cornell, 1988). During the Persian Gulf crisis, a memo circulated within the Forest Service urged the agency to take advantage of the public's fear of a loss of imported oil to push through approval. The memo's author pressed for relaxing existing procedures for environmental review and argued in favor of limiting public comment. Environmentalists were opposed to any attempt to drill in this land and argued that the area was home to the grizzly bear, an endangered species. They pointed to government studies that indicated drilling would disturb more than 7,000 acres of land and create air, water, and noise pollution (Baum, 1990).

The Blackfeet joined environmentalists in opposing oil exploration in the area. They shared the concern about the impact on the environment. But the Blackfeet were also concerned that it would upset their ability to practice their religion. Tribal leaders argued that the land was used as a place of spiritual renewal. Their sweat lodges were built along a creek for retreats as tribal members conducted traditional purification rites. There they make pilgrimages to the top of the mountains and fast in a practice known as "vision quests," conduct sun dances, and practice various other religious ceremonies. According to Tiny Man Heavy Runner, a chief of the Blackfeet, the idea of digging oil wells in this area would be as much of a sacrilege as digging a well in St. Patrick's Cathedral (Baum, 1990). The Forest Service contended that the Native Americans had not proved their case that the land is sacred. The Blackfeet failed to produce what government officials considered to be adequate documentation of their claims. However, they continued to press their claims in an alliance with environmentalists. To date, this has not begun.

The Blackfeet battle with oil companies and their governmental supporters is an example of cultural conflict—the result of two competing and distinctive worldviews. Developers view the natural world as separate from humans, who, to survive and thrive, must exploit the resources provided by that world. Furthermore, individuals derive their definitions of personal identity from the social and cultural world they inhabit, not from the natural world. The natural world is not sacred, but profane.

In stark contrast, the Blackfeet identify with their natural environment, seeing themselves as a part of it and thus finding their own identities in it. Any action that disrupts or profoundly alters the existing state of nature and the Blackfeet relation to it is condemned. From this perspective, such changes could destroy the distinct identity of the Blackfeet. Tribal elders attribute the ravages of alcoholism and drug abuse to a weakening of tribal identity. In their view, the exploitation of the region for oil and gas will exacerbate these problems and intensify the alienation experienced by many younger Blackfeet.

This particular conflict between proponents and opponents of economic development is an example of many similar battles between those who view land as a commercial resource and those who invest land with spiritual power. The Northern Cheyennes, for example, have waged a similar campaign against coal mining. Related concerns are fundamentally about the preservation of Native American identities. Some tribes, including the Crows and Navajos, have voiced their opposition to economic plans that would result in the influx of sizable numbers of nonNative Americans. Native Americans fear that such an influx would produce assimilative pressures that many tribal members want to resist (Cornell, 1988).

Land Disputes: The Legacy of Treaty Violations

The terms of many treaties that ceded lands occupied by Native Americans to whites have been followed. In other instances, violations have resulted in land disputes, many of which have persisted since the nineteenth century. As noted in the Chippewas case, the increased willingness of Native Americans to use the American legal system to redress injustices has resulted in several highly publicized court cases that had or continue to have far-reaching implications.

On the East Coast, a number of challenges were made to Native American land cessations that had taken place during the colonial period, involving Native Americans from tribes such as the Passamaquoddies, Penobscots, Wampanoag-Mashpee, and Narragansetts. For example, the Native Americans of Maine argued in federal court that they should be given title to millions of acres of land in the state. They based this claim on a 1790 federal law that required states to obtain the approval of the federal government prior to purchasing any Native American lands. According to the suit, Massachusetts (the state that at the time controlled what is now Maine) had failed to do so. If the court had ruled in the Native Americans' favor, the entire social and economic structure of Maine would have been placed in jeopardy. The apprehensions among the white citizenry of Maine heightened tensions. Rather than continuing a long, protracted legal battle, Native Americans opted for a negotiated settlement that provided them with monetary compensation for lost lands (Prucha, 1985).

A similar claim was made for much of Cape Cod, a major resort and tourist area. Like the Maine case, the basis for the claim rested on the legality of the state's original purchase of Native American land. The high property values of the Cape put the Native Americans in a position to make rather stiff demands for monetary compensation. In a parallel case, the Wampanoags unsuccessfully sought to reclaim land on Martha's Vineyard. Similar land claims have been made elsewhere along the Atlantic seaboard, in Rhode Island, New York, and South Carolina (Prucha, 1985). And these claims have not been confined to this region of the country. The Puyallup in Washington State negotiated a settlement that netted the tribe $162 million, and the Sioux were awarded $106 million for the Black Hills in South Dakota. The Southern Pacific Transportation Company agreed to pay the Walker River Paiutes $1.2 million to settle a land dispute that began a century ago (*New York Times*, 1984b, 1989, 1990b).

In some instances, land rather than money was awarded. This occurred during the early 1970s in the Alaska Native Claims Settlement, which gave 40 million acres of land to the Native Americans, Aleuts, and Eskimos (Dinnerstein, Nichols, and Reimers, 1990). Such land disputes are far from over. Numerous simmering controversies exist in various places throughout the nation. These include a dispute between the Chippewas in northwestern Minnesota and local white farmers over land ownership and the assertion of the Oneidas that they are the rightful owners of 5 million acres of land in central New York State.

Development Plans on Native American Reservations

Reservations were created in a way that made it difficult to incorporate them into the national economy. Not only were they located in areas generally remote from major transportation networks and manufacturing and commercial centers, but they usually had few natural resources that could make them profitable. In the previous section we focused on issues related to cultural conflict and the antidevelopmental logic that can be seen in some types of Native American-white conflict. This section explores some of the varied ways in which Native Americans have pursued economic development (Cornell and Kalt, 1995). Many reservation residents have not opposed development; rather, they have sought to find ways to control and channel it for the best interests of the tribe.

Stephen Cornell and Joseph Kalt (1998) point to several tribal success stories: (1) the Mississippi Choctaws have become one of the largest employers in the state, offering both manufacturing and public sector jobs; (2) the White Mountain Apaches have found a niche in forest products, skiing, and recreation; (3) the Salish and Kootenai tribes of the Flathead Reservation in Montana have found success in tourism, agriculture, and retail services; and (4) the Cochiti Pueblo in New Mexico have created a variety of successful tribal enterprises. They contend that "Economic development on Indian reservations is first and foremost a political problem. At the heart of it lie sovereignty and the governing institutions through which sovereignty can be effectively exercised." While these examples are exceptions to the rule, they are not alone, as the following discussions on exploiting natural resources and tourism and gaming indicate. Moreover, they reveal something of the political character of economic development.

Exploiting Natural Resources

Several tribes, especially in the Midwest and the West, occupy land containing valuable oil, coal, and other mineral resources that have been mined by white-owned companies. Native Americans generally believe that there has been rampant exploitation by these companies and that reservations have not been paid adequate royalties. In perhaps the most concerted attempt to rectify this situation, several dozen tribes founded the Council of Energy Resource Tribes (CERT) in 1975 to obtain better contracts with companies. Supplied with grant monies from the federal government, CERT employed skilled negotiators and rather quickly won a contract with Atlantic Richfield that provided the tribes $78 million in royalties for 20 years. Many subsequent contracts were also favorable to Native Americans. Government support for CERT waned after Ronald Reagan's election, however, and CERT proved to be far less successful in the 1980s than in the preceding decade (Dorris, 1981; Fixico, 1985; Ungeheuer, 1987).

Within tribal communities there was considerable dissent over the aggressive pro-developmental stance of CERT's leadership. Many questioned the impact of such a campaign on tribal cultures. AIM was as vigorous in its opposition to unbridled development as were various environmental groups, especially over the issue of uranium mining (Jorgensen, 1984; Feagin, 1984).

Efforts to find ways to end the endemic poverty of reservations continue. Five tribes—the Yakima Indian Nation in Washington, the Mescalero Apache tribe in New Mexico, Minnesota's Prairie Island Indian Community, and two tribes in Oklahoma—the Sac and Fox Nation and the Chickasaw Indian Nation—are among the seven applicants for Department of Energy grants given to sites willing to store thousands of tons of high-level nuclear waste on their land. Many consider this willingness as a sign of the economic desperation felt by tribal councils. As Keith Schneider (1992) has written, the request for grant proposals has "stirred political dissension and raised questions about whether the Government is taking advantage of hard economic times and rural poverty to gain a site for some of the nation's most dangerous industrial wastes."

Tourism and Gaming

Some tribes have promoted tourism to provide an economic base. In fact, tourism has been an important part of reservation economic life for some tribes for decades. However, it can only work in some places and depends on the accessibility of the reservation, the scenic character of the landscape, and so forth. Furthermore, even where tourism is well established, Native Americans are often disappointed with the economic returns it provides (M. E. Smith, 1982).

Tribes have attempted to find other ways out of a state of chronic poverty. Thus, the Moapa band of Paiute Native Americans in Nevada contemplated establishing a brothel on the reservation as a way of becoming economically self-sufficient (*New York Times*, 1984b). Taking advantage of the fact that state laws do not apply to reservations, many tribes have turned to organized gaming as a means of generating revenues for reservations. Initially, many tribes established bingo parlors, including the Mohawk Indians of Rooseveltown, New York, who built

A casino resort operated by the Mashantucket Pequot Tribal Nation, Mashantucket, Connecticut.

one of the nation's largest bingo parlors. Tribes throughout the country have constructed gambling casinos on tribal lands, including the Pequots and Seminoles in the East; the Chippewas, Oneidas, and Sioux in the Midwest; and the Navajo in the West. There are now more than 120 casinos and 220 high-stakes bingo games on Indian reservations, and, according to Gary Anders (1998: 99), "In 1996, Indian gaming exceeded $5 billion. . . . Casinos range from the palatial Foxwoods casino in Connecticut to trailers in remote locations offering a few slot machines." Revenue since 1996 has more than doubled.

A National Indian Gaming Commission was established to oversee and coordinate gaming ventures. In addition, the Indian Gaming Regulatory Act (IGRA) was passed in 1988 to provide an operating framework for such ventures (Anders, 1998; Stein, 1997). Supporters of gambling argue that it is a major industry and that Native Americans are in a position to benefit financially from entry into such ventures. Critics counter such claims by arguing that many Native Americans will be victimized by gaming. Furthermore, they are concerned about the potential for corruption and about the possible influence of organized crime (*New York Times*, 1992a).

Whatever the future of gambling on reservation lands, it is sometimes seen as viable where manufacturing has not been particularly successful. The Blackfeet have run a pen and pencil manufacturing plant, but in most instances, plans for industrial development either have not gotten started or have failed. In a review of three economic development plans formulated by Navajo, Zuni, and Standing Rock Sioux, David Vinje (1985: 167) observed, "Manufacturing is not viewed as the key to economic development in the current plans." Instead, the focus is on social service activities (health care, provision for the elderly, and so on) in the public sector, and on improving the level of commercial businesses—stores, restaurants, gas stations, and the like—on reservations. At the same time, many tribal leaders are aware of the fact that gambling may not prove to be a long-term solution to economic development. For that reason, many reservations are using the profits from gaming as start-up capital for other economic development plans and for improving the infrastructure of their reservations by building new housing, schools, hospitals, and so forth (Anders, 1998).

Quality of Life on Reservations

Reservations remain sites of persistent poverty and high levels of chronic unemployment and underemployment. Overall, the income of Native Americans has improved since the 1960s: Native Americans had a lower per capita income than blacks in 1969, but a higher income than blacks a decade later. Native Americans nonetheless lag far behind whites, especially Native Americans living on reservations. Overall, about one third of American Indians had incomes below the poverty line in the last half of the 1990s (U.S. Bureau of the Census, 1999). On 15 of the 16 most populated reservations, the proportion of families with incomes below the official poverty line ranged from a low of one third to more than one half (Snipp, 1989: 259). Since labor force participation is heavily tied to governmentally funded jobs, federal cutbacks in various programs during the past two decades have had a negative impact on reservation inhabitants. Reservation unemployment rates average 45 percent, with some reservations reporting rates as high as 80 percent (Anders, 1998).

Housing

The quality of reservation housing is considerably worse than that of housing for the general population. Overcrowding is a major problem. Housing units are more likely to lack running water, indoor plumbing, and electricity than is the case for whites and blacks. This is partly because rural housing in general is characterized by deficiencies in these amenities to a greater extent than urban housing.

An attempt to improve reservation housing in the 1960s and 1970s involved the BIA and the Department of Housing and Urban Development. Housing authorities modeled after the public housing program were created and controlled by tribes, the BIA, or both. New construction undertaken by these authorities resulted in an expansion of housing stock, which somewhat reduced overcrowding. It also provided to poor Native Americans subsidized housing in which rents were assessed in terms of a family's ability to pay.

Appreciable improvements were made in the overall housing stock on reservations. For example, the percentage of Native American homes with complete bathrooms increased from 72 percent in 1970 to 90 percent in 1980. Nonetheless, this figure was still below that for whites (97.8 percent) and blacks (93.6 percent). Furthermore, some reservations are poorer than others, so general figures do not reveal the actual depth of poverty in some locales. In 1980, on the Hopi reservation, 55.5 percent of households did not have indoor plumbing, while the figure was 53.5 percent for the Papago. In addition, 15.9 percent of housing units on reservations did not have electricity, 16.6 percent did not have refrigerators, and 55.8 percent were without telephones. Clearly, parity in housing had not been achieved by 1980. Since that time, further improvements have been stymied because Native American housing assistance programs were abolished during the Reagan administration (Snipp, 1989; Tippeconnic, 1990).

Health Issues

American Indians may be the least healthy racial group in the United States. The infant mortality rate is higher than average, and the life expectancy of Native Americans is about 10 years shorter than the national average. Death rates due to diseases including pneumonia, diabetes, and tuberculosis are higher for Indians than for other groups. The suicide rate slightly exceeds that of the general population, and the death rate due to homicide is nearly two times that of all racial groups. As Table 7.2 indicates, accidental deaths are more than twice as common for Native Americans as for all races (Indian Health Service, 1987). Compounding the problem is the inadequate provision of health care. For example, over a quarter of Native Americans lacked health in-

Table 7.2 Mortality Rates for Selected Causes (per 100,000)		
Cause of Death	**American Indians**	**All Races**
Cardiovascular disease	173.1	228.4
Malignant neoplasms	88.4	133.5
Accidents	81.3	35.0
Auto	42.0	19.1
Other	39.3	15.9
Liver disease and cirrhosis	30.7	10.0
Diabetes	20.6	9.5
Pneumonia and influenza	18.4	12.2
Homicide	14.5	8.4
Suicide	12.9	11.6
Tuberculosis	1.8	0.5

Source: Indian Health Service Chart Book Series (1987).

surance at the beginning of the twenty-first century (U.S. Bureau of the Census, 2000).

Most staggering is the fact that deaths due to alcoholism are five times greater for Native Americans as for all races (May, 1999). There is a high incidence of liver disease and cirrhosis, and alcohol abuse is also linked to accidental deaths, suicides, and homicides.

Over the past three decades, there has been a noticeable decrease in alcohol-related deaths, although alcoholism continues to be an extremely serious problem. Not surprisingly, in a public opinion survey of Native Americans conducted by the *Arizona Republic* (1987), substance abuse was identified as the greatest problem facing Native Americans today. A troubling dimension to this problem has recently received media attention: the incidence of fetal alcohol syndrome, a cluster of mental and physical defects suffered by infants of alcoholic mothers. This serious problem has resulted in one instance in the jailing of a pregnant alcoholic woman to ensure that she refrained from drinking while carrying her child.

Native Americans in the White Mind

When whites think of race relations, they think of black and white relations. More recently, the impact of immigration has made whites more conscious of population changes among both Hispanics and Asians. In contrast, among whites there is relatively little consciousness of developments within Native American communities except in white communities located near reservations. This is partly because Native Americans are more rural than other racial groups and thus are more invisible to most whites and partly because of the relatively small size of the Native American population.

Whatever the reasons, white attitudes toward Native Americans differ from those directed at other racial groups. In the nineteenth century, Native Americans were perceived as museum pieces, as part of a premodern world that was destined to disappear entirely. This general attitude has not disappeared even today. For example, if one looks at how Native Americans are depicted in American movies, it is clear that they are generally portrayed as an "entertaining anachronism" (Bataille and Silet, 1980). Films about Native Americans are seldom about their current circumstances; rather, they are mainly portrayals of Indians on the American frontier (Woll and Miller, 1987). Though about half of Native Americans now reside in cities, no film has been produced that explicitly examines the lives of urban American Indians.

Countless B movies depicted Native Americans as savage aggressors. These "cowboy-and-Indian" movies were the stock of matinees that shaped the attitudes of at least two generations of moviegoers. The frontier settlers were generally presented as the innocent victims of attacks in which women and children were routinely abducted, while men were the victims of brutal torture and death. These films rarely showed sensitivity to the fact that the western expansion of the nation entailed a form of colonial occupation, or that whites—soldiers and civilians—brutalized Native Americans and uprooted their lives in the process of conquest.

. Beginning as early as the late 1940s, however, several movies either reflected a more ambiguous understanding of white and Native American relations or offered a sympathetic treatment of Native Americans. In the 1950 film *Broken Arrow,* the Apache chief Cochise (played by the nonNative American Jeff Chandler) was presented as an advocate of peaceful relations with whites, and Apache culture was treated in a favorable manner—although the perspective was somewhat romanticized and not entirely accurate historically. Indicating a very different attitude than that held by the public and reflected by Hollywood regarding black and white interracial love, the film also had a romantic relationship between a frontiersman (James Stewart) and a Native American woman played by Debra Paget (Woll and Miller, 1987; Bataille and Silet, 1980).

In the 1960s several Hollywood films were highly critical of American society in general, reflecting the growing hostility over the Vietnam War and the more militant phase of the civil rights movement. Members of the youth counterculture, known at the time as hippies, became interested in Native American cultures. They saw the Native American as a valuable model for alternative lifestyles that were more in tune with nature and that fostered harmony and cooperation rather than individual competitiveness. Although Hollywood films did not necessarily embrace this view, several movies did turn the tables, portraying Native Americans in a favorable light and whites as the aggressive victimizers. This view could be seen, for example, in *Soldier Blue, A Man Called Horse, Tell Them Willie Boy Is Here,* and *Buffalo Bill and the Indians.* The film that perhaps best captured this sensibility was Arthur Penn's *Little Big Man.* Bataille and Silet (1980) considered the film to be a powerful indictment of white-dominated culture in America and summarized its main message in the following way:

> The slaughter of Custer and his men was seen as a perfectly justifiable revenge for the atrocities committed by the cavalry on a peaceful people. . . . Penn contrasts the organic culture of the Cheyenne with the confusing and destructive Anglo-Saxon society which is engulfing it. Civilization becomes disordered, hypocritical, self-seeking, and nihilistic with people living in constant fear and tension. The culture projects all of its hatred and insecurity onto its enemies.

Native Americans occupy an ambivalent place in the minds of whites. This is evident in such films as Kevin Costner's *Dances With*

Wolves (1990) and the animated *Pocahontas* (1995), which are intended to be sympathetic to Indian life and culture but manage to perpetuate various problematic stereotypes. Images of the noble savage, the victim of conquest, and peaceful and harmonious communities living intimately connected to the natural world continue to coincide with negative images of drunken, violence-prone, and lazy Native Americans living in disorganized and impoverished tribal units. NonNative Americans know little about people of mixed ancestry, especially those who, like Scott Momaday, have managed to remain connected to their Native American past while integrating into the outside society. Yet these people constitute a large and ever-growing component of the Native American population. If intermarriage rates continue to remain high, as is likely, they will become even more typical.

Uncertain Futures

The futures of mixed-bloods will probably be quite different than those of full-bloods. Although those who are only part Native American have frequently embraced assimilation, many of this group, like European Americans, will express their sense of being Native American in various manifestations of symbolic ethnicity. They will choose to be Native American on some occasions and downplay or conceal this part of their ancestry at other times. As with similar members of other ethnic groups, these Native Americans do not rely to any great extent on ethnic institutions, and their interpersonal relationships may be chiefly with nonNative Americans. They are assimilationists whose lives are shaped by the values of the dominant society. They are unwilling to let their Native American ancestry be an impediment to success, and not surprisingly they are better educated and far more upwardly mobile in socioeconomic terms than other Native Americans. They are urbanites with few, if any, ties to reservation residents.

Native Americans who have chosen to remain on or near reservations are more likely to be full-blooded. They differ from those involved in an assimilative symbolic ethnicity insofar as they are attempting to preserve not simply a sense of individual Native American identity but a viable communal life as well. They are undertaking this task while seeking to take advantage of those aspects of contemporary society that can help improve their lives. As C. Matthew Snipp (1989: 322) wrote, "That American Indians no longer wander the plains on horseback in search of wild game does not mean that there are no longer any 'real' Indians." Rather than treating what it means to be a Native American as unchanging, these native people have a more dynamic perspective that entails the construction of a Native American identity that preserves selective traditions while seeking ways to overcome economic isolation and deprivation.

This goal is not easily accomplished, as can be seen in recent developments in higher education. Beginning in 1968 on the Navajo's reservation in Tsaile, Arizona, tribes in 12 states opened colleges on Native American land. There are currently 24 tribal colleges and 2 run by the federal government. Most are junior colleges and some are not fully accredited. Four are four-year institutions, with Sinte Gleska University in Rosebud, South Dakota, also offering a master's degree in education. What these institutions are attempting to do is twofold: first, to provide skills that can assist students in finding jobs, and second, to instill a sense of pride and appreciation of Native American identity. There are attempts to teach using values more in tune with Native American culture, such as downplaying individual competition and promoting ways in which students can learn by working together on common tasks.

The results have been somewhat mixed. The dropout rate is quite high, and students who go on to four-year colleges off the reservation do not have a high rate of success. On the other hand, many graduates attribute their ability to acquire better jobs to the education they received at these institutions. Some outside observers have credited the colleges with impressive results in reaching native people who are not served by mainstream American educational institutions. The education offered has a practical character because administrators see their role as one of training professionals needed on reservations, and students focus on certain areas where they see genuine local job opportunities. According to Michael Marriott (1992: A13), "Topping the list are usually studies in land and resource management and human welfare and health services."

Summary

On reservations, the lives of Native Americans are shaped by the community, which is beset with many serious social problems. Native Americans' lives are also frequently characterized by internal conflict and dissent; corruption by tribal leaders is a common complaint and source of strain. Nonetheless, the reservation is home to many, and the familiarity of the reservation provides a sense of security not found elsewhere. Those who have left the reservation in search of employment in cities often return because of the loss of a sense of community. The problems they hoped to escape often follow them to cities, while the benefits of communal life do not. The fate of those who do not return has not been studied much, so we know very little about their circumstances. What we do know about reservation Native Americans is that most have not succeeded in becoming self-sufficient, so they continue to depend on the federal government playing a prominent role (Prucha, 1985). However, there are some indications that this situation is changing as economic self-determination has had a positive impact on some locales (Cornell and Kalt, 1995).

Key Terms

Indian Reorganization Act   *reservation*
intermarriage   *termination*
Red Power   *urbanization*

Questions for Discussion and Critical Thinking

1. Compare and contrast the Indian Reorganization Act and termination. What are the implications of these policies for Native Americans, and how did they respond to them? What is the relevance of urbanization to these policies?

2. Describe the key events associated with the Red Power movement. Compare and contrast this movement with its Black Power counterpart in the African American community.

3. Based on information presented in this chapter, what do you think the future holds for American Indians who continue to reside on reservations? ✦

Chapter 8

Latino Americans: Into the Mainstream or on the Margins?

Araceli Rodriguez was born in Fresno, California. Her parents came to the United States from Mexico during the early part of the last century. They settled in the California valley town known for food production, and like so many of other Mexicans they worked as agricultural laborers. Both of her parents worked in the fields as children. They became active in the United Farmworkers Union but managed to leave manual labor when they entered college. Today Araceli's parents are teachers, and she grew up in a middle-class family. She also wants to continue what she calls "the family tradition" by becoming an educator herself.

Alex Ramos was born in El Salvador but left in 1985 when he was only 4 years old. At that time, he was reunited with his father, who had migrated to California somewhat earlier. Traveling with his mother, his older brother, and several other unrelated men and women, they came across the U.S.-Mexican border with the help of a "coyote," or paid guide, who ferried the illegal immigrants into the country. His family made their way north to Los Angeles and settled in the growing Salvadoran community in the area. Today his father works as a gardener for a wealthy family in southern California. Alex's father expects and hopes that his children will go to college but worries about how he will finance their education.

Steven Diaz is a third-generation Cuban American. His grandparents left Cuba in the late 1960s when his father was an infant. They owned a successful business in Havana before the Cuban Revolution. Steven grew up in Florida and Texas. Although his family still has relatives in Cuba, his parents have not had much contact with them during the past four decades because of the ongoing political conflict between the Cuban and American governments. Steven is in graduate school, working on his MBA. While his parents have a successful business in the Cuban ethnic enclave in Miami, he does not think he will join them in the firm. Rather, he is looking forward to a job in corporate America. His parents are supportive of his goal, but they make it clear that they would like to see him marry a Cuban woman.

Maria Aguilar is a Puerto Rican American, born in New York City. Her parents came to the mainland over 50 years ago. Racially, she is *mulatto*, mixed race born of African, Spanish, and indigenous Puerto Rican roots. Being *mulatto* might allow her to transcend racial boundaries, but in American society, where race has historically been defined along a stark black/white dichotomy, she is most often perceived to be black rather than of mixed race. Maria is active in a New York City theater group whose actors explore issues of racial and ethnic identity in the Latino community.

As these examples illustrate, Latino Americans are highly diverse—ethnically, racially, and socioeconomically. The Latino population in the United States has grown dramatically since 1965 because of the combined impact of increased immigration levels and high fertility rates for most Hispanic groups. A decade ago, demographers predicted that Latinos would become the largest racial minority by 2050 (U.S. Bureau of the Census, 1992b). As it turns out, this dramatic outcome occurred considerably earlier. Nearly 13 million Hispanics arrived in the country between 1991 and 2000. Not surprisingly, the 2000 Census revealed that the Hispanic and African American populations were nearly equal in size (U.S. Bureau of the Census, 2001). Based on population estimates from July 1, 2001, the U.S. Bureau of the Census concluded that the Hispanic population had reached approximately 37 million, while blacks were slightly more than 36 million (Clemetson, 2003). Moreover, as Figure 8.1 indicates, Mexicans constitute 66.1 percent of the Latino population. Indeed, Mexicans are by far the largest group among all of the foreign-born in the United States (Perlmann and Waldinger, 1998). Migration is such a part of life in Mexico that, in the words of William Kandel and Douglas S.

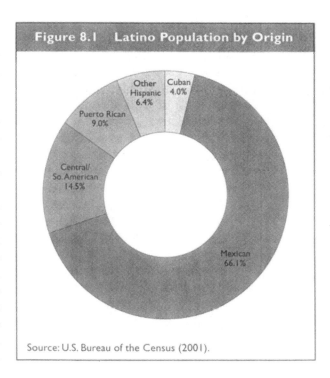

Figure 8.1   Latino Population by Origin

Other Hispanic 6.4%
Cuban 4.0%
Puerto Rican 9.0%
Central/So. American 14.5%
Mexican 66.1%

Source: U.S. Bureau of the Census (2001).

Massey (2002), it is possible to speak of a "culture of Mexican migration."

Latinos tend to be regionally concentrated, so they may have an even greater impact than they would if they were evenly dispersed throughout the country. The cultures, politics, and economies of some cities, particularly Miami and Los Angeles, have been profoundly altered by the Hispanic presence. Miami has become a truly bilingual city in only three decades, primarily because of the presence of Cubans. One consequence of this increase is that the city's black population is now a smaller percentage of the city's overall population than it was prior to 1960 (Portes and Stepick, 1993). The same transition has occurred in Los Angeles. The Latino—largely Mexican—population of Los Angeles County is now 38 percent, only 3 percentage points lower than the white population. Meanwhile, the black population has declined to 11 percent (Waldinger and Bozorgmehr, 1996).

Both Los Angeles and Miami have experienced major urban riots during the past quarter century: Miami in 1980 and Los Angeles in 1992. Each riot revealed that, unlike the essentially black and white character of the urban disorders of the 1960s, other groups were involved as well. The event that triggered the uprising in Miami's Liberty City was a jury's innocent verdict in a case in which police officers had been accused of beating a black motorcyclist to death. A larger underlying factor was that many blacks in Miami felt that the expanded Cuban American presence in the region had been detrimental to black interests. The Los Angeles riot has been described as the nation's first multiracial riot, involving blacks, whites, Asians, and Hispanics. The role of Mexicans is complicated, but as in Miami, clearly many blacks in Los Angeles believe that the growing Latino population has undermined their own place in the region (Sears, 1994).

Voices   Esther Báez

Our lives are totally different now, and so much has to do with what we have learned from the United States. It's both good and bad. When Javier told us that he wouldn't stand being tricked by politicians anymore or having to wait on long lines at city hall because they are so unorganized there, these were good things that he taught us about his life in the United States. But when people come back saying that they care more about themselves than about our community or that you can make a lot of money by selling drugs and that is okay, then we would rather not learn what the U.S. has to offer.

Esther Báez, a leader in her Dominican community, reflecting on the impact that transnational contacts have had on her city (Levitt, 2001: 54).

These statistics and events illustrate that the Hispanic presence in the United States is becoming more pronounced over time. This trend has international implications, as Mexico is one of the most important trade partners of the United States. The debate over the North American Free Trade Agreement (NAFTA) is an indication of the crucial economic ties between the nations. The strengths or weaknesses of the economies of the two nations at any particular time have had a direct bearing on the number of Mexicans who immigrated to the United States, legally or illegally. U.S. corporations, however, have found it beneficial to set up shop in Mexican border communities, as part of the Border Industrialization Program. These businesses are referred to as *maquiladora* **industries**. Typically, U.S.-manufactured parts are shipped to the Mexican plants, which have much lower labor costs, for assembly. The plants are owned either by U.S. firms or by Mexican firms under contract to the American companies. *Maquiladora* industries began in the mid-1960s and employed more than a quarter million persons by the late 1980s (Stoddard, 1987; Heyman 1991).

Latino Panethnic Unity or Ethnic Distinctiveness?

As noted in Chapter 1, two terms are now commonly used to describe Spanish-speaking people from the Western hemisphere: Hispanic and Latino. The latter term has been embraced most recently, especially by younger people who consider the term *Hispanic* to refer too directly to their descent from a colonized people. Some do not agree with this negative assessment and use the terms interchangeably. Both collective terms describe a number of highly diverse nationality groups (and we will continue to use the terms interchangeably). This chapter focuses on the three largest groups, which in descending order are Mexicans, Puerto Ricans, and Cubans. But these three do not encompass all of Latino America. The United States is home to 1.7 million immigrants from various nations in Central America, and another 1.4 million from South America. Other Hispanic groups that, according to the 2000 Census, have more than 750,000 persons include Dominicans, Salvadorans, Colombians, Guatemalans, Ecuadorians, Nicaraguans, Peruvians, Hondurans, and Panamanians (U.S. Bureau of the Census, 2001). There is considerable diversity among these groups. Some of the smaller ones are classic labor immigrants, with Dominicans representing the largest group in this category (Levitt, 2001). Others are political refugees who fled either communist or right-wing authoritarian regimes. Nicaraguans are an example of the former, while their neighbors in El Salvador are an example of the latter (Fernández-Kelly and Curran, 2001).

The federal government uses the Hispanic label when dividing the nation into major racial and ethnic groups. Some within the various

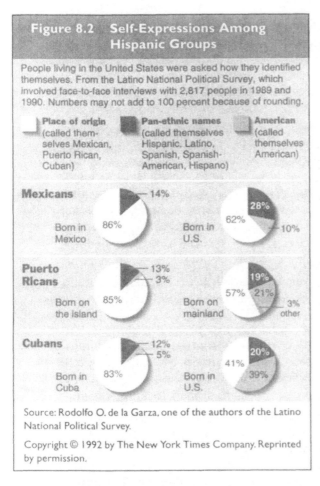

Figure 8.2 Self-Expressions Among Hispanic Groups

People living in the United States were asked how they identified themselves. From the Latino National Political Survey, which involved face-to-face interviews with 2,817 people in 1989 and 1990. Numbers may not add to 100 percent because of rounding.

Place of origin (called themselves Mexican, Puerto Rican, Cuban)

Pan-ethnic names (called themselves Hispanic, Latino, Spanish, Spanish-American, Hispano)

American (called themselves American)

Mexicans
Born in Mexico 86% — 14%
62% 28% 10%

Puerto Ricans
Born on the island 85% — 13% — 3%
57% 21% 19% 3% other

Cubans
Born in Cuba 83% — 12% — 5%
41% 20% 39%

Source: Rodolfo O. de la Garza, one of the authors of the Latino National Political Survey.

Copyright © 1992 by The New York Times Company. Reprinted by permission.

Hispanic communities have promoted a panethnic identity, seeing it as the basis for a powerful political alliance. According to a survey conducted in 1989 and 1990 by the Latino National Political Survey, however, the majority of people surveyed defined their identities in terms of national place of origin and not in panethnic terms.

Figure 8.2 illustrates this tendency, which is more pronounced for the immigrant generation than for subsequent generations. Mexicans born in the United States are most likely to use the label, but most individuals from the second and subsequent generations of both Puerto Ricans and Cubans choose to call themselves "American." David Gonzalez (1992a) found that Cubans were especially reluctant to lose their distinctive ethnic identity by using a panethnic label. Thus, he reports bumper stickers in Miami that read "No soy Hispano, soy Cubano" ("I am not Hispanic, I am Cuban"). Juan Flores (2000: 3) reports that despite some cross-group identification among Latinos, there is an important stake in their national identity: "If I'm Latino or Hispanic, then I am Dominican, or Puerto Rican, or Mexican American first."

The Bilingual Issue

After English, more people in the United States speak Spanish as a first language than any other language. In regions where Hispanics are concentrated, Spanish not only is spoken in the home but can be heard on the streets, in schools, in businesses, and in public facilities. Although the wave of immigration since 1965 has brought many other people who do not speak English or do not speak it as a first language—especially various Asian groups—the issue of **bilingualism** chiefly revolves around Spanish. It is worth noting that more people in the Western hemisphere speak Spanish than speak English. This fact has led some nativists to raise fears that the privileged role of English in the United States is being placed in jeopardy by the "invasion" of new immigrants.

Since the 1960s, language rights have evolved, partly as a result of pressure from legislative and judicial changes. In 1968 Congress passed the Bilingual Education Act, which supported research into programs that would help schoolchildren with little or no English language proficiency. Two years later the Department of Health, Education, and Welfare issued a regulation related to Title VI of the Civil Rights Act of 1964. The regulation declared that if a student was not able to participate effectively in a school's educational programs because of English language deficiencies, the school district was required to implement actions designed to remedy the deficiency. In several judicial decisions, notably *Serna v. Portales Municipal Schools* (1974) and *Lau v. Nichols* (1974), the courts upheld these regulations, while failing to rule conclusively on whether there is a constitutional right to bilingual education (Piatt, 1990).

Bilingual education programs have been in place for the past two decades. They have taken a variety of forms, from intensive English immersion programs to academic courses taught in the native tongue while instruction to develop English language proficiency is provided. Whatever their form, the regulatory intent has been to help students make a transition to fluency in English. Although many proponents of bilingualism have also sought to assist students in preserving their native tongue—thus becoming and remaining truly bilingual—this is not an explicit goal of such programs. Indeed, it has been assumed that in the long run, English would replace the native language. The implementation of bilingual programs has been extremely varied, and it is difficult to assess their effectiveness. Although much of the controversy over bilingualism has centered on education, language rights issues include the right to courtroom interpreters, the provision of multilingual voting ballots, the obligations of social service agencies to provide information in languages other than English, and equal access to broadcasting outlets (Piatt, 1990).

A reaction to bilingualism began to mount by the late 1970s. A key demand of those opposed to bilingualism was for an amendment to the Constitution that would declare English to be the official language of the United States. The organization chiefly responsible for spearheading this drive was U.S. English, founded by former U.S. Senator S. I. Hayakawa and Dr. John Tanton. The stated rationale was that the constitutional amendment would encourage assimilation. Spokespersons for U.S. English argued that proponents of bilingualism were hostile to assimilation and that this worked against the ability of nonEnglish-speaking immigrants to succeed economically in America. Such an amendment was introduced into Congress in 1981, 1984, and 1988, and in each instance, it was defeated. At the state level, however, "official English" legislation has been passed by 27 states (<www.us-english .org>).

Although states have passed official English legislation, in reality it is questionable how much it is enforced. For example, in the state of California, one may still get driver's information and voter pamphlets in several different languages. Phone answering systems routinely ask callers if they would prefer a Spanish menu, as do ATM machines and a host of other self-serve devices. We might also note the sociological significance of where the English-only legislation has received its strongest support: in states such as California and Florida. These are two states where the Hispanic population is growing (in California, there is also a substantial Asian immigrant population). Nativist sentiment springs up when the majority English-speaking population feels overwhelmed or threatened by the nonEnglish-speaking population. The majority population might express their concerns through the electoral process—namely, by passing discriminatory or anti-immigrant legislation. This may certainly be the case in places, such as California and Florida, where the traditional "majority" is no longer the majority in numbers.

Several prominent people served on the U.S. English board, including former television anchorperson Walter Cronkite, and it claimed a membership of 350,000. The group lost the endorsements of many earlier supporters, however, when it was revealed that Dr. Tanton had written in racist terms about the threat to the educated, English-speaking population from the rapid population growth of poor, uneducated nonEnglish-speaking people. To counter this perceived threat, he had advocated draconian measures to stop immigration and had proposed forced sterilization as a method of population control (Piatt, 1990). Although supporters then questioned the motives of U.S. English, many people continue to oppose bilingualism. Among them are some prominent individuals within the Hispanic community, including former Reagan aide Linda Chavez and writer Richard Rodriguez. Chavez (1991) considered the acquisition of English language to be a prerequisite for poor Latinos to move "out of the barrio."

This argument implies that it is necessary to learn English to succeed economically in America and that once one does speak the language, upward mobility will follow. Cubans are the most successful group, yet more than 46 percent of Cubans claim that they do not speak English well or at all. On the other hand, only 27 percent of Puerto Ricans, the Hispanic group with the lowest median income, claim that they do not speak English well (Bean and Tienda, 1987). These statistics suggest that much more than language determines the ability of ethnic groups to succeed in America. However, it is also clearly the case that by the second generation, English language proficiency is quite high, often with a simultaneous decline in proficiency in the native language

(Portes and Hao, 2002; Portes and Schauffler, 1996). At the same time, there is evidence that Latinos remain bilingual longer than their Asian counterparts. We explore some of the important factors that contribute to the differing experiences of the three largest Hispanic groups in the remainder of this chapter.

Cuban Americans

Cuba is only 90 miles from the U.S. coast, yet immigration levels remained relatively low until the 1950s. From the Spanish-American War in 1898 until 1959, Cuba was dependent on the United States, both politically and economically. The United States was responsible for ending Spanish control of Cuba, and subsequent Cuban governments relied heavily on American support. Although democratic government did not develop in Cuba, the economy developed throughout the first half of the twentieth century, which resulted in considerable foreign investment. It also permitted the growth of a class of wealthy entrepreneurs, many of whom created an essentially aristocratic lifestyle, and it produced a middle class of small business owners and educated professionals.

Although there was considerable poverty in Cuba because wealth was concentrated in a small segment of the population, the island was far from being the poorest of Caribbean nations. This is one major reason that emigration levels were so low until the late 1950s. Then, in little more than two decades—between the late 1950s and 1980—about 794,000 Cubans settled in the United States. The Cubans became the second largest Caribbean group to immigrate during this period, surpassed only by Puerto Ricans (Briquets and Perez, 1981; Pedraza-Bailey, 1992).

Under the dictatorship of Fulgencio Batista, Cuba was perceived as a tourist mecca, especially for those interested in gambling. Organized crime elements from the United States developed a warm relationship with the Batista regime, which allowed the creation of casinos owned by crime syndicates. The regime was characterized by its corruption. Not surprisingly, this situation stimulated organized dissent to the dictatorship. During this time a revolutionary movement headed by Fidel Castro waged a guerrilla campaign against the dictatorship. Prior to the overthrow of the regime in 1959, the number of immigrants to the United States began to rise as conflict escalated. Among the arrivals during the 1950s were people seeking employment, as well as those who had run afoul of the dictatorship and were political exiles.

The number of people emigrating from Cuba rose dramatically after 1960, when the revolutionaries attempted to recast Cuban society into a Marxist one. They sought to pattern themselves after the Soviet Union, which became Cuba's main financial patron. In so doing, the revolutionary government found considerable support among the nation's working classes and poor and intense opposition from the upper and the middle classes. When it became clear that the regime would not create a liberal democracy, anticommunists sought political refuge, overwhelmingly in the United States. This is interesting because Cuban emigrants opted not to go to Spanish-speaking countries with similar cultures. In the three years between 1959 and 1962, 155,000 Cuban immigrants arrived in the United States (Pérez, 1980; Daniels, 1990). These immigrants came largely from the more privileged classes and included landed aristocrats, political elites, wealthy entrepreneurs, and many members of the professional middle classes. Not surprisingly, members of this phase of the Cuban migration were often referred to as the "Golden Exiles," although many immigrants were also from the lower middle class or the working class.

This migration occurred during the height of the Cold War, and the presence of the Marxist government off the shore of Florida proved to be a powerful symbol of competing ideologies in the struggle between the United States and the Soviet Union (Pérez, 2001). Thus, the U.S. government received these political exiles warmly. The relationship between the United States and Cuba soured quickly. On January 3, 1961, President Dwight Eisenhower severed diplomatic relations with the Castro regime, which did not stop the flow of out-migration from Cuba. The Castro regime was ambivalent about emigration: The exodus of dissidents was a way of getting rid of potential troublemakers; however, the character of the migration resulted in a "brain drain" from the island nation (Boswell and Curtis, 1983).

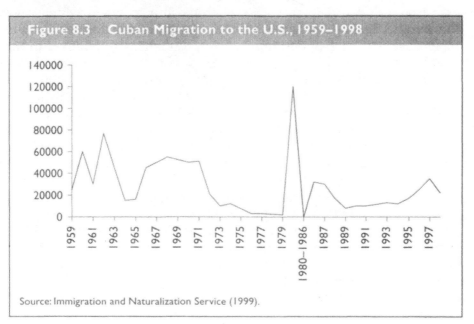

Figure 8.3 Cuban Migration to the U.S., 1959–1998

Source: Immigration and Naturalization Service (1999).

Many Cuban exiles thought that the Castro government could be toppled, and they hoped for a speedy return to their homeland. They viewed their stay in America as temporary, so they could justifiably be seen as irredentists. Some in the exile community began conspiratorial plans to overthrow Castro, and in this goal they found support within the U.S. government, especially in the C.I.A. Clandestine groups mobilized with the ambition of retaking their island home. Such activities culminated in the early days of President Kennedy's administration with the ill-fated Bay of Pigs invasion of Cuba in April 1961. The failure of the Bay of Pigs attack led to the imprisonment of more than 1,000 of the invading U.S. forces and proved to be a major foreign policy failure of the Kennedy administration (Boswell and Curtis, 1983).

Tensions between Cuba and the United States escalated when intelligence sources discovered Soviet missiles on the island. When President Kennedy demanded that the Soviet Union remove the missiles, a major international confrontation occurred. Recently unclassified documents reveal that during the Cuban missile crisis, the world stood at the brink of a nuclear war between the superpowers. This tiny island loomed large in the history of the Cold War, and, mainly for this reason, the Cuban immigrants in the United States were viewed far more positively than were their Hispanic counterparts from other countries.

One result of the missile crisis was the curtailment of air travel between Cuba and the United States and Cuba's suspension of legal emigration to the United States. This ban did not stop the exodus from Cuba, as more than 50,000 Cubans left between 1962 and 1965. Several thousand escaped to the mainland by boat or plane. The vast majority of those who left during these three years, however, did so by obtaining exit visas to third countries, the two most important of which were Mexico and Spain. This hiatus in legal migration ended in 1965 when Fidel Castro granted emigration rights to Cubans with relatives in the United States, and flights between the two nations resumed. Flights continued until 1973, during which time approximately 302,000 Cubans immigrated. They differed from those from the "Golden Exile" period: This group contained fewer middle-class professionals and considerably more lower-middle-class and working-class Cubans (Boswell and Curtis, 1983). In contrast with the earlier arrivals, who were essentially political immigrants, economic considerations also played a role for these "Freedom Flight" immigrants.

From 1973 to 1979, the numbers of immigrants declined significantly—only 38,000 arrived during this entire period. Included were 3,600 political prisoners who were released from Cuban jails in 1978. The final phase of mass migration, which Lisandro Pérez (2001) has characterized as "disorganized," occurred in 1980 when approximately 125,000 Cubans departed from Cuba through the port of Mariel and thus became known as the "Marielitos." Prior to this exodus, the Cuban government had relaxed travel regulations by permitting visits of

Cuban Americans to see family members. This was done to improve relations with the United States and to provide hard currency for the
Cuban economy. An unintended consequence of this policy was that
Cubans began to see firsthand that those who had left the country were
economically better off than those who remained. This situation fueled
increased resentment toward the regime.

One response that had major international reverberations was that
11,000 Cubans sought refuge in the Peruvian embassy in Havana. This
act triggered Castro's decision to allow emigration to the United States
as a way of alleviating internal criticism. The large number of Cubans
seeking to exit became an embarrassment for Castro. He responded by
including among the Marielitos a number of what he called "social
undesirables," which consisted of criminals, homosexuals, mental patients, and even some lepers (Boswell and Curtis, 1983). One estimate
of hard-core criminals among this group was 5,000. The presence of
these elements in this migration wave caused many Americans to respond unfavorably to their arrival, in stark contrast with the response
to the arrival of the two earlier groups. Although the impact of social
"undesirables" has often been overestimated, clearly the Marielitos differed from earlier arrivals in terms of social class, employment, and educational backgrounds. The Marielitos were poorer, with fewer occupational skills and lower educational attainment levels. The differences
between early and later arrivals paralleled the changes that occurred
among German immigrants in the nineteenth century.

Settlement Patterns

The 1.2 million people of Cuban descent are a highly concentrated
group geographically. Although Cubans can be found almost everywhere in the country, about 90 percent are found in only six states.
Florida has about 60 percent of the total, while New Jersey ranks second with about 20 percent. Metropolitan Miami is the undisputed center of Cuban American life. Other cities that have received relatively
large numbers of Cuban immigrants include New York City; Jersey City
and Newark, New Jersey; Chicago; and Los Angeles. A substantial number of Cubans who first settled in other cities because of the refugee resettlement program eventually moved to Miami (Boswell and Curtis,
1983).

More than 150,000 nonCuban Latinos reside in the Miami area;
they come from Mexico, Puerto Rico, the Dominican Republic, and several countries in Central and South America. In addition, there may be
as many as 50,000 French-speaking Caribbeans from Haiti. Cubans are
by far the largest of the recent immigrant groups to the metropolitan
area, however. At present, more than a half million Cubans live in the
Miami area, and only Havana has more Cuban residents than Miami.

The result of this mass influx is that Miami is now a genuinely multicultural and bilingual city. According to the U.S. Census, Hialeah (Florida) and Miami rank first and second in the nation in terms of the percentage of their populations that are foreign-born. For Hialeah the number is an astounding 72.1 percent, and for Miami it is 59.5 percent. In contrast, the figure for Los Angeles is 40.9 percent, while that for all other major U.S. cities is under 40 percent (U.S. Bureau of the Census, 2003).

Prior to 1960, Miami was an aging tourist city, but the influx of immigrants from the Caribbean and Latin America has transformed not only Miami proper but also many surrounding communities in Dade County. Indeed, a mayor of Miami described the city as a "boiling pot," and historian Raymond Mohl (1985: 52) considered the changes in this area to be a "twenty-year demographic revolution without precedent in American history."

Cubans are residentially concentrated in an area known as "Little Havana," which extends outside of Miami proper to include other municipalities in Dade County. A once-declining section of the metropolitan area has been rejuvenated with the creation of the Cuban ethnic community. A rich and varied institutional structure created by the Cuban American community includes social halls, political organizations, mutual aid societies, newspapers, radio and television stations, and literally thousands of businesses. Most Cuban Americans are Roman Catholic, and the size of the local archdiocese has grown tremendously. Church-related organizations play a prominent role in the Cuban American community. Some Cubans, however, are practitioners of *santeria*, a syncretistic religious cult that links elements of African religions to Catholicism (Pérez, 1980). Evangelical Protestantism has also made some inroads into Cuban America.

The Enclave Economy

Many ethnic groups have established businesses that have proved to be highly profitable for the owners (Portes and Sensenbrenner, 1998; Waldinger, 1994; Light, 1972). Edna Bonacich's (1973) "middleman minority" theory accounts for the success of these enterprises mostly because owners cooperate with other owners to limit competition and because the owners hire co-ethnics, to whom they pay low wages. Thus, in her view, ethnic economies can be avenues of success for ethnic entrepreneurs, but employees do not do as well as their counterparts in the larger or primary economy.

This argument was challenged by Kenneth Wilson and Alejandro Portes (1980), who, in a study of Cubans in Miami, argued that the **ethnic enclave economy** not only had proved to provide opportunities for entrepreneurial success but was also beneficial to workers. They concluded that workers did as well working in the enclave economy as they would have done working outside. Although the argument has been questioned when applied to other groups, such as the Chinese, Mexicans, and blacks, it appears that for the Cubans, the ethnic enclave has been beneficial to both owners and workers (Wilson and Martin, 1982; Sanders and Nee, 1987; Portes and Jensen, 1989; Model, 1992; Light and Gold, 2000). Portes and Stepick (1985) indicated that the existence of the ethnic enclave economy for Cubans in Miami and the lack of one for Haitians partially accounts for the fact that the former have fared better economically than the latter. On the other hand, the capacity of the enclave economy to produce success comparable to that in the economic mainstream should not be overstated, for, as Pérez (2001) suggests, it "may function not as a golden springboard for the second generation but as a basic safety net."

As early as 1972, Cubans owned more businesses than blacks in Miami, and the net worth of their enterprises was almost four times that of blacks. This is a reflection of Cubans nationally, who along with Koreans rank high in terms of levels of self-employment (Portes and Zhou, 1996). By the 1980s, the enclave economy of Miami consisted of more than 20,000 businesses. The vast majority were small businesses, including retail stores, gas stations, restaurants, cafes, pastry shops, pharmacies, and family-run grocery stores, or *bodegas*. There are Cuban-owned banks, construction companies, auto dealerships, and fishing fleets (Mohl, 1985). As with Cubans in Tampa early in the century, Miami contains numerous cigar factories. The garment industry employs the largest number of people, however—approximately 25,000. Traditionalist family definitions historically kept women out of the workforce, but more than half of Cuban American women work outside of the home. The garment industry attracts sizable numbers of them (Sullivan, 1984). In addition, many import-export businesses have linked the enclave economy to Latin American markets. Finally, "Little Havana" contains thousands of white-collar professionals, including doctors, pharmacists, lawyers, accountants, and the like.

The middle- and upper-class origins of the immigrants who arrived during the 1960s, combined with the impact of the enclave economy, make Cubans by far the most economically successful Hispanic group. In 2000, the average median household income for all Hispanics was $39,045, a figure well below the white nonHispanic median household income of $58,343. Part of the differences across Hispanic groups is explained by the differing rates of female participation in the labor force. When compared with Mexicans, and especially Puerto Ricans, more Cuban households rely on two incomes than one. Thus, the median family household income is greater for Cubans than for other Hispanic ethnic groups. In 2001 the median family household income for Cubans was $35,831, compared with Puerto Ricans at $31,752, and closer to Mexican family households at $35,293 (U.S. Bureau of the Census, 2002). Some observers have concluded that at the individual level,

Cuban American economic success has been somewhat exaggerated, but at the household level the success can be linked to what Pérez (1986) called the Cuban "family work ethic."

Political Participation

Cubans differ from other Hispanics both in levels of participation in politics and in their political orientations. Perhaps because Cubans view themselves as political refugees, and not economic migrants, they are considerably more active politically than other Hispanic groups. In contrast with Mexicans, Cubans have a high rate of naturalization, a prerequisite to involvement in American politics. In this regard, Cubans are more like recent Asian immigrants than other Hispanics (Puerto Rico is a special case because of the island's U.S. territorial status). Cubans also have a high rate of voter registration and turnout at elections (Portes and Mozo, 1985).

Cubans tend to be politically conservative. Their politics are shaped by their intense hostility to the Castro regime, so they have been fervently anticommunist. In contrast with Mexicans and Puerto Ricans, both of whom are overwhelmingly aligned with the Democratic party, Cuban Americans are chiefly identified with the Republican party. Although a relatively small immigrant group, the regional concentration of Cubans makes them a potent political force in southern Florida. It is estimated that Cuban Americans constitute 53 percent of all registered Republicans in the Miami area (Bouvier, 1992). In Ronald Reagan's two presidential electoral victories, Cubans in Miami may have cast in excess of 90 percent of their votes for him, and for both Bush presidents,

Table 8.1	Median Income of Hispanic Groups, 2001			
	Mexican	Puerto Rican	Cuban	Central/ South American
Median age of population	24.7 years	29 years	42.7 years	29.4 years
Males, money income	$19,581	$20,741	$19,910	$21,549
Females, money income	$12,289	$12,274	$11,501	$13,365
All household types	$33,574	$28,738	$27,564	$37,512
Family households	$35,293	$31,572	$35,831	$40,632

Source: U.S. Bureau of the Census (2002).

the Cuban vote was a critical part of their electoral strategies in Florida. It is not surprising that the national Republican party has been quite active in its efforts to court this particular immigrant group.

Cuban Americans have established powerful political action committees in the United Sates that have sought to influence foreign policy toward Cuba. The Cuban American National Foundation (CANF) was founded in the early 1980s by a wealthy group of Cuban businessmen. They have a political action committee that supports politicians that are anti-Castro and pro-democracy. Not only have they donated to both Republican and Democratic campaigns, in the 1980s they also pressured the Reagan and Bush administrations to enact embargoes on various activities by Americans who wanted to go to Cuba. CANF focuses on a variety of issues connected to Cuba in the hopes of discouraging Cuba's political influence on other countries in the Third World. According to Garcia (1996), CANF is one of the most popular organizations among Cuban exiles living in the United States. Besides its support of political activities, CANF is also involved in a number of humanitarian concerns, particularly those related to Cuban exiles in other countries, having scholarships and other funds available to help those in the exile community (Garcia, 1996).

At the local level, because Cubans have aligned themselves with conservative white business forces in the Miami area, tension exists between Cubans and blacks (Hero, 1992). Many African Americans see the political ascendancy and economic advancement of Cubans to be at least in part at their expense. Thus, for example, as the city became bilingual, many jobs in the service sector, even low-paying ones, often required Spanish-language skills. The result was that employers often chose Latino applicants instead of blacks. The tension between blacks and Cubans took violent form in the 1980 Liberty City riot. In New York and New Jersey, where Cubans are a smaller part of the Hispanic population, they have tended not to enter into political alliances or coalitions with Puerto Ricans, Dominicans, or other Latino groups.

Are Cubans Assimilating?

As we have seen with other ethnic groups who have sizable middle classes and have experienced upward mobility, the opportunities and temptations to assimilate increase over time. This may be the case with Cubans, but because they are only in the second generation, it is a bit early to discern with any precision what the future might hold.

Cubans in Miami have a vibrant ethnic community, so they are able to preserve much of their culture and to confine most of their social relations to the ethnic community. Thus, the ethnic community can serve as a buffer to prevent rapid assimilation. Cubans in other parts of the country, where the ethnic communities are not as large or institutionally complete, show greater indications of assimilationist tendencies.

But even in Miami, considerable generational change can be seen. The second generation uses English with far greater ease than their parents did. The transition to English is being accomplished by the mixture of the two languages into something referred to as "Spanglish." Younger Cubans have greater opportunities to interact with Anglos, especially in school. For those who go to college, and this group is growing, interpersonal relations outside of the Cuban community increase.

Even within the ethnic community, cultural change is seen. As we have noted, the role of women in the workforce challenged traditional family definitions. In addition, courtship practices have been liberalized. Young Cubans are no longer required to have chaperones when they go on dates, although Cuban Americans still have lower levels of premarital sexual intimacy than Anglos and other Hispanics do. Cuban families have relatively low fertility rates compared with the rates that characterized pre-Castro Cuba. Finally, exogamous marriages have begun to increase. Thus, Cuban Americans appear to be between two worlds: poised in many respects to enter the mainstream, while seeking to preserve not only their individual ethnic identities but their ethnic community as well. As Susan Eckstein and Lorena Barberia (2002) have illustrated, those more recently arrived Cubans who migrated largely for economic reasons are interested in preserving transnational ties to the homeland.

Puerto Ricans

Despite the fact that Puerto Rico is close to the U.S. mainland and the island's residents have had citizenship rights since 1917, which permitted unrestricted migration, mass migration from the island did not occur until after World War II. Because of their legal status as citizens, Puerto Ricans are not, strictly speaking, immigrants. One consequence of their distinctive status is that a "circular migration," or movement back and forth between the mainland and the island, has been common (Kitano, 1991). The relatively few Puerto Ricans in the country prior to World War II included a substantial percentage of political exiles, including socialists and nationalists. Mass migration was shaped largely by economic, and not political, factors, however. The economic stimulus to migrate was also influenced by demographic change. During the first four decades of the twentieth century, Puerto Rico's population doubled (Moore and Pachon, 1985). This situation overwhelmed the job market, contributed to poverty and unemployment, and served as a powerful incentive to emigrate.

Puerto Rico's status as a colony of the United States meant that for several decades its rulers and laws were imposed by the federal government. The president appointed the governor of the island, and all laws were established by the U.S. Congress. During the first several decades of U.S. rule, peasants and small farmers (*jíbaros*) lost much of the land they had held in the nineteenth century to large corporations that produced export crops, the most important being tobacco, coffee, and sugar. A professional class of *criollos* emerged that had ties to American corporations and was an important component of the island's population that supported the American presence. Ultimately, the island was primarily associated with one major export crop that was grown on large plantations owned by U.S. agricultural companies: sugar (Mintz, 1960). Poverty and debt were endemic features of life for the peasantry. The subsistence economy eroded as agricultural production became geared toward international markets. Thus, Puerto Rico lacked not only political autonomy, but economic independence as well.

During the New Deal era, progressive reformer Rexford Tugwell was appointed governor of Puerto Rico by Franklin D. Roosevelt. Unlike his predecessors, Tugwell encouraged economic development. He saw a need for reforms of the agrarian economy and encouraged investment in industrial development. Tugwell's tenure as governor extended until 1946, when a Puerto Rican was chosen for the position. In 1947 Congress passed the Elective Governors Act, which granted Puerto Ricans the right to choose their own governor. The following year Luis Muñoz Marin became the first elected governor. Congress permitted the island's residents to draft their own constitution and redefined Puerto Rico as a commonwealth (Daniels, 1990). Although this newly defined relationship with the United States did result in greater political autonomy, it was not without critics. Some residents wanted statehood, while others sought to create an independent nation. In 1952, radical nationalists attempted to assassinate President Harry S. Truman, and others fired shots in the U.S. House of Representatives.

Advocates of independence constitute a small minority of Puerto Ricans. For example, in a plebiscite held in 1967, less than 1 percent of voters supported the cause of nationhood. Statehood proponents have considerably more support, but in the same plebiscite, they mustered only 39 percent of the vote, while 60 percent of Puerto Ricans preferred to maintain their commonwealth status. The small minority of Puerto Ricans called *Independentistas* tend to refuse to vote in regular elections. They believe that freedom and independence cannot be voted on because the elections do not include independence as an option.

One reason for the continued support for commonwealth status is that individuals and businesses do not have to pay federal income taxes. This status does, however, set limits to political empowerment. So, for example, Puerto Ricans can serve in the U.S. military (and can be subject to the draft), but they cannot vote for president. Although they elect a Resident Commissioner to the House of Representatives, that person does not have voting rights. Overall, the issue of statehood versus commonwealth status versus independence is complicated by social conditions and by the colonial relationship between the United States and Puerto Rico that has existed for over 100 years.

Tugwell's desire to bring industry to Puerto Rico was shared by Muñoz, who initiated "Operation Bootstrap" in an attempt to introduce industry to the island, especially to areas that suffered from chronic poverty. This program was in effect from 1948 to 1965 and promoted industrialization at the expense of reforms in the agricultural sector. The result was rapid social change, including a precipitous drop in the percentage of people employed in agriculture—from 50 percent in 1940 to only 10 percent by 1970. Lured by tax incentives and the prospect of a cheap labor force, multinational corporations flocked to Puerto Rico after World War II. Leading the way were U.S. corporations, which by 1970 owned 80 percent of all industrial enterprises (Bonilla and Campos, 1981). With industrialization came rapid urbanization. The middle class grew, as did a huge government bureaucracy that employed 30 percent of the workforce by the mid-1970s.

Despite these profound changes, unemployment grew. Industrial jobs did increase, but they only kept pace with the growth of the working-age population. The decline in agricultural jobs meant that unemployment increased rather than decreased. One response to these social and economic dislocations was emigration to the mainland. That began in the late 1940s and became a mass exodus in the 1950s (Mills, Senior, and Goldsen, 1950; Senior, 1965). Bean and Tienda (1987: 24) observed, "So intense was the outflow of wage laborers that during the 1950s Puerto Rico provided the unusual spectacle of a booming economy with a shrinking labor force."

Settlement Patterns

During the 1940s, the annual number of Puerto Ricans who migrated was 18,700. In the following decade that number soared to 41,200 people per year—the peak of migration. By 1960 there were approximately 900,000 Puerto Ricans on the mainland. In the 1960s the annual rate of migration fell to 14,500. There were 1,429,396 Puerto Ricans on the mainland in 1970, 2 million in 1980, 1.9 million in 1990, and 3.4 million in 2000 (U.S. Bureau of the Census, 1992b, 2001; Sánchez-Ayéndez, 1988).

New York is to Puerto Ricans what Miami is to Cubans: the mainland location of choice. Although at least 75,000 Puerto Ricans are found as far west as California and in Illinois, Florida, Pennsylvania, and Massachusetts, the heaviest concentration is in the greater New York area, which extends into New Jersey and Connecticut. Sizable Puerto Rican communities have been created in a number of cities in this northeastern region, including Newark, Jersey City, and Patterson in New Jersey and Bridgeport and Hartford in Connecticut. By 1970, however, two-thirds of all Puerto Ricans resided in New York City.

Since then, New York Puerto Ricans have dispersed to other communities, but still approximately half of all Puerto Ricans on the mainland live in that city (U.S. Bureau of the Census, 1992b, 2001; Sowell, 1981a).

The earliest arrivals concentrated in the section of Manhattan that became known as Spanish Harlem (Sexton, 1966; Glazer and Moynihan, 1963). Harlem had become the large black ghetto in that borough of New York City, so Puerto Ricans lived in close proximity to African Americans. Over time, Puerto Ricans also established enclaves in the South Bronx and Brooklyn. In contrast with Cubans, immigrants from Puerto Rico were quite poor. They were generally peasants or young urban dwellers without prior experience in urban industries and thus without specialized skills that provided opportunities for economic advancement. In addition, the migration flow lacked a significant middle class. As a result, unlike Cubans, Puerto Ricans did not develop an enclave economy.

Economic Status

Instead, Puerto Ricans found work outside of the barrio. They were highly concentrated in low-paying blue-collar jobs and often found jobs working in service industries such as hotels, restaurants, and hospitals as bellboys, busboys, dishwashers, and orderlies. Many men found employment in industry as assembly-line operatives, while women early on found jobs in the garment industry. This situation changed over time as many textile firms left the Northeast in search of cheaper labor forces, either in the South or overseas. By the late 1970s, Puerto Rican women began to enter the clerical and sales workforces (Sowell, 1981a; Feagin, 1984).

Puerto Ricans on the mainland have not fared well economically compared with other Hispanic groups, but have struggled to climb the socioeconomic ladder. Given that Puerto Ricans live in cities where the cost of living is high, they have persistently been overrepresented at the lower end of the income spectrum. The Puerto Rican unemployment rate has over time exceeded the national rate, even exceeding the 20 percent mark at times during the economic recessions of the 1980s and 1990s. There are several reasons for chronic unemployment, underemployment, and poverty. Immigrants' lack of human and financial capital put them at a disadvantage from the beginning (Borjas, 2000). High school drop-out rates and a lack of adequate occupational training compounded this problem.

The Role of Race. Another compounding factor related to underemployment and unemployment is racial discrimination. Puerto Ricans frequently compete with African Americans for jobs, and it might have been assumed that the former would have fared better because the latter confronted racial discrimination in hiring practices. However, this has not been the case, because many Puerto Ricans have been doubly stigmatized as black Hispanics. Like many other Caribbeans, Puerto Ricans have historically treated race in terms of color gradations and have not used the stark black-white dichotomy that has characterized American race relations (Denton and Massey, 1989). They use various terms that recognize color gradations, such as *pardo, moreno, mulatto,* and *trigueño.* Clara Rodriguez (1989) differentiated the Puerto Rican and the American perspectives by making the observation:

> In Puerto Rico, racial classification was subordinate to cultural identification, while in the United States, racial identification, to a large extent, determined cultural identification. Thus, Puerto Ricans were first Puerto Ricans, then blanco/a (white), moreno/a (black), and so on, while Americans were first white or black, then Italian, Irish, West Indian, or whatever. (52)

That American society did not take account of color gradations frequently came as a shock to Puerto Ricans. This is vividly illustrated in Piri Thomas's *Down These Mean Streets* (1967), an autobiographical account of growing up in a world of crime and drugs in East Harlem. He recalled the following scene from prison: Engaged in a conversation with a fellow Puerto Rican in the lunch line, Thomas failed to realize that there were two lines, one for whites and one for blacks. The shock of being defined as black occurred when a prison guard pushed him into the black line and the other Puerto Rican into the white line. Thomas recounts that this externally imposed racial definition resulted in considerable confusion about his sense of self-identity and left him with a simmering rage at the American racial order.

The precise extent to which racial discrimination in hiring has impeded Puerto Rican economic advancement is difficult to measure. Some evidence suggests that those with darker skin have not fared as well as those with lighter skin, and the trigueños in the middle find that they confront considerable ambiguity about their racial standing (Fitzpatrick, 1987; Rodriguez, 1989). Moreover, at least one study suggested that darker-skinned Puerto Ricans, because of their greater marginality, are more likely to be involved in crime and various forms of deviant behavior (Berle, 1959).

Ethnic Competition for Jobs. In the past 20 years, the economic position of Puerto Ricans has improved slightly, with their median household income increasing. In 2001, the median household income for Puerto Ricans was $26,738 (U.S. Bureau of the Census, 2002). While Puerto Rican household income has increased, it is largely a result of women's labor force participation rates, even though Puerto Rican women have the lowest labor force participation rates among all women (Rivera-Batiz and Santiago, 1994). In comparison, Mexicans and Cubans showed greater overall increases in income. One explanation for the variations in economic improvement lies in regional economic conditions. The heavy concentration of Puerto Ricans in the northeastern states placed them in declining cities in the Rust Belt. As the industrial bases of these cities have declined, hundreds of thousands of unskilled and skilled union jobs have disappeared. Throughout the 1980s and 1990s, industrial growth has occurred in the Sunbelt states and in the West. These are destinations that have attracted relatively few Puerto Rican migrants.

Marta Tienda (1989) pointed out that Puerto Ricans have never been singled out as preferred workers in particular jobs (in contrast, for example, with Mexicans in agriculture), which puts them at a distinct disadvantage when job shortages occur. Comparatively lower levels of educational achievement and other aspects of human capital have translated into a competitive disadvantage in comparison with other groups (Tienda, 1999). In addition, being born in the United States (nativity) also appears to be a factor in accessing jobs (Pérez y Gonzalez, 2000). Thus, in comparison, blacks and Cubans have fared better than Puerto Ricans in the Northeast region.

In New York City the character of the Latino population has changed during the past three decades. First, it grew from 16.3 percent in 1970 to 30 percent in 2000 (U.S. Bureau of the Census, 2000). Although 30 years ago Puerto Ricans constituted the overwhelming majority of Hispanics, they now compose less than half of the city's total Latino population. That is because of the rise in immigration—legal and illegal—of Central Americans, South Americans, and more recently Mexicans (Kasinitz, Mollenkopf, and Waters, 2002). The Dominicans are by far the largest of the newer arrivals in New York. They rank second in number to Puerto Ricans, who often view the new arrivals as rivals for jobs and political influence. Part of the tension between Puerto Ricans and Dominicans is that the latter appear to be doing better economically, despite their relatively short stay in America. David Gonzalez (1992b: A11) observed that although both groups "live on the struggling side of success, the Dominicans have made substantial economic progress in a single entrepreneurial generation, buying up bodegas, restaurants, and livery-cab fleets around the city."

The Impact of Return Migration

The inability to gain a solid foothold in the American economy has prompted increasing numbers of Puerto Ricans to return to the island. Since the 1970s, the earlier circular migration has been replaced by a growing return migration. Those who return tend to be from two sectors of the ethnic community: older Puerto Ricans who want to spend their remaining years in their birthplace and younger Puerto Ricans who confront the highest levels of unemployment. In this regard, Puerto Ricans are a good example of global villagers intent on preserving transnational ties (Portes, 1996). The young returnees are primarily men (Sánchez-Ayéndez, 1988).

The decline in the number of young men relative to women can help explain the high proportion of female-headed households. The 53.3 percent figure of out-of-wedlock births is higher than for other Hispanic groups, second only to African Americans, and far exceeds the 14.9 percent for European Americans. In addition, Puerto Rican women have a lower level of participation in the labor force than other groups, so they are forced to rely solely on government assistance to a greater extent than other groups. The contrast between Puerto Ricans and blacks indicates that while 66 percent of Puerto Rican women are not in the labor force, only 49 percent of black women are not. Moreover, while only 28 percent of black female-headed households rely solely on some form of public assistance, the number is 57 percent for Puerto Ricans (Falcon, Gurak, and Powers, 1990; Rodriguez, 1989). This situation contributes significantly to the extremely low median income of Puerto Ricans noted earlier.

Another way to look at Puerto Rican migration between the mainland United States and the islands is as a "revolving door" (Pérez y Gonzalez, 2000) of back-and-forth immigration dictated by economic needs. As such, Puerto Ricans are **transnational immigrants.** Puerto Ricans may have two home bases, in Puerto Rico and on the mainland, where friends, family, and community provide social, psychological, and economic supports. When the U.S. economy booms, there is a greater out-migration from Puerto Rico to the United States; when the economy is bust, Puerto Ricans may return to their island home base until the economic conditions improve. The pattern of dual home bases is likely to continue as long as Puerto Rico continues to be economically dependent on the United States (Pérez y Gonzalez, 2000).

The Ethnic Community

Given the limited resources that immigrants brought with them and the relative lack of economic success of Puerto Ricans on the mainland, it is not surprising that the ethnic community is more fragile and less institutionally complete than that created by most other groups. The ability to return to Puerto Rico with ease has also weakened the ethnic community; people ambivalent about whether to remain on the mainland or return to the island are less likely to commit resources to institution building. Despite these limitations, however, an ethnic community has emerged.

A central feature of the community has been the role played by the family. In Puerto Rico, prior to changes brought about by Operation Bootstrap, the extended family was of central importance. Today the nuclear family has become more important, especially in child rearing. The role played by "fictive kin," people who, though not related to a family, will informally adopt children during periods of family crisis, is significant (Sánchez-Ayéndez, 1988). Further changes in family composition occurred on the mainland. Fitzpatrick (1987) identified four types of household structures among Puerto Rican Americans. In addition to the modified extended family (where relatives such as grandparents may live in the household or in close proximity) and the nuclear family, he added two others: (1) blended families, in which two parents are present but some of the children are biologically related to only one of the parents, and (2) female-headed households. The family, regardless of type, was viewed by Sánchez-Ayéndez (1988: 186) as the "primary support system for first- and second-generation Puerto Ricans in the United States."

As with the Mexicans earlier, informal self-help organizations—ranging from social clubs and after-hours clubs to athletic clubs for youth—have played an important role in assisting immigrants to adjust to their new environment. In addition, a number of formal organizations have been created, many initiated by members of the relatively small middle class. Most are local rather than national in scope. Among the most established organizations in New York are the Puerto Rican Merchants' Association, the Puerto Rican Forum, Aspira (an agency promoting higher education), the Puerto Rican Community Development Fund, a social service agency staffed largely by Puerto Rican social workers called the Puerto Rican Family Institute, and the Puerto Rican Legal Defense and Education Fund. Some of these organizations, as well as the National Puerto Rican Coalition founded to lobby in Washington, operate at the national level (Fitzpatrick, 1987; Padilla, 1987).

Puerto Ricans are nominally Roman Catholic, but their religious practice is that of a nontraditional folk religion, an amalgam of orthodox Catholicism and various forms of personalistic saint worship and spiritualism. Puerto Ricans have not been as committed to the institutional church as have some groups. On the mainland, they have tended to feel marginalized from American Catholicism due to its domination by Anglos. In the early years, most Puerto Rican parishes did not have Spanish-speaking priests, and although the church has changed this practice, that has not resulted in most Puerto Rican parishes being served by Puerto Rican priests. Many priests serving predominantly Puerto Rican congregations are Spanish-speaking Anglos. No prominent Puerto Rican clergy have risen to the rank of bishop (Daniels, 1990). No more than one-third of Puerto Ricans on the mainland are estimated to be members of Catholic congregations, while perhaps an additional 6 percent have joined various Protestant denominations (Fitzpatrick, 1987). In other words, a majority of Puerto Ricans are not involved with the institutional church. The church does have an important but somewhat limited role in the community.

Puerto Ricans have not created newspapers to the extent that most ethnic groups have. In fact, the main newspapers serving the Puerto Rican community in New York, including the influential *El Diario*, have not been owned or controlled by Puerto Ricans. Puerto Ricans have been involved in Spanish-language radio programming, and the availability of such programming has been an important source for creating and sustaining group identity. More recently, two Cuban-owned television stations have provided Spanish-language programming. For both radio and television, the programming is intended for all Latinos rather than specifically for Puerto Ricans (Fitzpatrick, 1987).

Some of the community's institutions were created with outside funding and were dependent for their existence on the continuation of such funding. This was especially true during the War on Poverty in the 1960s, when neighborhood organizations were created with money from the federal government. This reliance on outside financial support is evident in a number of ways. For example, in a comparison of Polish and Puerto Rican participation in an ethnic parade in Philadelphia, Jo Anne Schneider (1990) noted that while the Polish parade committee was self-supporting, the Puerto Rican group relied on contributions from such corporate donors as Goya, Coca-Cola, McDonald's, and American Airlines. In addition, indicating the Puerto Rican community's concerns about major social problems, their parade contingent included messages such as "Say No to Drugs" and "To Read Is Power." Schneider noted that while the sole focus of the Polish parade contingent was on ethnic pride, a major thrust of the Puerto Ricans' revolved around issues related to impoverishment: unemployment, crime, drugs, the lack of day care, and so forth. This is a clear indication that Puerto Ricans are experiencing **segmented assimilation,** in which part of the ethnic community is enmeshed in the culture of the streets, with all its attendant social problems (Rumbaut, 1996; Portes and Zhou, 1993).

Integration or Isolation?

Some ethnic groups have used politics as a means to establish contacts with the larger society and improve the circumstances of group members. Political involvement has had a limited impact on Puerto Ricans so far, however. They have been somewhat slow to become actively involved in politics. In the past, the major political parties ignored this potential voting bloc. The 1960s marked a period of greater political involvement, and as a leadership stratum arose, sometimes emerging from the training ground of the period's antipoverty programs, Puerto Rican leaders have been courted by local political parties. Puerto Ricans are primarily affiliated with the Democratic party. Although they remain underrepresented in elective offices and political appointments in New York City, their numbers have increased in recent years. The future is unclear, especially because Puerto Ricans are now a smaller part of Hispanic New York than in the past. In cities where they constitute a smaller percentage of the overall urban population, they are even less politically influential, although there is evidence of increased involvement in local and state politics, particularly in northeastern cities such as Hartford and Bridgeport, Connecticut, and Newark and Patterson, New Jersey (Hero, 1992; Moore and Pachon, 1985).

Relations with other Latinos and blacks have frequently been strained. Social interaction with Anglos is often limited, partly because of residential segregation. Thus, Puerto Ricans are far more marginalized and isolated from the rest of American society than Cubans. Nonetheless, those born on the mainland—the second generation—are beginning the process of creating an identity that reflects that their home is on the mainland and not back in Puerto Rico (Flores, 1985). In New York the second generation has been referred to as the "Nuyoricans," which shows the significance of New York City in the evolution of their definition of ethnic identity.

Unlike Cubans, Puerto Ricans do not appear to be poised to enter the mainstream. This is primarily because they have not been sufficiently successful in combating discrimination and in establishing the economic preconditions for ending their marginality.

Mexican Americans

In the middle and late twentieth century, as the Mexican American community evolved and its middle class expanded, immigration also continued. The Mexican American population continued to be extremely fluid and highly diverse, complicated by the continuous arrival of newcomers and the fact that the "preexisting Mexican American community serves as an important part of the context of reception for new immigrants" (López and Stanton-Salazar, 2001). Mexican America is unique in this regard (Kerr, 1984; Burma, 1954).

After World War II, Mexicans continued to enter the United States, attracted to higher wages than were available at home. The immigrants included both legal and undocumented individuals. An important component of this wave of immigration included those involved in the **bracero program,** which continued after the war.

Although the need for workers in defense industries had ended, the bracero program continued to supply contract laborers to employers, especially in agriculture. For example, by the end of the 1950s, 75 percent of sugar beets and 90 percent of cucumbers were being harvested by braceros (Valdes, 1991). Many Mexican Americans felt that they had been displaced by braceros in these jobs, and thus a demand to abolish the program gained support within the Mexican American community.

> ### Voices   Soraya Sanchez
>
> When she came to yell at me that first time, she tells me she is firing me, and I said to her, "You know what? You don't have to fire me, I won't work for you! Not for a million dollars! I'm quitting!". . . I said to her, "You know what? Now I'm no longer your maid, and you're no longer my boss, and you and I are equals! Now you are going to hear what I am going to say to you." I said to her, "I don't work for you. . . . You're the mother and not even you want to take care of your own children. Why I should have to worry? I hope," I said, "that you find a person who really understands your children, because not even you know how to understand them . . . I quit, I'm quitting, I'm quitting!" and I went out the door and I started packing my things.
>
> *Soraya Sanchez, a live-in domestic, describing the end of a conflict-ridden relationship with her employer (Hondagneu-Sotelo, 2001: 115–116).*

The program was finally terminated in 1964, but by then the number of new braceros was quite small.

Immigrant workers were particularly vulnerable to changes in the economy. They were welcomed when there was a demand for labor, but when their labor was not needed, as during the Depression, pressures mounted to deport them. Migratory push forces mounted in Mexico during the late 1940s and early 1950s. The population of the nation grew rapidly. Many Mexicans migrated to cities along the U.S. border, and from there many were attracted to the higher wages north of the border.

The dramatic increase in migration during this period was met with demands to restrict immigration. In 1954 the government initiated Special Force Operation—more popularly known as "Operation Wetback"—to stop illegal entry into the country. *Wetback* was a slang term for Mexicans who had entered the country illegally by crossing the Rio Grande River. To curtail such activities, the federal government began rounding up and repatriating undocumented aliens. In addition to those who had recently arrived in the country, many long-term illegal residents were also detected. Many legal aliens were also rounded up, thereby creating fear and anger in the Mexican American community. During the two-year period ending in 1956, the Immigration and Naturalization Service sought the deportation of 3.8 million Mexicans. Although only 63,000 were officially deported, more than 1 million returned to Mexico voluntarily to avoid deportation proceedings (Stoddard, 1973; Barrera, 1985).

By the end of the 1950s, the Mexican population in the United States had been reduced considerably; most who remained dated either their residency or that of their family to no later than the 1920s. In

A Mexican factory worker in Los Angeles.

other words, the most recent arrivals had returned to Mexico. This situation did not continue, however, as the net flow of immigration increased during the 1970s and 1980s. For example, the number of resident aliens with permanent status who arrived during the 1970s was approximately 640,000, nearly triple that of two decades earlier (Daniels, 1990).

The number of undocumented aliens who entered the country during the past two decades is difficult to ascertain. Many enter for short periods of time before returning to Mexico. Some come and go frequently. Government estimates of illegal aliens have suggested that the numbers may be as high as 6 to 8 million, and one estimate even put the figure at 10 to 12 million. These are politically motivated estimates designed to mobilize public sentiment about the presumed problem of **undocumented immigration.** More careful demographic estimates put the figure at between 1 and 3 million. A careful analysis of existing data by demographer David Heer (1990) resulted in an estimate of about 1.8 million undocumented Mexicans. Although these aliens can be found throughout the United States, they are heavily concentrated in the border states from Texas to California.

Organized campaigns to control undocumented immigration gained momentum during the 1970s and early 1980s. Legislation was proposed in Congress to reform current policies. Originally introduced by Republican Senator Alan Simpson and Democratic Representative Romano Mazzoli in 1982, a bill that was intended to give the federal government more power to control movement across the border was highly controversial. Mexican American groups, spearheaded by the League of United Latin American Citizens (LULAC) and the Mexican American Legal Defense Educational Fund (MALDEF), mobilized to defeat it. They contended that if enacted, the law would increase discrimination against all Hispanics, not only undocumented immigrants. Moreover, they argued that undocumented individuals had rights that would likely be violated. The proposed bill had foreign policy implications after the Mexican Senate registered its concerns about the legislation (DeConde, 1992; Gutierrez, 1991).

Nonetheless, prompted by President Reagan's claim that it was imperative that the United States regain control of its borders, a modified version of the bill, known as the Immigration Reform and Control Act, became law in 1986. It was the result of a delicate compromise designed to appease several interests and audiences simultaneously. The act did give the government greater power to control the Mexican border and also provided for a temporary-worker program, a key concern of the Southwest's agribusinesses. One provision imposed sanctions on employers who used illegal immigrants. To placate the opposition to the bill coming primarily from the Mexican American community, the act established an amnesty program. The program granted legal residency to all undocumented Mexicans who could prove that they had resided in the United States since January 1, 1982 (Hero, 1992). To date, the precise impact of the law is difficult to determine.

It is also difficult to determine the impact of undocumented immigration on the U.S. economy. Critics contended that illegal immigrants have a negative impact because they tend to drive down wages, and they place additional financial burdens on public institutions such as schools. This claim has been challenged by economist George Borjas (1990), however, who argued that immigrants do not appreciably lower earnings or reduce employment opportunities. Lawrence Fuchs (1990) argues that undocumented workers actually create additional jobs. Douglas Massey noted that without illegal immigrants, some businesses, including the garment industry, would probably relocate to a Third World country (CQ Researcher, 1992; see also Massey et al., 2002; Bouvier, 1992; Thomsen, 1993).

Chicano Politics

From the 1940s to the 1960s, Mexican Americans became more politically assertive and, especially in the Southwest, began to demand an enhanced role in local and regional politics. Reformers pressed for the election of Mexican American officials to city councils, school boards, state legislatures, and so forth. Although the number of Mexican American elected officials did increase during the 1950s and 1960s, the numbers remained comparatively low. One reason was the persistence of discrimination. Another reason was that Mexicans were somewhat slow to become naturalized citizens and were thus ineligible to vote.

LULAC continued to play a key role in efforts to end discrimination and to achieve economic equal opportunity. LULAC grew from only 46 local councils in 1932 to more than 150 by 1960. Other older groups, such as the Congress of Spanish-Speaking People and the Alianza Hispano-Americano, declined in significance but were replaced by new organizations. One of the most important civil rights organizations to emerge after World War II was the American G.I. Forum, which was founded in 1948 after a funeral home in Three Rivers, Texas, refused to provide burial services for Felix Longoria, a Mexican American veteran (Green, 1992). Mexican Americans who had served in the armed forces during the war expected past discrimination to end. When it was appar-

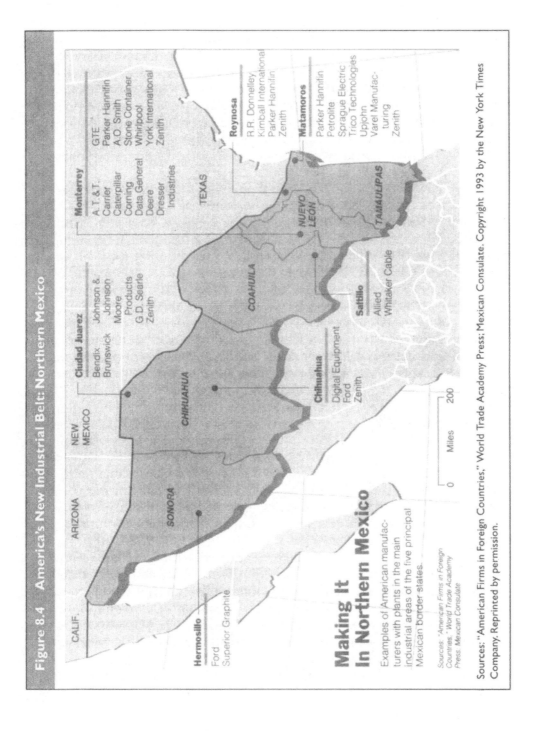

Figure 8.4 America's New Industrial Belt: Northern Mexico

**Making It
In Northern Mexico**

Examples of American manufacturers with plants in the main industrial areas of the five principal Mexican border states.

Sources: "American Firms in Foreign Countries," World Trade Academy Press; Mexican Consulate

CALIF.

ARIZONA

NEW MEXICO

Ciudad Juarez
Bendix
Brunswick
Johnson & Johnson
Moore Products
G.D. Searle
Zenith

Monterrey
A.T.&T.
Carrier
Caterpillar
Corning
Data General
Deere
Dresser Industries
GTE
Parker Hannifin
A.O. Smith
Stone Container
Whirlpool
York International
Zenith

Reynosa
R.R. Donnelley
Kimball International
Parker Hannifin
Zenith

Matamoros
Parker Hannifin
Petrolite
Sprague Electric
Trico Technologies
Upjohn
Varel Manufacturing
Zenith

Saltillo
Allied
Whitaker Cable

Chihuahua
Digital Equipment
Ford
Zenith

Hermosillo
Ford
Superior Graphite

SONORA

CHIHUAHUA

COAHUILA

NUEVO LEÓN

TAMAULIPAS

TEXAS

Miles 0 200

Sources: "American Firms in Foreign Countries," World Trade Academy Press; Mexican Consulate. Copyright 1993 by the New York Times Company. Reprinted by permission.

ent that past inequities had not ended, Mexican American veterans used patriotic symbols in their efforts to combat discrimination against them (Hero, 1992; Gomez-Quiñones, 1990; Stoddard, 1973).

At the same time, the Catholic church became more involved in the Mexican American community, promoting church-related activities that were designed to instill lessons in religion, ethics, and civic participation. Although the conservative sector of the Catholic church was especially concerned about the impact of atheistic communism on poor Mexicans, the more liberal elements in the church began to involve themselves in social reform. Liberals sought to alleviate the social problems besetting the Mexican American community (Gomez-Quiñones, 1990).

Some new organizations focused their energies on explicitly political objectives. Among the most important were the Los Angeles-based Community Service Organization (CSO), the Mexican American Political Association (MAPA), the Political Association of Spanish-Speaking Organizations (PASSO), and the American Coordinating Council on Political Education (ACCPE). Voter registration drives, promotion of Mexican American candidates for elective offices, and endorsement of various Anglo politicians seen as sympathetic to Mexican Americans constituted the major activities of these organizations (Moore, 1970).

A campaign in Crystal City, Texas, served as a symbol of the new ethnic politics. In this relatively small city of 10,000, the 25 percent of the population that was Anglo controlled the city both politically and economically, excluding from effective political participation the 75 percent of the population that was Mexican. This situation changed in 1963, when a slate of working-class Mexicans, endorsed by MAPA, won a landslide victory. The tensions in the community prior to the election were high, and Texas Rangers were dispatched to the city at the request of Anglo politicians. Mexicans saw the Rangers' presence as an attempt to intimidate Mexicans from going to the polls. The election received national attention, for it was the first time in the state's history that Mexican Americans had elected candidates from their community through the conventional political process (Stoddard, 1973).

Mexicans were overwhelmingly identified with the Democratic party. In his presidential campaign, John F. Kennedy actively courted Mexican Americans, seeing them as a potentially important voting bloc in some key electoral states, particularly Texas and California. Many middle-class Mexicans were actively involved in Viva Kennedy clubs. Nationally, Kennedy received approximately 85 percent of the Mexican vote (Gomez-Quiñones, 1990).

These political developments were not without problems. Many organizations suffered from internal conflict and from a lack of effective leaders. For example, the Mexican slate in Crystal City was voted out of office in 1965, and many local chapters of political action organizations were relatively short-lived. Although Mexican Americans made gains during the 1950s and 1960s in education, employment, status, and political representation, they were far from reaching parity with Anglo Americans. Historian Juan Gomez-Quiñones (1990) contended that because of the even greater gains in these areas experienced by Anglos, the gulf between the two may have increased. The optimistic expectations of the immediate postwar years gave way to bitterness and to a growing surge of militancy. Developments during the tumultuous decade of the 1960s have clear parallels with political activities in both the black and the Native American communities.

The movement that received the most widespread media attention nationally was the United Farm Workers (UFW), led by the CSO-trained Cesar Chavez. Like Martin Luther King, Chavez advocated nonviolence, but his organization was not strictly a civil rights organization like the Southern Christian Leadership Conference. Rather, it was a labor union that sought to unite Mexicans with other exploited laborers, including Filipinos, whites, and others.

Beginning in 1965, the UFW targeted selected large agribusiness concerns in California. It used strikes (*La Huelga*) and consumer boycotts—of lettuce and grapes—in an effort to obtain union recognition by growers and to end a century of "harvests of shame." Emerging at the height of the civil rights and antiwar movements, the UFW presented itself as an organization of high moral purpose and was quite successful in its effort to convey a favorable image of its cause in the mass media. The UFW received the support of several prominent liberal politicians on the national level, including Robert F. Kennedy and George McGovern, as well as Jerry Brown at the state level. It was also endorsed by the AFL-CIO. Powerful opponents of the UFW included the Teamsters' Union and Ronald Reagan (who at one point referred to striking workers as "barbarians") when he was governor of California. The UFW succeeded in obtaining union recognition from several major growers and entered into contract negotiations with them (Majka and Majka, 1982). Similar drives were initiated in other parts of the country, often with the support of the AFL-CIO (Valdes, 1991).

During the same period, more militant voices developed a new ethnic political expression that became known as **Chicanismo.** By identifying with the term *Chicano*, which up to the 1960s had been a derogatory expression applied to unskilled Mexican laborers, Mexicans fostered a positive collective self-image. This was intended to directly challenge the negative imagery harbored by many Anglos and was based on the conviction that Mexican Americans were the victims of conquest—not only economically exploited, but subjected to political oppression and deculturation. The Chicano movement addressed all three of these problems. The cultural aspect entailed an effort to recover and preserve the ancestral culture. In promoting this project, movement adherents were hostile to assimilationists. Moreover, by stressing the importance of *la raza* ("the race," a term signifying peoplehood), they emphasized collective goals rather than individual upward mobility (Moore and Pachon, 1985; Melville, 1983; Gutierrez and Hirsch, 1970; Steiner, 1970).

An urban expression of Chicano politics emerged in Denver under the leadership of Rodolfo ("Corky") Gonzales, who had gained familiarity with city politics through his work in Great Society antipoverty programs. Gonzales founded a civil rights organization called the Crusade for Justice, which sought to end discrimination in employment and housing. The Crusade for Justice organized a strike of high school students to protest the lack of attention paid to the special needs of Spanish-language students and also focused attention on police brutality. Many of the activists were young, including college and high school students as well as student dropouts. This was also the case with other organizations, such as the United Mexican American Students (UMAS), the Mexican American Youth Organization (MAYO), and the Brown Berets, a militant organization that modeled itself after the Black Panthers (Gomez-Quiñones, 1990; Moore and Pachon, 1985).

Another manifestation of the decade of dissent was the short-lived career of the *Alianza Federal de Mercedes* (Federal Alliance of Land Grants), founded in 1963 by the former Pentecostal preacher Reies Lopez Tijerina. The *Alianza* sought to reclaim land for Mexicans that it believed had been taken from them illegally. Tijerina engaged in political theater when he and his supporters seized a section of New Mexico's Kit Carson National Park and used this dramatic event to call attention to the history of land expropriation by Anglos. Although this event resulted in a negotiated settlement that conceded some of the park's land to 75 Hispanic families, the *Alianza*'s protests also resulted in violence, including a 1967 shootout between activists and the police at the Tierra Amarilla courthouse. Tijerina was convicted of destruction and assaulting law officers and was sent to prison for two years. Without his charismatic leadership, the *Alianza* began to crumble, and when Tijerina was released he no longer wanted to run the organization he had founded (Gomez-Quiñones, 1990).

In numerous southwestern communities with large Mexican populations, separatists conducted third-party election campaigns under the banner of *La Raza Unida* and, as in Crystal City, achieved some level of success. This success in turn prompted a number of Chicanos to attempt to establish a national, ethnically based third party. *La Raza Unida*'s political ideology was separatist, although its decision to be involved in conventional electoral politics moderated its militant tendencies. As with the more local efforts described earlier, the party declined in significance after the early 1970s, and by 1980 it was no longer a political force (Moore and Pachon, 1985; Montejano, 1999).

Actually, *Chicanismo* as a political ideology lost its appeal for many by the mid-1970s, which led many Mexican Americans to either enter or return to the liberal wing of the Democratic party, where they embraced the liberal reformism characteristic of the period before the 1950s. This resulted in a reinvigoration of some of the older organizations, such as LULAC, in a shift that Mario Barerra (1985) referred to as "retraditionalization." The difference was that by this time Mexican Americans were somewhat better positioned to demand a larger role in politics, at both the state and national levels. During the 1970s and 1980s, the number of Hispanics elected to political offices increased from fewer than 800 to nearly 3,400. The vast majority of these officials were Mexican Americans (Fuchs, 1990). One of the most successful younger Mexican American elected officials was Henry Cisneros. The former mayor of San Antonio, he had been mentioned as a potential vice presidential candidate. In January 1993, he joined the Clinton administration as the Secretary of Housing and Urban Development, but a subsequent personal scandal forced him to withdraw from the political limelight.

Mexican Americans persist in favoring the Democratic party in state and national elections, usually by 70 to 75 percent of the Mexican American vote. Nonetheless, since the 1980s Republicans have actively courted Mexican Americans. Perhaps as an indication of how important this constituency is, during the 2000 election, George Bush followed his Democratic counterpart Al Gore by addressing Mexican American audiences in Spanish. A sector of upper- and upper-middle-class conservative Mexican Americans have long supported the Republican party, although few have been elected to public office.

As a middle class has grown within the ethnic community, political strategists have posed the following question: "Will Mexicans vote like Jews or like Italians?" In other words, as Mexicans become wealthier, will they become more politically conservative, and therefore inclined to the Republican party, as Italians have done, or will they maintain their historical allegiance to the Democratic party, as Jews have done? In addition to economic factors, some believe that the strong emphasis placed on traditional social values means that Mexicans can be attracted to political conservatism. Two things work against this, however. The first is the tradition of collective action rather than the individualism preached by the political right. The second is a deeply entrenched belief among Mexicans that the government should establish programs to assist the general welfare of the citizenry (*The Economist*, 1990).

Although political affiliation remains an open question, current evidence does not suggest a shift to conservatism. In one test case, a former Reagan official, Linda Chavez, ran for a U.S. Senate seat in Maryland in 1986 and lost. She had campaigned on a platform that was opposed to affirmative action, bilingual education, and government welfare programs. Moreover, she was hostile to the politics of ethnic pride and preservation, urging instead actions designed to result in assimilation—including intermarriage (Chavez, 1991). Her political views remain a minority position within the Mexican American community. To date, Mexican Americans remain firmly in the Democratic camp, supporting liberal economic policies.

Socioeconomic Status

The Mexican American poverty rate is similar to that of blacks. The unemployment level, although not as high as that of blacks or Puerto Ricans, is nonetheless higher than that of nonHispanic whites. Mexican Americans complete fewer years of school than nonHispanic whites, blacks, and all other Hispanics (Bean and Tienda, 1987; Farley, 1990; Aponte, 1991). Mexican Americans are more likely to attend predominantly minority schools than blacks are (San Miguel, 1987; Orfield and Monfort, 1988). They have lower GPAs and do less well than other groups on standardized tests (Portes and Rumbaut, 2001). Mexican Americans are proportionately underrepresented among college students, and they have a higher drop-out rate than nonHispanics (Suarez-Orozco, 1998). Mexicans appear to be a distinctly disadvantaged group at present, despite the efforts of Chicano politics to combat prejudice and discrimination.

These statistics can be misleading, however. Many Mexicans are new arrivals and have not had time to gain a foothold in the economy. Moreover, like Puerto Ricans, Mexicans are more youthful than the American public at large (Cubans, by contrast, are older than not only other Hispanics, but nonHispanics as well). Since younger people tend to earn less than older people, it is not surprising that the median income of Mexicans is lower than the national average (Blank, 2001; Tienda, 1999; Bean and Tienda, 1987; Tienda and Lii, 1987; Sowell, 1981a).

Mexicans drop out of school to go to work. During periods of economic prosperity, Mexicans are more likely to remain in school, but during economically difficult times, when the principal wage earner may by unemployed, Mexican teenagers increasingly leave school to supplement the family income. Contrary to the view of the culture of poverty, which suggests that fatalism about one's economic prospects undermines the work ethic, many observers see the Mexicans as having a powerful work ethic. This image stands in stark contrast to the earlier negative stereotype of Mexicans as lazy. In their study of Los Angeles, Roger Waldinger and Michael Lichter discovered that employers often rated the Mexican work ethic favorably, in comparison not only to blacks but also to whites. As one of their respondents put it,

Latino food service workers.

Yes, the immigrants just want to work, work long hours, just want to do anything. They spend a lot of money coming up from Mexico. They want as many hours as possible. If I called them in for four hours to clean latrines, they'd do it. *They like to work.* (Waldinger and Lichter, 2003: 161)

Underlying this positive assessment is a view that Mexicans are particularly easy to exploit. Moreover, the authors discovered that many employers also held a conviction that Mexicans appeared content to remain in menial jobs rather than become upwardly mobile.

Work may not be seen as a means to upward mobility, but is it seen as an essential means for preserving the integrity of one's family. The centrality of the family among Mexicans contributes to their high rate of labor force participation. This commitment is connected to the high school drop-out rate, because the motive for exiting school is frequently to contribute financially to the family (Becerra, 1988; Williams, 1990). At the moment it is clear, as David López and Ricardo Stanton-Salazar (2001) put it, that Mexicans (as well as Central Americans) "play a well-defined if controversial role in the American economy. They do the dirty work in virtually all industries in California and the Southwest, and they are increasingly filling these roles throughout the country."

Undocumented workers are far more vulnerable than legal residents. Moreover, they have been the focus of much anti-immigrant sentiment. This was especially evident when **Proposition 187** was passed in California, as it called for the prohibition of granting public services and welfare programs to undocumented individuals, including the denial of the right of their children to attend public schools. While provisions of the proposition were subsequently struck down in the courts as unconstitutional, the campaign was vivid testimony to the hostility that many immigrants confront.

One study of Mexicans in the Los Angeles area revealed that 80.6 percent of Mexican men were currently in the labor force, compared with 66.7 percent for blacks and 76.2 percent for Anglos. Only 6 percent of Mexicans were receiving welfare payments, in contrast with 35 percent for blacks and 12 percent for nonHispanic whites. Furthermore, 53 percent of Mexican American households with children were two-parent households. The comparable figures for blacks and whites were 32 percent and 57 percent respectively (Meyer, 1992).

In addition, as with African Americans, the Mexican American middle class has expanded during the past two decades. The majority of these white-collar professionals work in service industries, about evenly split between private-sector and public-sector employment. Most of those in the middle class are from the third or subsequent generations. Often they have moved out of the central-city barrio. While there is evidence of movement into integrated white suburbs, many reside in middle-class neighborhoods that are predominantly Latino (Alba et al., 1999). This situation is partly a result of the persistence of housing discrimination and partly a result of choice (Hwang and Murdock, 1988). These are the most acculturated Mexicans, with the best English-language skills. But they also desire to maintain their ethnic background by continuing to shop in Mexican-owned shops and use the professional services of fellow ethnics—lawyers, accountants, doctors, and so forth. After 1982, when the problems of the Mexican economy intensified, middle-class professionals and skilled workers were among the newly arriving immigrants (Dinnerstein and Reimers, 1988; Moore and Pachon, 1985).

Current Economic Problems

The central-city barrios are home to the poorest Mexican Americans, and many new immigrants gravitate to these neighborhoods. Mexican American poverty is concentrated in these barrios (Moore and Pinderhughes, 1993). Workers are often exploited. For example, in Los Angeles Hispanics constitute a majority of the garment industry workforce. The sweatshops are often unsafe and unsanitary, and workers are expected to work long hours for very low wages. Edna Bonacich (1992) reported that some workers in these enterprises were being paid only $50 a week, while working 11-hour days, five or six days a week. This situation is not confined to Los Angeles; indeed, similar conditions exist in the garment industry in other cities along the border, such as El Paso. In the Midwest, Mexicans are being hired in meatpacking plants that have restructured to eliminate labor unions. This industry has the highest rate of job-related injuries. Thus, the industry is paying its workers considerably less than it did in the recent past and is greatly reducing or eliminating fringe benefits, while doing relatively little to reduce the dangers on the job (Delgado, 1993). Bonacich and Richard Appelbaum (2000) stress that these exploitive industries need to be seen in terms of the globalization of capital and within the context of "free trade" policies coming from the North American Free Trade Agreement (NAFTA).

But Mexican poverty is not just an urban phenomenon, for Mexicans continue to be an important source of agricultural labor. During the conservative political shift of the 1980s, many of the United Farm

Workers' labor contracts were terminated, and California Governor Dukmejian worked with growers to reduce the influence of organized labor in the fields. Thus, Mexicans continue to confront annual "harvests of shame." Subsequent governors have done little to change this situation.

Many immigrants from the last great wave of migration that began in the late nineteenth century lived impoverished lives, but their children and grandchildren experienced upward mobility into the middle class. The unanswered question is whether a similar intergenerational process of socioeconomic mobility will occur for Mexican immigrants or whether they will remain in the lowest tier of the economy. Reynolds Farley and Richard Alba (2002: 697) argue that while the evidence suggests that most immigrant groups are experiencing upward mobility, Mexicans (and Puerto Ricans) "are exceptions since third and higher generations, in the aggregate, have characteristics similar to those of the second generation."

The Problem of Marginalized Youth

It is within the economic context of poverty and lack of economic opportunity that an "oppositional" or "adversarial" culture has arisen (Perlmann and Waldinger, 1998). This is an example of *segmented assimilation*, in which immigrant youth are incorporated into the world of antisocial behavior and gang membership. Vigil (1988, 2002) explains the causes of gangs and gang membership as a result of "multiple marginality." Larger societal forces move young people toward gangs. Racism, cultural repression, immigrant status, and economic circumstances contribute to the situation in which individuals are marginalized in society (Vigil, 2002). Thus, gang membership is an important source of identity and camaraderie for those barrio youth who feel particularly estranged from the larger society (Moore, 1978; Moore and Vigil, 1987). Gang membership becomes a source of self-esteem or "honor" to the "homeboys." In her study of Chicano gang members in Chicago, Ruth Horowitz (1983: 81) wrote that honor "revolves around a person's ability to command deference in interpersonal relations." To command respect means that one cannot be perceived as weak. Any potential challenge or insult to the person's honor must be met directly, and often violently. The result is that gang membership entails a willingness to fight, and "gangbanging" (that is, fighting rival gangs) becomes a frequent occurrence. In recent years the consequences of fighting have gotten more serious as guns—including automatic weapons—have become an increasingly important part of the gang's arsenal. Gang activities often revolve around the use and sale of drugs and involvement in criminal activities. The problems of the barrio—gangs, school dropouts, and drugs—are, as Ray Hutchison (1992: 15) pointed out, "symptoms of declining economic opportunities."

Vigil's work on multiple marginality can be extended to explain why gangs emerge in other ethnic groups besides Latinos. He notes that gangs are present in all ethnic groups and are a result of complex historical and cultural factors that ethnic groups experience in similar yet distinctive ways. Gangs

A Latina factory worker with the Israeli owners.

are particularly present in immigrant communities, both Asian and Latino, where youth are vulnerable to the stresses of acculturation and generational conflict. African American youth in urban areas also experience marginality because of their social and economic position. This status, coupled with racism, places youth in these communities at high risk for gang membership (Vigil, 2002).

New Latino Immigration: Central and South America and the Caribbean

Although this chapter focused on the three largest Latino groups—Cubans, Puerto Ricans, and Mexican Americans—they are by no means the only components of the growing Hispanic American population. For instance, over 750,000 Dominicans from the Caribbean are concentrated in the greater New York area. Dominicans and Puerto Ricans share neighborhood space and ethnic enclaves. Costa Ricans, Guatemalans, Hondurans, Nicaraguans, Panamanians, and Salvadorans form the bulk of the 1.6 million people from Central America (see Table 8.2).

Many Central Americans left their homes because of political turmoil and sought political asylum in the United States. Similar to Dominicans who have settled near Puerto Rican enclaves, Central Americans have built neighborhoods close or next to Mexican American ethnic enclaves. Although the groups may share a common language, individuals still maintain their own national and ethnic identity. Finally, another 1.3 million individuals (or 3.8 percent of the Latino population) are of South American origin, with larger populations from Colombia, Ecuador, and Peru. The combination of Central and

South American and Caribbean Latino populations bring great social and economic diversity to this panethnic group defined by a shared language.

Table 8.2	Hispanic and Latino Population in the United States, 2000		
		Number	Percentage
Total Hispanic/Latino Population		35,305,818	100.0
Mexican		20,640,711	58.5
Puerto Rican		3,406,178	9.6
Cuban		1,241,685	3.5
Other Hispanic or Latino		10,017,244	28.4
Dominican		764,945	2.2
Central American (excludes Mexican)		1,686,937	4.8
Costa Rican		68,588	0.2
Guatemalan		372,487	1.1
Honduran		217,569	0.6
Nicaraguan		177,684	0.5
Panamanian		91,723	0.3
Salvadoran		655,165	1.9
Other Central American		103,721	0.3
South American		1,353,562	3.8
Argentinean		100,864	0.3
Bolivian		42,068	0.1
Chilean		68,849	0.2
Colombian		470,684	1.3
Ecuadorian		260,559	0.7
Paraguayan		8,769	0.0
Peruvian		233,026	0.7
Uruguayan		18,804	0.1
Venezuelan		91,507	0.3
Other South American		57,532	0.2

Source: U.S. Bureau of the Census (2000).

Summary

Latinos have become more prominent in American life in the recent past and, given current population growth projections, they will play an even greater role in shaping American society in the twenty-first century. The rapidity of recent developments makes it difficult to predict what the future will be like.

Clearly the major Hispanic groups have had rather different historical experiences in America. Although there is considerable diversity within each group, we can make some comparative generalizations about the three groups discussed in this chapter. Cubans appear to be poised to enter the mainstream, while Puerto Ricans remain on the margins. The Mexican American community exhibits a more radical disjuncture between those who are upwardly mobile and those who remain caught in poor barrios. The middle class has expanded, but poverty characterizes a sizable segment of the population, especially among the immigrant generation.

What does this mean for the future? Will Cubans preserve their ethnic enclave economy, or will younger Cubans move out of the ethnic community and into the larger society? Will intermarriage undermine Cuban American institutions? How will Cuban Americans respond to developments in the homeland? Will some, especially among the elderly, return to Cuba if communism ends?

In a similar vein, will Puerto Ricans find an economic niche? Will they begin to exert greater political influence in the northeastern cities where they are concentrated? What are the prospects for continued return migration to the island? What is the likelihood that Puerto Ricans will develop alliances with other Latino groups?

Finally, to what extent will the largest immigrant group reshape not only the social and political character of the American Southwest, but the culture as well? Will their political power expand? Will immigration increase or decrease? What will be the long-term impact of *maquiladora* industries? What will be the impact of the specific economic arrangements created by NAFTA and of larger forces of economic globalization?

These and countless other questions can only be answered in the future as these groups take their place in this country and the larger society responds to them.

Key Terms

bilingualism	*Proposition 187 (California)*
bracero program	*segmented assimilation*
Chicanismo	*transnational immigrants*
ethnic enclave economy	*undocumented immigration*
maquiladora *industries*	

Questions for Discussion and Critical Thinking

1. Compare and contrast the historical experiences and the current status of the two major Latino groups from the Caribbean: Cubans and Puerto Ricans.

2. Review the evolution of the Mexican American community, paying particular attention to the different kinds of organizations that members of this community have created. Which organizations have had the greatest impact, and why? How do these organizations reflect internal divisions based on class and generation?

3. Compare and contrast the impact of segmented assimilation on the three groups that are the focus of this chapter: Cubans, Puerto Ricans, and Mexicans. ✦

Chapter 9

Asian Americans: The Myth of the Model Minority

Jason Fong grew up in the Midwest. His great-grandfather came to the United States in 1916 as a "paper son," which meant that he had false papers that claimed he was the son of a San Francisco merchant. His real family name was Wong. His parents own a Chinese restaurant, a grocery story, and other properties in the suburbs of Chicago. Jason works for his family after school and during summer vacations. He plans to major in business and join the family businesses when he graduates from college.

Amy Sasaki grew up in California. She is a college biology major, planning a career in public health. When she was growing up, she thought of herself as being similar to her classmates at her predominantly white suburban high school. Only when she went to college did she become aware of the experiences her grandparents had gone through during World War II. She found out that they were interned in a relocation center called Heart Mountain, in the middle of Wyoming. She always wondered why they never talked about it. All she heard from her grandparents and parents was that it was important that she get good grades, and attend a competitive college, which would lead to a good job.

Thuy Nguyen was born in Vietnam. She and her mother have been in the United States for five years. They live with her father and brothers, who had emigrated from Vietnam in 1979. Her father was a schoolteacher before he left Vietnam; now he works in a small Vietnamese restaurant in southern California. Her mother works as a manicurist in a beauty salon. Thuy hopes to go to college, but she struggles to learn English and does not know whether there will be enough money for her to attend.

These stories illustrate some of the typical experiences of contemporary young Asian Americans. They are fictional composites that suggest some of the similarities and some of the differences that can be found in the Asian American experience. Asian Americans compose a

295

number of diverse ethnic groups whose origins are from East and South Asia (Fong, 2000). Socially and culturally these ethnic groups are very different from one another, yet throughout their history in the United States their members have experienced similar forms of prejudice and discrimination. The diversity in the Asian American population reflects the realities of global transmigration and the complex geopolitical relationships between countries in Asia and the United States.

In 1990, 6.9 million persons of Asian ancestry were reported by the U.S. Census, representing 2.9 percent of the nation's total population. By 2000, that population had increased to 11.9 million persons, or 4 percent of the entire population. This number included those who counted themselves as belonging to one or more specific Asian groups. This chapter will highlight the larger Asian groups: Japanese, Chinese, Korean, Filipino, Asian Indian, and Southeast Asian. There are also about three dozen other groups that cannot be detailed here, including groups with 150,000 or more members such as the Taiwanese, Pakistani, Cambodian, Laotian, Hmong, and Thai (U.S. Bureau of the Census, 2000). Hawaiians, who are Americans by conquest and annexation, are enumerated under a separate count as an indigenous group.

The term *Asian American* is, in fact, relatively new. In the past, Asian ethnic groups were referred to solely by their national origin. Beginning in the 1980s, the U.S. Census began to unify the several Asian national origin groups and Pacific Islanders (Hawaiian, Samoan, Tongan, Guamanian) into one panethnic category. Hence, the broad category of "Asian/Pacific Islander" was born. While this term may be useful for statistical purposes, the larger category tends to blur the differences among Asian ethnic groups.

This chapter resumes the history of the Japanese and Chinese in America since the watershed World War II period. There are similarities in the subsequent histories of the two groups, but the differences are especially pronounced. In addition to these groups, the rapidly expanding Korean and Filipino communities will be examined, followed by brief overviews of two panethnic communities: the Asian Indian and Southeast Asian. Although all of these groups can trace their histories to the early part of this century, they were very small until recently. They are, however, among the largest of the post-1965 immigrant groups. Again, although there are similarities among the groups, important differences must be recognized, for these differences suggest potentially rather divergent futures for these groups.

The Model Minority: Myth and Reality

Some Asians have proved to be economically successful in a relatively short time. Many are educated middle-class professionals who emigrated because of the perception of greater professional opportunities in America than could be reasonably expected at home. Many American-born Asians have experienced intergenerational upward mobility: Although they have entered the professional white-collar workforce, their parents may have worked as agricultural workers or unskilled laborers. In addition, many Asian students—including relatively recent immigrants—have done very well academically. Asian students, for example, have higher average scores than white students on the Scholastic Aptitude Test (SAT). For students whose family income exceeds $70,000, white students have an average composite SAT score of 998, while their Asian counterparts have an average of 1,066. The average score for Hispanics from the same income range is 932, and that for blacks is 854 (Hacker, 1992).

Table 9.1 Asian Population Growth			
Asian Ethnic Group	Growth Rate 1980–1990	Growth Rate 1990–2000	Percentage of Asian American Population
Chinese	104.1%	47.5%	23.7%
Filipino	81.6	30.3	18.1
Asian Indian	125.6	113.4	16.4
Vietnamese	125.3	89.2	11.0
Korean	134.8	35.1	10.5
Japanese	20.9	−9.4	7.8
Source: U.S. Bureau of the Census (2003).			

Since World War II, prejudice and discrimination directed at Asian Americans has gradually declined, and the images used to depict various Asian groups have shifted. Moon H. Jo and Daniel D. Mast (1993) noted that as the most negative stereotypes were toned down during the 1950s, the image that began to emerge was initially neutral, rather than positive. Asians were collectively described as being "compliant, quiet, and docile." They were seen positively as polite, obedient, and hardworking, and they were portrayed as exhibiting high levels of family loyalty and responsibility. Beginning in the 1960s, but escalating to a peak by the 1980s, the focus was on the economic and educational achievements of Asians. This resulted in the rather widespread depiction in the American media and in scholarly publications of examples of the Asian "success story." Jo and Mast (1993: 431) wrote, "The common theme of all these success stories is identified as Asian Americans' strong family and community ties, strong work ethic, academic excellence, self-sufficiency, low crime rate, and fewer requests for public assistance."

The characterization of Asian Americans as the **model minority** emerged out of this imagery (Hurh and Kwang, 1989). Without downplaying the genuine achievements of many Asian Americans who have succeeded in spite of the legacy of racism and the difficulties associated with acculturation, two features of the notion of a model minority are problematic and question the efficacy of the term. First, as this chapter will indicate, not all Asians have been successful. Not only have some groups been more successful than others, but also within each group significant sectors have not gained the foothold in the American economy that promises upward mobility. Some immigrant groups arrived with monetary and human capital that gave them a distinct advantage. Some groups settled in locales with expanding job opportunities, while others found themselves in places with fewer opportunities for economic advance. Some confronted intense competition from other groups, while others did not (Olzak, 1992). In short, many social structural and historical variables contribute to the likelihood of success, not simply the character of the members of any particular ethnic group.

Second, although some Asians have embraced the idea of the model minority—understandably preferring it to the negative images of the recent past—members of the dominant white society, not Asians, created the image. In part, the model minority serves an ideological purpose. It makes an invidious comparison between the "successful Asians" and those racial and ethnic groups that have not achieved eco-

Table 9.2 Metropolitan Areas With the Largest Asian Populations		
Metropolitan Area	**Asian American Population**	**Percent of Total Population**
Los Angeles	1,799,000	11.4%
New York	1,343,000	6.7
San Francisco	1,279,000	18.8
Honolulu	566,000	64.9
Washington, DC / Baltimore	373,000	5.1
Chicago	367,000	4.2
Source: U.S. Bureau of the Census (2003).		

nomic parity with whites and that continue to be viewed as second-class citizens—most notably, blacks. The term implicitly suggests that if blacks and less successful Hispanic groups such as Puerto Ricans and Mexicans would adapt the Asian work ethic and general lifestyle, they, too, would be successful. As such, the model minority concept contributes to the tendency to "blame the victim" (Takaki, 1989).

Japanese Americans

In the two decades after World War II, Japanese Americans managed a remarkable recovery from the devastating impact of the wartime internment (Ng, 2002). This recovery did not occur without considerable difficulty, however. Thousands of *Issei* lost the businesses and farms that they had owned, and they were unable—because of age, educational background, acculturation problems, and discrimination—to find work in either skilled blue-collar jobs or the expanding area of white-collar professional occupations. As a consequence, many turned to small business ownership and in particular to commercial gardening. For example, in Los Angeles, it is estimated that as late as 1960, as many as 75 percent of Japanese-owned businesses were contract-gardening related (Levine and Rhodes, 1981; Levine and Montero, 1973).

For the second generation, like the first, the internment was a nightmare. According to Harry H. L. Kitano (1988),

> One of the unstated but constant concerns of the Nisei is that an event similar to the wartime evacuation should not happen again. However, for a long period after the event, many Nisei remained silent concerning the violation of their civil liberties; instead, they concentrated on reestablishing themselves in financially secure

---

Voices ◆ Warren Furutani

Now even though I wasn't in camp, it's always a reference point for Japanese Americans. People will ask, "Were you in camp?" And of course I wasn't. That doesn't end the questioning, because they then ask if your parents were. If you tell them what camp your parents were in and if they were not themselves in that camp, then they ask if you know so-and-so who was in that camp. The point I am making is that the camp experience has had a direct impact on those of us who were born after the war because it is a constant reference and because it is a part of our history. [It is] something that impacts on us as individuals and as young people today.

Testimony of Warren Furutani before the Commission on Wartime Relocation and Internment of Civilians (Ng, 2002: 179).

positions, with the hope that economic gain would somehow take care of most problems. (269)

The *Nisei* did not generally follow in the footsteps of the immigrant generation. Rather than remaining in the ethnically based economic niche, the second generation instead entered the world of the white-collar middle class (Tsukashima, 1991). Even before World War II, they had used higher education—especially in technical fields such as engineering, pharmacy, and optometry—as a means of becoming upwardly mobile. William Petersen (1971) noted that by 1940, Japanese Americans had higher levels of educational attainment than whites, and this differential has persisted over the past half century.

As the ***Sansei,*** or third generation, entered the workforce, these trends continued. The Japanese almost reached income parity with whites by 1960, and a decade later their personal incomes were 11 percent above the national average and their family income averages were 32 percent greater (Sowell, 1981a). In many respects, the Japanese American experience parallels that of Jewish Americans: both confronted considerable prejudice and discrimination, were set apart from the dominant culture (the Jews by religion and the Japanese by race and to some extent religion), used education as a vehicle for economic advancement, and have higher educational attainment levels and average incomes than the general white population. But for the *Sansei,* because of their parents' experiences in the relocation camps, there was in addition a powerful parental emphasis placed on assimilating—working hard to fit into the mainstream by acting like typical middle-class white Americans (Ng, 1989).

Discrimination in the workforce has not been eliminated entirely. Another parallel with Jews is that both groups have tended to be excluded from top managerial or administrative positions in major corporate, financial, and educational institutions. There is evidence of a glass ceiling that upwardly mobile Japanese Americans bump into (Woo, 1999). Valued for their technical expertise, the Japanese are not similarly valued for their leadership capabilities. Thus, they are proportionately underrepresented in the ranks of high-level management (Kitano and Daniels, 1988).

The Third Generation and Beyond

The Japanese American population in 2000 was just under 796,700 (U.S. Bureau of the Census, 2000). Their population is the sixth largest of all Asian ethnic groups, a considerable decline in rank since 1965. The Japanese are the only Asian group that has not grown larger as a result of continued immigration from abroad. Thus, today's Japanese American community is primarily American-born.

Both the *Sansei* and ***Yonsei*** (fourth generation) came of age in a world markedly different from that of their grandparents. Ethnic an-

tagonism had declined, and most had not experienced the wartime incarceration. They were encouraged not to look at the painful past, but
instead to the future. They have not been the victims of persistent prejudice in the way their ancestors were. Moreover, they are the beneficiaries of the relative economic success of their parents, which among
other things provided them with the opportunity to pursue higher education (Lyman, 1977).

Growing numbers from subsequent generations have grown up in
racially integrated suburbs, where they are increasingly removed from
the institutions of the ethnic community (Osako, 1984; Lyman, 1986).
Of the 28 percent of Japanese Americans who do not live in the American West, the suburbanites have not tended to create ethnic organizations, and their involvement in urban ethnic institutions is relatively infrequent. This is somewhat different in the West, especially California
and Hawaii, where, because of the high concentration of Japanese,
there is evidence of greater ongoing contact with and involvement in
the ethnic community.

The third and subsequent generations were intent on fitting into
America and were willing to pattern their behaviors in ways that were
designed to assist in that process. Their parents tended to lead quiet,
conformist lives and got their children involved in what were seen as
wholesome middle-class activities, such as YMCA programs, scouting,
Little League baseball, and the like (Kitano, 1991). On the job, in
school, and in their neighborhoods, younger Japanese function in a
world that is largely middle class and white. Their knowledge of contemporary Japan is often quite limited. Many *Nisei* believe this has resulted in a loss of the inherited Japanese culture as well as a devalua-
tion of what they see as traditional character. In short, the *Sansei* and
later generations are Americanized in a way that the *Issei* and *Nisei*, as
well as most of their Asian counterparts, are not (Lyman, 1977).

An indication of this change is that Japanese Americans tend to
have few if any relationships with recent Japanese arrivals who are
temporarily working in the United States for Japanese firms. This contingent of Japanese, known as *Kai-sha*, are in the United States for
specified periods of time, after which the firms recall them to Japan. As
they are well aware, if they or their families appear to be too Americanized upon their return to Japan, not only will they have a difficult time
adjusting to the homeland, but their success with the company may be
threatened. Thus, they tend to avoid activities that promote
acculturative tendencies. A considerable cultural gulf separates these
temporary sojourners from contemporary Japanese Americans.

Changes in the Ethnic Community

Generational changes have had an impact on ethnic institutions.
The second generation initiated changes that posed a direct challenge

to the traditional family. For example, many of them embraced the American family model by endorsing individuals' rights to choose their own marital partners on the basis of romantic love. Marital ties were considered more important than ties to blood relations (Yanagisako, 1985). Decision-making in the family was shared more equitably by spouses, and, as Stanford M. Lyman (1977: 169) wrote, child-rearing practices followed "the white middle-class ethos of love, equality, and companionship. The principles of *Bushido* gave way to those of Dr. Spock." This trend toward a decidedly American family model is even more characteristic of the *Sansei* (Kitano, 1988).

A similar change characterizes religious institutions among Japanese Americans. Although many immigrants practiced Buddhism or Shintoism, a significant segment of the *Nisei* converted to Christianity, particularly to such Protestant denominations as Methodist and Presbyterian. This trend accelerated during World War II because the wartime hysteria resulted in equating allegiance to traditional Japanese religions with a loyalty to the Japanese government (Fukuda, 1990).

Since the 1960s, when members of the counterculture took a keen interest in Eastern religions, hostility to nonWestern religion has declined considerably, and renewed interest in Buddhism can be seen among Japanese Americans. At present, the largest organization of Buddhists is the Jodo Shinshu Buddhist Churches of America. It currently has between 60 and 70 temples and a membership of approximately 150,000. Not all members are Japanese—many other Asian groups are also represented. Although there are several small Buddhist groups, most Japanese Americans are not affiliated with Buddhist or Shinto religious institutions. As with the family, changes set in motion by the second generation have been pushed further by the *Sansei* and the *Yonsei*.

Although changes in the family and religion provide evidence of acculturation, in areas of the country where there are high concentrations of Japanese Americans, a sense of ethnic identity is preserved by various kinds of ethnically based group activities—such as sporting activities and community service projects—that foster friendships and other ingroup relationships. Even though there may be little traditional Japanese culture evident in the activities, they do preserve a sense of group identity (Kurashige, 2002).

Stephen S. Fugita and David J. O'Brien argued that for the California Japanese they studied in the late 1970s, while cultural assimilation was occurring, structural assimilation was not (Fugita and O'Brien, 1991; see also O'Brien and Fugita, 1991). It is uncertain whether this pattern will persist into the future. Moreover, the sites of their study— Gardena, Fresno, and Sacramento— are not typical of the communities where many Japanese Americans live insofar as they are communities with substantial Japanese American populations. As geographic dispersal in suburban America continues, it will likely have an impact on structural assimilation.

The *Nisei*-created Japanese American Citizens League (JACL) has continued to play a political role nationally. When the *Issei* were granted citizenship rights in 1952, the JACL conducted voter registration drives. The organization urged active involvement in mainstream American politics. This mostly meant working within the Democratic party. In Hawaii, and to a lesser extent California, a number of Japanese candidates have been elected to national political offices since Daniel Inouye's election to Congress when Hawaii became a state in 1959.

The JACL has also functioned as a civil rights organization. Shortly after World War II, members began to demand compensation for the losses they had suffered as a result of the wartime evacuation. Minimal payments were made for business and property losses in 1948, but these inadequate payments were not accompanied by an admission that the government had violated the constitutional rights of Japanese Americans. This acknowledgment had to wait until the Carter administration created a Commission on Wartime Relocation and Internment of Civilians (Hosokawa, 1982). The Commission's final report, issued in 1983, recommended that each surviving internee be paid a tax-exempt amount of $20,000, and it called for admitting that racial discrimination had caused this violation of civil liberties. After much delay, President Reagan signed the Civil Liberties Act of 1988, which formally ratified the Commission's recommendations. Actual payments did not commence until 1990. Although the Act can be viewed as too little too late, it ended a long quest for justice (Takahashi, 1997).

As this mobilized activity indicates, the ethnic community has by no means disappeared. But considerable evidence suggests that it no longer plays the prominent role in the lives of Japanese Americans that it did earlier in the century.

The Future of the Japanese American Community

In *Come See the Paradise* (1990), a film set in the 1930s and 1940s, a young *Nisei* woman falls in love with an Irish American labor organizer. Not only is the couple forced to confront the enforced separation brought about by the war, but they also have to deal with her family's intense opposition to an interracial marriage. Until this point, the intermarriage rate for Japanese Americans had been very low, probably less than 2 percent. After midcentury, however, the intermarriage rate of Japanese Americans began to rise dramatically (Spickard, 1989; Kitano et al., 1984).

Even during the earlier period, intermarriage rates were higher outside of the western states, where Japanese were spread geographically, and thus the likelihood of finding an ingroup marital partner was considerably lower than in areas of high concentration. In some of these regions, more than 50 percent of Japanese Americans were intermarrying by 1960. The rise in intermarriage was not confined to regions of sparse Japanese American settlement, however. For example, by the mid-1970s, the outgroup marriage rate in Los Angeles County exceeded 50 percent, and before the end of the decade it had risen to more than 60 percent (Kitano, 1988). By 1985, more than half of all Japanese American marriages in Hawaii were exogamous (Barringer, Gardner, and Levin, 1993; Nakamaru, 1993).

No evidence suggests that this pattern will be reversed. Indeed, just as with Jews, there are few impediments from the ethnic community or from parents to discourage intermarriages. Even if parents might prefer that their child marry a Japanese American, they largely allow their children to choose. If they did not do so, they think, quite rightly, that their children would likely defy their wishes. Thus, here is another instance of intermarriage by default (Kitano, 1988). The children of interracial marriages often felt a sense of marginality and ambiguity. Some have navigated this situation well, while others have not. Some have found themselves in environments that are supportive of their mixed identity, and thus they inhabit what Amy Iwaskai Mass (1992) called "the best of both worlds." For others, however, their marginality has been a source of strain.

What explains the high rate of intermarriage, and why would the Japanese American community be concerned about it? According to Milton Gordon's (1964) classic assimilation model, intermarriage is a crucial step in the assimilation process. However, this does not explain why it occurs. There are many complex reasons as to why the out-marriage rate is so high. Sociologists Larry H. Shinagawa and Gin Y. Pang (1990, 1996) point to the significance of **hypergamy,** which involves a person gaining social rank by marrying a person of higher status. They note that Japanese American women are more likely to choose non-Japanese spouses, maximizing their status by marrying individuals perceived to possess high levels of economic and social capital. There are those who believe that interracial marriage results from negative associations with other Japanese Americans and the lingering stigma attached to World War II. Others suggest that residential dispersion and exposure to white society play significant roles.

The prevalence of intermarriage raises the prospect of not only an erosion in the ethnic community but also a decline in the salience of ethnic identity. Within and without the Japanese American community, the question has been posed: Does intermarriage signal, as Mass (1992: 265) put it, "the end of the Japanese American community"? Although it is far too soon to see what the future portends, the possibility exists that, as Masako M. Osako (1984: 536) wrote, "Japanese-Americans may become the first nonwhites to merge biologically into the dominant American society."

Increasingly, interracial unions mean multiracial families. The presence of such families signals a need to redefine what it means to be Japanese American. In some instances, children of interracial marriages feel marginalized. But for many others, there is an increasing sense of pride and identity in being "hapa" (from the pidgin Hawaiian "hapa-haole" or "half-white"). They have begun to create a new social group that is defined not solely by the race of one parent but through a combination of both parents' ethnic and cultural backgrounds.

Chinese Americans

The 2000 Census reported 2.7 million Chinese in America. This represents a huge increase from the 77,504 figure recorded in 1940 (U.S. Bureau of the Census, 2000; Wong, 1988). One consequence of this dramatic population increase was that Chinatowns grew. Thus, Robert Park's (1950) prediction that Chinatown would disappear (made in the 1920s when the Chinese population hit its lowest level) did not happen. The increase was caused by a steady improvement in the sex ratio among Chinese Americans and by new immigration.

Pre-1965 Developments

Immigration took place in two stages. The first occurred during the two decades between 1945 and 1965, during which time growth was significant. Growth was far more modest, however, compared with the period after 1965. Because the Chinese were allies of the United States in World War II, the Chinese Exclusion Act of 1882 was repealed in 1943, and a token quota of 105 was established. After the war an act of Congress permitted 6,000 Chinese war brides of U.S. military personnel to enter the country, and this number was subsequently expanded to include wives and children of U.S. citizens. As a result of the revolutionary upheaval in China that culminated in the victory of communist forces led by Mao Tse-tung and the forced withdrawal of nationalist forces led by Chiang Kai-shek, several thousand Chinese were granted permanent resident status under the provisions of the Displaced Persons Act (Tong, 2000). The passage of the McCarran-Walter Act in 1952 marked the end of racial criteria in determining eligibility for immigration (Kitano and Daniels, 1988; Wong, 1988; Chen, 1980).

The Chinese American population grew to 236,084 by 1960. Immigration during this period played a major role in considerably redressing the skewed sex ratio. Women accounted for 9 out of every 10 immigrants between 1940 and 1960 (Wong, 1988); the sex ratio imbalance improved from 285.3 males per 100 females in 1940 to 134.5 males per 100 females in 1960.

The Growth of the Chinese Middle Class. Not all of the new immigrants gravitated to Chinatowns. Brides of servicemen, students, and others often lived outside of the ethnic enclave. At the same time, many residents also exited Chinatowns during the two decades after World War II. These individuals were largely from the English-speaking second generation who were prepared to take advantage of new opportunities available because of postwar prosperity.

Many entered colleges and universities to pursue professional training. More than 80 percent of college-educated Chinese Americans went into professional occupations rather than business ownership. Stanford M. Lyman observed that the Chinese were highly selective in their choice of occupations. They opted for careers in engineering, medicine, pharmacy, dentistry, optometry, and chemistry and tended to avoid positions in education and the law. They also exhibited a tendency to work for state and federal governmental organizations. This was, in Lyman's view, by design. The Chinese often had limited English-language skills, and they were concerned about prejudicial treatment from potential employers and clients. Thus, they selected careers that were seen as minimizing the problems associated with English profi-

A Chinese-Cambodian cook at work in Boston.

ciency and racism. Over time this trend has intensified, as the Chinese middle class is largely based on people in technical fields and independent professions while being underrepresented in managerial and proprietorial occupations (Lyman, 1974).

Entry into the middle class stimulated a movement out of Chinatown and into the suburbs. This meant that the Chinese middle class came into contact with the white middle class in a way that had not been possible a generation earlier. The movement to the suburbs frequently resulted in the clustering of Chinese in various suburban neighborhoods, however. Thus, many of New York's upwardly mobile Chinese located in Hempstead, Long Island, and those from Los Angeles moved to the San Gabriel Valley. Concerned that their children might lose much of their cultural heritage, the suburban middle class often established Chinese language schools and cultural centers to instill in their children an appreciation of their Chinese backgrounds (Zhou, 2002; Zhou and Logan, 1991).

One consequence of upward mobility was that Chinatowns got smaller. For example, by the late 1960s, only one of six Chinese Americans in Chicago lived in Chinatown, while the figure was one in four in New York City (Schaefer, 1988). As a result, the power of the ruling elite in Chinatowns eroded considerably. The middle class did not depend on this elite for their economic well-being, nor did they need to rely on them as mediators with the larger society.

Although Chinatowns remained tourist attractions, and thus continued to be economically viable, the community also continued to be beset with serious social problems. Poverty has been endemic. The Chinese American community is a divided one in which the successful tend to move out of Chinatown while those who have not made it remain. Housing problems include the prevalence of substandard units and a shortage of affordable units, resulting in overcrowding. Health care is inadequate—Chinatown residents suffer disproportionately from a number of serious illnesses and, in fact, are afflicted with one disease, tuberculosis, that is all but eradicated from the general population. Chinatowns have a serious suicide problem, as well as related mental health problems. Finally, crime, especially gang-related crime, has a negative impact on the community. Although often depicted in terms of juvenile delinquency, youth gangs are a perpetuation of the role historically played by the secret societies (Lyman, 1986; Lyman, 1974).

Homeland Politics. During the 1950s, most Chinese Americans supported the Chinese Nationalist cause and voiced their opposition to the communist takeover of the mainland. Since the People's Republic of China closed its doors to emigration, most Chinese arriving in the United States after 1949 were from either Hong Kong or Taiwan. These people were primarily hostile to the communist regime, which intensified anticommunist sentiment among Chinese in America. Given the political climate of the Cold War and in particular the resurgence of "yellow peril" hysteria during the armed conflict in Korea, Chinese Americans became concerned that the reduction in anti-Chinese prejudice might be short-lived. Their worst fears were that they might suffer a similar fate to that of the Japanese during World War II. Not surprisingly, the ruling elite in Chinatown sought to reassure the American public that Maoist sentiment was minimal, and they worked actively to suppress the little support that existed (Lyman, 1974).

Elements of the American political right wing with an interest in Asia—such as the publisher Henry Luce, Representative Walter H. Judd, and Senator William F. Knowland—organized what became known as the "China lobby." Its main goal was to topple the communist regime on the mainland and return Chiang Kai-shek's government-in-exile on the island of Taiwan to power. When Senator Joseph McCarthy began his anticommunist witch-hunt, he and his sympathizers began a campaign of vilification against government officials and others accused of "losing" and "betraying" China.

Many Chinese Americans believed it was all the more imperative to do what they could to express loyalty to the United States and opposition to international communism. Thus, the Chinese American leadership cooperated with the China lobby. As Alexander DeConde (1992:

150) noted, they used a variety of tactics "in the nation's Chinatowns to stimulate Chinese-American opposition to Mao Tse-tung's mainland regime."

Post-1965 Developments

The number of Chinese increased dramatically after 1965, as the Chinese became the third largest immigrant group during recent decades, surpassed only by Mexicans and Filipinos. Between 1960 and 1980 the Chinese population expanded more than threefold because of these new immigrants, or *San Yi Man*. In 1990 the Chinese were the largest Asian group. Most immigrants came from urban areas and included both Mandarin and Cantonese speakers. Some came from the People's Republic of China by way of Hong Kong; they left because of the political turmoil and bloody violence brought about by the Cultural Revolution. Most, however, came from Hong Kong or Taiwan and were motivated primarily by economic considerations (Takaki, 1989).

As a result, the Chinese American community was once again composed primarily of immigrants, as the first generation rose from 39 percent of the total group in 1960 to 63 percent by 1980. A majority of the new arrivals settled in either California or New York, thereby revitalizing the Chinatowns in those states (Gold, 1992). The Chinatown in New York City, for example, grew from about 15,000 to more than 100,000 residents. Although many immigrants gravitated to traditional urban Chinatowns, others settled in suburban areas.

The choice of residential location was largely determined by the individual's economic status. Takaki (1989: 425) reported that the "different class backgrounds of the new immigrants has led to the formation of a bipolar Chinese American community—one divided between a colonized working class and an entrepreneurial-professional middle class." The working-class immigrants are largely found in the traditional Chinatowns, while the more upwardly mobile and affluent have chosen suburbs. As one commentator put it, there is a major divide between the "Chinatown ghettos" and the "arriviste suburbs" (Awanohara, 1991). In New York City, reminiscent of the division between poor and affluent Jews at the turn of the century, the "Downtown Chinese" are employed in restaurants and the garment industry, while the "Uptown Chinese" are engaged in various professions and business enterprises (Kwong, 1987).

Many middle-class Chinese live in suburbs that are characterized by large numbers of Asians in general and Chinese in particular. Thus, in the New York metropolitan area, many middle-class Chinese live in multiethnic neighborhoods in Flushing and Elmhurst (Chen, 1992). In the Los Angeles area, Monterey Park has become known as the first suburban Chinatown (Fong, 1994). The majority of the community's citizens are of Chinese ancestry, and thus it has become known as "Little Taipei." Although the community elected its first Chinese American mayor during the 1980s, this ethnic transformation of Monterey Park produced a nativist backlash among some whites. Thus, Takaki (1989: 425) noted, "In 1986 a sign at a gas station near the city limits, for example, displayed two slant eyes with the declaration: 'Will the last American to leave Monterey Park please bring the flag.' "

Changing Chinatown: New York City. New York City's Chinatown, located in lower Manhattan, is the largest Chinese enclave not only in the United States but also in the Western Hemisphere. The population has grown so dramatically that it has spilled over into adjacent neighborhoods, including Little Italy. At present, approximately 150,000 Chinese inhabit Chinatown; perhaps as many as one in five are undocumented immigrants (Kinkead, 1992; Wong, 1982). As with other ethnic neighborhoods throughout the history of the United States, not all residents of Chinatown are Chinese; however, a sizable majority of them are. Perhaps 80 percent are foreign born. As with Little Italies a century ago, many streets are defined in terms of the homeland region or the diaspora country of the immigrants. Thus, Peter Kwong (1987: 41) observed, "Groups with different dialects concentrate in separate sections of Chinatown: Fukienese on Division Street, Burmese Chinese on Henry Street, Chinese from Taiwan on Centre Street, Vietnamese on East Broadway."

Residents find employment in a variety of businesses, but prominent among them are laundries, grocery stores, shops catering to tourists, and especially restaurants and the garment industry. Several thousand individuals, primarily male, are employed in the approximately 450 restaurants in Chinatown (Kwong, 1987). Chinese expansion in New York's garment industry since the mid-1960s has been remarkable. The 30 Chinese-owned firms in 1965 grew to about 500 firms within a little more than two decades, and the current 20,000 Chinese workers compose more than one-sixth of the city's apparel labor force.

Sociologist Roger Waldinger (1986) emphasized the importance of the departure from the industry by earlier immigrants and their offspring, chiefly Jews and Italians. Waldinger's survey of Jewish and Italian factory owners provides clues to their reasons for leaving the business as well as the disinclination of the children to take over from their parents. Central to this change is the perception of occupational alternatives. What has occurred is a process of ethnic succession in which the Chinese had an opportunity as competition with more established groups in the industry declined.

To explain why the Chinese have been particularly successful in getting into the industry, Waldinger (1986) suggested that various cultural and psychological forces have an impact, and he provided an interesting perspective on the particular motives of the Chinese by a comparison with another group that has made inroads into the industry, Dominicans. For the Chinese, entrepreneurship is perceived as the most realistic way to achieve social mobility, while for the Dominicans it is a means to escape the oppressive work routines of the manual laborer. This attitude suggests that the Chinese have goals similar to those of the Jews and Italians who preceded them in the industry and are thus likely to exit it if other occupational possibilities emerge. The influx of new immigrants has caused intense competition for jobs in these immigrant industries. Many workers are forced to rely on more than one job to survive economically. Working hours are generally long, and the pay is low (Kinkead, 1992: 66; Zhou and Logan, 1989).

Chinatown continues to thrive on tourist dollars because a highly romanticized and exotic image has been maintained. This gilded ghetto is still beset by many serious problems, including health problems. Kinkead (1992) reported that Chinatown suffers from a lower life expectancy and a high infant mortality rate because of such health problems as parasites, intestinal ailments, hepatitis, malnutrition, and anemia. The community also continues to suffer from high rates of mental illness and suicide.

This enclave economy, unlike the Cuban, exploits workers. Thus, the male-dominated restaurant industry and the female-dominated garment industry demand long work hours for very low pay (at or below minimum wage) and without the provision of fringe benefits. Employees, for example, are generally without health insurance, thereby compounding the health problems noted earlier. Housing also continues to be substandard, unsafe, unhealthy, overcrowded, and overpriced. Chinatown lacks adequate recreational facilities.

Crime has become a more serious problem and is intimately linked to the role of tongs, or youth gangs. Countless gangs currently operate in Chinatown, usually with a membership of between 30 and 50 members. Gangs pit different elements of the Chinese community against one another: Cantonese versus Mandarin, Hong Kong Chinese versus Taiwan Chinese, new arrivals versus youth who have been in America for some time, and so forth. They are involved in turf wars and a variety of criminal activities. Gangs routinely extort "protection" money from Chinatown businesses. Kinkcad (1992) wrote that more than 80 percent of Chinese restaurants and about two-thirds of all businesses indicate that regular protection payments are made to various gangs. Recently gangs have become involved in drug trafficking. The FBI estimates that as much as half of the heroin smuggled into the United States is under the control of criminal syndicates in Chinatown.

Traditionally, the ruling elite of Chinatown controlled the secret societies, or tongs. Whether they are able to do so effectively today is not clear. Nonetheless, the Chinese Consolidated Benevolent Association (CCBA) remains a powerful force in Chinatown, functioning as the unofficial governing body of the community, as in the past. Housed in a building on Mott Street, the CCBA's headquarters operates something like a city hall, with the president's role being seen—as in the nine-teenth century—as akin to that of a mayor.

Within the CCBA umbrella are two subdivisions that reflect the internal divisions in Chinatown: fongs, or village associations, and about 40 family associations, composed of people sharing last surnames. Both serve important functions, including organizing recreational activities and celebrations on Chinese holidays; running schools designed to provide cultural and language instruction to youth; promoting traditional religious practices associated with ancestor worship; and providing various services, including loans and jobs for new arrivals, credit clubs, translation services, and lodging for the elderly and unemployed. In addition, district associations settle disputes, thereby permitting Chinatown residents to avoid the American judicial system except as a last resort (Wong, 1982, 1987; Kuo, 1977).

The current role of the CCBA reflects the vitality of the traditional ethnic community. According to Bernard Wong (1987: 247), however, "the community is no longer controlled by the monolithic power structure of the CCBA and its affiliates." New organizations have been created, many by new immigrants and many with the support of federal and state funding. These include modern social service agencies such as the Chinatown Planning Council, the Chinatown Advisory Council, and the Chinese Health Clinic. More than 200 organizations have been created on the basis of educational backgrounds (such as alumni groups) and professional or business interests. The Organization of Chinese-Americans, for example, is a civil rights organization concerned with combating prejudice and discrimination (Wong, 1987).

What is significant about these new organizations is that they reflect a different orientation toward American society (Lin, 1998). Rather than seeking to keep Chinese isolated in ethnic communities, their purpose is to prepare Chinese for entry into the larger society. According to Wong (1987), there are two distinct orientations toward the larger society in contemporary Chinatown:

> Having lived in an era of intense racism against Chinese, old settlers came to feel that any intimate contacts with the larger society would invite trouble and they isolated, and still isolate, themselves from the mainstream of American society. Most of the new immigrants do not want to isolate themselves and the community from the larger society. On the contrary, they would like to see their community as an integral part of the city as well as of the wider U.S. society. Thus, Chinatown is not an "unmeltable" ethnic community. Rather, it is an assimilable community with an interest in changing its boundaries. (249)

At present, it is unclear how likely assimilation is. It depends on economic opportunities and options, as well as political and cultural factors. Thus, we can only speculate about if and how those boundaries might change. This being said, there is evidence that the second generation is far more acculturated than their parents' generation (Kibria, 2003).

Korean Americans

The 2000 Census reported that 1.2 million Koreans live in the United States, so Koreans continue to rank fourth in size among Asian groups (U.S. Bureau of the Census, 2000). The vast majority of Korean Americans are here as a result of post-1965 immigration. Indeed, the small size of the Korean American community that had been created by the first two waves of immigration—after the turn of the century and in the wake of the Korean War—meant that they had only a minimal impact on America's ethnic mix (Melendy, 1977). Between 1950 and 1965, only 18,797 Koreans were admitted into the country as permanent residents. In the three decades between 1970 and 2000, however, the Korean population increased dramatically. Koreans have settled in large numbers in a few major cities where their presence is especially felt: Los Angeles, New York, and Chicago.

During the period of mass migration, South Korea became an important economic force in Asia, with an expanding industrial base. In this context of economic expansion, what were the migratory push forces that contributed to the contemporary Korean diaspora? Korean immigration has been largely a middle-class phenomenon. In this regard, they are most like Cubans and Filipinos. Koreans are one of the most highly educated groups among the new immigrants. Many Koreans came to the United States not only with college degrees but also with various kinds of postgraduate professional credentials. One might assume that it is precisely this class that had the most to gain by South Korean industrialization, and indeed the professional middle class has grown. As In-Jin Yoon (1992) showed, however, the rapid expansion of a new urban middle class resulted in a situation in which many in this class experienced "a widening gap between their expectations of upward mobility and the limited opportunities available in South Korea."

The provisions of the 1965 Immigration Act facilitated Korean immigration to America, for it was precisely middle-class professionals who were accorded preferential treatment. The choice of the United States was also influenced by political and cultural ties that existed between the nations. Many institutions of higher education in Korea had been established by Christian missionaries from the United States, beginning in the last part of the nineteenth century, and many prominent Koreans have been educated in these institutions.

Many educated in these schools converted to Christianity—largely Protestant Christianity. This conversion provided an important cultural link to the United States (Min and Kim, 2002; Kitano and Daniels, 1988;

Kim, 1977). The political dimension became important in the years after the Korean War, when U.S. military and economic aid was a major factor in making the transition from an agrarian to a market-based industrial economy (Yoon, 1992; Cha, 1977). These factors merged with purely economic considerations to motivate members of Korea's educated middle class to emigrate.

In recent years, the class composition of Korean immigration has changed as middle-class immigration has tapered off, while the percentage of non-white-collar workers has increased (Yoon, 1992). As we have seen with Cubans recently and Germans a century ago, this pattern is not atypical. Many recent arrivals do not have the education or specific job skills that permit easy entry into the mainstream American economy. In addition, many from this cadre have more limited English-language proficiencies. As a result, they are far more dependent on the Korean ethnic economy for jobs than the earlier migrants were. They can also begin the adjustment process by relying on social networks and organizations established by the middle class (Kibria, 2003).

Immigrant Entrepreneurs

Many Koreans experienced an initial period of downward mobility (Kitano and Daniels, 1988). For some professionals, this was the inevitable consequence of the need to acquire additional educational training or recredentialing to enter American white-collar occupations. Koreans can be found in a range of professions but are especially concentrated in health care and education. The number of Koreans teaching in higher education is attested to by the existence of an academic organization called the Association of Korean Christian Scholars in North America (Kivisto, 1993). Although this move into the mainstream economy has been the route to upward mobility pursued by some, Koreans are disproportionately involved in small businesses.

In a study conducted by the U.S. Bureau of the Census (1984), Koreans ranked first among 17 recent immigrant groups in their rate of self-employment. The proportion of Koreans who were self-employed in 1980 was almost twice that of the U.S. average. Pyong Gap Min (1991) determined that the Census report undercounts the number of self-employed Koreans, and he contended that the rate of self-employment has actually increased since 1980. Won Moo Hurh and Kwang Chang Kim (1984) estimated that one-third of all Korean adults in Los Angeles are either owners or managers of small businesses, and other researchers have arrived at comparable percentages in other cites, such as New York and Atlanta (Kim, 1981; Min, 1988).

Self-employment means that immigrants own their own businesses. These businesses tend to be small enterprises that frequently involve families. Korean women have a very high labor-force participation rate, chiefly because they work in family-owned businesses.

Koreans own a wide range of small businesses, including grocery stores, fruit stands, flower shops, liquor stores, apparel shops, wig shops, repair shops, and restaurants. Although their businesses are visible in a number of cities where Koreans constitute a small group, they are particularly important in Los Angeles, New York, and Chicago. In these cities Koreans are involved in a wide range of business activities but are highly concentrated in a few businesses, including produce, liquor, and wigs. Los Angeles has the most highly developed enclave economy (Light and Bonacich, 1988; Kim, 1981; Kim and Hurh, 1985; Yoon, 1991).

Korean entrepreneurs frequently use ethnic resources when getting started in business. As with Chinese, Japanese, and West Indians, Koreans operate rotating credit associations, known in the Korean community as **Kye,** which provide start-up capital. Other ethnic resources that assist with entrepreneurial activities include loans from kin, friends, and Korean banks. In addition, informal ethnic networks provide information and advice. Although the role of ethnic resources is a crucial factor in explaining the high level of Korean business activity, not all Korean merchants rely on the ethnic community to get started. Many enter into business by investing their own personal savings, and others make use of loans from American banks. Yoon (1991) discovered that although ethnic resources do play an important role for many at the beginning of business formation, they become less important over time.

Interethnic Conflict

In contrast with Cubans, Koreans have established many businesses outside of the residential ethnic enclaves. The large Koreatown in Los Angeles and the smaller residential enclave in Chicago have many Korean businesses, but even more businesses are located outside of the ethnic neighborhood. In New York, Koreans live in various suburban areas but operate most of their businesses in the city.

Particularly significant to new forms of interracial conflict is the presence of Korean-owned businesses in black neighborhoods. By the early 1970s, Koreans had begun to operate businesses in black inner-city ghettos. In part this development can be seen as an example of ethnic succession, for until that point various European-origin groups, especially Jews, had been a prominent presence in ghettos. Jews and other white merchants, however, did not aspire to hand their businesses over to their children, who often went to college in preparation for entering the professional middle class. The urban upheavals of the late 1960s destroyed many of these businesses and prompted many merchants to leave the ghetto for good. Black entrepreneurs did not fill the economic void left by this mass departure, so there were opportunities for the newly arriving Korean immigrants. And they took advantage of the opportunities. There is evidence that Koreans have displaced black stores as well as white stores (Neufeld, 1990).

In Spike Lee's 1989 film *Do the Right Thing*, a trio of older black men bemoan the fact that the corner market is owned by Koreans and not by African Americans. As the racial tensions escalate, the Koreans become targets of black animosity. At the climax of the movie, the Italian-owned Sal's pizzeria is set ablaze, and as the crowd begins to move on the Korean market, the owner protests, proclaiming that he, too, is black. The message implies that America is ultimately divided between whites on the one hand and all people of color on the other. Whether the crowd agreed is never made clear. The store is spared from attack, however.

Considerable tension exists between blacks and Koreans (Hurh, 1998; Min, 1996). In a study of ethnic conflict in Chicago, Steven Neufeld (1990) found that black complaints about Korean (and other "outsider," such as Arab) merchants were widespread. At the most general level, the Koreans were considered to be exploiters. More specifically, people complained about the quality of merchandise, the high prices, refund and exchange policies, and disrespectful treatment of customers. Koreans were faulted for not hiring enough blacks and for not investing in the black community by failing to use black suppliers, banks, and so forth. Black community organizers had, at various times, attempted to press for changes by calling for boycotts of Korean-owned businesses. These efforts have proved to be futile. In Los Angeles, Korean-black tensions erupted in the case of Soon Ja Du, a female Korean storeowner. She was found guilty of the second-degree murder of Latasha Harlins, a 16-year-old girl who she believed was shoplifting (Min, 1996).

In contrast to the fictional riot of Lee's film, the 1992 Los Angeles riot that occurred in the wake of the Rodney King beating trial resulted in large-scale destruction of Korean businesses. More than 1,000 Korean businesses were destroyed, with an estimated price tag of $300 million (Burton, 1992). Koreans were viewed sympathetically as innocent victims by the public at large. In the aftermath of the riot, many of those who remained readily expressed bitter resentment at those who took part in the riot. Gun merchants reported a brisk trade in automatic weapons by those intent on being prepared for any future racial confrontations (Abelmann and Lie, 1995). At the same time, there is an ordinariness to many interactions between Korean shop owners and black customers (J. Lee, 2002). Perhaps like Jews a quarter century ago, they, too, will exit. Whether Koreans will continue doing business in black neighborhoods remains to be seen.

Korean Ethnic Churches

Koreans have created ethnic communities replete with charitable and mutual aid societies; senior citizen, handicapped, and youth centers; business and professional associations; musical societies; sports associations, which include judo and tae kwon do clubs; and other distinctly ethnic organizations (Lee, 1992).

One institution in particular is central to the Korean American community: the ethnic church (Min and Kim, 2002). Although Christianity is a minority religion in Korea—approximately 16 percent of Koreans are affiliated with Protestant churches and 5 percent with Roman Catholic churches—about 70 percent of Korean Americans report their religion as Christian. In other words, Korean immigrants have come disproportionately from the Korean Christian community. This statistic implies a class connection, because Christianity is more prevalent among the Korean middle class than among other classes. In addition, many Christian Koreans fled from North Korea during and before the Korean War and thus do not have especially strong ties to the South. This has probably made them more willing to emigrate than those from the South (Warner, 1992; Min, 1991; Hurh and Kim, 1990; Shin and Park, 1988; Kim, 1977).

Koreans have not generally joined existing Protestant or Catholic parishes. Instead, they have created over 2,000 ethnic congregations. Many of the congregations are quite small. For example, in New York City, the median number of members is 82 (Min, 1991). Some congregations meet in the parish halls of established American churches, at least during the congregation's formative period.

By remaining distinctive, religious affiliation served practical functions in helping Korean immigrants adjust to their new homeland. Min (1991) contended that one of the most important functions is to provide fellowship with other Koreans. Many churches provide the benefits of a primary group, and people derive their most intimate friendships from among the congregation's members. Larger parishes often create district meetings (*Kuyok Yebae*) in which church members in the same residential areas meet in members' homes for religious services and dinner parties.

By facilitating and encouraging such social relationships, churches reinforce the bonds of ethnic attachment. Korean churches also reinforce Korean culture. Church services, even children's services, are usually conducted in Korean, not English. The church is the key institution in programs designed to promote the retention of the Korean language among young people. In addition, the church is the place where many traditional cultural practices are enacted and where the preservation of traditional values is observed.

Adhesive Adaptation

One important value that Korean churches attempt to instill in young people is filial piety. This value is rooted in Confucianism, but it is reinforced by Korean Christianity. Filial piety grants parents a high degree of authority over their children, who are expected to defer to, respect, and show devotion to their parents. As Korean children encounter and interact with American youth, especially in school, many of them increasingly question the tradition of filial piety. Min and Min (1992) identified two major sources of intergenerational strain and conflict. The first is differences regarding traditional values. Children frequently complain that their parents are too traditional and are too strict, not permitting them the kind of freedom most American school-children take for granted. Korean parents often believe that their children do not work enough and do not expend sufficient effort to learn the Korean language and culture. The second source of tension is produced by the parental demand that children perform well in school. Some students think their parents' expectations are unrealistic and they resent the pressure to succeed.

However real the conflict between parents and school-aged youth is, it should not be overestimated. One reason is that Korean parents have also been Americanized, so they are not as traditional as their children might sometimes claim. They are engaged in what Hurh and Kim (1984) called a process of **adhesive adaptation,** meaning that Koreans are engaged in grafting onto the traditional culture certain aspects of American culture and social relations. In other words, rather than abandoning the ethnic past, they connect it to the present.

This concept is seen in the high labor force participation rate of Korean women, despite their traditional role in the household. Many Koreans explain this shift as the result of economic necessity: as with most struggling members of the middle class, two incomes are needed to support their lifestyle. Although adaptation has occurred, the essentially patriarchal structure of the family remains intact. Hurh and Kim (1984) noted that despite working outside of the home, women are still expected to perform most household work. Family decisions are still primarily made by men rather than shared (Um, 1992).

In another example of adhesive adaptation, changes in definitions of filial piety were detected in a study of elderly Koreans and their adult children (Kim and Hurh, 1992). The researchers noted that although both groups are committed to the ideal of filial piety, they have modified their understanding of what such piety means. Adult children tend to live separately from their aging parents, rather than taking them into their homes as would have been expected in the past. Many of the elderly continue to reside in the urban enclaves of initial settlement, while the children, having better economic situations than their parents, have moved to the suburbs. The adult children still visit and in other ways express their concern for their parents, but their expressions of piety have been modified.

Scenarios for the Future

Most Koreans are first- or second-generation ethnics, so they have not been in the United States for a long time. This means that the ethnic community, including churches and the family, continues to play a vital role in the adjustment process. Certain trends suggest that the future of Koreans might most resemble that of the Japanese. That is to say, Koreans may be assimilating to a greater degree than other Asian groups, such as the Chinese and the Vietnamese (Min, 1999).

First, by placing a premium on education, Koreans do not seem intent on handing ethnic enterprises on to their offspring. Rather, Koreans appear to want their children to become white-collar professionals. Although many college-educated Koreans have not obtained such jobs themselves, or have found themselves marginalized in various professions, they probably attribute this lack of success to language and cultural difficulties that the American-born will not confront (Shin and Chang, 1988a). White-collar jobs would promote entry into the mainstream and erode the institutional structure of the ethnic community.

Second, although most Korean marriages are endogamous, the rate of intermarriage for Koreans is higher than for some other Asian groups, and it is increasing. In a study of intermarriage patterns in the San Francisco-Oakland metropolitan area, Kumiko Shibuya (1992) found that for six Asian groups, the Japanese out-marriage rate was the highest at 47 percent, while the Chinese was the lowest at 17.2 percent. Slightly above the Chinese rate were the Vietnamese and Asian Indian. The Korean rate was 30.2 percent, close to the 33.6 percent reported for Filipinos. This suggests that Koreans are increasingly willing to look beyond the confines of the ethnic community for marital partners. Two points should be noted about this trend. First, most out-marriages take place between Koreans and members of other Asian groups. Second, women are four times more likely than men to marry a nonKorean. Korean women may be searching for more egalitarian marriages than they think are likely if they marry a Korean.

Filipino Americans

The Filipino immigration wave that began after 1965 resulted in a substantial increase in population during the three decades beginning in 1960, when the figure was 181,614. In 2000 there were 1,815,314 Filipinos in the United States (U.S. Bureau of the Census, 2000). These new arrivals differed considerably from those who came during the earliest immigration period, in both educational achievement and occupational backgrounds. To appreciate how different they were, a brief overview of pre-World War II immigration is necessary.

The earliest mass immigration began around 1910 and lasted for more than two decades, although the relatively small numbers meant that Filipinos did not have the impact that Chinese and Japanese immigrants did. Like their Chinese counterparts, this immigrant group was overwhelmingly composed of single males with few occupational skills and little education. Most were peasants, with no experience in an industrial setting. They were heavily concentrated in Hawaii and California, where many had been recruited by agricultural concerns such as the Hawaiian Sugar Planters Association (Bulosan, 1973 [1946]; Melendy, 1977; Kitano and Daniels, 1988). They worked under the padrone system and suffered from the economic exploitation inherent in that system. Although there were several instances when Filipino workers attempted to organize unions to improve their economic conditions, they nonetheless were frequently criticized by white workers for undercutting wage levels (Jiobu, 1988).

Voices **Carlos Bulosan**

When the fishing season in San Pedro was over, I left for a small agricultural town called Nipomo. I worked with pea pickers. I found a new release. The land has always been important to me. I felt my old peasant heritage returning with fresh nourishment. I knew that my future was linked with these tillers of the soil, from whose common source I had sprung.

I started a little workers' school and invited the pea pickers. They were shy at first, but as the days went by, they became more natural and bold. They were interested in American history. I traced the growth of democracy in the United States, illustrating the achievements of each epoch with the contributions of its dominant personality.

Then the old men who spoke little English began to participate in discussions. When I pointed out that the advance of democracy was related to the working man's struggle for better wages and living conditions, I felt a warm feeling of humanity grow inside me.

Writer and Filipino labor activist Carlos Bulosan describes his earliest organizing efforts with agricultural workers (Bulosan, 1973 [1946]: 311–312).

Economically based ethnic animosity was exacerbated because Filipino men, unlike other Asians, sought out the company of white women. One way this occurred was by an institution known as the taxi-dance hall, a place where Filipino men would pay to dance with white women. These halls, which were immensely popular with this bachelor society, were often fronts for prostitution. Interracial sexual relations—both commercial and intimate ones—intensified anti-Filipino sentiment.

Thus, when Filipino men began to marry white women in California, an effort was made to prevent such unions by invoking the state's antimiscegenation statute. When the state's Supreme Court determined that the law did not apply to Filipinos, who were defined as members of the Malay race, the state quickly amended the law to prohibit Malay unions with Caucasians. Similar laws were passed in Oregon, Nevada, and Washington. In stark contrast with other Asian groups, interracial intermarriages before 1950 were not uncommon among Filipinos (Kitano and Daniels, 1988). Although relatively little is known about these marriages, Barbara Posadas's (1981) study of Filipinos in Chicago found that most involved Filipino men and second-generation women from various Eastern European ethnic groups.

Hostility toward interracial marriages was widespread. For some it conjured the fear of racial degeneracy, as reflected in the words of a prominent anti-Asian nativist: "The Filipino tends to interbreed with near-moron white girls" (quoted in Melendy, 1977: 61). Filipinos were characterized as being unassimilable. They were depicted as being "primitive"—unintelligent, disease-carrying, lazy, and morally suspect. Moreover, they were, like other Asian groups, the periodic victims of racist violence, including serious attacks during the 1920s and 1930s in the California communities of Exeter, Watsonville, and Modesto (Jiobu, 1988; Pido, 1986).

The skewed sex ratio in the Filipino community and the termination of immigration caused the size of the community to decline over time. As Roger Daniels (1990: 358) wrote, "Between 1934 and the end of World War II, the Filipino population in the United States aged and dwindled, [while] the war years changed the image of the Filipinos to that of loyal allies against the Japanese." This image change was important in reducing levels of prejudice and discrimination. In this, the Filipino experience parallels that of the Chinese.

Immigration Since 1945

As with the Chinese and Koreans, the 1965 Immigration Act proved to be a watershed event in the Filipino community. A more limited wave of immigration took place between 1945 and 1965, during which the Filipino population in the United States almost doubled. The Philippines became independent in 1946, and during that year the immigrants became eligible for naturalization. The annual quota was raised to 100, and after 1954 to 1,300. More Filipinos were nonquota immigrants than quota. Many arrived with tourist or student visas and subsequently changed their immigrant status to remain in the country permanently. Many newcomers were women, which reduced the sex imbalance considerably. This situation resulted in the development of a sizable second generation (Melendy, 1980).

One unique group of immigrants constituted part of this immigration wave: the thousands of Filipinos, some in an organization known as the Philippine Scouts, who had served in the U.S. Navy. They were granted citizenship rights even before entering the United States, so many immigrated with their families (Daniels, 1990).

The post-1965 immigrants were quite different from their predecessors, and thus much about the Filipino American ethnic group changed dramatically during the last part of the twentieth century. Perhaps as many as two thirds of more recent immigrants were educated, white-collar professionals. In contrast, the earlier arriving immigrants and their offspring were and are characterized by relatively low levels of educational achievement and by their concentration in unskilled jobs in industry and agriculture. The newcomers were also better educated and trained than those who remained in the Philippines (Pido, 1986; Melendy, 1980).

Like the earlier immigrants, the post-1965 immigrants were primarily motivated by economic considerations. They believed that they could earn more in a professional occupation if they emigrated, rather than remaining in their birthplace. In an interview with Alfredo Muñoz (1971), one immigrant explained that a person could earn in a day in America what would be a month's salary in the Philippines. Thus, these immigrants are part of the "brain drain" from Third World countries (Rumbaut, 1991; Jasso and Rosenzweig, 1990).

Although a wide range of professions are represented among this group, including engineers, accountants, lawyers, and teachers, most immigrants are members of the health professions, including doctors, pharmacists, and nurses. About half of these immigrants are women, and nursing is by far the most common profession for them (Espiritu, 2002). During the 1970s, about 20 percent of nurses graduating from Philippine nursing schools emigrated to find work in the United States (Daniels, 1990). Some immigrants report instances of discrimination in hiring, difficulties with adapting to the new culture, and language problems.

Many professionals experienced a period of downward mobility, being forced to work in unskilled or semiskilled jobs while obtaining the credentials needed to resume their professions. This was least problematic for nurses because of acute nursing shortages in many public hospitals, different levels of licensing, and the fact that the nursing curriculum used in the Philippines was similar to that used in the United States. Thus, perhaps as many as 33 percent of all licenses issued to foreign nurses went to Filipinas (Melendy, 1980).

As with other Asian groups, Filipinos are highly concentrated in western states. The 1990 census revealed that 68.4 percent resided in this part of the country, most of them in two states: California and Hawaii (U.S. Bureau of the Census, 1992b). In this regard they are most like the Japanese. Although many earlier immigrants lived in rural areas or smaller cities in agricultural areas, the newer immigrants are highly concentrated in larger cities, especially Los Angeles, Honolulu, Chicago, and New York.

The Ethnic Community

Of the four major Asian groups, the Filipinos have created the least institutionally complete ethnic community. There are few "Little Manilas" in large cities. Although Filipinos in cities such as San Francisco and Los Angeles tend to cluster in neighborhoods with kin and friends, these neighborhoods have not developed into ethnic enclaves and have essentially disappeared. Rather than establishing mutual aid societies, fraternals, social halls, and the like, Filipinos tend to rely on more informal networks for assistance during difficult times (Yu, 1980). This reliance on informal relationships involving friends and relatives is reminiscent of the Mexican American community in an earlier stage of its development.

Unlike Koreans, Filipinos have not founded very many churches. Nominally Roman Catholic, Filipinos have been noted for their relative lack of involvement in American Catholicism. Those who are active join local parishes that are multiethnic rather than chiefly Filipino (Pido, 1986; Cordova, 1983). Thus, for Catholic Filipinos there is a rather minimal fusion of religious and ethnic identities that reinforces group distinctiveness and cohesiveness. Protestant churches do exist, but not as prevalently as among Koreans (Tizon, 1999). This group differs from Koreans (and other Asian groups) in yet another way: Very few Filipinos own small businesses (Min, 1987). The pre-1965 immigrants did not engage in entrepreneurship to a significant extent because of a lack of capital. The post-1965 immigrants have worked to get re-credentialed as quickly as possible to obtain professional employment, rather than opting for business ownership.

One reason for the lack of cohesion among Filipino Americans is that regional and linguistic loyalties transplanted from the Philippines have divided rather than united Filipinos in America. In the Philippines there are eight major languages, with about 200 different dialects. Immigrants who speak, as their first language, three of these languages are well represented: Tagalog (the most widely spoken and common language), Ilocano, and Visayan (Mangiafico, 1988; Pido, 1986). According to H. Brett Melendy (1980), most immigrants can speak both English and Tagalog. Thus, there is a linguistic basis for ethnic group unity. At present, however, regional differences remain sufficiently powerful to make such unity difficult.

Compounding these differences are political differences. During the regime of Ferdinand Marcos, expatriates in America remained acutely interested in **homeland politics.** Marcos had both supporters and detractors in America, and the level of animosity between the two sides made cooperative political undertakings infrequent. Partly for this reason, Filipinos have not been particularly successful in organizing politically in this country to advance their collective interests. Even after Marcos was driven from power in 1986 (as the evidence accumulated about the regime's high level of corruption) and the reformist Corazon Aquino became head of state, political differences persisted (Kitano and Daniels, 1988).

The ongoing instability of the Philippine political system is reflected in divisions within Filipino America: Some continue to support Aquino, while others are more sympathetic to some of her powerful political challengers. Although communist guerrillas have operated in the Philippines for decades and have had considerable success in controlling some areas of the country, few Filipino Americans are sympathetic to leftist revolutionary politics.

The second generation is now coming of age. These young adults have had little or no exposure to their homeland and are far more Americanized than their parents. It is not clear what the homeland means to them. Both at school and in the labor force, their worlds are shaped by their encounters with the larger society. The immigrant generation has made relatively minimal efforts to use language schools and cultural centers to preserve a distinctively Filipino American identity among the American-born (Espiritu, 2001).

This situation suggests that over time, Filipino Americans might be far less likely to maintain their ethnic identities than many other recent immigrant groups. Although racial distinctiveness may prove to impede inclusion into the larger society, it appears that Filipinos differ somewhat from other Asians in this regard. Both physical features and names make the Filipinos in some ways similar to Hispanic rather than Asian groups. The implications of their somewhat ambiguous identities are unclear, so it is too early to predict whether assimilation or exclusion is a more likely future outcome. As long as immigration continues, the situation will remain fluid (Tuan, 1999).

Other Asians

In addition to the four groups discussed above, the Asian population has grown in recent decades as a result of immigrants from the Indian subcontinent and Southeast Asia. We turn briefly to an examination of these two panethnic communities.

Indians have migrated throughout the world for over 2,000 years. Their presence in North America began as early as 1750, but they did not emigrate in significant numbers until the early twentieth century. These immigrants consisted of two groups: the first was composed of farmers and laborers, while the second contained middle-class students, elites, and political refugees. Although in the popular mind Indians were equated with Hinduism, in fact about two-thirds of those who immigrated to the United States in the early 1900s were of the Sikh faith, while the remainder were divided between Muslims and Hindus. They were predominantly male laborers who worked along the West Coast as far north as British Columbia. Substantial communities formed in areas of California's Sacramento and Imperial valleys, where because of a shortage of Indian women, the intermarriage rate with Mexican women was pronounced (Leonard, 1991).

Vietnamese Catholics celebrate the Feast of the Immaculate Conception.

Today the Indian population is the third largest Asian ethnic group in the United States. The population of close to 1.9 million exceeds that of the Japanese and Korean populations, which until recently were much larger. By far the greatest growth of the Asian Indian population has occurred since 1980 because of the increased demand for technical and professional workers (especially engineers and doctors) who may receive temporary worker H1-B visas. South Asian "guest" workers are in high demand in technology-related industries such as computing and engineering. Their increasing numbers in the past decade has been due to the growth of technology-related jobs and the perceived shortage of qualified American workers. Some South Asian Indian workers have tried to convert their status to permanent residents in the United States, but for many the recent downturn in high-tech industries has meant that their legal status is problematic.

The U.S. involvement in the Vietnam War led to the exodus of people from Vietnam, Cambodia, and Laos. Since the fall of Saigon in 1975, over 130,000 Vietnamese have sought refugee status in the United States. This first group is often referred to as "first wave" refugees. They consisted of South Vietnamese military officials, individuals who worked for the U.S. military or American companies based in South Vietnam, and anyone else who had the resources to leave before the fall. There was a massive effort to resettle and relocate this population of refugees elsewhere throughout the world, although a large number came to the United States.

Initially, the South Vietnamese were brought to refugee camps located in California, Florida, Pennsylvania, and Arkansas. The U.S. government and social service agencies, or "VOLAGs," worked to resettle the refugees in communities throughout the United States. The general policy was to disperse refugees into different communities rather than in one area, so that no one community or agency would be overly burdened. It was also thought that dispersal would help the assimilation process by forcing refugees to interact with nonrefugee populations. Refugee and resettlement officials and agencies were unaware of the social and cultural importance of extended family and community networks and did not anticipate the secondary migration that began to take place during the late 1970s and early 1980s.

By this time, the "second wave" refugees began arriving. Commonly referred to as the "boat people," this group left Vietnam, usually by a harrowing boat journey across the South China seas. They would have to fend off sea pirates, dehydration, and starvation, until being rescued or arriving in port. Unlike the earlier refugees, many of this group had spent years in Communist reeducation camps. Some left Vietnam for fear of persecution because they were ethnic Chinese. They came with few financial resources, and the U.S. government provided less refugee assistance. They did, however, encounter established communities of Vietnamese in places like San Jose and Westminster in California and Houston, Texas. Thus, "new" refugees moved into social networks established by the 1975 refugees, where many found work in the ethnic enclave.

Arriving at the same time were Cambodian (Khmer) refugees who were able to escape their country's "killing fields" and Hmong and Mien tribal groups from Laos. Many who came to the United States were unprepared for a lifestyle and culture different from the ones in their Southeast Asian homelands. These were rural and traditionalist peoples who had a difficult time adjusting to an urban industrial society.

Nazli Kibria's (1993) study of intergenerational and gender relations in Vietnamese families settled in Philadelphia during the 1980s points out how families adjusted to their new environments. She found that Vietnamese families did not retain the same family and kinship structures that would have been found earlier in Vietnam, in part because the war had disrupted family life and kinship relations. In the United States, despite changes in Vietnamese men's social status in America, they attempted to reassert traditional forms of patriarchal authority. At the same time, families were caught between maintaining traditional family power relations and adapting to the more egalitarian family structure of contemporary American society.

Beginning in the late 1980s, Vietnam began to relax its policies toward emigration. Thus, the Vietnamese immigrant population in the United States continues to grow, especially in areas with established communities such as Orange County and San Jose in California and parts of Texas and Florida. New migrants continue to reinforce ethnic ties among Vietnamese Americans, although with each successive generation, it will be a challenge to see how they become incorporated into the American social fabric.

Education and Occupation

The recent Asian immigrants can be divided into two groups of people: those who are highly educated, skilled, and upwardly mobile, and those who are low-skilled, with limited English-speaking ability, and employed in marginal or transitory businesses. This bimodal distribution of the Asian population makes it difficult to generalize about the success of Asians in American society. If we were to look at income, Asian Americans as a group have made noticeable gains in recent years. U.S. Census figures show a median family income of $41,251 for all Asian and Pacific Islander Americans, compared with $37,152 for whites, $22,429 for blacks, and $25,064 for Latinos. When we focus on different Asian ethnic groups, the Vietnamese rank the lowest at $30,550. However, this is still higher than incomes for African Americans and Hispanics. What explains this difference? One possible explanation is that Asian Americans are more concentrated in areas with a higher cost of living: California, New York, and Hawaii. Moreover, they are likely to reside in high-cost metropolitan areas in those states, which means that their median incomes may be higher, but so is the cost of living. Although the African American population is highly urbanized, it is also geographically dispersed, and a greater percentage live in rural areas as compared with Asians. This might account for lower median family incomes in the African American population.

In terms of jobs, a larger proportion of Asian Americans occupy both the lowest and highest tiers of the occupational hierarchy. To put it simply, more Asian Americans are in lower-status occupations than their European American counterparts, while simultaneously more Asians are in higher-status occupations than European Americans. This bimodal distribution tends to mask the inequalities experienced by sectors of the Asian American community. The bipolar distribution in occupation is also apparent in education. Asian American students tend to do better on standardized tests compared with all other students. But, they also receive some of the lowest scores on standardized tests. Thus, again, it is difficult to assess how successful Asian American students have been in education because of these divergent results. One thing is clear: Those at the top are applying in increasing numbers to the most highly selective colleges and universities in the country. As Dana Y. Takagi's study *The Retreat From Race: Asian-American Admissions and Racial Politics* (1993) indicates, this situation has led to competition with whites for valued slots and a debate over whether Asians should be excluded from race-based affirmative action plans.

Prejudice and Discrimination

Asian Americans continue to encounter prejudice and discrimination. Perhaps the best way to describe the persistent treatment of Asians in America, regardless of ethnicity, is as foreigners or strangers (Takaki, 1989; Tuan, 1999). American-born Asians are frequently asked, "Where are you from?" or commended for speaking such good English, regardless of how many generations their families have lived in the United States. A more malicious form of defining the Asian as an Other revolves around the long-lasting stereotype of the "yellow peril," implying that hoards of Chinese and Japanese would invade and overrun the United States.

A recent version of the yellow peril could be seen in the early 1980s, when Japan's economy was booming while the U.S. economy was struggling to compete with it. On the one hand, Japanese business success led to widespread interest in Japanese approaches to management and organization. On the other hand, because American manufacturers experienced stiff competition from Japanese firms, nativist attitudes surfaced in the form of the belief that the Japanese economy was responsible for America's economic troubles. Moreover, as the Japanese began to invest in businesses and real estate in the United States, a new version of yellow peril hysteria grew, which suggested that the Japanese "invasion" posed a threat not only to American jobs but to America's culture and social fabric as well.

In the midst of this tension, Asian Americans became targets. Perhaps the best-known incident of anti-Asian violence was the case of Vincent Chin. In 1982, Chin was beaten to death in an altercation with two unemployed white male autoworkers. These men were later tried and sentenced to a $3,700 fine and probation. The Asian American community was outraged by the leniency of the sentence and sought to try the men for violating Chin's civil rights. In a second trial, this time in federal court, the two were convicted and sentenced to serve prison sentences. A perverse irony in this case is that Chin was Chinese, not Japanese. This example illustrates that Asians tend to be lumped together into a single category in the minds of the prejudiced.

Since Chin's murder, several other incidents of racial violence have been directed at Asian Americans. In another case of mistaken identity, in 1989 Jim Loo was killed by two brothers who accused him of being Vietnamese (he, too, was Chinese), reviving the conflicts in American society brought about by the Vietnam War. In 1992, 19-year-old Lyuen Phan Nguyen, a Vietnamese premed student, was murdered in Coral Springs, Florida. Nguyen's attackers chased him around, calling him "chink" and "Vietcong" and shouting "Sayonara." He was severely beaten and never regained consciousness. In 1993, Sam Nhem, a Cambodian refugee, was beaten to death outside a housing project in Fall River, Massachusetts.

As these examples indicate, attitudes toward Asian Americans often reflect the ongoing dynamics of international relations. Leaders of various Asian American organizations monitoring the level of prejudice and discrimination have voiced concerns about the potential for a widespread revival of negative stereotypes. One particular case gave them pause for concern. In the spring of 1999, Dr. Wen Ho Lee, a Taiwanese-born, naturalized American citizen, was terminated from his job as a physicist at the Los Alamos National Laboratory in New Mexico. By December, the government had charged Dr. Lee with violating the Atomic Energy Act through mishandling important restricted data, a felony. He was placed in solitary confinement for nine months as he awaited trial. Although Lee had admitted to failing to report meetings with scientists from other countries, he denied passing classified information to others. Lee's handling of certain government documents on his computer was also questioned. Many in the Asian American community felt he was targeted because of his racial background, referring to Lee's handling of computer material as DWA or "Downloading While Asian."

Dr. Lee's case drew national attention and galvanized the Chinese American community. Many who shared Lee's similar social class and ethnic background were appalled at how he was treated and mistrusted, feeling that he had been targeted by federal officials because he was Asian. Lee has always denied being a spy, but after prolonged negotiations between his lawyers and the U.S. government he pled guilty to one of the 59 original charges brought against him. Late in 2000, Dr. Lee gained his freedom and received an apology for the way he was treated by the judge who ordered his initial detention.

Summary

Sociologist Yen Le Espiritu (1992) suggests that Asian Americans may be in the process of forging a core identity that is based not on national ethnic origins but their experiences in America as Asian—or in other words, a **panethnic identity.** A pan-Asian ethnic identity can be seen as the product of external factors that promote and facilitate group alliances and cohesion. When Asian Americans joined together to protest Vincent Chin's murder and the racial profiling of Wen Ho Lee, or to support the nomination of Bill Lann Lee for U.S. Attorney General, they established a sense of pan-Asian unity that is distinct from one that focuses on their own national or ethnic origins.

Evidence of a panethnic identity does not mean that particular ethnic identities have become less relevant. Differences within the Asian community remain significant. This chapter has revealed the diversity in the Asian American experience. It has done so by examining in depth four of the largest Asian groups in the United States—Japanese, Chinese, Korean, and Filipino—as well as briefly discussing immigrants from South and Southeast Asia. Although these groups do have many things in common, especially because the images and stereotypes used by many white Americans tend to lump all Asians together, this chapter reveals the significant differences that have created rather different experiences in America.

For example, Japanese Americans, unlike the other three groups, have not had large numbers of new immigrants arriving during the past quarter century, so there is comparatively less contact with and familiarity about the homeland. The life world of Japanese Americans is shaped by one world—America—rather than two. Moreover, comparatively speaking, the Japanese American community is an older one. Its educational attainment level and occupational status, combined with the high rate of intermarriage to whites, raises the possibility that assimilation might result in the end of the Japanese American ethnic community.

Street scene of San Jose's Chinatown.

The other three groups have grown because of recent immigration. Mass immigration in recent years has revitalized the Chinese American community, considerably expanded the number of Filipinos without strengthening the institutional fabric of the ethnic community, and created a variety of new institutions by Korean Americans. Unlike the Chinese, among the Korean and Filipino immigrants are large numbers of middle-class professionals, part of the Third World "brain drain." The different class compositions of the respective groups account to a considerable degree for the different levels of economic success discussed in this chapter. It is too soon to tell what the ultimate futures of these groups will be, but it is conceivable that if immigration declines, some of these groups may have a future similar to that of Japanese Americans.

Key Terms

adhesive adaptation	*model minority*
homeland politics	*panethnic identity*
hypergamy	Sansei
Kye	Yonsei

Questions for Discussion and Critical Thinking

1. In what ways is it appropriate to speak about Asians as a model minority? In what ways is it incorrect to use the blanket term? What is the ideological function of the model minority thesis?

2. Provide an overview of the similarities and differences between the historical experiences of the two oldest Asian groups in America: the Chinese and the Japanese. What accounts for the differences?

3. Yen Le Espiritu thinks that a pan-Asian identity is emerging that transcends the particular identities of the various Asian groups. Do you agree or disagree with this argument? Why? ✦

Chapter 10

Multicultural Prospects in Comparative Perspective

Ethnic relations in the United States have in profound and far-reaching ways been redefined during the past half century. The civil rights movement brought to an end the enforced segregation and racial subordination of the Jim Crow era. Comparable movements among American Indians, Latinos, and Asians have also resulted in the expansion of civil, political, and social rights for those groups. At the same time, the nation has increasingly become enmeshed in a global economy, which has resulted in a restructuring of the domestic economy. Manufacturing jobs have been exported overseas, resulting in a bifurcated economy that is composed of well-paying jobs at the top for those with adequate human and social capital and low-paying jobs at the bottom for those lacking in such resources. The new global economic order has triggered a wave of global immigration (Sassen, 1996).

During this period the United States has experienced the third great wave of immigration in the nation's history. Over 25 million newcomers have taken up residency in the country since 1965. The last decade of the twentieth century saw 9.1 million immigrants arrive, the largest number in the nation's history (surpassing the number in the previous record decade at the beginning of the twentieth century). We need to put this into perspective. When 8.8 million immigrants arrived in the country between 1901 and 1910, they entered a country with a population considerably smaller than today's 281 million, and thus they constituted a much larger percentage of the overall population. Nonetheless, the impact of contemporary migration is real and significant, especially since the migrants are so highly concentrated in a select number of states (California, New York, Texas, Florida, and Illinois have the highest levels).

While there are lessons to learn from the earlier waves of immigration and parallels that can be drawn between the past and present in terms of modes of immigrant adaptation and incorporation, commentators have also identified some salient differences that make the present unique. First, on the positive side, American society is more receptive to newcomers than it was a century ago (Perlmann and Waldinger, 1999). This is not to suggest that anti-immigration attitudes and overt discrimination aren't significant today; they definitely are (Jaret, 1999). However, as in the past, the nation's doors will remain open in part because employers want them open, and immigrants have more legal protections than they once did. Another important difference is that more newcomers today are middle-class professionals than was the case in the past. Today's economy has been described as an hourglass, where there are good jobs at the top and unskilled, low-paying jobs at the bottom. As the preceding chapters illustrate, immigrants can be found in all sectors of the economy. Thus, the new immigrants are more bimodal than their earlier counterparts, with some doing quite well economically and others struggling at the margins to gain a foothold in the American economy. For this reason it is particularly difficult to generalize about whether today's immigrants are making it in America (Zhou, 2001; Foner, 2000).

The presence of the new immigrants raises questions about the salience of race in the twenty-first century in general, and about the location of blacks in what some have described as a potentially new racial hierarchy (Alba and Nee, 2003; Gans, 1999). As we noted in earlier chapters, the historic racial division has been between whites and nonwhites, with the white/black divide serving to define the location of other groups on the nonwhite side of the divide. One possible scenario for the new century is that the color line is in the process of being redrawn. Herbert Gans (1999) suggests that it might be increasingly defined in terms of black and nonblack, which means that those defined as nonblack would be on the side of the racial divide inhabited by whites. Asians, in effect, would be perceived for all intents and purposes as white—as Mia Tuan (1999) characterizes it, "honorary whites." A similar definition would apply to Latinos. If so, this prospect is pessimistic insofar as it further serves to isolate blacks from other groups. One of the questions that this possibility raises is where dark-skinned immigrants from places such as the Caribbean would be located in this hierarchy. Would they be located on the side of the divide with American blacks? Mary Waters's (1999) research on West Indian immigrants has revealed that this is a concern voiced within these communities. Parents often encourage their children to maintain their Caribbean accents in order to effect a presentation of self that says, "We are different from American blacks."

Richard Alba and Victor Nee (2003) point out that while there are definitely reasons to think that this is where we are headed, there are also forces at play that could lead to a more positive outcome. They point to the growth of the black middle class, the small but nonetheless real rise in intermarriage between blacks and nonblacks, and the growing recognition of mixed-race persons in America, arguing that these factors can contribute to a more optimistic outcome by in various ways muting or downplaying the salience of race. We concur with them when they conclude that at the moment we can't know what the future will bring, but it will be the result of the admixture of both of these trends.

Complicating things even further is the fact that the rise of multicultural attitudes and policies and transnational practices might suggest that ethnic groups will persist long into the future. Unlike the European Americans who arrived a century ago and have now entered the twilight of ethnicity, for some of the new immigrants, as Alejandro Portes and Rubén Rumbaut (2001) contend, multiculturalism and transnationalism may contribute to "the high noon of ethnicity." If this is so, how it might affect blacks is yet another unanswerable question at the moment.

In the preceding nine chapters we provided a historically grounded and comparative analysis of the major ethnic groups in the United States. In this concluding chapter we turn to a comparison of the United States as a whole with other nations that are like it insofar as they can be defined economically as advanced capitalist industrial societies and politically as liberal democracies. The former means that in general terms standards of living are high, while the latter means that citizenship can be see as a potential vehicle, for individuals and groups, to fully participate as equals in the political process (Joppke and Morawska, 2003). However, socioeconomic inequalities persist in these nations, including inequalities along ethnic lines. Related to this situation is the fact that not everyone has achieved genuine citizenship status, and thus they are not equals in the political arena (Glenn, 2000). Ethnic relations in all of these nations arc framed by these realities.

The United States in Comparative Perspective

While in many ways the history of the United States is unique, in significant ways it resembles the experience of other nations. We are a **settler nation,** in which most people or their ancestors came from another nation. As we discussed in Chapter 1 and in the subsequent historical chapters, widely held images of the American nation stress that it is distinctive due to its heterogeneous identity. However, these images often belie a lack of familiarity with other nations. As a settler society, we are not alone, and thus it shouldn't be surprising that our experience in many ways closely parallels that of other settler nations, particularly Canada and Australia. In recent times, they too have become important destinations for migrants. In fact, as Figure 10.1 indicates, the foreign-born populations of these two nations as a percentage of the total labor force—24.6 percent in Australia and 19.2 percent in Canada—are larger than that of the United States, with an 11.7 percent figure.

However, settler nations are not the only immigrant-receiving nations. In fact, all of the advanced industrial nations have had large influxes of newcomers in recent decades, including all of Western Europe and Japan (Kivisto, 2002; Pearson, 2001). All are part of the global economy, having been transformed by the expansion of transnational capitalism and by the emergence and increasing significance of regional and international economic entities, such as the European Union and North American Free Trade Agreement (NAFTA), that are designed to regulate capitalist development. Their political systems have been transformed as well, as a result of the increasing importance of international bodies such as the United Nations and the proliferation of International Nongovernmental Organiza-

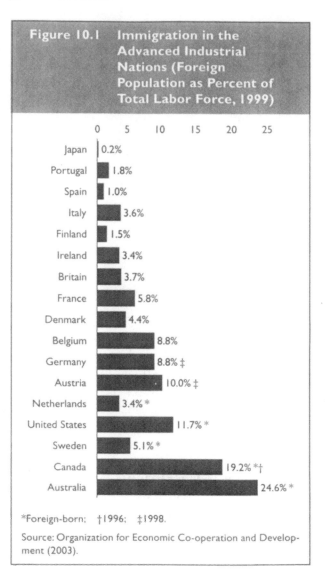

Figure 10.1   Immigration in the Advanced Industrial Nations (Foreign Population as Percent of Total Labor Force, 1999)

Japan	0.2%
Portugal	1.8%
Spain	1.0%
Italy	3.6%
Finland	1.5%
Ireland	3.4%
Britain	3.7%
France	5.8%
Denmark	4.4%
Belgium	8.8%
Germany	8.8% ‡
Austria	10.0% ‡
Netherlands	3.4% *
United States	11.7% *
Sweden	5.1% *
Canada	19.2% *†
Australia	24.6% *

*Foreign-born; †1996; ‡1998.

Source: Organization for Economic Co-operation and Development (2003).

tions (INGOs). Finally, the pace and intensity of cultural interchange is unlike that of any time in the past, with the result being the hybridization of cultures across national boundaries.

To locate the United States in this context, it is instructive to briefly examine the recent transformations of several major nations that have become genuinely multicultural in recent decades, dividing them into the settler nations of Canada and Australia and the largest western European nations, Britain, Germany, and France.

Settler Nations

Australia, Canada, and the United States share common origins as the products of British colonial expansion, and thus all share the imprint of English customs, culture, laws, and language. However, only the United States severed its political ties to Britain, while the other two nations remain part of the British Commonwealth, though for all intents and purposes they are independent nations. Although the three nations are relatively similar in terms of geographic size, Canada at 31 million and Australia at 19 million have far smaller populations that the United States. Both need population growth in order to sustain their modern economies. In the context of these historical and geographic realities, the governments of Canada and Australia have been international pioneers in establishing multicultural policies. These two nations are unique insofar as they have implemented explicit multicultural policies that speak to emerging national self-identities that not only are aware of ethnic diversity but also describe it as positive rather than as something to be overcome.

Canada: The Vertical Mosaic

Canada's population is similarly diverse to that of its larger neighbor to the south, and it, too, has had comparatively open immigration laws throughout its history. Nevertheless, Canadians have never viewed their nation as a melting pot. Rather, the most popular image is that of a vertical mosaic—which is a metaphor for the class character of the nation, within which ethnic differences are layered (Porter, 1965). The idea of a mosaic is located deep in the nation's history. The major reason that assimilationist metaphors did not take root in Canada was due to the fact that the birth of the nation was the product of a struggle between its two charter groups, the English and the French. Although the French lost out to English domination, they did become a significant force within Canadian society, particularly in the province of Quebec, where they are highly concentrated. The French confronted considerable prejudice and discrimination, along with the political and economic domination of British Canadians. The response of the Francophone, or French-speaking, community was to turn inward in an effort to protect its cultural heritage. The result was a deep rupture between the Anglophone and Francophone communities. Add to this the fact that the indigenous peoples of Canada—known today as First Nations people—were forced off of their ancestral lands and, similar to what occurred in the United States, experienced forced relocations, economic marginalization, and political oppression. Thus, the formative period of Canada was defined in terms of three discrete groups, and there was no expectation that they would assimilate.

In the twentieth century, immigration made Canada's ethnic composition more complex. Mass migration occurred later than in the United States, with waves of immigration occurring after World War I, after World War II, and again during the last decades of the century. The Immigration Act of 1910 and its 1919 amended version established the basis for a "white Canada." The clear preference was for settlers from Western Europe, with Eastern Europeans seen as less desirable but acceptable, while Asian immigration was to be severely restricted. During the first wave, arriving immigrants included Germans, Scandinavians, Dutch, Poles, Ukrainians, Italians, and Jews. After World War II, they included many displaced persons (DPs), political refugees who left the war-ravaged nations of Eastern Europe, particularly as communist regimes took over their homelands. However, larger numbers of the new arrivals were more traditional labor immigrants, with particularly large numbers of Italians, Greeks, Poles, and Portuguese arriving at this time. These groups became known collectively as the **third force** vis-à-vis the two charter groups.

The most recent wave of immigration has taken place in a more liberal environment, after Canada abolished its racist immigration policies of the past. The result was that the nation has seen a dramatic influx of immigrants from Asia and the Caribbean. The largest Asian groups are the Chinese, Indian, Pakistani, Filipino, and Vietnamese, while the largest Caribbean groups are from Jamaica, Trinidad and Tobago, and Haiti (Hawkins, 1989). As in the United States, these newcomers are geographically concentrated in certain locales. They are heavily concentrated in particular in three major cities, Toronto, Montreal, and Vancouver, but they can also be found in significant numbers in other large cities such as Edmonton, Calgary, Winnipeg, and Ottawa. Many of the most recent immigrants have entered the lowest tiers of the economy, finding employment in unskilled industrial work and in the service sector. In this regard, the segmented labor market is increasingly defined in racial terms. Others have found work in enclave economies, while yet another segment represents brain-drain immigrants, composed of educated professionals and entrepreneurs. The last segment is comparatively larger in Canada than in the United States because of Canada's immigration laws, which are more highly selective. Asians and blacks live in more residentially segregated neighborhoods than is the case for other ethnic groups, although the levels of segregation are generally lower than in American cities (Fong, 1996).

Although Canadians generally perceive their country to be tolerant and inclusive, there is ample evidence that many of the new racial minorities confront discrimination in various forms. Rita Simon and James Lynch (1999: 459–464) point out that although the Canadian public has a somewhat more favorable attitude about the current level of immigration than its American counterpart, the majority would nonetheless like to see fewer immigrants accepted into the country than current law allows. That being said, it's worth noting, as Seymour Martin Lipset (1990: 186) has, that Canada and the United States "remain more universalistic and socially heterogeneous in their immigration patterns than other white First World countries." Perhaps for this reason, there is reason to think that as these communities of new immigrants begin to acculturate and coalesce into political constituencies, they—both individually and as part of a reconfigured third force—have the potential to become an important factor in defining Canadian multiculturalism.

This last wave of immigrants began arriving at the same time that the Francophone community developed a potent ethnic nationalist—or as Walker Connor (1994) terms it, **ethnonationalist**—separatist movement in Quebec, which took political form with the formation of the Parti Québecois. The gestation period of the movement, known as the "Quiet Revolution," occurred in the 1960s. It was characterized by demands to end economic and social discrimination and to increase provincial (and thus French) power vis-à-vis that of the federal government. The Quiet Revolution was more about advancing the civil rights and the economic conditions of the Francophone community than in promoting a separatist agenda. However, a key aspect of its demands focused on preserving the French cultural heritage. This is what Canadian political philosopher Charles Taylor (1992) has called the "politics of recognition."

The Canadian government responded by addressing a key aspect of that heritage, the French language. Up to 1970, English was the official language of government and business. Prime Minister Pierre Trudeau pushed through the passage of the Official Language Act in 1970, thereby making Canada officially a bilingual nation. Around the same time the federal government also sought in symbolic terms to recast the stature of the two charter groups by replacing the flag that reflected the nation's ties to Britain (a modified Union Jack) with a neutral flag featuring a red maple leaf. By distancing itself from explicit reference to Britain in this symbol of national identity, Canada was making a concerted attempt to find a new common ground between the two charter groups (Evans, 1996).

These efforts at reconciliation did not placate Francophone nationalists, who over the next three decades attempted to up the ante. Militant separatists described Quebec as an internal colony and called for an armed struggle, a campaign that proved to be short-lived. Instead, the Parti Québecois sought to raise the independence issue through legitimate political means, seeking to press the federal government for further concessions that would grant greater provincial autonomy, while also preparing the electorate in the province for a referendum on whether to remain a part of Canada. The first vote took place in 1980, at which time it lost by a substantial 60–40 margin (Evans, 1996). In the aftermath of this defeat, the federal government once again attempted to diffuse separatist sentiment, pressing for what was known as the Meech Lake Accord, which would have kept Quebec in the confederation while according it the status of a "distinct society." This proposal created a backlash from Canada's other provinces, resulting in the accord's defeat. In a national referendum held in 1992, voters defeated another attempt, the Charlottetown Agreement, to treat Quebec as different from the other provinces. Then, a 1995 referendum asked Quebec's voters if they wanted to create a new sovereignty within the context of a partnership with Canada. In an extremely close vote, 50.6 percent of voters rejected the idea—including overwhelming majorities of both the English-speaking community and new immigrants.

In the early years of the twenty-first century, the separatist movement has lost ground compared with its position in the preceding quarter century. One of the ironies of the separatist campaign is that it occurred at a time when the socioeconomic status of French Canadians had improved dramatically, leading some researchers to conclude that, in terms of the two charter groups, the vertical mosaic as conceived earlier no longer exists (Lian and Matthews, 1998).

Coinciding with the rise of the French separatist movement and concurrent with the mobilization of Native Americans in the United States, a Red Power movement also developed in Canada during the 1960s. One of the ways it manifested was by attempting to revisit land claims and other treaty provisions; connected to this was a demand for greater political empowerment. Within Quebec, some First Nations groups have argued that if Quebec left the confederation, they should similarly be permitted to exit Quebec. Some tribes are currently campaigning in the Maritime Provinces for the right to engage in commercial fishing in protected areas, while similar campaigns over hunting rights are being waged elsewhere. Corporations exploring for oil and natural gas fields in lands controlled or claimed by First Nations tribes is another source of conflict. In the case of the Inuit, living in the remote northern regions of the country, the demand for greater political control over their own lives led to the agreement to create a new territory of 135,000 square miles of the eastern sector of the Northwest Territories. Called Nunavut (the term for "our land" in the Inuit language), the new territory began as a functional political entity in 1999.

As this overview suggests, the ethnic mosaic of Canada is a fractured one and serves to exacerbate the problematic nature of efforts aimed at forging an overarching Canadian national identity that will at once recognize ethnic diversity while transcending ethnic particularism. Canada, along with Australia, has been at the forefront of efforts to implement official governmental multicultural policies. The Canadian government's policies no longer call for assimilation into an Anglophone identity but rather suggest that cultural differences can and should persist over time. To that end, unlike the United States, Canada has been prepared to promote ethnic group rights, rather than only individual rights. In part, this policy is a reflection of the reality of politically mobilized ethnicity in the cases of Québecois nationalism and First Nations' rights advocates. However, the goal of multiculturalism is not to further divide Canada, but to keep it together. Whether it will succeed remains an unanswered question.

Australia: From Settler Country to Multicultural Nation

Since the 1970s, Australia has also been a "laboratory for multiculturalism" (Smolicz, 1997: 171). Over the past quarter century, it has dramatically revised its national policies regarding ethnic minorities and in so doing has become a nation officially committed to the preservation of ethnic diversity. What makes this transition all the more remarkable is that into the 1960s, Australia maintained an explicitly racist "White Australia" assimilationist position regarding immigration and continued its long history of political oppression, economic degradation, and cultural suppression of the nation's Aborigines.

In 1996, Prime Minister John Howard proposed a Parliamentary Statement on Racial Tolerance that was supported by the opposition leader and passed unanimously. The statement affirmed equal rights regardless of race or national origin, maintained a nonracially discriminatory immigration policy, and sought reconciliation with Aboriginals and a redressing of their disadvantaged socioeconomic status. It committed the nation to a policy of openness, tolerance, and a commitment to diversity (Department of Immigration and Multicultural Affairs, 2001). Out of this statement, an explicit policy was instituted in 1999, based on four core principles: civic duty, cultural respect, social equity, and productive diversity. The context within which this framework evolved is a reflection of two distinct but interrelated social realities: the evolution in the treatment of the original settlers toward the Aborigines and the growing inclusiveness that has shaped the development of immigration policies.

Australia's historical treatment of Aborigines was brutal. The earliest British settlers assumed that the native peoples would simply die out. When they didn't (although their population numbers did decline precipitously), an institutional system of reserves and mission settlements was created that served both to control and to marginalize the Aborigines. Rather than being granted citizenship rights, they became dependents or wards of the state, subject to its dictates. For example, Aborigines were required to seek state permission to move, marry, or get a job. They were an underprivileged caste in a class society, deprived of the same political, economic, and social rights as their white counterparts. Another aspect of the exploitation of the Aboriginal community was sexual. Despite laws prohibiting white-Aboriginal marriages, liaisons between white males and Aboriginal females were commonplace in the nineteenth and twentieth centuries. The societal recognition of a growing mixed-race community led the government to establish a draconian policy of seizing such children from their Aboriginal families and either placing them in orphanages or putting them up for adoption by white families—the rationale being that they were "saving" these children from a "doomed race." Begun in 1910, the policy did not officially end until 1970. These children became known within the Aboriginal community as the "lost generation." As the film *Rabbit Proof Fence* poignantly illustrates, this policy represents an especially bitter testimony to the oppression and exploitation of Aborigines.

In the 1960s, Aboriginal rights campaigns took off, inspired in part by the civil rights movement in the United States. In 1966 Aborigines obtained a guarantee that they were entitled to the same wages and work conditions as whites. In 1967, in an overwhelmingly affirmative vote in a national referendum, Aborigines were granted full citizenship. Inspired by these and similar victories, but concerned about the future of their culture, Aboriginal peoples began to demand not only redress for long-standing land claims, an end to discrimination, and remedies to the community's social problems, but also self-determination and the recognition of and respect for cultural differences. In other words, Aborigines were not prepared to equate citizenship with the loss of cultural identity and with the abandonment of ethnic attachments. In rejecting this equation, they became an important social force in advancing the shift from assimilation to multiculturalism as official government policy.

During the nineteenth century, the overwhelming majority of immigrants to Australia were from Britain and Ireland. During the early decades, the island continent was used as a prison colony, and as late as the 1830s almost 40 percent of the white occupants of Australia were convicts. Immigration policies paralleled those in Canada, giving preference to western Europeans, somewhat reluctantly accepting eastern and southern Europeans, and barring Asians. The last point was particularly significant for Australia, given its close proximity to millions of potential immigrants from various destinations in Asia. From the passage of the Immigration Restriction Act in 1901 until the 1960s, Australia defined itself legally and culturally as "White Australia." Whites who did enter the country were expected to assimilate, and what this meant for Australians was something akin to the melting pot. Everything changed dramatically in the 1960s. By the late 1950s reforms had begun to chip away at White Australia, and by 1966 it was officially dead. As Australia's economy became increasingly enmeshed in the regional Asian economy, the racism of the White Australia policy proved to be problematic in dealing with trade partners such as Japan.

During the last quarter of the twentieth century, the number of immigrants arriving from Britain and elsewhere in Western Europe declined dramatically. At the same time, the number of immigrants arriving from the former Soviet Union, the former Yugoslavia, the Baltic nations, and Poland increased. There have also been increases in new white arrivals from New Zealand and South Africa. However, complementing these immigrant groups are people of color from such places as Vietnam, India, the Philippines, the People's Republic of China, Hong Kong, Taiwan, India, Sri Lanka, Malaysia, Indonesia, and Fiji. Added to this are asylum seekers, some entering the nation illegally from such nations as Iran and Afghanistan.

Both assimilation and a racist immigration law gave way to a policy that encouraged integration (which meant recognition of cultural pluralism) and a racially inclusive approach to immigration. Beginning in 1972, the government embarked on a new approach to ethnic diversity. Influenced by developments in Canada, it embraced multiculturalism in place of integration. This approach was meant to apply to all of Australia, and in particular it was conceived not only in terms of immigration but also in terms of the Aboriginal community. While there is a clear similarity between integration and multiculturalism, there were significant differences as well. Part of making it possible to flourish entailed combating racism. With the passage of the Race Discrimination Act in 1975, the government assumed a more proactive role in protecting minority groups than it had in the past. Moreover, multiculturalism did not mean merely tolerating the presence of difference, but rather viewing the core of Australian identity as embedded in the notion of diversity. This view implied that Australian national identity, rather than being a fixed notion located in the past, was open, fluid, and future-oriented. In concrete terms, the government committed itself to helping to preserve and enhance ethnic identities, which included supporting the preservation of nonEnglish languages and heritages.

As with the United States and Canada, Australian critics of multiculturalism contend that the policy will inevitably lead to the "balkanization" or the "disuniting" of the society. However, as the New Agenda noted above indicates, multiculturalism is to be understood in relationship to "civic duty," which is the term used to locate cultural diversity within a framework of shared values and orientations as citizens. Multiculturalism in this sense encourages cultural pluralism, accepts structural pluralism, and necessitates civic assimilation. Simon and Lynch (1999: 460) contend that Australian government "policies are more proimmigrant than public opinion seems to support." That being said, however, while many Australians are critical of illegal immigrants and are concerned in various ways about adjustment problems that members of some groups experience, the majority of the public rejects the politics of the rear guard and embraces in principle the idea of multiculturalism (Beckett, 1995). It is difficult to predict how the concept of multiculturalism will evolve over time or to know what kinds of changes will transpire to reshape the meaning of Australian identity. Suffice it to say that with the shift from assimilation to multiculturalism, the nation has embarked on a potentially profound reconsideration of diversity and national identity.

Western Europe

Until relatively recently, the nations of Western Europe tended to be characterized by the emigration of their people to settler nations. However, during the past half century these nations have become major immigration-receiving sites. As a result, they display a diversity today quite unlike earlier periods in their histories. Moreover, since many of the new immigrants are people of color, the ethnic formations currently emerging are being shaped within a racialized crucible. In this respect, Western Europe is coming to resemble developments in the United States and the other settler states discussed above (Castles and Miller, 1993). At the same time, some of these nations are also confronting the challenges and conflicts that are the result of the renewed vitality of ethnonationalist movements. The impact of immigration can be seen in all three of Western Europe's largest nations: Britain, Germany, and France. Among these three nations, ethnonationalist movements are only significant in Britain. We look briefly at each of these nations.

Britain in a Postcolonial World

The end of World War II marked a watershed in British history. Although it was once the world's preeminent industrial power, the devastation of the war was the final contributing factor to its economic decline. It was still an important capitalist industrial economy, but its earlier position at the top was no more. At the same time, the British Empire, which had been the largest empire during the imperialist age, was progressively dismantled. Within this general context, what it meant to be British was posed from two quarters. First, Britain confronted challenges from resurgent ethnonationalist movements in Scotland, Wales, and Northern Ireland. Second, beginning in the 1950s, immigrants from Commonwealth countries began to enter the country in large numbers, making it for the first time a racially mixed, multiethnic nation.

In terms of ethnonationalist movements, three nationality groups long incorporated into the United Kingdom, but with historical memories of earlier independence, have questioned whether the current polit-

Voices	Anita Craven

When I was a lot younger it was a need to have an identity, a lot of us of mixed race didn't have an identity. Your mum was white and your dad was Black; a lot of us were brought up by our mothers who were white. So where is your identity? We all thought Black was being a color. And because we were all so fair [in colour] we could have pushed for "white." And the word "Black" was derogatory then, wasn't it? But now because the word "Black" is positive, it's different. I feel personally before that I didn't have an identity. . . . But at the end of the day, for my own personal identity, I need to say that I'm a Black woman. That's where I'm coming from.

Anita Craven, a mixed-race British woman (Christian, 2000: 35).

ical geography of Britain will continue to exist. In effect, Scotland, Wales, and Ireland represent Britain's—or more properly, England's—first colonies. Nationalist movements in these regions date back to the nineteenth century, but it is only in recent decades that they have taken political form. In the cases of Wales and Scotland, calls for independence have been heard since the 1960s, while in the case of Northern Ireland, the irredentist aspirations of the Irish Republican Army call for the reunification of Northern Ireland with the rest of Ireland.

Scottish nationalism has centered on the Scottish Nationalist Party (SNP), while in Wales the SNP's counterpart, Plaid Cymru, has advanced the ethnonationalist movement. In both cases, there are long-standing grievances with England and with the British government. Both regions have experienced serious economic difficulties with the decline of manufacturing and mining, a matter only offset in Scotland by the exploitation of North Sea oil off its coast. The stated goal of the SNP is to sever Scotland's ties from Britain and become an independent nation that is fully integrated into the European Union. Members of Plaid Cymru have voiced similar goals, though somewhat less forcefully. In both cases, the route to independence would be through legitimate political channels, at the ballot box and not as a result of armed violence. In this regard, they resemble the Parti Québecois. Both parties have sought to mobilize voter sentiment on behalf of this goal. As a strategy, both have pushed for greater regional autonomy, but especially with the SNP, this is seen as an interim step leading ultimately to complete independence (Guibernau, 1999).

For their part, the voters in Scotland and Wales have not evidenced a desire to make a complete break with Britain. While there is more support for independence in Scotland than in Wales, in both places only a minority supports it (at the moment no more that a quarter of the Scottish public supports independence, with a much smaller percentage in Wales). Far more voters are sympathetic to greater autonomy. Moreover, while economic and political considerations are central in Scotland, the Welsh are far more interested in preserving their culture, including the Welsh language.

The conservative government of Margaret Thatcher during the 1980s was adamantly opposed to these movements and resisted giving in to demands for greater autonomy. This resistance actually played into the hands of nationalists. When the New Labour government of Tony Blair came to power, a new policy promoting **devolution** was initiated, which in effect meant that Scotland and Wales would have far greater say in their own domestic affairs than they previously did. Substantial majorities in Scotland and Wales supported devolution in a 1997 referendum, which among other things called for the creation of a Scottish Parliament and a Welsh Assembly. Both institutions opened in 1999. They have considerable power regarding domestic issues, including agriculture, culture and sports, economic development, education, environment, fisheries and food, health, housing, justice, planning, roads, rural affairs, and social services.

The unanswered question, especially for Scotland, at the beginning of the twenty-first century is whether this new arrangement is the final achievement of ethnonationalists or will prove to be merely a step on the way to the breakup of Britain. Does a regional parliament mean that sufficient autonomy has been achieved to satisfy most voters, thereby taking the wind out of the sails of the independence movement? Or should it be seen as a victory that will serve as a stimulus for ethnonationalists to press for total political independence? In the short term, the ability of the independence movements to increase public support appears rather limited. However, the longer-term prospects are difficult to predict (Nairn, 1977, 2000).

Northern Ireland is far more problematic. Since the 1960s, the Irish Republican Army (IRA) and other radical groups have waged a guerrilla war against what they see as the British occupation of Ireland, during a protracted period known as "the troubles." Rooted in the Roman Catholic community, the IRA seeks to create a united and independent Ireland. Pitted against them are not only the military forces of Britain but also the Protestant majority of Northern Ireland that is adamantly opposed to union with the Irish Republic and from which comes militant armed groups that are part of the so-called loyalist community. For Irish Catholic nationalists, the conflict represents the unfinished business of achieving independence that began with the Easter Uprising in 1916, which led to the independence of the rest of Ireland. The Protestant community is intent on seeing that independence doesn't happen. The intractability of the conflict has led to recurrent waves of violence punctuated by uneasy calms. Over 3,600 people have been killed during this time.

Efforts aimed at a mediated peace settlement have been under way since the mid-1980s, during which time both the British and Irish governments have worked cooperatively in getting both sides of the conflict to the negotiating table. In 1998 the Belfast Agreement (popularly known as the Good Friday Agreement) was signed, in part due to the initiative of President Bill Clinton. The essence of the agreement is the implementation of an arrangement of consociational democracy, which as Michael Hechter (2000: 136) put it, means in effect that ethnic group leaders from both sides agree to "participate in decision making as a cartel." The agreement grants to the people of Northern Ireland the right to choose their collective future. They could presumably decide to become part of Ireland, remain part of Britain, or stake out a course as an independent nation. At this point it remains unclear which choice will be made and whether it will be accomplished democratically and peacefully or by violent means.

Concurrent with these ethnonationalist movements, Britain became an immigrant-receiving nation. At least symbolically, the beginning of this migratory movement occurred in 1948 when the *Empire Windrush* arrived at Tilbury Docks with 492 Jamaican passengers aboard. This event marked the commencement of a small but steadily growing stream of new nonwhite immigrants. The new arrivals came overwhelmingly from British Commonwealth nations, where they possessed the British passports that gave them ready access to the former empire's hub. The vast majority of the newcomers can be divided into three major panethnic groups based on their points of origin: the Caribbean, the Indian subcontinent, and Africa.

Cultural differences between these communities and the host society provoked an immediate anti-immigrant response in virtually all quarters of British society. Not only did these new arrivals raise anew questions about what it meant to be British in an increasingly multicultural society, but they also raised the specter of race. Paul Gilroy (1987) traces the shifting responses in Britain to the new people of color, focusing on the various reformulations of the category of "other" that have arisen in recent decades. During the first phase of immigration, nonwhite immigrants were uniformly referred to as black, reflective of the fact that the host society tended to treat all in a similar fashion. Although fewer than 100,000 immigrants had entered the country by 1960, racial tensions nonetheless escalated. Discrimination against immigrants in employment and housing was rampant, and there was considerable political pressure to stop new immigrants from arriving and to find ways of repatriating those already in the country (Holmes, 1988).

Today there is a greater tendency to refer to groups by their nation of origin or by their religion (Muslim, Hindu, and Sikh, for example), reflecting an appreciation of the differences among the various immigrant groups. Two panethnic labels have emerged that are commonly used: black (or Afro-Caribbean) and Asian. The former refers to immigrants from the Caribbean and Africa, while the latter refers in particular to the nations of the Indian subcontinent (India, Pakistan, Bangladesh, and Sri Lanka) and sometimes also to the Chinese.

At present, 1.6 percent of the British population is black. A comparison between blacks in Britain and the United States can be instructive. First, unlike their American counterparts, British blacks are relative newcomers. Second, they represent a considerably smaller percentage of the overall population than blacks in the United States. Third, while Afro-Caribbean residential enclaves can be found in major cities, there is far less residential segregation in Britain than in the United States. Finally, British blacks are also less segregated in other areas of social life, such as schools and workplaces.

As Afro-Caribbeans struggle to obtain an economic foothold in their new homeland, they confront the classical problems associated with poverty, unemployment, discrimination, low wage rates, and the like (Model, 1999). They are overrepresented in the ranks of the unskilled working class. While they report lower levels of self-employment than other groups, a black middle class has emerged and has continued to grow. However, since most middle-class job opportunities are located in the professional sector of the economy, educational attainment plays a major role in upward mobility. Here there is reason for concern about the future, since blacks have not fared as well as other groups in the classroom. They have the lowest scores of any ethnic group in standardized test results and have higher rates of academic failure than the general student population. In addition, blacks are far more likely to be expelled or suspended from school for behavioral problems. Some educationists have expressed fears that in some inner-city neighborhoods a black underclass in developing.

In this context, an ethnic community has developed, replete with a range of institutions that provide needed services to blacks. These include mutual aid societies, political organizations, cultural organizations, churches, and so forth. The general function of these organizations is to assist in the integration of Afro-Caribbeans into British society and in combating racism. Despite evidence of improving attitudes toward blacks and gains in their socioeconomic status, it is clear that racism has not disappeared. The racist murder of black student and aspiring architect Stephen Lawrence in 1993 was a reminder to the nation that, as Ian Hargreaves (1996) put it, "We have not put the racist devil behind us."

Asian immigrants occupy a somewhat different place in contemporary British society. In some respects, these immigrants look like a success story and insofar as they do, they bear a resemblance to recent Asian immigrants in the United States. While there is a tendency to overstate the level of economic success they have achieved, in fact this segment of the new immigrant population is doing better economically than blacks. At the same time, Asians have a higher unemployment rate than whites, tend to be located in the lower-paying sectors of the economy, and continue to confront discrimination in hiring and promotion practices. In contrast to Afro-Caribbeans, who speak English, language barriers also play a role in explaining economic disadvantage. It is also important to note that there are differences among Asian groups in terms of their economic circumstances. Indians in general are doing the best, with Bangladeshis at the other end of the spectrum, with the highest levels of unemployment and poverty (Mason, 1995).

Some Asians have found success in niche economies. Thus, many Indians own small newsstands, convenience shops, and restaurants. The Bangladeshi community has a high level of involvement in restaurants and in the wholesale leather industry. Paralleling this propensity to self-employment, these two groups also have the highest rates of homeownership of any group, including whites. At the same time, there is evidence that they often reside in substandard and overcrowded housing. In terms of educational attainment, Asians are doing comparatively well. In spite of language barriers and cultural differences, Asians as a whole are high achievers on standardized tests, and the number going on to university education is rising. There is evidence that many Asian parents are pressing their children to use education as a means for upward mobility, hoping that they will not remain in the ethnic enclave but will find employment in the British mainstream. As such, they are promoting the acculturation of their children. In other instances, the more acculturated children press their parents to allow them to be free of certain inherited cultural constraints, as the humorous film *Bend It Like Beckham* nicely illustrates. However it occurs, it is clear that a growing number of Asian families are overcoming traditionalist values about the roles of women and are increasingly coming to see the value of higher education for all of their children, regardless of gender.

At the same time, it is important to note that Asian groups are far more culturally distinctive than their Afro-Caribbean counterparts, in no small part because most are not Christians. Most Asians are Muslim, Hindu, or Sikh. The tension between Muslims and the host society has been far greater than the other two religions—tensions that have intensified since 9/11—because part of the Islamic community in Britain is attracted to, and in some instances actively supportive of, radical fundamentalism. Some in British society have questioned whether it is possible to integrate groups who harbor intolerant, antidemocratic, and illiberal worldviews.

At the same time, many in the second generation, Muslim and other, actually do identify with and want to be a part of the larger society. They, for example, share with white Britons fervent allegiances to particular soccer teams, and they have similar interests in popular music (Back, 1996). However, complicating the situation is the fact that tensions between Asians and whites spilled over in the summer of 2001 in a series of race riots, pointing to the fact that acculturation occurs within a society where extremist racism continues to cast its shadow.

As Britain enters the twenty-first century, a number of competing tendencies are evident. On the one hand, there are both traditional conservatives and extreme racists who seek to view Britishness as unchanging and exclusive—a perpetual reminder that "there ain't no black in the Union Jack" (Gilroy, 1987). At the same time, there are those who refuse to embrace British identity. Such a view is evident in the ethnonationalist movements in Scotland, Wales, and especially Northern Ireland, but it can also be found among some immigrants. However, a third position is also evident, one that seeks to foster a new multicultural sensibility that accords respect and tolerance for diversity while simultaneously seeking to redefine what it means to be British (Parekh, 2000b).

Germany: The Challenge of a 'Blood-and-Soil' Conception of Citizenship

Germany is at the moment home to as many foreigners on a per capita basis as Canada. The labor migrants and political refugees who have settled in Germany since the end of World War II reflect a major change in German migration patterns and raise important questions about the meaning of citizenship and of what it means to be German (Brubaker, 1992). For much of the past half century, Germany was divided between the capitalist and democratic Federal Republic of Germany (West Germany) and the Soviet-bloc nation, the German Democratic Republic (East Germany). West Germany experienced a postwar boom that made it the "economic miracle" of Western Europe.

The loss of lives during the war meant that the nation suffered from extreme labor shortages during its economic recovery. These were met in part by attracting immigrants of German ancestry, who were immediately granted citizenship. Although these newcomers found that adjusting to Germany was not easy, over time they were assimilated into the larger society (Castles and Miller, 1993). However, these immigrants were not enough to meet the demand for workers. As a result, immigrants began arriving from many other nations, including Italy, Spain, Portugal, Morocco, Algeria, and Tunisia. However, the two most important contributing nations proved to be Turkey and the former Yugoslavia.

Realizing the need for workers, the German government played an active recruitment role, entering into arrangements not unlike the bracero program in the United States. However, unlike those immigrants of German ancestry, these workers were denied the legal right of permanent residence. Instead, they were defined as *Gastarbeiter* (**guestworkers**), entering the country under a system of labor contracts for set periods of time. The underlying rationale for such an approach was due to the *jus sanguinis* definition of German citizenship, which meant that one could only be a German citizen if one's ancestors were ethnic Germans. In other words, citizenship was defined in ethnic terms, with a clear sense of who was eligible and who wasn't. This is sometimes referred to as a "blood-and-soil" view of national identity.

Guestworkers continued to be recruited into the early 1970s. Although they lived apart from the German population, relatively little open hostility was displayed toward them. This was primarily because low unemployment and economic good times facilitated a relatively tolerant society. Moreover, there was little direct competition between German and immigrant workers, since the latter performed the unskilled and low-paying jobs that German workers avoided. This situation changed when economic restructuring began and the need for new workers subsided. Indeed, unemployment became an issue, and with it a demand that guestworkers return to their homelands. Relatively few did return, and in fact, because of family reunification, the number of immigrants actually increased (Castles and Miller, 1993).

A new generation—the children of the guestworkers—was born on German soil and began to grow up with little or no contact with their parents' homelands. Germany officially contended that it was not a nation of immigration. It was, however, forced to confront the prospect of a category of permanent residents who were not citizens. A stark question confronted the nation: Should there be efforts to integrate immigrants into the fabric of German society, or should they be encouraged to remain in self-contained and segregated ethnic enclaves? Rather than formulating a national policy, it was determined that state governments should dictate their own policies. Thus, the conservative Bavaria constructed policies that promoted exclusion and held out the prospect that immigrants might return to their homelands, while liberal Berlin encouraged assimilation.

During the 1980s, the number of immigrants grew compared with the preceding decade, due in part to the influx of asylum seekers from various countries in Asia, Africa, and South America (Castles and Miller, 1993). The fall of the Berlin Wall in 1989 signaled the collapse of communism and set the stage for the reunification of Germany in the following year. One of the groups to enter Germany at this time from various places in Eastern Europe was the *Aussiedler*, composed of ethnic Germans whose ancestors had often lived for centuries outside of Germany. Although they could immediately qualify for citizenship, many of them experienced cultural shock as then entered a modern, affluent industrial society.

One of the demographic realities Germany faces is that without immigration, the German population will decline. Germany has an aging population and a low fertility rate, and projections indicate that without the infusions of new immigrants it could decline by as many as 10 million people by the year 2030. Thus, there is a need for new immigrants. At present, they constitute a small percentage of the overall population. Ethnic Germans represent 94 percent of the total population. Turks represent 2.5 percent, with the remaining 3.5 percent being divided among all the rest of the groups in the country. The Turkish presence is the most noticeable of all immigrant groups, in part because it is the largest and in part because the cultural differences are the most pronounced. As in Britain, the cultural differences often focus on religion. Since most Turks are Muslims, the tensions between Islam and the West serve to a large extent to account for the manifestations of cultural conflict between immigrants and the host society. The social distance between Turks and Germans is pronounced. Occupational location explains part of the distance, although it should be noted that upward mobility is occurring for some Turks, albeit slowly. Although Turks do not live in hypersegregated neighborhoods, residential segregation exists, reflecting the class location of Turks at the bottom of the social hierarchy.

Germany differs from Britain in terms of its definition of citizenship and its orientation toward the incorporation of immigrants. Ruud Koopmans and Paul Statham (1999) have described the German case as "ethnocultural exclusionist," in contrast to the British case, which they define as "multicultural pluralist." While these terms accurately characterize the differing national responses to ethnic diversity over much of the past half century, changes are under way in Germany as the nation haltingly moves closer to the British model. As it does so, however, it is meeting considerable resistance. In recent years, Germany has witnessed waves of overt prejudice and discrimination, including violence, directed at foreigners. Racist hostility toward immigrants is seen in its most virulent form among those on the extreme right, which includes the overlapping groups associated with neo-Nazism and skinheads. In general, anti-immigrant sentiment is high, and right-wing politicians have exploited this sentiment.

On the other hand, the political left has encouraged the nation to rethink its historic exclusionary immigration policies. In 1999, they managed to pass a new citizenship law that was more congruent not only with the policies of the European Union but also with the policies of other liberal democracies. The law in effect ends the *jus sanguinis* rules of the past and makes it possible for nonethnic Germans to become citizens and to otherwise fully integrate into German society. The new law has a *jus soli* element, which means that the children of immigrants born on German soil qualify to become citizens. Some have seen this change as an indication that Germany is now on the road to becoming a "multiethnic, multilingual, multifaith democratic polity" (Benhabib, 1999: 7). Others are less optimistic, contending that while this is an important step, it is only a first step in a long and difficult process of finding a way to incorporate immigrants into the society while simultaneously redefining what it means to be German.

The French Melting Pot

French national identity stands in stark contrast to the German version. France has its own version of the melting pot, which means in ideal terms that anybody who wants to become a citizen can do so provided that the person is willing to embrace the ideals and core values of the republic (Noiriel, 1996). In other words, rather than basing citizenship on an ethnic basis, the French opted for a civic definition based on a willingness of immigrants to assimilate (Brubaker, 1992). On the surface, it would thus appear that immigrants would have a much easier time being accepted and integrated into French society, compared with the German case. However, the reality is considerably more complicated, as recent immigrants to France have confronted high levels of anti-immigrant sentiment, revealing the limits of France's openness to newcomers.

Like Germany, France suffered from labor shortages after World War II and began to actively recruit migrant workers from the 1950s into the 1970s. However, unlike Germany, France did not separate work permits from residency permits, thus allowing immigrants to view themselves as permanent settlers rather than as labor sojourners (Hargreaves, 1995). These two decades represent the zenith of immigration in French history. Two regions contributed the largest number of immigrants: the Iberian peninsula and the northern African Maghreb region. In terms of the former, Portugal accounted for more immigrants than Spain. Both of these countries lagged behind the rest of western Europe economically and continued to live under authoritarian political regimes. Thus, emigrants from these two nations left for a mixture of economic and political reasons. Three nations from the Maghreb became important sources of immigration, as a whole providing the largest number of contemporary immigrants. In order of size they are Algeria, Morocco, and Tunisia. As a former colony that became independent in 1962 only after a brutal war of liberation that threatened the political stability of France, Algeria is singularly significant. A reflection of the distinctive character of the relationship of France to Algeria can be seen by the fact that before independence Algeria was typically referred to as *l'autre France* ("the other France"), and the colony was declared to be an integral part of France. Among the immigrants who came from Algeria was a group known as the *pieds-noir*. They were ethnically French, although they and their ancestors had lived outside of France for decades. This contingent of immigrants managed to blend into the population with relative ease. In contrast, Muslim Algerians did not, and neither did their counterparts from Morocco and Tunisia.

Sales promotion in Chinese-owned shop in Paris.

These regions were not the only places from which immigrants came. Italy, long a source of labor in France, continued to supply immigrants during the early phase of immigration. However, as the Italian economy improved, fewer and fewer Italians left their homeland to seek work in France. In addition, almost 340,000 immigrants from "Departments d'Outre-Mer" and "Territoires d'Outre-Mer" (DOM-TOM) arrived during this period. These immigrants were from some of the few overseas colonies or territories that France still controlled in the postcolonial era. Four nations from DOM-TOM provided the bulk of this segment of the immigrant population: the Caribbean nations of Guadeloupe and Martinique, and French Guyana and the island of Re-union in the Indian Ocean. On a smaller scale, immigrants from former French-speaking colonies in sub-Saharan Africa have also contributed to the overall ethnic mix, along with smaller numbers of Asians (in particular, Vietnamese) and Turks. As with the rest of the European Union nations, France ceased to actively recruit foreign workers by the early 1970s, although the number of immigrants arriving in the country has continued.

Given that the dominant religion of the Maghreb and Turkey is Islam, France is similar to the other nations in the region insofar as they are now confronting a growing Islamic presence. These particular immigrants are also defined as being racially distinct from the French population. The confluence of race and religion has had a pronounced impact on public opinion. Although the French saw themselves as an assimilationist nation, they were unprepared for the presence of large numbers of people of color and similarly large numbers of Muslims (Hargreaves, 1995). The far right wing focused its energies on immigration, contending that the new immigrants have created unemployment problems, housing shortages, a drain on the government treasury because of social service costs, and rising rates of crime and delinquency. Moreover, they are accused of threatening French culture. Because Muslim immigrants are perceived to be incapable of assimilation, the call is for these immigrants to be returned to their homelands. This has been the message of the National Front (FN) and its charismatic racist leader Jean-Marie le Pen since the 1970s. Le Pen's party has managed to attract between 10 and 15 percent of the vote in national elections since the 1980s. But the far right is not alone in being opposed to immigrants. The mainstream conservative parties, too, have embraced anti-immigration policies. But the FN has also managed to tap into electoral support on the left, whose working-class constituents in declining industrial regions have exhibited growing levels of xenophobia.

Opposition to the FN came from students, civil rights organizations, and the Catholic church, with the most visible challenge to the party being SOS-Racisme, a multiethnic movement promoting tolerance and acceptance. For its part, the mainstream left has sought in various ways to combat racism and discrimination while improving the economic circumstances of immigrant communities. At the same time, they have discouraged additional immigration, promoting a policy that Sami Nair (1996: 76) has referred to as "integration with closure."

Unlike Germany, France is not immune to ethnic nationalism. The Bretons, Basques, Occitans, and Corsicans have all exhibited ethnic nationalist claims, with ethnonationalism on the Mediterranean island of Corsica being the most consequential. A recent effort to grant to the citizens of Corsica greater regional autonomy was rejected by the voters. This would have been a first recognition of the desirability of forging a multicultural policy solution to this challenge to the integrity of the French nation, something akin to Britain's devolution policy. While the future is unclear, in general it is fair to say that ethnonationalism is comparatively weaker in France than in Britain or Canada.

The real battles over multiculturalism are being raised over the new immigrants, and in particular over those who are Muslim. There are currently 4 to 5 million Muslims in France, representing between 7 and 8 percent of the total population. This means that there are now more Muslims in France than Protestants or Jews, making Islam the second largest religion in France after Roman Catholicism. Muslims in general are overrepresented in unskilled manual-labor jobs, particularly those that the native French avoid. They have comparatively high unemployment rates, high school-dropout rates, and lower levels of educational attainment, and they tend to live in relatively segregated poor neighborhoods (Hargreaves, 1995). Add to this the fact that many leaders of mosques have taken political positions that are unpopular among the French and that such practices as female circumcision and polygamy have been introduced into the country, and the culture conflict between host society and newcomers has proven to be intense.

As in Britain, riots have broken out in some cities during the past two decades. While there is a fundamentalist presence among Muslims that has resulted, for example, in attacks on synagogues, it is also the case that many in the Islamic community are only nominally attached to Islam, especially among the second generation. The tensions between the more secular and the religious quarters of the community are humorously depicted in Mahmoud Zemmouri's film *100% Arabica*, which revolves around the battle of wills between a conniving imam of a local mosque and two raï musicians. The film captures the ambiguous situation of many in the second generation, who live between two cultural worlds and are quite willing to blend or hybridize them. Tensions increased in 2004 because of the government's decision to ban religious headscarves in public schools. Whether the French nation will encourage or discourage this form of multicultural integration will depend on the outcome of political struggles that have been under way in France since the 1970s.

A Multicultural America in the Twenty-First Century

What can we learn from these comparisons with other advanced industrial nations? One obvious conclusion is that the United States is not as unique as is sometimes thought. All of the major industrialized nations have become multicultural in recent decades and have had to confront the challenges posed by diversity. They have a shared need to simultaneously find ways of incorporating or assimilating people—both new immigrants and those minority groups that have historically been disenfranchised and marginalized—and ways of recognizing, permitting, and perhaps encouraging diversity. Second, ethnonationalism is a factor in some nations but not in others. Clearly Canada and Britain are the two nations that confront the possibility that the existing state will break up. Although France is not immune to ethnic nationalism, this factor poses less of a threat to the integrity of the existing nation. In contrast, ethnonationalism is not a factor of any real consequence in the United States, Australia, or Germany. Third, like the two other settler nations discussed in this chapter—Canada and Australia—a part of the ethnic matrix of the United States is composed of the indigenous peoples who inhabited the land before white settlers arrived from Britain. Whether they are Native Americans, First Nation peoples, or Aborigines, they have experienced a long and painful history of oppression and marginalization and in recent years have exhibited a political assertiveness that seeks redress for past economic and political abuses and protections for their vulnerable cultures.

The United States stands alone as the nation with a large racial minority that is the result of the slave trade. African Americans are the only group in any of the nations examined herein that are nonvoluntary migrants. The distinctive features of the legacy of slavery, the century-long form of racial oppression known as Jim Crow, and the long battle for justice that has shaped all of American history continues to frame the way ethnic identities and intergroup relations are defined for all of this nation's ethnic groups.

The detailed historical, structural, and comparative analyses of race and ethnic relations in America contained in the preceding nine chapters make it obvious that none of the images discussed in Chapter 1 adequately captures the nation's complexity: its diversity, the constant change, and the ever-present admixture of opportunity for some groups and denial of opportunity to others. For some groups, especially those of European origin, the nation does in many respects resemble a melting pot. But even for these groups, the melting pot metaphor oversimplifies a far more complicated situation, one in which ethnic identities continue to affect the present. For other groups, which have been excluded from full incorporation or have chosen to retain a distinct sense of ethnic identity, their social world perhaps more closely resembles a salad bowl or mosaic. Even so, much of their sense of personal identity is shaped by a shared American experience. Using the orchestra image, both beautiful harmonic melodies and a cacophony of harsh and competing sounds have been and continue to be heard.

American history involves a ceaseless interplay between diversity and unity, between adhering to discrete ethnic identities and embracing a sense of being a part of "one people." The contemporary debates over multiculturalism illustrate this well. On the one hand, some exponents of multiculturalism criticize the very notion of assimilation, decrying what they perceive to be the Eurocentrism of the concept. That is, they see the call for assimilation as entailing the loss of distinctive ethnic and racial identities by nonEuropeans. They emphasize differences rather than those things that Americans share in common. On the other hand, some critics of multiculturalism express concern that an overemphasis on differences tends to undermine a necessary sense of commonality and with it a common civic culture (Takaki, 1993b; West, 1993; Gitlin, 1993; Taylor et al., 1992; Schlesinger, 1992; Fuchs, 1990). In the middle are those seeking common ground by promoting liberal views of tolerance and inclusion, while simultaneously embracing a shared national identity. This is, in fact, the position taken by most advocates for multiculturalism as practice and as social policy in the United States and elsewhere. It operates with the assumption that neither embracing differences at the expense of similarities nor seeking to deny them is adequate. Neither romanticizing differences, as some multiculturalists tend to do, nor denigrating them, as those hostile to multiculturalism do, will help to overcome past legacies of injustice and provide the basis for a more equitable and humane society.

What is clearly a necessary prerequisite for establishing such a society is greater understanding. This includes understanding the internal dynamics of the ethnic groups that make up the composite American population. It involves understanding the nature of intergroup relations over time. It requires locating these groups and patterns of relationships in terms of the economic, political, and cultural character of the larger American society. It requires an appreciation of the long-term impact of racism in its many guises. In this book, we have analyzed the complexity and fluidity of a highly diverse society. Making sense of that complexity and fluidity is not easy. In a multicultural society such as ours, what does assimilation mean? How can we remain tied to ethnic groups while also being fully American? Are prejudice and discrimination decreasing or remaining constant? Are Americans committed to the notion of racial justice, or have they turned their back on it (Steinberg, 1995)? Some groups—including some recent arrivals—are doing relatively well and are becoming integrated into the American mainstream. Others—in particular African Americans and American Indians—continue to experience considerable adversity and are far from overcoming historical legacies of racial oppression.

This description of the American scene suggests two things. First, diversity will continue to characterize the nation well into the future. Second, because there is nothing fixed about ethnicity, including its racialized form, the inequality and oppression that have and continue to characterize intergroup relations are not inevitable. On the other hand, it remains clear that as we move into the twenty-first century—

100 years after W. E. B. Du Bois's famous prediction about the century just past—"the problem of the color line" is far from being resolved.

Key Terms

devolution
ethnonationalism
guestworkers
jus sanguinis

jus soli
settler nation
third force

Questions for Discussion and Critical Thinking

1. Compare and contrast the two settler states discussed in this chapter: Canada and Australia. In what ways are their multicultural experiences similar to and in what ways are they different from the American experience?

2. Compare and contrast the meaning of national identity in Germany and France. In what ways has immigration affected these meanings? While the ethnic definition of what it means to be German works against the incorporation of nonGerman ethnics, why has the civic nationalism of France not worked better to incorporate new immigrants?

3. List as many ways as you can think of in which the United States is similar to the other advanced industrial nations, and make another list of ways in which it is distinctive. With these two lists in mind, discuss what you think ethnic relations will look like 20 years from now. ✦

References

Abelmann, Nancy and John Lie. 1995. *Blue Dreams: Korean Americans and the Los Angeles Riots*. Cambridge, MA: Harvard University Press.

Abramson, Harold J. 1973. *Ethnic Diversity in Catholic America*. New York: John Wiley and Sons.

——. 1975. "The Religioethnic Factor and the American Experience." *Ethnicity* 2 (July): 165–177.

——. 1980. "Assimilation and Pluralism." 150–160 in *Harvard Encyclopedia of American Ethnic Groups*, edited by Stephan Thernstrom, Ann Orlov, and Oscar Handlin. Cambridge, MA: Harvard University Press.

Adamic, Louis. 1944. *A Nation of Nations*. New York: Harper.

Adorno, T. W., Else Frenkel-Brunswik, Daniel J. Levinson, and R. Nevitt Sanford. 1950. *The Authoritarian Personality*. New York: John Wiley and Sons.

Aho, James A. 1990. *The Politics of Righteousness: Idaho Christian Patriotism*. Seattle: University of Washington Press.

Alba, Richard D. 1981. "The Twilight of Ethnicity Among American Catholics of European Ancestry." *Annals* 454 (March): 86–97.

——. 1985a. *Italian Americans: Into the Twilight of Ethnicity*. Englewood Cliffs, NJ: Prentice-Hall.

——. 1985b. "Interracial and Interethnic Marriage in the 1980 Census." Paper presented at the 1985 meeting of the American Sociological Association.

——. 1990. *Ethnic Identity: The Transformation of White America*. New Haven, CT: Yale University Press.

Alba, Richard D., John R. Logan, and Brian J. Stults. 2000. "How Segregated Are Middle-Class African Americans?" *Social Problems* 47 (4): 543–558.

Alba, Richard D., John R. Logan, Brian J. Stults, Gilbert Marzan, and Wenquan Zhang. 1999. "Immigrant Groups in Suburbs: A Reexamination of Suburbanization and Spatial Assimilation." *American Sociological Review* 64 (3): 446–460.

Alba, Richard D. and Victor Nee. 2003. *Remaking the American Mainstream: Assimilation and Contemporary Immigration*. Cambridge, MA: Harvard University Press.

Alexander, Adele Logan. 1991. *Ambiguous Lives: Free Women of Color in Rural Georgia, 1789–1879*. Fayetteville: The University of Arkansas Press.

Allen, Irving Lewis. 1990. *Unkind Words: Ethnic Labeling From Redskin to WASP*. New York: Bergin & Garvey.

Allen, Theodore W. 1994. *The Invention of the White Race*, vol. 1, *Racial Oppression and Social Control*. London: Verso.

Allport, Gordon. 1958. *The Nature of Prejudice*. Garden City, NY: Doubleday.

Anders, Gary C. 1998. "Indian Gaming: Financial and Regulatory Issues." *Annuals*, AAPSS, 556: 98–108.

Anderson, Charles H. 1970. *White Protestant Americans: From National Origins to Religious Group*. Englewood Cliffs, NJ: Prentice-Hall.

Anderson, Elijah. 1990. *Streetwise: Race, Class, and Change in an Urban Community*. Chicago: The University of Chicago Press.

——. 2000. *Code of the Street*. New York: W.W. Norton.

Angelou, Maya. 1969. *I Know Why the Caged Bird Sings*. New York: Random House.

Ansell, Amy Elizabeth. 1997. *New Right, New Racism: Race and Reaction in the United States and Britain*. New York: New York University Press.

Anthias, Floya. 1990. "Race and Class Revisited—Conceptualizing Race and Racisms." *The Sociological Review* 38 (1): 19–42.

Aponte, Robert. 1991. "Urban Hispanic Poverty: Disaggregations and Explanations." *Social Problems* 38 (4): 516–528.

Appel, John. 1961. "Hansen's Third Generation 'Law' and the Origins of the American Jewish Historical Society." *Jewish Social Studies* 23 (January): 3–20.

Aptheker, Herbert. 1943. *American Negro Slave Revolts*. New York: Columbia University Press.

Archdeacon, Thomas. 1983. *Becoming American: An Ethnic History*. New York: The Free Press.

———. 1985. "Problems and Possibilities in the Study of American Immigration and Ethnic History." *International Migration Review* 19 (Spring): 112–134.

———. 1990. "Hansen's Hypothesis as a Model of Immigrant Assimilation." 42–63 in *American Immigrants and Their Generations: Studies and Commentaries on the Hansen Thesis After Fifty Years*, edited by Peter Kivisto and Dag Blanck. Urbana: University of Illinois Press.

Arendt, Hannah. 1974. *Rahel Varnhagen: The Life of a Jewish Woman*. New York: Harcourt Brace Jovanovich.

Arizona Republic. 1987. "Fraud in Indian Country." October 11: 34.

Auletta, Ken. 1982. *The Underclass*. New York: Random House.

Awanohara, Susumu. 1991. "Tyros, Triads, Tycoons: Chinatown Ghettos Versus Arriviste Suburbs." *Far Eastern Economic Review* 153 (July 18): 50–51.

Back, Les. 1996. *New Ethnicities and Urban Culture: Racisms and Multiculture in Young Lives*. New York: St. Martin's.

Baer, Hans A. and Merrill Singer. 1992. *African-American Religion in the Twentieth Century: Varieties of Protest and Accommodation*. Knoxville: The University of Tennessee Press.

Baily, Samuel L. 1983. "The Adjustment of Italian Immigrants in Buenos Aires and New York, 1870–1914." *The American Historical Review* 88 (2): 281–305.

Bailyn, Bernard. 1967. *The Ideological Origins of the American Revolution*. Cambridge, MA: The Belknap Press of Harvard University Press.

———. 1986. *Voyagers to the West: A Passage in the Peopling of America on the Eve of the Revolution*. New York: Alfred A. Knopf.

Baker, Ray Stannard. 1964 [1908]. *Following the Color Line: American Negro Citizenship in the Progressive Era*. New York: Harper Torchbooks.

Balch, Emily. 1910. *Our Slavic Fellow Citizens*. New York: Charities Publication Committee.

Banner-Haley, Charles T. 1994. *The Fruits of Integration: Black Middle-Class Ideology and Culture, 1960–1990*. Jackson: University Press of Mississippi.

Banton, Michael. 1983. *Racial and Ethnic Competition*. Cambridge, UK: Cambridge University Press.

———. 1987. *Racial Theories*. Cambridge, UK: Cambridge University Press.

———. 2001. "Progress in Ethnic and Racial Studies." *Ethnic and Racial Studies* 24 (2): 173–194.

Banton, Michael and Jonathan Harwood. 1975. *The Race Concept*. New York: Praeger.

Barkan, Elazar. 1992. *The Retreat of Scientific Racism: Changing Concepts of Race in Britain and the United States Between the World Wars*. Cambridge, UK: Cambridge University Press.

Barrera, Mario. 1979. *Race and Class in the Southwest*. Notre Dame, IN: University of Notre Dame Press.

———. 1985. "The Historical Evolution of Chicano Ethnic Goals: A Bibliographic Essay." *Sage Race Relations Abstracts* 10 (1): 1–48.

Barringer, Herbert, Robert W. Gardner, and Michael J. Levin. 1993. *Asians and Pacific Islanders in the United States*. New York: Russell Sage Foundation.

Barth, Fredrik, ed. 1969. *Ethnic Groups and Boundaries*. Boston: Little, Brown.

Barth, Gunther. 1964. *Bitter Strength: A History of the Chinese in the United States, 1850–1870*. Cambridge, MA: Harvard University Press.

Barton, Josef J. 1975. *Peasants and Strangers: Italians, Rumanians, and Slovaks in an American City, 1890–1950*. Cambridge, MA: Harvard University Press.

Basch, Linda, Nina Glick Schiller, and Christina Szanton Blanc. 1994. *Nations Unbound: Transnational Projects, Postcolonial Predicaments, and Deterritorialized Nation-States.* Basel, Switzerland: Gordon and Breach.

Bataille, Gretchen and Charles L. P. Silet. 1980. "The Entertaining Anachronism: Indians in American Film." 36–53 in *The Kaleidoscopic Lens: How Hollywood Views Ethnic Groups.* Englewood Cliffs, NJ: Jerome S. Ozer.

Baudrillard, Jean. 1988. *America.* London: Verso.

Baum, Dan. 1990. "Blackfeet Fight Oil Exploration on Sacred Land." *Denver Post,* December 16: 1–3.

Bayor, Ronald H. 1978. *Neighbors in Conflict: The Irish, Germans, Jews, and Italians of New York City, 1929–1941.* Baltimore: The Johns Hopkins University Press.

Bean, Frank D. and Marta Tienda. 1987. *The Hispanic Population of the United States.* New York: Russell Sage Foundation.

Becerra, Rosina M. 1988. "The Mexican American Family." 141–172 in *Ethnic Families in America: Patterns and Variations,* ed. Charles H. Mindel et al. New York: Elsevier.

Beckett, Jeremy. 1995. "National and Transnational Perspectives on Multiculturalism: The View From Australia." *Identities* 1 (4): 421–426.

Beer, William R. 1987. "Resolute Ignorance: Social Science and Affirmative Action." *Society* 24: 63–69.

Bell, Daniel. 1965. *The End of Ideology: On the Exhaustion of Political Ideas in the Fifties.* New York: Free Press.

——. 1973. *The Coming of Post-industrial Society: A Venture in Social Forecasting.* New York: Basic Books.

Bellah, Robert, Richard Madsen, William M. Sullivan, Ann Swidler, and Stephen M. Tipton. 1985. *Habits of the Heart: Individualism and Commitment in American Life.* Berkeley: University of California Press.

Benedict, Ruth. 1959. *Race: Science and Politics.* New York: The Viking Press.

Benhabib, Seyla. 1999. "Germany Opens Up." *The Nation,* June 21: 6–7.

Benjamin, Lois. 1991. *The Black Elite: Facing the Color Line in the Twilight of the Twentieth Century.* Chicago: Nelson-Hall.

Bensman, Joseph and Arthur J. Vidich. 1971. *The New American Society: The Revolution of the Middle Class.* Chicago: Quadrangle Books.

Berger, Bennett. 1960. *Working-Class Suburb: A Study of Auto Workers in Suburbia.* Berkeley: University of California Press.

Bergquist, James M. 1984. "German Communities in American Cities: An Interpretation of the Nineteenth-Century Experience." *Journal of American Ethnic History* 4 (Fall): 9–30.

Berle, Beatrice. 1959. *Eighty Puerto Rican Families in New York City.* New York: Columbia University Press.

Berlin, Ira. 1974. *Slaves Without Masters: The Free Negro in the Antebellum South.* New York: Pantheon Books.

——. 2003. *Generations of Captivity: A History of African-American Slaves.* Cambridge, MA: The Belknap Press of Harvard University Press.

Bernal, Martin. 1987. *Black Athena: The Afroasiatic Roots of Classical Civilization,* vol. 1. New Brunswick, NJ: Rutgers University Press.

Berry, Brewton. 1963. *Almost White.* New York: Macmillan.

Berthoff, Rowland. 1971. *An Unsettled People: Social Order and Disorder in American History.* New York: Harper & Row.

Billigmeier, Robert Henry. 1974. *Americans From Germany: A Study in Cultural Diversity.* Belmont, CA: Wadsworth.

Billington, Roy. 1938. *The Protestant Crusade 1800–1860: A Study of the Origins of American Nativism.* New York: Macmillan.

Blackwell, James E. 1985. *The Black Community: Diversity and Unity.* New York: Harper & Row.

Blake, Casey Nelson. 1990. *Beloved Community: The Cultural Criticism of Randolph Bourne, Van Wyck Brooks, Waldo Frank and Lewis Mumford.* Chapel Hill: The University of North Carolina Press.

Blalock, Hubert M. 1967. *Toward a Theory of Minority-Group Relations*. New York: John Wiley and Sons.

Blank, Rebecca. 2001. "An Overview of Trends in Social and Economic Well-Being by Race." 21–39 in *America Becoming: Racial Trends and Their Consequences*, vol.1, edited by Neil J. Smelser, William Julius Wilson, and Faith Mitchell. Washington, DC: National Academy Press.

Blassingame, John W. 1972. *The Slave Community: Plantation Life in the Antebellum South*. New York: Oxford University Press.

Blauner, Robert. 1969. "Internal Colonialism and Ghetto Revolt." *Social Problems* 16 (Spring): 393–408.

Blee, Kathleen. 2003. *Inside Organized Racism: Women in the Hate Movement*. Berkeley: University of California Press.

Blessing, Patrick J. 1980. "Irish." 524–545 in the *Harvard Encyclopedia of American Ethnic Groups*, edited by Stephan Thernstrom, Ann Orlov, and Oscar Handlin. Cambridge, MA: Harvard University Press.

Bloom, Jack M. 1987. *Class, Race, and the Civil Rights Movement*. Bloomington: Indiana University Press.

Blumberg, Rhoda Lois. 1984. *Civil Rights: The 1960s Freedom Struggle*. Boston: Twayne.

Blumer, Herbert. 1954. "What Is Wrong With Social Theory?" *American Sociological Review* 19: 3–10.

———. 1958. "Race Prejudice as a Sense of Group Position." *Pacific Sociological Review* 1: 3–7.

———. 1965. "The Future of the Color Line." 322–336 in *The South in Continuity and Change*, edited by John McKinney and E. T. Thompson. Durham, NC: Duke University Press.

Bobo, Lawrence. 1983. "Whites' Opposition to Busing: Symbolic Racism or Realistic Group Conflict." *Journal of Personality and Social Psychology* 45 (6): 1196–1210.

———. 2001. "Racial Attitudes and Relations at the Close of the Twentieth Century." 264–301 in *America Becoming: Racial Trends and Their Consequences*, vol. 1, edited by Neil J. Smelser, William Julius Wilson, and Faith Mitchell. Washington, DC: National Academy Press.

Bodnar, John. 1976. "Materialism and Morality: Slavic-American Immigrants and Education, 1890–1940." *The Journal of Ethnic Studies* 3 (4): 1–19.

———. 1982. *Workers' World: Kinship, Community, and Protest in an Industrial Society, 1900–1940*. Baltimore: The John Hopkins University Press.

———. 1985. *The Transplanted: A History of Immigrants in Urban America*. Bloomington: Indiana University Press.

Bodnar, John, Roger Simon, and Michael P. Weber. 1982. *Lives of Their Own: Blacks, Italians, and Poles in Pittsburgh, 1900–1960*. Urbana: University of Illinois Press.

Bogardus, Emory. 1933. "A Social Distance Scale." *Sociology and Social Research* 17 (January–February): 265–271.

———. 1934. *The Mexican in the United States*. Los Angeles: University of Southern California Press.

———. 1959. *Social Distance*. Yellow Springs, OH: Antioch Press.

Bolt, Christine. 1971. *Victorian Attitudes to Race*. London: Routledge and Kegan Paul.

———. 1987. *American Indian Policy and American Reform*. London: Unwin Hyman.

Bonacich, Edna. 1972. "A Theory of Ethnic Antagonism: The Split Labor Market." *American Sociological Review* 37: 547–559.

———. 1973. "A Theory of Middlemen Minorities." *American Sociological Review* 38 (4): 583–594.

———. 1980. "Class Approaches to Ethnicity and Race." *Insurgent Sociologist* 10 (2): 9–23.

———. 1992. "Alienation Among Asian and Latino Immigrants in the Los Angeles Garment Industry: The Need for New Forms of Class Struggle in the Late Twentieth Century." 165–180 in *Alienation, Society and the Individual*, ed. Feliz Geyer and Walter R. Heinz. New Brunswick, NJ: Transaction Publishers.

Bonacich, Edna and Richard P. Appelbaum. 2000. *Behind the Label: Inequality in the Los Angeles Apparel Industry*. Berkeley: University of California Press.

Bonilla, Frank and Ricardo Campos. 1981. "A Wealth of Poor: Puerto Ricans in the New Economic Order." *Daedalus* (110): 133–176.

Bonilla-Silva, Eduardo. 1997. "Rethinking Racism: Toward a Structural Interpretation." *American Sociological Review* 62 (3): 465–480.

———. 2003. *Racism Without Racists: Color-Blind Racism and the Persistence of Racial Inequality in the United States.* Lanham, MD: Rowman and Littlefield Publishers.

Borjas, George J. 1990. *Friends or Strangers: The Impact of Immigrants on the U.S. Economy.* New York: Basic Books.

———. 2000. "The Economic Progress of Immigrants." 15–49 in *Issues in the Economics of Immigration,* edited by George Borjas. Chicago: University of Chicago Press.

Boswell, Thomas D. and James R. Curtis. 1983. *The Cuban-American Experience: Culture, Images, and Perspectives.* Totowa, NJ: Rowman and Allanheld.

Bourne, Randolph. 1977. *The Radical Will: Selected Writings, 1911–1918.* New York: Urizen Books.

Bouvier, Leon F. 1992. *Peaceful Invasions: Immigration and a Changing America.* Lanham, MD: University Press of America.

Brace, Charles Loring. 1872. *The Dangerous Classes of New York and Twenty Years' Work Among Them.* New York: Wynkoop and Hallenbeck.

Bredemeier, Harry. 1955. *The Federal Public Housing Movement: A Case Study of Social Change.* Ph.D. dissertation, Columbia University.

Breton, Raymond. 1964. "Institutional Completeness of Ethnic Communities and the Personal Relations of Immigrants." *American Journal of Sociology* 70 (2): 193–205.

Briquets, Sergio Diaz and Lisandro Pérez. 1981. *Cuba: The Demography of Revolution.* Washington, DC: Population Reference Bureau, vol. 36, no. 1.

Broderick, Francis L. 1959. *W. E. B. Du Bois: Negro Leader in a Time of Crisis.* Stanford, CA: Stanford University Press.

Brodkin, Karen. 1998. *How Jews Became White Folks and What That Says About Race in America.* New Brunswick, NJ: Rutgers University Press.

Brown, Dee. 1970. *Bury My Heart at Wounded Knee.* New York: Holt, Rinehart, and Winston.

Brown, Francis J. and Joseph S. Roucek, eds. 1937. *Our Racial and National Minorities.* New York: Prentice-Hall.

Brown, Rupert. 1995. *Prejudice: Its Social Psychology.* Cambridge, MA: Blackwell.

Brown, Thomas N. 1966. *Irish-American Nationalism.* Philadelphia: J.B. Lippincott.

Brownlaw, Kevin. 1990. *Behind the Mask of Innocence.* New York: Alfred A. Knopf.

Brubaker, Rogers. 1992. *Citizenship and Nationhood in France and Germany.* Cambridge, MA: Harvard University Press.

Bugelski, B. R. 1961. "Assimilation Through Intermarriage." *Social Forces* 40 (December): 148–153.

Bukowczyk, John J. 1987. *And My Children Did Not Know Me: A History of the Polish-Americans.* Bloomington: Indiana University Press.

Bulosan, Carlos. 1973 [1946]. *America Is in the Heart: A Personal History.* New York: Harcourt, Brace, and Company.

Burma, John. 1954. *Spanish-Speaking Groups in the United States.* Durham, NC: Duke University Press.

Burt, Larry W. 1982. *Tribalism in Crisis: Federal Indian Policy, 1953–1961.* Albuquerque: University of New Mexico Press.

Burton, Jonathan. 1992. "Razed Hopes: Korean Americans Struggle to Rebuild After Riots." *Far Eastern Economic Review* 55 (October): 26–27.

Bush, Rod. 1999. *We Are Not What We Seem: Black Nationalism and Class Struggle in the American Century.* New York: New York University Press.

Butler, Jon. 1990. *Awash in a Sea of Faith: Christianizing the American Republic.* Cambridge, UK: Cambridge University Press.

Cahan, Abraham. 1896. *Yekl: A Tale of the New York Ghetto.* New York: D. Appleton and Company.

Calhoun, Craig. 1997. *Nationalism.* Minneapolis: University of Minnesota Press.

Callinicos, Alex. 1993. *Race and Class.* London: Bookmarks.

Camarillo, Albert. 1979. *Chicanos in a Changing Society: From Mexican Pueblos to American Barrios in Santa Barbara and Southern California, 1848–1930.* Cambridge, MA: Harvard University Press.

Carling, Alan. 1991. *Social Division.* London: Verso.

Carmichael, Stokely and Charles V. Hamilton. 1967. *Black Power: The Politics of Liberation in America.* New York: Random House.

Caroli, Betty Boyd. 1973. *Italian Repatriation From the United States, 1900–1914.* New York: Center for Migration Studies.

Caroli, Betty Boyd and Thomas Kessner. 1978. "New Immigrant Women at Work: Italians and Jews in New York City, 1880–1905." *The Journal of Ethnic Studies* 28 (Winter): 5: 21.

Carter, Stephen L. 1991. *Reflections of an Affirmative Action Baby.* New York: Basic Books.

Castles, Stephen and Mark J. Miller. 1993. *The Age of Migration: International Population Movements in the Modern World.* New York: The Guilford Press.

Cha, Marn J. 1977. "An Ethnic Political Orientation as a Function of Assimilation: With Reference to Koreans in Los Angeles." 191–203 in *The Korean Diaspora,* edited by Hyung-chan Kim. Santa Barbara, CA: ABC-Clio.

Chafe, William H., Raymond Gavins, and Robert Korstad. 2001. *Remembering Jim Crow: African Americans Tell About Life in the Segregated South.* New York: The New Press.

Champagne, Duane. 1992. *Social Order and Political Change: Constitutional Government Among the Cherokee, the Choctaw, the Chickasaw, and the Creek.* Stanford, CA: Stanford University Press.

Chan, Sucheng. 1991. *Asian Americans: An Interpretive History.* Boston: Twayne.

Chavez, John R. 1984. *The Lost Land: The Chicano Image of the Southwest.* Albuquerque: University of New Mexico Press.

Chávez, Linda. 1991. *Out of the Barrio: Toward a New Politics of Hispanic Assimilation.* New York: Basic Books.

Chávez, Lydia. 1998. *The Color Bind: California's Battle to End Affirmative Action.* Berkeley: University of California Press.

Chen, Hsiang-Shiu. 1992. *Chinatown No More: Taiwan Immigrants in Contemporary New York.* Ithaca, NY: Cornell University Press.

Chen, Jack. 1980. *The Chinese of America.* San Francisco: Harper & Row.

Chen, Shehong. 2002. *Being Chinese: Becoming Chinese American.* Urbana: University of Illinois Press.

Christian, Mark. 2000. *Multiracial Identity: An International Perspective.* London: Macmillan.

Churchill, Ward. 1999. "The Crucible of American Indian Identity: Native Tradition Versus Colonial Imposition in Postconquest North America." 39–67 in *Contemporary Native American Cultural Issues,* edited by Duane Champagne. Walnut Creek, CA: Alta Mira Press.

Cinel, Dino. 1981. "Between Change and Continuity: Regionalism Among Immigrants From the Italian Northwest." *Journal of Ethnic Studies* 9: 19–36.

———. 1982a. *From Italy to San Francisco: The Immigrant Experience.* Stanford, CA: Stanford University Press.

———. 1982b. "The Seasonal Emigrations of Italians in the Nineteenth Century: From Internal to International Destinations." *Journal of Ethnic Studies* 10: 43–68.

Clark, Dennis J. 1977. "The Irish Catholics: A Postponed Perspective." 48–68 in *Immigrants and Religion in Urban America,* edited by Randall M. Miller and Thomas D. Marzik. Philadelphia: Temple University Press.

Clark, Terry. 1975. "The Irish Ethnic and the Spirit of Patronage." *Ethnicity* 2: 305–359.

Clemetson, Lynette. 2003. "Hispanics Now Largest Minority, Census Shows." *New York Times,* January 22: A1, A19.

Cohen, Lizabeth. 1990. *Making a New Deal: Industrial Workers in Chicago, 1919–1939.* New York: Cambridge University Press.

———. 2003. *Consumer's Republic: The Politics of Mass Consumption in Postwar America.* New York: Alfred A. Knopf.

Cohen, Steven M. 1988. *American Assimilation or Jewish Revival?* Bloomington: Indiana University Press.

Cohen, Steven M. and Leonard J. Fein. 1985. "From Integration to Survival: American Jewish Anxieties in Transition." *The Annals of the American Academy of Political and Social Sciences* 480 (July): 75–88.

Coleman, James S., Thomas Hoffer, and Sally Kilgore. 1981. *Public Private Schools.* Chicago: National Opinion Research Center.

Coleman, James S., Sara D. Kelly, and John A. Moore. 1975. *Trends in School Segregation, 1968–1973.* Washington, DC: Urban Institute.

Coleman, James, Ernest Q. Campbell, Carol J. Hobson, James McPartlarl, Alexander Mood, Frederick D. Weinfield, and Robert L. York. 1966. *Equality of Educational Opportunity.* Washington, DC: Government Printing Office.

Collier, John. 1945. "United States Indian Administration as a Laboratory of Ethnic Relations." *Social Research* 12 (2): 265–303.

Collins, Randall. 2001. "Ethnic Change in Macro-Historical Perspective." 13–46 in *Problem of the Century: Racial Stratification in the United States,* edited by Elijah Anderson and Douglas S. Massey. New York: Russell Sage Foundation.

Commager, Henry Steele. 1977. *The Empire of Reason: How Europe Imagined and America Realized the Enlightenment.* Garden City, NY: Anchor Press.

Connell, K. H. 1950. *The Population of Ireland, 1750–1845.* London: Oxford University Press.

Connor, Walker. 1978. "A Nation Is a Nation, Is a State, Is an Ethnic Group, Is a . . ." *Ethnic and Racial Studies* 1 (4): 377–400.

———. 1994. *Ethnonationalism: The Quest for Understanding.* Princeton, NJ: Princeton University Press.

Conzen, Kathleen Neils. 1980. "Germans." 405–425 in *Harvard Encyclopedia of American Ethnic Groups,* edited by Stephan Thernstrom, Ann Orlov, and Oscar Handlin. Cambridge, MA: Harvard University Press.

———. 1985. "Peasant Pioneers: Generational Succession Among German Farmers in Frontier Minnesota." 259–292 in *The Countryside in the Age of Capitalist Transformation,* edited by Steven Hahn. Chapel Hill: University of North Carolina Press.

———. 1991. "Ethnic Patterns in America Cities: Historiographical Trends." Paper presented in Vaxjo, Sweden, May 31.

Conzen, Kathleen Neils, David A. Gerber, Ewa Morawska, George E. Pozzetta, and Rudolph J. Vecoli. 1990. "The Invention of Ethnicity: A Perspective From the USA." *Altreitalie* 3: 37–62.

Coon, Carleton S. 1965. *The Living Races of Man.* New York: Alfred A. Knopf.

Cordova, Fred. 1983. *Filipinos.* Dubuque, IA: Kendall-Hunt.

Cornell, Stephen. 1988. *The Return of the Native: American Indian Political Resurgence.* New York: Oxford University Press.

Cornell, Stephen and Joseph P. Kalt. 1995. "Where Does Economic Development Really Come From? Constitutional Rule Among the Contemporary Sioux and Apache." *Economic Inquiry* 33 (July): 402–426.

———. 1998. "Sovereignty and Nation-Building: The Development Challenge in Indian Country Today." *American Indian Culture and Research Journal* 22 (3): 187–214.

Cortés, Carlos. 1980. "Mexicans." 697–719 in *Harvard Encyclopedia of American Ethnic Groups,* edited by Stephan Thernstrom, Ann Orlov, and Oscar Handlin. Cambridge, MA: Harvard University Press.

Cottle, Thomas J. 1976. *Busing.* Boston: Beacon Press.

Covello, Leonard. 1972. *The Social Background of the Italo-American School Child.* Totowa, NJ: Rowan and Littlefield.

Cowell, D. D. 1985. "Funerals, Family, and Forefathers: A View of Italian-American Funeral Practices." *Omega* 16: 69–85.

Cox, Oliver C. 1948. *Caste, Class, and Race.* New York: Monthly Review Press.

CQ Researcher. 1992. *Illegal Immigration.* Washington, DC: Congressional Quarterly, April 24.

Cravens, Hamilton. 1978. *The Triumph of Evolution: American Scientists and the Hereditary-Environment Controversy, 1900–1941.* Philadelphia: University of Pennsylvania Press.

Creel, Margaret Washington. 1988. *"A Peculiar People": Slave Religion and Community—Culture Among the Gullahs.* New York: New York University Press.

Creelan, Paul and Robert Granfield. 1986. "The Polish Peasant and the Pilgrim's Progress: Morality and Myth in W. I. Thomas' Social Theory." *Journal for the Scientific Study of Religion* 25 (2): 162–179.

Crispino, James A. 1980. *The Assimilation of Ethnic Groups: The Italian Case.* Staten Island, NY: Center for Migration Studies.

Cronon, E. David. 1955. *Black Moses: The Story of Marcus Garvey and the Universal Negro Improvement Association.* Madison: University of Wisconsin Press.

Cross, William E., Jr. 1991. *Shades of Black: Diversity in African-American Identity.* Philadelphia: Temple University Press.

Curti, Merle, with the assistance of Robert Daniel, Shaw Livermore, Jr., Joseph Van Hise, and Margaret W. Curti. 1959. *The Making of an American Community: A Case Study of Democracy in a Frontier County.* Stanford, CA: Stanford University Press.

Curtin, Philip. 1969. *The Atlantic Slave Trade.* Madison: University of Wisconsin Press.

Dadrian, Vahakn N. 1989. "Genocide as a Problem of National and International Law: The World War I Armenian Case and Its Contemporary Legal Ramifications." *Yale Journal of International Law* 14 (2): 221–334.

Daniel, Pete. 1985. *Breaking the Land: The Transformation of Cotton, Tobacco, and Rice Cultures Since 1880.* Urbana: University of Illinois Press.

Daniels, Jessie. 1997. *White Lies: Race, Class, Gender, and Sexuality in White Supremacist Discourse.* New York: Routledge.

Daniels, Roger. 1972. *Concentration Camps, U.S.A., Japanese Americans and World War II.* New York: Holt, Rinehart, and Winston.

——. 1988. *Asian America: Chinese and Japanese in the United States Since 1850.* Seattle: University of Washington Press.

——. 1990. *Coming to America: A History of Immigration and Ethnicity in American Life.* New York: Harper Collins.

Danzger, Herbert M. 1989. *Returning to Tradition: The Contemporary Revival of Orthodox Judaism.* New Haven, CT: Yale University Press.

Dashefsky, Arnold, ed. 1976. *Ethnic Identity in Society.* Chicago: Rand McNally.

Davis, Allison, Burleigh B. Gardner, and Mary R. Gardner. 1941. *Deep South: A Social Anthropological Study of Caste and Class.* Chicago: The University of Chicago Press.

Davis, David Brion. 1966. *The Problem of Slavery in Western Culture.* Ithaca, NY: Cornell University Press.

Davis, F. James. 1991. *Who Is Black? One Nation's Definition.* University Park: Pennsylvania State University Press.

DeConde, Alexander. 1992. *Ethnicity, Race and American Foreign Policy.* Boston: Northeastern University Press.

de Crèvecoeur, J. Hector St. John. 1904 [1782]. *Letters From an American Farmer.* New York: Fox, Duffield.

Degler, Carl. 1991. *In Search of Human Nature: The Decline and Revival of Darwinism in American Social Thought.* New York: Oxford University Press.

Delgado, Héctor L. 1993. *New Immigrants, Old Unions: Organizing Undocumented Workers in Los Angeles.* Philadelphia: Temple University Press.

Deloria, Vine, Jr., ed. 1985. *American Indian Policy in the Twentieth Century.* Norman: University of Oklahoma Press.

Denton, Nancy A. and Douglas S. Massey. 1989. "Racial Identity Among Caribbean Hispanics: The Effect of Double Minority Status on Residential Segregation." *American Sociological Review* 54 (5): 790–808.

Department of Immigration and Multicultural Affairs, Australia. 2001. *Immigration: The Facts—Information Kit.* <www.immi.gov.au>.

Deutsch, Sarah. 1987. *No Separate Refuge: Culture, Class, and Gender on an Anglo-Hispanic Frontier in the American Southwest, 1880–1940.* New York: Oxford University Press.

di Leonardo, Micaela. 1984. *The Varieties of Ethnic Experience: Kinship, Class, and Gender Among California Italian-Americans.* Ithaca, NY: Cornell University Press.

Diner, Hasia R. 1983. *Erin's Daughters in America: Irish Immigrant Women in the Nineteenth Century.* Baltimore: The Johns Hopkins University Press.

Dinnerstein, Leonard, Roger L. Nichols, and David M. Reimers. 1990. *Natives and Strangers: Blacks, Indians, and Immigrants in America.* New York: Oxford University Press.

Dinnerstein, Leonard and David M. Reimers. 1988. *Ethnic Americans: A History of Immigration.* New York: Harper & Row.

Dobbs, Michael. 2004. "U.S. School Segregation Now at '69 Level: Study Shows 15-Year Decline." *Washington Post* January 18: A10.

Dollard, John. 1937. *Caste and Class in a Southern Town.* New Haven: Yale University Press.

Donaldson, Gordon. 1980. "Scots." 908–916 in *Harvard Encyclopedia of American Ethnic Groups,* edited by Stephan Thernstrom, Ann Orlov, and Oscar Handlin. Cambridge, MA: Harvard University Press.

Dore, R. F. 1959. *Land Reform in Japan.* New York: Oxford University Press.

Dorris, Michael A. 1981. "The Grass Still Grows, the Rivers Still Flow: Contemporary Native Americans." *Daedalus* 110 (Spring): 43–69.

Douglass, Frederick. 1993 [1845]. *Narrative of the Life of Frederick Douglass: An American Slave.* New York: Bedford Books of St. Martin's Press.

Douglass, William A. and John Bilbao. 1975. *Amerikanauk: The Basques in the New World.* Reno: University of Nevada Press.

Douglass, William A. and Stanford Lyman. 1976. "L'ethnie: Structure, processus, et saillance." *Cahiers Internationale de Sociologie* 61: 342–358.

Doyle, Bertram W. 1936. "The Etiquette of Race Relations—Past, Present, and Future." *Journal of Negro Education* 5: 191–208.

Drake, St. Clair and Horace R. Cayton. 1962 [1945]. *Black Metropolis: A Study of Negro Life in a Northern City.* New York: Harper & Row.

D'Souza, Dinesh. 1995. *The End of Racism.* New York: Free Press.

Duany, Jorge. 2002. *The Puerto Rican Nation on the Move: Identities on the Island and in the United States.* Chapel Hill: University of North Carolina Press.

Dubinin, N. P. 1956. "Race and Contemporary Genetics." 68–94 in *Race, Science and Society,* edited by Leo Kuper. Paris: The Unesco Press.

Dublin, Thomas. 1993. *Immigrant Voices New Lives in America, 1773–1986.* Urbana: University of Illinois Press.

Dubofsky, Melvyn. 1969. *We Shall Be All: A History of the Industrial Workers of the World.* Chicago: Quadrangle.

Du Bois, W. E. B. 1961 [1903]. *The Souls of Black Folk.* New York: Fawcett World Library.

———. 1969 [1896]. *The Suppression of the African Slave-Trade to the United States of America, 1638–1870.* New York: Schocken Books.

———. 1970 [1909]. *The Negro American Family.* Cambridge, MA: MIT Press.

———. 1973 [1935]. *Black Reconstruction in America.* New York: Atheneum.

Dunn, L. C. and Theodor Dobzhansky. 1952. *Heredity, Race, and Society.* New York: The New American Library.

Duster, Troy. 1990. *Backdoor to Eugenics.* New York: Routledge.

Early, Gerald, ed. 1993. *Lure and Loathing: Essays on Race, Identity, and the Ambivalence of Assimilation.* New York: The Penguin Press.

Eckstein, Susan and Lorena Barberia. 2002. "Grounding Immigrant Generations in History: Cuban Americans and Their Transnational Ties." *International Migration Review* 36 (3): 799–837.

The Economist. 1990. "American Survey," September 29: 41–42.

Edsall, Thomas Byrne and Mary D. Edsall. 1991. "Race." *The Atlantic Monthly* 267 (5): 53–86.

Elkins, Stanley M. 1959. *Slavery: A Problem in American Institutional and Intellectual Life.* Chicago: The University of Chicago Press.

Erdmans, Mary Patrice. 1998. *Opposite Poles: Immigrants and Ethnics in Polish Chicago, 1976–1990.* University Park: Pennsylvania State University Press.

Erickson, Charlotte. 1972. *Invisible Immigrants: The Adaptation of English and Scottish Immigrants in Nineteenth-Century America.* Coral Gables, FL: University of Miami Press.

——. 1980. "English." 319–336 in *Harvard Encyclopedia of American Ethnic Groups,* edited by Stephan Thernstrom, Ann Orlov, and Oscar Handlin. Cambridge, MA: Harvard University Press.

Erie, Steven P. 1988. *Rainbow's End: Irish-Americans and the Dilemmas of Urban Machine Politics, 1840–1985.* Berkeley: University of California Press.

Eschbach, Karl, Khalil Supple, and C. Matthew Snipp. 1998. "Changes in Racial Identification and the Educational Attainment of American Indians, 1970–1990." *Demography* 35 (February): 35–43.

Espiritu, Yen Le. 1992. *Asian American Panethnicity.* Philadelphia: Temple University Press.

——. 2001. " 'We Don't Sleep Around Like White Girls Do': Family, Culture and Gender in Filipina American Lives." *Signs* 26 (2): 415–440.

——. 2002. "Filipino Navy Stewards and Filipina Health Care Professionals: Immigration, Work, and Family Relations." *Asian and Pacific Migration Journal* 11 (1): 47–66.

Esposito, Luigi and John W. Murphy. 1999. "Desensitizing Herbert Blumer's Work on Race Relations: Recent Applications of His Group Position Theory to the Study of Contemporary Race Prejudice." *The Sociologist Quarterly* 40 (3): 397–410.

Evans, J. A. S. 1996. "The Present State of Canada." *The Virginia Quarterly* 72 (3): 213–225.

Ewen, Elizabeth. 1980. "City Lights: Immigrant Women and the Rise of the Movies." *Signs* 5 (3): 45–65.

Ezorsky, Gertrude. 1991. *Racism and Justice: The Case for Affirmative Action.* Ithaca, NY: Cornell University Press.

Fairchild, Henry Pratt. 1926. *The Melting Pot Mistake.* Boston: Little, Brown.

Faist, Thomas. 2000. *The Volume and Dynamics of International Migration and Transnational Social Spaces.* Oxford, UK: Oxford University Press.

Falcon, Luis M., Douglas T. Gurak, and Mary G. Powers. 1990. "Labor Force Participation of Puerto Rican Women in Greater New York City." *Sociology and Social Research* 74 (2): 110–117.

Fallows, Marjorie R. 1979. *Irish Americans: Identity and Assimilation.* Englewood Cliffs, NJ: Prentice-Hall.

Farber, Bernard, Charles H. Mindel, and Bernard Lazerwitz. 1988. "The Jewish American Family." 400–437 in *Ethnic Families in America: Patterns and Variations,* edited by Charles H. Mindel, Robert W. Habenstein, and Roosevelt Wright, Jr. New York: Elsevier.

Farley, John E. 1982. *Majority-Minority Relations.* Englewood Cliffs, NJ: Prentice-Hall.

Farley, Reynolds. 1984. *Blacks and Whites: Narrowing the Gap?* Cambridge, MA: Harvard University Press.

——. 1990. "Blacks, Hispanics, and White Ethnic Groups: Are Blacks Uniquely Disadvantaged?" *The American Economic Review* 80 (2): 237–241.

——. 1999. "Racial Issues: Recent Trends in Residential Patterns and Intermarriage." 85–128 in *Diversity and Its Discontents: Cultural Conflict and Common Ground in Contemporary American Society,* edited by Neil J. Smelser and Jeffrey C. Alexander. Princeton, NJ: Princeton University Press.

Farley, Reynolds and Richard Alba. 2002. "The New Second Generation in the United States." *International Migration Review* 36 (3): 669–701.

Farley, Reynolds and Walter R. Allen. 1989. *The Color Line and the Quality of Life in America.* New York: Oxford University Press.

Farley, Reynolds and William H. Frey. 1994. "Changes in the Segregation of Whites From Blacks During the 1980s: Small Steps Toward a More Integrated Society." *American Sociological Review* 59 (1): 23–45.

Farley, Reynolds, Toni Richards, and Clarence Wurdock. 1980. "School Desegregation and White Flight: An Investigation of Competing Models and Their Discrepant Findings." *Sociology of Education* 53: 123–139.

Farley, Reynolds, Howard Schuman, Suzanne Biachi, Diane Colasyto, and Shirley Hatchett. 1978. "Chocolate City, Vanilla Suburbs: Will the Trend Toward Racially Separate Communities Continue?" *Social Science Research* 7 (December): 319–344.

Fass, Paula S. 1989. *Outside In: Minorities and the Transformation of American Education.* New York: Oxford University Press.

Feagin, Joe R. 1984. *Racial and Ethnic Relations.* Englewood Cliffs, NJ: Prentice-Hall.

——. 1991. "The Continuing Significance of Race: Antiblack Discrimination in Public Places." *American Sociological Review* 56 (1): 101–116.

Feinberg, William E. 1985. "Are Affirmative Action and Economic Growth Alternative Paths to Racial Equality?" *American Sociological Review* 50 (4): 561–571.

Femminella, Francis X., ed. 1985. *Irish and Italian Interaction.* New York: Italian-American Historical Association.

Fenton, Steve. 1999. *Ethnicity: Racism, Class, and Culture.* London: Macmillan.

Ferber, Abby L. 1998. *White Man Falling: Race, Gender, and White Supremacy.* Lanham, MD: Rowman & Littlefield.

Ferguson, Ronald F. 1996. "Shifting Challenges: Fifty Years of Economic Change Toward Black-White Earnings Equality." 76–111 in *An American Dilemma Revisited: Race Relations in a Changing World,* edited by Obie Clayton, Jr. New York: Russell Sage Foundation.

——. 2001. "Test-Score Trends Along Racial Lines, 1971 to 1996." 348–390 in *America Becoming: Racial Trends and Their Consequences,* vol. 1, edited by Neil J. Smelser, William Julius Wilson, and Faith Mitchell. Washington, DC: National Academy Press.

Fernández-Kelly, Patricia and Sara Curran. 2001. "Nicaraguans: Voices Lost, Voices Found." 127–155 in *Ethnicities: Children of Immigrants in America,* edited by Rubén Rumbaut and Alejandro Portes. Berkeley and New York: University of California Press and the Russell Sage Foundation.

Ferraro, Thomas. 1993. *Ethnic Passages: Literary Immigrants in Twentieth-Century America.* Chicago: The University of Chicago Press.

Fischer, Claude. 1996. *Inequality by Design: Cracking the Bell Curve Myth.* Princeton, NJ: Princeton University Press.

Fischer, David Hackett. 1989. *Albion's Seed: Four British Folkways in America.* New York: Oxford University Press.

Fishel, Leslie H., Jr. and Benjamin Quarles. 1970. *The Black American: A Brief Documentary History.* Glenview, IL: Scott, Foresman.

Fisher, Alan M. 1979. "Realignment of the Jewish Vote?" *Political Science Quarterly* 94: 97–116.

Fisher, Robert. 1959. *Twenty Years of Public Housing.* New York: Harper and Brothers.

Fishman, Joshua, ed. 1966. *Language Loyalty in the United States.* The Hague: Mouton.

Fishman, Joshua, Michael H. Gertner, Esther G. Lowy, and William G. Milán. 1985. *The Rise and Fall of the Ethnic Revival.* Berlin: Mouton.

Fishman, Sylvia Barack. 1987. *Learning About Learning: Insights on Contemporary Jewish Education From Jewish Population Studies.* Research Report 2, Center for Modern Jewish Studies, Brandeis University.

Fitzhugh, George. 1854. *Sociology for the South: Or the Failure of Free Society.* Salem, NH: Ayer Company.

Fitzpatrick, Joseph P. 1980. "Puerto Ricans." 858–867 in *Harvard Encyclopedia of American Ethnic Groups,* edited by Stephan Thernstrom, Ann Orlov, and Oscar Handlin. Cambridge, MA: Harvard University Press.

——. 1987. *Puerto Rican Americans: The Meaning of Migration to the Mainland.* Englewood Cliffs, NJ: Prentice-Hall.

Fixico, Donald. 1985. "Tribal Leaders and the Demand for Natural Energy Resources on Tribal Lands." 42–78 in *The Plains Indians of the Twentieth Century,* edited by Peter Iverson. Norman: University of Oklahoma Press.

——. 1986. *Termination and Relocation: Federal Indian Policy, 1945–1960.* Albuquerque: University of New Mexico Press.

——. 1998. *The Invasion of Indian Country in the Twentieth Century: American Capitalism and Tribal Natural Resources.* Boulder: University Press of Colorado.

Fligstein, Neil. 1981. *Going North: Migration of Blacks and Whites From the South, 1900–1950.* New York: Academic Press.

Flores, Juan. 1985. " 'Que Assimilated Brother, Yo So Asimilao': The Structuring of Puerto Rican Identity in the U.S." *Journal of Ethnic Studies* 13 (3): 1–16.

——. 2000. *From Bomba to Hip-Hop: Puerto Rican Culture and Latino Identity.* New York: Columbia University Press.

Foerster, Robert S. 1919. *The Italian Emigration of Our Times.* Cambridge, MA: Harvard University Press.

Fogel, Robert William. 1989. *Without Consent or Contract: The Rise and Fall of American Slavery.* New York: W.W. Norton.

Fogel, Robert William and Stanley L. Engerman. 1974. *Time on the Cross: The Economics of American Negro Slavery.* Boston: Little, Brown.

Fogelson, Raymond D. 1998. "Perspectives on Native American Identity." 40–59 in *Studying Native America: Problems and Prospects,* edited by Russell Thornton. Madison: University of Wisconsin Press.

Foner, Eric. 1988. *Reconstruction: America's Unfinished Revolution, 1863–1877.* New York: Harper & Row.

Foner, Nancy. 2000. *From Ellis Island to JFK: New York's Two Great Waves of Immigration.* New Haven, CT: Yale University Press.

Fong, Eric. 1996. "A Comparative Perspective on Residential Racial Segregation: American and Canadian Experiences." *The Sociological Quarterly* 69 (4): 575–598.

Fong, Timothy P. 1994. *The First Suburban Chinatown: The Remaking of Monterey Park, California.* Philadelphia: Temple University Press.

——. 1998. *The Contemporary Asian American Experience: Beyond the Model Minority.* Upper Saddle River, NJ: Prentice-Hall.

——. 2000. "The History of Asian Americans." 13–30 in *Asian Americans: Experiences and Perspectives,* edited by Timothy P. Fong and Larry H. Shinagawa. Upper Saddle River, NJ: Prentice-Hall.

Formisano, Ronald P. 1991. *Boston Against Busing: Race, Class, and Ethnicity in the 1960s and 1970s.* Chapel Hill: University of North Carolina Press.

Foster, Morris W. 1991. *Being Comanche: A Social History of an American Indian Community.* Tuscon: University of Arizona Press.

Foucault, Michel. 1979. *Discipline and Punish: The Birth of the Prison.* New York: Vintage Books.

Fox-Genovese, Elizabeth and Eugene D. Genovese. 1983. *Fruits of Merchant Capital: Slavery and Bourgeois Property in the Rise and Expansion of Capitalism.* New York: Oxford University Press.

Francis, E. K. 1947. "The Nature of the Ethnic Group." *American Journal of Sociology* 52 (5): 393–400.

——. 1951. "Minority Groups—A Revision of Concepts." *British Journal of Sociology* 2: 219–229.

——. 1976. *Interethnic Relations: An Essay in Sociological Theory.* New York: Elsevier.

Frankenberg, Erica, Chungmei Lee, and Gary Orfield. 2003. "A Multiracial Society With Segregated Schools: Are We Losing the Dream?" Cambridge, MA: The Civil Rights Project, Harvard University.

Franklin, John Hope. 1967. *From Slavery to Freedom: A History of Negro Americans.* New York: Alfred A. Knopf.

Franklin, Raymond S. 1991. *Shadows of Race and Class.* Minneapolis: University of Minnesota Press.

Frazier, E. Franklin. 1939. *The Negro Family in the United States.* Chicago: The University of Chicago Press.

——. 1949. *The Negro in the United States.* New York: Macmillan.

——. 1957. *Black Bourgeoisie: The Rise of a New Middle Class in the United States.* New York: The Free Press.

——. 1963. *The Negro Church in America.* New York: Schocken Books.

Fredrickson, George M. 1981. *White Supremacy: A Comparative Study in American and South African History.* New York: Oxford University Press.

Freeman, Leonard. 1969. *Public Housing: The Politics of Poverty.* New York: Holt, Rinehart, and Winston.

Frideres, James S. 1996. *Native Peoples of Canada.* Scarborough, Ont.: Prentice-Hall of Canada.

Friedman, Lawrence. 1978. *Government and Slum Housing.* New York: Arno Press.

Fuchs, Lawrence H. 1990. *The American Kaleidoscope: Race, Ethnicity, and the Civic Culture.* Hanover, NH: Wesleyan University Press.

Fugita, Stephen S. and David J. O'Brien. 1991. *Japanese American Ethnicity: The Persistence of Community.* Seattle: University of Washington Press.

Fukuda, Yoshiaki. 1990. *My Six Years of Internment: An Issei's Struggle for Justice.* San Francisco: The Konko Church.

Fullinwider, Robert K. 1980. *The Reverse Discrimination Controversy.* Totowa, NJ: Rowman and Littlefield.

Furer, Howard B. 1972. *The British in America 1578–1970: A Chronology and Fact Book.* Dobbs Ferry, NY: Oceana Publications.

Gabbacia, Donna. 1988. *Militants and Migrants: Rural Sicilians Become American Workers.* New Brunswick, NJ: Rutgers University Press.

——. 2000. *Italy's Many Diasporas: Elites, Exiles, and Workers of the World.* Seattle: University of Washington Press.

——. 2002. *Immigration and American Diversity: A Short Introduction.* Malden, MA: Blackwell Publishing.

Gabbacia, Donna and Franca Iacovetta, eds. 2002. *Women, Gender, and Transnational Lives: Italian Workers of the World.* New Providence, NJ: BPR Publishers.

Gallagher, Charles. 2003. "Playing the White Ethnic Card." 145–158 in *White Out: The Continuing Significance of Racism,* edited by Ashley Doane and Eduardo Bonilla-Silva. New York: Routledge.

Gambino, Richard. 1974. *Blood of My Blood.* New York: Anchor Books.

Gans, Herbert. 1956. "American Jewry Present and Future." *Commentary* 21 (5): 422–430.

——. 1962. *The Urban Villagers: Group and Class in the Life of Italian-Americans.* Glencoe, IL: The Free Press.

——. 1967. *The Levittowners: Ways of Life and Politics in a New Suburban Community.* New York: Pantheon Books.

——. 1979. "Symbolic Ethnicity: The Future of Ethnic Groups and Cultures in America." 193–220 in *On the Making of Americans: Essays in Honor of David Riesman,* edited by Herbert J. Gans, Nathan Glazer, Joseph R. Gusfield, and Christopher Jencks. Philadelphia: University of Pennsylvania Press.

——. 1985. "Ethnicity, Ideology, and the Insider Problem." *Contemporary Sociology* 14 (3): 303–304.

——. 1992. "Comment: Ethnic Invention and Acculturation, A Bumpy-Line Approach." *Journal of American Ethnic History* 12 (1): 42–52.

——. 1999. "The Possibility of a New Racial Hierarchy in the Twenty-first Century United States." 371–390 in *The Cultural Territories of Race,* edited by Michèle Lamont. Chicago and New York: University of Chicago Press and the Russell Sage Foundation.

Garcia, Maria Cristina. 1996. *Havana USA: Cuban Exiles and Cuban Americans in South Florida, 1959–1994.* Berkeley: University of California Press.

Garcia, Mario T. 1981. *Desert Immigrants: The Mexicans of El Paso, 1880–1920.* New Haven, CT: Yale University Press.

——. 1989. *Mexican Americans: Leadership, Ideology, and Identity, 1930–1960.* New Haven, CT: Yale University Press.

Garcia, Richard A. 1991. *Rise of the Mexican Middle Class: San Antonio, 1929–1941.* College Station: Texas A&M University Press.

Garrow, David J. 1978. *Protest at Selma: Martin Luther King, Jr., and the Voting Rights Act of 1965.* New Haven, CT: Yale University Press.

Gedicks, Al. 1993. *The New Resource Wars: Native and Environmental Struggles Against Multinational Corporations.* Boston: South End Press.

——. 2001. *Resources Rebels.* Boston: South End Press.

Geertz, Clifford. 1973. *The Interpretation of Culture.* New York: Basic Books.

Gellner, Ernest. 1983. *Nations and Nationalism.* Ithaca, NY: Cornell University Press.

Genovese, Eugene D. 1972. *Roll, Jordan, Roll: The World the Slaves Made*. New York: Pantheon Books.

——. 1979. *From Rebellion to Revolution: Afro-American Slave Revolts in the Making of the Modern World*. Baton Rouge: Louisiana State University Press.

Gerstle, Gary. 2001. *American Crucible: Race and Nation in the Twentieth Century*. Princeton, NJ: Princeton University Press.

Geschwender, James. 1978. *Racial Stratification in America*. Dubuque, IA: William C. Brown.

Gibson, Campbell J. and Emily Lennon. 1999. "Historical Census Statistics on the Foreign-Born Population of the United States: 1850–1990." Population Division Working Paper No. 29, U.S. Bureau of the Census. Washington, DC: Government Printing Office.

Giddens, Anthony. 1973. *The Class Structure of the Advanced Societies*. New York: Harper & Row.

——. 1984. *The Constitution of Society: Outline of a Theory of Structuration*. Berkeley: University of California Press.

Giddings, Franklin Henry. 1893. *Philanthropy and Social Progress*. New York: Thomas Y. Crowell.

Gilroy, Paul. 1987. *"There Ain't No Black in the Union Jack": The Cultural Politics of Race and Nation*. Chicago: University of Chicago Press.

Gitlin, Todd. 1993. "The Rise of 'Identity Politics.'" *Dissent* (Spring): 172–177.

Glazer, Nathan. 1957. *American Judaism*. Chicago: The University of Chicago Press.

——. 1975. *Affirmative Discrimination: Ethnic Inequality and Public Policy*. New York: Basic Books.

——. 1985. "On Jewish Forebodings." *Commentary* 80 (2): 32–36.

——. 1997. *We Are All Multiculturalists Now*. Cambridge, MA: Harvard University Press.

Glazer, Nathan and Daniel P. Moynihan. 1963. *Beyond the Melting Pot*. Cambridge, MA: MIT Press and Harvard University Press.

——. 1975. "Introduction." 1–26 in *Ethnicity: Theory and Experience*, edited by Nathan Glazer and Daniel P. Moynihan. Cambridge, MA: Harvard University Press.

Gleason, Philip. 1964. "The Melting Pot: Symbol of Fusion or Confusion?" *American Quarterly* 16 (1): 20–46.

——. 1983. "Identifying Identity: A Semantic History." *Journal of American History* 69 (4): 428–453.

——. 1991. "Minorities (Almost) All: The Minority Concept in American Social Thought." *American Quarterly* 43 (3): 392–424.

——. 1992. *Speaking of Diversity: Language and Ethnicity in Twentieth-Century America*. Baltimore: The John Hopkins University Press.

Glenn, Evelyn Nakano. 1986. *Issei, Nisei, War Bride: Three Generations of Japanese American Women in Domestic Service*. Philadelphia: Temple University Press.

——. 2000. "Citizenship and Inequality: Historical and Global Perspectives." *Social Problems* 47 (1): 1–10.

Glenn, Norvall D. 1982. "Interreligious Marriage in the United States." *Journal of Marriage and the Family* 44: 555–565.

Glenn, Susan A. 1990. *Daughters of the Shtetl: Life and Labor in the Immigrant Generation*. Ithaca, NY: Cornell University Press.

Gobineau, Comte Arthur de. 1915 [1853–1855]. *The Inequality of Human Races*. London: Heinemann.

Goering, John M. 1971. "The Emergence of Ethnic Interests: A Case of Serendipity." *Social Forces* 48 (March): 379–384.

——. 1986. "Minority Housing Needs and Civil Rights Enforcement." 195–215 in *Race, Ethnicity, and Minority Housing in the United States*, edited by Jamshid A. Momeni. Westport, CT: Greenwood Press.

Goffman, Erving. 1961. *Asylums: Essays on the Social Situation of Mental Patients and Other Inmates*. Garden City, NY: Doubleday.

Golab, Caroline. 1977. *Immigrant Destinations*. Philadelphia: Temple University Press.

Gold, Steven J. 1992. "Chinese-Vietnamese Entrepreneurs in California." Paper presented at the annual meeting of the American Sociological Association, Pittsburgh, PA.

——. 1995. *From the Worker's State to the Golden State: Jews From the Former Soviet Union in California.* Boston: Allyn and Bacon.

——. 1997. "Transnationalism and Vocabularies of Motive in International Migration: The Case of Israelis in the United States." *Sociological Perspectives* 40 (3): 409–427.

——. 2002. *The Israeli Diaspora.* Seattle: University of Washington Press.

Goldscheider, Calvin. 1986. *Jewish Continuity and Change.* Bloomington: Indiana University Press.

——. 2003. "Are American Jews Vanishing Again?" *Contexts* 2 (1): 18–24.

Goldscheider, Calvin and Alan S. Zuckerman. 1984. *The Transformation of the Jews.* Chicago: The University of Chicago Press.

Goldstein, Sidney and Alice Goldstein. 1996. *Jews on the Move: Implications for Jewish Identity.* Albany: State University of New York Press.

Gomez-Quiñones, Juan. 1990. *Chicano Politics: Reality and Promise, 1940–1990.* Albuquerque: University of New Mexico Press.

Gonzalez, David. 1992a. "What's the Problem With 'Hispanic'? Just Ask a 'Latino.'" *New York Times,* November 15: E6.

——. 1992b. "Dominican Immigration Alters Hispanic New York." *New York Times,* September 1: A1, A11.

Goodwyn, Lawrence. 1978. *The Populist Movement.* New York: Oxford University Press.

Gordon, Milton M. 1964. *Assimilation in American Life: The Role of Race, Religion, and National Origins.* New York: Oxford University Press.

Goren, Arthur A. 1980. "Jews." 571–598 in *Harvard Encyclopedia of American Ethnic Groups,* edited by Stephan Thernstrom, Ann Orlov, and Oscar Handlin. Cambridge, MA: Harvard University Press.

Gossett, Thomas. 1965. *Race: The History of an Idea in America.* Dallas: Southern Methodist University Press.

Gotham, Kevin Fox. 2002. *Race, Real Estate, and Uneven Development: The Kansas City Experience, 1900–2000.* Albany: State University of New York Press.

Graham, Ian Charles. 1956. *Colonists From Scotland: Emigration to North America, 1707–1783.* Ithaca, NY: Cornell University Press.

Grant, Madison. 1916. *The Passing of the Great Race.* New York: C. Scribner's Sons.

Graves, Joseph L., Jr. 2001. *The Emperor's New Clothes: Biological Theories of Race at the Millennium.* New Brunswick, NJ: Rutgers University Press.

Greeley, Andrew M. 1971. *Why Can't They Be Like Us? America's White Ethnic Groups.* New York: E.P. Dutton.

——. 1974. *Ethnicity in the United States: A Preliminary Reconnaissance.* New York: John Wiley and Sons.

——. 1975. "A Model for Ethnic Political Socialization." *American Journal of Political Science* 19: 187–206.

——. 1988. "The Success and Assimilation of Irish Protestants and Irish Catholics in the United States." *Sociology and Social Research* 72: 229–236.

Greeley, Andrew and William C. McCready. 1975. "The Transmission of Cultural Heritages: The Case of the Italians and the Irish." 209–235 in *Ethnicity: Theory and Experience,* edited by Nathan Glazer and Daniel P. Moynihan. Cambridge, MA: Harvard University Press.

Greeley, Andrew, William C. McCready, and Gary Theisen. 1980. *Ethnic Drinking Subcultures.* New York: Praeger.

Green, George N. 1992. "The Felix Longoria Affair." *The Journal of Ethnic Studies* 19 (3): 23–49.

Greene, Victor R. 1968. *The Slavic Community on Strike.* Notre Dame, IN: University of Notre Dame Press.

——. 1975. *For God and Country.* Madison: Wisconsin State Historical Society.

——. 1980. "Poles." 787–803 in *Harvard Encyclopedia of American Ethnic Groups,* edited by Stephan Thernstrom, Ann Orlov, and Oscar Handlin. Cambridge, MA: Harvard University Press.

——. 1987. *American Immigrant Leaders 1800–1910: Marginality and Identity.* Baltimore: The Johns Hopkins University Press.

———. 1990. "Old-time Folk Dancing and Music Among the Second Generation, 1920–50." 142–163 in *American Immigrants and Their Generations*, edited by Peter Kivisto and Dag Blanck. Urbana: University of Illinois Press.

Griswold, Wendy and Nathan Wright. 2004. "Cowbirds, Locals, and the Dynamic Endurance of Regionalism." *American Journal of Sociology* 109 (6): 1411–1451.

Griswold del Castillo, Richard. 1979. *The Los Angeles Barrio, 1850–1890: A Social History.* Berkeley: University of California Press.

Grossman, James. 1989. *Land of Hope: Chicago, Black Southerners, and the Great Migration.* Chicago: The University of Chicago Press.

Guibernau, Montserrat. 1999. *Nations Without States: Political Communities in a Global Age.* Cambridge, MA: Polity Press.

Gutierrez, Armando and Herbert Hirsch. 1970. "The Militant Challenge to the American Ethos: 'Chicanos' and 'Mexican Americans.' " *Social Science Quarterly* 53 (March): 830–845.

Gutierrez, David G. 1991. "Sin Fronteras? Chicanos, Mexican Americans, and the Emergence of the Contemporary Mexican Immigration Debate, 1968; 1978." *Journal of American Ethnic History* 10 (4): 5–37.

Gutman, Herbert. 1976. *The Black Family in Slavery and Freedom, 1750–1925.* New York: Pantheon Books.

Gyory, Andrew. 1998. *Closing the Gate: Race, Politics, and the Chinese Exclusion Act.* Chapel Hill: University of North Carolina Press.

Hacker, Andrew. 1992. *Two Nations: Black and White, Separate, Hostile, Unequal.* New York: Charles Scribner's Sons.

Haines, Herbert H. 1988. *Black Radicals and the Civil Rights Mainstream, 1954–1970.* Knoxville: The University of Tennessee Press.

Handlin, Oscar. 1948. *Race and Nationality in American Life.* Boston: Little, Brown.

———. 1959. *Immigration as a Factor in American History.* Englewood Cliffs, NJ: Prentice-Hall.

———. 1970. *Boston's Immigrants.* New York: Atheneum.

———. 1973. *The Uprooted.* Boston: Little, Brown.

Handlin, Oscar and Lillian Handlin. 1982. *A Restless People: Americans in Rebellion, 1770–1787.* Garden City, NY: Anchor Press.

Hanke, Lewis. 1970. *Aristotle and the American Indians.* Bloomington: Indiana University Press.

Hannerz, Ulf. 1969. *Soulside: Inquiries Into Ghetto Culture and Community.* New York: Columbia University Press.

Hansen, Marcus Lee. 1938. "The Problem of the Third Generation Immigrant." Rock Island, IL: Augustana Historical Society.

———. 1940a. *The Atlantic Migration, 1607–1860: A History of the Continuing Settlement of the United States.* Cambridge, MA: Harvard University Press.

———. 1940b. *The Immigrant in American History.* Cambridge, MA: Harvard University Press.

Harding, Sandra, ed. 1987. *Feminism and Methodology.* Bloomington: Indiana University Press.

Hargreaves, Alec. 1995. *Immigration, "Race," and Ethnicity in Contemporary France.* London: Routledge.

Hargreaves, Ian. 1996. "We Have Not Put the Racist Devil Behind Us." *New Statesman* 128 (4460): 52.

Harlan, Louis. 1983. *Booker T. Washington: The Wizard of Tuskegee, 1901–1915.* New York: Oxford University Press.

Harney, Robert F. 1976. "The Italian Experience in the United States." 1–18 in *A Handbook for Teachers of Italian*, edited by Anthony Mollica. New York: American Association of Teachers of Italian.

Harney, Robert F. and J. Vincenza Scarpaci, eds. 1981. *Little Italies in North America.* Toronto: The Multicultural History Society of Ontario.

Harrington, Michael. 1962. *The Other America: Poverty in the United States.* Baltimore: Penguin Books.

Hartigan, John, Jr. 1999. *Class Predicaments of Whiteness in Detroit.* Princeton, NJ: Princeton University Press.

Hauptman, Laurence M. and James D. Wherry. 1990. *The Pequots in Southern New England: The Fall and Rise of an American Indian Nation.* Norman: University of Oklahoma Press.

Hawgood, John A. 1940. *The Tragedy of German America: The Germans in the United States of America During the Nineteenth Century—and After.* New York: G.P. Putnam's Sons.

Hawkins, Freda. 1989. *Critical Years in Immigration: Canada and Australia Compared.* Kingston and Montreal: McGill-Queen's University Press.

Hechter, Michael. 1986. "Rational Choice and the Study of Race and Ethnic Relations." 264–279 in *Theories of Race and Ethnic Relations,* edited by John Rex and David Mason. Cambridge, UK: Cambridge University Press.

——. 2000. *Containing Nationalism.* New York: Oxford University Press.

Hechter, Michael, Debra Friedman, and M. Appelbaum. 1982. "A Theory of Ethnic Collective Action." *International Migration Review* 16: 412–434.

Heer, David M. 1990. *Undocumented Mexicans in the United States.* Cambridge, UK: Cambridge University Press.

Heilman, Samuel C. and Steven M. Cohen. 1989. *Cosmopolitans and Parochials: Modern Orthodox Jewish America.* Chicago: The University of Chicago Press.

Heller, Scott. 1991. "Anthropologists Examine Commemorations of Columbus's Fateful Voyage." *The Chronicle of Higher Education* 38 (17): A9–A10.

Herberg, Will. 1955. *Protestant-Catholic-Jew: An Essay in American Religious Sociology.* Garden City, NY: Doubleday.

Hero, Rodney E. 1992. *Latinos and the U.S. Political System: Two-Tiered Pluralism.* Philadelphia: Temple University Press.

Herrnstein, Richard J. and Charles Murray. 1994. *The Bell Curve: Intelligence and Class Structure in American Life.* New York: The Free Press.

Herskovits, Melville J. 1941. *The Myth of the Negro Past.* New York: Harper and Brothers.

Hertzberg, Arthur. 1989a. *The Jews in America. Four Centuries of an Uneasy Encounter: A History.* New York: Simon and Schuster.

——. 1989b. "The End of American Jewish History." *New York Review of Books* 36: 26–30.

Heyman, Josiah McC. 1991. *Life and Labor on the Border: Working People of Northeastern Sonora, Mexico, 1886–1986.* Tucson: University of Arizona Press.

Higgs, Robert. 1978. "Landless by Law: Japanese Immigrants in California Agriculture to 1941." *Journal of Economic History* 38 (1): 205–225.

Higham, John. 1970. *Strangers in the Land.* New York: Atheneum.

——, ed. 1978. *Ethnic Leadership in America.* Baltimore: The Johns Hopkins University Press.

——. 1982. "Current Trends in the Study of Ethnicity in the United States." *Journal of American Ethnic History* 2 (1): 5–15.

——. 1999. "Cultural Responses to Immigration." 39–61 in *Diversity and Its Discontents,* edited by Neil J. Smelser and Jeffrey C. Alexander. Princeton, NJ: Princeton University Press.

Hill, Herbert. 1966. *Anger, and Beyond: The Negro Writer in the United States.* New York: Harper & Row.

——. 1973. "Anti-Oriental Agitation and the Rise of Working-Class Racism." *Transaction* 10 (2): 43–54.

Hirata, Lucie Cheny. 1975. "Free, Indentured, Enslaved: Chinese Prostitutes in Nineteenth Century America." *Signs* 5 (Autumn): 3–29.

Hirsch, Arnold R. 1998. *Making the Second Ghetto: Race and Housing in Chicago, 1940–1960.* Chicago: University of Chicago Press.

Hirschman, Charles. 1983. "America's Melting Pot Reconsidered." *Annual Review of Sociology* 9: 397–423.

"The Hispanic Population in the United States: March 1991." *Current Population Reports,* Series p. 20, no. 455. Washington, DC: Government Printing Office.

Hobsbawm, E. J. 1959. *Primitive Rebels: Studies in Archaic Forms of Social Movement in the 19th and 20th Centuries.* New York: W.W. Norton.

——. 1969. *Industry and Empire*. New York: Penguin Books.

——. 1983. "Introduction: Inventing Traditions." 1–14 in *The Invention of Tradition*, edited by Eric Hobsbawm and Terence Ranger. Cambridge, UK: Cambridge University Press.

——. 1991. "The Perils of the New Nationalism." *The Nation*, November 4: 537–556.

Hochschild, Jennifer. 1985. *Thirty Years After Brown*. Washington, DC: Joint Center for Political Studies.

——. 1995. *Facing Up to the American Dream: Race, Class, and the Soul of the Nation*. Princeton, NJ: Princeton University Press.

Hoffman, Abraham. 1974. *Unwanted Mexican Americans in the Great Depression: Repatriation Pressures, 1929–1938*. Tucson: University of Arizona Press.

Holli, Melvin G. 1981. "The Great War Sinks Chicago's German Kultur." 460–512 in *Ethnic Chicago*, edited by Peter d'A. Jones and Melvin G. Holli. Grand Rapids, MI: Eerdmans.

Holloway, Joseph E., ed. 1990. *Africanisms in American Culture*. Bloomington: Indiana University Press.

Holmes, Colin. 1988. *John Bull's Island: Immigration and British Society, 1871–1971*. London: Macmillan.

Holt, Hamilton, ed. 1991 [1906]. *Life Stories of Undistinguished Americans, as Told by Themselves* (introduction by Werner Sollors). New York: Routledge.

Hondagneu-Sotelo, Pierrette. 2001. *Doméstica: Immigrant Workers Cleaning Up and Caring in the Shadows of Affluence*. Berkeley: University of California Press.

Horowitz, Donald L. 1985. *Ethnic Groups in Conflict*. Berkeley: University of California Press.

Horowitz, Ruth. 1983. *Honor and the American Dream: Culture and Identity in a Chicano Community*. New Brunswick, NJ: Rutgers University Press.

Horton, Hayward Derrick and Melvin E. Thomas. 1998. "Race, Class, and Family Structure: Differences in Housing Values for Black and White Homeowners." *Sociological Inquiry* 68 (1): 114–136.

Hosokawa, Bill. 1982. *JACL in Quest in Justice*. New York: William Morrow.

Hout, Michael and Joshua R. Goldstein. 1994. "How 4.5 Million Irish Immigrants Became 40 Million Irish Americans: Demographic and Subjective Aspects of the Ethnic Composition of White Americans." *American Sociological Review* 59 (1): 64–82.

Howe, Irving. 1976. *World of Our Fathers*. New York: Harcourt Brace Jovanovich.

Hraba, Joseph. 1979. *American Ethnicity*. Itasca, IL: F.E. Peacock Publishers.

Hsu, Madeline Yuan-yin. 2000. *Dreaming of Gold, Dreaming of Home: Transnationalism and Migration Between the United States and South China, 1882–1942*. Stanford, CA: Stanford University Press.

Huggins, Nathan Irvin. 1971. *Harlem Renaissance*. New York: Oxford University Press.

Hughes, Everett C. 1943. *French Canada in Transition*. Chicago: The University of Chicago Press.

Hughes, Everett C. and Helen MacGill Hughes. 1952. *Where Peoples Meet: Racial and Ethnic Frontiers*. Glencoe, IL: The Free Press.

Hughes, Henry. 1854. *A Treatise on Sociology, Theoretical and Practical*. Philadelphia: Lippincott and Grambo.

Hurh, Won Moo. 1998. *The Korean Americans*. Westport, CT: Greenwood Press.

Hurh, Won Moo and Kwang Chang Kim. 1984. *Korean Immigrants in America: A Structural Analysis of Ethnic Confinement and Adhesive Adaptation*. Cranbury, NJ: Fairleigh Dickinson University Press.

——. 1989. "The 'Success' Image of Asian Americans: Its Validity and Its Practical and Theoretical Implications." *Ethnic and Racial Studies* 12 (4): 512–538.

——. 1990. "Religious Participation of Korean Immigrants in the United States." *Journal for the Scientific Study of Religion* 29 (March): 19–34.

Hurston, Zora Neale. 1978 [1937]. *Their Eyes Were Watching God*. Urbana: University of Illinois Press.

Hutchinson, Edward P. 1956. *Immigrants and Their Children, 1850–1950*. New York: John Wiley and Sons.

Hutchison, Ray. 1992. "Immigration and Family Networks in Chicago's Hispanic Community." Paper presented at the annual meeting of the American Sociological Association, Pittsburgh, PA.

Hwang, Sean-Shongend and Steve H. Murdock. 1988. "Residential Segregation and Ethnic Identification Among Hispanics in Texas." *Urban Affairs Quarterly* 23 (3): 329–345.

Hymowitz, Kay S. 1993. "Multiculturalism Is Anti-culture." *New York Times*, March 25: A15.

Iamurri, Gabriel A. 1951. *The True Story of an Immigrant.* Boston: Christopher Publishing House.

Ignatiev, Noel. 1996. *How the Irish Became White.* New York: Routledge.

Indian Health Service. 1987. *Chart Book Series.* Washington, DC: Department of Health and Human Services.

Isaacs, Harold R. 1975. *Idols of the Tribe: Group Identity and Political Change.* New York: Harper & Row.

Isajiw, Wsevolod W. 1979. *Definitions of Ethnicity. Occasional Papers in Ethnic and Immigration Studies.* Toronto: The Multicultural History Society of Ontario.

Ivey, Mike. 1990. "Report Targets Racism as Basis for Indian Treaty Rights Tension." *Capital Times* (Madison, WI), January 17: E14.

Jackson, Helen Hunt. 1881. *A Century of Dishonor.* Boston: Roberts Brothers.

Jacobson, Matthew Frye. 1998. *Whiteness of a Different Color: European Immigrants and the Alchemy of Race.* Cambridge, MA: Harvard University Press.

Jacoby, Tamara, ed. 2004. *Reinventing the Melting Pot: The New Immigrants and What It Means to Be American.* New York: Basic Books.

Jaret, Charles. 1979. "The Greek, Italian, and Jewish American Press: A Comparative Analysis." *Journal of Ethnic Studies* 7: 47–70.

——. 1999. "Troubled by Newcomers: Anti-Immigrant Attitudes and Action During Two Eras of Main Immigration to the United States." *Journal of Asian Ethnic History* 18 (3): 9–39.

Jarvenpa, Robert. 1985. "The Political Economy and Political Ethnicity of American Indian Adaptations and Identities." *Ethnic and Racial Studies* 8 (1): 29–48.

Jasso, G. and M. R. Rosenzweig. 1990. *The New Chosen People.* New York: Russell Sage Foundation.

Jaynes, Gerald David and Robin M. Williams, Jr., eds. 1989. *A Common Destiny: Blacks and American Society.* Washington, DC: National Academy Press.

Jen, Gish. 1991. *Typical American.* Boston: Houghton Mifflin.

Jenkins, J. Craig and Craig M. Eckert. 1986. "Channeling Black Insurgency: Elite Patronage and Professional Social Movement Organizations in the Development of the Black Movement." *American Sociological Review* 51 (December): 812–829.

Jennings, Francis. 1976. *The Invasion of America: Indians, Colonialism, and the Cant of Conquest.* New York: W.W. Norton.

Jiobu, Robert M. 1988. *Ethnicity and Assimilation: Blacks, Chinese, Filipinos, Japanese, Koreans, Mexicans, Vietnamese, and Whites.* Albany: State University of New York Press.

Jo, Moon H. and Daniel D. Mast. 1993. "Changing Images of Asian Americans." *International Journal of Politics, Culture and Society* 6 (3): 417–441.

Johnson, Troy, Duane Champagne, and Joane Nagel. 1997. "American Indian Activism and Transformation: Lessons From Alcatraz." 9–44 in *American Indian Activism*, edited by Troy Johnson, Joane Nagel, and Duane Champagne. Urbana: University of Illinois Press.

Jones, LeRoi. 1963. *Blues People: The Negro Experience in White America and the Music That Developed From It.* New York: William Morrow.

Jones, Maldwyn Allen. 1960. *American Immigration.* Chicago: University of Chicago Press.

——. 1980. "Scotch-Irish." 895–908 in *Harvard Encyclopedia of American Ethnic Groups*, edited by Stephan Thernstrom, Ann Orlov, and Oscar Handlin. Cambridge, MA: Harvard University Press.

Joppke, Christian and Ewa Morawska, eds. 2003. *Toward Assimilation and Citizenship: Immigrants in Liberal Nation States.* New York: Palgrave Macmillan.

Jordon, Winthrop D. 1968. *White Over Black: American Attitudes Toward the Negro, 1550–1812*. Chapel Hill: University of North Carolina Press.

Jorgensen, Joseph G. 1984. "Native American and Rural Anglos: Conflicts and Cultural Responses to Energy Developments." *Human Organization* 43 (Summer): 178–185.

Josephy, Alvin M., Jr. 1969. *The Indian Heritage of America*. New York: Alfred A. Knopf.

———. 1971. *The Nez Perce Indians and the Opening of the Northwest*. New Haven, CT: Yale University Press.

Kahn, Arcadus. 1978. "Economic Choices and Opportunities: The Jewish Immigrants, 1880–1914." *Journal of Economic History* 38 (March): 235–251.

Kallen, Horace M. 1924. *Culture and Democracy in the United States: Studies in the Group Psychology of the American People*. Salem, NH: Ayer Company.

Kamphoefner, Walter D. 1987. *The Westfalians: From Germany to Missouri*. Princeton, NJ: Princeton University Press.

Kandel, William and Douglas S. Massey. 2002. "The Culture of Mexican Migration: A Theoretical and Empirical Analysis." *Social Forces* 80 (3): 981–1004.

Kantowicz, Edward R. 1975. *Polish-American Politics in Chicago, 1888–1940*. Chicago: University of Chicago Press.

Kashima, Tetsuden. 1980. "Japanese-American Internees Return, 1945 to 1955: Readjustment and Social Amnesia." *Phylon* 41 (Summer): 107–115.

Kasinitz, Philip, John Mollenkopf, and Mary C. Waters. 2002. "Becoming American/Becoming New Yorkers: Immigrant Incorporation in a Majority Minority City." *International Migration Review* 36 (4): 1020–1036.

Katz, Daniel and Kenneth Braly. 1933. "Racial Stereotypes of One Hundred College Students." *Journal of Abnormal and Social Psychology* 28: 280–290.

Katz, Michael B. 1989. *The Underserving Poor: From the War on Poverty to the War on Welfare*. New York: Pantheon Books.

Katzman, David M. 1973. *Before the Ghetto: Black Detroit in the Nineteenth Century*. Urbana: University of Illinois Press.

Katznelson, Ira. 1981. *City Trenches: Urban Politics and the Patterning of Class in the United States*. New York: Pantheon Books.

Kaufman, Debra Renee. 1991. *Rachel's Daughter: Newly Orthodox Jewish Women*. New Brunswick, NJ: Rutgers University Press.

Kaups, Matti. 1986. "A Commentary Concerning the Legend of St. Urho." *Finnish Americana* 7: 13–17.

Kedourie, Eli. 1985. *Nationalism*. London: Hutchinson.

Keil, Charles. 1979. "Class and Ethnicity in Polish America." *Journal of Ethnic Studies* (Summer): 37–45.

Keil, Harmut and John B. Jentz, eds. 1983. *German Workers in Industrial Chicago, 1850–1910: A Comparative Perspective*. DeKalb: Northern Illinois University Press.

Kennedy, Ruby Jo Reeves. 1944. "Single or Triple Melting-Pot? Intermarriage Trends in New Haven, 1870–1940." *American Journal of Sociology* 49 (4): 331–339.

Kerr, Louise Año Nuevo. 1984. "Mexican Chicago: Chicano Assimilation Aborted, 1939–1954." 269–298 in *Ethnic Chicago*, edited by Melvin G. Holli and Peter d'A. James. Grand Rapids, MI: William B. Eerdmans.

Kessner, Thomas. 1977. *The Golden Door: Italian and Jewish Mobility in New York City, 1880–1915*. New York: Oxford University Press.

Kibria, Nazli. 1993. *Family Tightrope: The Changing Lives of Vietnamese Americans*. Princeton, NJ: Princeton University Press.

———. 2003. *Becoming Asian American: Second-Generation Chinese and Korean American Identities*. Baltimore, MD: The Johns Hopkins University Press.

Killian, Lewis M. 1970. "Herbert Blumer's Contributions to Race Relations." 179–190 in *Human Nature and Collective Behavior: Papers in Honor of Herbert Blumer*, edited by Tamotsu Shibutani. New Brunswick, NJ: Transaction Books.

———. 1975. *The Impossible Revolution, Phase II: Black Power and the American Dream*. New York: Random House.

———. 1984. "Organization, Rationality, and Spontaneity in the Civil Rights Movement." *American Sociological Review* 49 (December): 770–783.

——. 1991. "Gandhi, Frederick Douglass and Affirmative Action." *International Journal of Politics, Culture, and Society* 5 (2): 167–182.

Kilson, Martin. 1983. "The Black Bourgeoisie Revisited: From E. Franklin Frazier to the Present." *Dissent* 30 (Winter): 85–96.

Kim, Hyung-chan. 1977. "The History and Role of the Church in the Korean American Community." 47–63 in *The Korean Diaspora*, edited by Hyung-chan Kim. Santa Barbara, CA: ABC-Clio.

Kim, Illsoo. 1981. *New Urban Immigrants: The Korean Community in New York.* Princeton, NJ: Princeton University Press.

Kim, Kwang Chung and Won Moo Hurh. 1985. "Ethnic Resources Utilization of Korean Immigrant Entrepreneurs in the Chicago Minority Area." *International Migration Review* 19 (1): 82–111.

——. 1992. "Generation Differences in Korean Immigrants' Life Experiences in the United States." Paper presented at the American Sociological Association annual meeting, Pittsburgh, PA.

Kinkead, Gwen. 1992. *Chinatown: A Portrait of a Closed Society.* New York: HarperCollins.

Kinlock, Graham C. 1974. *The Dynamics of Race Relations: A Sociological Analysis.* New York: McGraw-Hill.

Kitano, Harry H. L. 1969. *Japanese Americans: The Evolution of a Subculture.* Englewood Cliffs, NJ: Prentice-Hall.

——. 1988. "The Japanese American Family." 258–275 in *Ethnic Families in America: Patterns and Variations*, edited by Charles H. Mindell, Robert W. Habenstein, and Roosevelt Wright, Jr. New York: Elsevier.

——. 1991. *Race Relations.* Englewood Cliffs, NJ: Prentice-Hall.

Kitano, Harry H. L. and Roger Daniels. 1988. *Asian Americans: Emerging Minorities.* Englewood Cliffs, NJ: Prentice-Hall.

Kitano, Harry H. L., Wai-tsang Yeung, Lynn Chai, and Herb Hatanaka. 1984. "Asian American Interracial Marriage." *Journal of Marriage and the Family* 46 (February): 179–190.

Kivisto, Peter. 1978. "Sumner on Race Relations: An Example of a Theoretical Short-Circuit in the Quest for Certitude." *Free Inquiry* 6 (2): 48–59.

——. 1984. *Immigrant Socialists in the United States: The Case of Finns and the Left.* Rutherford, NJ: Fairleigh Dickinson University Press.

——. 1986. "An Historical Review of Public Housing Policies and Their Impact on Minorities." 1–18 in *Race, Ethnicity, and Housing in the United States*, edited by Jamshid Momeni. Westport, CT: Greenwood Press.

——. 1989. "Overview: Thinking About Ethnicity." 11–23 in *The Ethnic Enigma*, edited by Peter Kivisto. Philadelphia: The Balch Institute Press.

——. 1990. "The Transplanted Then and Now: The Reorientation of Immigration Studies From the Chicago School to the New Social History." *Ethnic and Racial Studies* 13 (4): 455–481.

——. 1991. "What Did Americanization Mean for the Finns?" Paper presented at the Making of Finnish America Conference, University of Minnesota.

——. 1993. "Religions and the New Immigrants." 92–108 in *A Future for Religion? New Paradigms for Social Analysis*, edited by William H. Swatos, Jr. Newbury Park, CA: Sage Publications.

——. 2001. "Theorizing Transnational Immigration: A Critical Review of Current Efforts." *Ethnic and Racial Studies* 24 (4): 549–577.

——. 2002. *Multiculturalism in a Global Society.* Malden, MA: Blackwell.

——, ed. 2005. *Incorporating Diversity: Rethinking Assimilation in a Multicultural Age.* Boulder, CO: Paradigm Publishers.

Kivisto, Peter and Dag Blanck, eds. 1990. *American Immigrants and Their Generations.* Urbana: University of Illinois Press.

Kivisto, Peter and Ben Nefzger. 1993. "Symbolic Ethnicity and American Jews: The Relationship of Ethnic Identity to Behavior and Group Affiliation." *The Social Science Journal* 30 (1): 1–12.

Knottnerus, David and David Loconto. 2003. "Strategic Ritualization and Ethnicity: A Typology and Analysis of Ritual Enactments in an Italian Community." *Sociological Spectrum* 23 (4): 425–461.

Koopmans, Ruud and Paul Statham. 1999. "Challenging the Liberal Nation-State? Postnationalism, Multiculturalism, and the Collective Claims Making of Migrants and Ethnic Minorities in Britain and Germany." *American Journal of Sociology* 105 (3): 652–696.

Korman, Gerd. 1967. *Industrialization, Immigrants, and Americanizers: The View From Milwaukee, 1866–1921.* Madison: State Historical Society of Wisconsin.

Kosmin, Barry, Sidney Goldstein, Joseph Waksberg, Nava Lerer, Ariella Keysar, and Jeffrey Scheckner. 1991. *Highlights of the CJF 1990 National Jewish Population Survey.* New York: Council of Jewish Federations.

Kovel, Joel. 1970. *White Racism: A Psychohistory.* New York: Vintage Books.

Kristeva, Julia. 1993. *Nations Without Nationalism.* New York: Columbia University Press.

Krysan, Maria and Reynolds Farley. 2002. "The Residential Preferences of Blacks: Do They Explain Persistent Segregation?" *Social Forces* 80 (3): 937–980.

Kuo, Chia-Ling. 1977. *Social and Political Change in New York's Chinatown: The Role of Voluntary Associations.* New York: Praeger.

Kuper, Leo. 1975. *Race, Class, and Power: Ideology and Revolutionary Change in Plural Societies.* Chicago: Aldine Publishing.

Kurashige, Lon. 2002. *Japanese American Celebration and Conflict: A History of Ethnic Identity and Festival, 1934–1990.* Berkeley: University of California Press.

Kwoh, Beulah Ong. 1947. "The Occupational Status of American-Born Chinese Male Graduates." *American Journal of Sociology* 53 (3): 192–200.

Kwong, Peter. 1987. *The New Chinatown.* New York: Hill and Wang.

LaBarre, Weston. 1975. *The Peyote Cult.* New York: Schocken.

Lal, Barbara Ballis. 1983. "Perspectives on Ethnicity: Old Wine in New Bottles." *Ethnic and Racial Studies* 6 (2): 154–173.

———. 1986. "The 'Chicago School' of American Sociology, Symbolic Interactionism, and Race Relations Theory." 280–298 in *Theories of Race and Ethnic Relations,* edited by John Rex and David Mason. Cambridge, UK: Cambridge University Press.

———. 1990. *The Romance of Culture in an Urban Civilization.* London: Routledge.

Lamphere, Louise, ed. 1992. *Structuring Diversity: Ethnographic Perspectives on the New Immigration.* Chicago: The University of Chicago Press.

Landry, Bart. 1987. *The New Black Middle Class.* Berkeley: University of California Press.

Lane, Charles. 1994. "The Tainted Sources of *The Bell Curve.*" *New York Review of Books* December 1: 14–19.

Langer, Elinor. 1990. "The American Neo-Nazi Movement Today." *The Nation* (July 16/23): 82–107.

LaSorte, Michael. 1985. *LaMerica: Images of Italian Greenhorn Experience.* Philadelphia: Temple University Press.

Lavender, Abraham. 1977. *A Coat of Many Colors: Jewish Subcommunities in the Unites States.* Westport, CT: Greenwood Press.

Lavender, Abraham D. and John M. Forsyth. 1976. "The Sociological Study of Minority Groups as Reflected by Leading Sociological Journals: Who Gets Studied and Who Gets Neglected?" *Ethnicity* 3: 338–398.

Lazerwitz, Bernard and Louis Rowitz. 1964. "The Three-Generations Hypothesis." *American Journal of Sociology* 69 (March): 529–538.

Leacock, Eleanor Burke and Nancy Oestreich Lurie, eds. 1988. *North American Indians in Historical Perspective.* Prospect Heights, IL: Waveland Press.

Lee, Dong Ok. 1992. "Commodification of Ethnicity: The Sociospatial Reproduction of Immigrant Entrepreneurs." *Urban Affairs Quarterly* 28 (December): 258–275.

Lee, Erika. 2002. "The Chinese Exclusion Example: Race, Immigration, and American Gatekeeping, 1882–1924." *Journal of American Ethnic History* 21 (3): 36–62.

Lee, Jennifer. 2002. *Civility in the City: Blacks, Jews, and Koreans in Urban America.* Cambridge, MA: Harvard University Press.

Lee, Rose Hum. 1949. "The Decline of Chinatown in the U.S." *American Journal of Sociology* 54 (5): 425–433.

Legters, Lyman H. and Fremont J. Lyden, eds. 1994. *American Indian Policy: Self-Governance and Economic Development.* Westport, CT: Greenwood Press.

Lemann, Nicholas. 1991. *The Promised Land: The Great Black Migration and How It Changed America.* New York: Alfred A. Knopf.

Leonard, Karen. 1991. *Ethnic Choices: California's Punjabi-Mexican Americans.* Philadelphia: Temple University Press.

Levine, Edward M. 1966. *The Irish and Irish Politicians: A Study of Cultural and Social Alienation.* Notre Dame, IN: University of Notre Dame Press.

Levine, Gene N. and Darrel M. Montero. 1973. "Socioeconomic Mobility Among Three Generations of Japanese Americans." *Journal of Social Issues* 29 (2): 33–48.

Levine, Gene N. and Colbert Rhodes. 1981. *The Japanese American Community: A Three-Generation Study.* New York: Praeger.

Levine, Lawrence W. 1977. *Black Culture and Black Consciousness.* New York: Oxford University Press.

LeVine, Robert A. and Donald T. Campbell. 1972. *Ethnocentrism: Theories of Conflict, Ethnic Attitudes and Group Behavior.* New York: John Wiley and Sons.

Levitan, Sar. and Robert Taggart. 1976. *The Promise of Greatness.* Cambridge, MA: Harvard University Press.

Levitt, Peggy. 2001. *The Transnational Villagers.* Berkeley: University of California Press.

Lewis, David Levering. 1981. *When Harlem Was in Vogue.* New York: Alfred A. Knopf.

———. 2001. *W. E. B. DuBois: The Fight for Equality and the American Century, 1919–1963.* Topeka, KS: Sagebrush Educational Resources.

Lian, Jason Z. and David Ralph Matthews. 1998. "Does the Vertical Mosaic Still Exist? Ethnicity and Income in Canada." *The Canadian Review of Sociology and Anthropology* 35 (4): 461–481.

Lieberson, Stanley. 1985. "Unhyphenated Whites in the United States." 159–180 in *Ethnicity and Race in the U.S.A.: Toward the Twenty-First Century.* London: Routledge and Kegan Paul.

Lieberson, Stanley and Mary C. Waters. 1985. "Ethnic Mixtures in the United States." *Sociology and Social Research* 70: 43–52.

———. 1986. "Ethnic Groups in Flux: The Changing Ethnic Responses of American Whites." *The Annals of the American Academy of Political and Social Science* 487 (September): 79–91.

———. 1988. *From Many Strands: Ethnic and Racial Groups in Contemporary America.* New York: Russell Sage Foundation.

Liebman, Arthur. 1979. *Jews and the Left.* New York: John Wiley and Sons.

Liebman, Charles S. 1973. *The Ambivalent American Jew: Politics, Religion, and Family in American Jewish Life.* Philadelphia: The Jewish Publication Society of America.

Liebow, Elliot. 1967. *Tally's Corner: A Study of Negro Streetcorner Men.* Boston: Little, Brown.

Light, Ivan. 1972. *Ethnic Enterprise in America: Business and Welfare Among Chinese, Japanese, and Blacks.* Berkeley: University of California Press.

Light, Ivan and Edna Bonacich. 1988. *Immigrant Entrepreneurs: Koreans in Los Angeles, 1965–1982.* Berkeley: University of California Press.

Light, Ivan and Steven J. Gold. 2000. *Ethnic Economies.* San Diego, CA: Academic Press.

Limerick, Patricia Nelson. 1987. *The Legacy of Conquest: The Unbroken Past of the American West.* New York: W.W. Norton.

Lin, Jan. 1998. *Reconstructing Chinatown: Ethnic Enclave, Global Change.* Minneapolis: University of Minnesota Press.

Lincoln, C. Eric and Lawrence H. Mamiya. 1990. *The Black Church in the African American Experience.* Durham, NC: Duke University Press.

Lindemann, Albert S. 1991. *The Jew Accused: Three Anti-Semitic Affairs (Dreyfus, Beilis, Frank) 1894–1915.* Cambridge, UK: Cambridge University Press.

Lipset, Seymour Martin. 1963. *The First New Nation: The United States in Historical and Comparative Perspective.* New York: Basic Books.

————. 1990. *Continental Divide: Values and Institutions of the United States and Canada*. New York: Routledge.

Lipset, Seymour Martin and William Schneider. 1978. "The Bakke Case: How Would It Be Decided at the Court of Public Opinion?" *Public Opinion* (March/April): 38–44.

Lipsitz, George. 1998. *The Possessive Investment in Whiteness: How White People Profit From Identity Politics*. Philadelphia: Temple University Press.

Litwack, Leon F. 1979. *Been in the Storm So Long: The Aftermath of Slavery*. New York: Alfred A. Knopf.

Livingstone, Frank B. 1962. "On the Nonexistence of Human Races." *Current Anthropology* 3 (3): 279–281.

Lobo, Susan and Kurt Peters, eds. 2001. *American Indians and the Urban Experience*. Walnut Creek, CA: Alta Mira Press.

Lockhart, Audrey. 1976. *Some Aspects of Emigration From Ireland to the North American Colonies Between 1600 and 1775*. New York: Arno Press.

Lockwood, William W. 1954. *The Economic Development of Japan: Growth and Structural Change, 1868–1938*. Princeton, NJ: Princeton University Press.

Loewen, James W. 1988. *The Mississippi Chinese: Between Black and White*. Prospect Heights, IL: Waveland Press.

Long, Larry and Diane DiAve. 1981. "Suburbanization of Blacks." *American Demographics* 3: 16–44.

Lopata, Helena Znaniecki. 1994. *Polish Americans*, 2nd ed. New Brunswick, NJ: Transaction Publishers.

López, David E. and Ricardo D. Stanton-Salazar. 2001. "Mexican Americans: A Second Generation at Risk." 57–90 in *Ethnicities: Children of Immigrants in America*, edited by Rubén Rombaut and Alejandro Portes. Berkeley and New York: University of California Press and the Russell Sage Foundation.

López, Ian F. Haney. 2003. *Racism on Trial: The Chicano Fight for Justice*. Cambridge, MA: Harvard University Press.

Lopreato, Joseph. 1970. *Italian Americans*. New York: Random House.

————. 1990. "From Social Evolution to Biocultural Evolutionism." *Sociological Forum* 5 (2): 187–212.

Lopreato, Joseph and Timothy Crippen. 1999. *The Crisis in Sociology: The Need for Darwin*. New Brunswick, NJ: Transaction Publishers.

Luebke, Frederick L. 1990. *Germans in the New World: Essays in the History of Immigration*. Urbana: University of Illinois Press.

Lurie, Nancy O. 1968. "Historical Background." 49–81 in *The American Indian Today*. Baltimore: Penguin Books

Lyman, Stanford M. 1972. *The Black American in Sociological Thought*. New York: Capricorn Books.

————. 1974. *Chinese Americans*. New York: Random House.

————. 1977. *The Asian in North America*. Santa Barbara, CA: ABC-Clio.

————. 1984. "Interactionism and the Study of Race Relations at the Macro-sociological Level: The Contribution of Herbert Blumer." *Symbolic Interaction* 7 (1): 107–120.

————. 1986. *Chinatown and Little Tokyo: Power, Conflict, and Community Among Chinese and Japanese Immigrants in America*. Millwood, NY: Associated Faculty Press.

————. 1990a. "The Drama in the Routine: A Prolegomenon to a Praxiological Sociology." *Sociological Theory* 8 (2): 216–223.

————. 1990b. "Race, Sex and Servitude: Images of Blacks in American Cinema." *International Journal of Politics, Culture, and Society* 4 (1): 49–77.

————. 1991. "The Race Question and Liberalism: Casuistries in American Constitutional Law." *International Journal of Politics, Culture, and Society* 5 (2): 183–247.

————. 1992. *Militarism, Imperialism, and Racial Accommodation*. Fayetteville: The University of Arkansas Press.

————. 1994. *Color, Culture, Civilization: Race and Minority Issues in American Society*. Urbana: University of Illinois Press.

————. 1997. *Postmodernism and a Sociology of the Absurd and Other Essays on the "Nouvelle Vague" in American Social Science*. Fayetteville: University of Arkansas Press.

——. 1998. "Gunnar Myrdal's *An American Dilemma* After a Half Century: Critics and Anticritics." *International Journal of Politics, Culture, and Society* 12 (2): 327–389.

Lynd, Robert S. and Helen Merrell Lynd. 1929. *Middletown: A Study in American Culture.* New York: Harcourt, Brace.

——. 1937. *Middletown in Transition: A Study in Cultural Conflict.* New York: Harcourt, Brace.

Majka, Linda C. and Theo J. Majka. 1982. *Farm Workers, Agribusiness, and the State.* Philadelphia: Temple University Press.

Mangiafico, Luciano. 1988. *Contemporary American Immigrants: Patterns of Filipino, Korean, and Chinese Settlement in the United States.* New York: Praeger.

Mangione, Jerre. 1978. *An Ethnic at Large: A Memoir of America in the Thirties and Forties.* New York: G.P. Putnam's Sons.

Mann, Arthur. 1979. *The One and the Many: Reflections on the American Identity.* Chicago: The University of Chicago Press.

Marable, Manning. 1983. *How Capitalism Underdeveloped Black America: Problems in Race, Political Economy and Society.* Boston: South End Press.

Marcus, Jacob R. 1970. *The Colonial American Jew, 1492–1776,* 3 vols. Detroit, MI: Wayne State University Press.

Marger, Martin and Phillip Obermiller. 1983. "Urban Appalachians and Canadian Maritime Migrants: A Comparative Study of Emergent Ethnicity." *International Journal of Comparative Sociology* 24 (September/December): 229–243.

Marks, Carole. 1989. *Farewell—We're Good and Gone: The Great Black Migration.* Bloomington: Indiana University Press.

Marriott, Michael. 1992. "Indians Turning to Tribal Colleges for Opportunity and Cultural Values." *New York Times,* February 26: A13.

Mason, David. 1995. *Race and Ethnicity in Modern Britain.* Oxford, UK: Oxford University Press.

Mass, Amy Iwasaki. 1992. "Interracial Japanese Americans: The Best of Both Worlds or the End of the Japanese American Community?" 265–279 in *Racially Mixed People in America,* edited by Maria P. P. Root. Newbury Park, CA: Sage Publications.

Massey, Douglas S. and Nancy A. Denton. 1988. "Suburbanization and Segregation in U.S. Metropolitan Areas." *American Journal of Sociology* 94 (3): 592–626.

——. 1993. *American Apartheid: Segregation and the Making of the Underclass.* Cambridge, MA: Harvard University Press.

Massey, Douglas S., Jorge Durand, Nolan J. Malone, and Alfred J. Bush. 2002. *Beyond Smoke and Mirrors: Mexican Immigration in an Era of Economic Integration.* New York: Russell Sage Foundation.

Massey, Douglas S. and Eric Fong. 1990. "Segregation and Neighborhood Quality: Blacks, Hispanics, and Asians in the San Francisco Metropolitan Area." *Social Forces* 69 (1): 15–32.

Matthews, Fred H. 1978. *The Quest for Community: Robert Park and the Chicago School of American Sociology.* Montreal: McGill-Queen's University Press.

——. 1987. "Louis Wirth and American Ethnic Studies: The World of Enlightened Assimilationism, 1925–1950." 123–143 in *The Jews of North America,* edited by Moses Rischin. Detroit: Wayne State University Press.

May, Philip A. 1999. "The Epidemiology of Alcohol Abuse Among American Indians: The Mythical and Real Properties." 227–244 in *Contemporary Native American Cultural Issues,* edited by Duane Champagne. Walnut Creek, CA: Alta Mira Press.

Mayer, Egon. 1979. *From Suburb to Stetl: The Jews of Boro Park.* Philadelphia: Temple University Press.

——. 1980. "Processes and Outcomes in Marriages Between Jews and Non-Jews." *American Behavioral Scientist* 23: 487–518.

Mazón, Mauricio. 1984. *The Zoot-Suit Riots: The Psychology of Symbolic Annihilation.* Austin: University of Texas Press.

McAdam, Doug. 1982. *Political Process and the Development of Black Insurgency, 1930–1970.* Chicago: The University of Chicago Press.

——. 1988. *Freedom Summer.* New York: Oxford University Press.

McAuley, Christopher A. 2004. *The Mind of Oliver Cox.* Notre Dame, IN: University of Notre Dame Press.

McCarthy, John D. and Mayer N. Zald. 1977. "Resource Mobilization and Social Movements: A Partial Theory." *American Journal of Sociology* 82 (6): 1212–1241.

McKay, James. 1982. "An Exploratory Synthesis of Primordial and Mobilizationist Approaches to Ethnic Phenomena." *Ethnic and Racial Studies* 5 (4): 395–420.

McNickle, D'Arcy. 1962. *The Indian Tribes of the United States: Ethnic and Cultural Survival.* New York: Oxford University Press.

McPhail, Clark. 1971. "Civil Disorder Participation: A Critical Examination of Recent Research." *American Sociological Review* 36: 1058–1073.

McPherson, James M. 1982. *Ordeal by Fire: The Civil War and Reconstruction.* New York: Alfred A. Knopf.

McWilliam, Carey. 1948. *North From Mexico: The Spanish Speaking People.* Philadelphia: J.B. Lippincott.

Meier, August and Elliot Rudwick. 1973. *CORE, a Study of the Civil Rights Movement, 1942–1968.* New York: Oxford University Press.

Melendy, H. Brett. 1977. *Asians in America: Filipinos, Koreans, and East Indians.* Boston: Twayne Publishers.

——. 1980. "Filipinos." 354–362 in *Harvard Encyclopedia of American Ethnic Groups*, edited by Stephan Thernstrom, Ann Orlov, and Oscar Handlin. Cambridge, MA: Harvard University Press.

Melville, Margarita. 1983. "Ethnicity: An Analysis of Its Dynamism and Variability Focusing on Mexican/Anglo/Mexican American Interface." *American Ethnologist* 10 (2): 272–289.

Merton, Robert K. 1972. "Insiders and Outsiders: A Chapter in the Sociology of Knowledge." *American Journal of Sociology* 24 (1): 9–47.

——. 1976. *Sociological Ambivalence and Other Essays.* New York: Free Press.

Metzger, Isaac, ed. 1971. *A Bintel Brief: "A Bundle of Letters" to the Jewish Daily Forward.* New York: Doubleday.

Meyer, Michael. 1992. "Los Angeles 2010: A Latino Subcontinent." *Newsweek,* November 9: 32–33.

Miles, Robert. 1993. *Racism After "Race Relations."* London: Routledge.

Miller, Kerby A. 1985. *Emigrants and Exiles: Ireland and the Irish Exodus to North America.* New York: Oxford University Press.

Miller, Randall M. 1978. *Ethnic Images in American Film and Television.* Philadelphia: Balch Institute Press.

Mills, C. Wright. 1951. *White Collar: The American Middle Class.* New York: Oxford University Press.

Mills, C. Wright, Clarence Senior, and Rose Kohn Goldsen. 1950. *The Puerto Rican Journey: New York's Newest Immigrants.* New York: Harper & Row.

Min, Jay and Pyong Gap Min. 1992. "The Relationship Bewteen Korean Immigrant Parents and Children." American Sociological Association annual meeting, unpublished paper.

Min, Pyong Gap. 1987. "Filipino and Korean Immigrants in Small Business: A Comparative Analysis." *Amerasia* 13 (Spring): 53–71.

——. 1988. *Ethnic Business Enterprise: Korean Small Business in Atlanta.* New York: Center for Migration Studies.

——. 1991. "Cultural and Economic Boundaries of Korean Ethnicity: A Comparative Analysis." *Ethnic and Racial Studies* 14 (2): 225–241.

——, ed., 1995. *Asian Americans Contemporary Trends and Issues.* Thousand Oaks, CA: Sage.

——. 1996. *Caught in the Middle: Korean Communities in New York and Los Angeles.* Berkeley: University of California Press.

——. 1999. "A Comparison of Post-Intergenerational Mobility and Cultural Transmission." *Journal of American Ethnic History* 18 (3): 65–94.

Min, Pyong Gap and Jung Ha Kim, eds. 2002. *Religions in Asian America: Building Faith Communities.* Walnut Creek, CA: AltaMira Press.

Mintz, Sidney W. 1960. *Worker in the Cane: A Puerto Rican Life History.* New Haven, CT: Yale University Press.

Model, Suzanne. 1992. "The Ethnic Economy: Cubans and Chinese Reconsidered." *Sociological Quarterly* 33 (1): 63–82.

——. 1999. "Ethnic Inequality in England: An Analysis Based on the 1991 Census." *Ethnic and Racial Studies* 22 (5): 966–991.

Mohl, Raymond A. 1985. "An Ethnic 'Boiling Pot': Cubans and Haitians in Miami." *The Journal of Ethnic Studies* 13 (Summer): 51–74.

Momaday, N. Scott. 1976. *The Names: A Memoir.* New York: Harper & Row.

Montejano, David, ed. 1999. *Chicano Politics and Society in the Late Twentieth Century.* Austin: University of Texas Press.

Moore, Joan. 1970. *Mexican Americans.* Englewood Cliffs, NJ: Prentice-Hall.

——. 1978. *Homeboys.* Philadelphia: Temple University Press.

Moore, Joan and Harry Pachon. 1985. *Hispanics in the United States.* Englewood Cliffs, NJ: Prentice-Hall.

Moore, Joan and Raquel Pinderhughes, eds. 1993. *In the Barrios: Latinos and the Underclass Debate.* New York: Russell Sage Foundation.

Moore, Joan and James Diego Vigil. 1987. "Chicano Gangs: Group Norms and Individual Factors Related to Adult Criminality." *Aztlan* 18 (2): 27–44.

Moore, Michael. 1988. "Scapegoats Again: 'Hate Crimes' Against Asian Americans on the Rise." *The Progressive,* February 25: 9.

Moore, William. 1969. *The Vertical Ghetto.* New York: Random House.

Morawska, Ewa. 1985. *For Bread With Butter: The Life-Worlds of East Central Europeans in Johnstown, Pennsylvania, 1890–1940.* Cambridge, UK: Cambridge University Press.

——. 1989. "Labor Migrations of Poles in the Atlantic World Economy, 1880–1914." *Comparative Studies in Society and History* 31 (2): 237–272.

——. 1990. "The Sociology and Historiography of Immigration." 187–238 in *Immigration Reconsidered: History, Sociology, and Politics,* edited by Virginia Yans-McLaughlin. New York: Oxford University Press.

——. 1994. "In Defense of the Assimilation Model." *Journal of American Ethnic History* 13 (2): 76–87.

——. 1999. "The Sociology and History of Immigration: Reflections of a Practitioner." European University Institute Workshop on Reflections on Migration Research, Florence, May 20–21.

Morris, Aldon D. 1984. *The Origins of the Civil Rights Movement: Black Communities Organizing for Change.* New York: The Free Press.

Moynihan, Daniel Patrick. 1965. *The Negro Family: The Case for National Action.* Washington, DC: Office of Policy Planning and Research, United States Department of Labor.

Mucha, Janusz. 1984. "American Indian Success in the Urban Setting." *Urban Anthropology* 13 (4): 329–354.

Muñoz, Alfredo. 1971. *The Filipinos in the United States.* Los Angeles: Mountain View Publishers.

Murray, Charles. 1984. *Losing Ground: American Social Policy, 1950–1980.* New York: Basic Books.

Myrdal, Gunnar. 1944. *An American Dilemma: The Negro Problem and Modern Democracy.* New York: Harper and Brothers.

Nabokov, Peter, ed. 1991. *Native American Testimony: A Chronicle of Indian-White Relations From Prophecy to the Present, 1492–1992.* New York: Viking.

Nagel, Joane. 1994. "The Construction of Ethnicity: Creating and Recreating Ethnic Identity and Culture." *Social Problems* 41 (1): 152–176.

——. 1995. "American Indian Renewal: Politics and the Resurgence of Identity." *American Sociological Review* 60 (6): 947–965.

——. 1996. *American Indian Ethnic Renewal: Red Power and the Resurgence of Identity and Culture.* New York: Oxford University Press.

——. 2000. "Ethnicity and Sexuality." *Annual Review of Sociology* 26: 107–133.

Nagel, Joane and Susan Olzak. 1982. "Ethnic Mobilization in New and Old States: An Extension of the Competition Model." *Social Problems* 30 (1): 127–143.

Nahirny, Vladimir and Joshua Fishman. 1965. "American Immigrant Groups: Ethnic Identification and the Problem of Generations." *Sociological Review* 13 (November): 311–326.

Nair, Sami. 1996. "France: A Crisis of Integration." *Dissent* 43 (Summer): 75–78.

Nairn, Tom. 1977. *The Break Up of Britain.* London: New Left Books.

——. 2000. *After Britain.* London: Granta.

Naison, Mark. 1983. *Communists in Harlem During the Depression.* Urbana: University of Illinois Press.

Nakamaru, Robert Tsuneo. 1993. "Assimilation and the Japanese American Experience." Paper presented at the annual Illinois Sociological Association meeting, October 21, Rockford, IL.

Nash, Gary B. 1990. *Race and Revolution.* Madison, WI: Madison House.

National Jewish Population Survey. 2003. New York: United Jewish Communities.

National Opinion Research Center. 1991. *General Social Survey.* Chicago: National Opinion Research Center.

Nee, Victor and Brett Nee. 1973. *Longtime Californ': A Study of an American Chinatown.* New York: Pantheon Books.

Nee, Victor and Jimy Sanders. 2001. "Understanding the Diversity of Immigrant Incorporation: A Forms-of-Capital Model." *Ethnic and Racial Studies* 24 (3): 386–411.

Nee, Victor and Herbert Y. Wong. 1985. "Asian American Socioeconomic Achievement: The Strength of the Family Bond." *Sociological Perspectives* 28 (3): 281–306.

Nefzger, Ben and Peter Kivisto. 1990. "Studying the Changing Conditions of Jewish Life in a Middle-Sized American City." *Sociological Focus* 23 (3): 177–201.

Nelli, Humbert S. 1970. *The Italians in Chicago.* New York: Oxford University Press.

——. 1980. "Italians." 545–560 in *Harvard Encyclopedia of American Ethnic Groups,* edited by Stephan Thernstrom, Ann Orlov, and Oscar Handlin. Cambridge, MA: Harvard University Press.

——. 1983. *From Immigrants to Ethnics: The Italian Americans.* New York: Oxford University Press.

Nelson, Lowry. 1943. "Intermarriage Among Nationality Groups in a Rural Area of Minnesota." *American Journal of Sociology* 48 (5): 585–592.

Nettles, Michael T. and Gary Orfield. 2000. "Large Gains, Recent Reversals, and Continuing Inequality in Education for African Americans." 119–143 in *New Directions: African Americans in a Diversifying Nation,* edited by James S. Jackson. Washington, DC: National Policy Association.

Neufeld, Steven. 1990. "Ethnic Conflict and Community Mobilization: Arab-Owned and Korean-Owned Businesses in Predominantly Black Neighborhoods." Paper presented at the Midwest Sociogical Society annual meeting, Chicago, IL.

Newman, Katherine S. 2000. *No Shame in My Game: The Working Poor in the Inner City.* New York: Vintage.

Newman, William M. 1973. *American Pluralism: A Study of Minority Groups and Social Theory.* New York: Harper & Row.

New Yorker, February 15, 1993: 6.

New York Times. 1984a. "Sioux Indians in South Dakota Awaiting $606 million in Compensation." July 16: 17.

——. 1984b. "Moapa Band of Paiute Indians Proposes Setting Up a Brothel on Reservation." November 4: A31.

——. 1989. "Southern Pacific Transportation Company to Pay Walker River Paiutes $1.2 million." August 13: 26.

——. 1990a. "The Mosaic Thing." January 3, 1990: 20.

——. 1990b. "Puyallup Tribe Signs Away Claim to Much of Its Land." March 25: 33.

——. 1992a. "Gambling Is a Billion Dollar a Year Business." January 6: A17.

——. 1992b. "New York Irish March as Gay Group Protest," and "Proud to Be Gay and Irish, but Sad as Marchers Go By." March 18: A16.

——. 2003. "Survey Finds Slight Rise in Jews' Intermarrying." September 11: A13.

Ng, Wendy. 1989. "The Collective Memories of Communities." 103–112 in *Asian Americans: Comparative and Global Perspectives*, edited by Shirley Hune et al. Pullman: Washington State University Press.

——. 2002. *Japanese American Internment During World War II: A History and Reference Guide*. Westport, CT: Greenwood Press.

Niehardt, John G. 1961. *Black Elk Speaks: Being a Life Story of a Holy Man of the Oglala Sioux*. Lincoln: University of Nebraska Press.

Nielsen, Francois. 1985. "Toward a Theory of Ethnic Solidarity in Modern Society." *American Sociological Review* 50 (2): 133–149.

Noiriel, Gérard. 1996. *The French Melting Pot: Immigration, Citizenship, and National Identity*. Minneapolis: University of Minnesota Press.

Noriega, Chon. 1991. "Citizen Chicano: The Trials and Titillations of Ethnicity in the American Cinema, 1935–1962." *Social Research* 58 (2): 413–438.

Novak, Michael. 1972. *The Rise of the Unmeltable Ethnics: Politics and Culture in the Seventies*. New York: Macmillan.

O'Brien, Conor Cruise. 1991. "Nationalists and Democrats." *New York Review of Books*, August 15: 29–31.

O'Brien, David J. and Stephen S. Fugita. 1991. *The Japanese American Experience*. Bloomington: Indiana University Press.

Oliver, Lawrence J. 1987. " 'Great Equalizer' or 'Cruel Stepmother?' Image of the School in Italian American Literature." *Journal of Ethnic Studies* 15: 113–130.

Oliver, Melvin L. and Thomas M. Shapiro. 1995. *Black Wealth/White Wealth: A New Perspective on Racial Inequality*. New York: Routledge.

——. 2001. "Wealth and Racial Stratification." 222–251 in *America Becoming: Racial Trends and Their Consequences*, vol. 1, edited by Neil J. Smelser, William Julius Wilson, and Faith Mitchell. Washington, DC: National Research Council.

Olzak, Susan. 1992. *The Dynamics of Ethnic Competition and Conflict*. Stanford, CA: Stanford University Press.

Omi, Michael A. 2001. "The Changing Meaning of Race." 243–263 in *America Becoming: Racial Trends and Their Consequences*, vol. 1, edited by Neil J. Smelser, William Julius Wilson, and Faith Mitchell. Washington, DC: National Academy Press.

Omi, Michael and Howard Winant. 1986. *Racial Formation in the United States: From the 1960s to the 1980s*. New York: Routledge and Kegan Paul.

Orfield, Gary. 1983. *Public School Desegregation in the United States, 1968–1980*. Washington, DC: Joint Center for Political Studies.

Orfield, Gary and Franklin Monfort. 1988. *Change in the Racial Composition and Segregation of Large School Districts, 1867–1986*. Alexandria, VA: National School Boards Association.

Organization for Economic Cooperation and Development. 2003. *Trends in Interpersonal Migration*. <http://www.oead.org/documents>.

Ortiz, Vilma. 1986. "Changes in the Characteristics of Puerto Rican Migrants From 1955 to 1980." *International Migration Review* 20 (3): 612–628.

Orzell, Lawrence J. 1982. "The 'National Catholic' Response: Franciszek Hodur and His Followers, 1897–1907." 117–182 in *The Polish Presence in Canada and America*, edited by Frank Renkiewicz. Toronto: The Multicultural History Society of Ontario.

Osajima, Keith. 1988. "Asian Americans as the Model Minority: An Analysis of the Popular Press Image in the 1960s and 1980s." 163–174 in *Reflections on Shattered Windows: Promises and Prospects for Asian American Studies*, edited by Gary Y. Okihiro, Shirley Hune, Arthur A. Hansen, and John M. Liu. Pullman: Washington State University Press.

Osako, Masako M. 1984. "Japanese-Americans: Melting Into the All-American Pot?" 513–544 in *Ethnic Chicago*, edited by Melvin G. Holli and Peter d'A. Jones. Grand Rapids, MI: William B. Eerdmans.

Padilla, Felix. 1987. *Puerto Rican Chicago*. Notre Dame, IN: University of Notre Dame Press.

Parekh, Bhikhu. 2000a. *Rethinking Multiculturalism: Cultural Diversity and Political Theory*. London: Macmillan.

——. 2000b. *The Future of Multi-Ethnic Britain, Report of the Runnymede Trust Commission on the Future of Multi-Ethnic Britain.* London: Profile Books.

Parenti, Michael. 1967. "Ethnic Politics and the Persistence of Ethnic Identification." *American Political Science Review* 61: 717–726.

Park, Robert Ezra. 1950. *Race and Culture: The Collected Papers of R. E. Park.* Glencoe, IL: The Free Press.

Parkin, Frank. 1979. *Marxism and Class Theory: A Bourgeois Critique.* London: Tavistock.

Parot, Joseph. 1981. *Polish Catholics in Chicago, 1850–1920.* DeKalb: Northern Illinois University Press.

Parrillo, Vincent N. 1996. *Diversity in America.* Thousand Oaks, CA: Pine Forge Press.

Patterson, James. 1981. *Americans' Struggle Against Poverty.* Cambridge, MA: Harvard University Press.

Patterson, Orlando. 1982. *Slavery and Social Death: A Comparative Study.* Cambridge, MA: Harvard University Press.

Pattillo-McCoy, Mary. 1999. *Black Picket Fences: Privilege and Peril Among the Black Middle Class.* Chicago: University of Chicago Press.

Peach, Cheri. 1980. "Which Triple Melting Pot? A Re-examination of Ethnic Intermarriage in New Haven, 1900–1950." *Ethnic and Racial Studies* 3: 1–16.

Pearce, Roy Harvey. 1967. *Savagism and Civilization: A Study of the Indian and the American Mind.* Baltimore: The Johns Hopkins University Press.

Pearson, David. 2001. *The Politics of Ethnicity in Settler Societies: States of Unease.* New York: Palgrave.

Pedraza-Bailey, Silvia. 1990. "Immigration Research: A Conceptual Map." *Social Science History* 14 (1): 43–67.

——. 1991. "Women and Migration: The Social Consequences of Gender." *Annual Review of Sociology* 17: 303–325.

——. 1992. "Cubans in Exile, 1959–1989: The State of the Research." 24–36 in *Cuban Studies Since the Revolution,* edited by D. J. Fernandez. Gainesville: University Presses of Florida.

Pérez, Lisandro. 1980. "Cubans." 256–261 in *Harvard Encyclopedia of American Ethnic Groups,* edited by Stephan Thernstrom, Ann Orlov, and Oscar Handlin. Cambridge, MA: Harvard University Press.

——. 1986. "Immigrant Economic Adjustment and Family Organization: The Cuban Success Story Reexamined." *International Migration Review* 20 (1): 4–20.

——. 2001. "Growing Up in Cuban Miami: Immigration, the Enclave, and New Generations." 91–125 in *Ethnicities: Children of Immigrants in America,* edited by Rubén Rumbaut and Alejandro Portes. Berkeley and New York: University of California Press and the Russell Sage Foundation.

Pérez y Gonzalez, Maria. 2000. *Puerto Ricans in the United States.* Westport, CT: Greenwood Press.

Perlman, Robert. 1991. *Bridging Three Worlds: Hungarian-Jewish Americans, 1848–1914.* Amherst: The University of Massachusetts Press.

Perlmann, Joel and Roger Waldinger. 1998. "Are the Children of Today's Immigrants Making It?" *The Public Interest,* no. 132: 73–96.

——. 1999. "Immigrants, Past and Present: A Reconsideration." 223–238 in *The Handbook of International Migration: The American Experience,* edited by Charles Hirschman, Philip Kasinitz, and Josh DeWind. New York: Russell Sage Foundation.

Perlmann, Joel and Mary C. Waters, eds. 2002. *The New Race Question: How the Census Counts Multiracial Individuals.* New York: Russell Sage Foundation.

Pernicone, Nicholas. 1979. "Carlo Tresca and the Sacco-Vanzetti Case." *Journal of American History* 66: 535–547.

Persons, Stow. 1987. *Ethnic Studies at Chicago 1905–1945.* Urbana: University of Illinois Press.

Petersen, William. 1966. "Success Story: Japanese American Style." *New York Times* 9 January: V1–V20.

——. 1971. *Japanese Americans.* New York: Random House.

——. 1982. "Concepts of Ethnicity." 1–26 in *Concepts of Ethnicity*, William Peterson, Michael Novak, and Philip Gleason. Cambridge, MA: The Belknap Press of Harvard University Press.

Pettigrew, Thomas F. 1958. "Personality and Sociocultural Factors in Intergroup Attitudes." *Journal of Conflict Resolution* 2: 29–42.

——. 1979. "The Changing—Not Declining—Significance of Race." 111–116 in *The Caste and Class Controversy*, edited by Charles Vert Willie. Bayside, NY: General Hall.

Pettigrew, Thomas F. and Robert F. Green. 1976. "School Desegregation in Large Cities: A Critique of the Coleman White Flight Thesis." *Harvard Educational Review* 46 (February): 1–53.

Phillips, Ulrich B. 1918. *American Negro Slavery*. New York: D. Appleton.

Piatt, Bill. 1990. *Only English? Law and Language Policy in the United States*. Albuquerque: University of New Mexico Press.

Pido, Antonio J. A. 1986. *The Filipinos in America*. New York: Center for Migration Studies.

Pieterse, Jan Nederveen. 1992. *White on Black: Images of Africa and Blacks in Western Popular Culture*. New Haven, CT: Yale University Press.

Pincus, Fred L. 2003. *Reverse Discrimination: Dismantling the Myth*. Boulder, CO: Lynne Rienner Publishers.

Pinderhughes, Dianne. 1987. *Race and Ethnicity in Chicago Politics: A Reexamination of Pluralist Theory*. Urbana: University of Illinois Press.

Pinkney, Alphonso. 1984. *The Myth of Black Progress*. Cambridge, UK: Cambridge University Press.

——. 1987. *Black Americans*. Englewood Cliffs, NJ: Prentice-Hall.

Piore, Michael. 1979. *Birds of Passage: Migrant Labor and Industrial Societies*. Cambridge, UK: Cambridge University Press.

Piven, Frances Fox and Richard Cloward. 1971. *Regulating the Poor: The Functions of Public Welfare*. New York: Vintage Press.

Polenberg, Richard. 1980. *One Nation Divisible: Class, Race, and Ethnicity in the United States Since 1938*. New York: Viking Press.

Porter, John. 1965. *The Vertical Mosaic: An Analysis of Social Class and Power in Canada*. Toronto: University of Toronto Press.

Portes, Alejandro. 1996. "Global Villagers: The Rise of Transnational Communities." *American Prospect* 25 (March/April): 74–77.

Portes, Alejandro, Luis E. Guarnizo, and Patricia Landolt. 1999. "The Study of Transnationalism: Pitfalls and Promise of an Emergent Research Field." *Ethnic and Racial Studies* 22 (2): 217–237.

Portes, Alejandro and Lingxin Hao. 2002. "The Price of Uniformity: Language, Family and Personality Adjustment in the Immigrant Second Generation." *Ethnic and Racial Studies* 25 (6): 889–912.

Portes, Alejandro and Leif Jensen. 1989. "The Enclave and the Entrants: Patterns of Ethnic Enterprise Before and After Mariel." *American Sociological Review* 54 (6): 929–949.

Portes, Alejandro and Rafael Mozo. 1985. "The Political Adaptation Process of Cubans and Other Ethnic Minorities in the United States: A Preliminary Analysis." *International Migration Review* 19 (1): 35–63.

Portes, Alejandro and Rubén G. Rumbaut. 1990. *Immigrant America: A Portrait*. Berkeley: University of California Press.

——. 2001. *Legacies: The Story of the Immigrant Second Generation*. Berkeley and New York: University of California Press and the Russell Sage Foundation.

Portes, Alejandro and Richard Schauffler. 1996. "Language and the Second Generation: Bilingualism Yesterday and Today." 8–29 in *The New Second Generation*, edited by Alejandro Portes. New York: Russell Sage Foundation.

Portes, Alejandro and Julia Sensenbrenner. 1998. "Embeddedness and Immigration: Notes on the Social Determinants of Economic Action." 127–149 in *The New Institutionalism in Sociology*, edited by Mary C. Brinton and Victor Nee. New York: The Russell Sage Foundation.

Portes, Alejandro and Alex Stepick. 1985. "Unwelcome Immigrants: The Labor Market Experiences of 1980 (Mariel) Cuban and Haitian Refugees in South Florida." *American Sociological Review* 50 (4): 493–514.

——. 1993. *City on the Edge: The Transformation of Miami*. Berkeley: University of California Press.

Portes, Alejandro and Min Zhou. 1993. "The New Second Generation: Segmented Assimilation and Its Variants Among Post-1965 Youth." *Annals of the American Academy of Political and Social Science* 530 (November): 74–96.

——. 1996. "Self-Employment and the Earnings of Immigrants." *American Sociological Review* 61 (2): 219–230.

Posadas, Barbara M. 1981. "Crossed Boundaries in Interracial Chicago: Philpino American Families Since 1925." *Amerasia Journal* 8 (1): 31–52.

Powledge, Fred. 1991. *Free at Last? The Civil Rights Movement and the People Who Made It*. Boston: Little, Brown.

Pozzetta, George and Gary Mormino. 1986. *The Immigrant World of Ybor City*. Urbana: University of Illinois Press.

Princeton Religion Research Center. 1998. *Religion in America*, annual survey conducted by the Gallup Organization.

Prucha, Francis Paul. 1985. *The Indians in American Society: From the Revolutionary War to the Present*. Berkeley: University of California Press.

Pula, James S. and Eugene E. Dziedzic. 1990. *United We Stand: The Role of Polish Workers in the New York Mills Textile Strikes, 1912 and 1916*. New York: Eastern European Monographs.

Quan, Robert Seto. 1982. *Lotus Among the Magnolias: The Mississippi Chinese*. Jackson: University Press of Mississippi.

Radzialowski, Thaddeus. 1976. "The Competition for Jobs and Racial Stereotypes: Poles and Blacks in Chicago." *Polish American Studies* 33 (2): 5–18.

——. 1982. "Ethnic Conflict and the Polish Americans of Detroit, 1921–42." 195–207 in *The Polish Presence in Canada and America*, edited by Frank Renkiewicz. Toronto: The Multicultural History Society of Ontario.

Rainwater, Lee. 1970. *Behind Ghetto Walls: Black Family Life in a Federal Slum*. Chicago: Aldine Publishing.

Rainwater, Lee and William L. Yancey, eds. 1967. *The Moynihan Report and the Politics of Controversy*. Cambridge, MA: The MIT Press.

Ramella, Franco. 1991. "Emigration From an Area of Intense Industrial Development: The Case of Northwestern Italy." 261–274 in *A Century of European Migrations, 1830–1930*, edited by Rudolph J. Vecoli and Suzanne M. Sinke. Urbana: University of Illinois Press.

Raper, Arthur F. 1933. *The Tragedy of Southern Lynching*. Chapel Hill: University of North Carolina Press.

Redkey, Edwin S. 1969. *Black Exodus: Black Nationalist and Back-to-Africa Movements, 1890–1910*. New Haven, CT: Yale University Press.

Reed, Adolph L., Jr. 1986. *The Jesse Jackson Phenomenon: The Crisis of Purpose in Afro-American Politics*. New Haven: Yale University Press.

——. 1999. *Stirrings in the Jug: Black Politics in the Post-Segregation Era*. Minneapolis: University of Minnesota Press.

Report of the President's Commission on Housing. 1982. Washington, DC: Government Printing Office.

Rex, John. 1983. *Race Relations in Sociology Theory*. London: Routledge and Kegan Paul.

Ribuffo, Leo P. 1986. "Henry Ford and *The International Jew*. 175–190 in *The American Jewish Experience*, edited by Jonathan D. Sarna. New York: Holmes and Meier.

Rieder, Jonathan. 1985. *Canarsie: The Jews and Italians of Brooklyn Against Liberalism*. Cambridge, MA: Harvard University Press.

Riesman, David, with Nathan Glazer and Revel Denney. 1950. *The Lonely Crowd: A Study of the Changing American Character*. New Haven, CT: Yale University Press.

Riggs, Christopher K. 2000. "American Indians, Economic Development, and Self-Determination in the 1960s." *Pacific Historical Review* 69 (3): 431–463.

Riis, Jacob. 1971 [1890]. *How the Other Half Lives: Studies Among the Tenements of New York*. New York: Dover.

Rippley, LaVern J. 1984. *The German-Americans*. Lanham, MD: University Press of America.

Rischin, Moses. 1962. *The Promised City: New York's Jews, 1870–1914*. Cambridge, MA: Harvard University Press.

——. 1990. "Just Call Me John: Ethnicity as Mentalite." 64–82 in *American Immigrants and Their Generations: Studies and Commentaries on the Hansen Thesis After Fifty Years*, edited by Peter Kivisto and Dag Blanck. Urbana: University of Illinois Press.

Rivera-Batiz, Francisco, and Carlos E. Santiago. 1994. *Puerto Ricans in the United States: A Changing Reality*. Washington, DC: National Puerto Rican Coalition.

Rodriguez, Clara. 1989. *Puerto Ricans: Born in the U.S.A.* Boston: Unwin Hyman.

Rodriguez, Richard. 1981. *Hunger of Memory: The Education of Richard Rodriguez*. Boston: David R. Godine.

——. 1992. *Days of Obligation: An Argument With My Father*. New York: Viking.

Roediger, David R. 1991. *The Wages of Whiteness: Race and the Making of the American Working Class*. London: Verso.

Rokeach, Milton. 1960. *The Open and Closed Mind*. New York: Basic Books.

Rollins, Judith. 1986. "Part of a Whole: The Interdependence of the Civil Rights Movement and Other Social Movements." *Phylon* 47 (1): 61–70.

Romo, Ricardo. 1983. *East Los Angeles: History of a Barrio*. Austin: University of Texas Press.

Roosens, Eugene E. 1989. *Creating Ethnicity: The Process of Ethnogenesis*. Newbury Park, CA: Sage Publications.

Rose, Arnold. 1951. *The Roots of Prejudice*. Paris: UNESCO.

Rose, Arnold and Caroline Rose. 1948. *America Divided: Minority Group Relations in the United States*. New York: Alfred A. Knopf.

Rose, Peter I. 1968. *The Subject Is Race: Traditional Ideologies and the Teaching of Race Relations*. New York: Oxford University Press.

——. 1978. *"Nobody Knows the Trouble I've Seen": Some Reflections on the Insider-Outsider Debate*. Northampton, MA: Smith College.

Ross, Edward A. 1914. *The Old World in the New*. New York: Century.

Rossell, Christine H. 1976. "School Desegregation and White Flight." *Political Science Quarterly* 90 (Winter): 675–695.

——. 1988. "Is It the Busing or the Blacks?" *Urban Affairs Quarterly* 24 (1): 138–148.

Rothschild, Joseph. 1981. *Ethnopolitics: A Conceptual Framework*. New York: Columbia University Press.

Royce, Anya Peterson. 1982. *Ethnic Identity: Strategies of Diversity*. Bloomington: Indiana University Press.

Royce, Edward. 1993. *The Origins of Southern Sharecropping*. Philadelphia: Temple University Press.

Rumbaut, Rubén G. 1991. "Passages to America." 208–243 in *America at Century's End*, edited by Alan Wolfe. Berkeley: University of California Press.

——. 1995. "Vietnamese, Cambodian, and Laotian Americans." 232–270 in *Asian Contemporary Issues and Trends*, edited by P. G. Min. Thousand Oaks, CA: Sage.

——. 1996. "The Crucible Within: Ethnic Identity, Self-Esteem, and Segmented Assimilation Among Children of Immigrants." 119–170 in *The New Second Generation*, edited by Alejandro Portes. New York: Russell Sage Foundation.

——. 2005. "The Melting and the Pot: Assimilation and Variety in American Life." In *Incorporating Diversity: Rethinking Assimilation in a Multicultural Age*, edited by Peter Kivisto. Boulder, CO: Paradigm Publishers.

Ryan, William. 1971. *Blaming the Victim*. New York: Random House.

Sahlins, Marshall. 1972. *Stone Age Economics*. Chicago: Aldine-Atherton.

——. 1976. *The Uses and Abuses of Biology*. Ann Arbor: University of Michigan Press.

Salvemini, Gaetano. 1977. *Italian Fascist Activities in the United States*. New York: Center for Migration Studies.

Sánchez-Ayéndez, Melba. 1988. "The Puerto Rican American Family." 173–195 in *Ethnic Families in America*, edited by Charles H. Mindel, Robert W. Hubenstein, and Roosevelt Wright, Jr. New York: Elsevier.

Sandberg, Neil C. 1974. *Ethnic Identity and Assimilation: The Polish-American*. New York: Praeger.

——. 1986. *Jewish Life in Los Angeles*. Lanham, MD: University Press of America.

Sandefur, Gary D. 1986. "American Indian Intermarriage." *Social Science Research* 15 (December): 347–371.

Sanders, Jimy M. and Victor Nee. 1987. "Limits of Ethnic Solidarity in the Enclave Economy." *American Sociological Review* 52 (6): 745–767.

San Miguel, Guadalupe. 1987. *Let All of Them Take Heed: Mexican-Americans and the Campaign for Educational Equality in Texas, 1910–1981*. Austin: University of Texas Press.

Sarna, Jonathan. 1978. "From Immigrants to Ethnics: Toward a New Theory of 'Ethnicization.'" *Ethnicity* 5: 370–378.

——. 2004. *American Judaism: A History*. New Haven, CT: Yale University Press.

Sassen, Saskia. 1996. *Losing Control? Sovereignty in an Age of Globalization*. New York: Columbia University Press.

Savas, Emmanual. 1979. *Federal Housing Policy: An Agenda*. Unpublished manuscript.

Saxton, Alexander. 1971. *The Indispensable Enemy: Labor and the Anti-Chinese Movement in California*. Berkeley: University of California Press.

——. 1990. *The Rise and Fall of the White Republic: Class Politics and Mass Culture in Nineteenth-Century America*. London: Verso.

Schaefer, Richard T. 1988. *Racial and Ethnic Groups*. Glenview, IL: Scott, Foresman.

Schermerhorn, R. A. 1978. *Comparative Ethnic Relations: A Framework for Theory and Research*. New York: Random House.

Schlesinger, Arthur M., Jr. 1992. *The Disuniting of America: Reflections on a Multicultural Society*. New York: W.W. Norton.

Schneider, Jo Anne. 1990. "Defining Boundaries, Creating Contacts: Puerto Rican and Polish Presentation of Group Identity Through Ethnic Parades." *The Journal of Ethnic Studies* 18 (1): 33–57.

Schneider, Keith. 1992. "Grants Stir Interest in Nuclear Waste Site." *New York Times*, January 9: A10.

Schuman, Howard, Charlotte Steeh, and Lawrence Bobo. 1985. *Racial Attitudes in America: Trends and Interpretations*. Cambridge, MA: Harvard University Press.

Schuman, Howard, Charlotte Steeh, Lawrence Bobo, and Maria Krysan. 1997. *Racial Attitudes in America: Trends and Interpretations*. Revised edition. Cambridge, MA: Harvard University Press.

Schwartz, Michael. 1988. *Radical Protest and Social Structure: The Southern Farmers' Alliance and Cotton Tenancy, 1880–1890*. Chicago: The University of Chicago Press.

Schweninger, Loren. 1990. *Black Property Owners in the South, 1790–1915*. Urbana: University of Illinois Press.

Scott, Anne Firor. 1984. "On Seeing and Not Seeing: A Case of Historical Invisibility." *The Journal of American History* 71 (1): 7–21.

Scott, Franklin D. 1963. *The Peopling of America: Perspectives on Immigration*. Washington, DC: American Historical Association.

Scott, George M., Jr. 1990. "A Resynthesis of the Primordial and Circumstantial Approaches to Ethnic Group Solidarity: Towards an Explanatory Model." *Ethnic and Racial Studies* 13 (2): 147–171.

Scott, Rebecca J. 1994. "Defining the Boundaries of Freedom in the World of Cane: Cuba, Brazil, and Louisiana After Emancipation." *American Historical Review* 99 (1): 70–102.

Sears, David O. 1994. "Urban Rioting in Los Angeles: A Comparison of 1965 With 1992." 237–253 in *The Los Angeles Riots: Lessons for the Urban Future*, edited by Mark Baldassare. Boulder, CO: Westview Press.

Sears, David O. and Donald R. Kinder. 1985. "Whites' Opposition to Busing: On Conceptualizing and Operationalizing Group Conflict." *Journal of Personality and Social Psychology* 48 (5): 1141–1147.

See, Katherine O'Sullivan and William J. Wilson. 1988. "Race and Ethnicity." 223–242 in *Handbook of Sociology*, edited by Neil Smelser. Newbury Park, CA: Sage.

Senior, Clarence. 1965. *The Puerto Ricans*. Chicago: Quadrangle Books.

Sennett, Richard. 1998. *The Corrosion of Character: The Personal Consequences of Work in the New Capitalism*. New York: W.W. Norton.

Sexton, Patricia Cayo. 1966. *Spanish Harlem: Anatomy of Poverty*. New York: Harper & Row.

Shannon, William V. 1963. *The American Irish*. New York: Macmillan.

Shapiro, Herbert. 1988. *White Violence and Black Response: From Reconstruction to Montgomery*. Amherst: University of Massachusetts Press.

Sharfman, Harold. 1977. *Jews on the Frontier*. Chicago: Regnery.

Shepperson, Wilbur S. 1965. *Emigration and Disenchantment: Portraits of Englishmen Repatriated From the United States*. Norman: University of Oklahoma Press.

Sherif, Muzafer and Carolyn W. Sherif. 1953. *Groups in Harmony and Tension: An Integration of Studies in Intergroup Relations*. New York: Harper and Brothers.

Shibutani, Tamotso and Kian M. Kwan. 1965. *Ethnic Stratification: A Comparative Approach*. New York: Macmillan.

Shibuya, Kumiko. 1992. "Patterns and Determinants of Minority Intermarriage in the San Franciso-Oakland Metropolitan Area, 1980." Paper presented at the American Sociological Association annual meeting, Pittsburgh, PA.

Shils, Edward. 1975. *Center and Periphery: Essays in Macrosociology*. Chicago: The University of Chicago Press.

Shin, Eui Hang and Kyung-Sup Chang. 1988. "Peripheralization of Immigrant Professionals: Korean Physicians in the United States." *International Migration Review* 22 (4): 609–626.

Shin, Eui Hang and Hyung Park. 1988. "An Analysis of Causes of Schisms in Ethnic Churches: The Case of Korean-American Churches." *Sociological Analysis* 49 (3): 234–248.

Shinagawa, Larry H. and Gin Y. Pang. 1990. "Marriage Patterns of Asian Americans in California, 1980." 225–282 in *Income and Status Differences Between White and Minority Americans*, edited by Sucheng Chan. Lewiston, NY: Edwin Mellon Press.

——. 1996. "Asian American Pan-Ethnicity and Intermarriage." *Amerasia Journal* 22 (2): 127–152.

Shipler, David K. 1997. *A Country of Strangers: Blacks and Whites in America*. New York: Alfred A. Knopf.

Shklar, Judith N. 1991. *American Citizenship: The Quest for Inclusion*. Cambridge, MA: Harvard University Press.

Shoemaker, Nancy. 1999. *American Indian Population Recovery in the Twentieth Century*. Albuquerque: University of New Mexico Press.

Shokeid, Moshe. 1988. *Children of Circumstances: Israeli Emigrants in New York*. Ithaca, NY: Cornell University Press.

Sigelman, Lee and Susan Welch. 1991. *Black Americans' Views of Racial Inequality: The Dream Deferred*. Cambridge, UK: Cambridge University Press.

Silberman, Charles E. 1985. *A Certain People: American Jews and Their Lives Today*. New York: Summit Books.

Simmel, Georg. 1955. *Conflict and the Web of Group Affiliations*. New York: The Free Press.

Simon, Rita J. and James P. Lynch. 1999. "A Comparative Assessment of Public Opinion Toward Immigrants and Immigration Policies." *International Migration Review* 33 (2): 455–467.

Sinclair, Upton. 1906. *The Jungle*. New York: New American Library.

Sindler, Allen P. 1978. *Bakke, DeFunis, and Minority Admissions: The Quest for Equal Opportunity*. New York: Longman.

Singer, David, ed. 1988. *American Jewish Yearbook, 1989*. New York: American Jewish Committee.

Siu, Paul. 1952. "The Sojourner." *American Journal of Sociology* 58: 34–44.

Skardal, Dorothy Burton. 1974. *The Divided Heart: Scandinavian Immigrant Experience Through Literary Sources*. Lincoln: University of Nebraska Press.

Sklare, Marshall. 1971. *America's Jews*. New York: Random House.

——. 1972 [1955]. *Conservative Judaism: An American Religious Movement.* New York: Schocken.

Sklare, Marshall and Joseph Greenblum. 1967. *Jewish Identity on the Suburban Frontier.* New York: Basic Books.

Skrentny, John David. 1996. *The Ironies of Affirmative Action: Politics, Culture, and Justice in America.* Chicago: University of Chicago Press.

——. 2000. "The Origins and Politics of Affirmative Action." 269–286 in *Multiculturalism in the United States: Current Issues, Contemporary Voices,* edited by Peter Kivisto and Georganne Rundblad. Thousand Oaks, CA: Pine Forge Press.

Slayton, Robert A. 1986. *Back of the Yards: The Making of a Local Democracy.* Chicago: The University of Chicago Press.

Sleeper, Jim. 1990. *The Closest of Strangers: Liberalism and the Politics of Race in New York.* New York: W.W. Norton.

Smith, Anthony. 1981. *The Ethnic Revival.* Cambridge, UK: Cambridge University Press.

——. 1986. *The Ethnic Origins of Nations.* Oxford: Blackwell.

Smith, Charles V. and Lewis M. Killian. 1990. "Sociological Foundations of the Civil Rights Movement." 105–116 in *Sociology in America,* edited by Herbert Gans. Newbury Park, CA: Sage Publications.

Smith, Dorothy. 1990. *Texts, Facts, and Femininity.* London: Routledge and Kegan Paul.

Smith, J. Owens. 1987. *The Politics of Racial Inequality: A Systematic Comparative Macro-Analysis From the Colonial Period to 1970.* New York: Greenwood Press.

Smith, M. Estell. 1982. "Tourism and Native Americans." *Cultural Survival Quarterly* 6 (Summer): 10–12.

Smith, M. G. 1982. "Ethnicity and Ethnic Groups in America: The View From Harvard." *Ethnic and Racial Studies* 5 (1): 1–22.

Smith, Timothy L. 1969. "Immigrant Social Aspirations and American Education, 1880–1930." *American Quarterly* 21 (3): 523–543.

Smolicz, J. J. 1997. "Australia: From Migrant Country to Multicultural Nation." *International Migration Review* 31 (1): 171–186.

Sniderman, Paul M. and Thomas Piazza. 1993. *The Scar of Race.* Cambridge, MA: The Belknap Press of Harvard University Press.

Snipp, C. Matthew. 1989. *American Indians: The First of This Land.* New York: Russell Sage Foundation.

Sollors, Werner. 1981. "Theory of American Ethnicity, or: "?S Ethnic?/Ti and American/Ti, De or United (w) States S Sl and Theor?" *American Quarterly* 33 (3): 257–283.

——, ed. 1989. *The Invention of Ethnicity.* New York: Oxford University Press.

Solomon, Barbara Miller. 1956. *Ancestors and Immigrants: A Changing New England Tradition.* Cambridge, MA: Harvard University Press.

Solomos, John and Les Back. 1995. "Marxism, Racism, and Ethnicity." *American Behavioral Scientist* 38 (3): 407–420.

Sorin, Gerald. 1985. *The Prophetic Minority: American Jewish Immigrant Radicals, 1880–1920.* Bloomington: Indiana University Press.

Southern, David W. 1987. *Gunnar Myrdal and Black-White Relations: The Use and Abuse of An American Dilemma, 1944–1969.* Baton Rouge: Louisiana State University Press.

Sowell, Thomas. 1981a. *Ethnic America: A History.* New York: Basic Books.

——. 1981b. *Pink and Brown People and Other Controversial Essays.* Stanford, CA: Hoover Institution Press.

——. 1989. "Affirmative Action: A Worldwide Disaster." *Commentary* 88: 21–41.

Spicer, Edward H. 1962. *Cycles of Conquest: The Impact of Spain, Mexico, and the United States on the Indians of the Southwest.* Tucson: University of Arizona Press.

——. 1980. *The American Indians.* Cambridge, MA: The Belknap Press of Harvard University Press.

Spickard, Paul R. 1989. *Mixed Blood: Intermarriage and Ethnic Identity in Twentieth Century America.* Madison: University of Wisconsin Press.

Spindler, George and Louise Spindler. 1984. *Dreamers Without Power: The Menominee.* Prospect Heights, IL: Waveland Press.

Spitzberg, Irving J., Jr. 1987. *Racial Politics in Little Rock, 1954–1964.* New York: Garland.

Stack, Carol. 1974. *All Our Kin: Strategies for Survival in a Black Community.* New York: Harper & Row.

Stampp, Kenneth M. 1956. *The Peculiar Institution: Slavery in the Ante-bellum South.* New York: Alfred A. Knopf.

Stanton, William. 1960. *The Leopard's Spots: Scientific Attitudes Towards Race in America, 1815–1859.* Chicago: The University of Chicago Press.

Starr, Paul. 1992. "Social Categories and Claims in the Liberal State." *Social Research* 59 (2): 263–295.

Steele, Shelby. 1990. *The Content of Our Character: A New Vision of Race in America.* New York: St. Martin's Press.

Stein, Howard F. and Robert F. Hill. 1977. *The Ethnic Imperative: Examining the New White Ethnic Movement.*

Stein, Wayne J. 1997. "American Indians and Gambling: Economic and Social Aspects." 145–166 in *American Indian Studies,* edited by Dane Morrison. New York: Peter Lang.

Steinberg, Stephen. 1981. *The Ethnic Myth: Race, Ethnicity, and Class in America.* New York: Atheneum.

——. 1995. *Turning Back: The Retreat From Racial Justice in American Thought and Policy.* Boston: Beacon Press.

——. 2000. "Affirmative Action and Liberal Capitulation." 287–294 in *Multiculturalism in the United States: Current Issues, Contemporary Voices,* edited by Peter Kivisto and Georganne Rundblad. Thousand Oaks, CA: Pine Forge Press.

Steiner, Stan. 1968. *The New Indians.* New York: Dell.

——. 1970. *La Raza: The Mexican Americans.* New York: Harper & Row.

Stoddard, Ellwyn R. 1973. *Mexican Americans.* New York: Random House.

——. 1987. *Maquilla: Assembly Plants in Northern Mexico.* El Paso: Texas Western Press.

Stoddard, Lothrop. 1920. *The Rising Tide of Color Against White World-Supremacy.* New York: Charles Scribner's Sons.

Stone, John. 1985. *Racial Conflict in Contemporary Society.* Cambridge, MA: Harvard University Press.

Storti, Craig. 1991. *Incident at Bitter Creek: The Story of the Rock Springs Chinese Massacre.* Ames: Iowa State University Press.

Strauss, Anselm. 1991. *Creating Sociological Awareness: Collective Images and Symbolic Representation.* New Brunswick, NJ: Transaction Publishers.

Struyck, Raymond, Neil Mayer, and John A. Tuccillo. 1983. *Federal Housing Policy at President Reagan's Midterm.* Washington, DC: The Urban Institute Press.

Stuckey, Sterling. 1987. *Slave Culture: Nationalist Theory and the Foundation of Black America.* New York: Oxford University Press.

Suarez-Orozco, Marcelo M. 1998. *Crossings: Mexican Immigration in Interdisciplinary Perspectives.* Cambridge, MA: Harvard University Press.

Sullivan, Teresa A. 1984. "The Occupational Prestige of Women Immigrants: A Comparison of Cubans and Mexicans." *International Migration Review* 18 (4): 1045–1062.

Sumka, Howard. 1978. "Displacement in Revitalizing Neighborhoods: A Review and Research Strategy." 134–167 in *Occasional Papers in Housing and Community Affairs,* vol 2. Washington, DC: Department of Housing and Urban Development.

Sumner, William Graham. 1940 [1906]. *Folkways: A Study of the Sociological Importance of Usages, Manners, Customs, Mores, and Morals.* Boston: Ginn.

Sung, Betty Lee. 1967. *Mountain of Gold.* New York: Macmillan.

Swain, Carol M. 2001. "Affirmative Action: Legislative History, Judicial Interpretations, Public Consensus." 318–347 in *America Becoming: Racial Trends and Their Consequences,* vol. 1, edited by Neil J. Smelser, William Julius Wilson, and Faith Mitchell. Washington, DC: National Academy Press.

Swatez, Marc Jon. 1990. "United We Stand: The Merging of the German and Eastern European Jews in Chicago." Paper presented at the annual meeting of the Midwest Sociological Society, Chicago.

Taeuber, Karl B. 1983. *Racial Residential Segregation, 28 Cities, 1970–1980.* Working paper 83-12. Madison: Center for Demography and Ecology, University of Wisconsin.

Tajfel, Henri. 1969. "Cognitive Aspects of Prejudice." *Journal of Biosocial Science,* Supplement no. 1.

——. 1978. *The Social Psychology of Minorities.* London: Minority Rights Groups.

——. 1981. *Human Groups and Social Categories.* Cambridge, UK: Cambridge University Press.

Takagi, Dana Y. 1993. *The Retreat From Race: Asian-American Admissions and Racial Politics.* New Brunswick, NJ: Rutgers University Press.

Takahashi, Jere. 1997. *Nisei/Sansei: Shifting Japanese American Identities and Politics.* Philadelphia: Temple University Press.

Takaki, Ronald. 1979. *Iron Cages: Race and Culture in 19th-Century America.* New York: Alfred A. Knopf.

——. 1989. *Strangers From a Different Shore: A History of Asian Americans.* Boston: Little, Brown.

——. 1992. *The Retreat From Race: Asian-American Admissions and Racial Politics.* New Brunswick, NJ: Rutgers University Press.

——. 1993a. *A Different Mirror: A History of Multicultural America.* Boston: Little, Brown.

——. 1993b. "Multiculturalism: Battleground or Meeting Ground." *Annals of the American Academy,* AAPSS, 530: 109–121.

Taylor, Charles, with commentary by Amy Gutmann, Steven C. Rockefeller, Michael Walzer, and Susan Wolf. 1992. *Multiculturalism and 'The Politics of Recognition.'* Princeton, NJ: Princeton University Press.

Taylor, D. Garth, Paul B. Sheatsley, and Andrew M. Greeley. 1978. "Attitudes Toward Racial Integration." *Scientific American* 238 (June): 42–51.

Taylor, Philip. 1971. *The Distant Magnet: European Emigration to the U.S.A.* New York: Harper & Row.

Terry, Don. 1991. "Indian Treaty Accord in Wisconsin." *New York Times,* May 21: A8.

——. 1996. "In White Flight's Wake, a Town Tries to Keep Its Balance." *New York Times,* March 11: A6.

TeSelle, Sallie, ed. 1973. *The Rediscovery of Ethnicity.* New York: Harper & Row.

Thernstrom, Stephan. 1973. *The Other Bostonians.* Cambridge, MA: Harvard University Press.

Thernstrom, Stephan, Ann Orlov, and Oscar Handlin, eds. 1980. *Harvard Encyclopedia of American Ethnic Groups.* Cambridge, MA: Belknap Press of the Harvard University Press.

Thistlethwaite, Frank. 1960. "Migrations From Europe Overseas in the Nineteenth and Twentieth Centuries." XIe Congres International des Sciences Historiques, *Rapports* (Uppsala, Sweden) 5: 32–60.

Thomas, Melvin E. 1993. "Race, Class, and Personal Income: An Empirical Test of the Declining Significance of Race Thesis, 1968–1988." *Social Problems* 40 (3): 328–342.

Thomas, Piri. 1967. *Down These Mean Streets.* New York: Alfred A. Knopf.

Thomas, Robert K. 1968. "Pan-Indianism." 128–140 in *The American Indian Today,* edited by Stuart Levine and Nancy Oestreich Luine. Baltimore: Penguin Books.

Thomas, William I. 1909. *Source Book for Social Origins: Ethnological Materials, Psychological Standpoint, Classified and Annotated Bibliographics for the Interpretation of Savage Societies.* Boston: Badger.

Thomas, William I. and Florian Znaniecki. 1918. *The Polish Peasant in Europe and America.* New York: Alfred A. Knopf.

Thompson, Cooper, Emmett Schaefer, and Harry Brod. 2003. *White Men Challenging Racism: 35 Personal Stories.* Durham, NC: Duke University Press.

Thomsen, Craig. 1993. "After Making a Run for the Border: A Historical and Economic Analysis of Illegal Mexican Immigrants in the United States." Unpublished paper.

Thornton, Russell. 1987. *American Indian Holocaust and Survival: A Population History Since 1492.* Norman: University of Oklahoma Press.

——. 1990. *The Cherokees: A Population History.* Lincoln: University of Nebraska Press.

Tichenor, Daniel J. 2002. *Dividing Lines: The Politics of Immigration Control in America.* Princeton, NJ: Princeton University Press.

Tienda, Marta. 1989. "Puerto Ricans and the Underclass Debate." *Annals* 501 (January): 105–119.

——. 1999. "Immigration, Opportunity, and Social Cohesion." 129–146 in *Diversity and Its Discontents: Culture Conflict and Common Ground in Contemporary American Society*, edited by Neil J. Smelser and Jeffrey C. Alexander. Princeton, NJ: Princeton University Press.

Tienda, Marta and Ding-Tzann Lii. 1987. "Minority Concentration and Earnings Inequality: Blacks, Hispanics, and Asians Compared." *American Journal of Sociology* 93 (1): 141–165.

Tilly, Charles. 1990. "The Weight of the Past on American Immigration." Unpublished paper.

Tippeconnic, John W., III. 1990. "American Indians: Education, Demographics, and the 1990s." 249–257 in *U.S. Race Relations in the 1980s and 1990s*, edited by Gail E. Thomas. New York: Hemisphere.

Tizon, Orlando. 1999. "Congregation and Family: Changing Filipino Identities." Ph.D. dissertation, Loyola University.

Tocqueville, Alexis de. 1981 [1835]. *Democracy in America*. New York: The Modern Library.

Todorov, Tzvetan. 1984. *The Conquest of America: The Question of the Other*. New York: Harper & Row.

Tolnay, Stewart E. and E. M. Beck. 1992. "Racial Violence and Black Migration in the American South, 1910 to 1930." *American Sociological Review* 57 (1): 103–116.

Tomasi, Lydio F. 1978. *The Italian in America: The Progressive View, 1892–1914*. New York: Center for Migration Studies.

Tomasi, Silvano M. 1975. *Piety and Power: The Role of the Italian Parishes in the New York Metropolitan Area, 1880–1930*. New York: Center for Migration Studies.

Tong, Benson. 2000. *The Chinese Americans*. Westport, CT: Greenwood Press.

Tricarico, Donald. 1984. *The Italians of Greenwich Village*. New York: Center for Migration Studies.

——. 1989. "In a New Light: Italian-American Ethnicity in the Mainstream." 24–46 in *The Ethnic Enigma*, edited by Peter Kivisto. Philadelphia: Balch Institute Press.

Trommler, Frank and Elliott Shore, eds. 2001. *The German-American Encounter: Conflict and Cooperation Between Two Cultures*. New York: Berghahn Books.

Tsukashima, Ronald Tadao. 1991. "Cultural Endowment, Disadvantaged Status, and Economic Niche: The Development of an Ethnic Trade." *International Migration Review* 25 (2): 333–354.

Tuan, Mia. 1999. *Forever Foreigners or Honorary Whites? The Asian Ethnic Experience*. New Brunswick, NJ: Rutgers University Press.

Tuch, Steven A. and Jack K. Martin, eds. 1997. *Racial Attitudes in the 1990s: Continuity and Change*. Westport, CT: Praeger.

Tucker, William H. 1994. *The Science and Politics of Racial Research*. Urbana: University of Illinois Press.

Ueda, Reed. 1992. "American National Identity and Race in Immigrant Generations: Reconsidering Hansen's 'Law.' " *Journal of Interdisciplinary History* 22 (3): 483–491.

Um, Shin Ja. 1992. "Korean Married Immigrant Woman Working in the Dallas Garment Industry: Looking for Feminist Threads in Patriarchial Cloth." Paper presented at the Midwest Sociological Society annual meeting, Kansas City, MO.

Ungeheuer, Frederick. 1987. "A New Band of Tribal Tycoons." *Time* 129 (March 16): 56–59.

United Jewish Communities. 2002. http://www.ujc.org/njps.

U.S. Bureau of the Census. 1975. *Historical Statistics of the United States: Colonial Times to 1970*. Part 1. Washington, DC: Government Printing Office.

——. 1984. *1980 Census of the Population*, PC80-1-D1-A. Washington, DC: Government Printing Office.

——. 1986. *Projections of the Hispanic Population of the United States: 1983–2080*. Washington, DC: Government Printing Office.

——. 1989. *The Hispanic Population in the United States*, Current Population Reports, Series P-20, No. 438. Washington, DC: Government Printing Office.

——. 1991. "The Economic Status of Hispanics in the United States." *Current Population Reports.* Washington, DC: Government Printing Office.

——. 1992a. *The Black Population in the United States,* Current Population Reports, Series P-20, No. 462. Washington, DC: Government Printing Office.

——.1992b. *Detailed Ancestry Groups for States,* 1990 Census of Population, CP-S-1-2. Washington, DC: Government Printing Office.

——. 1999. *Census Bureau Facts for Features,* CB-99-FF.14. Washington, DC: Government Printing Office.

——. 2000. *Census Bureau Facts for Features,* CB-00-FF.13. Washington, DC: Government Printing Office.

——. 2001. "Diversity of the Country's Hispanics Highlighted." http://www.census.gov.

——. 2002. *Current Population Survey,* 2002. Ethnic and Hispanic Statistics Branch, Population Division. Washington, DC: Government Printing Office.

——. 2003. *The Foreign-Born Population: 2000.* Washington, DC: Government Printing Office.

U.S. Department of Housing and Urban Development. 1980. *Condominium Conversions.* Washington, DC: Government Printing Office.

U.S. Immigration and Naturalization Service. 1985. *Statistical Yearbook.* Washington, DC: Government Printing Office.

U.S. Public Health Services. 2001. *Trends in Indian Health.* Rockville, MD: Goverment Printing Office.

Valdes, Dennis Nodin. 1991. *Al Norte: Agricultural Workers in the Great Lakes Region, 1917–1970.* Austin: University of Texas Press.

Valentine, Charles A. 1968. *Culture and Poverty: Critique and Counter Proposals.* Chicago: The University of Chicago Press.

Valocchi, Steve. 1996. "The Emergence of the Integrationist Ideology in the Civil Rights Movement." *Social Problems* 43 (1): 116–130.

van den Berghe, Pierre L. 1965. *South Africa: A Study in Conflict.* Middletown, CT: Wesleyan University Press.

——. 1967. *Race and Racism: A Comparative Perspective.* New York: John Wiley and Sons.

——. 1970. *Race and Ethnicity: Essays in Comparative Sociology.* New York: Basic Books.

——. 1978. "Race and Ethnicity: A Sociobiological Perspective." *Ethnic and Racial Studies* 1 (4): 401–411.

——. 1981. *The Ethnic Phenomenon.* New York: Elsevier.

——. 1986. "Ethnicity and the Sociobiology Debate." 246–263 in *Theories of Race and Ethnic Relations,* edited by John Rex and David Mason. Cambridge, UK: Cambridge University Press.

——. 1990. "Why Most Sociologists Don't (and Won't) Think Evolutionarily." *Sociological Forum* 5 (2): 173–185.

Vander Zanden, James W. 1973. *American Minority Relations.* New York: Plenum.

Vecoli, Rudolph J. 1964. "Contadini in Chicago: A Critique of the Uprooted." *Journal of American History* 51: 404–417.

——. 1970. "Ethnicity: A Neglected Dimension of American History." 70–88 in *The State of American History,* edited by Herbert J. Bass. Chicago: Quadrangle Books.

——. 1979. "The Resurgence of American Immigration History." *American Studies International* (Winter) 17 (2): 46–66.

——. 1987. *Italian Immigration in Rural and Small Town America.* New York: Italian America Historical Association.

——. 1991. "Inter-ethnic Perspectives on American Immigration History." Paper presented in Vaxjo, Sweden, May 31.

Vidich, Arthur J. 1992. "Boston's North End: An American Epic." *Journal of Contemporary Ethnography* 21 (April): 80–102.

Vidich, Arthur J. and Joseph Bensman. 1958. *Small Town in Mass Society: Class, Power, and Religion in a Rural Community.* Princeton, NJ: Princeton University Press.

Vigil, James Diego. 1988. *Barrio Gangs: Street Life and Identity in Southern California.* Austin: University of Texas Press.

———. 2002. *A Rainbow of Gangs: Street Cultures in the Mega-city.* Austin: University of Texas Press.

Vinje, David. 1985. "Cultural Values and Economic Development on Reservations." 155–175 in *American Indian Policy in the Twentieth Century,* edited by Vine Delona, Jr. Norman: University of Oklahoma Press.

Vogel, Virgil J. 1972. *This Country Was Ours.* New York: Harper & Row.

Vogt, Evan Z. 1957. "The Acculturation of American Indians." *Annals of the American Academy of Political and Social Science* 311: 137–146.

Wacker, R. Fred. 1983. *Ethnicity, Pluralism, and Race: Race Relations Theory in America Before Myrdal.* Westport, CT: Greenwood Press.

Waddell, Jack O. and O. Michael Watson, eds. 1971. *The American Indian in Urban Society.* Boston: Little, Brown.

Wakatsuki, Yasuo. 1979. "Japanese Emigration to the United States." *Perspectives in American History* 12: 395–465.

Waldinger, Roger. 1986. *Through the Eye of the Needle: Immigrants and Enterprise in New York's Garment Trades.* New York: New York University Press.

———. 1994. "The Making of an Immigrant Niche." *International Migration Review* 28 (1): 3–30.

Waldinger, Roger and Mehdi Bozorgmehr, eds. 1996. *Ethnic Los Angeles.* New York: Russell Sage Foundation.

Waldinger, Roger and David Fitzgerald. 2004. "Transnationalism in Question." *American Journal of Sociology* 109 (5): 1177–1195.

Waldinger, Roger and Michael I. Lichter. 2003. *How the Other Half Works: Immigration and the Social Organization of Labor.* Berkeley: University of California Press.

Wallerstein, Immanuel. 1974. *The Modern World-System: Capitalist Agriculture and the Origins of the European World-Economy in the Sixteenth Century.* New York: John Wiley and Sons.

Ware, Caroline F. 1935. *Greenwich Village, 1920–1930.* Boston: Houghton Mifflin.

———. 1940. "Cultural Groups in the United States." 62–73 in *The Cultural Approach to History,* edited by Caroline F. Ware. New York: Gordon Press.

Warner, R. Stephen. 1992. "Religious Institutions Emerging Among New (Post-1965) Immigrant Groups in the U.S." Paper presented at the Midwest Sociological Society annual meeting, Kansas City, MO.

Washington, Booker T. 1963 [1901]. *Up From Slavery.* New York: Bantam Books.

Waters, Mary C. 1990. *Ethnic Options Choosing Identities in America.* Berkeley: University of California Press.

———. 1999. *Black Identities: West Indian Immigrant Dreams and American Realities.* Cambridge, MA: Harvard University Press and New York: Russell Sage Foundation.

———. 2000. "Immigration, Intermarriage, and the Challenges of Measuring Racial/Ethnic Identities." *American Journal of Public Health* 90 (11): 1735–1737.

Wattenberg, Ben. 1991. *The First Universal Nation: Leading Indicators and Ideas About the Surge of America in the 1990s.* New York: The Free Press.

Wax, Murray L. 1971. *Indian Americans: Unity and Diversity.* Englewood Cliffs, NJ: Prentice-Hall.

Waxman, Chaim I. 1983. *America's Jews in Transition.* Philadelphia: Temple University Press.

Weber, David J. 1973. *Foreigners in Their Native Land.* Albuquerque: University of New Mexico Press.

Weed, Perry. 1971. *The White Ethnic Movement and Ethnic Politics.* New York: Macmillan.

Weibel-Orlando, Joan. 1991. *Indian Country, L.A.: Maintaining Ethnic Community in a Complex Society.* Urbana: University of Illinois Press.

Weinberg, Sydney Stahl. 1988. *The World of Our Mothers.* Chapel Hill: University of North Carolina Press.

Weiss, Bernard, ed. 1982. *American Education and the European Immigrant.* Urbana: University of Illinois Press.

Wells, Robert V. 1975. *The Population of the British Colonies in America Before 1776: A Survey of Census Data.* Princeton, NJ: Princeton University Press.

West, Cornel. 1993. *Race Matters.* Boston: Beacon Press.

White, Ronald C., Jr. 1990. *Liberty and Justice for All: Racial Reform and the Social Gospel.* New York: Harper & Row.

Whyte, William Foote. 1943. *Street Corner Society: The Social Structure of an Italian Slum.* Chicago: The University of Chicago Press.

Wiley, Norbert. 1986. "Early American Sociology and the Polish Peasant." *Sociological Theory* 4 (Spring): 20–40.

Wilhelm, Sidney M. 1970. *Who Needs the Negro?* Garden City, NY: Doubleday.

Williams, Norma. 1980. *The Mexican American Family: Tradition and Change.* Dix Hills, NY: General Hall.

Williams, Rhonda. 2004. *The Politics of Public Housing: Black Women's Struggles Against Urban Inequality.* New York: Oxford University Press.

Williams, Richard. 1990. *Hierarchial Structures and Social Value: The Creation of Black and Irish Identities in the United States.* Cambridge, UK: Cambridge University Press.

Williams, Robin M., Jr. 1977. *Mutual Accommodation: Ethnic Conflict and Cooperation.* Minneapolis: University of Minnesota Press.

Williamson, Joel. 1980. *New People: Miscegenation and Mulattoes in the United States.* New York: The Free Press.

——. 1986. *A Rage for Order: Black-White Relations in the American South Since Emancipation.* New York: Oxford University Press.

Willie, Charles Vert. 1979. "The Inclining Significance of Race." 145–158 in *The Caste and Class Controversy,* edited by Charles Vert Willie. Bayside, NY: General Hall.

Wilson, Kenneth L. and W. Allen Martin. 1982. "Ethnic Enclaves: A Comparison of the Cuban and Black Economies in Miami." *American Journal of Sociology* 88 (1): 135–160.

Wilson, Kenneth L. and Alejandro Portes. 1980. "Immigrant Enclaves: An Analysis of the Labor Market Experiences of Cubans in Miami." *American Journal of Sociology* 86 (2): 295–319.

Wilson, William Julius. 1978. *The Declining Significance of Race: Blacks and Changing American Institutions.* Chicago: The University of Chicago Press.

——. 1987. *The Truly Disadvantaged: The Inner City, the Underclass, and Public Policy.* Chicago: The University of Chicago Press.

——. 1991. "Studying Inner-City Social Dislocations: The Challenge of Public Agenda Research." *American Sociological Review* 56 (1): 1–14.

——. 1996. *When Work Disappears: The World of the New Urban Poor.* New York: Alfred A. Knopf.

——. 1999. *The Bridge Over the Racial Divide: Rising Inequality and Coalition Politics.* Berkeley and New York: University of California Press and the Russell Sage Foundation.

Winant, Howard. 1999. "Whiteness at Century's End." 23–45 in *The Making and Unmaking of Whiteness,* edited by M. Wray. Durham, NC: Duke University Press.

——. 2000. "Race and Race Theory." *Annual Review of Sociology* 26: 169–185.

——. 2001. *The World Is a Ghetto: Race and Democracy Since World War II.* New York: Basic Books.

Winter, J. Alan. 1996. "Symbolic Ethnicity or Religion Among Jews in the United States: A Test of Gansian Hypotheses." *Review of Religious Research* 37 (3): 137–151.

——. 2002. "Consistency and Importance of Jewish Identiy and One's Own or One's Child's Intermarriage." *Review of Religious Research* 44 (1): 38–57.

Wirth, Louis. 1945. "The Problem of Minority Groups." 347–372 in *The Science of Man in the World Crisis,* edited by Ralph Linton. New York: Columbia University Press.

——. 1956 [1928]. *The Ghetto.* Chicago: The University of Chicago Press.

Wittke, Carl. 1939. *We Who Built America: The Saga of the Immigrant.* New York: Prentice-Hall.

——. 1952. *Refugees of Revolution: The German Forty-Eighters in America.* Philadelphia: University of Pennsylvania Press.

——. 1956. *The Irish in America.* Baton Rouge: Louisiana State University Press.

Woll, Allen L. and Randall M. Miller. 1987. *Ethnic and Racial Images in American Film and Television: Historical Essays and Bibliography.* New York: Garland.

Wong, Bernard. 1982. *Chinatown: Economic Adaptation and Ethnic Identity of the Chinese.* New York: CBS College.

——. 1987. "The Chinese: New Immigrants in New York's Chinatown." 243–271 in *New Immigrants in New York,* edited by Nancy Foner. New York: Columbia University Press.

Wong, Jade Snow. 1945. *Fifth Chinese Daughter.* New York: Harper and Brothers.

Wong, Morrison G. 1988. "The Chinese American Family." 230–257 in *Ethnic Families in America: Patterns and Variations,* edited by Charles H. Mindel, Robert W. Habenstein, and Roosevelt Wright, Jr. New York: Elsevier.

Woo, Deborah. 1999. *Glass Ceilings and Asian Americans: The New Face of Workplace Barriers.* Walnut Creek, CA: Alta Mira Press.

Woocher, Jonathan. 1986. *Sacred Survival: The Civil Religion of American Jews.* Bloomington: Indiana University Press.

Wood, Forrest G. 1990. *The Arrogance of Faith: Christianity and Race in America From the Colonial Era to the Twentieth Century.* New York: Alfred A. Knopf.

Woods, Robert A. 1903. *Americans in Process: A Settlement Study.* Boston: Houghton, Mifflin.

Woodson, Carter. 1968. *The Education of the Negro Prior to 1861.* New York: Arno Press.

Woodward, C. Vann. 1974. *The Strange Career of Jim Crow.* New York: Oxford University Press.

World Jewish Congress. 2003. http://www.wjc.org.il/communities/html.

Wright, Richard. 1937. *Black Boy: A Record of Childhood and Youth.* New York: Harper and Brothers.

Wrobel, Paul. 1979. *Our Way: Family, Parish, and Neighborhood in a Polish-American Community.* Notre Dame, IN: University of Notre Dame Press.

Yanagisako, Sylvia J. 1985. *Transforming the Past.* Stanford, CA: Stanford University Press.

Yancey, William L., Eugene P. Ericksen, and Richard N. Juliani. 1976. "Emergent Ethnicity: A Review and Reformulation." *American Sociological Review* 41 (3): 391–403.

Yancey, William L., Eugene P. Ericksen, and George Leon. 1985. "The Structure of Pluralism: 'We're All Italian Around Here, Aren't We, Mrs. O'Brien?' " 94–116 in *Ethnicity and Race in the U.S.A.: Toward the Twenty-First Century,* edited by Richard Alba. London: Routledge and Kegan Paul.

Yans-McLaughlin, Virginia. 1977. *Family and Community: Italian Immigrants in Buffalo, 1880–1930.* Ithaca, NY: Cornell University Press.

Yinger, J. Milton. 1985. "Ethnicity." *Annual Review of Sociology* 11: 151–180.

——. 1986. "Intersecting Strands in the Theorization of Race and Ethnic Relations." 20–41 in *Theories of Race and Ethnic Relations,* edited by John Rex and David Mason. Cambridge, UK: Cambridge University Press.

Yoon, In-Jin. 1991. "The Changing Significance of Ethnic and Class Resources in Immigrant Business: The Case of Korean Immigrant Business in Chicago." *International Migration Review* 25 (2): 303–332.

——. 1992. "The Social Origins of Korean Immigration to the United States, 1965–Present." Paper presented at the American Sociological Association annual meeting, Pittsburgh, PA.

Young, Donald. 1932. *American Minority Peoples: A Study in Racial and Cultural Conflicts in the United States.* New York: Harper and Brothers.

Yu, Elena S. H. 1980. "Filipino Migration and Community Organizations in the United States." *California Sociologist* 3 (Summer): 76–102.

Zangwill, Israel. 1909. *The Melting-Pot: A Drama in Four Acts.* New York: Macmillan.

Zelinsky, Wilbur. 2001. *The Enigma of Ethnicity: Another American Dilemma.* Iowa City: University of Iowa Press.

Zeul, Carolyn R. and Craig R. Humphrey. 1971. "The Integratives of Black Residents in Suburban Neighborhoods: A Reexamination of the Contact Hypothesis." *Social Problems* 18 (4): 462–474.

Zhou, Min. 2001. "Contemporary Immigration and the Dynamics of Race and Ethnicity." 200–241 in *American Becoming: Racial Trends and Consequences,* vol. 1., edited by Neil J. Smelser, William Julius Wilson, and Faith Mitchell. Washington, DC: National Academy Press.

——. 2002. "The Enclave Economy and Ethnic Social Structure: Sources of Social Capital in Facilitating the Education of Immigrant Children." Paper presented at the International Sociological Association meeting in Brisbane, Australia, July 11.

Zhou, Min and John R. Logan. 1989. "Returns on Human Capital in Ethnic Enclaves: New York City's Chinatown." *American Sociological Review* 54 (5): 809–820.

——. 1991. "In and Out of Chinatown: Residential Mobility and Segregation of New York City's Chinese." *Social Forces* 70 (2): 387–407.

Zorbaugh, Harvey. 1929. *The Gold Coast and the Slum.* Chicago: The University of Chicago Press.

Zunz, Olivier. 1982. *The Changing Face of Inequality: Urbanization, Industrial Development, and Immigrants in Detroit, 1880–1920.* Chicago: The University of Chicago Press.

——. 1985. "American History and the Changing Meaning of Assimilation." *Journal of American Ethnic History* 4 (2): 53–72.

Zweigenhaft, Richard L. and G. William Domhoff. 1991. *Blacks in the White Establishment? A Study of Race and Class in America.* New Haven, CT: Yale University Press. ✦

Photo Credits

Front Cover
(Top to bottom): Corbis images; Corbis images; Corbis images; Courtesy of Special Collections (Hauberg Collection), Augustana College.

Chapter 1
Page 5—courtesy of the Library of Congress; page 16— Steven J. Gold.

Chapter 2
Page 49—courtesy of the Swenson Center, Augustana College; page 59—Steven J. Gold; page 60—Steven J. Gold.

Chapter 3
Page 69—Survey Graphic; page 92—courtesy of the Library of Congress; page 97—courtesy of the Library of Congress.

Chapter 4
Page 109—courtesy of the Swenson Center, Augustana College; page 110—courtesy of the Library of Congress; page 125—courtesy of the Library of Congress; page 143—courtesy of Special Collections (Hauberg Collection), Augustana College.

Chapter 5
Page 160—Steven J. Gold.

Chapter 6
Page 197—Larry Fisher and the *Quad City Times;* page 210—Steven J. Gold; page 212—Wendy Ng; page 216—Steven J. Gold.

Chapter 7
Page 232—Steven J. Gold; page 244—courtesy of Mashantucket Pequot Tribal Nation.

Chapter 8
Page 279—Steven J. Gold; page 287—Steven J. Gold; page 290—Steven J. Gold.

Chapter 9
Page 306—Steven J. Gold; page 324—Steven J. Gold; page 329—Wendy Ng.

Chapter 10
Page 351—Steven J. Gold. ✦

Author Index

A, B, C

Abelmann, Nancy, 315
Abramson, Harold J., 42, 158
Adamic, Louis, 31
Adorno, T. W., 57
Aho, James A., 177
Alba, Richard D., 104, 106, 154, 161, 163, 164, 166, 167, 211, 288, 289, 332
Alexander, Adele Logan, 94
Allen, Irving Lewis, 58
Allen, Theodore, 52
Allen, Walter R., 204, 210
Allport, Gordon, 57
Anders, Gary, 245, 246
Anderson, Charles H., 72
Anderson, Elijah, 10, 219, 220
Angelou, Maya, 7, 8, 9, 11
Ansell, Amy, 178
Anthias, Floya, 46
Aponte, Robert, 286
Appel, John, 158
Applebaum, M., 47
Applebaum, Richard, 288
Aptheker, Herbert, 92
Archdeacon, Thomas, 13, 72, 158, 164
Arizona Republic, 248
Auletta, Ken, 220
Awanohara, Susumu, 308
Back, Les, 46, 347
Baer, Hans A., 189
Bailyn, Bernard, 68, 69, 70
Baker, Ray Stannard, 122
Balch, Emily, 110, 111
Banner-Haley, Charles T., 216
Banton, Michael, 30, 34, 35, 47
Barberia, Lorena, 268
Barkan, Elazar, 28, 35

Barrera, Mario, 129, 130, 278, 285
Barringer, Herbert, 304
Barth, Fredrik, 53
Barth, Gunther, 134
Barton, Josef J., 104
Basch, Linda, 55
Bataille, Gretchen, 248, 249
Baudrillard, Jean, 19
Baum, Dan, 240, 241
Bayor, Ronald H., 108
Bean, Frank D., 259, 269, 286
Becerra, Rosina M., 287
Beck, E. M., 127
Beckett, Jeremy, 341
Beer, William R., 201
Bell, Daniel, 151
Benedict, Ruth, 28, 35
Benhabib, Seyla, 350
Benjamin, Lois, 204
Bensman, Joseph, 152, 154
Berger, Bennett, 154
Berle, Beatrice, 272
Berlin, Ira, 86, 93, 94
Bernal, Martin, 87
Berry, Brewton, 15
Berthoff, Rowland, 68
Biachi, Suzanne, 210
Bilboa, John, 15
Billigmeier, Robert Henry, 78
Billington, Roy, 21
Blackwell, James E., 211
Blake, Casey Nelson, 22
Blalock, Hubert M., 32
Blanc, Christina Szanton, 55
Blanck, Dag, 63
Blank, Rebecca, 286
Blassingame, John W., 90, 91, 92
Blauner, Robert, 129
Blee, Kathleen, 176
Blessing, Patrick J., 73, 74
Bloom, Jack M., 185, 187

Blumberg, Rhoda Lois, 186, 188, 189, 190
Blumer, Herbert, 41, 52, 58, 120
Bobo, Lawrence, 174, 175, 194, 201, 204, 214
Bodnar, John, 54, 102, 103, 113
Bogardus, Emory, 130, 131
Bolt, Christine, 34, 83, 144, 145, 146
Bonacich, Edna, 46, 62, 63, 130, 264, 288, 314
Bonilla, Frank, 269
Bonilla-Silva, Eduardo, 40, 214, 217
Borgardus, Emory, 107
Borjas, George J., 271, 280
Boswell, Thomas D., 261, 262, 263
Bourne, Randolph, 22, 69
Bouvier, Leon F., 266, 280
Bozorgmehr, Mehdi, 255
Brace, Charles Long, 105
Braly, Kenneth, 107
Bredemeier, Harry, 207
Breton, Raymond, 53, 54, 80, 118
Briquets, Sergio Diaz, 260
Brod, Harry, 177
Broderick, Francis L., 123
Brodkin, Karen, 173
Brown, Dee, 143, 145
Brown, Frances J., 31
Brown, Rupert, 57, 58
Brown, Thomas N., 75
Brubaker, Rogers, 348, 350
Bugelski, B. R., 157
Bukowczyk, John J., 111, 114
Bulosan, Carlos, 319
Burma, John, 128, 277
Burt, Larry W., 227
Burton, Jonathan, 315

Bush, Rod, 189, 190
Butler, Jon, 80
Calhoun, Craig, 31
Callinicos, Alex, 46
Camarillo, Albert, 129
Campbell, Donald T., 57
Campos, Ricardo, 269
Carling, Alan, 53
Carmichael, Stokely, 189
Caroli, Betty Boyd, 104
Carter, Stephen L., 203
Castles, Stephen, 342, 348, 349
Cayton, Horace, 29, 127–128, 215
Cha, Marn J., 313
Chafe, William H., 184
Champagne, Duane, 238
Chan, Sucheng, 96
Chang, Kyung-Sun, 318
Chavez, John R., 96
Chavez, Linda, 259, 284, 285, 286
Chavez, Lydia, 200
Chen, Hsiang-Shiu, 308
Chen, Jack, 305
Chen, Shehong, 137
Christian, Mark, 342
Churchill, Ward, 233
Cinel, Dino, 104
Clark, Dennis J., 75
Clemetson, Lynette, 254
Cloward, Richard, 185
Cohen, Lizabeth, 112–113, 154, 168, 171
Cohen, Steven M., 117, 169, 170
Colaysto, Diane, 210
Coleman, James, 193, 194, 205
Collier, John, 146, 147, 226
Collins, Randall, 40
Commager, Henry Steele, 68
Connell, K. H., 73
Connor, Walker, 30, 31, 337
Conzen, Kathleen Neils, 52, 62, 78, 79, 80
Coon, Carleton S., 35
Cordova, Fred, 322
Cornell, Stephen, 82, 83, 86, 142, 144, 225, 227, 228, 230, 234, 235, 236, 237, 240, 241, 243, 252
Cortés, Carlos, 129
Cottle, Thomas, 193
Cowell, D. D., 106
Cox, Oliver C., 40, 46, 212
Cravens, Hamilton, 28

Creel, Margaret Washington, 89
Creelan, Paul, 28
Crippen, Timothy, 36
Crispino, James A., 157
Cronon, E. David, 124
Cross, William E., Jr., 40
Curran, Sara, 256
Curtin, Philip D., 87
Curtis, James R., 261, 262, 263

D, E, F

D'Souza, Dinesh, 178
Dadrian, Vahakn N., 41
Daniel, Pete, 127
Daniels, Jessie, 176, 261, 269, 275, 279, 300
Daniels, Roger, 74, 96, 97, 98, 111, 129, 136, 138, 141, 305, 312, 313, 319, 320, 321, 323
Danzger, Herbert M., 167
Dashefsky, Arnold, 47
Davis, Allison, 125, 126
Davis, F. James, 15
de Crèvecoeur, J. Hector St. John, 19
de la Garza, Rodolfo O., 257
DeConde, Alexander, 279, 307
Degler, Carl, 28
Delgado, Héctor L., 288
Deloria, Vine, Jr., 226
Denton, Nancy A., 209, 211, 219, 272
Department of Immigration and Multicultural Affairs, 339
Deutsch, Sarah, 129
di Leonardo, Micaela, 163, 166
DiAve, Diane, 210
Diaz, Porfirio, 130
Diner, Hasia, 74
Dinnerstein, Leonard, 84, 242, 288
Dobbs, Michael, 195
Dobzhansky, Theodore, 35
Dollard, John, 57, 125, 126
Domhoff, G. William, 216
Dore, R. F., 138
Dorris, Michael A., 244
Douglass, Frederick, 93
Douglass, William A., 15, 50
Doyle, Bertram, 125
Drake, St. Clair, 29, 127, 215

Du Bois, W. E. B., 91, 94, 119, 121, 122–123
Duany, Jorge, 133
Dubinin, N. P., 35
Dunn, L. C., 35
Duster, Troy, 35
Dziedzic, Eugene, 112
Early, Gerald, 10
Eckert, Craig, 185
Eckstein, Susan, 268
Edsall, Mary D., 178
Edsall, Thomas Byrne, 178
Elkins, Stanley, 89, 90
Engerman, Stanley L., 95
Erdmans, Mary Patrice, 157
Ericksen, Eugene, 50, 105, 159
Erickson, Charlotte, 71, 72
Erie, Steven P., 75
Eschbach, Karl, 233
Espiritu, Yen Lee, 321, 323, 328
Esposito, Luigi, 58
Evans, J. A., 337
Ewen, Elizabeth, 109
Ezorsky, Gertrude, 196
Fairchild, Henry Pratt, 21
Faist, Thomas, 56
Falcon, Luis M., 274
Fallows, Marjorie R., 75
Farber, Bernard, 116
Farley, John E., 31
Farley, Reynolds, 194, 204, 206, 209, 210, 211, 286, 289
Feagin, Joe R., 217, 244, 271
Fein, Leonard J., 169
Feinberg, William E., 199, 203
Femminella, Francis X., 106
Fenton, Steve, 40
Ferber, Abby L., 176
Ferguson, Ronald F., 205, 206
Fernández-Kelly, Patricia, 256
Ferraro, Thomas, 10
Fischer, Claude, 36
Fischer, David Hackett, 70
Fisher, Robert, 206
Fishman, Joshua, 155, 158, 171
Fitzgerald, David, 56
Fitzhugh, George, 87
Fitzpatrick, Joseph P., 133, 272, 275, 276
Fixico, Donald, 227, 228, 244
Fligstein, Neil, 127
Flores, Juan, 257, 277

Foerster, Robert S., 15, 104
Fogel, Robert William, 91, 95
Fogelson, Raymond D., 233
Foner, Eric, 121, 332
Fong, Eric, 296, 336
Fong, Timothy P., 308
Ford, Henry, 118
Formisano, Ronald P., 193
Forsyth, John M., 29
Foster, Morris W., 144
Foucault, Michel, 89
Fox-Genovese, Elizabeth, 89
Francis, E. K., 32, 37, 58
Frankenberg, Erica, 195
Franklin, John Hope, 94
Franklin, Raymond S., 178, 179
Frazier, E. Franklin, 29, 89, 90, 91, 92, 120, 215
Fredrickson, George M., 86, 87
Freeman, Leonard, 208
Frey, William H., 211
Friedman, Debra, 47
Friedman, Lawrence, 206
Fuchs, Lawrence H., 81, 82, 280, 285, 355
Fugita, Stephen S., 302
Fukuda, Yoshiaki, 302
Fullinwider, Robert K., 198
Furer, Howard B., 70

G, H, I

Gabaccia, Donna, 102, 104, 106
Gallagher, Charles, 166
Galton, Sir Francis, 34
Gambino Richard, 107
Gans, Herbert, 49, 51, 153, 154, .160, 162, 164, 169, 332
Garcia, Maria Christina, 267
Garcia, Mario T., 130, 132, 133
Garcia, Richard A., 132
Gardner, Burleigh, 125, 126
Gardner, Mary, 125, 126
Gardner, Robert W., 304
Garrow, David J., 187
Gavins, Raymond, 184
Gedicks, Al, 240
Geertz, Clifford, 45
Gellner, Ernest, 30
Genovese, Eugene D., 89, 90, 91, 92, 94
Gerstle, Gary, 63, 179

Geschwender, James, 124, 125
Gibson, Campbell J., 101
Giddens, Anthony, 61, 151
Giddings, Franklin Henry, 34
Gilroy, Paul, 345, 347
Gitlin, Todd, 355
Glazer, Nathan, 22, 23, 44, 45, 51, 55, 115, 117, 159, 169, 196, 198, 203, 271
Gleason, Philip, 19, 21, 31, 42, 45
Glenn, Evelyn Nakano, 139, 333
Glenn, Norvall D., 171
Gobineau, Comte Arther de, 33, 34
Goering, John, 159, 189
Goffman, Erving, 88, 89, 143
Golab, Caroline, 111
Gold, Steven J., 63, 167, 168, 265, 308
Goldscheider, Calvin, 114, 169, 171
Goldsen, Rose Kohn, 269
Goldstein, Alice, 169
Goldstein, Joshua R., 161
Goldstein, Sidney, 169
Gomez-Quiñones, Juan, 282, 283, 284
Gonzalez, David, 257, 273
Goodwyn, Lawrence, 124
Gordon, Milton M., 39, 42, 43, 212, 304
Goren, Arthur A., 114
Gossett, Thomas, 28
Gotham, Kevin Fox, 207, 211, 219
Graham, Ian Charles, 72
Granfield, Robert, 28
Grant, Madison, 21, 34
Graves, Joseph L., Jr., 35
Greeley, Andrew, 13, 32, 45, 154, 155, 156, 157, 173
Green, George N., 280
Green, Robert F., 194
Greenblum, Joseph, 119
Greene, Victor R., 54, 75, 110, 112, 158
Griswald del Castillo, Richard, 129
Griswold, Wendy, 165
Grossman, James, 127
Guarnizo, Luis E., 56
Guibernau, Montserrat, 15, 343
Gumplowicz, Ludwig, 47
Gurak, Douglas T., 274

Gutierrez, Armando, 284
Gutierrez, David G., 279
Gutman, Herbert, 91
Gyory, Andrew, 134
Hacker, Andrew, 198, 199, 203, 220, 297
Haines, Herbert H., 184, 185, 186, 188
Hamilton, Charles V., 189
Handlin, Oscar, 3, 15, 31, 38, 102, 103, 109
Hannerz, Ulf, 218
Hansen, Marcus Lee, 63, 71, 158
Hao, Lingxin, 260
Harding, Sandra, 33
Hargreaves, Ian, 346, 351, 352, 353
Harlan, Louis, 123
Harney, Robert F., 105
Harrington, Michael, 184
Hartigan, John, Jr., 175
Harwood, Jonathan, 35
Hatchett, Shirley, 211
Hauptman, Laurence M., 83
Hawkins, Freda, 336
Hechter, Michael, 47, 344
Heer, David, 279
Heilman, Samuel C., 117
Hero, Rodney E., 267, 277, 280, 282
Herrnstein, Richard, 35
Herskovits, Melville J., 89, 90
Hertzberg, Arthur, 116, 169
Heyman, Josiah, 130, 256
Higgs, Robert, 140
Higham, John, 46, 54, 63, 118
Hill, Robert F., 160
Hirata, Lucie Cheny, 135
Hirsch, Arnold R., 127
Hirsch, Herbert, 284
Hobsbawm, E. J., 30, 51, 89, 98
Hochschild, Jennifer, 195, 220
Hoffer, Thomas, 205
Hoffman, Abraham, 131
Holloway, Joseph E., 90
Holmes, Colin, 345
Holt, Hamilton, 11, 12, 103
Horowitz, Donald L., 30
Horowitz, Ruth, 289
Horton, Hayward Derrick, 211
Hosokawa, Bill, 303
Hout, Michael, 161
Howe, Irving, 116
Hraba, Joseph, 96

Hsu, Madeline Yuan-Yin, 137
Huggins, Nathan Irvin, 128
Hughes, Everett C., 3, 29, 88
Hughes, Helen MacGill, 3
Hughes, Henry, 88
Humphrey, Craig R., 193
Hurh, Won Moo, 298, 313, 314, 315, 317
Hutchinson, Edward P., 104
Hutchison, Ray, 290
Hwang, Sean-Shongend, 288
Iacovetta, Franca, 104
Ignatiev, Noel, 76
Isaacs, Harold, 45
Isajiw, Wsevolod, 38, 39
Ivey, Mike, 240

J, K, L

Jackson, Helen Hunt, 86
Jacobson, Matthew Frye, 69
Jacoby, Tamara, 19
Jaret, Charles, 116, 332
Jarvenpa, Robert, 231
Jasso, G., 321
Jaynes, Gerald David, 192, 194, 195, 197, 204, 206
Jen, Gish, 18
Jenkins, J. Craig, 185
Jennings, Francis, 83
Jensen, Arthur, 35
Jensen, Leif, 265
Jiobu, Robert M., 319, 320
Jo, Moon H., 297
Johnson, Troy, 238
Jones, LeRoi, 128
Jones, Maldwyn Allen, 77
Joppke, Christian, 333
Jordon, Winthrop D., 87
Jorgensen, Joseph G., 244
Josephy, Alvin M., 144, 145
Juliani, Richard, 50, 159
Kahn, Arcadus, 115
Kallen, Horace, 22
Kalt, Joseph P., 226, 243, 252
Kandel, William, 254
Kantowicz, Edward R., 112
Kashima, Tetsuden, 142
Kasinitz, Philip, 273
Katz, Daniel, 107
Katz, Michael B., 208
Katzman, David M., 214
Kaufman, Debra Renee, 167
Kaups, Matti, 164
Kedourie, Eli, 30
Kelly, Sara, 194
Kerr, Louis Año Nuevo, 277

Kessner, Thomas, 104, 105
Kibria, Nazli, 312, 313, 325
Kilgore, Sally, 205
Killian, Lewis M., 58, 182, 185, 190, 202
Kilson, Martin, 216
Kim, Hyung-chan, 313
Kim, Illsoo, 313, 314
Kim, Jung Ha, 312, 316
Kim, Kwang Chang, 313, 314, 317
Kinder, Donald, 194
Kinkead, Gwen, 309, 310
Kinlock, Graham C., 61
Kitano, Harry H. L., 96, 136, 139, 141, 268, 299, 300, 301, 302, 303, 304, 305, 312, 313, 319, 320, 323
Kivisto, Peter, 13, 29, 37, 46, 56, 63, 107, 169, 170, 171, 207, 313, 334
Knottnerus, David, 158
Koopmans, Ruud, 350
Korstad, Robert, 184
Kosmin, Barry, 168, 171
Kovel, Joel, 57
Kristeva, Julia, 30
Kroeber, Alfred L., 28
Krysan, Maria, 211
Kuo, Chia-Ling, 311
Kuper, Leo, 61
Kurashige, Lon, 302
Kwan, Kian M., 60
Kwang, Chang Kim, 298
Kwoh, Beulah Ong, 137
Kwong, Peter, 308, 309
LaBarre, Weston 145
Lal, Barbara Ballis, 29, 43, 47
Lamphere, Louise, 62
Landolt, Patricia, 56
Landry, Bart, 214, 215–216
Lane, Charles, 36
Langer, Elinor, 177
LaSorte, Michael, 104
Lavender, Abraham D., 29, 114
Lazerwitz, Bernard, 116, 158
Leacock, Eleanor Burke, 82
Lee, Chungmei, 195
Lee, Erika, 135
Lee, Jennifer, 315
Legters, Lyman H., 238
Lemann, Nicholas, 127
Lennon, Emily, 101
Leon, George, 105
Leonard, Karen, 324
Levin, Michael, 304
Levine, Edward M., 75

Levine, Gene N., 299
Levine, Lawrence W., 90
LeVine, Robert A., 57
Levitan, Sar, 209
Levitt, Peggy, 255
Lewis, David Levering, 123
Lian, Jason Z., 338
Lichter, Michael, 286, 287
Lie, John, 315
Lieberson, Stanley, 161, 162, 164
Liebman, Arthur, 118
Liebow, Elliot, 10, 218
Light, Ivan, 63, 137, 139, 140, 264, 265, 314
Lii, Ding-Tzann, 286
Limerick, Patricia, 233
Lin, Jan, 311
Lincoln, C. Eric, 90, 91, 184
Lindemann, Albert S., 118
Lipset, Seymour Martin, 68, 201, 336
Lipsitz, George, 173
Litwack, Leon F., 120
Livingstone, Frank, 35
Lobo, Susan, 230
Lockhart, Audrey, 72
Lockwood, William W., 138
Loconto, David, 158
Logan, John R., 211, 306, 310
Long, Larry, 210
Lopata, Helena Znaniecki, 113
López, David E., 277
López, Ian F. Haney, 132
Lopreato, Joseph, 36, 106
Lowie, Robert, 28
Lurie, Nancy Oestreich, 82, 144
Lyden, Fremont J., 238
Lyman, Stanford M., 43, 47, 48, 50, 58, 63, 95, 96, 98, 120, 122, 135, 136, 137, 139, 140, 141, 146, 182, 196, 301, 302, 306, 307
Lynch, James, 336, 341
Lynd, Helen Merrell, 127
Lynd, Robert S., 127
López, David, 287

M, N, O

Majka, Linda C., 283
Majka, Theo J., 283
Mamiya, Lawrence H., 90, 91, 184
Mangiafico, Luciano, 322

Mangione, Jerre, 6, 10, 11
Mann, Arthur, 20
Marable, Manning, 177
Marger, Martin, 15, 165
Marks, Carole, 127
Marriott, Michael, 251
Martin, Jack K., 204
Martin, W. Allen, 265
Mason, David, 346
Mass, Amy Iwaskai, 304
Massey, Douglas S., 209, 211, 219, 254–255, 272, 280
Mast, Daniel D., 297
Matthews, David Ralph, 338
Matthews, Fred H., 28, 43, 47
May, Philip A., 248
Mayer, Egon, 167, 172
Mayer, Neil, 209
McAdam, Doug, 183, 185, 186, 187, 188, 190, 191
McAuley, Christopher A., 40
McCarthy, John D., 185
McCready, William C., 154
McKay, James, 45
McNickle D'Arcy, 82, 143
McPhail, Clark, 190
McPherson, James M., 120
McWilliam, Carey, 130
Mead, Margaret, 28
Meier, August, 184
Melendy, H. Brett, 312, 319, 320, 321, 322
Melville, Margarita, 284
Merton, Robert, 13, 59
Meyer, Michael, 287
Miles, Robert, 46
Miller, Kerby A., 73
Miller, Mark J., 342, 348, 349
Miller, Randall M., 146, 248, 249
Mills, C. Wright, 151, 269
Min, Jay, 317, 318
Min, Pyong Gap, 312, 313, 315, 316, 317, 322
Mindel, Charles H., 116
Mintz, Sidney W., 269
Mitchell, Margaret, 88
Model, Suzanne, 265, 345
Mohl, Raymond, 264, 265
Mollenkopf, John, 273
Momaday, N. Scott, 9, 10, 250
Monfort, Franklin, 286
Montejano, David, 284
Montero, Darrel M., 299
Moore, Joan, 129, 130, 131, 132, 268, 277, 282, 284, 288, 289
Moore, John, 194

Moore, William, 208
Morawska, Ewa, 13, 27, 46, 111, 333
Mormino, Gary, 133
Morris, Aldon D., 184, 186
Moses, Robert, 205, 205
Moynihan, Daniel P., 22, 23, 44, 45, 51, 159, 218–219, 271
Mozo, Rafael, 266
Mucha, Janusz, 230, 231
Murdock, Steve H., 288
Murphy, John W., 58
Murray, Charles, 35, 221
Muñoz, Alfredo, 321
Myer, Dillon S., 226–227
Myrdal, Gunnar, 181, 182
Nabokov, Peter, 142, 145
Nagel, Joane, 52, 53, 54, 159, 235, 236, 238
Nahirny, Vladimir, 158
Nair, Sami, 352
Nairn, Tom, 344
Naison, Mark, 128
Nakamaru, Robert Tsuneo, 304
Nash, Gary, 94
Nee, Brett, 135
Nee, Victor, 62, 135, 265, 332
Nefzger, Ben, 169, 170
Nelli, Humbert S., 104, 105, 108
Nettles, Michael T., 204
Neufeld, Steven, 314, 315
Newman, Katherine, 10, 220
Newman, William M., 31, 43
Ng, Wendy, 141, 299, 300
Nichols, Roger L., 84, 242
Niehardt, John G., 145
Nielsen, Francois, 159
Noiriel, Gérard, 350
Novak, Michael, 23, 157
O'Brien, Conor Cruise, 31
O'Brien, David J., 302
Obermiller, Phillip, 15, 165
Odum, Howard, 28
Oliver, Lawrence J., 107
Oliver, Melvin, 217
Olzak, Susan, 40, 159, 298
Omi, Michael, 40, 173, 176, 177
Orfield, Gary, 194, 195, 196, 204, 205, 286
Organization for Economic Co-Operation and Development, 334
Orlav, Ann, 15, 38
Osako, Masako M., 301, 304

P, Q, R

Pachon, Harry, 132, 268, 277, 284, 288
Padilla, Felix, 275
Pang, Gin Y., 304
Parekh, Bhikhu, 55, 347
Parenti, Michael, 45
Park, Hyung, 316
Park, Robert E., 28, 29, 40, 43, 47, 58, 89, 175, 305
Parkin, Frank, 46
Parot, Joseph, 111
Parrillo, Vincent N., 55
Patterson, James, 208
Patterson, Orlando, 86
Pattilo-McCoy, Mary, 217
Pearce, Roy Harvey, 84
Pearson, David, 54, 159, 334
Pedraza-Bailey, Silvia, 54, 61, 260
Pérez y Gonzalez, Maria, 273, 274
Pérez, Lisandro, 260, 261, 262, 264, 265, 266
Perlman, Robert, 115
Perlmann, Joel, 15, 254, 289, 332
Pernicone, Nicholas, 108
Persons, Stow, 28
Peters, Kurt, 230
Petersen, William, 30, 300
Pettigrew, Thomas F., 58, 194, 214
Phillips, Ulrich B., 93
Piatt, Bill, 258, 259
Piazza, Thomas, 220
Pido, Antonia J. A., 320, 321, 322
Pincus, Fred L., 202
Pinderhughes, Dianne, 112, 128, 288
Pinkney, Alphonso, 94, 196, 200
Piven, Frances Fox, 185
Polenberg, Richard, 159
Porter, John, 335
Portes, Alejandro, 56, 255, 260, 264, 265, 266, 274, 276, 286, 333
Posadas, Barbara, 320
Powers, Mary G., 274
Powledge, Fred, 187
Pozzetta, George, 133
Prucha, Francis Paul, 225, 226, 227, 228, 236, 237, 242, 251
Pula, James, 112

Rainwater, Lee, 208, 219
Raper, Arthur F., 125
Ratzenhofer, Gustav, 47
Redkey, Edwin S., 124
Reed, Adolph L., 221
Reimers, David M., 84, 242, 288
Reuter, Edward B., 28
Rex, John, 62
Rhodes, Colbert, 299
Ribuffo, Leo P., 118
Richards, Toni, 194
Rieder, Jonathan, 159
Riesman, David, 152
Riggs, Christopher K., 228
Riis, Jacob, 105
Rippley, LaVern J., 77
Rischin, Moses, 19
Rivera-Batiz, Francisco L., 272
Rodriguez, Clara, 272, 274
Rodriguez, Richard, 7, 8, 11, 259
Roediger, David, 52
Rokeach, Milton, 57
Rollins, Judith, 189
Romo, Ricardo, 129, 131
Roosens, Eugene, 49, 50
Rose, Arnold, 32, 57
Rose, Caroline, 32
Rose, Peter, 14, 33
Rosenzweig, M. R., 321
Rossell, Christine H., 194, 195
Rothschild, Joseph, 159
Roucek, Joseph S., 31
Rowitz, Louis, 158
Royce, Anya Peterson, 47, 122
Royce, Edward, 122
Rudwick, Elliot, 184
Rumbaut, Ruben G., 19, 276, 286, 321, 333
Ryan, William, 219

S, T, U

Sahlins, Marshall, 37, 83
Salvemini, Gaetano, 108
San Miguel, Guadalupe, 286
Sanchez-Ayéndez, Melba, 269, 275
Sandberg, Neil, 156, 157, 171
Sandefur, Gary D., 232
Sanders, Jimy, 62, 265
Santiago, Carlos E., 272

Sarna, Jonathan, 50, 115, 117, 119
Sassen, Saskia, 331
Savas, Emmanual, 208
Saxton, Alexander, 81, 134
Scarpaci, J. Vincenza, 105
Schaefer, Emmett, 177
Schaefer, Richard T., 31, 306
Schauffler, Richard, 260
Schermerhorn, R. A., 32, 39, 41, 58
Schiller, Nina Glick, 55
Schlesinger, Arthur, Jr., 54, 355
Schlesinger, Arthur, Sr., 52
Schneider, Jo Anne, 276
Schneider, Keith, 244
Schneider, William, 201
Schuman, Howard, 174, 175, 201, 204, 210
Schwartz, Michael, 125
Scott, Anne Firor, 12
Scott, Franklin, 68
Scott, George M., Jr., 45
Scott, Rebecca J., 121
Sears, David, 194, 255
See, Katherine O'Sullivan, 57
Senior, Clarence, 269
Sennett, Richard, 152
Sensenbrenner, Julia, 264
Sexton, Patricia Cayo, 271
Shannon, William V., 75
Shapiro, Herbert, 125
Shapiro, Thomas, 217
Sharfman, Harold, 115
Sheatsley, Paul B., 173
Shepperson, Wilbur, 71
Sherif, Carolyn W., 58
Sherif, Muzafer, 58
Shibutani, Tamotso, 60
Shibuya, Kumiko, 318
Shils, Edward, 45
Shin, Eui Hang, 316, 318
Shinagawa, Larry H., 304
Shipler, David, 179
Shklar, Judith N., 63
Shoemaker, Nancy, 233
Shokeid, Moshe, 167
Sigelman, Lee, 201, 204, 210
Silberman, Charles E., 169
Silet, Charles L. P., 248, 249
Simmel, Georg, 47
Simon, Rita, 336, 341
Simon, Roger, 113
Sindler, Allen P., 198
Singer, Merrill, 189
Siu, Paul, 135
Skardal, Dorothy Burton, 10

Sklare, Marshall, 114, 115, 117, 119, 171
Skrentny, John David, 195
Slayton, Robert A., 113
Sleeper, Jim, 160
Smith, Anthony, 30, 158
Smith, Charles V., 182
Smith, Dorothy, 33
Smith, J. Owens, 95
Smith, M. E., 244
Smith, M. G., 40
Smith, Timothy L., 107
Smolicz, J. J., 339
Sniderman, Paul M., 220
Snipp, C. Matthew, 231, 232, 233, 246, 247, 250
Sollors, Werner, 37, 51
Solomon, Barbara Miller, 21
Solomos, John, 46
Sorin, Gerald, 117
Southern, David W., 181, 182
Sowell, Thomas, 60, 140, 196, 198, 203, 271, 286, 300
Spicer, Edward H., 142, 227, 228, 229, 230, 236
Spickard, Paul R., 172, 303
Spindler, George, 145
Spindler, Louise, 145
Spitzberg, Irving, Jr., 191
Stack, Carol, 219
Stampp, Kenneth M., 86, 88, 90
Stanton, William, 34
Stanton-Salazar, Ricardo D., 277, 287
Starr, Paul, 15
Statham, Paul, 350
Steeh, Charlotte, 174, 175, 201, 204
Steele, Shelby, 203
Stein, Howard F., 160
Stein, Wayne J., 245
Steinberg, Stephen, 46, 60, 178, 202, 202, 355
Steiner, Stan, 147, 284
Stepick, Alex, 255, 265
Stoddard, Ellwyn R., 95, 131, 256, 278, 282
Stoddard, Lothrop, 21
Stone, John, 34
Storti, Craig, 136
Strauss, Anselm, 19
Struyck, Raymond, 209
Stuckey, Sterling, 90, 94
Stults, Brian J., 211
Suarez-Orozco, Marcelo M., 286
Sullivan, Teresa A., 265

Sumka, Howard, 211
Sumner, William Graham, 13, 36, 37, 182
Sung, Betty Lee, 135
Supple, Khalil, 233
Swain, Carol M., 200
Swatez, Marc John, 119
Taeuber, Karl B., 210
Taggart, Robert, 209
Tajfel, Henri, 58
Takagi, Dana Y., 326
Takahashi, Jere, 303
Takaki, Ronald, 54, 85, 134, 135, 136, 138, 139, 142, 299, 308, 309, 327, 355
Taylor, Charles, 55, 337, 355
Taylor, D. Garth, 173
Taylor, Philip, 76
Terry, Don, 238, 240
TeSelle, Sallie, 158
Theisen, Gary, 154
Thernstrom, Stephan, 15, 38
Thistlethwaite, Frank, 61
Thomas, Melvin E., 211, 217
Thomas, Piri, 272
Thomas, Robert, 234
Thomas, William I., 28, 48, 109, 119
Thompson, Cooper, 177
Thomsen, Craig, 280
Thornton, Russell, 41, 85
Tichenor, Daniel J., 135
Tienda, Marta, 259, 269, 273, 286
Tilly, Charles, 61
Tippeconnic, John W., III, 247
Tizon, Orlando, 322
Tocqueville, Alexis de, 19, 69
Todorov, Tvetan, 67
Tolnay, Stewart E., 127
Tomasi, Lydio F., 105
Tomasi, Silvano M., 106
Tong, Benson, 305
Tricarico, Donald, 158
Trommler, Frank, 81
Tsukashima, Ronald Tadao, 300
Tuan, Mia, 323, 327, 332
Tuccillo, John A., 209
Tuch, Steven A., 204
Tucker, William H., 35
Turner, Frederick Jackson, 20
Ueda, Reed, 63
Um, Shin Ja, 317
Ungeheuer, Frederick, 244

V, W, X

Valdes, Dennis Nodin, 277, 283
Valentine, Charles A., 219
Valocchi, Steve, 186
Van den berg, Pierre, 36, 37, 45
Vander Zanden, James W., 31
Vecoli, Rudolph J., 12, 13, 18, 104, 105
Vidich, Arthur, 109, 152, 154
Vigil, James Diego, 289, 290
Vinje, David, 245
Vogel, Virgil J., 143
Vogt, Evan Z., 232
Wacker, R. Fred, 28, 182
Waddell, Jack O., 229
Wakatsuki, Yasuo, 139
Waldinger, Roger, 56, 254, 255, 264, 286, 287, 289, 309, 332
Wallerstein, Immanuel, 83
Ware, Caroline F., 37, 108
Warner, R. Stephen, 316
Warner, W. Lloyd, 37
Washington, Booker T., 123
Waters, Mary C., 15, 160, 161, 162, 163, 164, 166, 273, 332
Watson, O. Michael, 229
Wattenberg, Ben, 3
Wax, Murray L., 84, 85, 144, 145, 234
Waxman, Chaim I., 116, 169
Weber, David J., 129
Weber, Michael P., 113
Weed, Perry, 159
Weibel-Orlando, Joan, 234
Welch, Susan, 201, 204, 210
Wells, Robert V., 68
West, Cornel, 222, 355
Wherry, James D., 83
White, Ronald C., Jr., 122, 123
Whyte, William Foote, 10, 109
Wiley, Norbert, 28, 28
Wilhelm, Sidney M., 127
Williams, Rhonda, 208
Williams, Richard, 62, 86, 287
Williams, Robyn M., Jr., 3, 192, 194, 195, 197, 204, 206

Williamson, Joel, 121, 122, 123
Willie, Charles Vert, 214
Wilson, Kenneth L., 265
Wilson, William Julius, 57, 203, 212, 213, 214, 216, 217, 218, 219, 220, 221
Winant, Howard, 40, 46, 52, 173, 176, 177, 179
Winter, J. Alan, 169, 171
Wirth, Louis, 29, 32, 119
Wittke, Carl, 73, 75, 79
Woll, Allen L., 146, 248, 249
Wong, Bernard, 309, 311
Wong, Herbert Y., 135
Wong, Jade Snow, 8, 9, 10
Wong, Morrison G., 135, 305
Woo, Deborah, 300
Woocher, Jonathan, 117
Wood, Forrest G., 87
Woods, Robert A., 105
Woodson, Carter, 94
Woodward, C. Vann, 122
Wright, Nathan, 165
Wright, Richard, 8
Wrobel, Paul, 111
Wurdock, Clarence, 194

Y, Z

Yanagisako, Sylvia J., 302
Yancey, William, 50, 105, 159, 219
Yans-McLaughlin, Virginia, 105
Yinger, J. Milton, 35, 46, 48
Yoon, In-Jin, 312, 313, 314
Young, Donald, 31
Yu, Elena S. H., 322
Zald, Mayer N., 185
Zangwill, Israel, 20, 21
Zelinsky, Wilbur, 54
Zeul, Carolyn R., 193
Zhou, Min, 265, 276, 306, 310, 332
Znaniecki, Florian, 28, 109, 110
Zorbaugh, Harvey, 105
Zuckerman, Alan S., 114
Zunz, Olivier, 46
Zweigenhaft, Richard L., 216 ✦

Subject Index

A, B

Abolition, 94
Aborigines, 339, 339–340, 341, 354
Accidental death, 247, 248
Accommodation, 43, 45, 117
Acculturation, 144, 157, 225, 290, 298, 299, 301, 302, 336, 347
Adaptation, 316–317, 331
Addams, Jane, 20
Administration for Native Americans, 227–228
Admissions decisions (University), 199
Affirmative action, 7, 17, 175, 178, 195–204, 286, 326
  constitutional basis for, 196, 200
  implementation of, 197–198
  legal challenges to, 198–201
  political orientations, 201–202
  public opinion, 201–202
  unintended consequences, 202–204
Affirmative opportunity, 203
Afghanistan, 340
AFL-CIO, 283
Africa/Africans, 3, 19, 30, 44, 62, 63, 67, 81, 86, 87, 91, 114, 119, 120, 124, 345, 349
  culture, 90
  gender role, 91
  Maghreb region, 351, 352
  religions, 90, 91

sub-Saharan, 352
African Americans, 8, 11, 12, 15, 17, 23, 28, 31, 32, 35, 40, 42, 44, 55, 62, 63, 74, 101, 107, 112, 118, 121, 122, 130, 131, 136, 152, 159, 166, 173, 174, 177, 181–224, 229, 254, 255, 265, 332, 333, 354, 355
  as Afro-American, 15, 16
  citizenship for, 120, 121
  crime, 218
  development of community, 127–128
  dropout rates, 204, 208
  education, 121, 216, 218
  emancipation to Jim Crow, 120–128
  entrepreneurs, 217
  farmers, 124
  female-headed/single-parent households, 208, 209, 218, 219
  ghettoes (see also Ghettoes), 10, 12, 59, 63, 190, 207, 208, 214, 218
  housing, 207, 209, 218
  IQs, 35
  leadership in, 122–124, 185
  lower-middle class, 123
  middle class, 47, 121, 126, 185, 206, 211, 214–217, 218, 288, 346
  as Negroes, 15, 16, 122
  origin of culture, 89–91
  out-of-wedlock birthrate, 91
  poor, 47, 126, 185, 203, 206, 209, 217–221
  poverty rate, 206, 208
  presidential candidate, 175
  religions, 91

  as Sambos, 90
  sexual exploitation by whites, 92
  sexual relations with white women, 126
  socioeconomic position/status, 206, 123, 196
  standardized tests, 199
  stereotypes, 58
  suburban, 210, 211, 216
  under/unemployment, 166, 218
  upper class, 125, 126
  upward mobility, 126
  violence, 218
  violence against, 127
  voting, 186
  women, 8
  working class, 47, 123, 185, 203
Afro-Caribbeans, 345, 346, 347
Agribusiness, 280, 283
Agriculture, 104, 321
Aid to Families with Dependent Children (AFDC), 208, 218
AIDS, 220
Alabama, 184, 198, 200
  Birmingham, 186
  Montgomery, 186
  Selma, 186–187
  State police, 198, 200
  Tuskegee, 29, 187
Alaska natives, 229, 242
  Aleuts, 242
  Eskimos, 242
Albanians, 30, 42
Albion's Seed, 70
Alexander v. Holmes, 192
Algebra Project, The, 205
Algeria, 348, 351

Alianza Federal de Mercedes (Federal Alliance of Land Grants), 284
Alianza Hispano-Americano, 280
Alien Land Act (1913), 140
Alienation, 102, 103
All-weather bigots, 59
All-weather liberals, 59
Allan Bakke v. Regents of the University of California, 198, 199, 201
Alliance College, 113
Allotment system, 226
Amache, 141
Amalgamation, 43
America (*see* United States)
America, 146
American Airlines, 276
American Coordinating Council on Political Education (ACCPE), 282
American Federation of Labor (AFL), 112, 134
American flag, 22
American G.I. Forum, 280
American Indian (*see* Native American)
American Indian Defense Association, 147
American Indian Movement (AIM), 235, 236, 237, 238, 244
American Minority Peoples, 31
American Nazi movement, 177
American Revolution/Revolutionary War, 68, 79, 84, 93, 94
Americanization, 20, 22, 43, 76, 317
Amerindian (*see* Native Americans)
Amish, 15, 39, 53
An American Dilemma, 181
Anarchists, 79, 117
Ancestry, 9, 37, 39, 152, 161, 162, 167
Ancient Order of Hibernians, 165
And My Children Did Not Know Me, 114
Anderson v. S. F. Unified School District, 198
Anglo-Americans, 96
Anglo-Saxon Clubs, 124

Anglo-Saxon Protestants, 69
Anglophone, 335, 338
Antebellum era, 212
Anti-British sentiment, 73
Anti-Catholic attitude/prejudice, 73, 75, 77
Anti-Chinese activity, 136–137
Anti-Chinese sentiment, 41–42
Anti-immigrant legislation, 259, 345
Anti-Irish prejudice, 73, 76
Anti-Semitism, 20, 32, 115, 118–119, 153, 167, 169, 172, 176
Antimiscegenation laws/statutes, 120, 319
Anxiety, 155
Apaches, 143, 226, 243
Apartheid, 32
Appalachia, 15, 70, 165
Aquino, Corazon, 323
Arabs, 169, 315
Aramaic, 114
Aristotle, 95
Arizona, 95, 130, 133, 141
   Flagstaff, 230
   Phoenix, 170, 230
   Tsaile, 251
Arkansas, 142, 187, 324
   Little Rock, 187, 191
Armenians, 41
Arranged marriages, 109, 116, 139
Aryan Nation, 172
Aryans, 33
Ascription, 50
Asia, 3, 119, 312, 349
   Southeast, 323
Asian Americans/immigrants, 67, 81, 101, 130, 152, 189, 259, 266, 295–330, 331, 332, 346, 347
   American-born, 297
   community ties, 298
   diversity, 296
   education, 296, 297, 326
   gangs, 290
   job opportunities, 298
   metropolitan areas with, 298
   middle class, 296
   as the model minority, 296–299
   prejudice/discrimination, 327–328

   refugees, 324
   skilled, 326
   suburban, 211
   upward mobility, 297, 298, 326
   white-collar workers, 297
   work ethic, 298
   World War II, post, 297
Asian immigration, 336
Asian Indians, 296, 318
Asian/Pacific Islander, 296, 326
Asians, 62, 63, 120, 131, 136, 152, 248, 319, 336, 340, 345, 352
   Southeast, 62, 296
Aspira, 275
Assimilation, 42, 42–43, 54, 71, 78, 123, 141, 170, 172, 173, 175, 181, 227, 237, 250, 258, 267–268, 286, 300, 304, 318, 323, 325, 335, 338, 340, 341, 350, 354, 355
   attitude receptional, 42
   behavioral receptional, 42
   civic, 43, 341
   cultural, 43, 169
   definition of, 42
   resistance to, 225
   segmented, 276, 289
   straight-line, 154
   structural, 43, 169, 302
Assimilationist nations, 352
Assimilationists, 44, 46, 160, 227, 284, 335, 339
Association of Korean Christian Scholars in North America, 313
Asylum seekers, 349
Asylums, 88
Athletic associations/clubs, 79, 120, 155, 157, 275
Atlanta University, 121
Atlantic Richfield, 244
Atlantic Slave Trade, 87
Atomic Energy Act, 328
Attitudes, 53
Aussiedler, 349
Australia, 333, 334, 335, 338, 339–341, 354
Austria
   Vienna, 79
Authoritarianism, 155
Autobiographies, 10
Azerbaijan, 30
B'nai B'rith, 115, 132

Badger-Two Medicine region, 240
Baha'is, 39
Baker, Ella, 184
Balkanization, 341
Balkans, 30
Baltic nations, 340
Bangladesh, 345, 346
Banking, 68
Baptism, 106
Baptists, 39
Barbados, 68
Barrio, 132, 271, 288, 289
Barriozation, 129
Basques, 14, 30
Batista, Fulgencio, 133, 260
Bay Area American Indian Council, 230
Bay of Pigs, 262
Bear Flag banner, 96
Behavior, 45, 53
Behavioral differences, 27
"Behind Our Masks," 40
Belfast/Good Friday Agreement, 344
Belgium
Flemish, 158
Bell Curve, The, 35
Bend it Like Beckham, 347
Benedict, Ruth, 28
Benny, Jack, 117
Berlet, Chris, 177
Berlin Wall, 349
Beyond the Melting Pot, 22, 159
Bilingual education, 17, 258, 286
Bilingual Education Act, 258
Bilingualism, 257–260
Biological fusion, 21
Bison/buffalo, 9, 145
Black activism, 182
Black America, 214
Black Bourgeoisie, 215
Black Boy, 8
Black capitalism, 124
Black codes, 120
Black colleges, 184
Black Metropolis, 29
Black Metropolis, 128
Black nationalism, 124, 189–191
Black nationalists, 185
Black Panthers, 189, 190, 235, 284
Black Power, 189
Black Star Line, 124

Blackfeet Indians, 145
and oil exploration, 240–241
Blacks (*see* African Americans)
Blair, Tony, 343
Blue-collar workers, 151, 153, 271, 299
Blues, 128
Boas, Franz, 28
Boat people, 325
Bontac Igorrotes, 11
Border Industrialization Program, 256
Boycotts, 186, 283, 315
Boyz N the Hood, 220
Bracero program, 131, 277, 278, 348
Brain drain, 261, 321, 336
Breton, 30
Brice, Fanny, 117
Britain (*see* England)
British Commonwealth, 335
British Empire, 342
British immigrants, 67
Broken Arrow, 249
Bronzeville, 128
Brown Berets, 284
Brown v. Board of Education of Topeka, Kansas, 188, 191, 195, 200
Brown, Jerry, 283
Buddhism, 141, 302
Buffalo Bill and the Indians, 249
Bulosan, Carlos, 319
Bureau of Indian Affairs (BIA), 144, 226, 228, 229, 235, 236, 246
Burmese, 309
Bush, President George H. W., 177, 178, 195, 200, 202, 228, 266, 267
Bush, President George W., 177, 178, 195, 200, 202, 228, 266, 285
Bushido, 302
Business associations, 315
Busing, 175, 191–195
Báez, Esther, 255

C, D

Cajuns, 165
California, 95, 96, 130, 136, 138, 141, 160, 200, 253, 259, 270, 279, 282, 283,

287, 289, 301, 302, 303, 308, 319, 321, 324, 325, 326, 331
Alcatraz, 236
Chinatown, San Francisco, 8, 9, 11, 97, 136
Chinatown, San Jose, 328
Eureka, 136
Exeter, 320
Fresno, 253, 302
Gardena, 302
Humboldt County, 136
Imperial Valley, 324
Koreatown, Los Angeles, 314
Los Angeles, 131, 136, 139, 140, 156, 170, 194, 210, 221, 230, 234, 253, 255, 263, 264, 279, 282, 286, 287, 288, 299, 304, 306, 312, 313, 314, 315, 322
Modesto, 320
Monterey Park, 308, 309
Nipomo, San Pedro, 319
Oakland, 190, 230, 318
Orange County, 170, 325
Proposition 187, 287
Proposition 209, 200
Sacramento, 7, 302, 324
San Diego, 130, 170
San Francisco, 135, 136, 139, 170, 198, 230, 236, 318, 322
San Gabriel Valley, 306
San Jose, 162, 230, 325
Watsonville, 320
Watts, Los Angeles, 190
Westminster, 325
Cambodia, 296, 324
Cambodian (Khmer) refugees, 325, 327–328
Canada, 31, 42, 68, 84, 97, 333, 334, 335, 338, 340, 341, 348
Asians, 336
blacks, 336
British Columbia, 324
Calgary, 336
discrimination, 336
Edmonton, 336
Montreal, 336
national identity, 338
new immigrants, 338
Northwest Territory, 338
Ottawa, 336
Quebec (*see also* Quebec), 31, 335

Québecois, 158
Toronto, 336
Vancouver, 336
as a vertical mosaic, 335–338
white, 335
Winnipeg, 336
Cantonese, 308, 310
Cantor, Eddie, 117
Capital Religion Study, 167
Capitalism, 55, 113, 124, 190, 333
Caribbean, 86, 260, 264, 272, 290–291, 332, 336, 345, 352
French-speaking, 263
Carmichael, Stokely, 189
Carnegie Corporation, 181
Carnegie, Andrew, 181
Carter, President Jimmy, 167, 303
Caste society, 122, 125, 126, 127–128
Castro, Fidel, 61, 260
Catalonian, 30
Catholicism, 282
Catholicism, American, 76, 80
Catholics, German, 80, 153
Cavaliers, 70
Central Americans/immigrants, 254, 256, 263, 273, 287, 290–291
Central High School, 188
Central Intelligence Agency (CIA), 262
Cermak, Anton, 112
Chain migration networks, 111
Chandler, Jeff, 249
Chaney, James, 188
Charitable Irish Society of Boston, 75
Charitable societies, 315
Charlottetown Agreement, 337
Chavez, Cesar, 283
Chavez, Linda, 259, 285–286
Cherokees, 85, 143
Chevron Oil Corporation, 240
Cheyennes, 241, 249
Chicago School, 28, 29, 41
Chicanismo, 283, 285
Chicanos, 96
politics, 280–286
Chickasaw Indian Nation, 244
Chin, Vincent, 327

China, 138
Fujian Province, 96
Guangdong Province, 96
China lobby, 307
China, People's Republic of, 307, 340
Chinatown Advisory Council, 311
Chinatown Planning Council, 311
Chinatowns, 97, 139, 305, 306, 307, 308, 310
changing, 309–312
as an ethnic island, 135–136
and the outside world, 137–138
restaurants in, 309
tourist trade, 137, 310
Chinese, 3, 12, 18, 54, 325, 336, 345
intermarriage, 136
Chinese Americans as immigrants, 8–9, 15, 81, 96, 97, 98, 107, 137, 139, 153, 265, 296, 305–312, 314, 318, 327, 328
bachelor society, 135
as birds of passage, 97
citizenship, 137
clan (*hui kuan*), 98, 135–136
crime, 310
economic status, 308
education, 137
enclave economy, 310
ethnic community, 135, 311
family, 135, 311
gangs/tongs, 307, 310
health care, 307
health insurance, 310
immigration restriction, 134–138
and Japanese, 132–142
laundries, 136
merchant associations, 135
merchants, 97, 135
middle class, 137, 305–307, 306, 307, 308
new immigration, 305
post-1965, 308–312
poverty, 307
pre-1965, 305
prejudice/discrimination, 137, 306, 311
restaurants, 136, 295

rotating credit, 137
secret societies, 135
sex ratio, 305
speech/territorial associations (*hui kuan*), 98
students, 135
suburban, 306, 308
upward mobility, 306
village associations/fongs, 311
women, 135, 305
working class, 308
World War II, 137, 305
World War II, post, 306
Chinese Consolidated Benevolent Association (CCBA), 135, 310, 311
Chinese Exclusion Act of 1882, 17, 135, 305
Chinese Health Clinic, 311
Chinese language schools, 306
Chinese nationalists, 307
Chippewa spearfishing dispute, 238–240
Chippewas, 238, 239, 242, 243, 245
Choctaws, 243
Christian academies, 194
Christianity, 39, 90, 141, 302, 316, 347
Christianity, Orthodox, 39
Church, 103, 105, 111, 128, 184, 275, 275
Churches, 156, 201, 230, 346
bombings of, 188
Circular migration, 268
Circumstantialist perspective (of ethnicity), 45–46
Cisneros, Henry, 285
Cities, 321, 322
Citizenship, 3, 63, 69, 120, 133, 239, 333, 348
Civic culture, 355
Civic duty, 339
Civic participation, 45
Civil Liberties Act of 1988, 303
Civil Rights Act of 1866, 121, 210
Civil Rights Act of 1964, 188, 192, 198, 202
Title VI, 210, 258
Title VII, 197
Civil Rights Act of 1968
Title VIII, 210

Civil rights movement, 119–120, 159, 173, 176, 178, 183–191, 194, 216, 220, 221, 222, 234, 236, 249, 327, 331, 340, 352
   initiated events, 187
   tactics, 185
   white responses to, 187–188
Civil rights organizations, 200–201, 283, 303, 311
Civil War, 17, 67–99, 101, 103, 119–120, 124, 145
   Reconstruction, 101, 120, 121, 122
Civil War, post, 196, 212
Clans, 82
Clark, Mark, 190
Class, 214
Class differences, 46
Class differentiation, 212, 231
Class structure, 62, 126, 151, 214, 215
Cleaver, Eldridge, 190
Clinton, President Bill, 178, 195, 228, 285, 344
Coal miners, 111, 241
Coca-Cola, 276
Cochise, 143, 249
Cognitive theory, 58
Cold War, 151, 226, 261, 262, 307
Collective action, 50
College athletes, 199
Colleges/universities, 198, 199, 201
   black, 215, 216
   enrollment, 204
   legacy, 202
Collier, John, 146
Colonial America, 67–99, 69, 72, 83, 86, 103, 242
Colonial domination, 61
Colonists, 69
Colonized peoples, 62
Colorado, 95, 130, 141
   Denver, 170, 230, 284
Columbia University, 7, 119
Columbians, 256, 290
Come See the Paradise, 303
Commerce Department, 85
Commercial gardening, 299
Commission on Wartime Relocation and Internment of Civilians, 299, 303
Commonwealth nations, 345
Communal attachments, 102

Communism, 79, 117, 118, 305, 307, 323, 336, 349
Communist party, 128, 132
Communist reeducation camps, 325
Community boundaries, 38
Community Service Organization (CSO), 282, 283
Compulsory education laws, 106
Confederacy, 120
Confederate Hammerskins, 176
Conflict, 36, 43, 47, 48, 63
   cultural, 349
   generational, 290
Conformism, 155
Conformity, 152
Confucianism, 316
Congress, 207, 207, 221, 235, 258, 268, 279
Congress of Industrial Organizations (CIO), 112, 128
   International Union of Mine, Mill, and Smelter campaign, 133
Congress of Racial Equality (CORE), 184
Congress of Spanish Speaking People, 280
Connecticut, 245, 270
   Bridgeport, 157, 270, 277
   Connecticut River Valley, 83
   Hartford, 270, 277
   Mashantucket, 245
   New Haven, 207
Conquest, politics of, 95–96
Conservatives, 178, 200, 202, 205, 221, 227, 227, 266, 285, 288
Constraints, 4, 62
Consumerism, 154
Cooperatives, 72
Copts, 15
CORE-initiated Freedom Rides, 186
Cornish Americans, 165
Corporations, 151, 201, 256, 270, 338
Corresca, Rocco, 103
Corsicans, 30
Costa Ricans, 290
Costner, Kevin, 249
Cotton, 89, 126
Council housing, 206, 207

Council of Energy Resource Tribe (CERT), 244
Counter-Intelligence Program (COINTELPRO), 190
Counterculture, 176
Court challenges, 186
Court orders, 187
Courtroom interpreters, 258
Coyotes, 253
Craven, Anita, 342
Creek Indians, 85
Creek War of 1813, 84
criollos, 269
Croatians, 30
Cronkite, Walter, 259
Crow Indians, 241
Crusade for Justice, 284
Cuba, 17, 253
   Castro regime, 261, 262, 266
   Havana, 253, 263
   independence, 133
   nationalist movement, 133
   Peruvian Embassy, 263
   poverty in, 260
   pre-Castro, 268
Cuban American National Foundation (CANF), 267
Cuban Americans/immigrants, 128, 133, 152, 253, 254, 255, 259–268, 270, 272, 310, 312, 313, 314
   culture, 267
   economic success, 266
   elites, 261
   entrepreneurs, 260, 261
   lower-middle class, 261, 262
   middle class, 261
   naturalization, 266
   opportunities, 264
   political participation, 266–267
   professionals, 260
   settlement patterns, 263–264
   small business owners, 260
   upper class, 261
   white-collar, 265
   women, 133, 265, 268
   working class, 261, 262
Cuban exiles, 267
Cuban missile crisis, 262
Cuban Revolution, 253
Cuban-owned television, 276
Cubans, 11, 16, 61, 63, 256, 257, 259, 273, 277

Cullen, Countee, 128
Cultural anthropology, 28
Cultural attachments, 51
Cultural change, 268
Cultural conflict, 243
Cultural differences, 27, 35, 161, 347
Cultural fusion, 21
Cultural interaction, 55
Cultural organizations, 155, 346
Cultural pluralism, 22–23
Cultural respect, 339
Cultural Revolution, 308
Cultural syncretism, 163
Cultural transmission, 154–157
Culture, 6, 19, 38, 39, 50, 55, 60, 61, 67, 69, 130, 144, 160, 161, 164, 255, 267, 318
    British American, 78
Culture, American, 141, 317
Culture, shared, 37
Custer, General, 249
Daley, Richard, 112
Dances With Wolves, 249–250
Danish, 54
Danish immigrants, 156
Darwinism, 34
Dawes Act, 144–145, 146
Days of Obligation, 7
de Crévecoeur, J. Hector St. John, 78
de las Casas, Bartolomé, 95
de Sepúlveda, Juan Ginés, 95
de Tocqueville, Alexis, 69
Dearborn Independent, The, 118
Declining Significance of Race, The, 212
Deculturation, 283
Defense-plant jobs, 197
DeFunis v. Odegaard, 198
Degradation ceremony, 89
Deindustrialization, 213
Delaware Indians, 85
Democracy, 69, 261, 319, 333, 344
Democracy in America, 18, 69
"Democracy Versus the Melting Pot," 22
Democratic campaigns, 267
Democratic party, 75, 80, 108, 112, 159, 172, 178, 202, 266, 276, 282, 285, 286, 303
Democratic values, 4

Demonstrators, 188
Department of Energy, 244
Department of Health, Education, and Welfare, 192, 258
Department of Housing and Urban Development (HUD), 211, 246, 285
Department of Natural Resources, 239
Department of Transportation, 153
Departments d'Outre-Mer, 351
Derogatory expressions, 58
Derogatory jokes, 58
Desegregation (*see also* integration), 186, 194, 195
    judicial decisions/litigation, 192, 195
    school, 191–195
    white opposition to, 192–193
Devolution, 343, 353
DeWitt, General, 141
Dialect, 38, 322
Differential socialization, 155
Dinkins, David, 23
Discrimination, 56, 57, 59, 73, 119, 132, 136, 164, 167, 181, 185, 188, 196, 277, 280, 282, 296, 297, 300, 320, 327–328, 331, 335, 345, 350, 355
    sociology of, 58–60
Discrimination, employment/hiring, 4, 63, 230, 284, 299, 321, 345, 346
Discrimination, gender, 9
Discrimination, housing, 209, 210, 217, 284, 288, 345
Discrimination, institutional, 60, 63
Discrimination, racial, 9, 17, 197, 271, 272, 279, 300, 311, 352
Displaced persons (DPs), 336
Displaced Persons Act, 305
Diversity, 22, 23, 54–56, 114, 341, 342, 347, 350, 354
    ethnic, 335, 339
Do The Right Thing, 315
Doak, William, 131
Documentary resources, 10
Dominican Republic, 16, 263
Dominicans, 61, 255, 256, 267, 273, 290, 309, 310

Douglass, Frederick, 92, 93, 94, 123
Down These Mean Streets, 272
Downloading while Asian (DWA), 328
Dramatic associations, 79
Dreamer movement, 145
Drugs, 98, 220, 310
Drum Cult, 145
Drums Along the Mohawk, 146
Du Bois, William Edward Burghardt (W. E. B.), 122, 124, 182, 183, 356
Du, Soon Ja, 315
Duke, David, 176, 177
Dukmejian, Governor, 289
Dunkers, 77
Dutch, 82, 336
Dutch immigrants, 68, 152, 163
Dylan, Bob, 146

E, F

Easter Uprising, 344
Economic attainment, 161
Economic competition, 27
Economic opportunity, 6
Economic recession, 217
Economics, 47, 67, 71, 255
Economy
    agrarian, 62
    class-based, 81
    global, 331, 334
    industrial, 62
    southern, 126
Ecuadorians, 256, 290
Education, 70, 106–107, 137, 152, 182
    affirmative action, 196
Educational achievement/attainment, 45, 57, 155, 161, 204, 205, 346, 346, 347, 353
Educational levels, 62
Educational mobility, 156
Eisenhower, President Dwight D., 191, 226, 227, 261
El Congresso del Pueblo de Habla Espanola (the Spanish-Speaking Congress), 132
El Diario, 276
El Salvador, 253
Elective Governors Act, 269
Elites, economic, 50, 135

Elk v. Wilkins, 146
Elk, John, 146
Ellis Island, 110
Elm Haven, 207
Emancipation, 120, 214
Embargoes, 267
Emerson, Ralph Waldo, 20
Empire Windrush, 345
Employment, 62, 63, 102, 147, 188, 280
  affirmative action, 196, 199
Employment patterns, 38
England, 20, 30, 70, 83, 114, 207, 334, 335, 342, 343, 344, 347, 350, 351
  as Albion, 70
  colonial expansion, 334
  council estates, 206
  definition of citizenship, 350
  Industrial Revolution, 89
  middle class, 206
  New Labour government, 343
  North Midlands, 70
  in a postcolonial world, 342–347
English immigrants, 72, 107, 152, 155, 156, 163
English language, 7, 75, 230, 257, 258, 268, 288, 295, 313, 326, 335, 337, 346
English people, 54, 68, 78, 82, 335
  culture, 76
Enlightenment, 68
Entitlement programs, 203, 206
Environmentalists, 240, 241
Equal access, 59
Equal Employment Opportunity Commission (EEOC), 197
Equal opportunity, 196, 201, 280
  housing, 209–212
  employment, 197
Equal rights, 339
Equal Rights for Everyone, 239
Equality, 69, 71, 79, 80, 191
Equality, racial, 123, 176, 177, 213
Estonia, 30
Ethclass relations, 212
Ethnic Americans, 101–103
Ethnic boundaries, 53, 56

Ethnic commitment, 44
Ethnic communities, 102, 109, 116–117, 118, 152, 155, 159, 167, 264, 267, 268, 322–323
  middle class, 103
Ethnic competition, 48
Ethnic differences, 60–63, 335
Ethnic dimensions, 3–25
Ethnic enclave, 97, 104, 119, 152, 154, 157, 159, 193, 290, 306, 314, 322, 325, 345, 349
  economy of, 264–266
Ethnic groups, 14–16, 29, 30, 33, 37–41, 40, 50, 52, 256, 298, 333, 355
  affiliation, 48
  definition, 70
  formation, 46
  size, 156
  unity, 322
Ethnic hum, 164
Ethnic options, 162–163
Ethnic organizations, 160
Ethnic relations, 29, 36, 41–46, 331
Ethnic revival, 157–160
Ethnic studies, emergence of, 27–29
Ethnic traditions, 164
Ethnic/interethnic relations, 5, 24, 27–64
Ethnicity, 5, 10, 12, 13, 33, 37–41, 42, 46, 47, 48, 49, 50, 152, 153, 154, 156, 333
  biology and, 27, 28, 36, 45
  and class, 63
  definitions of, 37, 38, 39
  emergent, 50, 165
  invention of, 51–54, 56, 164–167, 234
  privatization of, 163–164
  relationship between race and, 15
  social construction of, 48–54
Ethnicity, political, 158–160
Ethnicity, twilight of, 154
Ethnicization, 50
Ethnocentrism, 13, 37
Ethnocultural exclusionists, 350
Ethnogenesis, 49–50
Ethnonationalism, 30, 337, 342, 343, 344, 347, 352, 353, 354

Eugenics, 34, 35, 36
Eurocentrism, 355
Europe, 3, 77, 79, 114
  Eastern, 34, 42, 52, 114, 115, 116, 117, 119, 336, 340, 349
  northwestern, 161
  settlers, 3
  south central, 161
  southern, 52, 340
  Western, 30, 34, 115, 334, 336, 340, 341–353
European Americans, 151–180, 156, 164, 171, 172, 333
  identity, 165–167
European colonization/settlements, 34, 81, 86
European immigrants, 19, 20, 21, 28, 32, 40, 62, 67, 250, 326
  Eastern, 23, 102, 112, 320
  southern, 23, 102, 112
  Western, 102
  working class, 21
European Union, 334, 343, 350
Europeans, 82, 87, 136
Euskaldunak, 15
Euskera, 15
Evangelical Lutheran Church, 240
Exclusion, 81–82, 167, 219, 323, 349
Experiences, ethnic, 6–14, 28
Experimental Housing Allowance Program, 209
Exploitation, economic, 219
Extreme insiderism, 13, 14
Factories, 104
Fair Employment Practices Commission, 183
Fair Housing Law, 189
  Title 8, 188
Family structure, 155
Famine, 97
Farnham Courts, 207
Fascism, 108, 183
Faubus, Governor Orval, 187, 191
Feast of the Immaculate Conception, 324
Federal Bureau of Investigation (FBI), 310
Federal District Court, 192, 327
Federal Housing Administration (FHA), 153, 210
Feet binding, 8

Fellowship of Reconciliation, 184
Female circumcision, 353
Fertility rates, 161, 254, 268, 349
Fictive kin, 274
Fiji, 340
Filial obedience/piety, 9, 316, 317
Filipino Americans/immigrants, 11, 283, 296, 308, 312, 318–323
  churches, 322
  discrimination/prejudice, 320, 321
  downward mobility, 321
  educational achievement, 318, 319, 321
  ethnic community, 322–323
  exploitation, 319
  naturalization, 320
  recredentialing, 322
  sex ratio, 320
  since 1945, 320–322
  small businesses and, 322
  unskilled jobs and, 321
  white-collar professionals, 321
  women, 320, 321
  World War II, pre, 318
Filipinos, 336
Fina Oil and Chemical, 240
Finance, 68
Financial sanctions, 192
Financiers, 124
Finland, 164
  Helsinki, 164
Finnish Americans, 164
Finns, 107, 165
Firefighters Local Union No. 1784 v. Stotts, 200
First Nations people, 335, 338, 354
First Quota Act (1921), 110
First wave refugees, 324
First-generation immigrants, 63, 275, 317
Fish-ins, 235
Fisk University, 121
Flint Knife, 145
Florida, 89, 133, 253, 259, 263, 266, 267, 270, 324, 325, 331
  Coral Springs, 327
  Dade County, 264
  Hialeah, 264

Liberty City, Miami, 255
Miami, 61, 63, 170, 254, 255, 257, 263, 264, 265, 266, 267, 268, 270
Tampa, 133, 265
Folklore, 38
Folkways, 22, 39, 70, 106
Folkways, 37
Fomoaley, Chief, 11
For Bread With Butter, 111
Forced relocation, 335
Forced sterilization, 259
Ford, Henry, 22, 118
Ford, John, 146
Forty-eighters, 79, 80
Fourth generation immigrants, 156, 162, 300
Fox Indians, 85
Foxwoods Casino, 245
France, 30, 83, 334, 342, 354
  Basques, 352
  Bretons, 352
  Corsicans, 352, 353
  definition of citizenship, 350
  l'autre, 351
  as a melting pot, 350–353
  Occitan, 158, 352
Francophone, 335, 337
Frank, Leo, 118
Franklin, Benjamin, 16, 78
Fraternal orders/societies, 72, 91, 115, 322
Fraud, 144
Freedman's Bureau, 120, 121
Freedom, 69, 70, 80
Freedom Flight immigrants, 262
Freedom rides, 188
Freedom Summer, 186, 188
French, 82, 335
  culture, 352
French Americans, 152, 156
French Canada, 29
French Canadians, 107
French Guyana, 352
French immigrants, 68, 163
French language, 337
French Revolution, 79
Freud, Sigmund, 57
Frontier, 96
Frustration-aggression theory (of prejudice), 57
Fugitive Slave Law, 94
Fukienese, 309
Fur trade, 83
Furutani, Warren, 299

G, H

G. I. Bill, 152
Gadsden Purchase, 96
Gambling/gaming, 98, 238, 244–246, 260
Gantt, Harvey, 202
Garment industry, 63, 104, 271, 288, 309, 310
Garrison, William Lloyd, 94
Garrity, Judge W. Arthur, 192
Garvey, Marcus, 122, 124, 189, 190
Gastarbeiter (guest workers), 348, 359
Geary Act, 135
Gemeinschaft, 37
Gender issues, 33, 47, 54
Generalizations, 13
Generational change, 158
Genocide, 41
Gentleman's Agreement (1907), 139
Geographic origin, 38
Georgia, 89
  Albany, 186
  Atlanta, 118, 170, 194, 313
German American/immigrants, 62, 67, 68, 72, 107, 141, 152, 156, 163, 263, 313
  economics, 77, 81
  as farmers, 78
  identity, 80
  interethnic encounters, 80–81
  intraethnic conflict, 79–80
  politics, 79, 80
  rate of literacy, 78
  religious divisions, 80
  social status, 81
  socioeconomic position, 78
German Democratic Republic (East Germany), 348
German language, 16
  middle high, 114
  newspapers, 78
German sociologists, 46–47
Germans, 39, 163, 336
  ethnic, 349
Germantowns/little Germanies, 79
Germany, 110, 114, 334, 342, 348–350, 349, 354
  Bavaria, 349
  Berlin, 79, 349
  blood and soil citizenship, 348, 349

Germany, Federal Republic of (West Germany), 348
Ghana, 124
Ghetto, The, 29
Ghettoes, 152, 159, 184, 310, 314
    rural, 227
    vertical, 208
Ghost Dance movement, 145, 236
Giago, Tom, 235
Gila River, 141
Glass ceiling, 300
Global transmigration, 296
Goals, collective, 284
Goals, Native American, 237, 238
Gold, 96–98
Golden Exiles, 261, 262
Golden Mean Society, 177
Gompers, Samuel, 134
Gone With the Wind, 88
Gonzales, Rodolfo "Corky," 284
Goodman, Andrew, 188
Gore, Al, 285
Gorras Blancas, 129
Governmental support/welfare programs, 218, 286
Goya, 276
Gratz v. Bollinger, 201
Great Britain (*see* England)
Great Depression, 127, 131, 133, 153, 206, 207
Great Migration, 127
Great Society, 208, 227, 228, 284
Greek immigrants, 130, 153
Greek Orthodox, 167
Greeks, 39, 70, 336
Green party, 240
Green v. New Kent Co., 192
Greenhorns, 116
Griffith, D. W., 146
Grizzly bear, 240
Grocery stores, 295
Group attachments, 36
Group boundaries, 15–16
Group definitions, 15–16
Group position, 56–60
Grutter v. Bollinger, 201
Guadeloupe, 352
Guamanians, 296
Guatemalans, 256, 290
"Guide to Understanding Chippewa Treaty Rights, A," 239
Gypsies, 41
H1-B visas, 324

Haiti, 263, 336
Haitians, 265
Halacha, 117
Hampton, Fred, 190
Hampton Institute, 121
Handicapped centers, 315
Hansen thesis, 158
Hapas, 305
Harlem Renaissance, 128
Harlins, Latasha, 315
Harvard Encyclopedia of American Ethnic Groups (HEAEG), 15, 38, 39
Harvard University, 119, 123, 203
    Civil Rights Project, 195
Hate, politics of, 176–178
Hawaii, 97, 138, 139, 301, 303, 304, 305, 319, 321, 326
    Honolulu, 322
Hawaiian Sugar Planters Association, 319
Hawaiians, 296
Hayakawa, Senator S. I., 258
Hayes, Ira, 146
Hayes, President Rutherford, 134
Head Start, 178, 204
Heart Mountain, 142, 295
Hebrew language, 114
Hegemony, 72
Helms, Senator Jesse, 202
Hereditary dispositions, 28
Heterogeneity, 3, 8, 19, 23, 32, 70, 101, 128, 333, 336
Hillbillies, 165
Hinduism, 324, 345
Hindus, 347
Hippies, 249
Hispanic settlement, 95
Hispanics, 11, 16, 32, 62, 81, 96, 101, 120, 152, 159, 189, 248, 253–293, 323, 326, 331, 332
    education, 129
    gangs, 290
    immigration, 128–134
    median income, 266
    poor, 129
    population/presence in the United States, 128–134, 291
    suburban, 211
    wealthy, 129
Historical conditions (of ethnicity), 45

History, shared, 39, 152
Hmong, 296, 325
Hoffman, Joyce, 163
Holland, 114
Hollywood, 146, 249
Holocaust, 41, 114, 167
Holt, Hamilton, 12
Homeland, 38, 55, 75, 79, 105, 108, 111, 156, 307–308, 322, 323, 336
Homeownership, 217, 346
Homicide, 247, 248
Homogeneity, 22
Homosexuality, 7, 33
Hondurans, 256, 290
Hong Kong, 307, 308, 310, 340
Hopi reservation, 246
Hopwood v. Texas, 200
Horton, Willie, 178
Host society, 56
Housing, 206–212, 310
    privatization, 209
    public ownership, 206
Housing Act of 1949, 206
Housing authorities, 207
Housing, public, 206–209, 218
    alternatives to, 208–209
    class-based inequalities, 208
    segregated, 207
    vertical ghettos, 208
    warehouses for the poor, 208
Housing Rights Act (1968), 188
Housing, subsidized, 206
Howard, Prime Minister John, 339
Howard University, 121, 195
Hughes, Langston, 128
Hull House, 20
Hungarian, 114
Hungary, 115
Hunger of Memory, 7
Hunting rights, 238
Hurricanes, 133
Hurston, Zora Neale, 128
Hutterites, 15, 39
Hypergamy, 304
Hyphenated Americans, 20

I, J

Iberian peninsula, 351
Idaho, 142

Identity Christians, 177
Identity, class, 152, 153
Identity, ethnic, 6–14, 44, 45, 46, 49, 50, 51, 113, 119, 152, 153, 156, 158, 160, 161, 162, 164, 166, 172, 233, 257, 290, 302, 304, 323, 354
attachment to, 162
collective, 53
discrete, 55
Identity, group, 50, 169
Identity, national, 55, 69, 290, 355
Identity, panethnic, 328
Identity, personal, 10, 342
Identity, racial, 39
Identity, regional, 165–166
Identity, religious, 167
Idolatry, 95
Illegal/undocumented immigration, 130, 135, 253, 277, 278, 279, 280, 280, 309, 341
Illinois, 270, 312, 331
Chicago, 20, 104, 105, 111, 112, 127, 128, 128, 130, 156, 157, 165, 170, 182, 190, 208, 211, 221, 230, 231, 263, 295, 306, 312, 314, 315, 322
Chinatown, Chicago, 306
Little Italy, Chicago, 105
Matteson, 211
Illiteracy, 21
Ilocano, 322
Immigrant generation, 141, 156, 300, 323
Immigrants, 3, 22, 39, 50, 55, 61, 68, 71, 72, 109
Immigrants, arriving, 288
Immigrants, involuntary, 62, 89
Immigrants, new, 310
Immigrants, voluntary, 31, 42, 62, 67, 89, 91, 95
Immigration Act (1910), 335
Immigration Act (1919), 335
Immigration Act (1965), 312, 320
Immigration/migration, 20, 61, 67, 84, 248, 259, 273, 325, 331
anti-immigration attitudes, 332
economic motives for, 74
global, 331

history of, 4–6
white supremacy and, 101–148
Immigration and Naturalization Service (INS), 130, 261, 278
Immigration policy/law, 42, 127, 134, 335, 336 341
Immigration Reform and Control Act, 279
Immigration Restriction Act (1901), 340
Immigration Restriction League, 34
Inclusion, 168
Income, 204
Incorporation, 42, 43, 61, 69, 89, 95, 115, 169, 331, 350, 354
Indentured servants, 70, 72, 93
Independentistas, 269
India, 340, 345
Indian agents, 144
Indian Allotment Act (*see* Dawes Act)
Indian, Asian, 324, 336, 346
women, 324
Indian Educational Assistance and Self-Determination (1975), 238
Indian Gaming Regulatory Act (IGRA), 245
Indian Health Service, 247
Indian New Deal, 146–147, 226
Indian Ocean, 352
Indian of All Tribes, 236
Indian Reorganization Act of 1934 (IRA), 147, 225–226, 227, 228
Indian Self-Determination Act (1975), 228
Indian subcontinent, 323, 345
Indian Wars, 9
Indigenous people/population, 69, 95, 354
Individualism, 69, 102
Indonesia, 340
Industrial Age, 47
Industrial America, 6
Industrial society, 151, 325
Industrialists, 124
Industrialization, 11, 44, 151, 312
Inequality, 35, 70, 123
Inequality of Human Races, The, 33

Inequality, racial, 200, 201, 203
Inequality, social, 4, 181
Infant mortality rate, 247, 310
Ingroups, 36, 56–60
Inouye, Daniel, 303
Insider-outsider debate, 13
Institution building, 274
Institutional completeness, 53–54, 56, 118
Institutional structure, 98
Institutions, community, 135
Institutions, ethnic, 103, 105, 111, 164, 301
Institutions, social, 61, 120, 346
Integration (*see also* Desegregation), 123, 124, 173, 182, 183, 188, 189, 190, 191, 192, 193, 195, 276–277
Integration, housing, 210
Integration, multicultural, 353
Integration, neighborhood/residential, 207, 211, 216
Integration, school, 175
Interethnic competition, 48
Interethnic conflict, 108, 314–315
Interethnic marriage, 163
Interethnic relations, 40
Intergenerational conflict/tension, 140, 317
Intergenerational flux, 170
Intergroup conflict, 194
Intergroup relations, 5, 14, 16–18, 36, 152, 354, 355
Intermarriage, 21, 24, 43, 45, 53, 114, 119, 154, 157, 161, 164, 169, 170, 171–173, 176, 231–233, 286, 304, 318, 324, 332
black-white, 232
laws against, 174
rate, 250, 303
International Nongovernmental Organizations (INGOs), 334
Interracial etiquette, 125
Interracial marriage, 120, 303, 320
Interracial unions, 305
Intertribal Friendship House, 230
Intraethnic conflict, 108
Intragroup relations, 5, 14, 31, 52
Inuit, 338

Inuit language, 338
Iran, 168, 340
Ireland, 164, 340, 343
  Great Famine, 73
Ireland, Northern, 70, 157,
  342, 343, 344, 347
Irish, 12, 15, 22, 163
Irish Americans/immigrants,
  62, 67, 68, 72, 72–77, 76,
  105, 107, 108, 111, 112,
  152, 155, 156, 157, 159,
  160, 165, 165, 192, 207,
  272
  adjustment, 73–75
  alcoholism, 74
  attacks on, 77
  crime/criminal activity, 74,
    75–76
  in domestic service, 74
  ghetto, 73, 74
  politics, 75, 77
  poor, 73, 74, 76
  sex ratio, 74
  stereotypes, 58
  violence, 74
  women, 74
Irish Catholics, 72, 73, 76, 77,
  80, 106, 165
Irish Lesbian and Gay Organization, 165
Irish names, 153
Irish Republican Army (IRA),
  164, 343, 344
Iroquois, 82, 84
Islam (*see also* Muslims) 39,
  352
Isolation, social, 137, 154,
  276–277
Israel, 114, 157, 167, 168, 169,
  172
Issei, 140, 141, 299, 301, 303
Italian Americans/immigrants,
  6–7, 10, 12, 15, 22–23, 44,
  54, 60, 101, 103–109, 111,
  130, 131, 141, 152, 153,
  155, 157, 159, 160, 163,
  165, 167, 192, 207, 272
  alcoholism, 107
  crime rate, 107
  divided loyalties of, 108
  education, 107
  ethnic community, 104–106
  family, 105, 108
  generational change among,
    108–109
  ghetto, 109
  housing, 207

mafia, 107
  politics, 108
  stereotypes, 58
  women, 104
  working class, 105–106
Italian language, 153, 154
Italian-language newspapers,
  105
Italians, 336
Italy, 6, 154, 348, 351
  Altavilla, 105
  Bagheria, 105
  Mezzogiorno, 103, 105
  Northern, 11, 103, 108
  Sambuca-Zabut, 105
  Sicily/Sicilians, 6, 11, 15,
    105
  southern, 104
  upward mobility, 107
Iwo Jima, 146
Jackson, Andrew, 84
Jackson, Jesse, 221, 222
Jamaica, 124, 336
Jamaicans, 345
Japan, 137, 138, 141, 334, 340
Japanese, 11
  and Chinese, 132–142
Japanese American Citizens
  League (JACL), 303
Japanese Americans/immi-
  grants, 138, 153, 296, 299–
  305, 314, 318, 321, 324,
  327
  agriculture, 140
  American born, 300
  changes in, 301–303
  child-rearing, 302
  citizenship, 303
  discrimination/prejudice,
    139, 140
  as domestics, 139
  education, 299, 300, 301
  ethnic community, 140–
    141, 301, 303, 304
  future of, 303–305
  gardening, 140
  generational differences,
    140–141
  identity, 141
  middle class, 300, 301, 302
  Pearl Harbor, 138
  Postwar era, 142
  religion, 302
  role of Japanese govern-
    ment in, 138–142
  rotating-credit system, 139
  sex ratio, 139

skills, 139
  stereotypes, 58
  suburban, 301
  women, 139
  World War I, 140
  World War II, 141–142,
    302, 304
  World War II, post, 299,
    303
  World War II, pre, 300
Japanese internment, 141–
  142, 299
Jazz, 128
Jemez, 10
Jessel, George, 117
Jewish Americans, 32, 107,
  157, 159, 160, 167–173
  civil rights movement, 185
  core population, 168–169
  identity, 171
  intermarriage, 171–173
  interpersonal relations,
    169–170
  socioeconomic terms, 167
  stereotypes, 58, 118
Jewish immigrants, 68, 101,
  105, 114–119, 160, 300
  culture, 118
  education, 119
  gender roles, 116
  German, 115, 116, 117
  labor/political organiza-
    tions, 117–118
  lower-middle class, 117
  as merchants, 115
  middle class, 117, 119
  post World War II, 119
  religious divisions, 117
  religious institutions, 116
  return migration rate, 116
  socioeconomic status, 117
  upward mobility of, 119
  working class, 119
Jewish Theological Seminary,
  117
Jews, 6, 23, 35, 39, 41, 60, 61,
  115, 167, 171, 336, 353
  activist, 170
  affiliated, 170
  Ashkenazim, 114
  as "Christ-killers," 115,
    118
  Conservative movement,
    117, 119
  Eastern European, 119
  German, 114, 119
  Hasidic, 53, 167

holiday, 170
inactives, 170
as International Jew, 118
as merchants, 63
Observant, 170
Orthodox, 115, 117, 119
Reform movement, 115, 117
Russian, 20
Sephardim, 114
as Shylocks, 118
Jibaros, 269
Jim Crow, 101, 120, 122, 177, 186, 188, 189, 191, 212, 219, 331, 354
Job opportunities, 130, 131, 221, 231, 346
Job training, 182
Jodo Shinshu Buddhist Churches of America, 302
Johnson, President Andrew, 120, 121
Johnson, President Lyndon B., 195, 200, 208, 227
Executive Order 11246, 197
Jolson, Al, 117
Jones v. Mayer, 210
Joseph, Chief, 142
Judd, Representative Walter H., 307
Julius Rosenwald Fund, 185
Jungle Fever, 220
Junior college, 251
Jus sanguinis, 348, 350
Jus soli, 350
Justice Department, 195

K, L

Kai-sha, 301
Kai-shek, Chiang, 305, 307
Kennedy, President John F., 185, 197, 227, 262, 282, 283
Executive Order 10925, 197
Executive Order 11063, 210
Keyes v. Denver School District No. 1, 192
Keynesian welfare state, 151
Kickapoo, 85
Kickbacks, 104
Killing fields, 325
Kin networks, 132
King, Martin Luther, Jr., 183, 184, 186, 189, 283

assassination of, 190
King, Rodney, 46, 315
Kinship, 38, 325
Kinship networks, 82
Kiowa tribe, 9, 10
Kirgizistan, 30
Klamath Indians, 227
Knights of the White Camelia, 125
Know-Nothing/American Party, 76
Knowland, Senator William F., 307
Kootenai, 243
Korea, 307, 312, 313, 316
Korean Americans/immigrants, 296, 312–318, 320, 324
churches, 315–316, 317
education, 312, 313, 317, 318
enclaves, 317
as entrepreneurs, 313–314
ethnic community, 317, 318
ethnic/enclave economy, 313, 314
family, 317
health care, 313
in black neighborhoods, 314, 315
middle class, 312, 313, 316, 317
post 1965, 312
recredentialing, 313
self-employment, 313
small businesses, 314
suburban, 317
upward mobility, 313
women, 313, 317, 318
Korean language, 316
Korean War, 312, 313, 316
Koreans, 11, 32, 63, 265
Kosovo, 42
Kroeber, Alfred L., 28
Ku Klux Klan (KKK), 118, 124, 125, 172, 176, 177, 188, 216, 235
Kuyok Yebae, 316
Kye, 314
La Huelga (*see* strikes)
La raza, 284
La Raza Unida, 284
Labor force/market, 130, 142, 213, 270
Labor migrants, 133, 348
Labor movement, 17, 116, 130
Labor organizations, 117–118
Labor sojourners, 351

Labor unions, 17, 72, 75, 103, 105, 106, 120, 198, 273
Labor-Zionists, 117
Lac Courte Oreilles, 239
Lace curtain Catholics/Irish, 73, 75
Lakota Indians, 226, 235, 236
Land claims, 238
Land grab, 144
Land ownership, 235
Landlords, 208
Landsmannschaften, 115, 116
Language, 22, 38, 39, 45, 70, 71, 114, 130, 290, 318, 321, 322, 323
Language barriers, 347
Language loyalty, 156
Laos, 324, 325
Laotians, 296
Latin America, 3, 264
Latin Americans, 11, 42
Latin Americans/immigrants, 67, 265
Latino National Political Survey, 257
Latino panethnic unity, 256–257
Latinos (*see* Hispanics)
Latvia, 30
Lau v. Nichols, 258
Lawrence, Stephen, 346
le Pan, Jean-Marie, 352
League of United Latin American Citizens (LULAC), 132, 279, 280, 285
Learning theory, 58
Leased Housing Program
section 23, 208, 209
section 8, 208, 209
Lebanon, 30
Lee, Spike, 216, 220, 315
Lee, Dr. Wen Ho, 328
Legal aliens, 278
Legislative decisions, 188–189
Leisure habits, 70
Letters From an American Farmer, 19
Lewis and Clark National Forest, 240
Liable to become a public charge (LPC), 131
Liberal capitulation, 202
Liberal whites, 185
Liberals, 59, 185, 202, 220, 227, 282
Liberty, 71, 79
Life expectancy, 247, 310

Life Stories of Undistinguished Americans, as Told by Themselves, The, 12
Lincoln, President Abraham, 120
Linnaeus, 33
Lithuania, 30, 115
Lithuanian immigrants, 62
Little Big Man, 249
Little Havana, 264, 265
Little Italies, 105
Little League baseball, 301
Little Taipei, 308–309
Lobbying, 184–189
Locke, Alain, 128
Lonely Crowd, The, 152
Longoria, Felix, 280
Loo, Jim, 327
Looting, 190
Los Alamos National Laboratory, 328
Louisiana, 122, 177
   Baton Rouge, 186, 194
   New Orleans, 122, 128
Louisiana Purchase, 85, 96
Lower-middle class, 159
Lowie, Robert, 28
Luce, Henry, 307
Lumbee Indians, 235
Lutheran Church, 153
Lynching, 8, 118, 125, 177, 183

M, N

Macedonians, 30
Machismo, 131
Macro level analyses, 5
Maine, 242
Malay race, 320
Malaysia, 340
Malcom X, 189
Man Called Horse, A, 249
Mandarin, 310
Mandarin speakers, 308
Mangione, Jerre, 6, 8, 9, 10, 11
Mango, 122
Manifest Destiny, 84
Mano Negro, 129
Manzanar, 141
Maoist sentiment, 307
Maquiladora industries, 256
March on Washington, DC, 182, 186
March on Washington, DC, pan-Indian, 235

Marcos, Ferdinand, 322, 323
Marginalization, 354
Marielitos, 17, 262, 263
Marin, Luis Muños, 269, 270
Marital status, 47
Maritime Provinces, 338
Marriage rates, 161
Marshall, Justice Thurgood, 200
Martinique, 352
Marxists, 44, 46–47, 261
Maryland, 72, 93, 285
   Baltimore, 105, 170
Mass communication, 183
Massachusetts, 108, 123, 242, 270
   Boston, 74, 77, 105, 153, 170, 192, 193
   Cape Cod, 242
   Cornerville, Boston, 109
   Fall River, 328
   Lawrence, 108
   Martha's Vineyard, 242
   Newburyport, 37
   South, Boston, 193
   West end, Boston, 153, 154
Mazzoli, Representative Romano, 279
McCarran-Walter Act (1952), 305
McCarthy, Senator Joseph, 307
McDonald's, 276
McGovern, George, 283
McKay Claude, 128
Mead, Margaret, 28
Meatpacking industry, 62, 111
Medical College Admissions Test (MCAT), 199
Meech Lake Accord, 337
Meharry Medical College, 184
Melting-Pot, The, 20
Mennonites, 77
Menominee Indians, 227
Mental illness, rates of, 310
Mentally disabled, 33
Merchant class, 72
Mescalero Apache, 244
Mestizas, 95
Methodists, 302
Metzger, Tom, 176, 177
Mexican American Legal Defense Educational Fund (MALDEF), 279
Mexican American Political Association (MAPA), 282

Mexican American Youth Organization (MAYO), 284, 324
Mexican Americans as immigrants, 7, 11, 15, 16, 62, 81, 95, 128, 131, 132, 152, 253, 254, 255, 256, 257, 266, 272, 273, 277–290, 308
   affirmative action, 200
   agriculture, 277
   amnesty program, 280
   delinquency, 132
   Depression, the 278
   discrimination/prejudice, 131, 286
   dropouts, 284, 286, 287, 290
   drugs, 290
   economics, 132, 278, 280
   education, 283
   employment, 283
   ethnic community/enclave, 132, 290
   exploitation of, 288
   gang membership, 289, 290
   labor, 131, 253
   marginalization of, 129
   middle class, 132, 253, 277, 282, 285, 289
   naturalization, 280
   politics, 132, 282, 283
   poverty, 132, 286, 288, 289
   repatriation, 131
   socioeconomic status, 286–288
   suburban, 288
   temporary worker program, 280
   unemployment, 286
   upper class, 285
   upper middle class, 285
   upward mobility, 284, 287, 289
   violence, 131
   working class, 282
   World War II, post, 277, 280
   youth, 132, 289–290
Mexican-American War, 128
Mexican War, 96
Mexicans, 96, 129, 265, 129–133
Mexico, 84, 262, 263
   Mexico City, 131
   northern, 281
Miami Indians, 85
Michigan, 104

Detroit, 111, 127, 130, 170, 194, 221
Lower Peninsula, 165
Upper Peninsula, 165
Micro-level analyses, 5
Middle class, 151, 152, 153, 183, 207, 213, 323, 332
Middle East, 39
Middle Easterners, 42
Middleman minority theory, 264
Mien tribal group, 325
Migrant workers, 351
Migrants, nonvoluntary, 354
Migratory status, 38
Militancy, 189–191
Mines, 104
Ming era, 97
Minidoka, 142
Minnesota, 104, 164, 238, 243, 244
Lake Superior, 238
Minneapolis-St. Paul, 230, 235
Minorities, 30, 55, 77, 107, 129, 198, 202, 339
Minority groups, 29, 31–33, 341
Missionaries, Catholic, 95, 312
Mississippi, 184, 186, 243
Mississippi River, 85
Missouri
Kansas City, 104
St. Louis, 104, 105, 127, 170, 208
Mixed bloods, 250
Mixed race children/people, 233, 333, 339, 342
Moapa, 244
Mob violence, 136
Modernization theorists, 44
Modified assimilationists, 44
Mohawk Indians, 244
Moieties, 82
Momaday, N. Scott, 9, 10, 250
Montana
Flathead reservation, 243
Montenegrins, 30
Montgomery Improvement Association, 186
Moravians, 77
Moreno, 272
Mores, 22, 39, 106, 109, 182, 216
Mormons, 15, 39
Morocco, 348, 351
Moses, Robert, 205

Moynihan Report, 218–219
Muhammad, Elijah, 189
Mulattos, 15, 39, 94, 122, 214, 254, 272
Multicultural pluralism, 350
Multiculturalism, 54–56, 331–356
American in twenty-first century, 353–356
critics of, 54
Musical societies, 315
Muslims, 39, 324, 345, 347, 349, 351, 353
Mussolini, Benito, 108
Mutual aid societies, 79, 91, 105, 111, 115, 116, 155, 157, 264, 315, 322, 346
Myrdal, Gunnar, 181, 182
Myth of the Negro Past, The, 89
Names, The, 9
Narragansetts, 242
Nation building, 67–72
Nation of Islam/Black Muslims, 189
National Association for the Advancement of Colored People (NAACP), 123, 124, 132, 182, 184, 185, 186, 200
National Association of Realtors, 211
National Committee Against Discrimination in Housing, 211
National Congress of American Indians (NCAI), 227, 234, 235
National Front (FN), 352
National Guard, 190, 191
National Indian Gaming Commission, 245
National Indian Youth Council (NIYC), 235
National Jewish Population Survey (NJPS), 168, 171, 172
National Opinion Research Center (NORC), 154, 174
National Puerto Rican Coalition, 275
National Urban League, 184
Nationalism, 30–31, 124, 268, 343, 352
Nationalist social movements, 158

Nationalities, 20, 30–31, 33, 70
Nations, 30–31
Nations of Nations, A, 31
Native American Party, 76
Native American Rights Fund, 238
Native American-white relations, structure of, 237
Native Americans, 3, 9–10, 15, 31, 40, 41, 42, 62, 67, 81, 82, 83, 84, 85, 86, 144, 152, 189, 225–252, 331, 338, 354, 355
acculturation of, 144–145
activism, 238
alcoholism/drug abuse, 146, 230, 241, 248
as American Indian or Amerindian, 16
as citizens, 85, 144, 146
church, 145
conflict period, 82, 84–85, 142
conversion to Christianity, 144, 145
court challenges, 238, 242
culture, 83, 244
displacement of, 84
draft, 146
economic considerations/development, 83, 228, 243, 250
education, 146, 251
employment, 146
ethnic communities, 233–234
European interaction with, 82, 83, 142
extended families, 82
federal government, 143, 225, 227, 234, 235, 236, 244, 251
films/movies, 248, 249
health care, 146, 245, 247
health insurance, 247–248
housing, 146, 246–247
identity, 226, 250, 251
income, 246
land disputes, 84, 227, 241–243
market period, 82, 83, 142
middle class, 10
middle passage, beyond the, 86–95
ongoing conflict, 238–243

political interests, 83, 234–238
poverty, 146, 230, 246
relocation, 85–86
reservation era, 142–147
self-determination, 144, 228
social organizations, 82
sovereignty, 243
subsidies, 246
treaties, 17, 85
tribal citizenship, 239
under/unemployment, 246
urbanization of, 228–231
World War II, 146
World War II, post, 226
Nativism, 76–77, 80, 113
Natural resources, 129, 238, 243, 243–244
Natural selection, 34
Nature of Prejudice, The, 57
Navajo, 10, 241, 245, 250
Nazi concentration camps, 89
Nazis, 41, 183
Near East, 114
Nebraska, 78
  Omaha, 127
Negro Family in the United States, The, 29
Negro Family: The Case for National Action, The, 219
Negro in the United States, The, 29
Neighborhood, 38, 120, 160, 164, 174, 193, 288, 314, 322
  integrated/multiethnic, 211, 308
  segregated, 209, 211, 353
Neo-ethnicity, 158
Neo-Nazi groups, 176, 177
Neoconservatives, 177, 178, 195, 200
Nepotism, 36
Nevada, 95, 244, 320
New Agenda, 341
New Black Middle Class, 215
New capitalism, 152
New Deal, 108, 151, 159, 182, 208, 226, 269
New Deal coalition, 172, 178, 202
New England, 104
New Jersey, 104, 263, 267, 270
  Jersey City, 263, 270
  Newark, 194, 263, 270, 277

Patterson, 108, 270, 277
New Mexico, 129, 130, 133, 243, 244, 328
  Albuquerque, 230
  Kit Carson National Park, 284
New Right, 177, 178
New World, 82
New York, 6, 104, 169, 171, 242, 243, 267, 270, 271, 275, 276, 290, 306, 308, 326, 331
  Albany, 163
  Brooklyn, 167, 271
  Buffalo, 111, 157
  Capital region, 163
  Chinatown, 97, 306, 308, 309
  Coney Island, 11, 167
  Elmhurst, 308
  Flushing, 308
  Greenwich Village, New York City, 108–109
  Harlem, New York City, 127, 128, 190, 271, 272
  Hempstead, 306
  Levittown, 153
  Little Italy, 309
  migrant farm workers, 133
  New York City, 22, 23, 61, 73, 74, 103, 105, 107, 111, 116, 128, 133, 159, 165, 170, 216, 221, 230, 254, 263, 270, 273, 276, 306, 308, 309, 312, 313, 314, 316, 322
  New York Mills, 112
  Queens, New York City, 167
  Rochester, 6, 8, 190
  Rockland County, 170
  Rooseveltown, 244
  Schenectady, 163
  South Bronx, New York City, 271
  Spanish Harlem, New York City, 271
  Troy, 163
New York Times, 165, 242, 244, 245, 257, 281
New Zealand, 340
Newfoundland, 68
Newspapers, 128, 155, 264, 276
Newton, Huey, 190
Nez Perce tribe, 142
Nguyen, Lyuen Phan, 327
Nhem, Sam, 327

Niagara Falls Conference (1905), 123
Nicaraguans, 256, 290
Niche economics, 346
Nisei, 140, 141, 142, 299, 300, 301, 302, 303
  442nd Regimental Combat Team, 142
Nixon, President Richard, 176, 198, 208, 228
No-no boys, 142
NonGovernmental Organizations (NGOs), 55
Nonviolent confrontation, 184–189, 234, 283
Nordic people, 34
Normative structure, 70
Norms, 51
North American Free Trade Agreement (NAFTA), 256, 288, 334
North Carolina
  Greensboro, 186
  Robeson County, 235
North Korea, 316
North Sea, 343
Norwegian Americans, 152, 156, 165
Nuclear waste, 244
Nunavut, 338
Nuns, 75, 106
Nurses, 321
Nuyoricans, 277

O, P

100% Arabica, 353
Occupational location, 50, 204
Occupational mobility, 156
Occupational status, 47
Octoroon, 122
Odum, Howard, 28
Office of Economic Opportunity (OEO), 227, 228
Official Language Act (1970), 337
Oglala Sioux, 145, 235, 236
Ohio, 78
  Cincinnati, 165
  Cleveland, 104, 111, 170, 210, 230
Oil companies, 241
Oklahoma, 10, 85, 244
  Oklahoma City, 230
  Tulsa, 230
Oklahoma City v. Dowell, 195

Old World in the New, The, 34
One-quarter blood quantum, 233, 239
Oneidas, 243, 245
Operation Bootstrap, 270, 274
Oppression, 13, 17, 36, 283, 339, 354
Oppression, racial, 355, 182, 183, 219
  resistance to, 91
Optionalists, 45
Order of the Star-Spangled Banner, 76
Order of United Americans, 76
Order, The, 177
Oregon, 227, 320
Organization of Chinese Americans, 311
Organizational differences, 27
Organizations, formal, 275
Organized crime, 245, 260
Organized labor, 112, 125, 130, 134, 166
Ottawas, 85
Our Racial and National Minorities, 31
Outgroups, 36, 56–60
Ozawa v. U.S., 140
Ozawa, Takao, 140
Padrone system, 130, 319
Paget, Debra, 249
Paiute, 145, 244
Pakistanis, 296, 336, 345
Palestinians, 169
Pan-Africanism, 124
Pan-Indian sensibility, 11, 233, 234
Panamanians, 256, 290
Papagos, 247
Paper son migration, 135, 295
Pardo, 272
Park, Robert E., 28, 29
Parks, Rosa, 186
Parliamentary Statement on Racial Tolerance, 339
Parochial schools, 76, 205
Parti Québecois, 337, 343
Passamaquoddies, 242
Passing of the Great Race, The, 34
Pearl Harbor, 137, 138, 141
Penn, Arthur, 249
Pennsylvania, 74, 111, 112, 270, 324
  Delaware Valley, 70
  Germantown, 77

Johnstown, 111
Philadelphia, 73, 74, 77, 105, 127, 162, 170, 190, 210, 221, 276, 325
Pittsburgh, 111, 165
Penobscots, 242
Peorias, 85
Pequot War of 1637, 83
Pequots, 83, 245
Permanent residents, 348, 349
Persian Gulf crisis, 240
Peru, 97
Peruvians, 256, 290
Peyote cult, 145
Phagan, Mary, 118
Philadelphia Plan, 198
Philippine Scouts, 320
Philippines, 320, 321, 322, 323, 340
Physically disabled, 33
Pick and shovel jobs, 104
Picture brides, 139
Pietists, 77, 80
Plaid Cymru, 343
Plains Indians, 145
Plantation, 88, 89, 94, 143
  slavery and, 88–89
Plessy vs. Ferguson, 122, 188
Plessy, Homer Adolphus, 122
Pluralism, 3, 42, 43–46, 54, 55, 81–82, 95, 341
  caste, 81
  sojourner, 81, 140
  structural, 341
  voluntary, 82
Pocahontas, 250
Pogroms, 115
Poland, 115, 340
Poles, 336
Police brutality, 190, 284
Police dogs, 188
Polish Americans/immigrants, 12, 28, 62, 101, 109–114, 152, 156–157, 163, 165, 167, 276
  Austro-Hungarian Poles, 110
  community, 111–113
  emigration, 110–111
  generational change, 113–114
  middle class, 113, 156
  political involvement, 112
  post World War I, 110
  post World War II, 113
  poverty, 111
  Russian, 110

  as sojourners, 110
  stereotypes, 58
  upward mobility, 113
  women, 111
  working class, 112, 156
Polish language, 113, 114
Polish National Alliance, 111
Polish Peasant in Europe and America, The, 28, 109
Polish Roman Catholic Union, 111
Political action committees, 267
Political Association of Spanish-Speaking Organizations (PASSO), 282
Political associations/organizations, 91, 117–118
Political campaigns, 4
Political exiles, 260, 268
Political influence/power, 56
Political machine, 75, 77, 112, 128
  Chicago democratic, 112
Political organizations, 264, 346
Political orientation, 45, 70
Political Process and the Development of Black Insurgency, 187
Politics of recognition, 337
Pollution, 240
Polygamy, 353
Polynesians, 19
Popular culture, 55
Portugal, 114, 348, 351
Portuguese, 114, 336
Posse Comitatus, 176–177
Postindustrial society, 151
Poston, 141
Potawatomis, 85
Poverty, 4, 21, 184, 221, 307, 345, 346
Poverty, culture of, 286
Poverty, feminization of, 218
Poverty, inner-city, 219–221
Powell, Colin, 222
Power, 36, 46, 52, 61, 62, 70, 144
Power, allocation of, 32
Power, distribution of, 4
Power, political, 17, 69, 221
Powerlessness, 13
Prairie Island Indian Community, 244
Prejudice, 9, 56, 87, 98, 132, 181, 296, 297, 300, 301,

311, 320, 327–328, 335, 350, 355
definition of, 57, 58
psychology of, 57–58
sociology of, 58–60
Presbyterians, 302
Prestige, 32
Priests, 75, 106, 111, 275
Primogeniture, 138
Primordialist perspective, 45, 48, 51
Princeton University, 107
Princeton Religious Review Center, 168
Prisons, 220
Private schools, 205
Productive diversity, 339
Professional associations, 315
Prohibition, 107
Projection, 57
Property taxes, 206, 211
Prostitution, 98, 319
Protect American Rights and Resources, 239
Protection money, 310
Protestants, 75, 76, 81, 90, 230, 275, 302, 312, 316, 322, 344, 353
"Protocols of the Learned Elders of Zion, The," 118
Pruitt-Igoe project, 208
Public School Desegregation in the United States, 196
Public schools, 76, 154, 188, 194, 205
Pueblo, 82, 243
Pueblo revolt, 96
Puerto Rican Community Development Fund, 275
Puerto Rican Family Institute, 275
Puerto Rican Forum, 275
Puerto Rican Legal Defense and Education Fund, 275
Puerto Rican Merchants' Association, 275
Puerto Ricans, 11, 23, 128, 133, 152, 254, 256, 257, 259, 260, 263, 265, 266, 267, 268–277, 271, 275, 286, 289, 290
agriculture, 270
blue collar jobs, 271
citizenship for, 268
as a colony, 268
drop-out rates, 271

economic position/status, 271–273
educational achievement, 273
ethnic community, 274–276
family, 274, 275
female-headed households, 274, 275
middle class, 271
political influence, 273, 276
poverty, 268, 271
return migration, 273–274
role of race, 271–272
service industry, 271
settlement patterns, 270–271
under/unemployment, 268, 270, 271, 273
women, 133, 271, 272, 274
World War II, post, 268, 270
Puerto Rico, 269, 270
Puritans, 70, 84
Puyallup, 242

Q, R

Quadroon, 122
Quakers, 70, 93, 230
Quebec, 337, 338, 343
Québecois, 30
Quinnipiac Terrace, 207
Quixano, David, 20
Quotas, 198, 201, 202
Québecois nationalists/separatists, 42, 338
Rabbit Proof Fence, 340
Race, 7, 29, 31, 33–37, 38, 40, 140, 173–178, 206, 213, 327, 332, 345
biology, 31, 35, 36, 40
definitions of, 40, 70
enduring significance of, 211–221
nineteenth-century racialist thought, 33–36
Race and Nationality in American Life, 31
Race Discrimination Act (1975), 341
Race relations, 29, 36, 40, 155, 181, 195, 213, 248
Race relations cycle, 43
Racial attitudes, 176

Racial boundaries, 173, 176
Racial dimensions, 3–25
Racial divisiveness, 176–178
Racial equity, 196
Racial etiquette, 187
Racial groups, 29, 30, 39–41, 256
Racial markers, 39
Racial separatism, 124
Racial slurs, 7
Racial theory, 33
Racism, 6, 8, 41, 136, 139, 175, 176, 177, 182, 193, 196, 201, 214, 215, 216, 221, 289, 298, 306, 311, 320, 340, 341, 347, 350, 352, 355
biological, 28
ideology of, 87–88
Rainbow Coalition, 222
Randolph, A. Philip, 182, 183, 184, 186
Rann, Emery, 184
Rational choice, 49, 50
Rational choice theory (of ethnicity), 47–49
Reagan, President Ronald, 147, 176, 177, 195, 200, 202, 209, 228, 244, 247, 266, 267, 279, 283, 303
Real estate industry, 207
Red Power Movement, 235–237, 338
Redlining, 211, 219
Refugees, 325, 336, 348
Religio-ethnic groups, 39
Religion, 19, 47, 70, 90, 155, 349
Religious affiliation, 153, 156
Religious freedom, 71, 77
Religious tolerance, 77
Relocation (Native American), 230
Report of the President's Commission on Housing, 209
Repression, 190, 289
Republican party, 75, 80, 108, 112, 121, 172, 177, 266, 267, 285
Resegregation, 195
Reservation system, 227, 228
Reservations, Indian, 11, 86, 246, 250, 251
development plans on, 243–246
elimination of, 227
health issues, 247–248

as a means of political
    containment, 143
quality of life on, 246–248
as total institutions, 143–
    144
Resident aliens, 279
Residential concentration, 156
Residential patterns, 50
Restaurant industry, 310
Restrictions, immigration, 141
Retraditionalism, 285
*Retreat From Race: Asian-
    American Admissions and
    Racial Politics, The,* 326
Reunion, island of, 352
Reuter, Edward B., 28
Revendal, Vera, 20
Reverse discrimination, 195,
    198, 202, 203
Revolution of 1910, 130
Rhode Island, 242
    Providence, 159
Rio Grande River, 278
Riots, 17, 127, 190, 255, 347,
    353
    Harlem, 190
    Liberty City (1980), 267
    Los Angeles (1992), 46,
        315
    Philadelphia (1844), 77
    Philadelphia (1964), 190
    Rochester, 190
    Watts, 190
*Rise of the Unmeltable Eth-
    nics, The,* 23
Ritual observance, 169, 171
Robert Taylor Homes, 208
Rochdale model, 72
Rodriguez, Richard, 7, 8, 11,
    259
Rohwer, 142
Roman Catholicism, 7, 75,
    106, 111, 129, 132, 153,
    157, 230, 264, 275, 316,
    322, 344, 353
    orthodox, 275
Romania, 115
Romanies (*see* Gypsies), 41
Roosevelt, President Franklin
    Delano, 141, 146, 182–183,
    197, 269
    Executive Order 8802, 183
    Executive Order 9066, 141
Roosevelt, President Theo-
    dore, 20, 123, 139
Rule of law, 4

Rural (communities), 62, 321,
    326
Rush, Benjamin, 78
Russia, 115, 118, 138, 167
    Odessa, 115
Russia, Czarist, 61
Russian immigrants, 168
Russian Revolution, 118
Russians, 20, 167
Rust Belt, 272
Rustin, Bayard, 184
Rwanda, 30

S, T

Sac and Fox Nation, 244
Sacco, Nicola, 108
Salish Indians, 243
Salvadorans, 256, 290
Sambos, 39, 122
Samoans, 296
San Francisco earthquake
    (1906), 135, 136
Sanchez, Soraya, 278
Sansei, 300, 301, 302
Santeria, 264
Sauk, 85
Savagism and Civilization, 84
Scandinavian immigrants, 156
Scandinavians, 81, 336
Scapegoats, 57, 131
Scholastic Aptitude Test (SAT),
    297
School Daze 216
Schwarzenau Brethren, 77
Schwerner, Mickey 188
Scotch-Irish, 70, 72, 73, 78,
    165
Scotch-Irish Americans 152
Scotland, 70, 342, 343, 344,
    347
Scottish 30, 68, 158
Scottish Americans 152
Scottish Nationalist Party, 343
Scottish Parliament, 343
Scouting, 301
Seale, Bobby, 190
Seasonal migrants, 104, 130
Secession, 42
Second generation immi-
    grants, 11, 108, 140, 153,
    154, 158, 259, 265, 267,
    268, 275, 277, 299, 300,
    301, 306, 312, 317, 320,
    323, 347, 353
Second wave refugees, 325

Secretary of War, 141
Segregation, legacy of, 191
Segregation, racial, 122, 175,
    183, 192, 210, 219, 331
    de facto 192, 215
    de jure 192
Segregation, residential, 174,
    206–212, 277, 345, 349–
    350
Self-determination, 340
Self-employment, 346
Self-identity, 22, 47, 50, 159,
    272, 335
Self-image, collective, 283
Seminoles, 85, 245
Senior citizen centers, 315
Separate but equal, 122, 188
Seperatism, 55, 189
September 11 (9/11), 347
Serbia, 42
Serbs, 30
*Serna v. Portales Municipal
    Schools,* 258
Service industry, 288
Settlement location, 62
Settlement patterns, 38
Settler nations, 333, 334–335,
    342
Sexuality, 70
Shanty Irish, 73
Sharecropping, 205
Shawnees, 85
Shelley v. Kramer, 210
Shintoism, 302
Shtetl, 116
Sicilian immigrants, 105
Sickle-cell anemia, 35
Sikhs, 324, 345, 347
Silk workers strike (1916), 108
Simpson, O. J., 197
Simpson, Senator Alan, 279
Singing clubs, 79
Sinhalese, 30
Sinte Gleska University, 251
Sioux, 242, 245
Sit-ins, 186
Six Companies, 135
Skin color, 7, 39, 126, 272
Skinheads, 172, 176
Slave quarters, 145
Slave revolts, 17, 92
Slave ships, 90
Slave trade, 3, 62, 87, 91, 354
Slaveholders, 34
Slavery, 34, 80, 83, 86, 87, 89,
    120, 123, 196, 197, 205
    challenges to, 94–95

legacy of, 354
as the peculiar institution, 88
the plantation and, 88–89
as a total institution, 88, 89
Slaves, 85, 94, 120
community of, 91–92
educating former, 121
escaped, 93
free, 93, 94
Slaves, freed, 120
Slavocracy, 94
Slavs, 112
Slot racket migration, 135
Slovenes, 30
Soccer, 347
Social class, 47, 54, 175, 194, 211, 213
Marxism and, 46–47
Social clubs, 111, 275
Social construction, 49–54
Social control, 125, 185
Social democratic account, 221
Social differences, 35
Social disorganization, 74
Social engineering, 182
Social environment, 5, 36
Social Gospel movement, 123
Social halls, 264, 322
Social hierarchy, 59, 61, 350
Social interactions/relations, 5, 46, 164, 277, 317
Social networks, 220
Social organization, 82, 120
Social policy, 181, 221
Social problems, 76, 128, 146, 220, 307
Social Security, 203
Social service agencies, 258, 311
Social structure, 4–6, 45, 51, 60, 61, 164, 221
Socialism, 80, 117, 124, 147, 268
Socialization, 57, 58, 194
Society of Friends (*see* Quakers)
Sociobiology, 36–37, 48
Sociocultural approach (to ethnicity), 28
Socioeconomic mobility, 45, 155
Sociology of the South, 88
Soldier Blue, 249
Solidarity Movement, 156, 157

Soulside, 218
South Africa, 32, 340
South America, 86, 263, 349
South Americans, 254, 256, 273
South Americans/immigrants, 290–291
South Carolina, 89, 242
Charlestown, 93, 122
Gullahs, 89
South Dakota, 145
Black Hills, 242
Rosebud, 251
South Korea, 312, 316
Southern Christian Leadership Conference (SCLC), 184, 283
Southern Farmers' Alliance, 124
Southern Pacific Transportation Company, 242
Southern race relations, 124–127
"Southern Town," 125
Soviet Union (former), 30, 167, 168, 183, 260, 261, 262, 340
Spain, 30, 95, 114, 262, 348, 351
Basques, 158
Spanglish, 268
Spanish, 82, 114
Spanish Americans, 14
Spanish conquistadors, 95
Spanish culture, 95
Spanish Inquisition, 114
Spanish (language), 7, 257, 258, 276, 285
Spanish-American War, 133, 260
Special Force Operation/Operation Wetback, 278
Split labor market, 62, 130
Spock, Dr., 302
Sports associations, 315–316
Sri Lanka, 30, 340, 345
St. George's Society, 72
St. Patrick's Day, 162, 164, 165
St. Urho's Pub, 164
Stagecoach, 146
Standard of living, 21
Standardized tests, 199, 286, 326, 346, 347
Stanford University, 7
State Department, 85
Statue of Liberty, 21
Status, 36
Steel production, 111

Stereotypes, 58, 59, 80, 90, 107, 131, 146, 194, 250, 286, 327, 328
Stewart, James, 249
Straight out of Brooklyn, 220
Stratification, class, 214
Stratification, ethnic, 60
Street Corner Society, 10
Streetcorner men, 218
Strikebreakers, 130
Strikes, 283, 284
Structure, household, 275
Student Nonviolent Coordinating Committee (SNCC), 185
Subcommunities, ethnic, 153
Subgroups, 31
Suburbs, 17, 119, 206, 210, 308
schools, 194
Sugar, 133, 269
Suicide rate, 247, 248, 307, 310
Sun Yi Man, 308
Supratribal organization, 238
Supratribalism, 234
Swann v. Charlotte-Mecklenberg, 192
Sweat lodges, 241
Sweatshops, 288
Swedes, 33, 165
Swedish Americans, 49, 107, 152, 156
Swedish Americans as immigrants, 61
Symbolic ethnicity, 160–164, 166, 167, 169, 232, 250
Symbolic interactionalism, 41
Symbolic racism, 194
Symbols, 38
Synagogues, 353
Syracuse University, 6
Syrians, 12
Tadzhikistan, 30
Tae kwon do, 316
Tae-tung, Mao, 305
Taft, President William Howard, 123
Tagalog, 322
Taiping Rebellion, 97
Taiwan, 307, 308, 340
Taiwanese, 309, 310
Tally's Corner, 10, 218
Tamils, 30
Tanton, Dr. John, 258, 259
Taxi-dance hall, 319
Tay-Sachs, 35

Teamsters' Union, 283
Teenage pregnancy, 220
Tell Them Willie Boy is Here,
    249
Temperance, 80
Temporary work, 130, 132
Tenant farmers, 125
Tenant labor, 125
Tenement (buildings), 105
Tennessee
    Fayette county, 186
    Haywood county, 186
    Memphis, 200
Termination, Native Ameri-
    can, 226–227, 229, 234
    alternatives to, 227–228
Territoires d'Outre-Mer (DOM-
    TOM), 351, 352
Territorial cloistering, 54
Texas, 95, 96, 130, 133, 253,
    279, 282, 325, 331
    Brownsville, 130
    Crystal City, 282, 284
    Dallas, 170, 230
    Houston, 170, 210, 325
    San Antonio, 285
    Three Rivers, 280
Texas Rangers, 130, 282
Texas, Republic of, 96
Textile industry, 133, 271
Textile workers strike (1912),
    108, 112
Textile workers strike (1916),
    112
Thai, 296
Thatcher, Margaret, 343
Theocracy, 71
Third force, 336, 337
Third generation, 107, 154,
    156, 158, 160, 162, 253,
    288, 300, 300–301
Third parties, 284
Third World, 30, 213
Thomas, Justice Clarence, 200
Thomas, Piri, 272
Thomas, W. I., 28
Tijerina, Reies Lopez, 284
Tilbury Docks, 345
Till, Emmett, 183
Time, 137
Timid bigots, 59
Tiny Man Heavy Runner, 241
Tobacco, 126, 133
Tobago, 68
Tongans, 296
Toomer, Jean, 128
Topaz, 142

Tourism, 244–246
Trade union movement, 80, 81
Trade unions (*see* Labor un-
    ions)
Traditions, 38, 51, 53
Trail of Broken Treaties march,
    236
Trail of Tears, 85
Trans-national America, 22
Transcontinental railroad, 97
*Transformation of the Jews,
    The,* 114
Transformative organizations,
    238
Transnational capitalism, 334
Transnational immigrants, 168,
    274
Transnationalism, 54–56, 274,
    333
Transplantation, 103
Transplanted, The, 102
Treaties, 239, 240, 338
    violations, 241–243
Treatise on Sociology, 88
Treaty of Guadalupe Hidalgo,
    96
Treaty of Paris (1763), 83
Tresca, Carlo, 108
Tri-racial isolates, 15
Tribal colleges, 251
Tribal elders, 241
Tribal governments/officials,
    17, 226, 229, 237
Tribal identity, 241
Tribal organizations, 144, 225,
    238
Tribal sovereignty, 238
Tribble brothers, 239
Tribes, Native American, 82,
    145, 225, 226, 234
Trigueño, 272
Trinidad, 16
Trinidad and Tobago, 336
Truancy, 107, 208
Trudeau, Prime Minister Pi-
    erre, 337
Truman, President Harry S.,
    183, 197, 269
Tse-tung, Mao, 308
Tuberculosis, 307
Tucker, Sophie, 117
Tugwell, Rexford, 269, 270
Tule Lake, 141
Tunisia, 348, 351
Turkey, 348, 352
Turkmenistan, 30
Turks, 41, 107, 131, 349, 352

Turner, Frederick Jackson, 20
Tuskegee Institute, 123

U, V

UNESCO, 35
Ukranians, 336
Underclass, 213
Underground Railroad, 94
Unemployment rates, 183,
    213, 345, 346, 348, 353
United Brethren, 77
United Farm Workers, 283,
    288–289
United Farmworkers Union,
    253
United Jewish Communities,
    168
United Mexican American
    Students (UMAS), 284
United Nations, 334
United States
    antebellum period, 81
    East Coast 153, 242, 245
    ethnic, 18–24
    Great Lakes region, 156
    as a kaleidoscope, 19, 23
    as a melting pot, 19–22,
        23, 24, 44, 354
    Midwest, 61, 78, 104, 107,
        115, 124, 130, 153, 171,
        172, 243, 245, 288
    military, 201, 269
    as a mosaic, 19, 23, 354
    nineteenth-century migra-
        tion, 71–72
    North, 94, 122
    Northeast, 85, 103, 172,
        271, 273
    post Revolution, 71
    post World War II, 18
    pre-Revolutionary, 70
    Rocky Mountain states, 141
    as a salad bowl, 19, 24, 42,
        44, 354
    South, 8, 11, 29, 87, 89, 90,
        93, 122, 127, 127, 128,
        172, 176, 183, 186, 187,
        191, 192, 205, 214, 271
    Southeast, 85
    Southwest, 10, 96, 131, 280,
        287
    Sunbelt states, 273
    as a symphonic orchestra,
        19, 22, 354

West, 136, 171, 172, 243, 273, 301
United States Census, 79, 101, 103, 110, 130, 133–134, 161–162, 167, 229, 230, 232, 246, 248, 254, 256, 264, 269, 271–273, 291, 296, 297, 298, 300, 305, 312, 313, 318, 326
United States Constitution, 258
Fifteenth Amendment, 121
Fourteenth Amendment, 121
Thirteenth Amendment, 120, 196
United States Court of Appeals, 239
Fifth District, 200
United States Department of Housing and Urban Development (HUD), 211
United States Department of Justice, 197
United States Department of Labor, 219
United States Forest Service, 240
United States Housing Act of 1937, 206
United States Navy, 320
United States Supreme Court, 122, 140, 146, 188, 192, 195, 199, 200, 201, 210
United States v. Paradise, 200
United States-Mexican border, 253
United Steel Workers Union, 199
Universal Negro Improvement Association (UNIA), 124
University of Alabama Citizens Council, 188
University of California at Berkeley, 7
University of California, Davis, 198
University of Chicago, 28, 37, 119
University of Michigan, 200
University of Texas Law School, 200
University of Washington Law School, 198
Unprejudiced discriminators, 59

Unprejudiced nondiscriminators, 59
Unskilled labor/workers, 62, 104, 111, 321
Uprooted, The, 102
Uptown Jews, 116
Upward mobility, 74, 106–107, 346, 347, 349
Urban industrial settings, 130
Urban infrastructure, 153
Urban Institute, 209
Urban League, 182
Urban renewal, 207
Urbanization, 228–234, 326
Ursuline convent, 77
Utah, 95, 142
Salt Lake City, 230
Uzbekistan, 30
Values, 6, 38, 45, 51, 60, 70, 285, 347
Vanzetti, Bartolomeo, 108
Vatican, 77
Vesey, Denmark, 93
Veteran's Administration (VA), 153, 210
Vietnam, 325, 326, 340
Saigon, 324
South, 324
Vietnam War, 176, 249, 324, 327
anti-war movement, 189
Vietnamese, 336, 352
Catholics, 324
Vietnamese Americans/immigrants, 295, 309, 318, 327
Virginia, 70
Visas, 131, 320
Visayan, 322
Vision quests, 241
Viva Kennedy clubs, 282
VOLAGs, 324
Voluntary associations/organizations, 75, 128
Voter registration, 186, 188, 266, 303
Voting, 121, 188, 258
Voting Rights Act, 188
Voucher/choice plans, 205

W, X

Wales, 70, 342, 343, 347
Walker, David, 94
Walker River Paiutes, 242
Wall Street, 118
Wallace, George, 188

Wampanoag, 242
War Department, 85
War of 1812, 71
War on Poverty, 208, 220, 276
Washington (state), 242, 244, 320
Seattle, 136, 139, 230
Tacoma, 136
Washington, Booker T., 29, 122, 123, 124, 182
Washington, DC, 20, 20, 127, 170, 218
Washington, George, 84
WASP hegemony, 67–99
Watt, Secretary James, 147
Wealth, 32, 36, 70, 71, 217
Weber, Brian, 199
Weber v. Kaiser Aluminum and Chemical Corporation, 199
Welsh, 30, 158
Welsh Assembly, 343
Welsh immigrants, 72
Welsh language, 343
West Indians, 272, 314, 332
West Indies, 72, 83, 128
Wetbacks, 278
White Anglo Saxon Protestants (WASPs), 32, 34
White Aryan Resistance (WAR), 176
White domination, reassertion, 121–122
White flight, 193–195, 211
White supremacist groups/organizations, 172, 188
terrorist acts, 177
White supremacy, 8, 101–148, 124, 173, 176
White-collar jobs/workers, 151, 153, 213, 299, 313
Whites, 15, 32, 33, 68, 93, 119, 120, 125, 128, 173, 174, 175–176, 177, 181, 184, 198, 201, 204, 283, 332, 346
affirmative action, 202
economic status, 206
farmers, 124
federal government, 175
landowning class, 120–121
lower-middle class, 192
middle class, 192, 203, 207, 216, 217, 220, 306
Native Americans and, 248–250
poor, 176

socioeconomic parity with, 178

suburbanization and, 152–154

women, 319

working class, 176, 192, 203, 207

Wilkins, Roy, 182

Wisconsin, 227, 238, 239

Milwaukee, 111

Wisconsin Alliance for Rights and Resources, 239

Women, 33, 162, 163, 218, 347

Wong, Jade Snow, 8, 9, 10, 11, 137

Woolworth store, 186

Working class, 62, 159, 346

World War I, 124, 127, 131, 131

World War I, post, 335

World War I, pre, 214

World War II, 127, 131, 146, 197

World War II, post, 107, 173, 178, 183, 184, 207, 213, 335, 336, 342, 348, 351

World War II, pre, 108

Wounded Knee, 145, 235, 236

Wovoka, 145

Wright, Richard, 8

Wyoming, 95, 142

Rock Springs, 136

Xenophobia, 352

Y, Z

Yakima Indian Nation, 244

Yale (University), 119, 202

Law School, 200

Yellow peril, 307, 327

Yeshiva, 117

Yiddish language, 114, 116

YMCA programs, 301

Yonsei, 300, 302

Youth centers, 315

Youth of Hitler, 176

Yugoslavia, former, 340, 348

Za chlebem immigrants, 110

Zemmouri, Mahmoud, 353

Zionist Occupied Government (ZOG), 177

Zoroastrians, 39

Zuni, 245 ✦

CPSIA information can be obtained at www.ICGtesting.com
Printed in the USA
BVOW031613070212

282160BV00002B/1/P